FOOD&WINE annual cookbook
an entire year of recipes **2003**

FOOD & WINE MAGAZINE

EDITOR IN CHIEF Dana Cowin
CREATIVE DIRECTOR Stephen Scoble
EXECUTIVE FOOD EDITOR Tina Ujlaki

FOOD & WINE ANNUAL COOKBOOK 2003

EDITOR Kate Heddings
ART DIRECTOR Patricia Kelleher Sanchez
DESIGNER Andrew Haug
PRODUCTION COORDINATOR Tanya Saltzman
PRODUCTION ASSOCIATE Griffin Plonchak
COPY EDITOR Lisa Leventer
EDITORIAL ASSISTANT Jennifer Murphy
PRODUCTION MANAGER Stuart Handelman

SENIOR VICE PRESIDENT, CHIEF MARKETING OFFICER Mark V. Stanich
VICE PRESIDENT, BRANDED PRODUCTS Bruce Rosner
DIRECTOR, BRANDED SERVICES AND RETAIL Marshall Corey
MARKETING MANAGER Bruce Spanier
OPERATIONS MANAGER Phil Black
BUSINESS MANAGER Doreen Camardi

COVER
PHOTOGRAPH BY James Merrell
FOOD STYLING BY Alison Attenborough

FLAP PHOTOGRAPHS
DANA COWIN PORTRAIT BY Andrew French
KATE HEDDINGS PORTRAIT BY Emily Wilson

AMERICAN EXPRESS PUBLISHING CORPORATION
Copyright 2003 American Express Publishing Corporation

ISBN 0-916103-82-X
ISSN 1097-1564

Published by American Express Publishing Corporation
1120 Avenue of the Americas, New York, New York 10036

Manufactured in the United States of America

FOOD&WINE annual cookbook
an entire year of recipes 2003

FOOD&WINE
BOOKS

n Express Publishing Corporation, New York

contents | 2003

8 hors d'oeuvres

24 first courses

122 beef, lamb + game

146 pork + veal

8 breakfast + brunch

an entire year of recipes

38 salads

54 soups

74 pasta

92 poultry

164 fish

184 shellfish

202 vegetables

222 potatoes,
grains + more

272 tarts, pies
+ fruit desserts

288 cakes, cookies
+ other desserts

318 sauces
+ condiments

330 beverages

foreword

Writing the introduction to FOOD & WINE's annual cookbook gives us a chance to reflect on the past year. What kinds of recipes were people becoming more eager for? What did they want to avoid? Where did our trend radar point us? As we compiled the chapters, a few things became quite clear: In 2002 the magazine published more fast recipes than ever before—you'll see that we've highlighted them at the beginning of each chapter. It was also a banner year for fish; we believe the 69 recipes here reflect our readers' overwhelming desire to eat lighter and our editors' growing confidence that more good fish is available. A few standouts: Fillet of Sole with Capers, Almonds and Lemon (p. 178); Scallop and Corn Bacon Burgers with Spicy Mayo (p. 196); and Crabby Carolina Rice (p. 200).

And you'll see an abundance of desserts. Could it be the natural outgrowth of the cocooning trend? After all, more people are taking comfort in staying at home, and what could be more comforting than the smell of cookies baking? Anyone looking for the perfect chocolate chip cookie, for example, will find the recipe here: Pierre Hermé's Chocolate Chocolate Chip Cookies (p. 301).

But there are more changes in the 2003 annual than simply the balance of recipes. We've added many features to the book that we think will make it more inspiring—and useful. One of the most significant is the wine glossary. F&W contributing editor Elin McCoy has created a concise guide, defining the major grapes and genres and recommending a style of wine (in addition to specific bottles) to accompany each recipe. We've also expanded our indexes with a listing of F&W editors' favorite recipes and 12 special menus. A new section on entertaining should give you stylish ideas for your next dinner party.

We'd love to know what you think of the improvements. And if you have ideas on how to make next year's cookbook even better, we'd be delighted to hear them. Please e-mail us at dana@foodandwine.com or cookbookcomments@foodandwine.com.

Dana Cowin

Editor in Chief
FOOD & WINE Magazine

Kate Heddings

Editor
FOOD & WINE Cookbooks

CAMEMBERT BAKED IN ITS BOX, P. 14

hors d'oeuvres

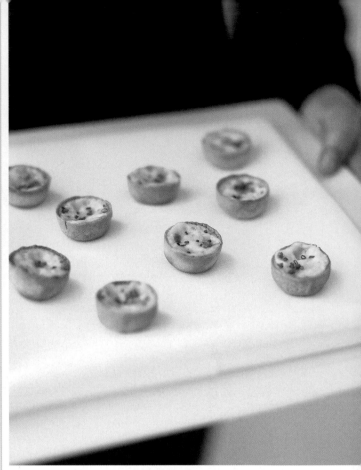

PARMESAN-RICE CRISPS

MUSHROOM POMPONNETTES

Parmesan-Rice Crisps

MAKES 8 LARGE CRISPS ● ●

These lacy crackers, which are made with just three ingredients—brown rice, wild rice and Parmesan cheese—don't taste like anything you would find in a health-food store. They're rich and incredibly crunchy. Break them up and scatter over salads or soups, or serve them as a cocktail snack.

- 1 cup brown rice
- ¼ cup wild rice
- ¾ cup freshly grated
  Parmesan cheese

Salt and freshly ground pepper

1. Bring a large saucepan of water to a boil. Add both the brown rice and the wild rice to the boiling water, cover and cook over low heat until the rice mixture is very soft, about 55 minutes. Drain the rice mixture and spread it on a platter, then let cool completely.

2. In a food processor, pulse the cooled rice mixture until coarsely chopped and sticky. Scrape the chopped rice mixture into a bowl and stir in the grated Parmesan until well blended. Season the rice mixture with salt and pepper.

3. Preheat the oven to 450°. Line a large cookie sheet with parchment paper. Scoop ½ cup of the rice mixture onto one half of the prepared cookie sheet and pat it into a disk. Cover the rice disk with plastic wrap, then press or roll it out to a very thin 7-by-10-inch rectangle. Repeat on the other half of the cookie sheet.

4. Bake the rice crisps in the lower third of the oven for about 12 minutes, or until crisp and golden. Using a spatula, carefully transfer the parchment paper with the crisps to a wire rack and let the crisps cool completely. Repeat with the remaining rice. —*Marcia Kiesel*

MAKE AHEAD The baked rice crisps can be stored at room temperature in an airtight container for up to 2 days; carefully layer the crisps between sheets of wax paper. If necessary, recrisp the crackers on a baking sheet in a preheated 350° oven.

Farmhouse Cheddar and Fig Crackers

MAKES ABOUT 36 CRACKERS ● ●

Because farmhouse Cheddars are aged longer than their factory-produced counterparts—over a year versus 90 days—they have a complex flavor and sharp bite that comes through brilliantly when cooked as well as when eaten plain. The textures of Cheddars from different artisans vary from smooth and creamy to crumbly and dry, which makes Cheddar an extremely versatile cheese in the kitchen.

3 large dried figs, preferably Calimyrna

Boiling water

1¾ cups all-purpose flour

1 stick (4 ounces) unsalted butter, at room temperature

¼ pound extra-sharp farmhouse Cheddar cheese, preferably from England, Canada or Vermont, grated (1¼ cups)

2 teaspoons kosher salt

½ teaspoon freshly ground pepper

1 large egg, lightly beaten

1. In a small heatproof bowl, cover the figs with boiling water and let soak until softened, about 20 minutes. Drain the figs and pat dry with paper towels. Slice off the tough stems, then cut the figs into ½-inch dice.

2. In a food processor, combine the flour, butter, Cheddar cheese, kosher salt and pepper and pulse until the mixture resembles coarse meal. Scrape the mixture into a large bowl and add the figs and egg. Using your hands, work the dough until it comes together.

3. Scrape the dough onto a large piece of plastic wrap and pat it into a 12-by-2-inch rectangular log. Wrap the log tightly and refrigerate until firm, at least 1 hour, or overnight.

4. Preheat the oven to 375°. Butter 2 large baking sheets. Cut the log of cracker dough crosswise into ¼-inch-thick slices. Arrange the slices at least 1 inch apart on the prepared baking sheets. Bake the Cheddar crackers for about 12 minutes, or until they are golden brown and slightly firm. Carefully transfer the crackers to a wire rack. Let cool completely, then serve.

—*Marcia Kiesel*

MAKE AHEAD The dough can be tightly wrapped in plastic and refrigerated for up to 2 days, or wrapped in plastic then in aluminum foil and frozen for up to 1 month. The crackers can be stored at room temperature in an airtight container for up to 2 days.

WINE Dry, fruity sparkling wine.

Mushroom Pomponnettes

MAKES 36 POMPONNETTES ●

At his Manhattan restaurant Daniel, Daniel Boulud makes these popular bite-size mushroom quiches in individual molds, but mini-muffin pans are a perfect substitute.

PASTRY

1 cup all-purpose flour

6 tablespoons unsalted butter, cut into pieces and chilled

⅛ teaspoon salt

1 large egg, lightly beaten

FILLING

1 cup dried porcini mushrooms (1 ounce)

2 cups boiling water

1 tablespoon unsalted butter

1 tablespoon extra-virgin olive oil

1 garlic clove, minced

Salt and freshly ground pepper

1 tablespoon finely chopped flat-leaf parsley

½ cup heavy cream

1 large egg

1 large egg yolk

½ cup shredded imported Fontina cheese (2 ounces)

1 tablespoon snipped chives

1. MAKE THE PASTRY: In a food processor, pulse the flour with the butter and salt until the mixture resembles coarse meal. Pour the beaten egg evenly over the mixture and pulse several times, just until evenly moistened. Transfer the pastry to a work surface and gather it into a ball. Flatten the pastry into a disk, wrap in plastic and refrigerate for at least 30 minutes.

2. Preheat the oven to 350°. On a lightly floured work surface, roll out the pastry to a 14-inch round a scant ⅛ inch thick. Using a 2¼-inch round cookie cutter, stamp out as many rounds as possible. Reroll the scraps and stamp out more rounds.

3. Line the cups of three 12-cup mini-muffin pans with the pastry rounds, pressing the pastry into the molds. Refrigerate until firm.

4. Cut out thirty-six 2-inch squares of foil and line the pastry with them. Bake for about 15 minutes, or until the shells are dry. Remove the foil and let the shells cool. Leave the oven on.

5. MEANWHILE, MAKE THE FILLING: In a heatproof medium bowl, soak the porcini in the boiling water until softened, about 20 minutes. Lift the porcini out of the soaking liquid and pat dry, then finely chop them.

6. In a medium skillet, melt the butter in the olive oil. When the foam subsides, add the porcini and cook over moderately high heat, stirring occasionally, until golden, about 3 minutes. Add the garlic and cook, stirring frequently, until fragrant, about 1 minute longer. Season with salt and pepper and stir in the chopped parsley. Transfer the porcini mushroom mixture to a medium bowl and let cool, then whisk in the cream, whole egg, egg yolk and Fontina until incorporated.

7. Spoon the mushroom custard into the pastry shells and sprinkle with the chives. Bake at 350° for about 15 minutes, or until set. Let the pomponnettes cool slightly before serving.

—*Daniel Boulud*

MAKE AHEAD The baked pomponnettes can be refrigerated overnight and rewarmed in a 325° oven.

WINE Dry, rich Champagne.

---

ingredient tip

farmhouse cheddar

WHEN SERVING THE CHEDDAR AND FIG CRACKERS on the opposite page, try the incredibly rich, aged extra-sharp Cheddar from Cabot Creamery of Montpelier, Vermont. The company has been in operation since 1919 (888-792-2268; www.cabotcheese.com).

hors d'oeuvres

Gougères

MAKES ABOUT 30 GOUGÈRES ●

Instead of spooning the gougère batter onto a baking sheet before baking, you could use mini-muffin tins. These delicate cheese puffs have a thin, creamy center.

1⅓ cups all-purpose flour, plus more for sprinkling
1 cup water
6 tablespoons unsalted butter, cut into tablespoons
¾ teaspoon salt
5 large eggs
1 cup shredded Gruyère cheese (3 ounces)

1. Preheat the oven to 400°. Sprinkle 2 large rimmed baking sheets with flour.

2. In a medium saucepan, combine the water with the butter and salt and bring to a boil over moderate heat until the butter melts. Add the 1⅓ cups of flour and beat constantly with a wooden spoon until a smooth, thick paste forms. Continue beating until the dough pulls away from the side of the pan and forms a ball, about 1 minute. Remove the pan from the heat and let the dough cool slightly, about 10 minutes. Add 4 of the eggs, 1 at a time, beating well after each addition. Stir in the cheese.

3. Drop rounded tablespoons of the dough onto the prepared sheets, about 1 inch apart. Beat the remaining egg in a small bowl. Brush the gougères with the beaten egg and bake for about 30 minutes, or until puffed and browned. Transfer the gougères to a platter and serve warm. —*Chantal Leroux*

MAKE AHEAD The gougères can be frozen for up to 1 month. Reheat in a 350° oven.

Red Pepper, Garlic and Pecorino Gougères

MAKES ABOUT 60 GOUGÈRES ●

1 large red bell pepper—stemmed, seeded, deribbed and cut into 1-inch pieces
½ cup water
2 garlic cloves, very finely chopped
6 tablespoons unsalted butter, cut into pieces
¾ teaspoon salt
¼ teaspoon freshly ground pepper
1 cup all-purpose flour
4 large eggs
½ cup freshly grated Pecorino Romano cheese

Pinch of cayenne pepper

1. Preheat the oven to 425°. Butter 2 large baking sheets.

2. In a food processor, puree the red bell pepper with the water and garlic until the mixture is as smooth as possible, about 2 minutes. Strain the pepper puree through a fine sieve set over a measuring cup, pressing hard on the solids with the back of a spoon to extract as much of the pepper juice as possible; you should have 1 cup. Stir in a little more water if necessary.

3. Transfer the red pepper juice to a medium saucepan. Add the butter, salt and pepper and cook over low heat until the butter melts. Add the flour and beat with a wooden spoon until the dough is smooth and shiny and pulls away from the side of the pan, about 2 minutes. Scrape the gougère dough into a large bowl. Using an electric mixer at medium speed, beat in the eggs, 1 at a time, beating well between additions. Beat in the grated Pecorino Romano and the cayenne.

4. Drop rounded teaspoons of the dough about 1 inch apart onto the prepared baking sheets. Bake the gougères on the upper and middle racks of the oven for about 20 minutes, or until puffed and browned; shift the baking sheets from top to bottom and back to front halfway through baking. Serve the gougères hot, warm or at room temperature. —*Melissa Clark*

MAKE AHEAD The gougères can be made up to 1 day ahead and stored in an airtight container. Rewarm in a 350° oven before serving.

Artichoke-Arugula Soufflé Squares

12 SERVINGS ●

Another option for serving these airy artichoke squares is to set them on mini cocktail toasts.

Olive oil, for brushing
4 scallions, cut into thirds
3 garlic cloves
1 cup packed arugula leaves
Two 6-ounce jars marinated artichoke hearts—drained, rinsed and patted dry
6 large eggs
½ teaspoon freshly grated nutmeg
¼ teaspoon freshly ground pepper
Tabasco sauce
½ pound sharp Cheddar cheese, shredded (2 cups)
Coarse salt, for sprinkling (optional)

1. Preheat the oven to 350°. Brush a 9-inch-square baking pan with olive oil. Line the pan with parchment or wax paper and oil the paper.

2. In a food processor, pulse the scallions with the garlic cloves and arugula leaves until they are finely chopped. Add the artichoke hearts and pulse until coarsely chopped.

3. In a large bowl, whisk the eggs until frothy. Whisk in the nutmeg, pepper and a dash of Tabasco. Add the eggs to the processor along with the Cheddar and pulse just to combine; the mixture should be chunky.

4. Pour the soufflé mixture into the prepared pan and smooth the surface with a spatula. Bake the soufflé for 30 minutes, or until a tester inserted in the center comes out clean. Transfer to a rack and let cool slightly.

5. Turn the soufflé out onto a cutting board and carefully peel off the parchment paper. Cut the artichoke-arugula soufflé into small squares and serve warm or at room temperature, sprinkled with coarse salt. —*Melissa Clark*

MAKE AHEAD The soufflé squares can be made up to 2 hours ahead and served at room temperature.

Cheese-Fried Piquillo Toasts

4 SERVINGS ● ◦

Produced in the Navarra region of Spain, piquillo peppers are cooked over a wood fire, then hand-peeled; the haunting smokiness deepens the piquillo's natural flavor and highlights its subtle heat. It's possible to approximate the flavor of piquillos by using roasted red bell peppers and a pinch of hot paprika, but nothing really duplicates it.

Eight ⅓-inch-thick slices crusty Italian
    bread, crusts removed
Extra-virgin olive oil, for brushing
1 large garlic clove, halved
¼ cup mild goat cheese, softened
Kosher salt and freshly ground pepper
3 ounces Manchego or Parmesan
    cheese, grated (about 1 cup)
8 medium piquillo peppers

1. Preheat the oven to 375°. Arrange the bread on a large baking sheet, brush with olive oil and bake for about 8 minutes, or until golden brown. Rub the hot toasts with the garlic.

2. In a small bowl, season the goat cheese with salt and pepper and mix until creamy. Spread a thin layer of the goat cheese over each toast.

3. Spread the Manchego in a shallow bowl. Dredge the peppers in the cheese to generously coat. In a large nonstick skillet, cook the peppers over moderate heat, turning once with a spatula, until richly browned and crusty, about 2 minutes per side. Using a spatula, scrape the peppers from the pan, transfer to the toasts and serve. —*Marcia Kiesel*

MAKE AHEAD The recipe can be prepared through Step 1 and stored overnight in an airtight container.

WINE Dry, crisp sparkling wine.

Chicken Liver Crostini with Beet Salsa

10 SERVINGS

Twenty ¼-inch-thick baguette slices
¼ cup plus 2 tablespoons
    extra-virgin olive oil
1 small beet
¼ cup finely diced red onion
3 teaspoons red wine vinegar
Salt and freshly ground pepper
1 tablespoon finely
    diced tomato
2 tablespoons finely
    chopped radicchio
1 pound chicken livers, trimmed
    and halved
1 teaspoon minced fresh ginger
⅛ teaspoon ground cloves
⅓ cup unsweetened apple juice

1. Preheat the oven to 350°. Lightly brush the baguette slices with the 2 tablespoons of olive oil and arrange on a baking sheet. Toast the slices for 15 minutes, or until golden and crisp.

2. Meanwhile, in a small saucepan, cover the beet with cold water and bring to a boil. Cook over moderate heat until tender when pierced with a knife, about 20 minutes. Drain and let cool. Peel the beet and cut it into ¼-inch dice.

3. In a medium bowl, combine the onion with 2 teaspoons of the vinegar and a generous pinch each of salt and pepper and let stand for 20 minutes. Stir in the beet, tomato, radicchio and 1 tablespoon of the olive oil. Let the beet salsa stand at room temperature for at least 1 or up to 3 hours.

4. In a large, heavy skillet, heat 2 tablespoons of the olive oil until shimmering. Add the chicken livers, season with salt and pepper and cook over high heat, turning once or twice, until browned, about 1 minute; transfer to a plate. Add the remaining 1 tablespoon of olive oil to the skillet along with the ginger and cloves and cook, stirring, until fragrant. Add the apple juice and the remaining 1 teaspoon of red wine vinegar and cook, scraping up the browned bits from the bottom of the pan, until thickened, about 3 minutes. Return the chicken livers to the skillet, season with salt and pepper and toss gently until the livers are just rosy within, about 1 minute longer. Cut the chicken livers into 1½-inch pieces.

5. Arrange the crostini on a large platter and top with the sautéed chicken livers. Spoon the pan drippings over the livers, then carefully garnish with the beet salsa. Serve the chicken liver crostini immediately. —*Peter Gordon*
WINE Dry, medium-bodied Pinot Gris.

Roasted Pearl Onion Crostini

MAKES ABOUT 36 CROSTINI ◦

For a festive look, you can use a combination of red and white pearl onions.

2 pounds red pearl onions
6 tablespoons extra-virgin olive oil
Salt and freshly ground pepper
1 thin baguette, preferably onion,
    cut into ¼-inch-thick slices
½ cup freshly grated
    Parmesan cheese
1 tablespoon balsamic vinegar

1. Preheat the oven to 450°. Bring a large saucepan of water to a boil. Add the pearl onions and blanch for 30 seconds; drain and let cool slightly. Peel the pearl onions and trim off the roots.

2. On a large rimmed baking sheet, toss the blanched pearl onions with 2 tablespoons of the olive oil and season generously with salt and pepper. Roast the pearl onions in the preheated oven for about 20 minutes, stirring once or twice, until the onions are caramelized and softened.

---

ingredient tip

best jarred peppers

WHOLE PIQUILLO PEPPERS When making the *Cheese-Fried Piquillo Toasts* on this page, try the smoky peppers from Organic Farming, which are packed in sea salt and fresh lemon juice, rather than in citric acid. To find the name of a local retailer, call The Cheese Works, 973-962-1202.

3. Meanwhile, brush a large baking sheet with 1 tablespoon of oil. Arrange the baguette slices on the sheet. Brush with the remaining 3 tablespoons of olive oil. Sprinkle the Parmesan over the slices and bake for 7 minutes, or until the cheese is melted and the bread is crisp; transfer to a platter.

4. Sprinkle the onions with the vinegar; season with salt and pepper. Mound the onions on the cheese toasts and serve warm or at room temperature.
—*Melissa Clark*

Pierogi Crostini with Two Toppings

6 SERVINGS ● ●

  2 dozen fresh, precooked potato pierogi (see Note)
Olive oil
  1 cup chopped tomato
  ¼ small red onion, thinly sliced
  1 medium jalapeño, seeded and thinly sliced
Salt and freshly ground pepper
  1 pound large shiitake mushrooms, stems discarded
  ¼ cup thinly sliced scallions
  1 cup sour cream

1. Light a grill. Arrange the potato pierogi on a large baking sheet and brush generously with olive oil. In a small bowl, mix the chopped tomato with the sliced onion and jalapeño. Season the tomato mixture with salt and pepper.

—— *dictionary* ——
italian toast defined

BRUSCHETTA are thin slices of toast rubbed with garlic cloves, drizzled with extra-virgin olive oil and served warm. **CROSTINI** are little toasts brushed with olive oil and sometimes spread with cheese or other toppings.

2. Brush the shiitake mushroom caps with olive oil and season with salt and pepper. Grill the mushroom caps over a medium-hot fire until tender and nicely browned, about 4 minutes per side. Thinly slice the mushrooms and transfer to a medium bowl. Toss the mushrooms with the scallions.

3. Grill the pierogi over a medium-hot fire until they are browned and crisp, about 2 minutes per side. Transfer the pierogis to a large platter and spread with the sour cream. Spoon the mushroom topping over half of the pierogi and spoon the tomato salsa over the rest. Serve hot. —*Marcia Kiesel*

NOTE If you use frozen pierogi that are not precooked, you must boil them first, then drain and let cool completely before grilling.

Warm Olives with Sesame Seeds and Oregano

8 SERVINGS ● ●

  1 tablespoon sesame seeds
  2 tablespoons extra-virgin olive oil
  ¾ pound Niçoise olives or other full-flavored brine-cured black olives, rinsed and dried
  1 tablespoon finely chopped oregano

1. In a medium skillet, toast the sesame seeds over moderate heat, stirring frequently, until golden, about 1½ minutes. Transfer to a plate.

2. Heat the olive oil in the skillet. Add the olives and oregano and cook over low heat, stirring, just until heated through. Stir in the sesame seeds, transfer to a bowl and serve. —*Ana Sortun*

Sweet-and-Sour Indian Snack

4 SERVINGS ● ●

Street carts throughout Bombay serve this spicy Indian snack, which is called Bhel Puri, in newspaper cones.

  1 medium red potato, peeled and cut into ½-inch dice
  ¼ cup coriander-mint chutney (see Note)

  ¼ cup tamarind chutney (see Note)
  1 tablespoon fresh lime juice
  1 teaspoon chaat masala (see Note)
  1 small onion, minced
  1 cup finely diced, peeled and seeded cucumber
  ½ cup finely diced red apple, such as Gala or McIntosh
  ½ cup coarsely grated green or unripened mango
  2 cups plain unsweetened puffed rice
  ½ cup Indian crisp chickpea noodles (see Note)

1. Bring a small saucepan of salted water to a boil. Add the diced potato and simmer over moderate heat until just tender, about 5 minutes. Drain the potato and let cool.

2. In a large bowl, mix the coriander-mint chutney and the tamarind chutney with the lime juice and the chaat masala. Stir in the onion, cucumber, apple, green mango and boiled potato. Fold in the puffed rice and chickpea noodles and serve the spicy snack at once. —*Floyd Cardoz*

NOTE These ingredients can be found at Indian and Middle Eastern markets.

Camembert Baked in Its Box

2 SERVINGS ●

One 8½-ounce Camembert, unwrapped, in its wooden box
  1 garlic clove, halved
Dry white wine, for sprinkling
Cooked baby new potatoes and pickled vegetables, for serving

Preheat the oven to 400°. Rub the rind of the Camembert with the garlic. Poke half a dozen tiny holes in the rind and sprinkle with the wine. Cover with the box lid. Transfer to a pie plate and bake for about 25 minutes, or until the cheese is molten beneath the rind. Serve the cheese in its box with the potatoes and pickled vegetables.
—*Nigel Slater*

WARM OLIVES WITH SESAME SEEDS AND OREGANO

hors d'oeuvres

Fresh Goat Cheese and Crispy Shallot Dip

MAKES ABOUT 2 CUPS ●

- 1 pound large shallots, thinly sliced
- 1½ cups peanut oil, for frying
- 6 pita breads, split horizontally

Salt

Cayenne pepper

- ½ pound fresh goat cheese, at room temperature
- ½ cup sour cream
- ½ cup whole milk
- 2 tablespoons chopped flat-leaf parsley

1. Preheat the oven to 350°. In a medium saucepan, bring the shallots and oil to a boil. Cook over moderately low heat, stirring, until the shallots are deep golden, about 18 minutes. Strain the shallots, then drain on paper towels and let cool. Reserve the shallot oil.

2. Brush the rough side of the pitas with some of the shallot oil and arrange on baking sheets, oiled side up. Reserve the remaining oil for another use. Sprinkle the pitas with salt and cayenne and bake for 10 minutes, or until golden and crisp. Let cool, then break into large pieces.

3. In a food processor, puree the goat cheese with the sour cream and milk. Season with salt and cayenne; process until smooth. Transfer to a bowl. Stir in three-quarters of the shallots and the parsley. Top with the remaining shallots and serve with the pita crisps.

—*Grace Parisi*

MAKE AHEAD The crispy shallots and pitas can be stored in airtight containers for 3 days; the goat cheese mixture can be refrigerated for 3 days.

Creamy Spinach-and-Shrimp Dip

MAKES ABOUT 2½ CUPS ● ● ●

This is a variation on spinach-and-cream cheese dip, a cocktail party classic.

- ¼ cup cilantro leaves
- 2 scallions, cut into thirds
- 1 garlic clove, minced
- 1 jalapeño, chopped
- One 10-ounce package frozen chopped spinach, thawed and squeezed dry
- ½ cup mayonnaise
- 4 ounces cream cheese (½ cup)
- 1 tablespoon fresh lime juice

Salt

- ¾ pound cooked shrimp, coarsely chopped

In a food processor, pulse the cilantro, scallions, garlic and jalapeño until finely chopped. Add the spinach, mayonnaise, cream cheese, lime juice and salt to taste and process until smooth. Add the shrimp and pulse until finely chopped. Transfer the dip to a bowl and refrigerate until chilled before serving.

—*Melissa Clark*

MAKE AHEAD The dip can be refrigerated for up to 1 day.

Egyptian Spiced Carrot Puree

8 SERVINGS ● ● ●

The Egyptian spice blend known as *dukka* includes toasted ground cumin, coriander and sesame seeds; this version adds toasted coconut. The carrot dish here is traditionally eaten by first dipping bread in oil and then in the *dukka* before spooning the puree on top. It's typical of North Africa's *qimia*—a version of tapas or meze.

- ¼ cup blanched almonds or hazelnuts
- ¼ cup coriander seeds
- 2 tablespoons cumin seeds
- 2 tablespoons sesame seeds
- ¼ cup unsweetened dried shredded coconut

Salt and freshly ground pepper

- 2 pounds carrots, cut into 2-inch lengths
- 6 tablespoons extra-virgin olive oil, plus more for serving
- 2 tablespoons white wine vinegar
- 4 teaspoons *harissa* (see Note)
- 1 teaspoon ground cumin
- ½ teaspoon ground ginger

Torn pita bread or thinly sliced baguette, for serving

1. In a dry, medium skillet, toast the almonds over moderate heat, stirring occasionally, until golden, about 4 minutes. Transfer the almonds to a work surface to cool, then finely chop. Add the coriander and cumin seeds to the skillet and toast over moderate heat, stirring, until fragrant, about 2 minutes. Transfer to a spice grinder and let cool completely, then coarsely grind. In a medium bowl, mix the chopped almonds with the spices.

2. Add the sesame seeds to the skillet and toast over moderate heat, stirring frequently, until golden, about 1½ minutes. Transfer the sesame seeds to the spice grinder. Toast the coconut in the skillet over moderate heat, stirring constantly, until golden, about 1 minute. Transfer to the grinder and let cool completely. Grind the sesame seeds and coconut to a coarse powder. Add to the almond-spice mixture and season with ½ teaspoon each of salt and pepper.

3. In a large saucepan, cover the carrots with water and bring to a boil. Reduce the heat to moderate and simmer until tender, about 20 minutes. Drain the carrots and return them to the saucepan. Cook for 30 seconds over medium heat, shaking the pan, to dry the carrots thoroughly. Remove from the heat and coarsely mash the carrots with a fork. Stir in the 6 tablespoons of olive oil, the vinegar, *harissa*, ground cumin and ginger. Season with salt and pepper. Transfer the carrot puree to a bowl and serve with torn pita, olive oil and the spice mixture on the side.

—*Ana Sortun*

NOTE *Harissa* is a fiery Tunisian spice paste. It is available in jars and tubes at Middle Eastern groceries as well as many specialty food shops.

MAKE AHEAD The spiced carrot puree can be prepared up to 2 days ahead. Refrigerate the carrots and store the spice mixture at room temperature; let the carrots return to room temperature before serving.

Chickpea Puree with Cumin Oil

12 SERVINGS ● ● ●

- 1 teaspoon cumin seeds
- ¾ cup extra-virgin olive oil
- Two 15-ounce cans chickpeas, drained
- 1 tablespoon minced garlic
- 1 tablespoon fresh lemon juice
- Salt
- 2 tablespoons chopped cilantro
- Carrot, zucchini or cucumber rounds, cut into ¼-inch-thick slices, for serving

1. In a small skillet, toast the cumin seeds over moderate heat, shaking the pan frequently, until fragrant, about 2 minutes. Add the olive oil and cook over low heat for 30 seconds. Transfer the cumin oil to a bowl and let cool.

2. In a food processor, puree the chickpeas, garlic and lemon juice; season with salt. With the machine on, gradually pour in all but 2 tablespoons of the cumin oil, leaving most of the seeds in the bowl; puree until smooth. Add the cilantro and pulse just until combined. Spoon the chickpea puree into a serving bowl. Drizzle with the reserved cumin oil and seeds; serve with the vegetables. —Melissa Clark

MAKE AHEAD The chickpea puree can be refrigerated for up to 1 day.

Armenian Bean and Walnut Pâté

8 SERVINGS ● ●

You can mold the pâté in a terrine or bowl lined with plastic wrap if you prefer a different shape.

- 1 cup dried red kidney beans (6 ounces)—picked over, soaked overnight and drained, or 2½ cups canned red kidney beans, rinsed and drained
- ½ small white onion, minced
- 1 bay leaf
- 6 cups water
- ¾ cup walnuts (3 ounces)
- 4 tablespoons unsalted butter, softened
- ¼ teaspoon minced garlic
- 1 tablespoon minced dill
- 1 tablespoon minced basil
- 1 tablespoon minced flat-leaf parsley
- Salt and freshly ground pepper
- Armenian string cheese and baguette slices or torn pita, for serving

1. In a medium saucepan, combine the dried beans, onion and bay leaf. Add the water and bring to a boil. Reduce the heat to moderate and simmer until the beans are tender, 1¼ to 1½ hours. Drain the beans in a colander and discard the bay leaf. Let cool completely.

2. Preheat the oven to 350°. Spread the walnuts in a pie plate and bake for about 7 minutes, or until lightly toasted. Transfer the walnuts to a food processor and let them cool completely. Add the cooked dried or drained canned kidney beans, butter and garlic and pulse until the mixture is smooth. Add the dill, basil and parsley, season with salt and pepper and pulse the bean pâté just until blended.

3. Scrape the bean pâté onto a long sheet of plastic wrap and shape it into a 12-by-2-inch log. Wrap the log in the plastic and refrigerate until chilled, at least 1 hour. Cut the bean pâté into ¼-inch-thick slices and serve with the string cheese and baguette slices or pita bread. —Ana Sortun

MAKE AHEAD The pâté can be refrigerated for up to 3 days.

Bagna Cauda with Crudités

12 SERVINGS ●

Bagna cauda is Italian for "hot bath" and refers to a pungent anchovy and olive oil dip. Since the solids in bagna cauda fall to the bottom, it is best set out in a shallow dish or a fondue pot. You can vary the vegetables for the crudités and also serve toasted bread chunks.

- 2 pounds asparagus, ends trimmed
- 2 bunches broccoli rabe (about 3 pounds), trimmed
- 1 stick (4 ounces) unsalted butter, cut into pieces
- ¾ cup extra-virgin olive oil
- One 3-ounce can flat anchovy fillets, drained and finely chopped
- ¼ cup minced garlic (about 8 cloves)
- Salt and freshly ground pepper
- 3 fennel bulbs, cut into thin wedges
- 1 pint grape or cherry tomatoes

1. Fill 2 large bowls with ice water. Bring a large pot of salted water to a boil. Add the asparagus and cook over moderately high heat until it is crisp-tender, 2 to 3 minutes. Transfer the asparagus to a bowl of ice water to cool; drain well and pat dry.

2. Return the water in the pot to a boil. Add the broccoli rabe and cook over moderately high heat until crisp-tender, about 2 minutes; drain. Immediately plunge the broccoli rabe into the other bowl of ice water to cool. Drain well and pat dry.

3. In a medium saucepan, melt the butter in the olive oil over moderately low heat. Add the anchovy fillets and minced garlic and cook, stirring occasionally, until the garlic is fragrant and opaque, 2 to 3 minutes. Season with salt and pepper. Pour the bagna cauda into a heatproof dish or a fondue pot. Arrange the asparagus, broccoli rabe, fennel and tomatoes on a platter and serve with the warm bagna cauda. —Melissa Clark

cooking tip

drying spinach

WHEN SQUEEZING SPINACH DRY for Creamy Spinach-and-Shrimp Dip, lay out the spinach on a plate and top with another plate. Hold the plates together upright and press on them to extract the liquid. Another strategy: Squeeze out excess liquid by pressing the spinach in a potato ricer.

PORT-GLAZED WALNUTS WITH STILTON

BASIL LEAVES STUFFED WITH CHÈVRE AND PINE NUTS

Spiced Caramelized Cauliflower Florets

12 SERVINGS ● ○

- 1 large head of cauliflower (about 3 pounds), cut into florets
- 4 tablespoons unsalted butter, melted
- 1 teaspoon sugar
- ½ teaspoon salt
- ½ teaspoon freshly ground pepper
- ½ teaspoon sweet paprika
- ½ teaspoon hot paprika
- ¼ teaspoon cinnamon

Coarse salt, for sprinkling

Preheat the oven to 500°. In a large bowl, toss the cauliflower with the butter. In a small bowl, combine the sugar, salt, pepper, sweet and hot paprika and the cinnamon. Add the spices to the cauliflower and toss until evenly coated. Spread the cauliflower florets on a baking sheet in a single layer. Roast for about 20 minutes, stirring once or twice, until the florets are crisp-tender and caramelized. Mound the florets on a serving platter or in a colorful glass bowl and sprinkle with coarse salt. Serve the cauliflower hot or warm, with toothpicks. —*Melissa Clark*

Basil Leaves Stuffed with Chèvre and Pine Nuts

MAKES 20 HORS D'OEUVRES ●

- ½ cup pine nuts
- 4 ounces soft goat cheese, at room temperature
- 2 tablespoons heavy cream

Salt and freshly ground pepper

- 20 large unblemished basil leaves, about 3 inches long
- 1 medium tomato, finely chopped

Extra-virgin olive oil, for drizzling

1. In a small, dry skillet, toast the pine nuts over low heat, shaking the pan occasionally, until golden and fragrant, about 3 minutes; let cool.

2. In a small bowl, mix the goat cheese with the heavy cream and season with salt and pepper.

3. Spread 1 teaspoon of the cheese on each basil leaf. Sprinkle with the pine nuts, pressing them into the cheese. Scatter the chopped tomato on top. Pinch each leaf together near the center to form slightly rounded bowls. Drizzle lightly with olive oil and serve.
—Kathy Gunst

Port-Glazed Walnuts with Stilton

12 SERVINGS ● ●

The best way to enjoy this recipe is to cut off small chunks of the Stilton and dip them in the port syrup.

2½ cups walnut halves (9 ounces)
¾ cup sugar
¾ cup ruby port
½ teaspoon freshly ground pepper
1 bay leaf
One 1-pound wedge of Stilton cheese

I. Preheat the oven to 350°. Spread the walnuts on a rimmed baking sheet and toast for about 8 minutes, or until lightly browned.
2. Meanwhile, in a large saucepan, combine the sugar, port, pepper and bay leaf and bring to a boil. Cook over moderate heat, stirring occasionally, until slightly thickened, 3 to 4 minutes. Discard the bay leaf.
3. Add the walnuts to the saucepan, stirring to evenly coat them. Using a slotted spoon, drain the nuts very well. Line a baking sheet with parchment and spread the walnuts on it in a single layer. Bake for about 12 minutes, stirring once, until the nuts are mostly dry; let cool. Separate any that stick together.
4. Meanwhile, simmer the syrup over low heat until it is thick enough to coat the back of a spoon, about 3 minutes.
5. Set the Stilton on a serving platter and place the walnuts in a separate bowl. Drizzle the port syrup over the cheese and serve with the nuts.
—Melissa Clark

MAKE AHEAD The nuts can be stored in an airtight container for up to 1 day. The port syrup can be refrigerated for up to 1 day; rewarm before serving.

Smashed Potatoes with Caviar

MAKES 30 HORS D'OEUVRES ●

30 small Yukon Gold potatoes, about 2 inches in diameter, scrubbed
Salt
1¼ cups sour cream
6 ounces salmon caviar
¼ cup snipped chives

I. In a large pot of salted water, bring the potatoes to a boil. Cook the potatoes over moderately high heat until tender when pierced with a fork, about 30 minutes. Drain and pat dry.
2. Working with 1 potato at a time and using a small plate, press down to flatten the potatoes to a ¾-inch thickness, keeping them intact.
3. Arrange the smashed potatoes on large serving platters. Season the potatoes with salt. Top each with a dollop of sour cream and 1 teaspoon of salmon caviar. Garnish with the chives and serve at once. *—Jennifer Rubell*

MAKE AHEAD The potatoes can be boiled up to 6 hours ahead and kept at room temperature. Cover the potatoes loosely with foil and rewarm them in a 325° oven for 10 to 15 minutes before smashing and serving.

WINE Dry, rich Champagne.

Tostones with Smoked Salmon

4 SERVINGS

Tostones—fried, smashed plantain slices—are a variation on the toast used for the familiar hors d'oeuvre of smoked salmon and herbed cream. Soaking the plantain slices may seem like an unnecessary step, but it helps remove some of their starchiness and keeps them white.

2 large green plantains (about 10 ounces each)
6 cups water
Kosher salt
2 cups vegetable oil, for frying
⅓ cup sour cream
2 tablespoons finely chopped dill, plus dill sprigs for garnish
2 teaspoons fresh lime juice

6 ounces thinly sliced smoked salmon, cut into 12 even pieces
Paper-thin lime slices, quartered, for garnish

I. Cut off both ends of the plantains and score them lengthwise, then peel off the skin. In a large bowl, combine the water with 1 teaspoon of salt. Add the plantains and let soak for 30 minutes. Drain and pat dry with paper towels. Cut each plantain on the diagonal into 6 slices about 1½ inches thick.
2. In a large skillet, heat the oil to 275°. Add the plantain slices and fry, stirring, for 2 minutes. Transfer the plantain slices to paper towels and let cool slightly. Reserve the oil in the skillet.
3. Wrap each plantain slice in a dampened paper towel and use a meat pounder to gently pound it into a ¼-inch-thick oval.
4. In a small bowl, using a spoon, stir to combine the sour cream with the chopped dill and lime juice.
5. Reheat the oil to 375°. Add the flattened plantain slices and fry, turning once, until golden and crisp, about 2 minutes. Drain the tostones on paper towels, then sprinkle with salt.
6. Dollop 1½ teaspoons of the herbed sour cream on each tostone. Top with a slice of smoked salmon, garnish with a dill sprig and lime slice and serve.
—Eric Ripert

MAKE AHEAD The recipe can be prepared through Step 4 up to 4 hours in advance. Refrigerate the herbed sour cream, but keep the plantains at room temperature.

WINE Dry, crisp sparkling wine.

Grilled Chicken Wings and Livers with Balsamic-Mustard Glaze

6 SERVINGS

6 pounds chicken wings, tips removed and reserved for stock
5 large garlic cloves, 4 coarsely chopped and 1 halved
2 jalapeños, seeded and chopped

1 cup Dijon mustard

½ cup plus 2 tablespoons
balsamic vinegar

¼ cup extra-virgin olive oil,
plus more for brushing

1 pound large chicken
livers, trimmed

2 tablespoons hot sauce

Salt and freshly ground pepper

6 large, thick slices of country bread

I. Using poultry shears or a chef's knife, cut the chicken wings in half at the joints; set the drumettes in a large shallow baking dish. With the shears, snip off the strips of fat along each side of the other wing pieces. Add the pieces to the drumettes.

2. In a mini-processor, combine the chopped garlic with the jalapeños, ¼ cup of the mustard, 2 tablespoons of the vinegar and ¼ cup of the olive oil. Process until smooth.

3. Toss ½ cup of the marinade with the wings. In a small bowl, toss the chicken livers with the remaining ¼ cup of marinade. Cover and refrigerate the wings and livers for 6 hours or for up to 2 days.

4. Light a grill. To make the glaze, in a medium bowl, whisk the remaining ¾ cup of mustard and ½ cup of balsamic vinegar with the hot sauce.

5. Thread the chicken wings without crowding onto pairs of parallel 12-inch skewers; keep the drumettes and the other chicken wing pieces on separate sets of skewers. Thread the livers onto double skewers, leaving ½ inch between them. Season the chicken wings and livers with salt and pepper.

6. Brush the chicken livers with the glaze and grill over a hot fire, brushing frequently with the balsamic glaze, until browned and crisp, about 2 minutes per side. Clean the grill with a wire brush if necessary, then brush the bread with olive oil and grill the slices over the hot fire until toasted. While still hot, rub the bread on both sides with the halved garlic clove. Serve immediately with the chicken livers.

7. Brush the chicken wings with the glaze and grill over a medium-hot fire, brushing generously with the glaze and turning for even browning, until cooked through and crisp, about 8 minutes per side. Serve at once. —*Marcia Kiesel*

MAKE AHEAD The marinated chicken wings and livers can be refrigerated for up to 2 days. The mustard-balsamic glaze can be refrigerated overnight.

WINE Light, fruity Pinot Noir.

Grilled Chorizos with Salsa

12 SERVINGS ●

4 large plum tomatoes (1 pound),
finely chopped

2 medium onions, finely chopped

2 tablespoons minced cilantro

1 garlic clove, minced

1 jalapeño, seeded and minced

2 tablespoons fresh lemon juice

Salt

12 crusty rolls (2 ounces each), split

Extra-virgin olive oil, for brushing

6 small chorizos (1¼ pounds)

I. In a medium bowl, mix the tomatoes, onions, cilantro, garlic, jalapeño and lemon juice and season with salt.

2. Light a grill or preheat a grill pan. Brush the rolls with olive oil and toast them on the grill or in the grill pan over moderate heat. Grill the chorizos until browned, about 20 minutes. Let the chorizos cool slightly, then cut each on the diagonal into 12 thin slices. Top each roll half with 3 slices of chorizo and 1 tablespoon of salsa and serve. —*Bernardita Del Campo Correa*

MAKE AHEAD The salsa can be refrigerated for up to 4 hours.

WINE Round, supple, fruity Syrah.

Crisp Sausage Cakes with Red Wine Prunes

MAKES 2 DOZEN PATTIES ●

1 cup dry red wine

5 thyme sprigs, plus more
for garnish

Salt and freshly ground pepper

8 pitted prunes, quartered

1 pound sweet Italian sausage,
casings removed

1 garlic clove, very finely chopped

1 tablespoon chopped basil

1 teaspoon chopped sage

2 teaspoons extra-virgin olive oil

I. In a small saucepan, combine the wine with the 5 thyme sprigs and a pinch each of salt and pepper. Simmer over moderate heat for 4 minutes. Add the prunes and cook until syrupy, about 6 minutes longer. Discard the thyme sprigs and let the syrup cool.

2. In a large bowl, mix the sausage with the garlic, basil, sage and a large pinch of pepper; knead until combined. Form the mixture into 1-inch patties.

3. Heat the olive oil in a large skillet until shimmering. Add the sausage patties and cook over moderate heat until cooked through and well browned on both sides, about 8 minutes. Drain on paper towels.

4. Arrange the patties on a platter and top each with a prune piece. Skewer with toothpicks, garnish the platter with thyme and serve. —*Melissa Clark*

Swedish Meatballs

MAKES ABOUT 60 MEATBALLS ● ●

2 slices of white bread,
crusts removed

1 cup whole milk

2 tablespoons unsalted butter

3 tablespoons vegetable oil

1 medium onion, minced

¾ teaspoon ground cumin

¼ teaspoon cayenne pepper

1 pound ground pork

1 pound ground beef

2 teaspoons celery salt

1½ teaspoons kosher salt

1 large egg, lightly beaten

1 cup heavy cream

Freshly ground black pepper

I. In a large bowl, cover the bread with the milk and soak until very soft, 5 minutes. In a medium skillet, melt 1 tablespoon of the butter in 1 tablespoon of the vegetable oil until shimmering.

Add the onion and cook over low heat, stirring, until softened, 5 minutes. Add the cumin and cayenne and cook until fragrant, 1 minute. Let cool.

2. Add the ground pork and beef to the soaked bread. Gently mix in the cooked onion, celery salt, kosher salt and beaten egg until thoroughly combined. Refrigerate until firm, about 30 minutes.

3. Shape the meat mixture into 1-inch meatballs. In a large skillet, melt the remaining tablespoon of butter in the remaining 2 tablespoons of vegetable oil. Add the meatballs and cook over moderately high heat, turning occasionally, until browned and cooked through, 8 minutes; reduce the heat to moderately low if the meatballs begin to brown too quickly. Drain on paper towels.

4. Pour off the fat from the skillet, add the cream and scrape up any browned bits from the pan. Simmer over moderately low heat until reduced by one-third, about 4 minutes. Season with salt and black pepper. Return the meatballs to the sauce and simmer for 2 minutes before serving. —*Fredrika Stjärne*

MAKE AHEAD The meatballs can be refrigerated overnight in their sauce.

Mini Meatballs with Yogurt-Mint Sauce

MAKES ABOUT 4 DOZEN

MEATBALLS ● ●

1½ tablespoons extra-virgin olive oil
1 pound ground lamb
½ cup minced onion
¼ cup plus 2 tablespoons
   dry bread crumbs
2 extra-large eggs
2 tablespoons chopped mint
2 tablespoons fresh lemon juice
¼ teaspoon cinnamon
¼ cup chopped dill
1 tablespoon plus 1 teaspoon
   minced garlic
Salt
One 8-ounce container Greek yogurt
   or plain whole-milk yogurt
1 tablespoon milk

1. Preheat the broiler. Brush a rimmed baking sheet with the olive oil.

2. In a bowl, combine the lamb, onion, bread crumbs, eggs, mint, lemon juice, cinnamon, 1 tablespoon of the dill, 2 teaspoons of the garlic and 1 teaspoon of salt; knead until combined. Shape into 1¼-inch meatballs. Arrange the meatballs on the oiled baking sheet and broil as close to the heat as possible for 6 minutes, turning the pan halfway through, until firm and lightly browned.

3. In a small bowl, whisk the yogurt with the remaining 3 tablespoons of dill and 2 teaspoons of garlic; whisk in the milk and season with salt. Transfer the meatballs to a plate and serve at once with the sauce. —*Melissa Clark*

MAKE AHEAD The recipe can be prepared up to 1 day ahead. Reheat the meatballs before serving.

Manchurian Pork-and-Zucchini Dumplings

MAKES ABOUT 4 DOZEN
DUMPLINGS ●

1 medium zucchini, cut into
   ¼-inch dice
Kosher salt
½ pound ground pork
1 celery rib, cut into ¼-inch dice
2 scallions, minced
1½ tablespoons soy sauce
1 tablespoon Chinese cooking wine
   (Shao-Hsing) or dry sherry
1 tablespoon vegetable oil, plus
   more for pan-frying
1 package gyoza wrappers

1. In a colander, toss the zucchini with ½ tablespoon of salt and let stand for 30 minutes. Rinse the zucchini under cool water; squeeze and pat dry. Transfer to a bowl. Add the pork, celery, scallions, soy sauce, Chinese cooking wine and 1 tablespoon oil; mix well.

2. Line a baking sheet with wax paper. On a work surface or in your palm, moisten the edge of 1 gyoza wrapper with water; cover the rest of the gyoza wrappers with a damp kitchen towel.

Spoon a level teaspoon of the pork filling into the center of the wrapper. Fold the wrapper over the filling to form a half-moon. Pinch the wrapper in the center, then pleat the edges to seal. Transfer the dumpling to the prepared baking sheet and cover with a damp kitchen towel. Repeat with the remaining wrappers and filling.

FOR STEAMED DUMPLINGS: Line a large steamer basket or several bamboo steamer trays with damp cheesecloth or lettuce leaves. Arrange the dumplings, not allowing them to touch, in a single layer on the cheesecloth. Set the steamer basket over 1 inch of simmering water in a large saucepan. Cover and steam until the filling is cooked through and the wrappers are tender, 10 to 15 minutes. Serve at once.

FOR PAN-FRIED DUMPLINGS: Heat a very thin film of vegetable oil in each of 2 large nonstick skillets. Arrange the dumplings in the pans, pleated sides up, in concentric circles; do not overcrowd the pans. Add enough water to the pans to reach halfway up the sides of the dumplings and bring to a boil.

entertaining tip

big dinners

STICK WITH WHAT YOU KNOW A big party is not the occasion to experiment.

INCLUDE JUST ONE "STAR" DISH Keep the rest of the menu straightforward.

PLAN AHEAD Focus on recipes that can be prepared in advance; avoid dishes that require last-minute work.

MINIMIZE THE INGREDIENTS Save on shopping and prep time (and free up needed counter space) by using recipes that call for only a few ingredients.

KEEP YOUR COOL Serving piping-hot food to 30 people is likely to be stressful; opt instead for recipes that offer leeway on serving temperature.

hors d'oeuvres

Cover partially and cook until the water has evaporated and the dumplings are crisp and browned on the bottom, about 15 minutes. Serve at once.
—*Michelle Shih*

MAKE AHEAD The uncooked dumplings can be frozen for up to 1 month. Do not thaw before steaming or pan-frying.

SERVE WITH Soy sauce mixed with a little rice vinegar.

Hazelnut Shrimp in Endive Leaves

MAKES 36 HORS D'OEUVRES ● ● ●

Endive leaves make pretty edible scoops for all kinds of savory fillings. And, they won't get soggy as they sit.

- 3 tablespoons hazelnuts
- 2 garlic cloves, smashed, plus ½ teaspoon minced garlic
- 1 pound large shrimp, shelled and deveined
- ¼ cup fresh lemon juice

Salt and freshly ground pepper
- ¼ cup hazelnut oil
- 2 tablespoons extra-virgin olive oil
- 2 tablespoons finely chopped basil
- 2 tablespoons chopped celery leaves
- 1 scallion, halved lengthwise and thinly sliced crosswise
- 3 large Belgian endives, leaves separated

1. Preheat the oven to 375°. In a pie plate, toast the hazelnuts for about 10 minutes, or until fragrant and browned. Transfer the hot nuts to a kitchen towel and rub them together to remove the skins. Let cool, then coarsely chop.

2. Meanwhile, bring a medium saucepan of salted water to a boil with the smashed garlic. Add the shrimp and cook until opaque, about 2 minutes. Drain and let cool; discard the garlic.

3. In a bowl, whisk the lemon juice with the minced garlic, ½ teaspoon of salt and a generous pinch of pepper. Whisk in the hazelnut and olive oils, then stir in the basil, celery leaves, scallion and 2 tablespoons of the hazelnuts.

4. Coarsely chop the shrimp and add to the dressing. Season with salt and pepper and toss to coat.

5. Arrange the endive leaves on a large platter and spoon the shrimp salad onto them. Sprinkle with the remaining 1 tablespoon of hazelnuts and serve.
—*Melissa Clark*

MAKE AHEAD The recipe can be prepared through Step 4 and refrigerated for up to 2 hours.

Citrus-Pickled Shrimp

10 SERVINGS ● ●

Don't worry if the shrimp appear undercooked after being boiled for just 1 minute. They will finish "cooking" overnight in the tangy citrus marinade.

- 2 tablespoons Old Bay Seasoning
- 3 pounds large shrimp, shelled and deveined
- 6 bay leaves, crumbled
- ½ cup fresh lemon juice
- ½ cup fresh orange juice
- 3 garlic cloves, minced
- 2 tablespoons extra-virgin olive oil
- 1 medium onion, thinly sliced
- 2 tablespoons crushed mustard seeds
- 1 tablespoon kosher salt
- ¾ teaspoon crushed red pepper
- ½ teaspoon celery seeds
- ½ teaspoon turmeric

1. Add the Old Bay Seasoning to a large pot of water, cover and bring to a boil. Add the shrimp and cook over moderate heat, stirring, until they just start to curl, about 1 minute. Drain and spread on a large rimmed baking sheet. Let cool to room temperature.

2. In a large resealable plastic bag, mix the bay leaves with the lemon and orange juices, garlic, olive oil, onion, mustard seeds, salt, crushed pepper, celery seeds and turmeric. Add the shrimp and seal; refrigerate overnight.

3. Transfer the shrimp and marinade to a large shallow bowl and serve.
—*Robert Stehling*

WINE Dry, crisp sparkling wine.

Chicken Croquettes

MAKES 16 CROQUETTES

Let the chicken mixture chill completely before forming it into croquettes so they will keep their shape when fried.

- 2 tablespoons unsalted butter
- 2 tablespoons extra-virgin olive oil
- 2 cups minced roasted chicken
- ½ cup finely chopped Serrano ham or prosciutto (2 ounces)
- ½ teaspoon freshly grated nutmeg

Salt and freshly ground pepper
- ¼ cup all-purpose flour, plus more for dredging
- ¾ cup plus 2 tablespoons whole milk
- 2 large eggs
- 1 cup fine, dry bread crumbs

Vegetable oil, for frying
Lemon wedges, for serving

1. In a skillet, melt the butter in the olive oil. Add the chicken, ham, nutmeg and a large pinch each of salt and pepper. Cook over moderate heat, stirring, for 3 minutes. Stir in ¼ cup of the flour; gradually whisk in ¾ cup of the milk. Simmer for 3 minutes, stirring. Scrape into a bowl and let cool. Cover and refrigerate until chilled, at least 1 hour.

2. Divide the croquette mixture into 16 equal portions. Using wet hands, roll the portions into oval croquettes.

3. Preheat the oven to 325°. In a shallow bowl, beat the eggs with the remaining 2 tablespoons of milk. Spread the bread crumbs and some flour in 2 more shallow bowls. Dredge each croquette first in the flour, then dip in the egg; coat the croquettes with bread crumbs and transfer to a platter.

4. In a small saucepan, heat ½ inch of vegetable oil until shimmering. Fry 4 croquettes at a time, turning twice, until golden brown, about 3 minutes. Transfer the croquettes to a wire rack set over a baking sheet and keep warm in the oven while frying the rest. Serve immediately, with lemon wedges.
—*Joseph Jiménez de Jiménez*

WINE Medium-bodied, round Pinot Blanc.

CHICKEN CROQUETTES

GRILLED ANTIPASTO WITH GARLICKY BEAN DIP, P. 32

first courses

GOLDEN GRATINÉED SHELLFISH

SPICY MUSSELS WITH GINGER AND LEMONGRASS

Golden Gratinéed Shellfish

8 SERVINGS

- 7 tablespoons unsalted butter
- 4 garlic cloves, finely chopped
- 1 large shallot, finely chopped
- 1½ tablespoons Dijon mustard
- 5 cups fresh white bread crumbs (7 ounces)
- 1½ tablespoons finely chopped thyme

Salt and freshly ground pepper

- ½ cup dry white wine
- 2 bay leaves
- 3 dozen medium mussels (1½ pounds), scrubbed and debearded
- 3 dozen medium littleneck clams, shucked, on the half shell, empty shells reserved
- 3 dozen medium shrimp, shelled and deveined

1. Preheat the oven to 500°. Melt the butter in a medium skillet. Add the garlic and shallot and cook over low heat until softened, 5 minutes. Transfer to a bowl and let cool. Stir in the mustard. Add the bread crumbs and thyme, season with salt and pepper and toss well.

2. In a saucepan, bring the wine to a boil with the bay leaves. Add the mussels, cover and cook over high heat until they open, 1 to 2 minutes. Transfer to a bowl; strain the cooking liquid into a cup and add a pinch of salt. Set the mussels on the half shell on a baking sheet; discard the empty shells.

3. Set the clams on the half shell on a baking sheet. Put a shrimp in each empty clam shell and arrange on a baking sheet. Spoon ¼ teaspoon of the mussel liquid over each mussel, clam and shrimp. Mound 2 teaspoons of bread crumbs on the seafood in each shell.

4. Position 2 sheets of shellfish on a rack in the upper third of the oven and bake for 5 minutes, or until browned. Repeat with the third sheet. Serve immediately. —*Marcia Kiesel*

VARIATION Spread the steamed mussels and raw clams and shrimp in a gratin dish. Sprinkle with the seasoned bread crumbs and bake at 500° until browned. Toss with cooked linguine, olive oil and some of the mussel liquid.

WINE Dry, rich Champagne.

Grilled Oysters Casino

12 SERVINGS ● ● ●

Oysters add a twist to the eastern seaboard classic clams Casino. Have your fishmonger shuck them for you.

- 24 shucked oysters, on the half shell
- 4 thick slices of smoky bacon
- 2 tablespoons unsalted butter
- ¼ cup finely diced red bell pepper

¼ cup finely diced green bell pepper
¼ cup finely diced onion
Salt and freshly ground pepper
1 tablespoon chopped
  flat-leaf parsley
Lemon wedges, for serving

1. Arrange the oysters on a large baking sheet and refrigerate. In a medium skillet, cook the bacon over moderate heat, turning occasionally, until crisp, about 5 minutes. Transfer to paper towels to drain, then cut crosswise into 1-inch lengths.

2. Melt the butter in a saucepan. Add the bell peppers and onion; cook over moderately high heat, stirring often, until softened, 5 minutes. Season with salt and pepper and stir in the parsley. Let cool slightly, spoon over the oysters and top with the bacon.

3. Light a grill or preheat the oven to 500°. Using tongs, transfer the oysters to the grate and grill over a moderately low fire for 7 to 10 minutes, or until just cooked through. Alternatively, roast the oysters on a baking sheet in the oven. Transfer to a platter and serve at once with lemon wedges.
—*David Page and Barbara Shinn*

MAKE AHEAD The recipe can be made through Step 2 and chilled for 5 hours.
WINE Dry, light, crisp Champagne.

Escargots in Herbed Cream
4 SERVINGS

For a more rustic version of this dish, serve the snails with a warm baguette instead of in the puff pastry shells.

4 frozen puff pastry shells, thawed
2 tablespoons unsalted butter
2 large shallots, minced
½ cup minced flat-leaf parsley
½ cup minced cilantro
¼ cup minced chives
2 tablespoons minced tarragon
Salt and freshly ground pepper
Two 7-ounce cans large snails
  (about 3 dozen), rinsed
½ cup dry white wine
1 cup heavy cream

1. Preheat the oven to 400°. Set the pastry shells on a baking sheet and bake in the center of the oven for about 25 minutes, or until puffed and browned. Cut out the scored tops and reserve. Scoop out any unbaked dough and bake the shells for 10 minutes longer. Transfer to a rack and let cool.

2. Meanwhile, melt the butter in a large skillet. Add the shallots and cook over low heat until softened but not browned, about 4 minutes. Add the parsley, cilantro, chives and tarragon, season with salt and pepper and cook over moderate heat until fragrant, about 3 minutes. Add the snails and cook for 1 minute. Add the wine and simmer for 3 minutes. Add the cream and simmer until thickened, about 5 minutes. Season with salt and pepper.

3. Spoon the snails and their sauce into the puff pastry shells, top with the lids and serve. —*Chantal Leroux*

MAKE AHEAD The snails can be prepared 1 hour ahead and gently reheated.
WINE Subtle, complex white Burgundy.

Steamed Mussels with Smoky Bacon
4 SERVINGS ● ●

¼ pound thick-sliced lean smoked
  bacon, cut into ½-inch pieces
2 large shallots, thinly sliced
1 large jalapeño, thinly sliced
  crosswise, with seeds
Salt and freshly ground pepper
½ pound plum tomatoes,
  coarsely chopped
½ cup dry white wine
2 tablespoons ketchup
3½ pounds medium mussels,
  scrubbed and debearded
2 tablespoons fresh lime juice
2 tablespoons unsalted butter
¼ cup chopped cilantro
Crusty bread, for serving

1. In a large enameled cast-iron casserole, cook the bacon over moderate heat until crisp, about 8 minutes. Pour off all but 2 tablespoons of the fat.

Add the shallots and jalapeño, season with salt and pepper and cook, stirring occasionally, until softened but not browned, about 4 minutes. Add the tomatoes and cook for 3 minutes. Add the wine and ketchup and simmer until reduced by half, about 4 minutes. Increase the heat to high and add the mussels. Cover and cook, shaking the pan a few times, until the mussels open, about 5 minutes. Discard any mussels that do not open.

2. With a slotted spoon, transfer the cooked mussels to 4 large shallow serving bowls. Remove the casserole from the heat and stir in the lime juice, butter and cilantro until the butter is melted. Ladle the sauce over the mussels and serve at once with bread.
—*Michael Romano*

Spicy Mussels with Ginger and Lemongrass
4 SERVINGS ● ●

2 tablespoons canola oil
2 tablespoons finely grated
  peeled fresh ginger
2 tablespoons minced fresh
  lemongrass, tender inner
  white bulb only
1 jalapeño, partially seeded
  and minced
2½ pounds mussels, preferably
  from New Zealand, scrubbed
  and debearded
¼ cup water
1 teaspoon light brown sugar
1 teaspoon Asian fish sauce
1 teaspoon unsalted butter
2 tablespoons minced cilantro

1. Heat the canola oil in a large, deep skillet. Add the ginger, lemongrass and jalapeño and cook over high heat until fragrant, about 1 minute. Add the mussels and water and toss to coat. Cover and cook, shaking occasionally, until the mussels open, about 5 minutes. Using a slotted spoon, transfer the mussels to a large, deep bowl; discard any mussels that do not open.

2. Carefully pour any accumulated mussel liquid back into the skillet. Stir in the brown sugar, Asian fish sauce, unsalted butter and minced cilantro. Pour the pan sauce over the steamed mussels and serve immediately.

—*Annabel Langbein*

SERVE WITH Crusty bread, steamed spinach and lime wedges.

WINE Lively, assertive Sauvignon Blanc.

Tuna Carpaccio with Citrus-Ginger Dressing

4 SERVINGS ● ●

Look for the freshest sushi-grade tuna available to make this raw dish.

- ½ cup fresh orange juice
- 1 tablespoon plus 1 teaspoon fresh lemon juice
- 1½ teaspoons red wine vinegar
- 1 teaspoon soy sauce
- 1 tablespoon minced jalapeño
- 1 teaspoon finely grated fresh ginger
- 2 tablespoons plus 1 teaspoon extra-virgin olive oil

Salt and freshly ground pepper

- 1 tablespoon sesame seeds

One 8-ounce sushi-grade tuna fillet, cut ½ inch thick

- 4 large radishes, sliced paper-thin

I. In a saucepan, combine the orange and lemon juices and boil over high heat until reduced to ⅓ cup, about 7 minutes. Transfer to a bowl; let cool.

---

cooking tip

slicing tuna

SLICING RAW TUNA NEATLY CAN BE A HARD TASK TO PULL OFF—the flesh is tender and difficult to work with. One trick is to freeze the fish first, which hardens it enough to make slicing (or dicing) much easier. Then refrigerate the tuna to bring it back to the right temperature before serving.

Stir in the vinegar, soy sauce, jalapeño and ginger. Whisk in the olive oil and season with salt and pepper.

2. In a small, dry skillet, toast the sesame seeds over moderately high heat, shaking the pan frequently, until golden, 2 to 3 minutes.

3. Cut the tuna into 4 equal pieces. Place 1 piece of tuna between 2 sheets of plastic and pound to a ⅛-inch thickness. Remove the top sheet of plastic and invert the tuna onto a plate. Repeat with the remaining tuna.

4. Stir the dressing and spoon it over the tuna. Garnish with the radishes and sesame seeds and serve.

—*Terrance Brennan*

Ten-Minute Smoked Salmon with Avocado-Radish Salad

6 SERVINGS ● ● ●

This recipe uses a superquick method for hot-smoking; it cooks and smokes fish fillets in just 10 minutes. You can serve this smoked salmon hot off the grill, at room temperature or even chilled the next day. Try hot-smoking fillets from other rich, oily fish, such as bluefish, bonito and Spanish mackerel, for equally good results.

- 2 tablespoons soy sauce
- 1 tablespoon mustard
- 1 teaspoon sugar

One 1¼-pound center-cut skinless salmon fillet, cut crosswise into 6 portions

- 1 cup small hardwood chips, such as hickory or apple
- 4 woody herb stems and sprigs, such as rosemary, thyme or winter savory
- ¼ cup mayonnaise
- 1 tablespoon fresh lime juice

Salt and freshly ground pepper

- 6 radishes, thinly sliced
- 2 medium cucumbers—peeled, halved, seeded and thinly sliced
- 1 avocado—peeled, pitted and cut into 1-inch slices
- ½ small red onion, thinly sliced

I. In a shallow glass baking dish, blend the soy sauce with the mustard and sugar. Add the salmon and turn to coat. Refrigerate for 2 to 3 hours.

2. Light a grill. If using charcoal, scatter the wood chips and herbs over the coals. If using a gas grill, place the wood chips and herbs in a smoker box or scatter over the heat bars. Place a large double layer of foil over the center of the grill. Arrange the salmon pieces on the foil. Cover the grill and smoke the salmon until just cooked through, about 10 minutes.

3. In a large bowl, mix the mayonnaise with the lime juice and season with salt and pepper. Gently fold in the radishes, cucumbers, avocado and onion.

4. Using thick oven mitts, carefully lift the foil from the grill. With a thin spatula, transfer the salmon to plates and serve with the avocado-radish salad.

—*Marcia Kiesel*

MAKE AHEAD The hot-smoked salmon can be refrigerated overnight.

WINE Dry, medium-bodied Pinot Gris.

Citrus-Marinated Scallops and Roasted Red Pepper

6 SERVINGS ●

- 18 ounces sea scallops, cut into ¾-inch dice
- ¼ cup fresh lemon juice
- 3 tablespoons fresh grapefruit juice
- 3 tablespoons fresh orange juice
- 2 tablespoons grapeseed oil
- 1 tablespoon almond or hazelnut oil
- 1 Thai chile or jalapeño, seeded and minced

Salt and freshly ground pepper

- 1 red bell pepper

I. In a medium bowl, toss the scallops with the citrus juices, grapeseed and almond oils and chile and season lightly with salt and pepper. Cover and refrigerate until the scallops are opaque, 45 minutes to 1 hour.

2. Meanwhile, roast the bell pepper directly over a gas flame or under the broiler, turning, until charred all over.

Transfer the pepper to a bowl, cover and let steam for 10 minutes. Peel the pepper and cut it into ½-inch dice.

3. Add the roasted pepper to the scallops, season with salt and pepper and stir. Serve the scallops in large spoons, small bowls or scallop shells set on a bed of ice. —*Jean-Georges Vongerichten*

WINE Lively, assertive Sauvignon Blanc.

Sea Scallop Tiradito

8 SERVINGS ● ●

Tiradito is a Peruvian seviche-style dish. This version is extremely simple but requires the freshest scallops you can find. The rocoto chili paste called for here is a South American specialty, but any chili paste will do.

- 12 large diver scallops
- 1 tablespoon vegetable oil
- Chili paste, preferably rocoto
- 24 small cilantro leaves
- 1 teaspoon fresh lemon juice
- Sea salt

Cut each scallop in half horizontally. Set a large skillet over high heat for 3 minutes. Add the vegetable oil and heat until smoking. Add the scallop slices to the skillet and sear for 1 minute. Arrange 3 scallop slices, seared side up, on each plate, overlapping them slightly. Garnish each slice with a dot of chili paste and a cilantro leaf. Sprinkle the scallops with the lemon juice and sea salt and serve immediately. —*Nobu Matsuhisa*

Saffron Shrimp and Stuffed Cherry Peppers

4 SERVINGS

- ½ cup dry white wine
- ½ cup water
- 2½ tablespoons extra-virgin olive oil
- Large pinch of saffron threads
- Kosher salt
- 1 pound medium shrimp, shelled and deveined
- 2 anchovy fillets, minced
- 2 small garlic cloves, minced
- Freshly ground pepper

TUNA CARPACCIO WITH CITRUS-GINGER DRESSING

CITRUS-MARINATED SCALLOPS AND ROASTED RED PEPPER

ROASTED PEPPERS STUFFED WITH TUNA AND CAPERS

WARM WHITE BEAN AND CALAMARI SALAD

16 mildly hot Italian red
     cherry peppers
½ cup fresh corn kernels
1 large egg
1 large egg yolk
¼ cup heavy cream
¼ cup milk
3 tablespoons grated
     Manchego cheese

I. MAKE THE SAFFRON SHRIMP:
In a large saucepan, combine the wine, water and olive oil. Crumble in the saffron, add a pinch of salt and bring to a boil. Add the shrimp and simmer over moderate heat for 2 minutes. Transfer the shrimp to a shallow baking dish and let cool. Simmer the cooking liquid until reduced to ¾ cup, about 12 minutes; let cool slightly. Stir in the anchovies and garlic and season with salt and pepper. Pour the cooking liquid over the shrimp and refrigerate for 2 to 3 hours.

2. MAKE THE STUFFED PEPPERS:
Preheat the oven to 350°. Cut the tops off the cherry peppers and reserve; remove the seeds and membranes. Season the insides of the peppers with salt and turn upside down to drain on paper towels for 10 minutes.

3. In a small saucepan, boil the corn kernels in water until almost tender, about 3 minutes; drain. In a bowl, whisk the whole egg with the yolk and ½ teaspoon of salt. Whisk in the cream and milk, then whisk in the grated cheese.

4. On a baking sheet, add a teaspoon of the corn to each pepper, then fill with the custard. Bake for 30 minutes, or until set. Serve the peppers warm with the reserved tops and the shrimp.
—*Marcia Kiesel*

SERVE WITH Manchego cheese, green olives, Serrano ham and bread.
WINE Tangy, crisp Vernaccia.

Piquillo Peppers Stuffed with Shrimp and Wild Mushrooms
4 SERVINGS ● ●

Piquillos (slightly sweet and spicy roasted peppers) are most typically used in Basque cuisine, where they are stuffed with pureed salt cod and served with a rich cream sauce. The recipe here, however, was inspired by the cooking of the non-Basque parts of Rioja, where these delicate peppers are often filled with a creamy shrimp-and-mushroom stuffing and served with a quick and rustic tomato sauce. The best-quality jarred piquillos are available at specialty markets. For firmer peppers, look for brands packed only in salt and water, with no added citric acid.

¼ cup extra-virgin olive oil, plus
     more for brushing
5 garlic cloves, 3 minced
     and 2 thinly sliced

1 small onion, minced

1 pound oyster mushrooms, stems discarded and large mushrooms halved

Salt and freshly ground pepper

½ pound medium shrimp— shelled, deveined and cut into ½-inch pieces

2 tablespoons all-purpose flour

¾ cup whole milk

2 tablespoons chopped flat-leaf parsley

2 tablespoons fine, dry bread crumbs

1½ teaspoons sweet pimentón (see Note)

2 large egg yolks

8 large piquillo peppers from a jar, drained

½ pound plum tomatoes, finely chopped

1. Preheat the oven to 350°. Lightly brush a medium shallow baking dish with olive oil. In a large skillet, heat 3 tablespoons of the olive oil. Add the minced garlic and the onion and cook over moderately low heat, stirring occasionally, until softened, about 4 minutes. Add the mushrooms and season with salt and pepper. Cover and cook over moderately low heat until softened and just golden, about 7 minutes. Add the shrimp and cook, stirring, just until opaque, about 2 minutes. Stir in the flour and then the milk and bring to a simmer, stirring constantly, until smooth. Stir in the parsley, bread crumbs and pimentón and season with salt and pepper. Stir in the egg yolks and remove from the heat. Continue to stir until the egg yolks are fully incorporated and the stuffing is thick, 1 to 2 minutes. Let cool.

2. Make a lengthwise slit down one side of each piquillo pepper. On a work surface, spread open the peppers and spoon the shrimp-and-mushroom stuffing into the center of each, overfilling them slightly. Close the pepper around the stuffing, as neatly as possible.

Transfer the stuffed piquillo peppers to the prepared baking dish, seam side down, and bake for about 15 minutes, or until they are heated through.

3. Meanwhile, in a small skillet, heat the remaining 1 tablespoon of olive oil. Add the sliced garlic and cook over low heat until golden, about 3 minutes. Add the tomatoes and cook over moderate heat, stirring occasionally, until a thick sauce forms, about 12 minutes. Season with salt and pepper.

4. Using a spatula, carefully transfer the stuffed piquillos to plates. Spoon the tomato sauce over them and serve. —*Joseph Jiménez de Jiménez*

NOTE Pimentón, smoked Spanish paprika, is available at specialty food stores in sweet and hot varieties.

MAKE AHEAD The unbaked stuffed peppers can be refrigerated overnight. Bring to room temperature before baking.

WINE Bright, fruity rosé.

Roasted Peppers Stuffed with Tuna and Capers

8 SERVINGS ● ●

Instead of serving a whole stuffed pepper per person, which would be too daunting for an hors d'oeuvre, Giorgio Rivetti makes petite portions by cutting the peppers in half and wrapping them around the tuna stuffing.

8 medium red and yellow bell peppers

¾ cup mayonnaise

4 anchovy fillets, minced

3 tablespoons chopped capers

2 tablespoons chopped flat-leaf parsley

2 teaspoons white wine vinegar

Two 6-ounce cans Italian tuna in olive oil, drained and flaked

Salt and freshly ground pepper

Extra-virgin olive oil, for drizzling

1. Preheat the oven to 450°. Put the bell peppers on a baking sheet and roast in the upper third of the oven until charred all over and just tender. Let cool slightly, then peel, halve, core and seed them.

2. In a medium bowl, blend the mayonnaise with the anchovy fillets, capers, chopped parsley and vinegar. Using a rubber spatula, gently fold in the flaked tuna until combined. Season the tuna stuffing with salt and pepper.

3. Lay open the roasted pepper halves skinned side down on a work surface. Spread 2 tablespoons of the tuna stuffing on each one and roll up the peppers. Transfer the pepper rolls to a serving platter, drizzle with olive oil and serve. —*Giorgio Rivetti*

MAKE AHEAD The recipe can be prepared through Step 2 and refrigerated overnight; refrigerate the peppers and stuffing separately. Stuff the peppers with the tuna just before serving.

Warm White Bean and Calamari Salad with Garlic Bruschetta

8 SERVINGS ● ●

Italian heirloom cannellini beans, as well as over 20 other varieties, can be ordered through Beppe chef Cesare Casella's Republic of Beans Web site, www.trulytuscan.com.

2 cups dried cannellini or Great Northern beans (about ¾ pound), soaked overnight in cold water and drained

3 garlic cloves, lightly smashed

Salt

¼ cup extra-virgin olive oil, plus more for drizzling

---

cooking tip

buying squid

WHEN BUYING SQUID (calamari) for the *White Bean and Calamari Salad* on this page, look for those that are small and whole with bright eyes and a good smell. Squid is inexpensive and cooks quickly, making it a great seafood for weeknight meals. It can be refrigerated, airtight, for up to 2 days.

first courses

1¼ pounds cleaned small squid,
     bodies cut into ½-inch rings,
     tentacles cut into 1-inch pieces
12 large sage leaves, chopped
One 28-ounce can peeled Italian plum
     tomatoes—drained, seeded
     and chopped
½ teaspoon crushed red pepper
1 tablespoon finely chopped
     flat-leaf parsley
Toasted slices of country bread,
     rubbed with garlic and olive oil

1. In a large saucepan, cover the beans with 2 quarts of water and add the garlic. Bring to a boil, then cook the beans over moderate heat until barely tender, about 30 minutes. Season with salt. Continue cooking the beans until tender, about 10 minutes. Drain the beans; reserve 1½ cups of their cooking liquid. Discard the garlic.

2. Meanwhile, in a large, deep skillet, heat ¼ cup of the olive oil until shimmering. Add the squid and sage and cook over moderate heat, stirring occasionally, until the squid whitens, about 5 minutes. Add the tomatoes and crushed red pepper and season with salt. Cook over moderately low heat, stirring occasionally, until the sauce is slightly thickened, 20 minutes. Add the beans and their reserved cooking liquid and simmer until the squid is tender and the sauce becomes a thick gravy, about 10 minutes longer. Stir in the chopped parsley.

3. Arrange the garlic-rubbed bruschetta on plates and spoon the bean and squid salad on top. Drizzle with olive oil and serve hot, warm or at room temperature. Alternatively, spoon the salad onto plates, drizzle with oil and serve with the garlic bruschetta alongside.
—*Cesare Casella*

MAKE AHEAD The bean and squid salad can be prepared through Step 2 and refrigerated overnight. Reheat the salad gently over moderately low heat, adding a few tablespoons of water before serving if it appears dry.

Grilled Antipasto with Garlicky Bean Dip

6 SERVINGS ● ○

Served with grilled country bread, this antipasto easily becomes a light main course. The bocconcini should be eaten hot off the grill, while still soft enough to spread on the bread. To prevent sticking, lightly oil the grate before grilling the bocconcini.

One 19-ounce can cannellini beans,
     drained and rinsed
2 small garlic cloves, minced
2 tablespoons fresh lemon juice
2 tablespoons extra-virgin olive oil,
     plus more for brushing
½ cup chopped basil
Salt and freshly ground pepper
6 small Italian frying peppers or
     Cubanelle peppers
4 medium zucchini, cut lengthwise
     into ¼-inch-thick slices
Two 1-pound eggplants, cut
     lengthwise into ½-inch-
     thick slices
2 dozen anchovy fillets
2 dozen marinated bocconcini
     (about ¾ pound)
2 large beefsteak tomatoes
     (1 pound each), cut crosswise
     into ½-inch-thick slices
Grilled country bread, for serving

1. In a food processor, combine the beans with the garlic, lemon juice and 2 tablespoons of the olive oil. Process until smooth, then scrape into a bowl. Fold in the basil and season with salt and pepper.

2. Light a grill. Brush the peppers and the zucchini and eggplant slices with olive oil and season with salt and pepper. Wrap an anchovy fillet around each of the bocconcini and thread the balls onto six 8-inch skewers.

3. Grill the frying peppers and the sliced zucchini and eggplant over a medium-hot fire until lightly charred and tender, about 2 minutes per side for the zucchini and 4 minutes per side for the peppers and the eggplant slices. Trans-fer the grilled vegetables to a large platter and spread the bean dip on the zucchini and eggplant slices.

4. Lightly brush the tomato slices with olive oil and season with salt and pepper. Grill until tender, about 1 minute per side. Transfer the tomatoes to the platter. Lightly oil the grate. Grill the skewered bocconcini for 1 minute, turning once, or just until beginning to melt; transfer the skewers to the platter. Serve the antipasto with the remaining white bean dip and the grilled bread.
—*Marcia Kiesel*

MAKE AHEAD The white bean dip can be covered and refrigerated overnight.
WINE Lively, assertive Sauvignon Blanc.

Peruvian Bean Cakes with Cucumber-Radish Salad

4 SERVINGS

Dried, peeled fava beans are available at Middle Eastern markets, or you can substitute another ½ cup of chickpeas for the fava beans.

½ cup dried chickpeas, soaked
     overnight in cold water
     and drained
6 cups water
4 bay leaves
½ cup dried, split and peeled
     fava beans
¼ cup plus 1 tablespoon
     vegetable oil
1 medium yellow onion,
     finely chopped
1 jalapeño, seeded and minced
1 tablespoon minced garlic
1 teaspoon ground cumin
1 teaspoon turmeric
3 tablespoons whole milk
Salt and freshly ground pepper
3 tablespoons extra-virgin olive oil
2 tablespoons fresh lemon juice
8 red radishes, thinly sliced
1 large cucumber—peeled,
     halved lengthwise, seeded
     and cut crosswise into
     ¼-inch-thick slices
½ small red onion, thinly sliced

In France, the role of the affineur, or cheese ager, is considered to be as essential as that of the cheesemaker. "To put it at its most basic, the cheesemaker makes the cheese, while the affineur gives it taste," says Bernard Antony, affineur to many Michelin three-star chefs. Here's a look at his craft and a crash course on cheese basics.

Every Cheese Has Its Season

The raw material for cheese is, of course, milk. "Cheese is seasonal, just like most agricultural products," Antony explains. "The best cheeses come from cows that graze on the first grass of spring and the last grass of fall. Winter milk from stabled, hay-fed animals makes for less flavorful cheese. The most delicious exception is Vacherin Mont d'Or, which is at its peak in January and February." To ensure quality, the French government has passed laws regulating the months during which certain kinds of cheese can be made. For instance, producers can make Salers, a huge semifirm cow's-milk cheese, only from May until late September, when the milk tastes of the mountain flowers that grow in the Massif Central.

Class Consciousness

There's no legal classification for cheeses, but affineur Pierre Androuët helps educate his clients by grouping cheeses into families. Fresh cheeses are simply uncooked and unaged curd that may be molded into shapes (for example, fresh goat cheese) or left loose (cottage cheese). Having been sprayed with or exposed to mold, bloomy-rind cheeses are white and velvety on the outside and ripen from the rind inward (Camembert). Washed-rind cheeses have been washed or rubbed and are often strong, with an orangey crust (Reblochon). Natural-rind cheeses have not been sprayed with mold or washed (Morbier). Blue cheeses are marbled with blue or green mold (Roquefort). Uncooked, pressed cheeses are made from curd that has been pressed in molds in order to expel the whey (Mimolette). Cooked, pressed cheeses are made from curd that has been heated and then pressed (Gruyère).

Age Matters

How long do you age a cheese? "Until it is ready," says Pascal Vittu, the cheese sommelier at Daniel. The affineur will know exactly when a cheese is at the peak of its flavor and texture and is ready to consume. For example, at twelve months Mimolette, a firm, Edam-like cow's-milk cheese from the north of France, is an unassuming little cheese, perfect as a salad garnish. Allow it to age for 24 months, however, and it develops a caramel-like richness and texture, with all the complexity to stand up to an equally complex red wine. A Brie or a Camembert, on the other hand, might be as good as it will ever be after one or two months.

The Perfect Cheese Plate

The traditional cheese plate contains a cross section of types, from mild to sharp and simple to complex, including cow, sheep and goat varieties. Vittu typically selects four or five cheeses from Pierre Androuët's major families. Antony takes a contrarian view: "The essential point is perfect maturation and the order in which the cheeses are eaten," he says. "It is possible to serve a single cheese or a selection of cheeses from the same family—at different ages, perhaps, or from different producers."

Wine Pairing

When it comes to matching wine with cheese, the rule used to be that if you were going to serve one bottle, it should be a full-bodied red. Pascal Vittu, who makes pairing suggestions thousands of times a year, agrees that for the strongest and most pungent cheeses, red is often the best choice. But the tannins in red wine can overwhelm more delicate cheeses. "Most of the time, a white wine goes better," Vittu says. "The freshness of a Sauvignon Blanc, for instance, is nice with a simple, gentle-tasting cheese, like a chèvre."

¼ cup mint leaves
¼ cup crumbled feta cheese,
preferably French
Roasted Pepper–Caper Aioli
(p. 325)

1. In a saucepan, combine the chick-peas with 4 cups of the water and 2 of the bay leaves and bring to a boil. Reduce the heat to low and simmer until tender, about 50 minutes. In another saucepan, combine the favas with the remaining 2 cups of water and 2 bay leaves and bring to a boil. Reduce the heat to low and simmer until the favas are tender, about 30 minutes.

2. Drain the chickpeas and fava beans and let cool. Discard the bay leaves. In a food processor, combine the beans and pulse them until coarsely ground.

3. In a medium saucepan, heat ¼ cup of the vegetable oil. Add the yellow onion and cook over moderate heat until softened, about 5 minutes. Add the jalapeño and garlic and cook, stir-ring, until fragrant, about 3 minutes longer. Add the cumin and turmeric and cook for 3 minutes. Stir in the beans and milk and season with salt and pep-per. Remove from the heat and let cool. Form into eight ¼-inch-thick patties.

4. In a large, nonstick skillet, heat the remaining 1 tablespoon of vegetable oil. Add the bean cakes and cook over moderate heat until browned, about 3 minutes per side. Drain on paper towels.

---

dictionary

greek cheese

KASSERI CHEESE (used in the *Red Pepper and Onion Tarts with Dates and Fried Cheese* on p. 36) is a sharp and salty Greek cheese that's made from sheep or goat's milk. Kasseri cheese is often used in saganaki, a traditional Greek appetizer, for which it's fried and served with pita bread.

---

5. In a medium bowl, whisk the olive oil with the lemon juice and season with salt and pepper. Add the radishes, cucumber, red onion, mint and feta and toss. Serve the bean cakes warm with the salad and pass the Roasted Pepper–Caper Aioli at the table.
—*Andrew DiCataldo*
MAKE AHEAD The bean mixture can be refrigerated for 3 days before frying.

Fontina-Taleggio Fonduta with Baked Potato Chips
4 SERVINGS ●
Melted cheese is fantastic in any form. Served in crocks with easy, homemade chips may be its best incarnation.

1 pound Yukon Gold potatoes, peeled and cut into ⅛-inch-thick slices on a mandoline
2 tablespoons extra-virgin olive oil
Salt and freshly ground pepper
5 ounces Fontina cheese, shredded (1 cup)
5 ounces Taleggio cheese, shredded (1 cup)
White truffle oil, for drizzling (optional)

1. Preheat the oven to 450°. Soak the potato slices in cold water for 5 min-utes. Drain the slices and pat dry with paper towels.

2. Transfer the potato slices to 2 large rimmed baking sheets and toss each batch with 1 tablespoon of the olive oil. Arrange the slices on the sheets side by side without overlapping and sea-son with salt and pepper. Bake for about 8 minutes, or until the potatoes begin to turn golden brown; as they brown, transfer the potato chips to a rack with a spatula.

3. Reduce the oven temperature to 350°. In a medium bowl, mix the shredded Fontina and Taleggio cheeses, then divide them among individual gratin dishes. Bake the cheese for about 7 minutes, or until bubbling. Drizzle with truffle oil and serve immediately with the baked potato chips.
—*Roberto Marchetti*

Fontina-Gorgonzola Fonduta
8 SERVINGS ●
The Rivetti family likes to serve this fonduta, the Piedmontese version of cheese fondue, with roasted potatoes and sautéed mushrooms as well as toasted bread.

1¾ pounds Italian Fontina cheese, rind discarded and cheese cut into ½-inch dice
4 tablespoons unsalted butter
4 large eggs, beaten
2 large egg yolks
1 cup milk
¼ pound Gorgonzola dolce cheese, crumbled
Grilled or toasted baguette slices, for serving

1. In a medium saucepan, bring 1 inch of water to a boil. In a medium stain-less steel bowl, combine the Fontina cheese with the butter, eggs, egg yolks, milk and Gorgonzola cheese.

2. Set the bowl over the saucepan and cook the fonduta mixture over low heat, stirring the cheeses constantly with a wooden spoon, until they are melted and smooth, about 10 minutes. Pour the fonduta into individual shallow bowls and serve at once with the grilled baguette slices alongside.
—*Giorgio Rivetti*

Alsatian Potato and Bacon Tart
MAKES ABOUT 24 SQUARES ● ●
6 ounces meaty slab or thick-cut bacon, cut into ¼-inch pieces
1 medium onion, thinly sliced
1 medium baking potato, peeled and coarsely shredded
2 teaspoons sherry vinegar
2 teaspoons snipped chives
1 teaspoon chopped sage
Salt and freshly ground pepper
½ pound homemade or prepared pizza or bread dough, thawed if frozen
¼ cup crème fraîche
⅛ teaspoon freshly grated nutmeg

1. Preheat the oven to 500°. In a large, heavy skillet, cook the bacon over moderate heat until lightly browned around the edges, about 3 minutes; drain. Add the onion to the skillet and cook over moderate heat until lightly browned, about 2 minutes. Add the potato and cook, stirring, for 3 minutes; add a little water to the pan if the potato begins to stick. Stir in the vinegar, chives and sage and season with salt and pepper; remove from the heat.

2. On a lightly floured surface, roll out the dough to a 10-by-13-inch rectangle. Transfer to a lightly floured baking sheet, stretching it back into the rectangle.

3. Stir the crème fraîche and nutmeg into the potato mixture and spread it over the dough, leaving a ½-inch border all around. Scatter the bacon on top. Bake the tart for 12 minutes, or until the edges are browned. Cut into squares and serve hot. —*Melissa Clark*
MAKE AHEAD The tart can be baked earlier in the day; reheat before serving.

Open-Face Onion, Goat Cheese and Pine Nut Tart

6 TO 8 SERVINGS ●

Don't be put off by the long list of ingredients. All of the elements of this delicious tart can be prepared ahead and then the tart can be assembled a few hours before serving. A handful of pitted small black olives can be scattered over the top of the tart before baking.

PASTRY

2 cups all-purpose flour
Pinch of salt
2 large egg yolks
3 tablespoons olive oil
4 tablespoons cold unsalted butter, cut into small pieces
5 tablespoons cold water

FILLING

1½ pounds yellow onions, very thinly sliced
3 tablespoons extra-virgin olive oil, plus more for brushing
1 pound Swiss chard

FONTINA-GORGONZOLA FONDUTA

ALSATIAN POTATO AND BACON TART

One 1-inch cinnamon stick

8 whole cloves

½ teaspoon ground ginger

½ teaspoon freshly grated nutmeg

¼ teaspoon freshly ground pepper

Salt

½ pound fresh goat cheese

8 ounces crème fraîche

¼ cup pine nuts

I. MAKE THE PASTRY: In a food processor, pulse the flour with the salt. Add the egg yolks and the olive oil and pulse until combined. Add the butter and continue pulsing just until the mixture resembles coarse meal. With the machine on, slowly add the water and process just until the dough comes together. Transfer the dough to a sheet of plastic wrap and pat it into a disk. Wrap the disk and refrigerate for at least 30 minutes.

2. MAKE THE FILLING: In a large skillet, stir the onions with 3 tablespoons of the olive oil until thoroughly coated. Cover and cook the onions over moderately low heat, stirring occasionally, until they are very soft, about 30 minutes. Reduce the heat to low if the onions begin to brown.

3. Uncover the skillet. Increase the heat slightly and continue cooking, stirring frequently, until the onions become a rich golden brown, about 30 minutes longer. Remove the skillet from the heat.

---

cooking tip

peeling roasted peppers

HERE'S AN EASY WAY TO GET THE SKIN OFF ROASTED PEPPERS. After roasting, place the peppers in a plastic bag to steam. Wait a half hour, then massage the peppers in the bag to remove the blackened skin and seeds. Take the peppers out of the bag.

---

4. Meanwhile, bring a large pot of water to a rolling boil. Strip the chard leaves from the ribs, leaving the leaves as intact as possible; reserve the ribs for another use. Blanch the chard leaves in the boiling water until softened, 1½ to 2 minutes. Drain the leaves and refresh them under cold running water. Drain again and pat thoroughly dry.

5. In a spice grinder, combine the cinnamon stick with the cloves, ginger, nutmeg and pepper and grind to a powder. Add 1¼ teaspoons of the spice mixture to the onions and stir until evenly incorporated; reserve the remaining mixture for another use. Season with salt.

6. In a small bowl, using a wooden spoon, lightly beat the goat cheese with the crème fraîche and 1 teaspoon of salt until smooth.

7. Preheat the oven to 400°. Set the disk of dough between 2 large sheets of wax paper and roll out to a 12-by-15-inch rectangle. Transfer the pastry to a 9-by-12-inch ceramic baking dish at least 1½ inches deep. Line the pastry with the chard leaves, allowing them to extend beyond the pastry overhang.

8. Using a spatula, spread the goat cheese mixture over the chard in an even layer. Spread the spiced onions over the cheese and sprinkle with the pine nuts. Fold the extended chard leaves and the pastry over the onion filling. Brush the pastry and the chard leaves with olive oil.

9. Bake the tart for about 40 minutes, or until the pastry is golden. Transfer to a rack and let cool for at least 30 minutes before serving warm or at room temperature. —*Kate Hill*

NOTE This savory onion tart can also be assembled and baked free-form on a large rimmed baking sheet.

MAKE AHEAD The recipe can be prepared through Step 6 up to 1 day ahead; refrigerate all of the components separately.

WINE Lively, assertive Sauvignon Blanc.

Red Pepper and Onion Tarts with Dates and Fried Cheese

8 SERVINGS

Slices of Halloumi, a slightly sweet cow's milk cheese from Cyprus, can be used instead of Greek Kasseri. Alternatively, you can sprinkle crumbled feta cheese over the individual pita tarts, although the texture will be different from the slightly springy, mozzarella-like Kasseri. For round tarts, use a biscuit cutter to stamp out circles from the pita breads before spreading them with the onion-pepper mixture.

2 tablespoons unsalted butter

2½ tablespoons extra-virgin olive oil

2 medium white onions, thinly sliced

Salt and freshly ground pepper

2 medium red bell peppers

2 Medjool dates, pitted and sliced

1 tablespoon sesame seeds, lightly toasted

½ teaspoon poppy seeds

2 large pocketless pita breads, lightly toasted

¼ pound Kasseri cheese, sliced ¼ inch thick and cut into sixteen ½-by-2-inch rectangles

½ cup all-purpose flour

I. In a deep, medium skillet, melt 1 tablespoon of the butter in 1 tablespoon of the olive oil. Add the onions and cook over high heat, stirring occasionally, until softened, about 5 minutes. Reduce the heat to moderately low and continue cooking, stirring occasionally, until the onions are browned, about 30 minutes; add a little water to the pan if the onions seem dry. Remove the pan from the heat and season the onions with salt and pepper.

2. Meanwhile, roast the red bell peppers directly over a gas flame or under the broiler until softened and charred all over. Transfer the peppers to a medium bowl, cover with plastic wrap and let stand for 15 minutes. Discard the peel, core and seeds from the peppers and cut them into ½-inch-wide strips.

Return the peppers to the bowl, add the dates, sesame, poppy seeds and ½ tablespoon of the olive oil and toss to combine. Season with salt and pepper.

3. Spread the sautéed onions on the toasted pitas and top with the red pepper mixture. Quarter the pitas and arrange on a platter.

4. Dredge the cheese in the flour and shake off any excess. In a medium nonstick skillet or grill pan, melt the remaining 1 tablespoon of butter in the remaining 1 tablespoon of oil. Fry the cheese over moderately high heat, turning once, until golden, 4 minutes. Top each tart with 2 pieces of fried cheese and serve. *—Ana Sortun*

Farmer's Salad with Bacon and Walnuts

4 SERVINGS ●

This salad often includes such lusty ingredients as smoked duck breast and sautéed chicken gizzard confit. By all means, add these mail-order specialties, available from D'Artagnan (800-327-8246), or try adding sautéed chicken livers.

- 6 ounces lean slab bacon, sliced ⅓ inch thick and cut into 1-inch sticks
- 2 slices firm white bread, cut into ½-inch cubes
- ½ cup coarsely chopped walnuts
- 2 tablespoons red wine vinegar
- 1 garlic clove, minced
- 2 tablespoons extra-virgin olive oil
- 1 tablespoon walnut oil

Salt and freshly ground pepper
- 4 cups mesclun (¼ pound)
- 12 cherry tomatoes, halved
- ¼ cup minced chives

1. Preheat the oven to 350°. In a medium skillet, cook the bacon over moderately low heat until lightly browned and crisp, about 8 minutes. Drain on paper towels.

2. Spread the bread cubes and walnuts on 2 baking sheets and bake for about 8 minutes, or until browned and crisp.

3. In a large salad bowl, whisk the vinegar with the garlic and olive and walnut oils; season with salt and pepper. Add the mesclun, tomatoes and chives and toss to coat. Add the bacon, croutons and walnuts, toss well and serve. *—Chantal Leroux*

Garlicky Marinated Eggplant

6 SERVINGS ● ●

- 3 narrow eggplants (¾ pound each), peeled and cut lengthwise into ¼-inch-thick slices

Kosher salt

About ⅔ cup pure olive oil
- 2 large garlic cloves, minced
- 2 tablespoons finely chopped mint
- 1 tablespoon finely chopped oregano
- 1½ tablespoons extra-virgin olive oil

1. Sprinkle the eggplant slices on both sides with 1 tablespoon of kosher salt. Arrange the slices on a wire rack set over a rimmed baking sheet and let stand for 30 minutes.

2. Blot the eggplant slices with paper towels. In a large nonstick skillet, heat 2 tablespoons of the pure olive oil until shimmering. Add 4 or 5 slices of eggplant and cook over high heat, turning occasionally, until tender and well browned, about 6 minutes. Transfer the eggplant to a wire rack lined with paper towels and blot off any excess oil. Repeat with the remaining eggplant slices and pure olive oil.

3. In a bowl, combine the garlic, mint, oregano and a pinch of salt. Arrange 4 eggplant slices in a layer in a small ceramic or glass dish. Sprinkle with 1 teaspoon of the herb mixture, then drizzle with 1 teaspoon of the extra-virgin olive oil. Repeat with the remaining eggplant, herbs and oil. Press a sheet of plastic directly on the eggplant; let stand at room temperature for at least 2 hours or refrigerate for up to 2 days. Let return to room temperature before serving. *—Benedetta Vitali*

SERVE WITH Crusty Italian bread.

Herbed Ricotta with Roasted Peppers

6 SERVINGS ●

It's essential to use fresh unsalted ricotta for Vitali's subtly spicy vegetarian antipasti.

- 3 medium red bell peppers
- 3 medium yellow bell peppers
- ½ cup extra-virgin olive oil
- 6 tablespoons finely chopped flat-leaf parsley
- 1 large garlic clove, minced

Salt and freshly ground pepper
- 1 pound fresh ricotta
- 1 tablespoon finely chopped mint leaves
- 1 tablespoon finely chopped jalapeño
- ½ teaspoon thyme leaves

Crusty bread, for serving

1. Preheat the oven to 425°. Set the peppers in a large roasting pan and roast for about 30 minutes, turning occasionally, until blackened in spots and softened. Transfer the peppers to a bowl, cover with plastic wrap and let stand for 30 minutes.

2. Peel, core and seed the peppers, then cut them into ½-inch-wide strips. In a bowl, toss the peppers with ¼ cup of the olive oil, 3 tablespoons of the parsley and half of the garlic; season with salt and pepper.

3. In a medium bowl, whisk the ricotta until creamy. Whisk in the remaining ¼ cup of olive oil, 3 tablespoons of parsley and half of the garlic along with the mint, jalapeño and thyme; season with salt and pepper.

4. Mound the herbed ricotta in the center of a plate. Arrange the pepper strips on top of and around the ricotta. Spoon the pepper juices on top and serve with crusty bread alongside.
—Benedetta Vitali

MAKE AHEAD The recipe can be prepared several hours ahead and refrigerated; refrigerate the peppers and ricotta separately. Bring to room temperature before finishing the dish.

OAK LEAF LETTUCE SALAD WITH CABRALES AND RED GRAPES, P. 40

salads

ARUGULA AND MINT SALAD

SUMMER GREENS AND HERBS WITH BEETS

Arugula and Mint Salad

6 SERVINGS ● ●

- ¼ teaspoon fennel seeds
- 1 tablespoon red wine vinegar
- ½ tablespoon Dijon mustard

Kosher salt and freshly
  ground pepper

- 2 tablespoons extra-virgin olive oil
- 4 cups curly green-leaf lettuce
- 4 cups young arugula leaves
- 20 mint leaves

In a mortar or spice grinder, coarsely grind the fennel seeds. In a small bowl, whisk the ground fennel with the red wine vinegar and Dijon mustard; season with salt and pepper. Gradually add the olive oil, whisking until the dressing is emulsified. In a bowl, toss the lettuce with the arugula and mint. Add the dressing and season with additional salt and pepper. Toss well and serve.
—*Amanda Hesser*

Oak Leaf Lettuce Salad with Cabrales and Red Grapes

8 SERVINGS ●

Any pungent blue cheese, such as Roquefort or Gorgonzola, can be substituted for the Spanish Cabrales cheese called for here. Chef Ben Ford likes to serve this salad European style, after the main course.

- ⅓ cup pine nuts
- 2 tablespoons sherry vinegar
- 2 tablespoons Shallot Confit (p. 128), plus 5 tablespoons of the reserved shallot oil
- 1 teaspoon honey
- ½ teaspoon kosher salt
- 1 pound red and green oak leaf lettuce (about 16 cups)
- 6 ounces Cabrales cheese, crumbled (1½ cups)
- 1½ cups seedless red grapes, halved

Freshly ground pepper

1. Preheat the oven to 350°. Spread the pine nuts in a metal pie plate and bake for about 8 minutes, or until lightly toasted. Transfer the pine nuts to a plate and let cool.

2. In a large bowl, whisk the vinegar with the Shallot Confit, honey and salt. Slowly whisk in the shallot oil until the dressing is emulsified. Add the lettuce, cheese and grapes and toss to coat. Season the salad with salt and pepper, sprinkle with the pine nuts and serve.
—*Ben Ford*

MAKE AHEAD The dressing can be refrigerated overnight.

Salade Guarnaschelli with Oregano Vinaigrette

6 SERVINGS ● ●

- ¼ cup plus 2 tablespoons extra-virgin olive oil
- 3 tablespoons balsamic vinegar

1 tablespoon red wine vinegar

2 garlic cloves, minced

1 tablespoon chopped oregano

Pinch of sugar

Salt and freshly ground pepper

2 Belgian endives, cored and cut crosswise ½ inch thick

1 head Boston lettuce, torn into bite-size pieces

1 small head radicchio, torn into bite-size pieces

In a large salad bowl, combine the olive oil with the balsamic and red wine vinegars, garlic, oregano and sugar. Season the vinaigrette with salt and pepper. Add the endives, lettuce and radicchio and toss to coat with the vinaigrette. Serve at once.

—*Maria Guarnaschelli*

Summer Greens and Herbs with Roasted Beets and Hazelnuts

4 SERVINGS

¾ pound medium red or golden beets (about 3), scrubbed

¼ cup unseasoned rice vinegar

2 tablespoons water

1 cup hazelnuts (about 4 ounces), lightly toasted

1 tablespoon simple syrup (see Note)

Sea salt and freshly ground pepper

Twelve ¼-inch-thick baguette slices

½ cup extra-virgin olive oil

¼ pound blue cheese, such as Roquefort, at room temperature

8 loosely packed cups mesclun (about 6 ounces)

¼ cup flat-leaf parsley leaves

3 tablespoons tarragon leaves

3 tablespoons chervil leaves

3 tablespoons snipped chives

1. Preheat the oven to 500°. In a small baking dish, toss the beets with 2 tablespoons of the vinegar and the water. Cover the dish with foil and bake for about 1 hour, or until tender. Let cool, then peel the beets and cut them into ¼-inch wedges. Reduce the oven temperature to 350°.

2. In a small bowl, toss the hazelnuts with the simple syrup and ¾ teaspoon each of salt and pepper. Transfer to a parchment-lined baking sheet and bake for 25 minutes, or until the syrup-covered nuts are shiny and dry. Let cool. Leave the oven on.

3. Brush both sides of the baguette slices with 2 tablespoons of the olive oil. Arrange on a baking sheet and bake for 10 minutes, or until lightly toasted. Let cool, then spread with the blue cheese.

4. In a large bowl, whisk the remaining 2 tablespoons of rice vinegar and 6 tablespoons of olive oil until blended. Season with salt and pepper. Add the mesclun, parsley, tarragon, chervil, chives, beets and hazelnuts and toss to coat. Transfer the salad to plates and serve with the Roquefort toasts.

—*Michael Leviton*

NOTE To make simple syrup, combine equal parts of sugar and water and simmer over moderate heat to dissolve the sugar. Refrigerate any leftover syrup.

WINE Soft, off-dry Riesling.

Arugula, Fennel and Dried Plum Salad

6 SERVINGS ● ○

¼ cup pine nuts

2 tablespoons balsamic vinegar

1 tablespoon red wine vinegar

¼ cup extra-virgin olive oil

Salt and freshly ground pepper

1 small head radicchio, leaves torn into 2-inch pieces

1 bunch arugula (4 ounces)

1 small fennel bulb—halved lengthwise, cored and sliced paper-thin crosswise

1 cup pitted dried plums (prunes), quartered

3 ounces fresh goat cheese, crumbled

1. In a small skillet, toast the pine nuts over moderate heat, shaking the pan, until golden brown, about 2 minutes; transfer to a plate to cool.

2. In a small bowl, whisk the balsamic and red wine vinegars with the olive oil; season with salt and pepper.

3. In a large bowl, toss the radicchio with the arugula, fennel, dried plums and pine nuts. Add the vinaigrette and toss. Transfer the salad to a platter, scatter the goat cheese on top and serve. —*Joanne Weir*

WINE Lively, assertive Sauvignon Blanc.

Spinach and Orange Salad with Parmesan Pecans

12 SERVINGS ● ○

2 cups pecan halves

2 tablespoons unsalted butter, melted

1 tablespoon honey

2 tablespoons freshly grated Parmesan cheese

Salt and freshly ground pepper

3 tablespoons fresh lemon juice

2 tablespoons minced shallots

1 tablespoon Dijon mustard

6 tablespoons extra-virgin olive oil

4 medium navel or blood oranges

1 pound baby spinach

1 cup Sicilian green olives, pitted and chopped

1. Preheat the oven to 375°. Toast the pecans on a baking sheet for 5 minutes. Transfer the nuts to a bowl, toss with the butter, honey, Parmesan and a generous pinch each of salt and pepper, then spread on the sheet and bake for 4 minutes, or until golden. Let cool.

2. In a small bowl, whisk the lemon juice with the shallots and mustard. Whisk in the oil and season with salt and pepper.

3. With a sharp knife, peel the oranges, removing all of the bitter white pith. Halve the oranges lengthwise, then slice crosswise ¼ inch thick.

4. In a large salad bowl, toss the baby spinach with the dressing, olives, pecans and oranges and serve at once.

—*Grace Parisi*

Parsley Salad

8 SERVINGS ● ●

- ¼ cup verjus (see Note)
- ¼ cup extra-virgin olive oil
- Pinch of crushed red pepper
- Salt and freshly ground black pepper
- 4 cups flat-leaf parsley leaves (from ½ pound of parsley)
- 2 medium tomatoes, diced
- 1 medium red onion, thinly sliced

In a large bowl, mix the verjus, olive oil and crushed red pepper. Season with salt and black pepper. Add the parsley, tomatoes and onion, toss and serve.
—*Paula Wolfert*

NOTE Verjus is the juice of unripened grapes. It's available at large supermarkets and specialty food shops.

Winter Vegetable Salad with Bagna Cauda Dressing

6 SERVINGS ●

- 18 baby carrots
- 2 medium fennel bulbs, cut into thin wedges
- ½ pound broccoli rabe, large stems discarded
- 5 tablespoons unsalted butter
- ½ cup extra-virgin olive oil
- 1 to 1½ tablespoons chopped anchovies
- 1 tablespoon minced garlic
- 1 teaspoon thyme leaves
- ¼ cup fresh lemon juice
- Salt and freshly ground pepper
- 1 medium red onion, thinly sliced
- 1 dried red chile, finely chopped
- 2 Belgian endives, separated into spears
- 18 small radishes with tops

1. In a large saucepan of boiling salted water, blanch the baby carrots for 2 minutes. Using a slotted spoon, transfer the carrots to a colander and refresh under cold running water. Drain the carrots well and transfer to a plate. Repeat the process with the fennel wedges and broccoli rabe.

2. In a small saucepan, melt the butter in ¼ cup plus 2 tablespoons of the olive oil. Add the chopped anchovies and cook over low heat, stirring, for 4 minutes. Add the garlic and ½ teaspoon of the thyme leaves and cook until the garlic is golden, about 3 minutes. Add the lemon juice and season with salt and pepper. Remove the bagna cauda dressing from the heat.

3. Heat the remaining 2 tablespoons of olive oil in a large skillet. Add the red onion, the remaining ½ teaspoon of thyme leaves and the red chile and cook over moderately high heat, stirring occasionally, just until the onion softens, about 2 minutes. Add the fennel wedges and broccoli rabe and cook, stirring, just until heated through, about 3 minutes longer. Stir in the bagna cauda dressing. Transfer the vegetables to a large shallow bowl. Add the carrots, endives and radishes. Season the winter vegetable salad with salt and pepper, toss well and serve.
—*Suzanne Goin*

SERVE WITH Mozzarella bruschetta.
WINE Dry, light, refreshing Soave.

Asparagus Salad with Roasted Peppers and Goat Cheese

8 SERVINGS ● ●

- 2 pounds medium asparagus, tough ends removed
- 2 red bell peppers
- 2 tablespoons white wine vinegar
- 2 tablespoons capers, drained
- 1 tablespoon Dijon mustard
- 2 teaspoons chopped tarragon or dill
- 1 garlic clove, very finely chopped
- ½ small red onion, finely chopped
- Salt and freshly ground pepper
- ¼ cup plus 2 tablespoons extra-virgin olive oil
- 2 ounces soft mild goat cheese
- 12 Niçoise or Calamata olives, pitted and chopped
- Shavings of Parmigiano-Reggiano cheese (optional)

1. In a large pot of boiling salted water, cook the asparagus until bright green and tender, about 3 minutes; transfer to a colander and refresh under cold water. Drain and pat dry.

2. Roast the peppers directly over a gas flame or under the broiler, turning, until charred all over. Transfer to a medium bowl, cover with plastic wrap and let steam for 10 minutes. Peel the peppers, discarding the cores and seeds, and cut them into ¼-inch-wide strips.

3. In a medium bowl, stir together the vinegar, capers, mustard, tarragon, garlic and onion; season with salt and pepper. Whisk in the olive oil.

4. Arrange the asparagus on a serving platter. Lay the roasted pepper strips over the asparagus and drizzle with half of the vinaigrette. Crumble the goat cheese on top. Garnish with the chopped olives and the Parmigiano shavings and serve, passing the remaining vinaigrette at the table. —*Gary Danko*

MAKE AHEAD The recipe can be prepared through Step 3 up to 8 hours ahead. Refrigerate the asparagus, peppers and vinaigrette separately.

─ *health note* ─

super spears

ASPARAGUS CAN GIVE OTHER PRODUCE AN INFERIORITY COMPLEX. Assistant professor of horticulture Anusuya Rangarajan of Cornell University explains that the stalks contain more of the antioxidant glutathione—one of the most potent cancer fighters around—than any fruit or any other vegetable. Asparagus is also a source of folic acid, a B vitamin that helps protect against cervical cancer, heart disease and some birth defects. In addition, it's low in calories, with only about four per spear. For maximum health benefits, Rangarajan advises, "Buy fresh and steam lightly."

ASPARAGUS SALAD WITH ROASTED PEPPERS AND GOAT CHEESE

ZUCCHINI CARPACCIO

"RED HOT" BEET SALAD WITH GOAT CHEESE TOASTS

Zucchini Carpaccio

4 SERVINGS ● ○

¼ cup extra-virgin olive oil
2 tablespoons fresh lemon juice
Salt and freshly ground pepper
1 pound small green and yellow zucchini, sliced ⅛ inch thick on the diagonal with a mandoline
1 bunch arugula (¼ pound), large stems discarded
1 ounce Parmesan, shaved (1 cup)

In a medium bowl, whisk the olive oil with the lemon juice and season with salt and pepper. Add the zucchini and toss well; let stand for 3 minutes. Arrange the zucchini slices, overlapping them slightly, on a platter. Add the arugula to the bowl and toss with the dressing, then mound on the zucchini. Scatter the Parmesan over the top and serve.
—*Jean-Georges Vongerichten*

Watercress and Mint Salad with Walnuts

8 SERVINGS ● ○

2 cups walnut halves
2 teaspoons ground cumin
2 teaspoons ground coriander
½ cup extra-virgin olive oil
¼ cup fresh lemon juice
2 large garlic cloves, minced
Salt and freshly ground pepper
1 pound watercress, stemmed
2 cups fresh mint leaves
Seeds from 1 large pomegranate

1. Preheat the oven to 350°. Spread out the walnuts on a small baking sheet and toast for about 10 minutes, or until lightly browned and fragrant.
2. In a small skillet, toast the cumin and coriander over moderate heat until fragrant, about 30 seconds. Transfer the spices to a small bowl to cool. Stir in the olive oil, lemon juice and garlic and season with salt and pepper.
3. In a large bowl, toss the watercress with the mint leaves, walnuts and the dressing. Sprinkle the pomegranate seeds over the salad and serve.
—*Marcia Kiesel*

"Red Hot" Beet Salad with Goat Cheese Toasts

4 SERVINGS ● ●

The fiery little candies called red hots inspired this salad, in which beets get spiked with cayenne pepper and sweetened with maple syrup.

- 8 medium beets (1¾ pounds), scrubbed
- 1 cup pure maple syrup
- 1¼ teaspoons cayenne pepper
- 2 tablespoons red wine vinegar
- 2 tablespoons extra-virgin olive oil
- 1 garlic clove, minced

Salt

- Twelve ¼-inch-thick baguette slices, toasted
- ½ cup fresh goat cheese (4 ounces)
- 1 teaspoon poppy seeds
- 4 heads Bibb lettuce (3 ounces each), leaves separated

ı. In a saucepan, cover the beets with water and bring to a boil. Simmer over moderate heat until tender, about 25 minutes. Transfer the beets to a plate and let cool, then peel and cut into ½-inch dice. Reserve 2 cups of the cooking liquid in the saucepan.

2. Add the maple syrup to the pan and boil over moderately high heat for 5 minutes. Stir in the beets and cayenne and simmer over moderate heat until the beets are sweet and hot, about 30 minutes. Using a slotted spoon, transfer the beets to a plate. Boil the cooking liquid until slightly thickened, about 8 minutes. Return the beets to the pan and let cool to room temperature.

3. In a small bowl, whisk 2 tablespoons of the beet syrup with the vinegar, olive oil and garlic and season with salt. Spread each toast with 2 teaspoons of goat cheese; sprinkle with poppy seeds.

4. In a bowl, toss the lettuce with the beets and vinaigrette. Mound the salad on plates, set the goat cheese toasts alongside and serve. —*Marcia Kiesel*

MAKE AHEAD The recipe can be prepared up to 1 day ahead through Step 2 and refrigerated.

Fennel and Bell Pepper Slaw

30 SERVINGS ● ● ●

- 1½ teaspoons caraway seeds
- ½ cup fresh lemon juice
- 1½ tablespoons sugar

Sea salt

- 6 large fennel bulbs—halved, cored and thinly sliced lengthwise
- 2 medium red bell peppers, very thinly sliced lengthwise
- 1 medium green bell pepper, very thinly sliced lengthwise

Freshly ground pepper

ı. In a small skillet, toast the caraway seeds over moderate heat, shaking the pan, until fragrant, about 2 minutes. Let cool, then coarsely grind.

2. Combine the lemon juice, sugar and a large pinch of salt. In a bowl, mix the fennel and peppers. Add the lemon juice mixture and caraway. Season with salt and pepper; serve. —*Jennifer Rubell*

MAKE AHEAD Refrigerate the dressing and vegetables separately overnight.

Tangy Broccoli Salad with Buttermilk Dressing

4 SERVINGS ●

- 1 small garlic clove, coarsely smashed

Kosher salt

- 2 teaspoons extra-virgin olive oil
- 2 teaspoons Dijon mustard
- ½ cup buttermilk
- ¾ teaspoon herbes de Provence

Freshly ground pepper

- 1 pound broccoli, cut into 1-inch florets, stems peeled and thinly sliced
- 4 ounces thickly sliced bacon, cut crosswise into ¼-inch strips
- 1 medium sweet onion, such as Vidalia or Walla Walla, halved lengthwise and thinly sliced crosswise
- ½ cup crumbled Roquefort cheese (about 2 ounces)

taste test balsamic vinegars		
PRODUCT	**F&W COMMENT**	**INTERESTING BITE**
Progresso $2	"Nice fruitiness. You can actually taste the grape here."	This low-cost American brand is made with selected grapes imported from Modena.
Villa Manodori $35	"Sweet and raisiny."	Modena chef Massimo Bottura blended balsamic vinegar with aged wine vinegar to create a vinegar specifically for use in cooking.
La Vecchia Dispensa Condimento Balsamico $39	"Smoky, oaky and full-bodied."	*Dispensa* means "cupboard" or "pantry" in Italian.

1. In a small bowl, mash the garlic with a large pinch of salt. Whisk in the olive oil and mustard, then whisk in the buttermilk in a thin stream. Add the herbes de Provence and a pinch of pepper and let the dressing stand for 30 minutes.
2. Meanwhile, steam the broccoli florets until crisp-tender, about 5 minutes. Plunge the florets into a bowl of ice water. Drain well and pat dry.
3. In a medium skillet, cook the bacon over moderately high heat until browned, about 5 minutes; drain.
4. In a large bowl, toss the broccoli florets and stems with the sliced onion and the dressing. Sprinkle with the Roquefort and bacon and serve.
—*Damon Lee Fowler*

Avocado Salad with Jalapeños
30 SERVINGS ● ◐

12 ripe Hass avocados—halved, pitted and cut into ½-inch wedges
6 tablespoons fresh lime juice
Salt and freshly ground pepper
1 cup cilantro leaves
3 large red or green jalapeños—stemmed, seeded and thinly sliced

Arrange the avocados on a large platter. Sprinkle with the lime juice and season with salt and pepper. Sprinkle with the cilantro and jalapeños and serve. —*Jennifer Rubell*

---

pantry news
true feta

GREECE, BULGARIA AND FRANCE ALL MAKE FETA CHEESE. Greek feta is salty and crumbly, while Bulgarian and French are creamy and less salty. The European Commission has ruled that only feta made in Greece can be labeled "feta"; the other countries have five years to rename their cheeses.

Autumn Salad of Persimmon, Pears, Grapes and Pecans
6 SERVINGS ●

½ cup pecan halves (2 ounces)
2 tablespoons sherry vinegar
1 tablespoon walnut or hazelnut oil
3 tablespoons extra-virgin olive oil
Salt and freshly ground pepper
2 small heads frisée (14 ounces), torn
1 Fuyu persimmon, thinly sliced crosswise
1 red Bartlett pear—halved, cored and thinly sliced
1 green pear, such as Anjou or Comice—halved, cored and thinly sliced
1 cup red seedless grapes
1 cup green seedless grapes

1. Preheat the oven to 375°. Spread the pecans in a pie plate and toast for 8 minutes, or until golden and fragrant. Let the nuts cool, then coarsely chop.
2. In a small bowl, whisk together the sherry vinegar, walnut oil and olive oil; season with salt and pepper.
3. In a large bowl, toss the frisée with the persimmon, pears and grapes. Add the vinaigrette and toss. Transfer the salad to a platter, garnish with the pecans and serve. —*Joanne Weir*

Grilled Red Onion, Celery and Parsley Salad
4 SERVINGS ● ● ●

3 tablespoons extra-virgin olive oil, plus more for brushing
2 medium red onions, thinly sliced, slices kept intact
6 tender inner celery ribs, thinly sliced
2 cups flat-leaf parsley leaves
2 tablespoons red wine vinegar
Salt and freshly ground pepper

1. Preheat a cast-iron grill pan or skillet and lightly brush with olive oil. Add the onion slices and cook over moderate heat, turning once, until lightly charred but still crisp-tender, about 5 minutes. Transfer to a bowl and let cool.

---

2. Add the celery and parsley to the onions and toss to separate the rings. In a small bowl, whisk the vinegar with the 3 tablespoons of olive oil and season with salt and pepper. Add the dressing to the salad, toss well and serve. —*Traci Des Jardins*

MAKE AHEAD The salad can be refrigerated for 2 hours. Serve cold or at room temperature.

Watermelon and Tomato Salad with Spicy Feta Sauce
8 SERVINGS ● ◐

Ana Sortun likes to blend sweet and spicy flavors, a combination she finds is a defining part of Arabic cuisine. Sortun's vegetarian watermelon salad with jalapeño-accented feta dressing exemplifies the hot-and-sweet mix.

1 large jalapeño
6 ounces feta cheese
¼ cup hot water
5 tablespoons extra-virgin olive oil
Salt and freshly ground pepper
Twelve ½-inch-thick wedges of seedless watermelon, rind removed
1 pint grape tomatoes, halved
1 tablespoon finely sliced basil

1. Roast the jalapeño directly over a gas flame or under the broiler until charred all over. Transfer to a bowl, cover with plastic and let stand for 10 minutes. Peel, stem and seed the jalapeño and transfer to a blender. Add the feta, hot water and ¼ cup of the olive oil and process until very smooth. Scrape the feta sauce into a bowl and season with salt and pepper.
2. Arrange the watermelon and tomatoes on a large platter, scatter the basil on top and drizzle with the remaining 1 tablespoon of olive oil. Season with salt and pepper; serve with the feta sauce. —*Ana Sortun*

MAKE AHEAD The spicy feta sauce can be stored in the refrigerator for up to 2 days. Let return to room temperature before serving.

WATERMELON AND TOMATO SALAD WITH SPICY FETA SAUCE

salads

Lemony Avocado and Celery Salad

12 SERVINGS ● ○

¼ cup plus 2 tablespoons extra-virgin olive oil

¼ cup fresh lemon juice

2 small garlic cloves, minced

Salt and freshly ground pepper

6 heads Bibb lettuce (1½ pounds), leaves separated

6 celery ribs, peeled and thinly sliced on the diagonal

4 avocados, cut into ¼-inch wedges

2 medium red or green bell peppers, cut into thin sticks

In a small bowl, whisk the olive oil with the lemon juice and garlic and season with salt and pepper. In a large bowl, toss the lettuce with half of the lemon dressing and mound the leaves on a platter. Add the celery, avocados, bell peppers and the remaining lemon dressing to the large bowl and toss to coat. Mound the dressed vegetables on the lettuce and serve.

—Bernardita Del Campo Correa

Heirloom Tomato Salad with Parmesan Anchovy Toasts

4 SERVINGS ● ○

1 pound heirloom tomatoes, cut into 1-inch wedges

¼ cup plus 2 tablespoons extra-virgin olive oil

2 tablespoons red wine vinegar

Salt and freshly ground pepper

1 bunch arugula (4 ounces)

Four ½-inch-thick slices of Tuscan or peasant bread

1 tablespoon anchovy paste

½ cup freshly grated Parmesan cheese

1. Preheat the broiler. In a large bowl, toss the tomato wedges with ¼ cup of the olive oil and the red wine vinegar. Season the tomatoes with salt and pepper. Add the arugula and toss again. Transfer the tomato salad to a large serving platter.

2. Set the bread slices on a small baking sheet and brush them all over with the remaining 2 tablespoons of olive oil. Broil the bread slices until golden, about 30 seconds. Flip the toasts, spread them with the anchovy paste and sprinkle them with the Parmesan cheese. Broil the toasts for about 1 minute, until the cheese is melted and lightly browned. Serve the toasts with the tomato salad. —Terrance Brennan

Farro Salad with Tomatoes and Herbs

12 SERVINGS ○ ●

Farro, an ancient Italian grain with a wonderfully chewy texture, is available at specialty shops and Italian markets.

1¼ pounds farro (about 3 cups)

2 quarts water

Salt

2 large garlic cloves, very finely chopped

¼ cup balsamic vinegar

½ cup extra-virgin olive oil

Freshly ground pepper

1¼ pounds tomatoes, seeded and chopped

1 medium sweet onion, such as Walla Walla, finely chopped

½ cup snipped chives

½ cup finely chopped flat-leaf parsley

1. In a large saucepan, cover the farro with the water and bring to a boil. Cover and simmer over moderately low heat until barely tender, about 20 minutes. Add 1 tablespoon of salt and simmer until tender, about 10 minutes longer. Drain well, then transfer to a large bowl and let cool.

2. In a medium bowl, mash the garlic with a pinch of salt until it becomes a puree. Whisk in the balsamic vinegar and then the olive oil. Season the dressing with pepper.

3. Add the tomatoes, onion, chives and parsley to the farro. Add the dressing, season with salt and pepper and toss, then serve. —Giada De Laurentiis

MAKE AHEAD The salad can be refrigerated overnight. Bring to room temperature before serving.

Garden Vegetable Panzanella

4 SERVINGS ● ○

This rustic Tuscan salad is used to rescue stale bread. Very fresh tomatoes, cucumber and bell pepper are the heroes here.

Three ½-inch-thick slices of Tuscan bread, crusts removed and bread cut into ½-inch dice (5 cups)

2 tablespoons red wine vinegar

Salt

¼ cup extra-virgin olive oil

Freshly ground pepper

3 medium tomatoes, cut into 1-inch pieces

1 small cucumber—peeled, seeded and cut into ½-inch pieces

½ medium red or yellow bell pepper, cut into ½-inch strips

1 celery rib, cut into ½-inch pieces

3 scallions, white and tender green parts only, thinly sliced

4 ounces button mushrooms, trimmed and thinly sliced (2 cups)

¼ cup torn basil leaves

1. Preheat the oven to 300°. Spread the bread on a baking sheet and toast for 10 minutes, or until dry but not browned. Let cool, then transfer to a large bowl.

2. In a small bowl, mix the vinegar with 1 teaspoon of salt until the salt dissolves. Slowly whisk in the olive oil and season with pepper.

3. Dip your fingers in water and flick them over the bread several times, tossing it with your hands until all the pieces are lightly moistened. Add the tomatoes, cucumber, bell pepper, celery, scallions, mushrooms and dressing and toss until evenly coated. Season the salad with salt and pepper, garnish with the basil and serve. —Pino Luongo

WINE Lively, assertive Sauvignon Blanc.

Chickpea Salad with Red Pepper Confetti

30 SERVINGS ● ● ●

Three 19-ounce cans of chickpeas,
    drained and rinsed
  4 small red bell peppers, minced
1¼ cups parsley leaves, chopped
1¼ cups cilantro leaves, minced
  5 teaspoons minced garlic
2½ teaspoons ground cumin
2½ tablespoons extra-virgin olive oil
  ¼ cup fresh lemon juice
Salt and freshly ground pepper

Toss all of the ingredients in a large
bowl and serve. —*Jennifer Rubell*

MAKE AHEAD The salad can be made up
to 6 hours ahead.

Roasted Leek and Potato Salad

4 SERVINGS ● ● ●

  4 medium leeks, white and
    tender green parts only,
    halved lengthwise
  1 pound fingerling or baby
    Yukon Gold potatoes,
    halved lengthwise
  ¼ cup plus 2 tablespoons
    extra-virgin olive oil
Salt and freshly ground pepper
  2 tablespoons red wine vinegar
  1 tablespoon plus 1 teaspoon
    whole-grain mustard
  2 teaspoons chopped
    drained capers
  2 cups mixed baby greens
  4 hard-cooked eggs, quartered or
    thickly sliced

I. Preheat the oven to 425°. On a large
rimmed baking sheet, toss the leeks
and potatoes with 2 tablespoons of oil;
season with salt and pepper. Arrange the
leeks and potatoes on the baking sheet,
cut side down, and roast on the bottom rack of the oven for 20 minutes,
or until the leeks are lightly browned
and tender. Transfer the leeks to a work
surface and cut them crosswise into 2-
inch lengths. Continue to roast the
potatoes for about 10 minutes longer,
or until they are browned and tender.

CHICKPEA SALAD WITH RED PEPPER CONFETTI

ROASTED LEEK AND POTATO SALAD

2. In a small bowl, whisk the remaining ¼ cup of oil with the vinegar, mustard and capers and season with salt and pepper. In a medium bowl, toss the greens with 1 tablespoon of the vinaigrette and arrange on 4 plates. Put the leeks and potatoes in the bowl and toss with all but 2 tablespoons of the vinaigrette. Arrange the leeks and potatoes on the greens. Garnish the salads with the eggs, drizzle the remaining vinaigrette on top and serve. —*Marcia Kiesel*
WINE Light, fruity Pinot Noir.

Salad of Potatoes, Green Beans, Zucchini and Herbs

4 SERVINGS ● ● ●

Four ¼-pound red potatoes
½ pound green beans
Four ¼-pound zucchini, halved lengthwise and cut crosswise into ¼-inch-thick slices
⅓ cup extra-virgin olive oil
¼ cup coarsely chopped basil
2 tablespoons coarsely chopped flat-leaf parsley
1 tablespoon plus 2 teaspoons balsamic vinegar
1 garlic clove, minced
1 tablespoon coarsely chopped dill
1 teaspoon coarsely chopped oregano
½ teaspoon coarsely chopped thyme
Salt and freshly ground pepper

---

dictionary

defining yam

WHAT'S THE DIFFERENCE BETWEEN SWEET POTATOES AND YAMS? True yams are scaly, dry, starchy tubers native to Asia and Africa and rare in the United States. Sweet potatoes are American tubers with moist orange or pale yellow flesh; the dark-skinned varieties are sometimes called yams.

---

1. Steam the potatoes in a basket over simmering water until tender, about 25 minutes. Transfer to a plate and let cool completely. Peel the potatoes, then cut them into ¼-inch-thick slices.

2. Meanwhile, add the green beans to the steamer and cook for 3 minutes. Scatter the zucchini over the green beans and steam until both are just tender, about 3 minutes longer. Spread the beans and zucchini out on a baking sheet and let cool completely.

3. In a small bowl, combine the olive oil with the basil, parsley, vinegar, garlic, dill, oregano and thyme and season with salt and pepper. In a medium bowl, toss the potatoes with all but 2 tablespoons of the herb vinaigrette, then transfer the potato salad to a platter. Add the beans, zucchini and remaining vinaigrette to the bowl and toss to coat. Mound the beans and zucchini on the potatoes and serve.

—*Graziella Dionisi*

MAKE AHEAD The salad can be made up to 4 hours ahead; let stand at room temperature.

WINE High-acid, savory Vermentino.

Roasted Sweet Potato and Onion Salad

6 SERVINGS ●

2 pounds medium sweet potatoes—peeled, quartered lengthwise and cut crosswise into ½-inch-thick slices
1 teaspoon finely chopped thyme
5½ tablespoons extra-virgin olive oil
Kosher salt to taste
1 tablespoon white wine vinegar
1½ teaspoons honey
1½ teaspoons molasses
6 small yellow onions (1¼ pounds), cut crosswise into ½-inch-thick slices
½ teaspoon cumin seeds
Pinch of crushed red pepper
2 garlic cloves, sliced
¾ cup fresh orange juice
½ pound arugula

1. Preheat the oven to 375°. On a rimmed baking sheet, toss the sweet potatoes, thyme, 1 tablespoon of the olive oil and salt. Spread in an even layer and roast for 30 minutes per side.

2. Meanwhile, in a large cast-iron skillet, mix 1½ tablespoons of the olive oil with the vinegar, honey and molasses; season with salt. Spread the onion slices in the skillet and bake until browned, about 20 minutes per side; transfer to a plate. Reserve the juices in the skillet.

3. In a small saucepan, toast the cumin seeds and crushed pepper over moderate heat. Transfer to a spice mill and let cool; grind to a powder. In the same pan, heat the remaining 3 tablespoons of olive oil over moderate heat. Add the garlic and cook until golden.

4. Set the reserved skillet over moderate heat, add the garlic, garlic oil, orange juice and spices and simmer for 5 minutes, scraping up the browned bits from the bottom; season with salt. Mound the arugula on plates and top with the sweet potatoes and onions. Drizzle the vinaigrette over the salad and serve. —*Mory Thomas*

Greek Bean-and-Beet Salad with Skordalia

8 SERVINGS ● ●

This boldly flavored salad was inspired by the time Jim Botsacos spent in Greece—as well as by his passion for garlic. Since its three main components easily stand on their own, he often serves them as separate dishes for a mezze-style buffet. Gigandes are available at Middle Eastern markets, but large lima, Great Northern or cannellini beans are fine substitutes.

1 pound gigandes, soaked overnight in cold water and drained
1 medium onion, quartered
1 bunch flat-leaf parsley stems, plus 2 tablespoons finely chopped leaves

ROASTED SWEET POTATO AND ONION SALAD

9 medium garlic cloves, 6 lightly
   smashed, 3 minced
2 bay leaves
8 black peppercorns
Kosher salt
½ cup extra-virgin olive oil
2½ tablespoons fresh
   lemon juice
1 small red onion, minced
2 large celery ribs, finely chopped
Freshly ground pepper
8 small red or golden beets
   (about 2 ounces each), trimmed
½ cup red wine vinegar
Skordalia (recipe follows)
Warmed pita bread, cut into triangles,
   for serving

1. In a large saucepan, cover the beans with 3 quarts of cold water. Wrap the quartered onion, flat-leaf parsley stems, smashed garlic cloves, bay leaves and peppercorns in a large square of cheesecloth and tie with kitchen string; add to the beans.

2. Bring the beans to a boil over high heat, then reduce the heat to moderately low and simmer until almost tender, about 30 minutes. Season with salt and cook until tender, about 10 minutes longer. Drain the beans and let cool slightly.

3. In a large bowl, whisk the olive oil with the lemon juice. Add the red onion, celery, minced garlic, chopped parsley and the cooked beans. Season with pepper and toss gently. Cover with plastic wrap and let stand at room temperature for 3 hours.

4. Meanwhile, in a large saucepan, combine the beets with the vinegar and 1 tablespoon of salt. Add enough water to reach 3 inches above the beets; bring to a simmer. Cook until tender, about 30 minutes. Cool the beets in their cooking liquid. Drain the beets, then peel and quarter them.

5. Transfer the beets to plates and top with the beans and dressing. Serve with the Skordalia and warm pita.
—Jim Botsacos

MAKE AHEAD The recipe can be prepared through Step 4; refrigerate the bean salad and beets separately for up to 2 days. Return to room temperature before serving.

SKORDALIA
MAKES ABOUT 4 CUPS ● ●

This garlicky potato and almond dip is also fabulous with toasted pita, bagel chips or crisp vegetables. For an even lighter and fluffier texture, use a standing mixer to blend the potato with the other ingredients here.

1 medium baking potato
   (about 6 ounces)
½ cup blanched whole almonds
6 large garlic cloves,
   coarsely chopped
1½ cups vegetable oil
⅓ cup white wine vinegar
1 cup sparkling water
Salt and freshly ground
   white pepper

1. In a medium saucepan, cover the potato with cold water and bring to a boil. Cook until tender, about 20 minutes. Let cool slightly, then peel and coarsely mash.

2. In a food processor, pulse the almonds with the garlic until minced. Add the potato and pulse just until combined. With the machine on, add the vegetable oil in a slow stream. Add the vinegar and process until blended. With the machine on, add the sparkling water in a slow, steady stream and process until the Skordalia is creamy. Season with salt and white pepper. —J.B.

MAKE AHEAD The Skordalia can be refrigerated for up to 2 days. Let the Skordalia return to room temperature before serving.

Lebanese Chicken Salad
4 SERVINGS ●

Don't be put off by the chicken salad's long ingredient list. Everything is available at supermarkets, and the salad is easy to assemble.

CHICKEN
½ cup extra-virgin olive oil
½ cup cilantro leaves
3 tablespoons fresh lemon juice
2 large garlic cloves, chopped
1 teaspoon ground cumin
1 teaspoon ground sumac or
   1 teaspoon fresh lemon juice
½ teaspoon ground coriander
½ teaspoon cayenne pepper
8 skinless, boneless chicken thighs
   (about 1½ pounds)
SALAD
2 large pita breads, split
   horizontally
2 tablespoons fresh lemon juice
2 teaspoons white wine vinegar
1 teaspoon Dijon mustard
⅓ cup canola oil
⅓ cup extra-virgin olive oil
Salt and freshly ground pepper
1 large romaine lettuce heart, cut
   crosswise into 1-inch strips
1 pound ripe tomatoes, cored and
   cut into ½-inch dice
½ small European cucumber—
   peeled, halved lengthwise,
   seeded and cut into ½-inch dice
½ cup flat-leaf parsley leaves
½ cup purslane or watercress
   leaves
2 tablespoons chopped mint
1½ teaspoons ground sumac or 1½
   teaspoons fresh lemon juice

1. COOK THE CHICKEN: In a blender, combine the olive oil, cilantro, lemon juice, garlic, cumin, sumac, coriander and cayenne and puree until smooth. Pour the marinade into a large resealable plastic bag. Add the chicken thighs, seal the bag and turn to coat with the marinade. Refrigerate for at least 4 hours, or overnight.

2. Light a grill or preheat a grill pan. Remove the chicken from the marinade; reserve the marinade. Grill the thighs over a medium-hot fire, turning occasionally and brushing with the marinade until browned and cooked through, about 18 minutes. Transfer to a plate.

3. MAKE THE SALAD: Preheat the oven to 300°. Bake the pitas directly on the rack for 10 minutes, or until dry and crisp but not browned. Let cool, then break into 1-inch pieces.

4. In a bowl, whisk the lemon juice with the vinegar and mustard. Slowly whisk in the canola and olive oils until emulsified. Season with salt and pepper.

5. In a bowl, toss the lettuce, tomatoes, cucumber, parsley, purslane, mint and sumac with ½ cup of the dressing. Add the pita and toss; add more dressing if necessary. Season with salt and pepper. Transfer the salad to a platter, top with the chicken and pass the remaining dressing separately. —*Michael Leviton*
WINE Light, spicy Pinot Grigio.

Smoked Chicken and Jicama Salad with Tarragon Dressing
6 SERVINGS ● ●

- 3 tablespoons red wine vinegar
- 1 tablespoon Dijon mustard
- 1 medium shallot, very finely chopped
- ½ cup vegetable oil
- ½ cup sour cream
- 3 tablespoons chopped tarragon
- Salt and freshly ground pepper
- 2 whole smoked chicken breasts (about 2 pounds), skin discarded and meat cut into thin strips (see Note)
- 3 Belgian endives—cored, halved crosswise and thinly sliced lengthwise
- 1 cucumber—peeled, halved, seeded and thinly sliced
- ½ large red onion, halved lengthwise and thinly sliced crosswise
- 1 medium jicama (¾ pound), peeled and cut into matchsticks
- ½ cup oil-packed sun-dried tomatoes, thinly sliced
- 2 bunches arugula (½ pound), stemmed
- ¼ cup snipped chives

1. In a blender or food processor, blend the vinegar with the mustard and shallot until combined. With the machine on, slowly add the vegetable oil until the dressing is emulsified. Blend in the sour cream. Transfer the dressing to a small bowl and stir in the chopped tarragon. Season the tarragon dressing with salt and pepper.

2. In a large bowl, toss the smoked chicken with the endives, cucumber, onion, jicama and sun-dried tomatoes. Add the tarragon dressing, season with salt and pepper and toss well. Arrange the arugula on plates and top with the chicken salad. Garnish the salads with the snipped chives and serve.
—*Ann Chantal Altman*

NOTE If smoked chicken is unavailable, 1½ pounds of smoked turkey can be substituted.

Cornish Hen Salad with Scotch Bonnet Vinaigrette
4 SERVINGS ●

Scotch bonnet chiles are some of the hottest—and fruitiest—in the world. The oil in the vinaigrette brings out the chiles' fruity side while cooling the fire.

- 2 Cornish hens (about 1½ pounds each)
- 4 medium carrots
- 2 tablespoons pure olive oil
- Salt and freshly ground pepper
- 2 tablespoons Scotch bonnet sauce (see Note)
- 1 tablespoon vegetable oil
- 2 teaspoons white wine vinegar
- ⅛ teaspoon ground allspice
- 8 medium red radishes, halved and cut into ⅛-inch-thick slices
- One 2½-ounce package radish sprouts
- ½ cup roasted, salted cashews, halved lengthwise

1. Preheat the oven to 350°. Put the hens and carrots in a roasting pan, rub them with the olive oil and season with salt and pepper. Roast in the upper third of the oven for 1 hour, then transfer the carrots to a plate to cool. Continue roasting the hens for about 15 minutes longer, or until the cavity juices run clear. Transfer the hens to a platter and let cool to room temperature.

2. Meanwhile, pour the hot pan juices into a measuring cup and skim the fat. Strain the juices into a small saucepan and bring to a simmer over moderate heat. Cook until reduced to 2 tablespoons, about 4 minutes. Pour the reduction back into the measuring cup and let cool to room temperature. Stir in the hot sauce, vegetable oil, vinegar and allspice and season the vinaigrette with salt and pepper.

3. Remove the meat from the hens and pull it apart into thick shreds. Cut the carrots into 2-by-⅓-inch sticks. In a large bowl, toss the cornish hen meat with the carrots, radishes, sprouts, and cashews. Add the Scotch bonnet vinaigrette and toss again, to coat. Mound the salad on plates and serve.
—*Marcia Kiesel*

NOTE Use a thick Scotch bonnet sauce for more character. Some excellent brands are Ricky's Red Hot, Coyote Cocina Howlin' Hot Sauce and Matouk's Hot Calypso Sauce.

MAKE AHEAD The recipe can be prepared up to 1 day ahead through Step 2. Refrigerate the Cornish hens and vinaigrette separately.

WINE Soft, off-dry Riesling.

---

pantry tip
storing lettuce

TO KEEP LETTUCE FRESH FOR LONG PERIODS, soak the leaves in ice water for 15 minutes, then spin them until they're completely dry. Wrap them in paper towels and seal them in a plastic bag, squeezing as much air out of the bag as possible. Lettuce stored this way should keep for at least 2 weeks.

SPRING VEGETABLE SOUP, P. 58

soups

ASPARAGUS VICHYSSOISE

FRESH TOMATO SOUP WITH CRAB GUACAMOLE

Asparagus Vichyssoise

4 SERVINGS ● ●

1½ tablespoons olive oil

2 leeks, white and light green parts only, sliced

1 quart vegetable stock, canned low-sodium broth or water

Salt and freshly ground pepper

1¾ pounds medium asparagus, tips cut to 1 inch, stems chopped

3 cups spinach (3½ ounces)

4 teaspoons nonfat plain yogurt

Edible flowers, for garnish (optional)

ı. Heat the olive oil in a medium saucepan. Add the leeks and cook over moderately low heat, stirring often, until softened, about 6 minutes. Add the stock, season with salt and pepper and bring to a boil. Add the asparagus stems and cook over moderately low heat until tender, about 6 minutes. Add the spinach and cook for 3 minutes.

2. Puree the soup in a blender. Refrigerate until chilled, at least 2 hours or overnight. Season with salt and pepper. **3.** Cook the asparagus tips in a medium saucepan of boiling salted water until barely tender, about 4 minutes. Drain and rinse in cold water. Drain again and pat dry. Ladle the soup into bowls and garnish with the asparagus tips, yogurt and flowers. —*Hubert Keller*

MAKE AHEAD The vichyssoise and asparagus tips can be refrigerated separately overnight.

Fresh Tomato Soup with Crab Guacamole

4 SERVINGS ● ●

2 pounds tomatoes

¼ cup plus 4 teaspoons extra-virgin olive oil

1 tablespoon balsamic vinegar

Salt and freshly ground pepper

½ pound Peekytoe or backfin crabmeat, picked over

2 tablespoons finely chopped red onion

1½ teaspoons finely chopped basil leaves

1 teaspoon very finely chopped jalapeño

1 tablespoon fresh lime juice

1 ripe Hass avocado, coarsely chopped

ı. Bring a large saucepan of water to a boil and prepare an ice-water bath in a large bowl.

2. Using a small paring knife, make a shallow X in the bottom of each tomato. Plunge the tomatoes into the boiling water for 10 seconds. Using a slotted spoon, transfer the tomatoes to the ice-water bath. Peel the tomatoes, then remove the core and the seeds; reserve the ice-water bath.

3. In a blender, puree the tomatoes with ¼ cup of the olive oil and the vinegar until smooth. Transfer to a bowl and season with salt and pepper. Set the bowl in the ice-water bath to chill the soup.

4. In a bowl, combine the crabmeat with the onion, basil, jalapeño and lime juice. Gently fold in the chopped avocado and season with salt and pepper. Ladle the tomato soup into shallow bowls and drizzle with the remaining 4 teaspoons of olive oil. Mound the crab guacamole in the center of each bowl of soup and serve. —*Terrance Brennan*

Yin-Yang Tomato Soup

4 SERVINGS ● ●

This recipe is made by pairing red and yellow tomato soups, but preparing it with only one type of tomato would also be delicious.

- 2 pounds ripe yellow tomatoes, quartered
- ¼ cup torn basil leaves, plus 4 basil sprigs
- 1 tablespoon extra-virgin olive oil
- 1 tablespoon honey (optional)
- 1 tablespoon fresh lemon juice (optional)

Salt and freshly ground pepper

- 2 pounds ripe red tomatoes, quartered

1. In a food processor or blender, puree the yellow tomatoes with 2 tablespoons of the basil leaves; strain through a coarse sieve. Whisk in ½ tablespoon of the olive oil, ½ tablespoon of the honey and ½ tablespoon of the lemon juice. Season with salt and pepper. Transfer to a pitcher and refrigerate until chilled, about 1 hour. Repeat with the red tomatoes and the remaining basil leaves, olive oil, honey and lemon juice. Season with salt and pepper.

2. Whisk each soup until smooth. At the same time, pour both soups from opposite sides into shallow bowls. Garnish with the basil sprigs and serve. —*Michel Nischan*

Tomato Acqua Cotta

6 SERVINGS ● ●

Acqua cotta, or "cooked water," is a rustic Italian vegetable soup; the vegetables vary depending on who is making the soup and what the season is.

- ½ cup dried porcini mushrooms (½ ounce)
- 6 cups water, 1 cup lukewarm
- 2 tablespoons extra-virgin olive oil
- 1 large red onion, finely chopped
- 1 celery rib, finely chopped
- 1 carrot, finely chopped
- 2 parsley sprigs, finely chopped
- 2 garlic cloves, finely chopped
- 1 tablespoon tomato paste

One 16-ounce can tomato puree

- 2 tablespoons coarsely chopped basil
- 2 medium zucchini, cut into ¼-inch dice

Salt and freshly ground pepper

- ¼ cup freshly grated Pecorino Romano cheese

1. In a small heatproof bowl, soak the porcini in the 1 cup of lukewarm water until softened, about 20 minutes. Drain the porcini, reserving the soaking liquid. Rinse the porcini, then coarsely chop them.

2. In a large saucepan, heat the olive oil. Add the onion, celery, carrot, parsley and garlic, cover and cook over low heat, stirring once or twice, until softened, about 10 minutes. Whisk in the tomato paste and the porcini and their soaking liquid, stopping when you reach the grit at the bottom. Simmer over moderate heat until almost all of the liquid has evaporated, about 5 minutes. Add the remaining 5 cups of water, the tomato puree and 1 tablespoon of the chopped basil. Cook the soup for 20 minutes. Add the diced zucchini and cook until crisp-tender, about 5 minutes. Season with salt and pepper. Stir in the remaining 1 tablespoon of basil. Ladle the soup into bowls and serve with the grated Pecorino Romano. —*Anna Teresa Callen*

Pickled Eggplant and Summer Lettuce Soup

4 SERVINGS ● ●

PICKLED EGGPLANT

- 1 pound Japanese eggplants, sliced into ¼-inch rounds

Kosher salt

- 1 cup extra-virgin olive oil
- 3 tablespoons sherry vinegar
- 3 tablespoons balsamic vinegar
- 4 garlic cloves, smashed
- ½ teaspoon crushed red pepper

Freshly ground pepper

LETTUCE SOUP

- ¼ cup extra-virgin olive oil
- 2 medium leeks, white part only, finely chopped
- 2 garlic cloves, very finely chopped

One 2-ounce Yukon Gold potato, peeled and finely chopped

- ½ cup finely chopped fennel bulb
- ½ pound hearts of romaine, thinly sliced crosswise
- 3 heads Bibb lettuce (about 9 ounces), thinly sliced
- 3 cups vegetable stock or broth
- 1 cup coarsely chopped flat-leaf parsley
- 2 teaspoons fresh lemon juice

Salt and freshly ground pepper

- ¼ cup fresh ricotta, preferably sheep's or goat's milk
- ¼ cup coarsely grated ricotta salata (2 ounces)
- 1 tablespoon minced chives
- 2 small tomatoes, cut into thin wedges
- 1 cup baby lettuces
- 2 tablespoons toasted pine nuts

1. MAKE THE PICKLED EGGPLANT: Arrange the eggplant slices in a single layer on 2 large baking sheets and sprinkle all over with 2 tablespoons of kosher salt. Let the eggplant slices stand for 3 hours. Thoroughly rinse the eggplant and then transfer the slices to a clean kitchen towel. Squeeze the eggplant slices dry.

soups

2. In a glass or ceramic jar, mix the olive oil with the sherry and balsamic vinegars, garlic and crushed pepper; season with salt and pepper. Add the eggplant, cover and refrigerate for 2 days.

3. MAKE THE LETTUCE SOUP: In a large saucepan, heat 1 tablespoon of the olive oil. Add the leeks, garlic, potato and fennel. Cover and cook over low heat until tender, about 10 minutes. Add the romaine and Bibb lettuces and toss just until wilted, about 30 seconds. Transfer to a blender. Add the vegetable stock, parsley and the remaining 3 tablespoons of olive oil and puree. Strain the soup through a fine sieve into a medium bowl. Stir in the lemon juice and season with salt and pepper. Refrigerate the lettuce soup until chilled.

4. In a small bowl, blend the fresh ricotta with the ricotta salata and chives and season with salt and pepper.

5. Ladle the soup into bowls. Garnish with eggplant rounds and tomato wedges. Using 2 spoons, form the cheese mixture into 8 quenelles and place 2 in each bowl. Scatter the baby lettuces and pine nuts over and serve.

—Dan Barber and Mike Anthony

MAKE AHEAD The pickled eggplant can be refrigerated for up to 1 month. The soup and the ricotta topping can be refrigerated separately overnight.

Spring Vegetable Soup

4 SERVINGS ● ○

¼ pound pasta, such as farfalloni or orecchiette

1 tablespoon unsalted butter

1 tablespoon extra-virgin olive oil

1 large leek, white and tender green part only, thinly sliced

6 cups chicken stock or canned low-sodium broth

½ pound sugar snap peas, halved diagonally

10 ounces baby spinach

1 tablespoon fresh lemon juice

2 teaspoons lemon zest

Salt and freshly ground pepper

1. In a large pot of boiling salted water, cook the pasta until almost al dente; drain. Transfer to a bowl and cover.

2. In a large saucepan, melt the butter in the olive oil. Add the leek; cook over moderately high heat until tender, about 1 minute. Add the stock, cover and bring to a simmer. Add the sugar snaps and cook over moderate heat until just tender, about 2 minutes. Stir in the pasta, spinach, lemon juice and lemon zest; season with salt and pepper. Cook just until the spinach is wilted, about 2 minutes. Ladle into bowls and serve.

—Wendy Kalen

WINE Medium-bodied, round Pinot Blanc.

Vegetable Stracciatella

4 SERVINGS ● ○

Stracciatella means "little rag," which is exactly what the beaten eggs look like once they're cooked in the soup.

5 cups chicken stock or canned low-sodium broth

3 garlic cloves, thinly sliced

1 small carrot, finely shredded

1 celery rib, cut into matchsticks

½ pound baby spinach, shredded

3 tablespoons minced parsley

2 tablespoons freshly grated Parmesan cheese, plus more for serving

2 large eggs

Salt and freshly ground pepper

1. In a large saucepan, combine the stock and garlic and bring to a boil. Add the carrot and celery, cover and cook over moderately high heat until the celery is crisp-tender, about 4 minutes. Add the spinach, parsley and the 2 tablespoons of Parmesan and simmer for 2 minutes.

2. Beat the eggs in a bowl and pour them into the soup. Cook over moderately low heat for 30 seconds, gently stirring with a fork until threads appear. Season with salt and pepper. Ladle the soup into bowls and serve with additional Parmesan cheese.

—Diane Rossen Worthington

Fresh Shell Bean Soup with Pistou

4 SERVINGS ● ● ●

SOUP

2 pounds fresh cranberry beans, shelled (2 cups), see Note

Salt

8 parsley stems

4 thyme sprigs

1 bay leaf

1 slice of bacon

2 tablespoons extra-virgin olive oil

1 medium onion, finely diced

2 garlic cloves, thinly sliced

1 medium carrot, cut into ¼-inch dice

1 medium celery rib, cut into ¼-inch dice

6 cups chicken stock or canned low-sodium broth

2 medium tomatoes—peeled, seeded and cut into ¼-inch dice

3 ounces thin green beans, cut into ¼-inch dice (½ cup)

¼ cup finely chopped flat-leaf parsley

1 tablespoon fresh lemon juice

½ teaspoon finely grated lemon zest

Freshly ground pepper

PISTOU

8 large basil leaves

1 small garlic clove, halved

¼ cup extra-virgin olive oil

Salt and freshly ground pepper

CROUTONS

2 tablespoons extra-virgin olive oil

1 cup diced (¼ inch) crustless country bread

2 tablespoons finely chopped flat-leaf parsley

Salt and freshly ground pepper

1. MAKE THE SOUP: In a medium saucepan, cover the cranberry beans with 1 inch of water and bring to a boil. Reduce the heat to low, cover partially and simmer the beans until almost tender, about 20 minutes. Season with salt and continue cooking until the beans are tender, about 5 minutes longer. Drain the beans.

2. Bundle the parsley stems, thyme sprigs and bay leaf in the slice of bacon and tie together with kitchen string. Heat the olive oil in a medium saucepan. Add the onion and garlic and cook over low heat, stirring occasionally, until softened, about 8 minutes. Add the carrot and celery and cook until softened, about 8 minutes. Add the cranberry beans, bacon bundle, stock, tomatoes and green beans and bring to a boil. Cover partially, reduce the heat to low and simmer for 10 minutes. Stir in the chopped parsley, lemon juice and lemon zest and season the soup with salt and pepper.

3. MAKE THE PISTOU: In a saucepan of boiling water, blanch the basil leaves for 5 seconds. Drain and rinse the basil under cold water. Squeeze dry and finely chop.

4. In a mortar, pound the garlic to a paste. Add the basil and pound together. Stir in the olive oil and season with salt and pepper.

5. MAKE THE CROUTONS: Heat the olive oil in a large skillet. Add the diced bread and cook over moderate heat, stirring often, until starting to crisp, about 2 minutes. Add the chopped parsley and cook, stirring, until the bread is browned and crisp, about 3 minutes longer. Season with salt and pepper and transfer to a plate.

6. Reheat the shell bean soup and discard the bacon bundle. Ladle the soup into individual bowls and drizzle with the pistou. Serve at once, passing the croutons at the table. —*Mark Sullivan*

NOTE Any combination of fresh shell beans can be used in this soup. Cooking time will vary according to the bean variety that you choose.

MAKE AHEAD The recipe can be prepared up to 1 day ahead. Refrigerate the soup and pistou separately. The croutons can be stored overnight in an airtight container. Rewarm the soup and let the pistou come to room temperature before serving.

Pasta e Fagioli with Roasted Red Peppers and Swiss Chard

4 SERVINGS ● ○ ●

2 tablespoons extra-virgin olive oil
1 medium onion, coarsely chopped
1 carrot, coarsely chopped
1 pound red Swiss chard, stems and inner ribs discarded, leaves cut crosswise into 1-inch ribbons
Two 15-ounce cans small white beans, drained
5 cups chicken or vegetable stock or canned low-sodium broth
½ cup coarsely chopped roasted red peppers, drained if jarred
¼ cup finely chopped flat-leaf parsley
¾ cup broken fine egg noodles
2 teaspoons balsamic vinegar
Salt and freshly ground pepper
Freshly grated Parmesan cheese, for serving

1. In a medium saucepan, heat the olive oil until shimmering. Add the onion and carrot and cook over moderately high heat, stirring occasionally, until lightly browned, about 5 minutes. Add the Swiss chard leaves and cook, stirring, until wilted. Add the beans, stock, red peppers and 3 tablespoons of the parsley and bring the soup to a simmer. Cover partially and simmer the soup until the vegetables are tender, about 15 minutes.

2. Meanwhile, bring a medium saucepan of salted water to a boil. Add the broken egg noodles and cook until al dente. Drain the noodles well.

3. Using a slotted spoon, transfer half of the vegetables to a blender along with a bit of the broth; puree until smooth. Return the puree to the soup. Add the cooked noodles and the balsamic vinegar, season with salt and pepper and simmer for 2 minutes. Stir in the remaining 1 tablespoon of chopped parsley, ladle the soup into bowls and serve at once, passing the grated Parmesan cheese at the table. —*Diane Rossen Worthington*

Root Vegetable Soup with Lentils and Gruyère

8 SERVINGS ● ●

½ cup green lentils
Salt
¼ pound pancetta, sliced ¼ inch thick and finely diced
6 garlic cloves, minced
2 carrots, finely diced
2 celery ribs, finely diced
1 onion, finely diced
1 medium red potato, finely diced
½ cup finely diced peeled celery root
½ cup finely diced peeled butternut squash
½ finely diced peeled rutabaga
1 bay leaf
Freshly ground pepper
2½ quarts chicken stock or canned low-sodium broth
2 tablespoons chopped parsley
1 tablespoon chopped thyme
¼ pound Gruyère cheese, thinly shaved

1. In a saucepan, cover the lentils with 1 inch of water and add a large pinch of salt. Cover and bring to a boil. Simmer over low heat, stirring, until the lentils are tender, about 20 minutes. Drain.

2. In a saucepan, cook the pancetta over moderately low heat until most of the fat is rendered, about 8 minutes. Add the garlic, carrots, celery, onion, potato, celery root, squash, rutabaga and bay leaf and cook over moderately high heat for 2 minutes, stirring to coat. Season with salt and pepper and cook until the vegetables are softened, about 3 minutes. Add the stock and bring to a boil. Reduce the heat to low and simmer until the vegetables are tender, about 20 minutes. Discard the bay leaf.

3. Stir in the lentils, parsley and thyme and season with salt and pepper. Ladle the soup into bowls, top with Gruyère and serve piping hot. —*Paul Kahan*

MAKE AHEAD The soup can be refrigerated for up to 3 days.

soups

Carrot and Sweet Potato Soup

4 SERVINGS ● ●

- 4 carrots, cut into 2-inch chunks
- 1 pound sweet potatoes, peeled and cut into 1-inch chunks
- 4 tablespoons unsalted butter
- 1 medium onion, thinly sliced
- 1½ tablespoons tomato paste
- 6½ cups hot chicken stock or canned low-sodium broth

Salt and freshly ground white pepper

- 1 tablespoon fresh lemon juice
- 2 tablespoons finely chopped flat-leaf parsley

Garlic croutons, for serving

1. In a food processor, pulse the carrots and sweet potatoes until minced.
2. Melt 2 tablespoons of the butter in a medium saucepan. Add the onion, cover and cook over moderately high heat, stirring occasionally, until softened. Add the carrots and sweet potatoes, cover and cook until just beginning to soften, about 2 minutes. Add the tomato paste and 5 cups of the stock and bring to a boil. Cover partially and cook over moderate heat until the vegetables are tender, about 15 minutes.
3. In a blender, puree the soup in batches until smooth. Return to the saucepan, season with salt and white pepper and stir in the remaining 1½ cups of hot stock and the lemon juice. Swirl in the remaining 2 tablespoons of butter and the parsley and serve with croutons. —Diane Rossen Worthington

MAKE AHEAD The soup can be refrigerated for up to 2 days.

Sweet Potato and Apple Soup

6 SERVINGS ● ●

- 1¾ pounds sweet potatoes, peeled and cut into 1-inch dice
- 1 small parsnip, peeled and cut into 1-inch dice
- 2 garlic cloves, coarsely chopped
- 2 tablespoons extra-virgin olive oil

Salt to taste

- 6 cups vegetable stock or low-sodium broth
- 1 cup apple cider
- 1 teaspoon green Tabasco sauce

Finely diced Granny Smith apple and minced parsley, for garnish

1. Preheat the oven to 375°. On a baking sheet, toss the sweet potatoes with the parsnip, garlic, olive oil and salt. Bake for 45 minutes, or until tender.
2. In a blender, puree half of the vegetables with 3 cups of the stock; transfer to a saucepan. Repeat with the remaining vegetables and stock. Add the cider and Tabasco and heat through. Season with salt. Serve with the diced apple and parsley. —Mory Thomas

MAKE AHEAD The soup can be refrigerated for up to 2 days.

Butternut Squash Soup with Popcorn and Sage

4 SERVINGS ● ●

- 2 teaspoons ground coriander
- 1 teaspoon sugar
- ½ teaspoon cayenne pepper

Salt

- 2½ pounds butternut squash, peeled and cut into 2-inch chunks
- 1 tablespoon extra-virgin olive oil
- 1¼ cups hot water
- 3 tablespoons unsalted butter
- 12 fresh sage leaves
- 1 cup popped popcorn, for garnish

1. Preheat the oven to 475°. Mix the coriander, sugar, cayenne and 2 teaspoons of salt. In a roasting pan, toss the squash with the oil and spices; roast for 35 minutes, until tender and browned.
2. Transfer the squash to a food processor. Add the water and puree until smooth. Transfer the soup to a saucepan, season with salt and keep warm.
3. In a saucepan, melt the butter over moderate heat. Add the sage and cook until crisp, about 1 minute. Transfer the sage to a paper towel. Continue to cook the butter over moderate heat until fragrant and browned, about 3 minutes. Ladle the soup into bowls. Drizzle with the sage butter, top with the fried sage and popcorn and serve. —Scott Ehrlich

Velvety Beet Soup

8 SERVINGS ● ●

- 3 pounds medium red beets
- 2 large parsnips
- 2 large carrots

One ¾-pound celery root

- 4 tablespoons unsalted butter
- ½ cup water

Salt and freshly ground white pepper

- 7 cups chicken stock
- ¼ cup balsamic vinegar

Green Tabasco sauce

1. Preheat the oven to 375°. Wrap the beets in 2 sheets of heavy-duty foil. Roast on a baking sheet for 1½ hours, or until tender. Let cool in the foil.
2. Peel the parsnips, carrots and celery root; cut into ¼-inch dice. In a large skillet, melt the butter in the water. Add the diced vegetables and cook over moderate heat until almost tender, about 8 minutes. Season with salt and white pepper and remove from the heat.
3. Peel and quarter the beets. Working in batches, in a blender, puree the beets and stock until smooth. Transfer to a large saucepan. Stir in the vinegar; season with salt, white pepper and Tabasco. Add the vegetables and simmer over moderate heat for 5 minutes before serving. —Mory Thomas

MAKE AHEAD The soup can be refrigerated for up to 2 days.

SERVE WITH Crème fraîche.

Broccoli-Leek Soup with Lemon-Chive Cream

4 SERVINGS ● ●

- 1 tablespoon unsalted butter
- 1 tablespoon extra-virgin olive oil
- 2 medium leeks, white and tender green parts only, finely chopped
- 1½ pounds broccoli, stems peeled and sliced ½ inch thick, florets cut into 1-inch pieces
- 3 garlic cloves, thinly sliced
- 5 cups chicken stock or canned low-sodium broth

Salt and freshly ground white pepper

- ½ cup sour cream

BUTTERNUT SQUASH SOUP WITH POPCORN AND SAGE

CREAMY SCALLION-MUSHROOM SOUP

YELLOW PEPPER SOUP WITH ASPARAGUS

Finely grated zest of 1 lemon
2 tablespoons fresh lemon juice
¼ cup snipped chives
¼ cup grated Parmesan cheese

1. In a saucepan, melt the butter in the oil. Add the leeks and cook over moderately high heat until softened, about 3 minutes. Stir in the broccoli, garlic and stock, season with salt and pepper and bring to a boil. Cover partially; simmer until the broccoli is tender, 20 minutes.

2. In a bowl, mix the sour cream, lemon zest and juice, chives and Parmesan. Season with salt and white pepper.

3. Transfer the soup to a blender and puree in batches until smooth. Stir in half of the lemon-chive cream. Ladle the soup into shallow bowls and serve the remaining lemon-chive cream on the side.

—*Diane Rossen Worthington*

MAKE AHEAD The soup can be refrigerated for up to 1 day.

Chicory-Leek Soup

8 SERVINGS ● ●

6 tablespoons unsalted butter
2 large leeks, white and tender green parts only, chopped
½ teaspoon celery seeds
½ teaspoon caraway seeds
6 pounds chicory, tough outer leaves discarded, the rest chopped
2½ quarts chicken stock
2 tablespoons apple cider vinegar
2 tablespoons mild honey
Salt and freshly ground white pepper

1. Melt the butter in a saucepan. Add the leeks and celery and caraway seeds and cook over moderate heat until the leeks soften, about 10 minutes. Transfer to a bowl and wipe out the saucepan.

2. Meanwhile, prepare an ice-water bath. In a large pot of boiling salted water, blanch the chopped chicory in batches until tender, 1½ to 2 minutes.

Transfer the chicory to the ice bath to cool. Drain and squeeze dry, then add to the leeks and toss.

3. Working in batches, in a blender, puree the vegetables and stock. Strain the soup through a coarse sieve into the saucepan; bring to a simmer. Stir in the vinegar and honey. Season with salt and white pepper and serve.

—*Mory Thomas*

MAKE AHEAD The soup can be refrigerated for up to 2 days.

SERVE WITH Sourdough croutons and dollops of fresh goat cheese.

Creamy Garlic Soup

4 TO 6 SERVINGS ●

Be sure to use the plumpest, freshest garlic you can find.

1½ tablespoons duck fat or
1 tablespoon extra-virgin olive oil and ½ tablespoon unsalted butter

1 whole plump head of garlic, cloves peeled and chopped

1 medium onion, chopped

4 plump shallots, chopped

1 tablespoon unbleached all-purpose flour

1½ quarts water

Salt and freshly ground pepper

3 large egg yolks

About 1 tablespoon white wine vinegar

12 to 16 slices of a baguette, toasted

3 tablespoons finely snipped chives

I. In a medium skillet, melt the duck fat over moderately low heat. Add the garlic, onion and shallots and stir to coat thoroughly with duck fat. Cook, stirring frequently, until the vegetables are thoroughly softened but not browned, about 12 minutes; if the garlic begins to brown, turn down the heat. Stir in the flour and cook gently for 5 minutes, stirring frequently; again, take care not to let the vegetables brown.

2. Meanwhile, in a large saucepan, bring the water to a boil. Season generously with salt and pepper. Scrape the sautéed vegetables into the saucepan and simmer for 35 minutes. Transfer the hot soup to a blender and puree, in batches if necessary. Return the soup to the saucepan.

3. In a small bowl, beat the egg yolks with 1 tablespoon of the wine vinegar. Whisk a few tablespoons of hot soup into the egg yolks to warm them, then whisk the yolks into the soup in the saucepan. Whisk the soup over moderately low heat just until it begins to look creamy; do not let the soup boil or the eggs will curdle. Season the soup with salt and pepper and add a little more vinegar if desired. Ladle the hot soup into bowls, garnish with the toasted bread and the chives and serve.

—Kate Hill

MAKE AHEAD The garlic soup can be prepared through Step 2, covered and refrigerated for up to 2 days. Bring to a bare simmer before proceeding.

Creamy Scallion-Mushroom Soup

8 SERVINGS ● ●

6 tablespoons unsalted butter

2 pounds scallions (about 5 bunches)—1 scallion julienned, the rest coarsely chopped

Salt and freshly ground pepper

2 tablespoons all-purpose flour

5 cups chicken stock or canned low-sodium broth

1 pound white mushrooms, very thinly sliced

1 cup packed flat-leaf parsley leaves

½ cup heavy cream

I. Melt the butter in a large saucepan. Add the chopped scallions and season with salt and pepper. Cover and cook over low heat, stirring occasionally, until softened, about 10 minutes. Add the flour and cook, stirring, until incorporated. Gradually stir in the stock and bring to a boil, then simmer over low heat for 10 minutes.

2. Remove the pan from the heat and stir in three-quarters of the mushrooms and all of the parsley. Working in batches, puree the soup in a blender until smooth. Return the soup to the pan and stir in the cream. Season with salt and pepper and warm gently over low heat. Ladle the soup into bowls, garnish with the remaining mushroom slices and the julienned scallion and serve. —Maria Guarnaschelli

MAKE AHEAD The soup can be refrigerated for up to 2 days.

Yellow Pepper Soup with Asparagus

4 SERVINGS ● ● ●

2½ cups water

4 asparagus, trimmed and cut into 2-inch-long matchsticks

3 yellow bell peppers—stemmed, seeded and cut into 1-inch pieces

1 large Idaho potato, peeled and cut into 1-inch pieces

1 large onion, cut into 1-inch pieces

3 garlic cloves

1½ teaspoons sugar

1 teaspoon salt

¼ teaspoon freshly ground pepper

2 tablespoons unsalted butter

2 tablespoons extra-virgin olive oil

I. Bring ½ cup of the water to a boil in a small saucepan. Add the asparagus and cook until barely tender, about 1 minute. Set a strainer over a heatproof bowl and drain the asparagus, reserving the cooking water.

2. In a saucepan, combine the peppers with the potato, onion, garlic, sugar, salt, pepper and the remaining 2 cups of water; bring to a boil. Add the asparagus cooking water, cover and simmer over moderate heat for 30 minutes.

3. Pass the pepper soup through a food mill set over a clean saucepan. Add the butter and olive oil and, using an immersion blender, blend the soup until smooth. Reheat the soup if necessary. Ladle into shallow bowls, garnish with the asparagus and serve immediately.

—Jacques Pépin

MAKE AHEAD The soup can be refrigerated for up to 1 day.

health note

the curry cure

MANY OF THE SPICES IN MADRAS CURRY POWDER (see *Curried Carrot and Leek Soup* recipe on p. 64) have curative properties. Cumin, cinnamon, coriander and fenugreek are all digestives, and vitamin C-rich chiles can help ward off colds. Research from the National Institute of Nutrition in Hyderabad, India, suggests that diabetics supplement drug treatment with fenugreek seeds, which help lower blood sugar. It also found that turmeric contains curcumin, a potent antioxidant; a teaspoon a day may help prevent certain kinds of cancer.

soups

Curried Carrot and Leek Soup

6 SERVINGS ● ● ●

2 tablespoons unsalted butter

1 tablespoon olive oil

1 tablespoon Madras curry powder

8 medium carrots, thinly sliced

3 large leeks, white and tender green parts, thinly sliced

2½ cups chicken stock or low-sodium broth

Salt and freshly ground pepper

1½ cups water

I. In a skillet, melt the butter in the oil over moderate heat. Add the curry and stir until fragrant, 45 seconds. Add the carrots and cook until just tender, about 7 minutes. Add the leeks and cook until beginning to brown, about 4 minutes. Add the stock and bring to a boil; simmer over low heat for 4 minutes. Season with salt and pepper.

2. Puree the soup in a blender or food processor. Return to the saucepan, add the water and rewarm. —*Wendy Kalen*

MAKE AHEAD The soup can be refrigerated for up to 2 days.

Zucchini Soup with Basil

8 SERVINGS ● ● ●

CROUTONS

2 tablespoons unsalted butter

⅓ cup basil leaves, finely chopped

Two ½-inch-thick slices of country bread, cut into ½-inch dice

Salt and freshly ground pepper

SOUP

3 tablespoons unsalted butter

3 tablespoons extra-virgin olive oil

3 celery ribs, peeled and diced

1 medium onion, minced

1 bay leaf

½ teaspoon chopped thyme leaves

1½ pounds small zucchini, cut into ½-inch pieces

3 cups chicken stock or canned low-sodium broth

Salt and freshly ground pepper

8 small basil leaves, for garnish

I. MAKE THE CROUTONS: In a large skillet, melt the butter over moderately high heat. Stir in the basil, then add the bread cubes and toss to coat with the butter. Season with salt and pepper. Cook, stirring, for about 3 minutes, or until the bread cubes are lightly toasted and crispy. Transfer to a plate.

2. MAKE THE SOUP: In a large, heavy saucepan, melt the butter in the olive oil. Add the celery, onion, bay leaf and thyme and cook over low heat, stirring occasionally, until the onion is soft, about 20 minutes. Increase the heat to moderate. Stir in the zucchini and stock, season with salt and pepper and simmer the soup until the zucchini is soft, about 10 minutes. Discard the bay leaf.

3. Working in batches, puree the soup in a blender until smooth. Return the soup to the saucepan and reheat gently. Season with salt and pepper. Ladle the soup into bowls, top with the croutons and basil leaves and serve. —*Gary Danko*

MAKE AHEAD The soup can be refrigerated for up to 1 day.

WINE Fruity, low-oak Chardonnay.

Fire-Roasted Tomato Bisque

4 SERVINGS ● ●

4 tablespoons unsalted butter

1 medium onion, finely chopped

1 medium carrot, finely chopped

1 celery rib, finely chopped

2 garlic cloves, finely chopped

3 tablespoons all-purpose flour

4 cups chicken stock or canned low-sodium broth

Two 14½-ounce cans diced fire-roasted tomatoes, drained

3 tablespoons tomato paste

2 teaspoons sugar

¼ cup heavy cream

Salt and freshly ground white pepper

½ cup garlic or cheese croutons, for garnish (optional)

I. In a medium saucepan, melt 2 tablespoons of the butter. Add the chopped onion, carrot, celery and garlic, cover and cook over moderately high heat, stirring occasionally, until the vegetables are just beginning to brown, about 5 minutes. Sprinkle the flour over the vegetables and stir over low heat for 1 minute, or until the flour is fully incorporated. Add the chicken stock, tomatoes, tomato paste and sugar and bring to a boil. Cover partially and cook the soup over moderate heat, stirring occasionally, until the vegetables are tender, 15 minutes.

2. Transfer half of the soup to a blender and puree until smooth. Return the puree to the saucepan, add the heavy cream and cook until the soup is just heated through. Season the soup with salt and white pepper and swirl in the remaining 2 tablespoons of butter. Ladle the soup into bowls, garnish with croutons and serve at once. —*Diane Rossen Worthington*

MAKE AHEAD The soup can be refrigerated for up to 2 days.

Bulgur and Fava Bean Soup

6 SERVINGS ● ●

This hearty soup, made from the kinds of basic grains and legumes every Tunisian housewife has in her larder, is remarkably easy to put together. The seasonings, added at the end of the cooking time, give the soup depth.

1 cup dried chickpeas (6 ounces), soaked overnight and drained

¾ cup coarse bulgur (5 ounces), rinsed

---

cooking tip

blender basics

AN IMMERSION BLENDER IS A GREAT TOOL for pureeing soups that you want to leave slightly chunky. It's also one that's much easier to clean up when you're finished. The F&W test kitchen prefers using regular blenders for smoother purees, even if that means more to wash up at the end.

BULGUR AND FAVA BEAN SOUP

soups

1 cup small dried split fava beans
(6 ounces)
2 quarts water
1 cup extra-virgin olive oil, plus
more for serving
2 tablespoons tomato paste
1 tablespoon *harissa*
1 tablespoon Tabil (p. 328)
2 teaspoons sweet paprika
3 garlic cloves, minced
Salt

In a large, heavy saucepan, combine the chickpeas, bulgur, favas, water and 1 cup of olive oil and bring to a boil. Simmer over low heat, stirring occasionally, until the chickpeas and fava beans are completely broken down, about 4 hours. Stir in the tomato paste, *harissa,* Tabil, paprika and garlic and simmer the bean soup for 5 minutes longer. Season the bean soup with salt and serve, passing extra olive oil at the table. —*Nancy Harmon Jenkins*

MAKE AHEAD The soup can be refrigerated for up to 2 days.

Hearty Mushroom and Oat Groat Soup
8 SERVINGS ● ●
The oat groats need to soak overnight, so plan accordingly.

½ ounce dried mushrooms (½ cup)
¾ cup boiling water
¼ cup olive oil
3 medium leeks, white and light
green parts, quartered lengthwise
and thinly sliced crosswise
2 garlic cloves, minced
1 pound mixed fresh mushrooms
6 cups vegetable stock or canned
low-sodium broth
½ cup oat groats, soaked overnight
and drained
2 medium carrots, thinly sliced
1 medium parsnip, thinly sliced
1 tablespoon balsamic vinegar
½ teaspoon minced thyme
½ teaspoon minced rosemary
Salt and freshly ground pepper
2 tablespoons minced parsley

1. In a heatproof bowl, soak the dried mushrooms in the boiling water until softened, about 20 minutes. Remove the mushrooms and reserve the liquid separately. Thinly slice the mushrooms.
2. Heat the oil in a large soup pot. Add the leeks and garlic and cook over moderately low heat, stirring, until lightly browned, about 5 minutes. Thinly slice the fresh mushrooms and add them and the reconstituted mushrooms to the pot. Cook, stirring, until the liquid has evaporated, about 10 minutes. Add the reserved mushroom liquid and the stock, oat groats, carrots, parsnip, balsamic vinegar, thyme and rosemary and bring to a simmer. Cover and cook over moderately low heat until the oat groats are tender, about 35 minutes. Season with salt and pepper and stir in the parsley. Serve piping hot. —*Suki Hertz*

MAKE AHEAD The soup can be refrigerated for up to 1 day.

Tortilla Soup with Cheese and Ancho Chiles
4 SERVINGS ●
2 medium ancho chiles—stemmed,
seeded and torn into small pieces
1 tablespoon vegetable oil
1 small white onion, finely
chopped
2 garlic cloves, minced
One 14½-ounce can peeled
whole tomatoes
5 cups chicken stock or canned
low-sodium broth
½ teaspoon dried oregano
¼ teaspoon dried thyme
¼ teaspoon dried marjoram
Salt
1⅓ cups broken tortilla chips
(½-inch pieces)
5 ounces queso fresco or Muenster
cheese, cut into ½-inch dice
(1 cup)
⅓ cup sour cream, for garnish
1 tablespoon chopped
flat-leaf parsley, for garnish
Lime wedges, for serving

1. In a medium bowl, soak the ancho chiles in very hot water until softened, about 10 minutes. Drain the ancho chiles and pat them dry.
2. Meanwhile, heat the vegetable oil in a small skillet. Add the onion and garlic and cook over moderate heat, stirring occasionally, until the onion softens, about 10 minutes. Transfer the cooked onion and garlic to a blender. Add one-third of the ancho chiles and the tomatoes with their juices and blend for 1 minute. Strain the mixture into a medium saucepan. Add the stock, oregano, thyme and marjoram and bring to a boil, then simmer for 10 minutes. Season the soup with salt.
3. Divide the broken tortilla chips, cheese and remaining ancho chiles among 4 soup bowls. Ladle the soup on top. Garnish the tortilla soup with a generous dollop of sour cream and the chopped parsley and serve immediately with lime wedges. —*Jim Peyton*

Lentil and Swiss Chard Soup
6 SERVINGS ● ● ●
1 cup brown lentils, rinsed
4 cups water
4 cups chicken stock or
low-sodium broth
Salt
3 tablespoons olive oil, plus more
for serving (optional)
1 large onion, finely chopped
Pinch of crushed red pepper
4 garlic cloves, finely chopped
½ cup coarsely chopped cilantro
1 bunch green Swiss chard
(1¼ pounds), ribs removed and
reserved for another use, leaves
coarsely chopped
⅓ cup fresh lemon juice
Freshly ground pepper

1. In a medium saucepan, combine the lentils with the water, stock and 1½ teaspoons of salt and bring to a boil. Cover partially and cook over moderately low heat until the lentils are barely tender, about 25 minutes.

2. Meanwhile, heat the 3 tablespoons of olive oil in a large skillet. Add the onion, crushed pepper and a pinch of salt and cook over moderately high heat, stirring occasionally, until the onion is lightly browned, 7 to 8 minutes. Add the garlic and cilantro and cook for 1 minute. Gradually add the chard leaves to the skillet and cook, stirring occasionally, until wilted, about 3 minutes longer.

3. Add the chard mixture to the lentils, cover partially and simmer until thickened, about 15 minutes. Stir in the lemon juice and season with salt. Ladle the lentil soup into bowls, season with pepper and olive oil and serve.
—*Tasha Prysi*

Chickpea Soup with Seared Monkfish and Thyme

4 SERVINGS ● ●

- 2 tablespoons plus 1 teaspoon extra-virgin olive oil, plus more for drizzling
- 1 medium onion, finely chopped
- 2 garlic cloves, minced
- 1 rosemary sprig
- 1 sage sprig
- ½ cup finely chopped pancetta (2 ounces)
- ½ pound dried chickpeas, soaked overnight and drained
- ½ cup dry white wine
- 5 cups fish stock or water or 2½ cups bottled clam juice diluted with 2½ cups water
- 2 canned Italian plum tomatoes, finely chopped

Salt and freshly ground pepper

- 1 pound trimmed monkfish fillet, cut into ⅓-inch medallions
- 1 teaspoon thyme leaves

1. Heat 2 tablespoons of the olive oil in a large saucepan. Add the onion, garlic, rosemary, sage and half of the pancetta and cook over low heat, stirring occasionally, until the onion has softened, about 5 minutes. Add the chickpeas and cook, stirring, for 2 more minutes.

Add the wine and simmer until almost evaporated, about 4 minutes. Add the fish stock and tomatoes, cover partially and simmer over low heat until the chickpeas are tender, about 2 hours.

2. Discard the rosemary and sage sprigs from the chickpeas. Transfer 1 cup of the chickpeas with some of the liquid to a food processor and puree; stir the puree into the soup and season with salt and pepper.

3. Heat the remaining 1 teaspoon of olive oil in a large skillet. Add the remaining ¼ cup of chopped pancetta and cook over low heat, stirring often, until all the fat is rendered, about 7 minutes. Remove the pancetta and save for another use. Season the monkfish medallions with salt and pepper and sprinkle with the thyme. Add half of the medallions to the skillet and cook over moderate heat until lightly browned, about 2 minutes per side. Transfer to a plate and repeat with the remaining monkfish. Ladle the soup into shallow bowls. Arrange 3 or 4 monkfish medallions in each bowl, drizzle with olive oil and serve. —*Andrea Buscema*

WINE Bright, fruity rosé.

White Bean Soup with Asparagus and Peas

8 SERVINGS ●

A flavorful broth is critical to a soup as simple as this, so use a rich stock. If you don't have time to make your own, pick one up from a specialty food store.

- 1 cup dried cannellini or Great Northern beans—picked over, rinsed, soaked overnight in cold water and drained

Salt

- 3 quarts rich chicken stock, preferably homemade
- ½ pound farfalle pasta
- ½ pound asparagus, cut on the diagonal into 1½-inch lengths
- 1 cup frozen baby peas
- 2 tablespoons minced flat-leaf parsley
- 1 tablespoon finely chopped mint
- 1 teaspoon finely chopped thyme
- 1 teaspoon finely chopped oregano
- 1 teaspoon finely grated lemon zest
- 1 tablespoon fresh lemon juice

Freshly ground pepper

Freshly grated imported Pecorino cheese, for serving

1. In a large saucepan, cover the white beans with enough water to reach 2 inches above them and bring to a boil. Reduce the heat to moderate and simmer the beans for 30 minutes. Add a generous pinch of salt and cook until the beans are tender, 15 to 20 minutes longer. Drain the beans.

2. In a large saucepan, bring the chicken stock to a boil. Add a pinch of salt and the farfalle pasta and cook over high heat until barely al dente, about 12 minutes. Add the asparagus pieces and beans and cook until the asparagus is crisp-tender, about 3 minutes. Add the peas, parsley, mint, thyme, oregano, lemon zest and lemon juice. Simmer until the vegetables are just tender and the pasta is al dente, 2 to 3 minutes longer. Season with salt and pepper. Ladle the soup into bowls and serve, passing the cheese at the table.
—*Joanne Weir*

MAKE AHEAD The recipe can be prepared through Step 1 and refrigerated overnight.

---

cooking tip

fish stock

TO MAKE A BASIC FISH STOCK, combine 2 pounds of fish heads and bones (from nonoily fish) with 1 sliced onion, 2 bay leaves and a few sprigs of parsley and thyme. Cover with cold water and simmer for 30 minutes, skimming often. Strain and use immediately or freeze for 2 months.

soups

Black-Bean Soup Augier

6 SERVINGS ● ●

SOUP

- 1 pound dried black beans, picked over and rinsed
- 2 quarts water
- 6 cups chicken stock or canned low-sodium broth
- ¾ pound red potatoes, peeled and cut into ½-inch dice
- 2 cups chopped fresh or drained canned tomatoes
- 1 cup coarsely chopped onion
- ½ cup chopped cilantro stems
- ½ teaspoon dried thyme

Salt

- ½ cup extra-virgin olive oil
- 3 garlic cloves, minced
- 1½ tablespoons red wine vinegar

Tabasco

GARNISHES

Chopped onion

- 2 hard-cooked eggs, chopped
- 2 small bananas, sliced

Cilantro leaves and small sprigs

Extra-virgin olive oil

Red wine vinegar

Tabasco

I. MAKE THE SOUP: Put the black beans in a large pot, cover with cold water and let stand for 1 hour. Drain the beans. Rinse the pot; add the beans with the water, stock, potatoes, tomatoes, onion, cilantro stems, thyme and 1 teaspoon of salt and bring to a boil.

Reduce the heat to low and cook, stirring occasionally, until the beans are tender and the soup has thickened, about 2½ hours.

2. Transfer 3 cups of the cooked beans to a food processor and puree until smooth. Stir the puree back into the soup. If the soup is too thick, thin it with a little water. Stir in the olive oil, garlic and vinegar, season with salt and Tabasco and bring to a boil.

3. PREPARE THE GARNISHES: Put the onion in a colander and rinse under cold water; pat dry. Put the onion, eggs, bananas and cilantro in separate bowls. Set out the olive oil, vinegar and Tabasco. Ladle the soup into bowls and serve accompanied by the garnishes.

—Jacques Pépin

MAKE AHEAD The soup can be refrigerated for up to 3 days. Reheat gently.

Mexican Black Bean Soup with Sausage

4 SERVINGS ● ● ●

- 2 tablespoons extra-virgin olive oil
- 1 medium onion, finely chopped
- 3 garlic cloves, very finely chopped
- 1 canned chipotle chile, seeded and finely chopped
- 1 teaspoon ground cumin
- 1 teaspoon dried oregano

Two 15-ounce cans black beans, drained

- 3 cups chicken stock or canned low-sodium broth
- ¾ pound smoky cooked sausage, such as andouille or kielbasa, thinly sliced
- 2 tablespoons fresh lime juice
- 2 tablespoons very finely chopped cilantro

Salt and freshly ground pepper

Sour cream and lime wedges, for serving

I. In a medium saucepan, heat the oil until shimmering. Add the onion; cook over moderate heat, stirring occasionally, until softened, about 3 minutes.

Add the garlic along with the chipotle, cumin and oregano and cook, stirring, until fragrant, 2 minutes. Add the black beans and chicken stock and simmer, partially covered, for 15 minutes. Using a potato masher, coarsely crush some of the beans.

2. Meanwhile, heat a large skillet over high heat. Add the sausage and cook until browned, stirring occasionally, about 5 minutes. Add the sausage to the beans, along with the lime juice and cilantro; season with salt and pepper. Simmer the soup for 2 minutes to allow the flavors to blend. Ladle the soup into bowls and serve, passing the sour cream and lime wedges separately.

—Diane Rossen Worthington

Caldo Verde

6 SERVINGS ● ● ●

Although this classic Portuguese soup is simple to make, it requires the highest quality chorizo, a spicy and chewy smoked sausage. It's also best with a leafy kale, such as Russian kale or Tuscan cavolo nero.

- 2 tablespoons extra-virgin olive oil, plus more for drizzling
- 2 garlic cloves, minced
- 1 large Spanish onion, chopped
- 6 ounces chorizo, cut into ¼-inch-thick slices
- 2 quarts water
- 1 pound Yukon Gold potatoes, peeled and cut into 1-inch chunks

Salt and freshly ground pepper

- 1 pound kale, stems discarded and leaves finely shredded

I. Heat the 2 tablespoons of olive oil in a large enameled cast-iron casserole. Add the garlic, onion and half of the chorizo and cook over low heat, stirring occasionally, until the onion is softened, about 8 minutes. Add the water and potatoes. Season with a large pinch each of salt and pepper and bring to a boil. Simmer the soup over low heat until the potatoes are tender, about 15 minutes.

---

kitchen tip

chilling soup

TO CHILL A LARGE AMOUNT OF SOUP OR STOCK QUICKLY, place a clean plastic bottle of frozen water into the pot. Once the soup has cooled, simply remove the bottle. For smaller batches of soup, submerge zip-top bags filled with ice cubes or ice packs into the soup and remove when chilled.

BLACK-BEAN SOUP AUGIER

GREEK CHICKEN SOUP

2. Using an immersion blender, process the soup to a coarse puree. Bring the soup to a boil. Add the kale and simmer until it is wilted, about 3 minutes. Stir in the remaining half of the chorizo and simmer for 5 minutes. Season with salt and pepper and serve in bowls, drizzled with olive oil. —*Taylor Fladgate*
MAKE AHEAD The soup can be refrigerated for 2 days.
WINE Aromatic, zesty Albariño.

Greek Chicken Soup

8 SERVINGS ●
Three 3-pound chickens, halved
 5 quarts cold water
 5 large carrots (about 1 pound),
  1 halved lengthwise and 4 cut
  into ½-inch dice
 5 celery ribs (about 1 pound),
  1 halved lengthwise and
  4 cut into ½-inch dice
 5 large flat-leaf parsley sprigs,
  plus 2 tablespoons finely
  chopped parsley
 2 bay leaves
 1 teaspoon whole peppercorns
 1 tablespoon unsalted butter
 1 large Spanish onion, quartered
  through the root end
Salt
 2 pounds large Yukon Gold
  potatoes, peeled and cut into
  ½-inch dice
Freshly ground pepper
Lemon wedges, for serving

1. Cut the breasts off the chickens and discard the skin. Cut the breast meat into 1-inch pieces and reserve in the refrigerator.
2. Put the remaining chicken halves in a large soup pot. Add the water, carrot and celery halves, parsley sprigs, bay leaves and peppercorns.

3. Melt the butter in a skillet. Add the onion and cook over moderately high heat until browned, about 5 minutes; add to the pot. Season with salt; bring to a boil. Skim and simmer over moderately low heat until the chicken falls off the bone and the broth is flavorful, about 3½ hours. Let cool slightly.
4. Strain the broth into a saucepan and skim off the fat. Bring the broth to a boil. Add the diced celery and cook for 3 minutes. Add the diced carrots and cook for 5 minutes. Add the potatoes and cook for 5 minutes. Season the reserved breast meat with salt and pepper, add it to the soup and simmer until it is cooked through and the vegetables are tender, about 5 minutes. Season the soup with salt and pepper, sprinkle with the chopped parsley and serve in bowls. Pass the lemon wedges at the table. —*Johannes Sanzin*

soups

Chicken and Sweet-Potato Chowder

4 SERVINGS ● ●

- 2 tablespoons unsalted butter
- 1 pound skinless, boneless chicken breast and thighs, cut into 1-inch pieces
- 1 medium onion, finely chopped
- 3 medium leeks, white and light green parts only, thinly sliced
- 2 large sweet potatoes, peeled and cut into ½-inch dice
- 3 cups chicken stock or canned low-sodium broth
- 2 tablespoons sliced fresh sage
- 1 tablespoon minced flat-leaf parsley
- 1 bay leaf

Salt and freshly ground white pepper
- 1 cup whole milk

1. Melt the butter in a large saucepan. Add the chicken and cook over moderately high heat, stirring, until golden, about 2 minutes. Transfer to a plate. Add the onion and all but 1 tablespoon of the leeks and cook, stirring often, until softened, about 5 minutes. Add the sweet potatoes and cook for 3 minutes. Return the chicken to the pan. Add the stock, 1 tablespoon of the sage, the parsley, bay leaf, salt and white pepper and bring to a boil. Cover and simmer over moderately low heat until the chicken is white throughout and the potatoes are tender, about 10 minutes.

2. Using a slotted spoon, transfer 1½ cups of the sweet potatoes to a food processor and puree until smooth. Return the puree to the saucepan. Stir in the milk and season with salt and pepper. Simmer the chowder for 3 minutes, then discard the bay leaf. Spoon the sweet-potato chowder into bowls and serve hot, garnished with the remaining 1 tablespoon each of leeks and sage. —*Damon Lee Fowler*

MAKE AHEAD The chowder can be refrigerated for up to 1 day.

WINE Ripe, creamy-textured Chardonnay.

Creamy Mushroom Soup with Chicken

4 SERVINGS ● ●

- 1 quart chicken stock or canned low-sodium broth
- 1 ounce dried shiitake or porcini mushrooms
- 4 tablespoons unsalted butter
- 1 medium onion, finely chopped
- ¾ pound cremini mushrooms, thinly sliced

Salt and freshly ground white pepper
- ¼ cup all-purpose flour
- 2 teaspoons soy sauce
- 1 pound skinless, boneless chicken breasts, cut into ¾-inch pieces
- 1 cup half-and-half
- 3 tablespoons tawny port or dry sherry
- 2 tablespoons finely chopped flat-leaf parsley

1. In a medium saucepan, bring the chicken stock to a boil with the dried mushrooms. Cover the saucepan and remove from the heat.

2. Melt the butter in another medium saucepan. Add the onion and cook over moderately high heat, stirring, until softened, about 3 minutes. Add the sliced cremini and cook until tender and their liquid has evaporated, about 5 minutes. Season the cremini with salt and white pepper and stir in the flour. Strain the stock into the saucepan, pressing hard on the solids with the back of a spoon. Stir the soy sauce into the mushroom soup, cover partially and simmer until slightly thickened, about 10 minutes.

3. Transfer half of the mushroom soup to a blender or food processor and puree until smooth. Return the puree to the saucepan. Add the chicken and simmer until cooked through, 3 to 4 minutes. Stir in the half-and-half and port and simmer the soup for 1 minute longer. Stir in the parsley, ladle the soup into bowls and serve right away. —*Diane Rossen Worthington*

MAKE AHEAD The soup can be refrigerated for up to 1 day.

Seafood Stew with Anchovy Aioli

4 SERVINGS ● ●

- 2 tablespoons extra-virgin olive oil
- 1 medium onion, finely chopped
- 1 medium carrot, finely chopped
- 4 garlic cloves, minced
- ½ cup dry white wine
- 1 cup bottled clam juice

One 28-ounce can diced peeled tomatoes with their juices
- 1 tablespoon tomato paste diluted in ½ cup water

Two 2-inch-long strips of orange zest
- 1½ teaspoons anchovy paste

Salt and freshly ground pepper
- ¼ cup mayonnaise

Cayenne pepper
- ¾ pound shelled and deveined large shrimp, cut into 1-inch pieces
- ¾ pound sea scallops, halved or quartered if large

1. Preheat the oven to 350°. In a medium saucepan, heat the olive oil until shimmering. Add the onion, carrot and three-fourths of the garlic and cook over moderately high heat, stirring occasionally, until softened, about 3 minutes. Add the wine and cook until evaporated, about 3 minutes. Stir in the clam juice, the tomatoes and their juices, the diluted tomato paste, orange zest and ½ teaspoon of the anchovy paste; season with salt and pepper. Simmer over moderately high heat until reduced by half, about 15 minutes.

2. Discard the zest. Transfer half of the soup to a blender and coarsely puree. Return the puree to the saucepan.

3. In a small bowl, stir the mayonnaise with the remaining garlic and 1 teaspoon of anchovy paste. Season with cayenne.

4. Return the soup to a gentle boil. Add the shrimp and scallops and simmer until just cooked through, about 3 minutes. Serve in deep bowls; pass the aioli at the table. —*Diane Rossen Worthington*

SERVE WITH Toasted baguette slices.

Gumbo-Style Crab Soup with Okra and Tomatoes

10 SERVINGS ● ●

This more delicate cousin of New Orleans gumbo is a spicier version of the crab soup Charleston is known for.

4 tablespoons unsalted butter
2 large onions, finely chopped
6 celery ribs, finely chopped
1 red bell pepper, finely chopped
2 tablespoons minced garlic
1 teaspoon thyme leaves
½ teaspoon crushed red pepper
Salt and freshly ground pepper
½ cup dry red wine
One 28-ounce can Italian plum tomatoes, drained and coarsely chopped, juices reserved
3 bay leaves
2½ quarts fish stock or light chicken stock or 1½ quarts bottled clam juice mixed with 1 quart water
1½ pounds fresh or thawed frozen okra, sliced crosswise ½ inch thick (6 cups)
1½ pounds lump crabmeat, picked over to remove cartilage
½ cup chopped basil
Tabasco sauce

1. In a large, heavy pot, melt 2 tablespoons of the butter. Add the onions and cook over low heat, stirring occasionally, until softened, about 10 minutes. Add the celery, bell pepper, garlic, thyme and crushed pepper. Season with salt and pepper and cook until the vegetables are softened, about 10 minutes. Add the wine and boil over moderately high heat until reduced to a syrup, about 1 minute. Add the tomato juices and bay leaves and boil until reduced by half, about 4 minutes. Add the stock, bring to a boil and simmer over low heat for 30 minutes.

2. In a large skillet, melt the remaining 2 tablespoons of butter. Add the okra, season with salt and pepper and cook over moderately high heat, stirring a few times, until browned, about 4 minutes. Add the tomatoes and bring to a boil. Stir the okra and tomatoes into the soup and simmer over low heat for 30 minutes longer. Discard the bay leaves.

3. Add the crabmeat to the soup and simmer until just heated through. Stir in the basil and season with salt, pepper and Tabasco. Ladle the soup into shallow bowls and serve. —*Robert Stehling*

MAKE AHEAD The soup can be prepared through Step 2 and refrigerated in an airtight container for up to 2 days. Reheat gently before proceeding.

WINE Light, spicy Pinot Grigio.

Spicy Red Lentil Coconut Soup with Shrimp Dumplings

10 SERVINGS ●

Red lentils make a hearty addition to this surprisingly tangy and fragrant Asian-style coconut soup.

SOUP

2 teaspoons fennel seeds
2 teaspoons cumin seeds
2 teaspoons coriander seeds
¼ cup peanut oil
3 carrots, coarsely shredded
2 red onions, halved lengthwise and thinly sliced crosswise
1 medium leek, white and tender green parts only, thinly sliced
4 garlic cloves, minced
2 teaspoons minced fresh ginger
1 small fresh red chile, seeded and minced
5 cups water
2¾ cups unsweetened coconut milk
6 kaffir lime leaves or six 1-inch strips of lime zest
¾ cup red lentils
Salt and freshly ground pepper

DUMPLINGS

2 small garlic cloves, smashed
¼ cup cilantro leaves
¼ cup mint leaves
1 pound large shrimp, shelled and deveined
1 tablespoon cornstarch

road test blenders		
PRODUCT	F&W COMMENT	INTERESTING BITE
Waring Pro Bar Blender	"It performs the basic liquefying function very well."	The unique cloverleaf shape of the carafe pulls food into the center of the vortex and onto the blades.
Oster In2itive Blender	"Nice, tight cover seal and very well balanced."	An LCD screen displays built-in recipes for 40 foods and drinks, such as salsas, smoothies and batters.
KitchenAid Ultra Power Blender	"The design is better. It used to be easy to open the bottom accidentally."	The blender is virtually silent when in use, thanks to an extra-powerful motor.

CREAMY NORTH FORK CLAM CHOWDER

HOT AND SOUR SHRIMP SOUP WITH JASMINE RICE

1 tablespoon plus 2 teaspoons Asian fish sauce, plus more for serving

½ teaspoon Asian sesame oil

¼ cup fresh lime juice

½ cup finely chopped cilantro

1. MAKE THE SOUP: In a skillet, toast the fennel, cumin and coriander seeds over moderate heat until fragrant, about 2 minutes; let cool. Transfer to a spice grinder and finely grind the spices.

2. In a casserole, heat the oil until shimmering. Add the carrots, onions, leek, garlic, ginger and chile and cook over moderately high heat until softened and lightly browned, about 5 minutes. Add the ground spices and cook until fragrant, about 2 minutes. Add the water, coconut milk and lime leaves and bring to a boil. Stir in the lentils; simmer over low heat, stirring, until tender, about 20 minutes. Season with salt and pepper.

3. MAKE THE DUMPLINGS: In a food processor, combine the garlic, cilantro and mint and pulse until finely chopped. Add the shrimp and pulse until coarsely chopped. Transfer the mixture to a bowl and stir in the cornstarch, 1 tablespoon of fish sauce and the sesame oil. Refrigerate for 30 minutes.

4. Using moistened hands, roll teaspoons of the shrimp mixture into balls; arrange on a plastic wrap–lined plate.

5. Add the dumplings and the 2 teaspoons of fish sauce to the casserole and simmer just until the dumplings are slightly pink and cooked, about 5 minutes. Remove the lime leaves. Stir in the lime juice and cilantro and serve with the fish sauce. *—Peter Gordon*

MAKE AHEAD The soup and shrimp balls can be prepared through Step 4 and refrigerated separately overnight.

WINE Lively, assertive Sauvignon Blanc.

Creamy North Fork Clam Chowder

12 SERVINGS ●

1½ cups dry white wine

1½ cups water

2½ dozen cherrystone clams

1½ pounds baking potatoes, peeled and cut into ½-inch dice

Kosher salt

8 thick slices of smoky bacon, cut into ¼-inch dice

1 large onion, finely chopped (1½ cups)

6 large celery ribs, finely chopped

2 small bay leaves

6 tablespoons all-purpose flour

3 cups whole milk

1½ cups heavy cream

2 tablespoons chopped dill

2 tablespoons chopped flat-leaf parsley

Tabasco sauce

1. In a large pot, bring the wine and water to a boil. Add the clams, cover and cook over moderately high heat, shaking the pot a few times, until the clams open, about 8 minutes. Transfer the clams to a bowl and let cool slightly; discard any clams that do not open. Remove the clams from their shells and coarsely chop them. Strain the cooking liquid and reserve. Rinse out the pot.

2. In a medium saucepan, cover the potatoes with water and bring to a boil. Season generously with salt and simmer over moderate heat until tender, about 8 minutes. Drain.

3. Add the bacon to the large pot and cook over low heat, stirring occasionally, until the fat has been rendered, about 7 minutes. Add the onion, celery and bay leaves and cook until the vegetables soften, about 8 minutes. Add the flour and cook for 2 minutes, stirring constantly. Slowly stir in the milk until smooth, then stir in the cream. Pour in the reserved cooking liquid, stopping before you reach the grit on the bottom. Bring the clam chowder to a simmer over moderate heat, then reduce the heat to low and simmer for 15 minutes, stirring occasionally.

4. Add the potatoes to the chowder and cook until heated through. Add the chopped clams and simmer for 5 minutes. Stir in the dill and parsley and season with salt and Tabasco. Ladle into soup bowls and serve piping hot. —*David Page and Barbara Shinn*

MAKE AHEAD The clam chowder can be refrigerated for up to 2 days. Reheat gently before serving.

Cellophane Noodle and Meatball Soup

4 SERVINGS ● ●

- 5 ounces ground pork
- 2 tablespoons minced cilantro stems and leaves
- 2 medium garlic cloves, minced
- 3 cups chicken stock
- 4 ounces soft tofu, cut into 1-inch dice
- 3 cups chopped Chinese cabbage
- 2 ounces dried cellophane noodles, cut into 3-inch lengths
- 3 tablespoons low-sodium soy sauce

Freshly ground pepper

- 2 medium scallions, chopped
- ½ cup chopped celery leaves

1. In a large bowl, gently mix the ground pork with the cilantro and garlic. Shape the mixture into 16 meatballs.

2. In a large saucepan, bring the chicken stock to a boil. Add the meatballs and simmer over moderate heat until no longer pink on the outside, about 2 minutes. Add the diced tofu and the chopped Chinese cabbage and simmer for 2 minutes longer. Add the cellophane noodles and soy sauce. Season the soup generously with freshly ground pepper and simmer for 3 minutes longer. Stir in the chopped scallions and the chopped celery leaves. Ladle the soup into warmed bowls and serve piping hot. —*Sompon and Elizabeth Nabnian*

Hot and Sour Shrimp Soup with Jasmine Rice

4 SERVINGS ● ●

The fresh, sophisticated flavors of this Vietnamese-style soup belie how quick and easy it is to make. The fragrant jasmine rice helps temper the boldly flavored broth.

1¼ cups Thai jasmine rice, rinsed

Water

- 1 pound medium shrimp, shelled and deveined, shells reserved
- 2 tablespoons vegetable oil
- 2 large garlic cloves, thinly sliced
- 2 teaspoons crushed red pepper
- ¼ pound snow peas, julienned
- 1 medium tomato, cut into thin wedges
- ¼ cup Asian fish sauce
- ¼ cup coarsely chopped cilantro
- ¼ cup fresh lime juice
- ½ teaspoon finely grated lime zest
- ½ teaspoon freshly ground pepper
- 1 large scallion, thinly sliced

1. In a saucepan, cover the rice with 1¾ cups of water and bring to a boil. Cover and simmer over very low heat for 12 minutes. Remove from the heat without lifting the lid and let stand, covered, for 5 minutes. Using a fork, fluff the rice, then cover and set aside.

2. Meanwhile, in a medium saucepan, cover the shrimp shells with 4 cups of water and bring to a boil. Simmer over low heat for 10 minutes. Strain the broth and return it to the saucepan.

3. Heat the oil in a small skillet. Add the garlic; cook over low heat until golden, about 2 minutes. Add the crushed red pepper. Scrape the garlic oil into a bowl.

4. Bring the shrimp broth to a boil. Add the snow peas and tomato and simmer over moderately high heat for 1 minute. Add the shrimp and cook just until opaque throughout and curled, about 1 minute. Stir in the garlic oil, fish sauce, cilantro, lime juice, lime zest, pepper and scallion. Spoon the rice into deep bowls, ladle the soup over it and serve. —*Marcia Kiesel*

Red Miso Soup

4 SERVINGS ● ●

3½ cups Dashi (p. 176)
- 2 tablespoons plus 1 teaspoon red miso paste
- ½ pound silken tofu, drained and cut into ½-inch cubes
- ½ cup coarsely chopped cremini mushrooms
- 2 tablespoons chervil or cilantro leaves

In a medium saucepan, bring the Dashi to a boil over moderately high heat. Whisk in the miso paste, then add the tofu and mushrooms and bring to a simmer. Ladle the soup into bowls, sprinkle with the chervil and serve. —*Kazuo Yoshida*

PENNE WITH VEAL RAGÙ, P. 88

pasta

LINGUINE FINE WITH ZUCCHINI, BASIL AND DILL

LAZY LINGUINE WITH TOMATOES AND HERBS

Penne with Cherry Tomatoes, Olives and Pecorino

4 SERVINGS ●

Salt

- 1 pound penne
- ½ cup plus 1 tablespoon extra-virgin olive oil
- 1 cup basil leaves
- ½ cup flat-leaf parsley leaves
- 2 garlic cloves, halved
- 2 teaspoons coarsely chopped thyme
- 2 teaspoons coarsely chopped marjoram
- 1½ pounds cherry tomatoes— halved, seeded and quartered
- ⅓ cup Calamata olives, pitted and coarsely chopped
- 1 cup coarsely grated Tuscan Pecorino cheese (3 ounces)

Freshly ground pepper

1. Bring a large pot of water to a boil. Add salt, then add the penne and cook until al dente. Drain the penne and toss with 1 tablespoon of the olive oil. Let cool to room temperature.

2. Meanwhile, in a blender, puree the basil, parsley, garlic, thyme and marjoram with the remaining ½ cup of olive oil. Scrape the herb puree into a bowl and season with salt.

3. In a large bowl, toss the penne with the herb puree to coat. Add the cherry tomatoes and Calamata olives and let stand at room temperature for at least 10 minutes to develop flavor. Just before serving, add the Pecorino to the penne, season with pepper and toss well.
—Graziella Dionisi

MAKE AHEAD The pasta can be assembled up to 2 hours ahead. Toss well before serving.

WINE Dry, light, refreshing Soave.

Linguine Fine with Zucchini, Basil and Dill

4 SERVINGS ● ●

Linguine fine is a thinner strand of noodle than the more common linguine.

- ¾ pound linguine fine
- ½ cup coarsely chopped dill
- ½ cup coarsely chopped basil leaves
- 2 garlic cloves, halved
- ¼ cup plus 2 tablespoons extra-virgin olive oil
- 6 scallions, cut into ½-inch lengths
- 1½ pounds small zucchini, cut into 2-by-¼-inch-long sticks

Salt and freshly ground pepper

- ½ cup freshly grated Tuscan Pecorino cheese (1½ ounces)

1. Cook the linguine fine in a large pot of boiling salted water until al dente. Reserve ¼ cup of the pasta cooking water, then drain the pasta.

2. Meanwhile, in a food processor, puree the dill with the basil, garlic and 3 tablespoons of the olive oil. In a large, deep skillet, heat the remaining 3 tablespoons of olive oil. Add the scallions and cook over low heat, stirring occasionally, until softened, about 10 minutes. Spread the zucchini on top of the scallions, cover and cook until the zucchini are al dente, about 6 minutes.

3. Add the pasta to the skillet along with the reserved pasta cooking water, season with salt and pepper and toss. Add the herb puree and the Pecorino and toss well. Transfer to a bowl and serve. —*Graziella Dionisi*

MAKE AHEAD The herb puree can be refrigerated overnight.

WINE Tangy, crisp Vernaccia.

Lazy Linguine with Cherry Tomatoes and Herbs
6 SERVINGS ● ● ●

- 1 pound linguine
- 1 pint cherry tomatoes, halved
- 2 large garlic cloves, minced
- ½ cup roughly torn basil
- ⅓ cup finely chopped flat-leaf parsley
- 1 tablespoon finely chopped marjoram
- 1 jalapeño, seeded and finely chopped
- ⅓ cup extra-virgin olive oil

Kosher salt and freshly ground pepper

1. In a large pot of boiling salted water, cook the pasta until al dente. Drain and cool under cold running water. Shake off any excess water and pat the linguine dry with paper towels.

2. In a large bowl, toss the cherry tomatoes with the garlic, basil, parsley, marjoram, jalapeño and olive oil and season with salt and pepper. Add the pasta, toss well and serve.

—*Benedetta Vitali*

MAKE AHEAD The pasta can be refrigerated for 3 hours. Let return to room temperature before serving.

WINE Lively, assertive Sauvignon Blanc.

Wagon Wheels with Broccoli and Parmesan Cheese
4 SIDE-DISH SERVINGS ● ● ●

Gale Gand's son, Gio, thinks wagon wheels, or rotelle, are the most fun pasta here. Any other pasta shape, such as penne or fusilli, can be used instead.

Salt
- 2 cups small broccoli florets
- ½ pound wagon-wheel pasta
- ½ cup chicken stock or low-sodium broth
- 2 tablespoons unsalted butter
- ¼ cup freshly grated Parmesan cheese, plus more for serving

Freshly ground pepper

1. In a large saucepan of boiling salted water, cook the broccoli until crisp-tender, about 5 minutes. Transfer the broccoli to a bowl with a slotted spoon.

2. Bring the water back to a boil. Add the wagon wheels and cook until al dente. Drain well in a colander.

3. Return the pasta to the saucepan. Add the chicken stock and butter and cook over moderately high heat, stirring gently, until some of the stock is absorbed. Stir in the broccoli and the ¼ cup of Parmesan, season with salt and pepper and toss. Serve immediately, with additional Parmesan. —*Gale Gand*

Bucatini with Pecorino and Coarse Pepper
4 SERVINGS ●

- 1 pound bucatini, broken in half
- 6 tablespoons extra-virgin olive oil
- 1 tablespoon very coarsely ground black pepper
- 1 tablespoon very coarsely ground white pepper
- 1 cup coarsely chopped cherry tomatoes
- 1¾ cups freshly grated Pecorino Romano cheese (6 ounces)

Salt

Cook the bucatini in a large pot of boiling salted water until al dente. Reserve ½ cup of the pasta cooking water; drain the bucatini and return it to the pot.

Add the olive oil, black and white pepper and the reserved pasta water. Add the cherry tomatoes and 1½ cups of the cheese, season with salt and toss well. Transfer to a large warmed bowl and sprinkle with the remaining cheese. Serve at once. —*Roberto Marchetti*

WINE Dry, light, refreshing Soave.

Chickpea and Swiss Chard Fideos with Orange Aioli
8 SERVINGS ●

Fideos (thin dried wheat noodles usually sold in coils) were introduced to Spain by the Moors and are used in Middle Eastern and Spanish dishes.

- 2 tablespoons vegetable oil
- ½ large white onion, chopped
- 1 carrot, coarsely chopped
- 4 garlic cloves, smashed
- 1 teaspoon ground coriander
- 1 teaspoon ground fennel seeds
- 1 tablespoon unsweetened cocoa powder

Pinch of saffron threads
- 1 bay leaf
- 4 plum tomatoes, coarsely chopped
- 3 medium ancho chiles—stemmed, seeded and cut into 2-inch pieces
- 2½ quarts water

Salt and freshly ground pepper
- 3 tablespoons extra-virgin olive oil
- 1 pound dried fideos or angel hair coils, broken into 2-inch lengths
- 1¼ pounds green Swiss chard, stems discarded and leaves chopped

One 15-ounce can of chickpeas, drained and rinsed

Orange Aioli (recipe follows)

1. In a large pot, heat the vegetable oil until shimmering. Add the onion, carrot and garlic and cook over moderate heat, stirring, until the vegetables just start to brown, about 5 minutes. Stir in the coriander, fennel, cocoa, saffron and bay leaf; cook for 10 seconds. Add the tomatoes, anchos and water and bring to a boil over high heat. Reduce the heat to moderate and simmer for 25 minutes. Discard the bay leaf.

pasta

2. Working in batches if necessary, puree the vegetable broth in a blender until smooth. Strain into a clean pot. Season the broth with salt and pepper and bring to a boil over high heat. Cook until reduced to just 8 cups.

3. In a large, deep skillet, heat the olive oil until shimmering. Add the pasta and cook over moderate heat, stirring, until golden, 5 minutes. Stir in the Swiss chard by handfuls, adding more as it wilts. Add the broth and bring to a boil over high heat. Cook over moderate heat, stirring occasionally, until the pasta is almost tender and most of the broth has been absorbed, about 15 minutes. Add the chickpeas and cook, stirring, until heated through and the broth has been almost completely absorbed by the pasta, about 3 minutes longer. Stir in 2 tablespoons of the Orange Aioli, season with salt and pepper and serve with the remaining aioli. —*Ana Sortun*

MAKE AHEAD The recipe can be prepared through Step 2 and refrigerated for up to 2 days. Reheat before proceeding with the dish.

ORANGE AIOLI
MAKES ABOUT 1¼ CUPS ● ●

- 1 large garlic clove, minced
- 1 teaspoon finely grated orange zest
- 1 teaspoon Dijon mustard
- 1 cup mayonnaise
- ¼ cup extra-virgin olive oil
- 1 tablespoon fresh lemon juice

Salt

Cayenne pepper

In a mini food processor, combine the garlic with the orange zest and mustard and pulse to combine. Add the mayonnaise and process until smooth. With the machine on, gradually add the olive oil and process until emulsified. Scrape the aioli into a small bowl. Stir in the lemon juice and season with salt and cayenne. —*A.S.*

MAKE AHEAD The aioli can be refrigerated for up to 3 days.

Mustard Spaetzle with Chives
4 SERVINGS

- 4 large eggs, at room temperature
- ¾ cup milk
- 3 tablespoons Dijon mustard
- 1 tablespoon snipped chives
- 1 teaspoon salt
- ¼ teaspoon freshly grated nutmeg
- 2 cups all-purpose flour
- 4 tablespoons unsalted butter

1. In a medium bowl, beat the eggs with the milk, mustard, chives, salt and nutmeg. Add the flour and stir until a sticky batter forms.

2. Scrape one-third of the batter into a large colander with ¼-inch holes. Working over a large pot of boiling salted water, scrape the batter across the colander bottom with a rubber spatula to press it through the holes. Gently stir the simmering spaetzle. Press the remaining batter through in 2 batches; stir and simmer the spaetzle until cooked through but slightly chewy, 1 to 2 minutes. Drain in a clean colander.

3. In a large skillet, melt the butter over moderately high heat. Add the spaetzle and cook, stirring, until thoroughly coated. Transfer the spaetzle to a bowl and serve right away. —*Gale Gand*

MAKE AHEAD The spaetzle can be prepared through Step 2 several hours ahead and sautéed just before serving.

Sweet Potato Gnocchi with Apple Cider Sauce
6 SERVINGS ●

- 3 pounds sweet potatoes— scrubbed, peeled and cut into 2-inch chunks

Salt

- 2 cups apple cider
- ¾ cup plus 2 tablespoons all-purpose flour
- 2 large egg yolks, beaten

Freshly ground pepper

- 2 tablespoons unsalted butter
- 2 garlic cloves, finely chopped
- 4 sage leaves, coarsely chopped

1. In a saucepan, cover the sweet potatoes with water, add salt and bring to a boil. Cover and simmer until tender, about 30 minutes; let cool slightly.

2. In a small saucepan, simmer the cider over moderately high heat until reduced to ½ cup, about 20 minutes.

3. Puree the sweet potatoes in a food processor. Transfer 3⅓ cups of the puree to a large bowl. Lightly beat in the flour and yolks; season with salt and pepper. Spoon the dough into a pastry bag fitted with a ½-inch round tip. Working in 3 batches over a large saucepan of simmering water, pipe out the dough, cutting it into ¾-inch lengths. Cook the gnocchi for 45 seconds. Using a slotted spoon, transfer the gnocchi to a baking sheet.

4. In each of 2 large skillets, melt 1 tablespoon of the butter. Add half the gnocchi to each and cook over moderate heat until golden, about 2 minutes. Add the garlic and sage and cook for 1 minute. Stir in the reduced cider and serve. —*Mory Thomas*

Green Olive Gnocchi with Green Olive Sauce
6 SERVINGS ●

Don't be tempted to leave out the cream here—it adds an amazing dimension.

- 1 pound medium red potatoes, scrubbed
- 1⅓ cups chicken stock or canned low-sodium broth
- ½ cup heavy cream
- 1½ cups all-purpose flour

Fine sea salt

- ½ pound green Sicilian olives, pitted and coarsely chopped
- 4 tablespoons unsalted butter, melted
- 1 tablespoon extra-virgin olive oil
- 1 large onion, finely chopped
- 3 garlic cloves, minced
- 3 tablespoons chopped parsley

Freshly ground pepper

- ¼ cup plus 2 tablespoons freshly grated Parmesan cheese

1. In a medium saucepan, cover the potatoes with water and bring to a boil. Cook over moderately high heat until tender, about 25 minutes. Drain and let cool slightly, then peel the potatoes. Meanwhile, in a medium saucepan, boil the stock until reduced to ⅔ cup, about 15 minutes. Transfer to a bowl and stir in the cream. Wipe out the saucepan.

2. In a large bowl, combine the flour with 1 teaspoon of salt and half of the olives. Pass the potatoes through a ricer set over the bowl with the flour. Add the butter and stir until a stiff dough forms. Turn the dough out onto a lightly floured work surface and knead it gently until smooth, 2 or 3 minutes. Quarter the dough. On an unfloured work surface, roll each piece of dough into a ½-inch-thick rope. Cut the ropes into 1-inch lengths and transfer the gnocchi to a lightly floured baking sheet.

3. Heat the oil in the medium saucepan. Add the onion and garlic, cover and cook over moderately low heat, stirring, until softened, about 8 minutes. Add the cream mixture and boil until reduced slightly, about 5 minutes. Add the remaining olives and 2 tablespoons of the parsley and season with salt and pepper. Cover and keep warm.

4. In a large pot of boiling salted water, cook the gnocchi over moderately high heat, stirring very gently, until they begin to rise to the surface. Cook the gnocchi for 1 minute longer, until just tender. Gently drain the gnocchi and return them to the pot. Add the green olive sauce and ¼ cup of the Parmesan, season with pepper and stir gently over moderate heat for 1 minute. Transfer the gnocchi to a serving platter, sprinkle with the remaining 1 tablespoon of parsley and 2 tablespoons of Parmesan and serve. —*Maggie Beer*

VARIATION The green olive gnocchi can be tossed with brown butter, chopped fresh sage leaves and Parmesan instead of the olive sauce.

WINE Tart, low-tannin Barbera.

MUSTARD SPAETZLE WITH CHIVES

SWEET POTATO GNOCCHI WITH APPLE CIDER SAUCE

CHILLED CAPELLINI WITH CLAMS AND CAVIAR

Handmade Pasta with Tomato and Artichoke Sauce

4 SERVINGS ● ●

This pasta is our simplified adaptation of the pici that Michael Romano makes. Pici is a Tuscan pasta that is laboriously rolled by hand, strand by strand.

PASTA

- 2 cups all-purpose flour, plus more for dusting

Pinch of kosher salt

- 3 large eggs
- 2 tablespoons extra-virgin olive oil, plus more for rubbing

Coarse cornmeal, for dusting

SAUCE

- 1 lemon, halved
- 4 medium artichokes
- 1 cup chicken stock or canned low-sodium broth
- 1 cup dry white wine
- 2 garlic cloves, minced
- 2 tablespoons tomato paste
- 1 tablespoon extra-virgin olive oil
- ¼ teaspoon crushed red pepper

Salt and freshly ground pepper

- ½ cup freshly grated Pecorino Romano cheese
- 2 tablespoons chopped fresh basil
- 1 tablespoon chopped parsley

I. MAKE THE PASTA: In a food processor, pulse the flour with the salt a few times. In a medium bowl, beat the eggs with the olive oil. With the machine on, pour in the eggs and process until a smooth, sticky dough forms. Scrape the dough out onto a lightly floured work surface and knead until smooth. The dough will be soft and still slightly tacky. Transfer the dough to a medium bowl and rub the surface with olive oil. Cover with plastic wrap and let stand at room temperature for at least 30 minutes.

2. Divide the dough in half. On a lightly floured surface, roll out 1 piece to a rectangle about ⅛ inch thick. Cut the dough in half. Using a pizza cutter, cut the dough into 6- to 8-inch-long strands about ⅓ inch wide. Dust 2 large baking sheets with cornmeal.

Carefully lay the strands on the sheets and sprinkle the strands with cornmeal to prevent sticking. Repeat with the remaining dough. Cover and set aside at room temperature.

3. MAKE THE SAUCE: Fill a large bowl with water and squeeze a lemon half into it. Working with 1 artichoke at a time, snap off the outer leaves. Using a sharp knife, cut off the top two-thirds of the leaves and trim the base and stem. Using a melon baller or teaspoon, scoop out the furry choke. Rub the artichoke heart all over with the remaining lemon half. Slice the heart ¼ inch thick and put in the bowl of lemon water. Repeat with the remaining 3 artichokes.

4. Drain the artichokes. In a medium saucepan, combine the artichokes with the stock, wine, garlic, tomato paste, olive oil and crushed pepper; season with salt and pepper and bring to a boil. Simmer over low heat, stirring a few times, until the artichokes are just tender and the sauce has thickened slightly, about 30 minutes. Season the sauce with salt and pepper and keep warm.

5. Bring a large pot of salted water to a boil. Add the pasta and cook, stirring, until al dente, about 5 minutes. Drain and transfer to a large, wide pasta bowl. Spoon the sauce over the pasta and toss well. Sprinkle with the Pecorino, basil and parsley and serve at once.
—Michael Romano

MAKE AHEAD The pasta dough can be refrigerated overnight. Bring to room temperature before rolling out.

WINE Lively, assertive Sauvignon Blanc.

Fresh Herb Couscous

4 SERVINGS ● ●

- 1 cup mixed chopped herbs, such as parsley, basil, chives and tarragon
- 1 large garlic clove, quartered
- 1¼ cups boiling water
- 1 tablespoon unsalted butter
- 1 cup instant couscous
- ½ teaspoon salt

I. In a mini food processor, combine the herbs, garlic and ¼ cup of the boiling water and process to a paste.

2. In a saucepan, melt the butter. Add the couscous and salt, stirring to coat. Stir in the herb paste and the remaining 1 cup of boiling water, cover and set aside for 10 minutes. Fluff the herb couscous and serve. —Jacques Pépin

Chilled Capellini with Clams and Caviar

4 FIRST-COURSE SERVINGS ● ● ●

- 5 tablespoons extra-virgin olive oil
- 2 garlic cloves, coarsely chopped
- 2 bay leaves
- 1 cup dry white wine
- 3 dozen small littleneck clams, scrubbed
- ½ pound capellini
- 2 tablespoons fresh lemon juice
- 3 tablespoons minced chives

Salt and freshly ground pepper

- 1¾ ounces osetra caviar

I. In a saucepan, heat 3 tablespoons of the oil. Add the garlic and bay leaves and cook over moderately high heat until fragrant but not browned, about 1 minute. Add the wine and bring to a boil. Add the clams, cover and steam until they start to open, about 4 minutes. Transfer each clam as it opens to a bowl. Pour the cooking liquid into a measuring cup, stopping before you reach the grit at the bottom. Remove the clams from their shells and cover.

2. In a large pot of boiling salted water, cook the capellini until al dente, about 3 minutes. Drain and rinse under cold water until chilled, then drain again.

3. In a bowl, whisk the reserved cooking liquid with the lemon juice and the remaining 2 tablespoons of oil. Add the chives and clams and season with salt and pepper. Add the capellini and toss to coat. Divide the pasta among 4 shallow bowls. Using a long fork, twist the capellini into knots. Pour the sauce on top, garnish with the clams and caviar and serve. —Fabio Trabocchi

Fettuccine with Shrimp, Zucchini and Basil

6 SERVINGS ●

- 1 pound medium shrimp, shelled and deveined, shells reserved
- 2 cups water
- 1 celery rib, thinly sliced
- 1 carrot, thinly sliced
- Salt
- 1 pound fresh fettuccine or 1¼ pounds dried fettuccine
- 5 tablespoons extra-virgin olive oil
- 1 pound small zucchini, cut into ¼-inch-thick slices
- 2 large garlic cloves, very thinly sliced
- ¼ cup tomato sauce
- 10 large basil leaves, roughly torn into pieces
- 1 teaspoon very finely chopped oregano
- Crushed red pepper
- 12 small zucchini blossoms, stems and pistils removed, petals roughly torn
- Freshly ground pepper

I. In a small saucepan, cover the shrimp shells with the water. Add the celery and carrot and boil over high heat until the liquid has reduced to 1 cup, about 20 minutes. Strain the stock through a fine sieve into a small bowl, pressing hard on the solids with the back of a spoon to extract the liquid. Season the shrimp stock with salt.

---

cooking tip

pasta water

CHEFS FREQUENTLY USE PASTA COOKING WATER TO ADD BODY TO PASTA SAUCES. To do this, set aside about ½ cup of the hot water once the pasta has finished cooking. Toss the pasta and sauce together in a pot over low heat; then mix in the water, little by little, until it is absorbed.

---

2. In a large pot of boiling salted water, cook the fettuccine until just barely al dente. Drain the fettuccine, reserving ¼ cup of the pasta cooking water.

3. In a large, deep skillet, heat 3 tablespoons of the olive oil until shimmering. Add the sliced zucchini and garlic and cook over high heat, stirring frequently, until the zucchini is just softened and beginning to brown, about 5 minutes. Add the shrimp stock, fettuccine, shrimp, tomato sauce, basil, oregano and the remaining 2 tablespoons of olive oil. Add a pinch of crushed pepper and simmer over moderate heat, tossing constantly, until the shrimp are pink and the sauce is nearly absorbed, about 4 minutes. Add the torn zucchini blossoms and toss just until they are wilted. Stir in the reserved pasta cooking water and season the fettuccine generously with salt and pepper. Transfer the fettuccine to a large serving bowl and serve immediately. —*Benedetta Vitali*
WINE Tangy, crisp Vernaccia.

Spaghetti with Scallops, Sun-Dried Tomatoes and Olives

4 SERVINGS ●

- 1 cup coarse fresh bread crumbs
- 3½ tablespoons extra-virgin olive oil
- Salt and freshly ground pepper
- 2 tablespoons chopped black olives, such as Calamata
- 2 tablespoons chopped oil-packed sun-dried tomatoes
- 1 tablespoon balsamic vinegar
- ¾ pound spaghetti
- 1½ pounds sea scallops
- ½ cup dry white wine
- 1 cup finely chopped tomatoes
- ⅓ cup grated ricotta salata (1 ounce)
- 2 tablespoons chopped basil leaves

I. Preheat the oven to 400°. On a rimmed baking sheet, toss the bread crumbs with 1 tablespoon of the olive oil and season with salt and pepper. Bake the bread crumbs for 12 minutes, or until browned and crisp.

2. In a small bowl, combine the olives, sun-dried tomatoes, balsamic vinegar and ½ tablespoon of the olive oil.

3. In a large pot of boiling salted water, cook the spaghetti until al dente. Meanwhile, in a large skillet, heat the remaining 2 tablespoons of olive oil until shimmering. Season the scallops with salt and pepper and cook over high heat until well browned on the bottom, about 3 minutes. Turn the scallops and cook until just done, about 1 minute longer. Transfer the scallops to a large plate. Add the wine to the skillet and cook, scraping up any browned bits, until reduced to ¼ cup, about 3 minutes. Pour in any accumulated juices from the scallops and remove from the heat.

4. Drain the spaghetti and transfer it to a large, shallow serving bowl. Add the pan sauce, the olive-and-sun-dried-tomato mixture and the chopped tomatoes and toss well; season with salt and pepper. Arrange the scallops on top of the spaghetti, scatter the ricotta salata, basil and bread crumbs on top and serve. —*Marcia Kiesel*
WINE High-acid, savory Vermentino.

Pasta with Mussels

4 SERVINGS ●

Artisanal pasta has the character to be an equal partner to any sauce it's paired with, thanks in large part to the local mineral-rich water and specially milled flour it's made with. Bronze-coated dies give the pasta a wonderfully coarse texture that helps sauces cling; slow-drying the pasta over several hours or even days also results in a comforting chewiness.

- 2 cups dry white wine
- 4 bay leaves
- 4 pounds small mussels, scrubbed and debearded
- Pinch of saffron threads
- 3 tablespoons unsalted butter, melted
- 2 tablespoons extra-virgin olive oil
- 4 large garlic cloves, thinly sliced

Before opening L'Impero, his elegant Italian restaurant in Manhattan's Tudor City neighborhood, chef Scott Conant spent three months exploring his Neapolitan roots—his mother's family still lives in Benevento. "I went everywhere and ate everything," he says. Here, Conant shares his tips for all things pasta-related.

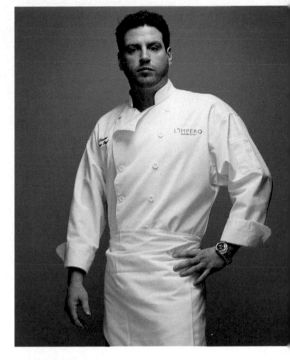

FW: What's the appropriate ratio of pasta to boiling water?
SC: For every pound of pasta, use a gallon of water.

FW: At what point should I add salt to the boiling water?
SC: Add the salt to the water before you bring it to a boil. Then, as the water heats up, try it; it should taste a bit like broth.

FW: What's the best way to tell when my pasta is ready?
SC: It's about trial and error: I require my staff to try every dish they prepare before sending it out of the kitchen. That said, taste the pasta as it's cooking. If you like it al dente, drain it when the pasta still has a bit of resistance, a bit of bite.

FW: How can I make my potato gnocchi tender—but not mushy?
SC: There are two important things to keep in mind. Avoid overcooking the potatoes and resist the temptation to add too much flour at the beginning. Instead, test the potatoes for doneness while you're cooking them and keep adjusting the amount of flour as you go along.

FW: What can I use to enhance the flavor of meatballs?
SC: My mother makes fabulous meatballs using raisins, bread crumbs, fresh parsley, fresh Parmesan cheese and a touch of oregano.

FW: Which canned tomatoes, if any, do you use?
SC: I like the ones from an Italian company called LaValle (penmac.com), but I try to use only fresh tomatoes. Like many New York restaurateurs and shop owners, I order my tomatoes from Lucky's Real Tomatoes (luckytomatoes.com); you can visit their Web site to find out which stores in your area carry them.

FW: Any tips for pasta salads?
SC: I'm not a big fan of pasta salads, but one that I do like is orzo with mixed vegetables and crumbled feta cheese in a vinaigrette. I also like couscous with tomatoes, grilled zucchini and mint.

FW: What brands of pasta do you recommend?
SC: Definitely Setaro, which you can find on-line (bienmanger.com) and Giuseppe Cocco (penmac.com). Supermarket brands like De Cecco and Barilla are also good to have on hand in your pantry.

FW: My lasagna is always so dull; what can I use to make it better?
SC: Use buffalo ricotta, high-quality tomatoes and fresh basil.

FW: What new tricks did you pick up when you were in Italy?
SC: My experience there was less about learning tricks than about seeing cooks letting their ingredients really shine. I remember eating an amazing strigoli dish, a short, thick pasta in squid ink with a shellfish reduction, bread crumbs and tomatoes. None of the ingredients were manipulated; nothing was too fussy. It was invigorating to see how powerful simple cooking can be. I was so impressed by that strigoli dish that I actually added a version of it to the menu here.

FW: So, what's the most important thing to keep in mind when making pasta?
SC: One thing that's good to do is to save the pasta cooking water and use it for your sauce. With its neutral flavor and high starch content, it's perfect for balancing the flavor and thickness of your sauce.

FW: Is twirling spaghetti with your fork and spoon tacky?
SC: I grew up using a fork and a piece of bread to eat mine. That might be even more tacky, but for me that's the only way to eat pasta.

FW: What's your favorite pasta?
SC: Nothing beats a fabulous, simple bowl of spaghetti with tomato and basil. When that dish is done right, it's hands-down the best.

pasta

½ teaspoon crushed red pepper
1 tablespoon fresh lemon juice
¾ pound artisanal Italian spaghetti
or linguine
Salt and freshly ground pepper

1. In a large pot, combine the white wine with the bay leaves and bring to a boil. Add the mussels, cover and cook over high heat, shaking the pan a few times, until the mussels open, about 5 minutes. Drain the mussels in a colander set over a medium bowl. Pour the mussel broth into a glass measuring cup. Crumble the saffron threads into the mussel broth.

2. Discard any unopened mussels. Remove the mussels from their shells and place in a bowl. Pour the melted butter over the mussels and toss to coat. Cover with plastic wrap.

3. Heat the extra-virgin olive oil in a large, deep skillet. Add the thinly sliced garlic and cook over low heat just until golden brown, about 4 minutes. Add the crushed red pepper and cook for 1 minute longer. Slowly pour in the reserved mussel broth, stopping when you reach the grit at the bottom of the glass measure. Add the lemon juice and simmer over moderately high heat until the sauce is reduced to about 1 cup, about 8 minutes.

4. In a large pot of boiling salted water, cook the spaghetti just until al dente. Drain the pasta well.

---

cooking tip

crushing garlic

CRUSHING AND MINCING OR CHOP-PING GARLIC RELEASES MORE OF ITS ESSENTIAL OILS than simply slicing it. The easiest way to crush a clove is to place it on a work surface, lay the flat side of a knife on top and whack the knife with your fist. Garlic is also easier to mince after it's been crushed.

---

5. Add the buttered mussels and the hot spaghetti to the mussel sauce and toss over low heat until the pasta is uniformly coated. Season with salt and pepper. Transfer to warmed shallow bowls and serve at once. —*Marcia Kiesel*
MAKE AHEAD The recipe can be prepared through Step 3 and refrigerated separately overnight.
WINE Flinty, high-acid Chablis.

Portuguese-Style Linguine with Clams, Chorizo and Tomatoes
4 SERVINGS ●

1 tablespoon extra-virgin olive oil
¾ pound chorizo, cut into
¼-inch-thick slices
1 large onion, thinly sliced
Pinch of cayenne pepper
2 dozen littleneck clams, scrubbed
4 medium tomatoes,
coarsely chopped
4 garlic cloves, minced
½ cup shredded basil leaves
1 cup dry white wine
¾ pound linguine
Salt and freshly ground pepper

1. Preheat the oven to 450°. Heat the olive oil in a large, deep ovenproof skillet. Add the chorizo and onion and cook over moderate heat, stirring occasionally, until the onion softens and the chorizo begins to brown, about 5 minutes. Stir in the cayenne. Arrange the clams in the skillet and scatter the tomatoes, garlic and ¼ cup of the basil on top. Add the wine and roast in the oven, uncovered, for 5 minutes. Stir the clams and roast for about 20 minutes longer, or until most of the clams have opened.

2. Meanwhile, cook the linguine in a pot of boiling salted water until al dente.

3. Drain the pasta and transfer it to a large serving bowl. Pour the chorizo clam sauce over the linguine, season with salt and pepper and toss to combine. Garnish the linguine with the remaining ¼ cup of basil and serve.
—*Kathy Gunst*

Spaghetti alla Pirata
4 TO 6 SERVINGS ● ●

2 tablespoons extra-virgin olive oil
3 garlic cloves, smashed
1 pound mussels, scrubbed
and debearded
1 pound cockles or Manila
clams, scrubbed
¾ cup dry white wine
2 cups canned tomato puree
1 tablespoon tomato paste
¼ teaspoon crushed red pepper
Salt and freshly ground pepper
1 pound cleaned small squid,
cut into ½-inch rings
¼ cup heavy cream
1 pound spaghetti
¼ cup torn basil leaves

1. In a large flameproof casserole, heat the olive oil until shimmering. Add the garlic and cook over moderate heat, stirring, until golden, about 2 minutes. Add the mussels, cockles and wine. Cook over high heat, stirring, until some of the shells are open and the liquid has reduced by half, about 3 minutes. Add the tomato puree, tomato paste, crushed red pepper and a pinch each of salt and pepper; bring to a boil. Cook over high heat until the sauce thickens slightly, about 5 minutes. Stir in the squid, return the sauce to a boil and cook just until the squid is firm and opaque, about 30 seconds. Add the cream, reduce the heat to moderate and simmer for 1 minute. Season with salt and pepper.

2. Using a slotted spoon, transfer the seafood to a platter. Boil the sauce over moderate heat until reduced by half, about 10 minutes.

3. Meanwhile, cook the spaghetti in a large pot of boiling salted water until al dente; drain. Stir the spaghetti into the sauce and cook over moderate heat for 1 minute. Return the seafood to the pasta and toss well. Transfer the spaghetti to plates, garnish with the basil and serve. —*Pino Luongo*
WINE Fruity, low-oak Chardonnay.

Linguine with Seafood Sauce

12 SERVINGS ●

Two 28-ounce cans peeled Italian
  plum tomatoes
 2 tablespoons extra-virgin
  olive oil
 2 large garlic cloves, smashed
 2 cups bottled clam juice
  (16 ounces)
 2 large thyme sprigs
 4 large basil leaves
Pinch of sugar
Salt and freshly ground pepper
 2 pounds cleaned baby squid,
  bodies sliced crosswise into
  ½-inch rings, large
  tentacles halved
1½ pounds thin linguine
 2 pounds mussels, scrubbed
  and debearded
 3 dozen cockles—scrubbed,
  soaked in cold water for
  2 hours and drained
 1 pound medium shrimp, shelled
  and deveined
Crushed red pepper

1. Puree the plum tomatoes in a food processor or blender. Strain them through a fine sieve set over a large bowl; discard the tomato seeds.

2. In an enameled cast-iron casserole, heat the oil until shimmering. Add the garlic and cook over moderately high heat until fragrant, about 30 seconds. Add the tomatoes, clam juice, thyme, basil and sugar. Season with salt and pepper and bring to a boil. Cook over moderately low heat until reduced by one-third, about 45 minutes. Add the squid and cook over low heat until very tender, about 45 minutes longer.

3. In a large pot of boiling salted water, cook the linguine until al dente. Drain the pasta well and return it to the pot.

4. Add the mussels and cockles to the tomato sauce, cover and cook over moderately high heat until most of the shells have opened, 3 to 5 minutes. Add the shrimp and cook until they are pink and firm, about 2 minutes longer.

Discard any unopened mussels and cockles. Pour the sauce over the pasta and toss over high heat for 2 minutes. Transfer the pasta and sauce to a large bowl, sprinkle with crushed red pepper and serve. —*Grace Parisi*

MAKE AHEAD The tomato-seafood sauce can be prepared through Step 2 and refrigerated overnight. Bring to a simmer before proceeding.

WINE Dry, light, refreshing Soave.

Linguine with Hard-Cooked Eggs and Anchovies

6 SERVINGS ●

 5 large eggs
 1 pound linguine
 4 tablespoons unsalted butter
¼ cup extra-virgin olive oil
 4 ounces oil-packed anchovies,
  drained and finely chopped
 3 garlic cloves, finely chopped
 2 tablespoons small capers,
  drained and rinsed
 2 tablespoons red wine vinegar
½ cup chopped flat-leaf parsley
½ teaspoon freshly ground pepper

1. Put the eggs in a saucepan and cover with cold water. Bring to a boil over moderate heat, then simmer over low heat for 10 minutes and drain. Transfer the eggs to a bowl of ice water to chill before peeling. Split the eggs and remove the yolks. Reserve the whites for another use. Press the yolks through a fine-mesh sieve into a small bowl.

2. In a large pot of boiling salted water, cook the linguine until al dente; reserve ⅓ cup of the pasta cooking water; drain.

3. Meanwhile, in a large nonstick skillet, melt the butter in the olive oil. Add the anchovies and garlic and cook over moderately low heat for 3 minutes. Add the yolks, capers and vinegar and cook just until heated through, 1 minute.

4. Add the pasta to the skillet with the reserved pasta water, parsley and pepper. Toss and serve. —*Ann Chantal Altman*

taste test jarred pasta sauces		
PRODUCT	**F&W COMMENT**	**INTERESTING BITE**
Rao's Homemade Vodka Sauce	"The cream rounds out the flavor. An improvement over other jarred sauces."	Rao's, a tiny red-sauce restaurant in New York's East Harlem, is perhaps the city's toughest reservation.
Dell'Amore Portobello Mushroom Sauce	"The flavor is subtle, and the texture comes close to homemade."	The company found porcini mushrooms overpowering; Portobellos, they decided, have a softer edge.
Barilla Green and Black Olive Sauce	"The olives in this are really top-quality."	Barilla didn't call this sauce "puttanesca" out of concern that customers might find the Italian name "confusing."

PAPPARDELLE WITH ZUCCHINI, ANCHOVIES AND MINT

Pappardelle with Zucchini, Anchovies and Mint

6 SERVINGS ● ●

- 4 ounces anchovies, drained and minced
- ¼ cup finely chopped mint
- 2 tablespoons snipped chives
- ¼ cup plus 2 tablespoons extra-virgin olive oil
- 4 large garlic cloves, thinly sliced
- ¼ teaspoon crushed red pepper
- 1½ pounds medium zucchini, thinly sliced lengthwise

Coarse sea salt

- 1 pound pappardelle

Freshly grated Parmesan cheese and lemon wedges, for serving

1. In a large bowl, mix the anchovies, mint, chives and 2 tablespoons of the oil.

2. In a large skillet, heat the remaining ¼ cup of oil until shimmering. Add the garlic and crushed red pepper; cook over moderate heat until the garlic is lightly golden, about 3 minutes. Add the zucchini, season with salt and cook over moderately high heat, tossing, until crisp-tender, about 5 minutes.

3. Cook the pappardelle in a pot of boiling salted water until al dente. Drain, reserving ½ cup of the pasta water. Return the pasta to the pot. Add the zucchini and the reserved pasta water and toss over moderate heat. Transfer the pasta to the bowl with the anchovies and herbs, season with salt and toss well. Serve, passing the Parmesan and lemon at the table. —*Melissa Clark*

Linguine with Fresh Tuna, Tomatoes and Lemon

4 SERVINGS ●

Marinating tuna and chopped tomatoes in wine, lemon zest and olive oil for an hour makes a fresh, simple pasta sauce. The sautéed tomatoes add depth of flavor with little effort.

- 2 tablespoons pine nuts
- 1 pound tuna steak, cut into ½-inch dice
- ½ cup dry white wine
- ½ teaspoon finely grated lemon zest
- ½ pound cherry tomatoes, coarsely chopped
- ¼ cup extra-virgin olive oil
- ¼ cup chopped fennel fronds
- ½ teaspoon crushed red pepper
- 1 pound linguine

Salt and freshly ground pepper

1. In a small skillet, toast the pine nuts over moderate heat, shaking the pan, until lightly browned, about 2 minutes. Transfer to a medium bowl. Add the tuna, wine, lemon zest, ½ cup of the cherry tomatoes and 2 tablespoons each of the olive oil and fennel fronds. Cover and refrigerate for 1 hour.

2. Heat the remaining 2 tablespoons of olive oil in a large, deep skillet. Add the crushed red pepper and the remaining cherry tomatoes and cook over low heat, stirring occasionally, until the sauce is flavorful, about 10 minutes.

3. Meanwhile, cook the linguine in boiling salted water until al dente. Reserve ¼ cup of the pasta cooking water, then drain the linguine.

4. Add the tuna mixture and the remaining 2 tablespoons of fennel fronds to the skillet and cook over low heat, stirring, just until the tuna starts to whiten, about 1½ minutes. Remove the skillet from the heat. Add the linguine and the reserved pasta cooking water and toss well. Season with salt and pepper and serve at once. —*Maria Paolillo*

WINE Bright, fruity rosé.

Penne with Tuna and Capers

4 SERVINGS ● ●

- ¾ pound penne rigate
- ¼ cup extra-virgin olive oil
- 3 garlic cloves, smashed

One 6½-ounce can or jar of olive oil–packed tuna, drained and flaked

- ¼ cup dry white wine
- ¼ cup drained capers
- 2 tablespoons finely chopped flat-leaf parsley

Salt and freshly ground pepper

1. Cook the penne in boiling salted water until al dente. Drain the pasta, reserving ½ cup of the pasta water.

2. Meanwhile, in a large skillet, heat the olive oil until shimmering. Add the garlic and cook over moderately high heat until golden, about 2 minutes. Add the drained tuna; cook for 1 minute. Add the wine, capers and 1 tablespoon of the parsley; season with salt and pepper. Cook the sauce until the wine has nearly evaporated, about 2 minutes longer. Add the penne and the reserved pasta water and cook, stirring, for 1 minute. Season with pepper, sprinkle with the remaining 1 tablespoon of parsley and serve. —*Pino Luongo*

WINE High-acid, savory Vermentino.

Tuna with Pasta and Frisée

4 SERVINGS ● ● ●

In America, canned tuna is considered kids' food—the more mayonnaise you can mash into it, the better. But in Mediterranean countries, tuna is treated with real culinary respect. That's why the best brands use whole, meaty pieces of center-cut fillet packed in luscious virgin olive oil. Unlike American tuna packed with water or vegetable oil in cans (which sometimes impart a slightly metallic aftertaste), the best imported tuna comes in glass jars, which protect the clean, fresh, delightfully complex flavor.

---

cooking tip

anchovies

ALWAYS START WITH A FRESH CAN OR JAR OF ANCHOVIES, because exposure to air can bring out a strong fishy taste. Once opened, anchovies keep for about 2 days. To decrease fishiness, soak the anchovies in whole milk for 10 minutes, then pat them dry with paper towels.

pasta

½ pound pasta, such as fusilli, quadrefiore or radiatore

⅓ cup plus 1 tablespoon extra-virgin olive oil

8 large fresh water chestnuts, peeled, or 1 small Granny Smith apple, peeled and cut into ½-inch chunks

4 large scallions, thinly sliced

¼ cup fresh lemon juice

3 garlic cloves, minced

Salt and freshly ground pepper

6 cups (packed) chopped frisée (10 ounces)

1 jar (8 to 10 ounces) imported tuna packed in olive oil, drained and broken into large chunks with a fork

1. In a large pot of boiling salted water, cook the pasta until al dente. Drain well and toss with 1 tablespoon of the extra-virgin olive oil.

2. In a saucepan of boiling salted water, blanch the water chestnuts for 1 minute. Drain and slice ¼ inch thick.

3. In a large bowl, mix the remaining ⅓ cup of olive oil with the scallions, lemon juice and garlic. Season with salt and pepper. Add the pasta, frisée, tuna and the water chestnuts or apple; toss well and serve. —*Marcia Kiesel*

WINE High-acid, savory Vermentino.

Penne with Veal Ragù

6 SERVINGS

1 tablespoon extra-virgin olive oil

1 pound ground veal

¾ pound mild pork sausage with fennel seeds, casings removed

Kosher salt and freshly ground pepper

1 small fennel bulb—halved, cored and finely diced, fronds reserved

1 medium carrot, finely diced

1 garlic clove, smashed

1 cup whole milk

1 cup dry white wine

1 cup canned peeled Italian tomatoes, drained and crushed

3 tablespoons tomato paste

1 tablespoon chopped marjoram

½ cup beef stock or canned low-sodium broth

¾ pound penne

Mixture of freshly grated Pecorino Romano and Parmigiano-Reggiano cheese, for serving

1. In a large skillet, heat the olive oil until shimmering. Add the veal and sausage and season with salt and pepper. Cook over moderately high heat, stirring occasionally and breaking the meat into walnut-size pieces, until just browned, about 20 minutes. Add the fennel, carrot and garlic and cook until the vegetables begin to soften, about 4 minutes.

2. Add the whole milk and simmer until reduced by three-quarters, about 5 minutes. Add the wine, tomatoes, tomato paste and marjoram and cook until reduced by half. Add the stock, season with salt and pepper and simmer over low heat until the liquid has reduced by three-quarters, about 20 minutes.

3. In a large pot of boiling salted water, cook the penne until al dente; drain. Add the penne to the veal sauce and cook over moderate heat, stirring to coat the penne with the sauce. Divide the penne among 6 bowls, sprinkle with the reserved fennel fronds and serve, passing the cheese at the table. —*Amanda Hesser*

Rigatoni with Pork Ragù and Fresh Ricotta

4 SERVINGS ●

This deeply flavored ragù would make a delicious dish just tossed with pasta, but when paired with sweet, fresh ricotta cheese, it's outstanding. Sheep's milk ricotta from the countryside outside Rome can be mail-ordered from Buonitalia, located in New York City's Chelsea Market (212-633-9090).

2 tablespoons extra-virgin olive oil

1 medium onion, finely chopped

½ cup coarsely chopped basil, plus 4 tiny basil sprigs for garnish

¼ cup coarsely chopped mint

1 tablespoon coarsely chopped sage

1 teaspoon minced rosemary

1 pound ground pork

Salt and freshly ground pepper

½ cup red wine

One 28-ounce can Italian plum tomatoes, crushed with their liquid

¼ teaspoon fennel seeds

1½ cups fresh whole-milk ricotta

¼ cup milk

1 teaspoon minced marjoram

1 pound rigatoni

1. Heat the olive oil in a large saucepan. Add the onion, chopped basil, mint, sage and rosemary and cook over low heat, stirring occasionally, until the onion has softened, about 7 minutes. Add the ground pork, season with salt and pepper and cook over moderate heat, breaking up the pork, until the meat is mostly white. Add the wine and cook until almost evaporated, about 4 minutes. Add the tomatoes with their liquid and simmer over low heat for 1 hour, stirring occasionally. Stir in the fennel seeds and season with salt and pepper.

2. In a bowl, stir the ricotta, then stir in the milk and marjoram and season with salt and pepper. Spoon the ricotta into shallow pasta bowls.

3. Cook the rigatoni in boiling salted water until al dente, then drain. Add the pasta to the ragù and simmer, stirring, for 1 minute; season with salt and pepper. Spoon the pasta into the bowls, garnish with the basil sprigs and serve. —*Andrea Buscema*

MAKE AHEAD The pork ragù can be refrigerated for up to 3 days.

WINE Tart, low-tannin Barbera.

Orecchiette with Brussels Sprouts and Bacon

6 SERVINGS ● ● ●

This hearty pasta dish is truly perfect in autumn, when Brussels sprouts are at their peak of flavor.

½ cup hazelnuts (2 ounces)

2½ cups chicken stock or canned low-sodium broth

Salt

1 pound Brussels sprouts, halved or quartered if large

¾ pound orecchiette

3 slices of thick-cut bacon, cut into 1-inch pieces

4 tablespoons unsalted butter

1 cup freshly grated Parmigiano-Reggiano cheese (3 ounces)

Freshly ground pepper

1. Preheat the oven to 375°. Spread the hazelnuts out in a pie plate and toast for about 8 minutes, or until fragrant. Let the hazelnuts cool, then coarsely chop them.

2. In a small saucepan, boil the chicken stock over moderately high heat until reduced to ¾ cup, about 15 minutes; keep warm.

3. Bring a large pot of salted water to a boil. Add the Brussels sprouts, cover and cook until crisp-tender, about 5 minutes. Using a slotted spoon, remove the Brussels sprouts and pat them dry. Return the water to a boil. Add the orecchiette and cook until al dente, 12 to 15 minutes; drain.

4. Meanwhile, in a large, deep skillet, cook the bacon over moderately high heat until crisp, about 6 minutes. Transfer the bacon to paper towels to drain. Add the butter to the skillet and cook over moderately high heat until browned and nutty, about 3 minutes. Add the Brussels sprouts and hazelnuts and cook until heated through, about 2 minutes. Add the orecchiette along with the reduced chicken stock and simmer, stirring occasionally, until the sauce is slightly absorbed, about 2 minutes. Stir in ½ cup of the Parmigiano cheese, season with salt and pepper and transfer to a large serving bowl. Garnish the pasta with the bacon and the remaining ½ cup of cheese and serve. —*Joanne Weir*

WINE Complex, savory Chianti Classico.

Pasta with Sausage, Basil and Mustard

4 SERVINGS ● ●

1 pound penne or medium shells

1 tablespoon extra-virgin olive oil

8 hot Italian sausages, meat removed from casings and crumbled (about 1½ pounds)

¾ cup dry white wine

¾ cup heavy cream

3 tablespoons grainy mustard

Pinch of crushed red pepper

1 cup thinly sliced basil

Cook the pasta in a large pot of boiling salted water until al dente; drain. Meanwhile, heat the oil in a large, deep skillet. Add the sausage and brown over moderately high heat, about 5 minutes. Add the wine and simmer, scraping up the browned bits, until reduced by half, about 5 minutes. Add the cream, mustard and crushed red pepper and simmer for 2 minutes. Remove from the heat, add the pasta and basil and toss to coat. Serve at once. —*Nigel Slater*

WINE Rich, velvety Merlot.

Singapore-Style Macaroni

4 SERVINGS ● ○

1 tablespoon tamari

1 tablespoon dry sherry

1¾ teaspoons curry powder

1 teaspoon cornstarch

1 teaspoon sugar

1 teaspoon Asian sesame oil

Freshly ground pepper

2 skinless, boneless chicken thighs, cut into ½-inch pieces

½ pound medium shrimp—shelled, deveined and cut into ½-inch pieces

½ pound elbow macaroni

2 tablespoons corn or peanut oil

Salt

1 garlic clove, minced

1 teaspoon finely grated fresh ginger

½ jalapeño, seeded and minced

2 scallions, thinly sliced crosswise

1 small carrot, finely chopped

1 tablespoon oyster sauce

¾ cup chicken stock or canned low-sodium broth

1 tablespoon small basil leaves

1. In a small bowl, combine the tamari, sherry, curry powder, cornstarch, sugar and sesame oil. Season with pepper. Pour all but 1 tablespoon of the marinade into a medium bowl. Add the chicken and toss to coat with the marinade. Add the shrimp to the small bowl and coat with the marinade. Cover both and refrigerate for 20 minutes.

2. In a saucepan of boiling salted water, cook the macaroni until al dente; drain.

3. In a large nonstick skillet, heat 1 tablespoon of the corn oil. Add the shrimp and season with salt. Cook over moderately high heat until the shrimp is just cooked through and turns opaque, about 2 minutes. Transfer to a plate.

4. Heat the remaining 1 tablespoon of oil in the skillet. Add the chicken and season with salt. Cook over moderate heat, stirring, until lightly browned, about 4 minutes. Add the garlic, ginger, jalapeño, scallions and carrot and cook, stirring, until fragrant, about 3 minutes. Add the oyster sauce and stir well. Add the chicken stock and simmer for a few minutes. Add the macaroni and shrimp and stir until heated through. Transfer to a platter, sprinkle with the basil and serve. —*Madhur Jaffrey*

ingredient tip

best dried pasta

MARTELLI PASTAS The Martellis make four fabulously chewy pastas— penne, spaghetti, spaghettini and maccheroni—in the tiny Tuscan town of Lari. You can purchase the pasta from Zingerman's (888-636-8162 or www.zingermans.com).

BAKED RIGATONI WITH MUSHROOMS AND PROSCIUTTO

THREE-CHEESE BAKED PASTA

Baked Rigatoni with Mushrooms and Prosciutto

6 SERVINGS ●

Unlike most pasta dishes, which are best served immediately, this rigatoni is perfect for preparing ahead and heating just before serving. To make this recipe for 12, double it and bake it in two 9-by-13-inch baking dishes.

- 1 stick (4 ounces) unsalted butter
- 6 tablespoons all-purpose flour
- 1 quart whole milk
- ½ cup homemade or store-bought tomato sauce

Pinch of freshly grated nutmeg

Salt and freshly ground pepper

- 10 ounces white mushrooms, stems discarded and caps coarsely chopped
- 1 medium onion, finely chopped
- ¼ pound thickly sliced prosciutto, finely chopped

- 1 pound rigatoni
- ½ pound imported Fontina cheese, coarsely shredded

1. Preheat the oven to 350°. In a large saucepan, cook 6 tablespoons of the butter over moderately high heat until lightly browned, about 2 minutes. Whisk in the flour over high heat until foaming. Whisk in the milk and bring the white sauce to a simmer over moderate heat, whisking frequently. Cook until thickened and no floury taste remains, about 10 minutes. Stir in the tomato sauce and nutmeg and season with salt and pepper. Remove from the heat.

2. Melt the remaining 2 tablespoons of butter in a skillet. Add the mushrooms and cook over high heat until dry and just beginning to brown, about 8 minutes. Add the chopped onion and cook until softened, 5 minutes. Stir the mushrooms and prosciutto into the sauce.

3. In large pot of boiling salted water, cook the rigatoni until barely al dente, about 8 minutes. Drain the pasta and return it to the pot. Add the tomato sauce and all but ½ cup of the Fontina and toss well. Transfer the pasta to a 9-by-13-inch glass or ceramic baking dish. Sprinkle the reserved ½ cup of Fontina over the top.

4. Cover the rigatoni loosely with foil and bake for about 30 minutes, or until heated through. Remove the foil and continue baking until the pasta is golden brown on top and bubbling, about 15 minutes longer. Serve hot.

—*Giada De Laurentiis*

MAKE AHEAD The recipe can be prepared ahead through Step 3. Cover the baking dish with plastic wrap and refrigerate the pasta overnight. Bring to room temperature before baking.

WINE Simple, fruity Chianti.

Three-Cheese Baked Pasta

6 SERVINGS

¼ cup extra-virgin olive oil

4 red bell peppers, thinly sliced

1 large onion, thinly sliced

6 garlic cloves, 4 halved, 2 minced

Salt

1 teaspoon chipotle powder

One 28-ounce can plum tomatoes, drained and juices reserved

3 cups fresh ricotta cheese

¾ cup freshly grated Parmesan cheese

½ cup shredded fresh mozzarella

Freshly ground pepper

1 pound trenne or rigatoni

1 tablespoon melted unsalted butter

1. In an enameled cast-iron casserole, heat the oil. Add the peppers, onion, halved garlic and a pinch of salt. Cover and cook over moderate heat until the vegetables soften, 15 minutes. Add the chipotle powder and cook uncovered, stirring, until the vegetables are lightly browned, 5 minutes. Add the tomatoes and their juices, cover and simmer over low heat for 20 minutes. Scrape the sauce into a food processor and puree. Wipe out the casserole. Strain the sauce into it and season with salt; keep warm.

2. Preheat the oven to 375°. Butter a 10-by-14-inch glass baking dish. In a bowl, mix the ricotta with the minced garlic, ½ cup of the Parmesan and the mozzarella. Season with salt and pepper.

3. Cook the pasta in a large pot of boiling salted water until almost al dente. Drain and return to the pot; toss with 2 cups of the sauce. Spread the pasta in the baking dish, top with the ricotta mixture and drizzle with the butter. Sprinkle the remaining ¼ cup of Parmesan on top. Cover the pasta with foil and bake for 25 minutes, or until hot.

4. Preheat the broiler. Uncover the pasta and broil 4 inches from the heat for 2 minutes, or until browned on top. Let stand for 5 minutes, then serve with the remaining sauce. —*Marcia Kiesel*

Soba in Green Tea with Chicken and Snow Peas

4 SERVINGS ● ○

To make green tea, steep leaves for 2 to 3 minutes in very hot—but not boiling—water. Brewing it longer makes tea taste bitter; for stronger flavor, use more tea.

3 tablespoons soy sauce

1½ tablespoons mirin

1 tablespoon minced peeled ginger

½ teaspoon Asian sesame oil

¾ pound skinless, boneless chicken breasts, cut crosswise into thin strips

½ pound soba noodles

3 cups brewed green tea

¼ pound snow peas, cut lengthwise into thin strips

1 medium leek, white and light green parts, halved lengthwise and thinly sliced crosswise

2 tablespoons umeboshi vinegar (see Note)

2 tablespoons coarsely chopped cilantro

1. In a medium bowl, combine the soy sauce with the mirin, ginger and sesame oil. Add the chicken and turn to coat. Let stand for 10 minutes.

2. Meanwhile, in a large saucepan of boiling salted water, cook the soba noodles until just tender, about 5 minutes. Drain the noodles; transfer to a large bowl and cover.

3. In the same saucepan, bring the green tea to a simmer. Add the chicken, snow peas and leek and cook over moderately low heat until the chicken is just white throughout, about 3 minutes. Stir in the vinegar, cilantro and noodles. Ladle the soba into bowls and serve. —*Suki Hertz*

NOTE Umeboshi vinegar is made with pickled plums and has a salty, tangy flavor. It is available at health food stores. For this recipe, you can substitute 1 tablespoon of rice vinegar mixed with 1 tablespoon of soy sauce and ½ teaspoon of kosher salt.

Cold Soba Noodle Salad with Cucumber and Shiitake

4 SERVINGS ● ○

1 pound shiitake mushrooms, stems discarded

8 scallions

3 tablespoons peanut oil

Salt and freshly ground pepper

3 tablespoons light soy sauce

2 teaspoons freshly grated ginger

2 teaspoons minced garlic

1 teaspoon Asian sesame oil

½ teaspoon rice vinegar

½ teaspoon chili oil

7 ounces soba noodles

1 large cucumber—peeled, halved, seeded and cut into thick matchsticks

2 teaspoons black sesame seeds (optional)

1. Light a grill or preheat a grill pan. In a large bowl, toss the shiitake mushrooms and the scallions with the peanut oil and season with salt and pepper. Grill the mushrooms over moderate heat, turning once, until cooked through and tender, about 4 minutes; transfer to a plate. Grill the scallions, turning once, until softened and blackened in spots, about 2 minutes; add them to the mushrooms. Let the mushrooms and scallions cool, then thinly slice them and return to the plate.

2. In a small bowl, whisk the soy sauce with the ginger, garlic, sesame oil, rice vinegar and chili oil.

3. Bring a large saucepan of salted water to a boil. Add the soba noodles and cook until al dente, about 5 minutes; drain. Transfer the noodles to a large bowl. Add the mushrooms, scallions, cucumber and dressing and toss well. Sprinkle with the sesame seeds and serve. —*Wendy Kalen*

MAKE AHEAD The recipe can be prepared through Step 2 up to 8 hours ahead. Cover and let stand at room temperature.

WINE Bright, citrusy Riesling.

BACON-ROASTED TURKEY WITH SWEET-ONION GRAVY, P. 115

poultry

THAI CHICKEN WITH MUSHROOMS AND GREEN BEANS

SMOTHERED CHICKEN

Thai Chicken with Mushrooms, Green Beans and Basil

4 SERVINGS ● ● ●

1½ tablespoons oyster sauce

1 tablespoon Asian fish sauce

1 teaspoon sugar

2½ tablespoons vegetable oil

½ pound green beans, cut into 2-inch lengths

3 scallions, white and light green parts only, cut into 1-inch lengths

2 large garlic cloves, minced

½ teaspoon salt

¾ pound skinless, boneless chicken breast cutlets, pounded thin and cut into strips

¼ pound small mushrooms, stemmed and quartered

½ cup drained canned baby corn, cut into 1-inch lengths

2 jalapeños, seeded and sliced

1 loosely packed cup torn basil

1. In a small bowl, mix the oyster sauce with the fish sauce and sugar.

2. In a wok, heat ½ tablespoon of the oil over high heat until smoking. Add the beans and stir-fry until crisp-tender, about 5 minutes. Transfer to a plate.

3. Add the remaining 2 tablespoons of oil to the wok and heat until smoking. Add the scallions, garlic and salt and stir-fry until the garlic is lightly golden, about 45 seconds. Add the chicken in 3 batches, pausing between additions, and stir-fry until the chicken just barely turns white, about 2 minutes. Add the mushrooms, corn, jalapeños and beans and stir-fry until the vegetables are crisp-tender, 2 to 3 minutes. Add the oyster sauce mixture and stir-fry until the chicken is cooked through, about 2 minutes longer. Stir in the basil, transfer to a platter and serve. —*Joyce Jue*
WINE Bright, citrusy Riesling.

Vietnamese Lemongrass Chicken with Caramel Sauce

4 SERVINGS ● ● ●

1 cup lukewarm water

½ cup sugar

2 tablespoons fresh lemon juice

¼ cup Asian fish sauce

2 teaspoons cornstarch

1 teaspoon freshly ground pepper

1½ pounds skinless, boneless chicken thighs, cut into ¾-inch dice

3 tablespoons vegetable oil

6 stalks of fresh lemongrass, tender white inner bulbs only, smashed and minced (about ¼ cup)

½ medium onion, very thinly sliced lengthwise

4 garlic cloves, minced

2 teaspoons very finely chopped fresh ginger

1   medium carrot, cut into very
    thin matchsticks
⅛   teaspoon cayenne pepper
¼   cup chicken broth

1. In a small saucepan, combine ½ cup of the water with the sugar and bring to a boil over high heat. Boil without stirring until an amber caramel syrup forms, 6 to 8 minutes. Remove from the heat and carefully pour in the remaining ½ cup of water. Boil until the caramel is syrupy, about 4 minutes longer. Swirl in the lemon juice. Transfer the caramel sauce to a medium bowl.
2. In a bowl, mix 2 tablespoons of the fish sauce with the cornstarch and pepper; add the chicken and stir to coat.
3. In a wok, heat 2 tablespoons of the oil until smoking. Add the lemongrass, onion, garlic and ginger and stir-fry over high heat until the garlic is golden, about 2 minutes. Add the remaining 1 tablespoon of oil. Add the chicken and stir-fry until the chicken turns white, about 3 minutes. Add the carrot, the remaining 2 tablespoons of fish sauce, the cayenne and 3 tablespoons of the caramel sauce and cook over moderate heat, stirring, until the chicken is glazed, about 4 minutes. Stir in the broth, simmer for 30 seconds and serve.
—*Joyce Jue*
WINE Soft, off-dry Riesling.

Smothered Chicken
6 SERVINGS
1   stick (4 ounces) unsalted butter
Two 3-pound chickens, each cut
    into 8 pieces
Salt and freshly ground pepper
2   large Spanish onions,
    finely chopped
4   thyme sprigs
2   bay leaves
¼   cup chicken stock or canned
    low-sodium broth

1. Melt the butter in a large, deep skillet. Season the chicken pieces all over with salt and ground pepper. Add half of the chicken pieces to the skillet.

Cook the chicken over moderate heat until golden brown, about 4 minutes per side; transfer to a large plate. Repeat the process with the remaining chicken. Add the onions to the skillet and cook over moderate heat, stirring occasionally, until lightly browned, about 8 minutes.
2. Spoon off all but 1 tablespoon of the butter from the skillet. Return the chicken to the skillet, add the thyme and bay leaves, cover tightly and simmer over very low heat until the chicken breast pieces are just white throughout, about 40 minutes. Transfer the breast pieces to a large plate and cover to keep warm. Continue simmering the chicken in the skillet until cooked through, about 15 minutes longer.
3. Stir in the stock and return the chicken breast pieces to the skillet. Season the chicken sauté generously with salt and pepper and serve.
—*Maria Guarnaschelli*
WINE Subtle, complex white Burgundy.

Chicken in Creamy Tomatillo Sauce
4 SERVINGS ●
¾   pound fresh tomatillos—husked,
    rinsed and quartered
½   cup beer, such as a pale lager
2   medium canned chipotle chiles,
    stemmed and seeded
2   garlic cloves, minced
½   tablespoon rice vinegar
1   teaspoon sugar
1   teaspoon dried oregano
2   tablespoons vegetable oil, plus
    more for brushing
Salt
Four 6-inch corn tortillas
1   tablespoon extra-virgin olive oil
4   skinless, boneless chicken breast
    halves (about 1½ pounds)
Freshly ground pepper
2   tablespoons unsalted butter
¼   cup heavy cream
¼   pound mozzarella cheese,
    shredded (1 cup)

1. Preheat the oven to 200°. In a food processor, puree the tomatillos with the beer, chipotles, garlic, vinegar, sugar, oregano, 2 tablespoons of the vegetable oil and 1 teaspoon of salt.
2. Heat a medium skillet. Brush both sides of the tortillas with vegetable oil and cook over moderate heat, 1 at a time, turning once, until crisp, about 3 minutes. Transfer to a baking sheet and keep warm in the oven.
3. Heat the olive oil in a large skillet. Season the chicken with salt and pepper and cook over moderately high heat, turning once, until golden brown on both sides and just cooked through, about 15 minutes. Transfer to a plate.
4. Melt the butter in the large skillet. Add the tomatillo sauce and heavy cream and cook over moderately high heat, stirring frequently, until the sauce thickens, about 8 minutes. Season with salt and pepper.
5. Lay a tortilla on each plate. Slice the chicken breasts and arrange on the tortillas. Sprinkle with the mozzarella, spoon the sauce on top and serve.
—*Jim Peyton*

Sautéed Chicken with Mushroom-Dill Cream Sauce
4 SERVINGS ●
4   boneless chicken breast
    halves with skin, tenderloins
    removed (see Note)

---

shopping tip
smart buy

BUYING CHICKEN BREASTS ON THE BONE is much less expensive than buying boneless breasts. Besides, boneless breasts are usually sold without the skin—and you may want that skin! Use a sharp knife to cut the meat off the bones, then reserve the bones for making stock.

Salt and freshly ground pepper

2 tablespoons unsalted butter

1 tablespoon vegetable oil

½ pound cremini mushrooms, cut into ⅛-inch-thick slices

1 large shallot, minced

½ cup dry white wine

2 tablespoons Cognac

1 cup heavy cream

½ cup chicken stock or canned low-sodium broth

2 tablespoons Dijon mustard

2 tablespoons minced dill

1. Season the chicken breasts with salt and pepper. In a large skillet, melt 1 tablespoon of the butter in the vegetable oil. Add the chicken breasts, skin side down, and cook over moderately high heat, without turning, until lightly browned, about 4 minutes. Cover the skillet and continue cooking the chicken over moderate heat until the skin is crisp, about 4 minutes. Uncover, turn the chicken and cook over moderately low heat until the chicken is just white throughout, about 6 minutes. Transfer the chicken to a large plate and cover loosely with foil.

2. Pour off the fat from the skillet and add the remaining 1 tablespoon of butter. Add the mushrooms and shallot and cook over moderate heat, stirring, until softened, about 4 minutes. Add the wine and Cognac and simmer over moderately high heat until almost dry, about 3 minutes. Add the cream and stock and simmer until thickened, about 8 minutes. Stir in the mustard and dill and season with salt and pepper. Add the chicken to the sauce, skin side up, along with any accumulated juices. Simmer over low heat until the chicken is warmed through, about 2 minutes. Spoon the sauce onto plates, top with the chicken and serve.

—Michael Romano

NOTE You can have your butcher bone the chicken breasts for you.

SERVE WITH Buttered egg noodles.

WINE Ripe, creamy-textured Chardonnay.

Chicken Tonnato with Arugula, Tomatoes and Olives

6 SERVINGS ●

Tonnato (from the Italian word *tonno,* which means tuna) can refer to any number of dishes made with that fish.

6 skinless, boneless chicken breast halves (about 2½ pounds)

4 cups fat-free chicken broth

1 small carrot, thinly sliced

One 6-ounce can olive oil–packed tuna, drained

4 oil-packed anchovy fillets

½ cup mayonnaise

⅔ cup sour cream

Salt and freshly ground pepper

3 bunches arugula (¾ pound), stemmed

1 pint grape tomatoes, halved

½ cup pitted Gaeta olives

1 tablespoon capers, drained

Lemon wedges and crusty bread, for serving

1. In a Dutch oven or enameled cast-iron casserole, cover the chicken with the broth, add the carrot and bring to a boil over high heat. Reduce the heat to moderately low, cover and simmer the chicken until just cooked through, about 15 minutes. Transfer the chicken to a plate to cool. Increase the heat to high and continue to cook the carrot until tender, about 10 minutes.

2. Using a slotted spoon, transfer the carrot to a food processor. Add the tuna, anchovies and mayonnaise and process until smooth. Add the sour cream and ¼ cup of the chicken broth, season with salt and pepper and blend the tonnato sauce until very smooth.

3. Slice the chicken diagonally ¼ inch thick. Pour about ½ cup of the sauce onto a serving platter. Top with the arugula and sliced chicken. Pour the remaining sauce over the chicken and garnish with the tomatoes, olives and capers. Serve the tonnato with lemon and crusty bread. *—Ann Chantal Altman*

WINE Lively, assertive Sauvignon Blanc.

Chicken with Cherry Tomato Pesto Sauce

6 SERVINGS ● ○

3 cups loosely packed basil and flat-leaf parsley leaves

2 garlic cloves

1 tablespoon pine nuts

1 teaspoon drained capers

1 teaspoon balsamic vinegar

1 pint cherry tomatoes, halved

¼ cup plus 2 tablespoons extra-virgin olive oil

Salt and freshly ground pepper

6 skinless, boneless chicken cutlets (about 6 ounces each)

1. In a food processor, combine the herbs with the garlic, pine nuts, capers, vinegar and 12 cherry tomato halves; pulse until chopped. Add 3 tablespoons of the olive oil and pulse just until pureed. Season with salt and pepper.

2. Heat 1½ tablespoons of the remaining olive oil in each of 2 large skillets. Season the chicken with salt and pepper and cook over high heat, turning once, until golden on both sides, about 5 minutes. Transfer to a platter, cover loosely with foil and keep warm.

3. Return 1 of the skillets to the heat, add the remaining tomatoes and cook over high heat just until heated through, about 1 minute; season with salt and pepper. Spoon the tomatoes over the chicken and serve the pesto on the side. *—Melissa Clark*

WINE Lively, assertive Sauvignon Blanc.

Sautéed Chicken with Garlic and Parsley

4 SERVINGS

1 stick (4 ounces) unsalted butter

2 tablespoons extra-virgin olive oil

One 3½-pound chicken, quartered, drumsticks and thighs separated

Salt and freshly ground pepper

1 cup dry white wine

4 garlic cloves, thinly sliced

1 cup coarsely chopped flat-leaf parsley

2 teaspoons fresh lemon juice

1. In a large cast-iron skillet or heavy casserole, melt 4 tablespoons of the butter in the olive oil over moderately high heat. Rub the chicken generously with salt and pepper. Add the chicken to the skillet, skin side down, and cook until golden and crispy, about 4 minutes. Turn the chicken and reduce the heat to moderate, then cover and cook, turning the chicken once or twice, until the juices run clear, 40 to 45 minutes.

2. Transfer the chicken to a platter and remove all but 1 tablespoon of fat from the skillet. Increase the heat to high, add the wine and simmer, scraping up the browned bits from the bottom, until reduced by half, about 7 minutes. Add the garlic and parsley to the skillet and cook over moderately high heat for about 5 minutes. Cut the remaining 4 tablespoons of butter into small chunks and gradually whisk them into the sauce. Add the lemon juice and season with salt and pepper. Pour the sauce over the chicken and serve.
—Nigel Slater

WINE Round, rich Sauvignon Blanc.

Chicken in Tarragon Cream Sauce
8 SERVINGS ●

There's an explanation for why French chefs still cook nineteenth-century recipes: They can be truly wonderful, like this creamy poached chicken. By today's standards, this dish seems impossibly rich, but you must try it once, at least, to know why people have been eating it for two hundred years.

- 10 tarragon stems, plus
    2 tablespoons leaves
- 2 quarts rich chicken stock
- 1½ quarts heavy cream
- 1 bottle dry white wine, preferably a French Sauvignon Blanc
- Salt and freshly ground pepper
- Two 3½-pound chickens—each cut into drumsticks, thighs and breast halves on the bone
- ½ pound baby carrots

1. Tie the tarragon stems in a bundle. In a large pot, combine the stock, cream, wine and tarragon stems. Bring to a boil and season lightly with salt and pepper. Add the chicken and bring to a boil, skimming. Reduce the heat to low and simmer, stirring, until the breasts are cooked through, 20 minutes. Transfer to a platter; cover with foil.

2. Continue to simmer the leg pieces until cooked through, about 20 minutes longer. Add the leg pieces to the breasts on the platter and cover with foil. Simmer the sauce over low heat until it has reduced by half, about 1½ hours. Discard the tarragon stems.

3. Meanwhile, in a medium saucepan of boiling salted water, cook the carrots until tender, about 4 minutes. Drain.

4. Return the chicken to the sauce. Add the carrots and simmer over low heat for 5 minutes. Season with salt and pepper. Garnish with the tarragon leaves and serve in shallow bowls.
—Pascal Chaupitre

MAKE AHEAD The poached chicken can be refrigerated in the sauce overnight. Reheat gently.

WINE Round, rich Sauvignon Blanc.

Kentucky Pan-Fried Chicken
6 TO 8 SERVINGS

- 1 cup evaporated whole milk or buttermilk
- 2 large eggs, lightly beaten
- Salt and freshly ground pepper
- 2 cups all-purpose flour
- 1½ pounds lard
- Two 3- to 4-pound chickens, each cut into 8 pieces, wing tips removed

1. In a bowl, mix the milk with the eggs, 1 teaspoon of salt and ½ teaspoon of pepper. In a large, sturdy plastic bag, mix the flour with 1 teaspoon of salt.

2. Divide the lard between 2 large cast-iron skillets and heat to 350° over moderate heat. (Alternatively, heat half the lard in 1 large skillet and fry the chicken in batches, adding the remaining lard as needed.)

3. Dip the chicken pieces in the egg mixture, turning to coat. Transfer the chicken to the bag of flour; shake to coat.

4. Divide the chicken between the skillets; don't crowd the pieces. Fry, turning occasionally, until dark golden and crisp, about 15 minutes for the wings, 20 minutes for the other pieces. Transfer the chicken to a rack set over paper towels to drain, then pat with paper towels and keep warm in the oven while you fry the remaining chicken; serve hot.
—Ramey's Diner, Whitesburg, Kentucky

SERVE WITH Hot sauce.

WINE Light, fruity Beaujolais.

Coq au Vin with Coconut Milk
4 SERVINGS ●

Coconut milk adds an exotic richness to this traditional Burgundian chicken stew and rounds out the flavors.

- One 4-pound chicken, cut into 8 pieces
- 2 bottles dry, light-bodied red wine
- 4 thick strips of bacon, cut crosswise into ½-inch-thick slices
- 2 carrots, finely chopped
- 2 garlic cloves, coarsely chopped

pairing tip

wine guide

LIGHT-MEAT BIRDS With game hens, chicken and turkey, which can be dry, look for light to medium-rich wines with juiciness and verve: New World Sauvignon Blancs and Chardonnays, dry rosés, European Rieslings and Pinot Blancs, dry Champagnes and sparkling wines and light reds such as Pinot Noir and Beaujolais.

DARK-MEAT BIRDS Earthier, fattier birds like duck, goose, quail and pheasant demand more robust wines: rich French or California Chardonnays, bigger Pinot Noirs, Rhône reds, Zinfandels and Syrahs.

1 onion, finely chopped

1 celery rib, finely chopped

⅓ cup Cognac or brandy

¼ cup vegetable oil

3 flat-leaf parsley sprigs

2 oregano sprigs

1 bay leaf

Salt and freshly ground pepper

3 tablespoons all-purpose flour

1 cup unsweetened coconut milk

1. In a bowl, combine the chicken, wine, bacon, carrots, garlic, onion, celery, Cognac and 2 tablespoons of the oil. Tie the parsley, oregano and bay leaf into a bundle and add it to the bowl. Cover and refrigerate overnight.

2. The next day, drain the chicken and vegetables, reserving the marinade and herb bundle. Pat the chicken and bacon dry with paper towels. Season the chicken with salt and pepper and dust with 1½ tablespoons of the flour. In an enameled cast-iron casserole, heat 1 tablespoon of the oil. Add half of the chicken and brown over moderately

high heat, about 5 minutes per side; transfer to a plate. Reduce the heat to moderate and repeat with the remaining 1 tablespoon of oil and chicken.

3. Add the reserved vegetables and bacon to the casserole and cook over low heat, stirring occasionally, until the vegetables are softened, about 12 minutes. Stir in the remaining 1½ tablespoons of flour, then add the reserved marinade and herb bundle and bring to a boil over high heat. Using a long match, ignite the liquid. When the flames subside, return the chicken pieces to the casserole and simmer over low heat until the breasts are just cooked through, about 15 minutes. Transfer the breast pieces to a plate and cover loosely with foil. Continue to simmer the chicken legs until very tender, about 45 minutes longer. Add the legs to the breast pieces.

4. Boil the sauce over moderately high heat until reduced by one-third, about 15 minutes. Discard the herb bundle and add the coconut milk. Simmer over moderately high heat until slightly thickened, about 7 minutes. Season with salt and pepper and return the chicken to the casserole. Cover and simmer over low heat, turning the chicken a few times, until hot, about 5 minutes.

—Eric Ripert

MAKE AHEAD The stew can be refrigerated overnight. Reheat gently.

SERVE WITH Boiled potatoes or noodles.

WINE Ripe, creamy-textured Chardonnay.

Grilled Texas Chicken

4 SERVINGS ●

4 whole chicken legs, skinned

Sea salt and freshly ground pepper

2 tablespoons annato seeds

¼ cup plus 2 tablespoons olive oil

1 cup fresh carrot juice

2 tablespoons sherry wine vinegar

3 bay leaves

3 thyme sprigs

3 garlic cloves, crushed

1½ serrano chiles, sliced into rounds

1. Season the chicken legs with salt and pepper. In a large skillet, cook the annato seeds in the olive oil over moderate heat until the oil is a deep brick red, about 5 minutes.

2. Strain the annato oil into a 9-by-13-inch baking dish. Add the carrot juice, vinegar, bay leaves, thyme, garlic and chiles. Add the chicken and turn to coat. Refrigerate for 6 hours or overnight.

3. Preheat the oven to 375°. Preheat a grill pan. Grill the chicken in the grill pan over moderate heat for 4 minutes, turning once. Transfer to a rimmed baking sheet and cook for 30 minutes, or until the juices run clear; serve hot.

—Paula Disbrowe

WINE Ripe, creamy-textured Chardonnay.

Curried Chicken with Chickpeas and Potatoes

4 SERVINGS ●

¼ cup vegetable oil

4 whole chicken legs, separated into drumsticks and thighs

Kosher salt and freshly ground pepper

1 medium onion, finely chopped

2 garlic cloves, minced

1 teaspoon grated fresh ginger

2 teaspoons ground coriander

1 teaspoon ground cumin

¼ teaspoon turmeric

¼ teaspoon cayenne

1 cup crushed tomatoes

1 cup water

One 19-ounce can chickpeas, drained and rinsed

1 pound medium red potatoes (about 4), peeled and quartered

1 tablespoon chopped cilantro

Steamed rice, for serving

1. In a skillet, heat the oil. Season the chicken with salt and pepper. Add half to the skillet; cook over moderately high heat until browned, about 4 minutes per side. Transfer the chicken to a plate. Repeat with the remaining chicken.

2. Add the onion to the skillet and cook over moderately high heat, stirring, until just browned, about 5 minutes.

---

cooking tips

grilling birds

PREPARE EXTRA COALS. Remove a few hot coals with tongs before you start cooking. Put them in a chimney starter and cover them with fresh charcoal. If your fire dies down, you can add the reserved red-hot coals.

ADD FLAVOR BY SCATTERING DRIED HERB CLIPPINGS—both sprigs and whole stems—over the coals. Or toss on cinnamon sticks, allspice berries and fennel seeds for a more intense flavor.

PREVENT FLARE-UPS by marinating and basting carefully so oil won't drip.

DON'T WASTE GOOD COALS. If they're still glowing, you can wrap vegetables in foil and throw them on the grill to roast, leaving the lid on. It's okay to leave them there until the embers die.

Add the garlic and ginger and cook, stirring, until fragrant, about 1 minute. Add the coriander, cumin, turmeric and cayenne and cook, stirring, for 1 minute. Add the crushed tomatoes, water, chickpeas and 1 teaspoon of salt. Add the chicken pieces and any juices. Nestle in the potatoes and bring to a boil. Cover and simmer over low heat, turning the chicken and potatoes once, until the chicken is cooked through and the potatoes are tender, about 25 minutes. Spoon the curry onto a platter and sprinkle with the cilantro. Serve at once with steamed rice. —*Madhur Jaffrey*
WINE Soft, earthy Rioja.

Coconut Curry Chicken
6 TO 8 SERVINGS ●
This chicken curry recipe makes ample sauce for spooning over vegetables, rice or noodles.

- 15 medium dried red chiles, such as Kashmiri, Guajillo or New Mexico, stemmed and seeded
- 1 cup boiling water
- 10 medium garlic cloves, halved
- 3 stalks of fresh lemongrass, tender white inner bulbs only, minced
- One 3-inch piece of fresh ginger, peeled and chopped
- 2 medium shallots, coarsely chopped
- ½ cup chopped cilantro stems and leaves, plus sprigs for garnish
- 1 tablespoon dried shrimp paste
- 1 teaspoon curry powder
- ½ teaspoon kosher salt
- Three 14-ounce cans unsweetened coconut milk
- 1 cup chicken stock
- ½ cup Asian fish sauce
- ½ cup soy sauce
- ¼ cup sugar
- 8 whole chicken legs, separated

I. In a medium heatproof bowl, soak the dried chiles in the boiling water until softened, about 20 minutes. Drain the chiles well; reserve the soaking

CURRIED CHICKEN WITH CHICKPEAS AND POTATOES

GRILLED TEXAS CHICKEN

liquid. In a food processor, combine the chiles, garlic, lemongrass, ginger, shallots, chopped cilantro, shrimp paste, curry powder and salt and process to a smooth paste.

2. Skim 1 cup of the thick cream from the top of the canned coconut milk. In a large enameled cast-iron casserole, cook the coconut cream over moderate heat, stirring, until it becomes oily, about 5 minutes. Add the chile paste and fry over moderately high heat, stirring, until fragrant, about 2 minutes. Add the chicken stock, fish sauce, soy sauce and sugar. Stir in the reserved chile soaking liquid and the remaining coconut milk and bring to a boil. Add the chicken and simmer over low heat, stirring occasionally, until cooked through, about 30 minutes. Serve the chicken curry garnished with cilantro.

—Sompon and Elizabeth Nabnian

MAKE AHEAD The chicken can be refrigerated overnight. Reheat gently.

WINE Lively, assertive Sauvignon Blanc.

Goan Chicken Curry

4 SERVINGS ●

- ½ cup tamarind pulp with seeds (4 ounces)
- 1 cup boiling water
- 10 black peppercorns
- 6 dried red chiles, such as Kashmiri or New Mexico, seeded
- 1 tablespoon coriander seeds
- 1 teaspoon cumin seeds
- One 1½-inch piece of cinnamon stick
- 2 tablespoons vegetable oil
- One 3½-pound chicken, cut into 8 pieces
- Salt and freshly ground pepper
- 1 large onion, minced
- 5 garlic cloves, minced
- 1½ tablespoons finely grated fresh ginger
- 1 teaspoon turmeric
- 2 fresh hot green chiles, such as jalapeños, seeded and minced
- 3 cups water
- 1 cup unsweetened coconut milk

1. In a heatproof bowl, soak the tamarind pulp in the boiling water, covered, until softened, 30 minutes. Strain through a coarse sieve; discard the seeds.

2. Meanwhile, in a small skillet, combine the peppercorns, dried red chiles, coriander seeds, cumin seeds and cinnamon and toast over moderate heat until fragrant, 1 minute. Transfer to a spice grinder to cool. Grind to a fine powder.

3. Heat the oil in a large enameled cast-iron casserole. Season the chicken with salt and pepper. Add half of the chicken to the casserole and cook over moderately high heat until browned, about 4 minutes per side. Transfer to a plate and repeat with the remaining chicken.

4. Pour off all but 2 tablespoons of the fat from the casserole. Add the onion and cook over moderately low heat, stirring occasionally, until softened, about 6 minutes. Add the garlic, ginger, turmeric, ground spices and green chiles. Cook, stirring, until fragrant, 3 minutes.

5. Stir the water and the strained tamarind pulp into the casserole. Return the chicken to the casserole and bring to a boil, then simmer over low heat for 20 minutes. Transfer the chicken breasts to a plate. Add the coconut milk and simmer for 20 minutes longer. Transfer the remaining chicken to the plate and simmer the sauce until very flavorful, about 8 minutes. Season with salt and pepper. Return the chicken to the sauce. Simmer the chicken until heated through before serving.

—Sonali Rao

MAKE AHEAD The chicken curry can be refrigerated overnight. Reheat gently.

SERVE WITH Steamed white rice.

WINE Spicy New World Gewürztraminer.

Basil Chicken Curry with Coconut Rice

4 SERVINGS ●

- 1½ cups basmati rice
- 2¼ cups water
- 1 teaspoon canola oil
- Salt

- ½ cup shredded unsweetened coconut
- 2 tablespoons extra-virgin olive oil
- 2 tablespoons minced fresh ginger
- 1½ pounds skinless, boneless chicken breasts, cut into 3-by-½-inch strips
- Freshly ground pepper
- 1 medium onion, chopped
- One 14-ounce can unsweetened coconut milk
- 1 cup chicken stock or canned low-sodium broth
- 1½ tablespoons Thai green curry paste
- ⅓ cup plus 2 tablespoons coarsely chopped basil leaves
- 3 tablespoons minced cilantro
- 3 scallions, white and light green parts only, cut into 2-inch lengths
- Freshly ground pepper
- ½ cup chopped dry-roasted peanuts
- Sliced avocado and mango, for serving

1. In a medium saucepan, bring the rice, water, canola oil and a pinch of salt to a boil; cover. Simmer over low heat for 15 minutes.

2. Meanwhile, in a medium skillet, toast the coconut over moderately low heat, stirring, until golden, about 5 minutes. Transfer to a plate and let cool.

3. In a large skillet, heat 1 tablespoon of the olive oil. Add 1 tablespoon of the ginger and cook over moderately high heat until fragrant, about 30 seconds. Add the chicken, season with salt and pepper and cook until lightly browned, about 5 minutes. Transfer to a bowl.

4. Add the remaining 1 tablespoon of oil to the skillet. Add the onion and the remaining 1 tablespoon of ginger; cook over moderate heat for 5 minutes, stirring frequently. Add the coconut milk, stock and curry paste and bring to a boil, stirring. Simmer the sauce for 5 minutes, until thickened. Add the chicken, ⅓ cup of the basil, 2 tablespoons of the cilantro and the scallions; simmer until the chicken is cooked through, 5 minutes. Season with salt and pepper.

During a Web chat on foodandwine.com, FOOD & WINE's talented Test Kitchen supervisor, Marcia Kiesel, shared simple tips and smart techniques for everything to do with chicken: chicken salad, chicken livers and even the best cheese for chicken cordon bleu. Her suggestions should make the ubiquitous bird seem more inspiring.

FW: Can you offer any tips for preparing chicken salad?
MK: During the summer, I like to combine poached chicken with a grain like bulgur, then dress it with lemon, olive oil, herbs and red onion. At the last minute, I add some halved grapes. It's very refreshing. I also like to prepare a Vietnamese-style chicken salad: Poach a whole Cornish hen, then toss the meat with sliced onion, lime juice, fish sauce, basil and cilantro.

FW: When roasting chicken, how do I keep the breast from drying out before the thighs are cooked?
MK: When it comes to roasting, I prefer using small chickens, ones that are about three pounds. They're just big enough for two people. I season the chicken with salt and pepper, rub it with butter or oil, put a lot of butter under the breast skin and roast it at 400 degrees for approximately one hour. I don't truss it, because the legs roast more quickly when they're open. I also make sure to baste the bird a few times while roasting it, until the skin is very crisp.

FW: How can I give roasted chicken a Southwestern flavor?
MK: Fresh poblano chiles are ideal since they have a complex flavor, which becomes even more intense when they're roasted. They have just enough heat and a lot of sweetness and are a perfect complement to chicken as well as pork. Roast and peel the poblanos, then slice and toss them with olive oil and salt and pepper, to use as a garnish.

FW: Do you recommend electric rotisseries for cooking chicken?
MK: Rotisseries are excellent for roasting chicken. They ensure that it will cook and crisp evenly, and they're easy—and fun—to use.

FW: What about chicken livers?
MK: I love chicken livers! I fry them with onion and tomato and fold them into an omelet, or, for breakfast, sauté them with balsamic vinegar and eat them on toast. You can also add chicken livers to stuffing or gravy. Oh, I could go on and on...

FW: And stuffing chicken breasts?
MK: Instead of cutting a pocket, I prefer to stuff boneless breasts under the skin. Carefully loosen the skin from the breast, keeping it intact. Then stuff it with whatever you're in the mood for—pesto, herbed ricotta cheese, sun-dried tomatoes, sliced ham, sautéed onions—and smooth the top. Sauté the breast skin side down to brown it, then turn it skin side up and finish it in the oven.

FW: What's the best cheese to use for chicken cordon bleu?
MK: Gruyère or Emmentaler work beautifully. Both are much more flavorful than domestic Swiss.

FW: What wines go with chicken?
MK: That depends on how you prepare the chicken. Simple roasted chicken with herbs tastes great with an herbal or rich white, like a French or a California Chardonnay. For a sweet, spicy chicken, try a big, oaky, buttery Chardonnay or sparkling wine. A chicken stew with bacon and tomato goes well with Beaujolais, and a chicken salad with vegetables or fruit works wonderfully with a rosé.

FW: Any suggestions for quick, simple chicken dinners?
MK: Chicken wings are great when you're pressed for time, and everyone loves them! Throw them on a sheet pan, toss them with lots of salt and pepper or seasonings and roast them in the oven at 425 degrees until they're crisp and brown. You can make an Asian version with soy, sesame and chili oil, or cook them with jerk spices. Cutlets are another quick alternative: Sauté them, remove them from the skillet, then add lemon juice, wine and capers to the pan. Boil the liquid until it's reduced by half, return the cutlets to the pan and swirl in some butter.

ROAST CHICKEN WITH OVEN-DRIED TOMATO VINAIGRETTE

5. Transfer the rice to a bowl; sprinkle with the toasted coconut. Transfer the chicken to another bowl. Garnish with the remaining 2 tablespoons of basil, 1 tablespoon of cilantro and the peanuts. Serve the avocado and mango on the side. —*Kathy Gunst*

WINE Lively, assertive Sauvignon Blanc.

Roast Chicken with Oven-Dried Tomato Vinaigrette

6 SERVINGS

Three 3-pound chickens, rinsed
Salt and freshly ground pepper
  3 lemon halves
  6 shallots, peeled
  6 garlic cloves, peeled
1½ bunches (1½ ounces) tarragon, plus 1 tablespoon finely chopped tarragon leaves
  6 large thyme sprigs
  ¼ cup plus 1 tablespoon extra-virgin olive oil
1½ teaspoons herbes de Provence
  1 cup water
24 Oven-Dried Tomatoes (p. 329)
  1 tablespoon Dijon mustard
  1 tablespoon whole-grain mustard
3½ tablespoons sherry vinegar
  1 teaspoon honey
Tabasco sauce

1. Preheat the oven to 375°. Season the chicken cavities generously with salt and pepper. Tuck a lemon half, 2 shallots, 2 garlic cloves, ½ bunch of tarragon and 2 thyme sprigs into each chicken cavity. Tie the legs together with kitchen string. Set the chickens in a large roasting pan or on a rimmed baking sheet. Rub the chickens all over with the 1 tablespoon of olive oil and season with the herbes de Provence, salt and pepper.

2. Roast the chickens in the middle of the oven for 30 minutes. Add ½ cup of the water to the roasting pan and roast the chickens for about 50 minutes longer, basting them occasionally with the pan juices; rotate the roasting pan as necessary to cook the birds evenly.

The chickens are done when the juices run clear when a thigh is pierced with a knife or when an instant-read thermometer inserted in one of the thighs registers 165°.

3. Preheat the broiler. Broil the chickens for about 5 minutes, rotating the roasting pan, until their skin is golden and crisp. Transfer the chickens to a large cutting board.

4. Pour any pan juices into a small saucepan and skim off the fat. Set the roasting pan over 2 burners, add the remaining ½ cup of water and simmer over moderate heat, using a wooden spoon to scrape up any browned bits on the bottom of the pan. Add the liquid to the pan juices in the saucepan and boil until reduced to ½ cup, about 5 minutes. Keep the pan juices warm.

5. Peel 12 of the oven-dried tomato halves and coarsely chop them. In a medium bowl, mix the tomatoes with the Dijon and whole grain mustards, vinegar, honey, warm pan juices and the 1 tablespoon of chopped tarragon. Whisk in the remaining ¼ cup of olive oil and season the vinaigrette with Tabasco, salt and pepper.

6. Spoon half of the oven-dried tomato vinaigrette onto a large platter. Quarter each of the chickens and arrange the pieces on the platter. Arrange the 12 remaining oven-dried tomato halves around the chicken and serve right away, passing the remaining tomato vinaigrette at the table. —*Tim Goodell*

WINE Bright, fruity Beaujolais.

Chicken Tikka with Cucumber Raita

6 SERVINGS ●

Tikka is the Indian version of shish kebabs. If you want to replicate the look of traditional Indian barbecue, add a few drops of red food coloring to the chicken marinade.

2¼ pounds boneless, skinless chicken breasts, cut into 1½-inch cubes

  3 garlic cloves, minced
  5 teaspoons minced fresh ginger
1½ teaspoons salt
  ¾ cup plain whole-milk yogurt
  ½ cup vegetable oil mixed with 1 tablespoon Chinese mustard
  2 tablespoons fresh lemon juice
  2 teaspoons ground cumin
  1 teaspoon ground mace
  1 teaspoon ground nutmeg
  1 teaspoon ground cardamom
  1 teaspoon turmeric
  1 teaspoon cayenne pepper
  1 teaspoon freshly ground black pepper
Vegetable oil, for the grill
Lemon wedges, thinly sliced red onion and chopped cilantro, for serving
Cucumber Raita (recipe follows)

1. Soak six 12-inch bamboo skewers in warm water for 30 minutes. Thread the chicken onto the skewers and set in a shallow glass baking dish.

2. On a cutting board, use the side of a large knife to mash the garlic, ginger and salt to a paste. In a bowl, whisk the paste with the yogurt, mustard oil, lemon juice, cumin, mace, nutmeg, cardamom, turmeric, cayenne and black pepper. Pour the marinade over the chicken; turn to coat. Cover and refrigerate for 3 to 4 hours, turning occasionally.

3. Light a grill. Lightly oil the grate. Grill the chicken over a medium-hot fire for about 4 minutes per side, or until it is cooked through and golden. Serve with the lemon wedges, red onion, cilantro and Cucumber Raita. —*Steven Raichlen*

WINE Lively, assertive Sauvignon Blanc.

CUCUMBER RAITA

MAKES ABOUT 3½ CUPS ● ● ●

  2 small garlic cloves, minced
Salt
  2 cups plain whole-milk yogurt
  ½ cup sour cream
  1 medium cucumber—peeled, halved, seeded and chopped

1 tomato, seeded and chopped

¼ cup chopped mint leaves

½ teaspoon cumin seeds, lightly
toasted and chopped

Freshly ground pepper

On a cutting board, use the side of a large knife to mash the garlic with a large pinch of salt to a paste. In a medium bowl, mix the garlic paste with the yogurt, sour cream, cucumber, tomato, mint and cumin. Season with salt and pepper and serve. —*S.R.*

Curried Chicken and Red Pepper Kebabs

6 SERVINGS ● ◐

3 skinless, boneless chicken
breast halves (1 pound), cut
into 1-inch pieces

2 red bell peppers, cut into
1-inch pieces

½ cup soy sauce

2 tablespoons extra-virgin olive oil

2 teaspoons Madras curry powder

2 tablespoons unsalted
butter, melted

1. Soak 12 wooden skewers in cold water for 15 minutes. Thread the chicken, alternating with the peppers, onto the skewers. Transfer to a baking dish.

2. In a small bowl, whisk the soy sauce with the olive oil and curry powder. Pour the marinade over the kebabs and let marinate for 10 minutes or for up to 1 hour, turning several times.

---

equipment tip

rack roasting

BIRDS ARE OFTEN ROASTED ON A RACK in order to allow a crispy skin to develop all over. If you don't own a rack, lay thick carrots or large stalks of celery in your roasting pan and set the bird on top of them. You can also make a quick and easy rack by rolling up long sheets of aluminum foil.

---

3. Meanwhile, light a grill or preheat a grill pan. Grill the kebabs over moderately high heat until golden brown, about 6 minutes. Remove from the grill, brush with the melted butter and serve. —*Bernardita Del Campo Correa*

WINE Bright, fruity rosé.

Honey-Marinated Chicken with Grilled Fennel

4 SERVINGS ◉

½ cup mild honey, such as clover, or
dark honey, such as buckwheat

2 teaspoons Worcestershire sauce

1 teaspoon fennel seeds,
slightly crushed

Kosher salt

1½ pounds thinly sliced
chicken cutlets

Freshly ground pepper

1 large fennel bulb (about
1¼ pounds)—halved, cored
and cut lengthwise into
¼-inch-thick slices

Vegetable oil, for brushing

1. In a shallow glass baking dish, mix the honey with the Worcestershire sauce, crushed fennel seeds and 1 teaspoon of kosher salt. Season the chicken cutlets with salt and pepper and add them to the honey marinade. Turn the chicken cutlets to coat well. Let stand at room temperature for 30 minutes, turning once.

2. Heat a large cast-iron grill pan or skillet. Lightly brush the fennel slices with vegetable oil and season with kosher salt and pepper. Arrange the fennel slices in the grill pan, loosely cover with a sheet of foil and cook over low heat, turning once, until nicely browned, about 22 minutes. Transfer the fennel to a platter.

3. Place the chicken in the grill pan and cook over moderate heat, turning once, until golden and just cooked through; reduce the heat if the cutlets brown too quickly. Arrange the chicken cutlets over the grilled fennel and serve. —*Gene Opton*

Honey-Glazed Chicken Drumsticks

6 SERVINGS ●

18 chicken drumsticks

2¼ teaspoons salt

2¼ teaspoons freshly
ground pepper

2¼ teaspoons Chinese
five-spice powder

4 garlic cloves, minced

¼ cup chopped cilantro

3 tablespoons Asian sesame oil

Vegetable oil, for the grill

6 tablespoons honey, warmed

1. Make 3 crosswise slashes down to the bone on the meaty part of each drumstick. Put the chicken in a large shallow baking dish.

2. In a small bowl, mix the salt, pepper, five-spice powder, garlic and cilantro. Add the sesame oil and stir into a paste. Rub the paste into the slashes in the chicken and spread any remaining paste over the skin. Cover and refrigerate the chicken for 2 hours.

3. Light a grill. Lightly oil the grate. Grill the chicken over a medium-hot fire, turning occasionally, for about 35 minutes, or until just cooked through. Brush the drumsticks with the honey and continue grilling until golden brown, about 1 minute per side. Serve hot. —*Steven Raichlen*

MAKE AHEAD The drumsticks can be refrigerated overnight.

WINE Soft, off-dry Riesling.

Roast Spice-Brined Chicken

4 SERVINGS

4 quarts cold water

1 cup kosher salt

¼ cup sugar

1 medium onion, chopped

8 thyme sprigs

6 garlic cloves, crushed

6 allspice berries, crushed

2 bay leaves

2 teaspoons peppercorns, cracked

One 3½- to 4-pound chicken

¼ cup extra-virgin olive oil

1. In a large pot, bring 1 quart of the water with the salt and sugar to a simmer, stirring. Off the heat, add the remaining 3 quarts of water, the onion, thyme, garlic, allspice, bay leaves and peppercorns; let cool completely. Add the chicken to the brine and cover with a plate to keep it submerged. Refrigerate for 4 hours.

2. Preheat the oven to 500°. Remove the chicken from the brine and pat dry inside and out. Set the chicken in a heavy roasting pan and rub it with the olive oil. Roast on the bottom shelf of the oven for 20 minutes, turning the pan and basting the chicken 4 times. Turn the oven down to 450° and roast for 20 minutes longer, basting occasionally, until a thermometer inserted in the thigh registers 165°. Let the chicken stand for 10 minutes, then carve and serve with its juices. —*Traci Des Jardins*
WINE Light, fruity Beaujolais.

Roasted Marjoram Chicken
4 SERVINGS ●

 4 chicken breast halves, on the
   bone (about ½ pound each)
Kosher salt and freshly
   ground black pepper
 1 tablespoon plus 1 teaspoon
   sweet paprika
 ⅛ teaspoon cayenne pepper
 ⅓ cup plus 2 tablespoons
   extra-virgin olive oil
 ⅓ cup raw unsalted
   sunflower seeds
 ½ cup coarsely chopped
   marjoram leaves
 ½ cup coarsely chopped
   flat-leaf parsley
 ½ teaspoon fresh lemon juice
Buttered egg noodles, for serving

1. Preheat the oven to 400°. Season the chicken breasts with salt and black pepper, then sprinkle all over with the paprika and cayenne.

2. In a large skillet, heat 2 tablespoons of the olive oil until shimmering. Add the chicken breasts, skin side down.

Cook the chicken over moderately high heat just until the skin is crisp, about 2 minutes; turn the breasts over. Transfer the skillet to the oven and bake the chicken for 25 minutes, or just until cooked through.

3. Meanwhile, in a small skillet, cook the sunflower seeds over moderate heat, stirring occasionally, until lightly browned, about 4 minutes. Transfer the seeds to a plate to cool. In a blender or food processor, blend the remaining ⅓ cup of olive oil with the marjoram, parsley and lemon juice. Add the toasted sunflower seeds, season with salt and puree the sauce until smooth, about 2 minutes.

4. Set the chicken on plates and top with the sauce. Serve at once with buttered egg noodles. —*Scott Ehrlich*
WINE Soft, earthy Rioja.

Roast Chicken with Shallots and Dried Cranberries
4 SERVINGS ●

One 4-pound chicken
 1 tablespoon unsalted
   butter, softened
Salt and freshly ground pepper
 1 bottle (750 ml) French
   hard cider
 8 small shallots, peeled
 ½ cup dried cranberries
 6 whole cloves
 ¾ cup dry vermouth,
   preferably French
 1 tablespoon extra-virgin olive oil
 ¼ cup pine nuts
 1½ tablespoons fresh lemon juice
One 10-ounce bag baby spinach

1. Preheat the oven to 375°. Put the chicken in a small roasting pan and rub the skin all over with the butter. Generously season the chicken inside and out with salt and pepper. Roast the chicken for 1 hour and 15 minutes, or until the juices tipped out of the cavity run clear. Transfer the chicken to a carving board and cover loosely with foil; let stand for 10 minutes.

2. Meanwhile, in a medium saucepan, combine the hard cider with the shallots, dried cranberries, cloves and a pinch of salt. Bring the mixture to a boil, then simmer over low heat until the cranberries are softened, about 5 minutes. With a slotted spoon, transfer the cranberries to a medium bowl. Continue to simmer the shallots until they are tender, about 20 minutes longer. Strain the mixture into a smaller saucepan and transfer the shallots to the bowl with the cranberries; discard the cloves. Boil the cider over moderately high heat until reduced to ½ cup, about 15 minutes.

3. Pour off the fat from the chicken-roasting pan and set the pan over 2 burners on the stove. Add ½ cup of the vermouth and simmer over moderately low heat, scraping up any browned bits from the bottom of the pan with a wooden spoon, about 2 minutes. Add the reduced hard cider and any accumulated juices from the chicken and simmer, stirring frequently, until the sauce is reduced to ¾ cup, about 3 minutes longer. Season the sauce with salt and pepper. Pour the cider sauce into a small saucepan and keep warm over low heat.

4. In a large skillet, heat the olive oil. Add the pine nuts and cook over moderate heat, shaking the pan occasionally, until golden, about 1 minute. Add the remaining ¼ cup of vermouth and the lemon juice and boil over moderately high heat until reduced to 2 tablespoons, about 2 minutes. Add the baby spinach and cook, stirring frequently, until just wilted, about 2 minutes. Stir in the cooked cranberries and shallots and heat through. Season the sauce with salt and pepper.

5. Carve the roasted chicken and arrange the pieces on a platter. Serve the shallot-and-spinach mixture alongside, passing the sauce at the table.
—*Marcia Kiesel*
WINE Rich, earthy Pinot Noir.

SKILLET CHICKEN WITH SUMMER SUCCOTASH

LEMON-HERB CHICKEN WITH VEGETABLES

Lemon-Herb Chicken with Roasted Vegetables and Walnuts

4 SERVINGS ●

1 lemon

One 3- to 3½-pound chicken

12 sage leaves

¼ cup flat-leaf parsley leaves

Salt and freshly ground pepper

2 large thyme sprigs

3 garlic cloves

3 tablespoons extra-virgin olive oil

1 cup Brussels sprouts (5 ounces)

2 medium beets (½ pound), peeled and cut into eighths

2 medium turnips (½ pound), peeled and cut into eighths

1 cup small pearl onions, peeled

1 cup baby carrots

1 cup chicken stock or canned low-sodium broth

1 tablespoon unsalted butter

⅓ cup walnuts, lightly toasted and chopped

I. Preheat the oven to 300°. Halve the lemon crosswise. Cut 3 very thin slices from 1 half; halve the slices. Squeeze 1 tablespoon of juice from the other lemon half and reserve. Carefully loosen the skin over the chicken breasts and thighs; do not tear the skin. Stuff the lemon slices, 8 of the sage leaves and the parsley under the skin. Season the cavity with salt and pepper; stuff with the remaining lemon, 3 sage leaves, 1 thyme sprig and 2 garlic cloves. Rub 1 tablespoon of the oil over the chicken; season with salt and pepper. Tie the legs together with kitchen string.

2. Coat the bottom of a roasting pan with the remaining 2 tablespoons of oil. Set the chicken in the pan, breast side down, and roast for 10 minutes.

3. Meanwhile, in a small saucepan of boiling water, blanch the Brussels sprouts for 2 minutes. Drain and let cool slightly, then halve.

4. Add the Brussels sprouts to the roasting pan along with the beets, turnips, onions, carrots and the remaining sage leaf, thyme sprig and garlic clove and season with salt and pepper. Roast with the chicken for 1 hour. Add ¾ cup of the chicken stock to the pan and roast the chicken and vegetables for 20 minutes longer.

5. Increase the oven temperature to 450°. Turn the chicken breast side up and baste with the pan juices. Continue roasting for about 10 minutes longer, or until the bird is well browned and an instant-read thermometer inserted in the thickest part of the thigh registers 165°. Transfer the chicken to a platter and cover loosely with foil.

6. Continue roasting the vegetables for another 10 minutes, or until tender. Transfer the vegetables to the platter and cover loosely with foil. Set the roasting pan over a burner and bring the pan juices to a boil. Add the remaining ¼ cup of stock and the reserved lemon juice and bring to a simmer over moderately high heat, scraping up the browned bits from the bottom of the pan. Remove the pan from the heat and swirl in the butter. Season the jus with salt and pepper; transfer to a warmed gravy boat. Carve the chicken. Sprinkle the walnuts over the chicken and vegetables and serve with the jus.
—*Michael Schlow*

WINE Ripe, creamy-textured Chardonnay.

Macedonian Lemon Chicken

4 SERVINGS

This simple grilled chicken marinates overnight, so plan accordingly.

  1 cup plain nonfat yogurt
 ⅓ cup fresh lemon juice
  3 garlic cloves, crushed with salt
  1 teaspoon sweet paprika
 ½ teaspoon hot Hungarian paprika
Pinch of ground allspice or cinnamon
Salt and freshly ground pepper
  8 chicken thighs

I. Set a paper towel–lined strainer over a bowl. Spoon in the yogurt and let drain overnight in the refrigerator to ½ cup.
2. In a medium bowl, combine the lemon juice, garlic, sweet and hot paprika, allspice, salt and pepper. Coat the chicken thighs with the marinade, cover and refrigerate overnight. Bring to room temperature before roasting.
3. Preheat the oven to 500°. Brush the chicken with the drained yogurt. Set the chicken thighs skin side up on a greased rimmed baking sheet and roast for about 25 minutes, until cooked through. Turn on the broiler. Broil the chicken 4 inches from the heat for about 5 minutes, until well browned. Serve hot or warm. —*Paula Wolfert*

WINE Lively, assertive Sauvignon Blanc.

Chicken Braised with Lemon and Garlic

6 SERVINGS ●

 25 garlic cloves, peeled (2 heads)
  6 whole chicken legs, skinned
Salt and freshly cracked pepper
  5 thyme sprigs
  1 lemon, all skin and white pith cut off and the fruit thinly sliced
  1 bay leaf
  1 cup hot chicken stock
 ⅓ cup white wine
1½ tablespoons all-purpose flour

I. Preheat the oven to 450°. Cook the garlic in a small saucepan of boiling water for 10 minutes, then drain. In an 8-by-11-inch roasting pan, season the chicken legs with salt and pepper and scatter the garlic, thyme, lemon slices and bay leaf around them. Whisk the stock, then the wine into the flour and pour over the chicken. Cover tightly with foil, bring to a boil on the stove, then braise in the oven for 20 minutes. Reduce the oven temperature to 350°, remove the foil and turn the legs. Braise for about 1 hour and 10 minutes longer, or until tender.
2. Transfer the chicken and garlic to a platter. Skim the fat off the sauce and simmer until slightly reduced, about 10 minutes. Serve with the chicken.
—*Tasha Prysi*

WINE Dry, mineral-flavored Chenin Blanc.

Skillet Chicken with Summer Succotash

6 SERVINGS ●

  6 cups fresh corn kernels (about 9 ears)
 ¼ vanilla bean
  2 tablespoons fresh lemon juice
  2 tablespoons chopped tarragon
  2 teaspoons finely grated lemon zest
Salt and freshly ground pepper
  2 tablespoons grapeseed oil or extra-virgin olive oil
Four 6-ounce skinless, boneless chicken breast halves
  4 carrots, cut into ¼-inch dice
 ½ Spanish onion, finely chopped
  1 pound baby lima beans, shelled
Lemon wedges, for serving

I. In a vegetable juicer, juice 4 cups of the corn; strain the juice through a fine sieve into a small saucepan. Add the vanilla bean and cook over low heat, stirring often, until thickened, about 25 minutes. Add the lemon juice, 1 tablespoon of the tarragon and the lemon zest and season with salt and pepper.
2. Heat ½ tablespoon of the oil in a large nonstick skillet. Season the chicken breasts generously with salt and pepper, add to the skillet and cook over moderately high heat until browned, about 6 minutes per side. Transfer to a plate.
3. In the same skillet, heat 1 tablespoon of the oil. Add the carrots and cook over moderate heat for 5 minutes. Add the onion and cook for 5 minutes. Add the lima beans and cook for 4 minutes. Transfer the vegetables to a bowl.
4. In the same skillet, heat the remaining ½ tablespoon of oil. Add the remaining 2 cups of corn and stir to coat with the oil. Cook over moderately high heat, stirring once, until browned, about 5 minutes. Stir in the corn sauce, the remaining 1 tablespoon of tarragon and the reserved vegetables. Slice the chicken and serve with the succotash and lemon wedges. —*Michel Nischan*

WINE Medium-bodied, round Pinot Blanc.

Roast Chicken with Olives and Yogurt

4 SERVINGS ●

This tangy and flavorful chicken is Italian home cooking at its best.

One 4-pound chicken
Salt and freshly ground pepper
  1 lemon, halved
  2 thyme sprigs, plus 1 teaspoon coarsely chopped thyme
 15 Calamata olives, pitted
  5 garlic cloves, 2 halved and 3 minced

5 tablespoons extra-virgin olive oil

¼ cup coarsely chopped flat-leaf parsley

2 tablespoons coarsely chopped capers

1 tablespoon finely grated lemon zest

1 tablespoon fresh lemon juice

1 teaspoon coarsely chopped rosemary

1 teaspoon coarsely chopped marjoram

¼ cup plus 2 tablespoons yogurt

1. Preheat the oven to 350°. Set the chicken in a small roasting pan and season the cavity with salt and pepper. Cut 1 lemon half into quarters and add them to the cavity along with the thyme sprigs, 6 of the olives and the 2 halved garlic cloves. Squeeze the remaining lemon half over the chicken, rub it with 2 tablespoons of the olive oil and season with salt and pepper. Tie the legs together.

2. Cover the pan with foil and roast the chicken for 45 minutes. Remove the foil and baste the chicken. Increase the oven temperature to 500° and roast the chicken in the upper third of the oven for about 15 minutes longer, or until it is golden and the juices in the cavity run clear.

3. Pour the juices from the cavity into the roasting pan, transfer the chicken to a carving board and cover loosely with foil. Pour the pan juices into a measuring cup and skim off the fat.

4. In a medium skillet, heat the remaining 3 tablespoons of olive oil. Add the 3 minced garlic cloves and cook over low heat until fragrant, about 3 minutes. Add the pan juices, parsley, capers, lemon zest, lemon juice, rosemary, marjoram, chopped thyme and the remaining 9 olives and cook, stirring, for 1 minute. Remove from the heat and stir in the yogurt. Season with salt and pepper. Carve the chicken and serve with the herb sauce. —*Graziella Dionisi*
WINE High-acid, savory Vermentino.

Moroccan Couscous-Stuffed Chicken Breasts

4 SERVINGS

½ cup pine nuts

3 tablespoons olive oil

1 cinnamon stick, broken in half

½ teaspoon ground cumin

½ teaspoon ground coriander

⅓ cup couscous

½ cup boiling chicken stock or canned low-sodium broth

8 small dried apricot halves, coarsely chopped

1 tablespoon chopped parsley

Salt and freshly ground pepper

4 boneless chicken breast halves with skin, pounded to an even thickness

1 tablespoon *harissa* (optional)

1. Preheat the oven to 375°. In a small dry skillet, toast the pine nuts over moderate heat, shaking the pan, until browned, about 3 minutes.

2. Heat 1 tablespoon of the olive oil in a small saucepan. Add the cinnamon stick, cumin and coriander and cook over moderate heat, shaking the pan, for 1 minute. Turn off the heat, add the couscous and boiling stock, cover and let stand for 5 minutes. Stir in the toasted pine nuts, apricots and parsley. Season with salt and pepper. Let cool to room temperature, then remove the cinnamon stick.

3. Using your fingers, loosen the chicken breast skin. Stuff the couscous under the skin, pressing it into an even layer.

4. In a small bowl, mix the *harissa* with 1 tablespoon of the olive oil. Brush the chicken skin with the *harissa* oil and season with salt and pepper.

5. Heat the remaining 1 tablespoon of olive oil in a large ovenproof skillet. Add the chicken, skin side down, and cook over moderately high heat until browned, about 4 minutes. Turn the chicken. Transfer the skillet to the oven and roast the chicken for about 10 minutes, or until white throughout. Serve at once. —*Alison Attenborough*

SERVE WITH Roasted red onions and sautéed greens.

VARIATION Double the couscous and stuff it into the cavities of four 1¼-pound Cornish hens. Truss the hens, brush with the *harissa* oil and roast at 350° for 1 hour.

WINE Simple, fruity Chianti.

Spice-Crusted Chicken Breasts with Lemon-Cucumber Raita

6 SERVINGS ●

2½ tablespoons coriander seeds

2½ tablespoons cumin seeds

2½ tablespoons fennel seeds

½ seedless cucumber, unpeeled and coarsely shredded

1¼ cups plain whole-milk yogurt

1 tablespoon finely grated lemon zest

1 garlic clove, minced

⅛ teaspoon cayenne pepper

Salt and freshly ground pepper

Six 6-ounce boneless chicken breast halves, with skin

¼ cup extra-virgin olive oil

1. Preheat the oven to 350°. In a small dry skillet, toast the coriander, cumin and fennel seeds over moderate heat, shaking the pan, until golden and fragrant, about 3 minutes. Transfer to a spice grinder and let cool. Grind the seeds to a fine powder.

2. Spread the shredded cucumber on several layers of paper towel and blot dry with more paper towels. Transfer the cucumber to a medium bowl and stir in the yogurt, lemon zest, garlic, cayenne and 1 teaspoon of the toasted spice mixture; season the raita with salt and pepper.

3. Brush the chicken with 2 tablespoons of the olive oil and season with salt and pepper. Sprinkle the remaining spice mixture all over the breasts. Heat 2 large ovenproof skillets over moderately high heat and add 1 tablespoon of olive oil to each. Add 3 of the breasts to each skillet, skin side down, and cook until golden, about 4 minutes.

Turn the breasts and continue cooking for another 3 minutes. Transfer the skillets to the oven and bake the chicken for about 8 minutes, or until just cooked through. Serve the chicken warm, with the raita. —*Joanne Weir*

WINE Lively, assertive Sauvignon Blanc.

Sautéed Chicken Livers with Onions and Port

4 SERVINGS ●

3 tablespoons unsalted butter
1 medium red onion, quartered through the core
Kosher salt and freshly ground pepper
¼ cup plus 2 tablespoons port wine
¼ cup plus 2 tablespoons fresh orange juice
1 pound chicken livers, trimmed and halved, 2 halves finely chopped
½ teaspoon Dijon mustard
All-purpose flour, for dredging
Paprika
6 ounces baby spinach

I. In a large skillet, melt 1 tablespoon of the butter. Add the onion quarters and cook over moderately high heat, turning occasionally, until they are golden brown all over, about 15 minutes. Transfer the onion quarters to a plate. Season the onions with salt and pepper and keep warm.

2. Pour the port into the skillet and simmer over high heat until reduced by half, about 3 minutes. Add the orange juice and cook until reduced by half, about 2 minutes. Stir in the finely chopped chicken liver, reduce the heat to low and simmer until just cooked, about 1 minute. Remove the skillet from the heat. Stir in the mustard, season the sauce with salt and pepper and keep warm.

3. Spread the flour on a large plate and season generously with paprika, salt and pepper. Dredge the remaining halved chicken livers in the seasoned flour, shaking off any excess.

4. Melt the remaining 2 tablespoons of butter in a large skillet. Add the livers and cook over moderately high heat, stirring occasionally, until pink in the center, about 5 minutes. Transfer to paper towels to drain.

5. Arrange the spinach on a serving platter. Top with the onion quarters and chicken livers, drizzle the sauce over the top and serve. —*Scott Ehrlich*

WINE Soft, earthy Rioja.

Country Chicken and Mushroom Pie

6 SERVINGS ●

This homey chicken potpie is ideal for entertaining because all the work can be done in advance; the pie can be popped in the oven before serving.

FILLING

Four ¾-pound chicken breast halves on the bone, with skin
Salt and freshly ground pepper
1 quart chicken stock or canned low-sodium broth
4 tablespoons unsalted butter
½ pound mixed wild mushrooms, any tough stems discarded, mushrooms thickly sliced
¼ cup all-purpose flour
¾ cup heavy cream
2 tablespoons finely chopped flat-leaf parsley
1 teaspoon minced thyme
PASTRY
2 cups all-purpose flour
½ teaspoon salt
2 sticks (½ pound) unsalted butter, cut into ½-inch pieces and chilled
½ cup sour cream
1 large egg, lightly beaten with ¼ cup milk

I. MAKE THE FILLING: Preheat the oven to 425°. Put the chicken breasts in a medium roasting pan and season generously with salt and pepper. Roast the chicken for about 20 minutes, or until it is partially cooked. Discard the skin and shred the breast meat. Leave the oven on.

2. Meanwhile, in a medium saucepan, boil the stock until reduced to 2 cups, about 15 minutes; keep warm.

3. Melt the butter in a large, deep skillet. Add the mushrooms, season with salt and pepper and cook over high heat, stirring occasionally, until softened and golden, about 6 minutes. Sprinkle the flour over the mushrooms and cook, stirring, until evenly coated. Add the reduced stock and the cream and whisk until thickened, about 3 minutes. Add the shredded chicken, parsley and thyme and season the filling with salt and pepper; let cool.

4. MAKE THE PASTRY: In a food processor, pulse the flour with the salt. Add the butter and pulse until the mixture resembles coarse meal. Add the sour cream and pulse just until the pastry comes together. Turn the pastry out onto a lightly floured surface and divide it into thirds; pat two of the thirds into 1 disk and the remaining third into another disk. Wrap the disks in plastic and refrigerate them until firm, at least 30 minutes.

5. On a lightly floured surface, roll out the larger piece of pastry to a 15-inch round. Transfer the pastry to a deep 10-inch glass pie plate. Spoon the chicken filling into the pastry and brush the rim with the egg wash. Roll out the remaining pastry to an 11-inch round and carefully lay it on top of the filling.

cooking tip

bird basics

NOT ALL CHICKENS COOK ALIKE. Younger chickens, such as broilers, capons, fryers, roasters and Rock Cornish hens, are best when baked, fried, roasted, grilled or sautéed. Older birds, like hens and stewing chickens, benefit from moist-heat cooking methods, like stewing and braising.

Press the edges of the pastry to seal and trim the overhang to 1 inch. Fold the overhanging pastry dough under itself and crimp it decoratively to seal. Cut 4 slashes in the top crust and brush with the egg wash.

6. Bake the chicken potpie for about 20 minutes, or until the pastry is lightly golden. Lower the oven temperature to 350° and continue baking for about 40 minutes longer, or until the top and bottom crusts are golden and the filling is bubbling. Cover the pie loosely with foil if the top crust browns too quickly. Let the chicken potpie stand for 15 minutes before serving.
—*Maggie Beer*

MAKE AHEAD The chicken potpie can be prepared ahead through Step 5. Cover and refrigerate for up to 6 hours before baking.

WINE Round, rich Sauvignon Blanc.

Country Captain

4 SERVINGS

This curried chicken dish reflects the diverse culinary influences on the southern port city of Charleston, South Carolina, by blending the French-inspired flavors of Creole cooking with the spices of India.

- ½ **cup blanched whole almonds**
- ½ **cup all-purpose flour**
- 1½ **tablespoons sweet paprika**
- **Kosher salt and freshly ground pepper**
- One 4-pound chicken, cut into 8 pieces
- 3 **tablespoons vegetable oil**
- 2 **tablespoons unsalted butter**
- 2 **green bell peppers, finely chopped**
- 1 **large onion, finely chopped**
- ½ **cup minced flat-leaf parsley**
- 2 **garlic cloves, minced**
- 2 **teaspoons curry powder**
- ½ **teaspoon ground mace**
- One 28-ounce can Italian tomatoes, chopped, juices reserved
- ½ **cup chicken stock**
- ¼ **cup dried currants**

1. Preheat the oven to 325°. Toast the almonds in a pie plate for about 6 minutes, until golden. Let the almonds cool, then coarsely chop.

2. In a shallow bowl, mix the flour with the paprika, 2 teaspoons of salt and ½ teaspoon of pepper. Dredge the chicken pieces in the seasoned flour, shaking off any excess.

3. In a large skillet, heat 2 tablespoons of the vegetable oil until shimmering. Add half of the chicken and cook over moderately high heat until browned, about 8 minutes. Transfer to a plate. Add the remaining 1 tablespoon of oil to the skillet and repeat with the remaining chicken.

4. Pour off the oil from the skillet, then melt the butter in it. Add the bell peppers, onion and parsley; cook over low heat, stirring, until the vegetables soften, 12 minutes. Add the garlic, curry powder and mace; cook, stirring, until fragrant, 4 minutes. Add the tomatoes, their juices and the stock; simmer over low heat for 15 minutes. Add the currants. Season with salt and pepper.

5. Transfer the sauce to a 9-by-13-inch glass baking dish. Add the chicken, skin side up. Cover with foil and bake for 30 minutes, or until the breasts are just cooked through. Transfer the breasts to a plate and cover with foil. Bake the remaining chicken for 1 hour longer, or until tender and the sauce is thickened. Return the breasts to the sauce and bake for 5 minutes longer, until heated through. Sprinkle the almonds on top and serve. —*Marcia Kiesel*

MAKE AHEAD The baked chicken can be refrigerated overnight.

SERVE WITH Steamed white rice.

WINE Light, zesty, fuity Dolcetto.

Spicy Chicken and Rice

4 SERVINGS

Medium-grain Spanish rice, such as Valencia, is naturally creamy, so it nicely absorbs the flavors of this classic Spanish dish.

- 4 **garlic cloves, halved**
- **Kosher salt**
- 3 **tablespoons extra-virgin olive oil**
- One 3½ pound chicken, cut into 8 pieces
- ¼ **cup plus 2 tablespoons chopped cilantro**
- 2 **large poblano chiles**
- 2 **ounces lean, smoky bacon, cut into ¼-inch dice**
- 1 **medium onion, finely chopped**
- 1 **large jalapeño, seeded and minced**
- 1½ **cups medium-grain Spanish rice, such as Valencia or Bomba**
- ½ **cup dry sherry**
- One 14-ounce can whole peeled tomatoes, crushed, juices reserved
- 2 **cups chicken stock or canned low-sodium broth**
- **Lime wedges, for serving**

1. In a mortar, pound the garlic to a paste with ½ teaspoon of salt. Stir in 1 tablespoon of the olive oil. In a large bowl, combine the chicken pieces with the garlic paste and ¼ cup of the cilantro; toss to coat. Let stand at room temperature for 30 minutes.

2. Roast the poblanos over an open flame or under the broiler until charred all over. Transfer to a bowl, cover with plastic wrap and let steam for 5 minutes. Stem, peel and seed the poblanos, then cut them crosswise into ½-inch-wide strips.

3. Preheat the oven to 350°. Heat the remaining 2 tablespoons of oil in an enameled cast-iron casserole. Add half of the chicken and cook over moderate heat until golden. Transfer to a plate. Repeat with the remaining chicken.

4. Add the bacon to the casserole and cook over moderately low heat until the fat begins to melt, about 2 minutes. Add the onion and jalapeño and cook, stirring, until softened, about 5 minutes. Add the rice and stir over moderate heat until well coated with fat, about 3 minutes. Add the sherry and

COUNTRY CAPTAIN

boil, stirring, until absorbed, about 2 minutes. Add the tomatoes and their juices, the poblanos, stock and 1 teaspoon of salt, then bring to a boil.

5. Tuck the chicken into the rice, cover and bake for 35 minutes, or until the rice is tender and the stock absorbed. Let stand, covered, for 10 minutes. Sprinkle with the remaining 2 tablespoons of cilantro; serve with lime wedges. —*Marcia Kiesel*

MAKE AHEAD The recipe can be prepared through step 2 and refrigerated separately overnight.

WINE Tart, low-tannin Barbera.

Rooster Gumbo with Tomatoes and Okra

MAKES ABOUT 2½ GALLONS ●
A very large roasting chicken is a fine substitute for the rooster.

- 6 quarts chicken stock or canned low-sodium broth
- 2 pounds meaty ham hocks
- 2 bay leaves
- 1¼ cups plus 2 tablespoons vegetable oil
- One 6-pound rooster or roasting chicken, quartered
- ½ cup Jan's Spice Mix (p. 328)
- 2 cups all-purpose flour
- 6 celery ribs, cut into ½-inch dice
- 2 large Spanish onions, cut into ½-inch dice
- 4 jalapeños, seeded and thinly sliced
- 2 large red bell peppers, cut into ½-inch dice
- 2 large yellow bell peppers, cut into ½-inch dice
- 2 large poblano chiles, cut into ½-inch dice
- 2 pounds okra, cut into ½-inch-thick slices
- 6 garlic cloves, minced
- 1½ pounds plum tomatoes, chopped
- ½ pound andouille sausage, cut into ¼-inch-thick slices
- 6 large scallions, white and light green parts, thinly sliced
- One 1¼-ounce jar filé powder (scant ½ cup; see Note)
- Salt

1. In a large stockpot, bring the stock, ham hocks and bay leaves to a boil. Cover and keep at a slow, steady simmer over low heat.

2. In a very large, deep skillet, heat 1¼ cups of the oil until shimmering. Season the chicken quarters all over with ¼ cup of Jan's Spice Mix. Working in 2 batches, sear the chicken over moderate heat until deeply browned, about 5 minutes per side. Transfer to a plate.

3. Add the chicken to the stock, cover and simmer until cooked through, about 30 minutes for the breasts and 50 for the legs. As the chicken is done, transfer it to a bowl. Continue to simmer the ham hocks until tender, 10 minutes longer, then transfer to the bowl. Skim the fat from the stock and keep warm.

4. Meanwhile, pour the oil from the deep skillet into a large cast-iron skillet. Heat the oil. Whisk in the flour and cook over moderately high heat, whisking constantly, until a deep brown roux forms, about 8 minutes. Scrape the roux into a heatproof bowl.

5. In the very large, deep skillet, heat the remaining 2 tablespoons of oil. Add the celery and onions and cook over moderately low heat, stirring occasionally, until slightly softened, about 12 minutes. Add the jalapeños, bell peppers and poblanos and cook, stirring occasionally, until softened, about 10 minutes. Add the okra, garlic and the remaining ¼ cup of Jan's Spice Mix and cook over moderate heat, stirring, until fragrant, about 5 minutes. Add the tomatoes and simmer until most of the liquid has evaporated, about 5 minutes.

6. Whisk the roux into the warm stock and simmer over low heat, whisking until smooth. Stir in the cooked vegetables and simmer for 30 minutes, skimming the fat occasionally.

taste test mail-order turkey

PRODUCT	F&W COMMENT	INTERESTING BITE
Willie Bird Smoked Turkey (877-494-5592; 800-541-2233)	"Very natural turkey flavor— juicy, tender and not too much smoke."	Each year, the Willie Bird ranch in Sonoma County loses 500 of its free-ranging turkeys to coyotes and eagles.
Nueske's Applewood Smoked Turkey (800-392-2266)	"Moist, with a nicely balanced flavor, but a bit too heavy on the salt."	Nueske gives away three prizes a month: a ham, bacon and a Nueske Breakfast Trio. Go to www.nueske.com for details.
Nodine's Whole Smoked Turkey (800-222-2059)	"Juicy, with mild smokiness, but tastes just like ham."	Nodine's also sells dog treats, such as smoked beef bones and pigs' ears.

7. Meanwhile, pull the meat from the chicken and ham hocks and cut it into 1-inch pieces. Add the meat to the gumbo along with the andouille and simmer for 10 minutes. Add the scallions, whisk in the filé powder and simmer for 5 minutes. Season the gumbo with salt and serve. —*Jan Birnbaum*

NOTE Filé powder is a Creole seasoning made from ground dried sassafras leaves. It is typically used to flavor and thicken gumbos and other stews. It is available at specialty markets.

MAKE AHEAD The dish can be refrigerated for 3 days or frozen for 2 months.

SERVE WITH Steamed white rice.

WINE Tart, low-tannin Barbera.

Roasted Capon Stuffed with Veal and Smoked Ham

8 SERVINGS ●

The decadent stuffing—it wouldn't be out of place to add a couple of diced black truffles—is more a condiment than a side dish. A few tablespoons will complement the moist bird and deeply flavored pan juices.

- ½ **ounce dried porcini mushrooms (½ cup)**
- 1 **cup boiling water**
- 3 **tablespoons unsalted butter, 1 tablespoon softened**
- 1 **large carrot, finely chopped**
- 1 **medium onion, finely chopped**
- ¼ **pound calf's liver, cut into ½-inch dice**

Kosher salt and freshly ground pepper

- ½ **pound ground veal**
- ¼ **pound cooked smoked ham, cut into ¼-inch dice**
- 2 **large eggs, beaten**

One 8-pound capon

- 1 **cup dry red wine, preferably Barbera d'Asti**
- 1 **cup chicken stock or low-sodium broth**
- ½ **cup water**

1. Preheat the oven to 350°. In a heatproof bowl, soak the porcini in the boiling water until softened, 20 minutes.

Rub the porcini to remove any grit, then lift them out of the soaking liquid and finely chop. Reserve the liquid.

2. Melt 2 tablespoons of the butter in a medium skillet. Add the carrot and half of the onion and cook over low heat, stirring occasionally, until the vegetables are softened, about 8 minutes. Add the calf's liver, season with salt and pepper and cook until it is no longer pink on the outside, about 2 minutes. Stir in the chopped porcini. Transfer the mixture to a medium bowl and let cool completely. Add the ground veal, ham, eggs, 1 teaspoon of salt and ½ teaspoon of pepper. Mix the stuffing with your hands until blended.

3. Spoon the stuffing into the cavity of the capon and tie the legs together. Transfer the capon to a roasting pan and rub with the tablespoon of softened butter. Pour the wine over the capon and season with salt and pepper. Add the remaining onion to the pan and roast the capon for about 45 minutes, or until the wine has almost evaporated, basting once halfway through. Add the stock to the pan and baste again. Roast for 2 hours longer, or until an instant-read thermometer inserted in the inner thigh registers 160°.

4. Transfer the capon to a carving board and let rest for 10 minutes. Meanwhile, strain the pan juices into a small saucepan. Set the roasting pan over 2 burners, add the water and simmer over moderate heat for 3 minutes, scraping up the browned bits from the bottom of the pan. Add the reserved mushroom soaking liquid, stopping before you reach the grit at the bottom. Add the pan juices to the saucepan, season with salt and pepper and keep warm over low heat. Spoon the stuffing into a warmed bowl. Carve the capon and serve with the stuffing and pan juices. —*Giorgio Rivetti*

MAKE AHEAD The recipe can be made through Step 2 and refrigerated overnight.

WINE Light, fruity Beaujolais.

Glazed Cornish Hens with Garlicky Radicchio

4 SERVINGS ●

The ginger preserves in the glaze make these hens particularly piquant, but any citrus preserves will do.

Four 1¼-pound Cornish hens

- 16 **cilantro sprigs**

Salt and freshly ground pepper

- 1 **medium orange, zest finely grated and orange quartered**
- ¼ **cup extra-virgin olive oil**
- 1 **tablespoon plus 1 teaspoon cumin seeds, crushed**
- ⅔ **cup fresh orange juice**
- ¼ **cup honey**
- ¼ **cup ginger preserves**
- ½ **teaspoon cayenne pepper**
- 6 **garlic cloves, slivered**
- 1¾ **pounds radicchio, cut into 1-inch pieces**

1. Preheat the oven to 400°. Using your fingertips, carefully loosen the breast skin of each hen; tuck the cilantro sprigs under the skin. Season the cavities with salt and pepper and tuck an orange quarter into each one. Set the hens on a baking sheet, rub them with 1 tablespoon of the olive oil and season with salt and pepper. Roast the hens for 60 to 70 minutes, or until the juices run clear when a thigh is pierced. Remove from the oven and preheat the broiler.

2. In a medium skillet, toast the cumin over moderate heat, shaking the pan, until fragrant, about 1 minute. Stir in the orange juice, honey, ginger preserves, cayenne and orange zest and cook until syrupy, about 4 minutes. Brush the glaze all over the birds.

3. Broil the hens for about 2 minutes, until browned all over. Transfer the hens to a serving platter and keep warm; reserve the pan juices.

4. In a large skillet, heat the remaining 3 tablespoons of olive oil until shimmering. Add the garlic and cook over moderate heat, stirring, until golden, about 3 minutes. Add the radicchio and cook, stirring, until wilted, 3 minutes.

Stir in any reserved pan juices, season the radicchio with salt and pepper and cook for 1 minute longer.

5. Spoon the radicchio onto plates, top with the hens and serve. —*Wendy Kalen*

WINE Full-bodied, fragrant Viognier.

Roasted Cornish Game Hens with Toasted Bread Crumbs

6 SERVINGS

- 1 cup coarse bread crumbs
- Six 1- to 1¼-pound Cornish game hens, halved
- ½ cup extra-virgin olive oil
- Salt and freshly ground pepper
- ¼ cup chopped flat-leaf parsley
- 2 tablespoons white wine vinegar
- 2 anchovy fillets, rinsed and chopped
- 1 tablespoon drained capers, chopped
- 1 tablespoon finely grated lemon zest
- 1 garlic clove, minced
- 1 scallion, thinly sliced
- ½ teaspoon chopped rosemary
- ½ teaspoon chopped thyme

1. Preheat the oven to 450°. Spread the bread crumbs on a rimmed baking sheet and toast for 5 minutes, or until they are golden brown. Let the bread crumbs cool.

2. Arrange the hen halves skin side up on a large rimmed baking sheet. Brush the hens with 2 tablespoons of the olive oil and season generously with salt and pepper. Roast the hens for 30 to 35 minutes, or until golden brown and an instant-read thermometer inserted into a thigh registers 170°.

3. Meanwhile, in a medium bowl, whisk the remaining 6 tablespoons of olive oil with the parsley, vinegar, anchovies, capers, lemon zest, garlic, scallion, rosemary and thyme; season with salt and pepper. Add the bread crumbs and toss to coat. Arrange the hens on a platter, top with the bread crumbs and serve. —*Joanne Weir*

WINE Complex, silky red Burgundy.

Roasted Poussins with Anchovy-Mustard Pan Sauce

6 SERVINGS

You can easily substitute two 3½-pound chickens for the six poussins here; the cooking time will be about 20 minutes longer.

- Six 1-pound poussins
- Sweet paprika
- 2 tablespoons unsalted butter, softened
- Salt and freshly ground pepper
- 1 tablespoon all-purpose flour
- 1 cup chicken stock or canned low-sodium broth
- 2 large shallots, minced (about ½ cup)
- 2 anchovy fillets, mashed
- 2 tablespoons whole-grain mustard
- 2 tablespoons minced chives
- 1 tablespoon chopped flat-leaf parsley
- 1 teaspoon chopped thyme

1. Preheat the oven to 425°. Rub the poussins all over with paprika and 1 tablespoon of the butter. Season with salt and pepper. Truss the poussins by simply tying the legs together with string. Set the poussins in a large shallow metal roasting pan. Roast the poussins in the upper third of the oven for 1 hour, or until nicely browned and the juices from the cavities run clear.

2. Meanwhile, in a small bowl, mix the remaining 1 tablespoon of butter with the flour until a smooth paste forms.

3. Transfer the poussins to a large platter, draining their juices into the roasting pan. Pour the pan juices into a glass measuring cup and skim the fat; reserve 1 tablespoon of the fat.

4. Set the roasting pan on 2 burners. Add the chicken stock and bring to a boil over moderately high heat, scraping up the browned bits from the bottom of the pan. Pour the stock into the glass measuring cup.

5. Heat the reserved 1 tablespoon of fat in a medium saucepan. Add the shallots and cook over low heat, stirring, until softened, about 5 minutes. Add the liquid in the measuring cup and bring to a simmer over moderate heat. Whisk in the anchovies, mustard and flour paste and whisk until the sauce is smooth and slightly thickened, about 3 minutes. Remove the pan from the heat, stir in the herbs and season with salt and pepper. Pour the sauce into a warmed gravy boat.

6. Cut the strings from the poussins and transfer them to plates. Pass the anchovy-mustard sauce at the table. —*Jan Birnbaum*

WINE Dry, medium-bodied Pinot Gris.

Bacon-Roasted Turkey with Sweet-Onion Gravy

12 SERVINGS

- ½ pound bacon (not too lean), chopped
- ¼ cup chopped flat-leaf parsley
- 1½ tablespoons thyme leaves, plus 1 thyme sprig
- Salt and freshly ground pepper
- One 16- to 18-pound turkey, giblets (liver, gizzard and heart) reserved for Dirty Turkey Rice Purloo (p. 237)
- 6 celery ribs, coarsely chopped
- 4 carrots, coarsely chopped
- 2 large white onions, chopped
- 1 large sweet onion, such as Spanish Sweets, thinly sliced
- 1 large garlic clove, smashed

cooking tip

better bacon

MANY RECIPES CALL FOR CHOPPED BACON, like the *Bacon-Roasted Turkey* on this page. An easy way to chop bacon is to freeze it when raw; that way it can be cut into a neat, even-sized dice. Another bacon tip: When cutting thin slices of bacon, use kitchen shears in place of a knife.

¾ **cup all-purpose flour**

1 **quart Rich Turkey Stock (p. 237), chicken stock or canned low-sodium broth**

1. Preheat the oven to 350°. In a food processor, combine the chopped bacon, parsley, thyme leaves, ¼ teaspoon of salt and ½ teaspoon of pepper; process until a paste forms.

2. Using your fingers, gently separate the turkey skin from the breast and legs. Season the turkey cavities with salt and pepper. Carefully spread the bacon paste under the loosened skin and press gently on the outside of the skin to evenly distribute. Season the outside of the turkey with salt and pepper and tie the legs together tightly with kitchen string.

3. Scatter the celery, carrots and white onions in a large roasting pan and set the turkey on top. Tightly cover the bird with 2 sheets of oiled foil and roast on the lowest rack of the oven for 2½ hours. Remove the foil and continue to roast for about 1 hour, or until the turkey is browned and an instant-read thermometer inserted in the inner thigh registers 170°. Transfer the turkey to a carving board, cover loosely with foil and let rest for at least 30 minutes or for up to 1 hour.

4. Meanwhile, strain the pan juices into a bowl. Skim off the fat; pour ¼ cup of the fat into a large, deep skillet. Add the sweet onion and thyme sprig and cook over moderately high heat until the onion is browned, about 5 minutes. Add the garlic, then stir in the flour. Gradually add the stock, whisking constantly, until smooth. Whisk in the reserved pan juices and simmer the gravy over low heat, whisking often, until no floury taste remains, about 15 minutes. Discard the thyme and garlic. Season the gravy with salt and pepper and transfer to a gravy boat.

5. Cut the string from the turkey legs and carve the bird. Serve with the onion gravy. —*Robert Stehling*

MAKE AHEAD The turkey can be prepared through Step 2 and refrigerated overnight. Bring the bird to room temperature before roasting.

WINE Full-bodied, fragrant Viognier.

Teriyaki-Glazed Turkey with Shallot Gravy

12 SERVINGS ●

½ **cup low-sodium soy sauce**

¼ **cup mirin**

¼ **cup sake**

2 **tablespoons rice vinegar**

2 **tablespoons light brown sugar**

1 **tablespoon grated fresh ginger**

1 **teaspoon cornstarch dissolved in 1 tablespoon water**

One 16-pound fresh turkey

1½ **pounds large shallots, peeled**

Salt and freshly ground pepper

6 **tablespoons unsalted butter, softened**

¼ **cup extra-virgin olive oil**

1 **cup water**

2 **cups Rich Turkey Stock (p. 237)**

2 **tablespoons all-purpose flour**

1. Preheat the oven to 500°. In a saucepan, combine the soy sauce, mirin, sake, vinegar, brown sugar and ginger. Add the cornstarch slurry and bring to a boil over high heat. Cook, stirring, until glossy and slightly thickened, 3 minutes. Transfer the teriyaki sauce to a bowl.

2. Set the turkey in a large roasting pan; scatter the shallots around it. Season the turkey cavities and skin with salt and pepper. In a small bowl, blend 4 tablespoons of the butter with the olive oil and brush some over the turkey.

3. Roast the turkey for 30 minutes, or until golden. Baste with the butter mixture and add the water to the roasting pan. Reduce the oven temperature to 325° and roast the turkey for 1 hour, basting twice with the remaining butter mixture; loosely cover the bird with foil if the breast browns too quickly.

4. Pour half of the teriyaki sauce into a bowl; baste the turkey with some of it. Roast the turkey for 1½ hours longer,

basting with the sauce from the bowl every 30 minutes; the turkey is done when the skin is lacquered and an instant-read thermometer inserted in an inner thigh registers 170°. Transfer to a carving board; let rest for 45 minutes.

5. Meanwhile, strain the pan juices into a bowl, skim off the fat and reserve the shallots. Set the roasting pan over 1 burner. Add the shallots back to the pan and cook over high heat, stirring, until browned, about 3 minutes. Add the pan juices, Rich Turkey Stock and the reserved teriyaki sauce. Bring to a boil, scraping up any browned bits from the bottom of the pan.

6. Strain the pan sauce into a medium saucepan, reserving the shallots. Boil the sauce over high heat until reduced by a third, 30 minutes. In a bowl, mix the remaining 2 tablespoons of butter with the flour until smooth. Whisk the flour paste into the sauce and boil, whisking constantly, until the gravy is thickened, about 5 minutes. Add the shallots, season with salt and pepper and transfer to a warmed gravy boat. Carve the turkey and serve with the shallot gravy. —*Grace Parisi*

WINE Bright, fruity rosé.

Roast Turkey with Cherry Salsa

4 SERVINGS ●

1½ **pounds boneless turkey breast**

1 **teaspoon olive oil**

Salt and freshly ground pepper

2 **tablespoons orange marmalade**

¾ **pound sweet cherries, pitted**

1 **Granny Smith apple, finely diced**

½ **small red onion, chopped**

¼ **cup toasted pecans, chopped**

1 **jalapeño, finely chopped**

2 **teaspoons grated fresh ginger**

1. Preheat the oven to 375°. In a roasting pan, rub the turkey breast with the olive oil; season with salt and pepper. Roast in the oven for 40 minutes, or until cooked through. Brush the turkey with the marmalade and broil until lightly charred, about 5 minutes.

2. Combine the cherries, apple, onion, pecans, jalapeño and ginger and season with salt. Slice the turkey and serve with the cherry salsa. —*Wendy Kalen*
WINE Light, zesty, fruity Dolcetto.

Imperial Turkey with Curry Gravy

12 SERVINGS

The turkey needs to marinate for at least two hours or overnight. Please note that this recipe requires a turkey injector.

- 2/3 cup plus 2 tablespoons extra-virgin olive oil
- 1/4 cup Madras curry powder
- One 15-pound fresh turkey
- 15 tablespoons unsalted butter
- Kosher salt
- 2 cups fruity white wine, such as Vouvray
- 3 large shallots, minced
- 5 cups Rich Turkey Stock (p. 237)
- 1/2 cup all-purpose flour
- 1 tablespoon fresh lime juice
- 2 tablespoons chopped cilantro

1. In a small saucepan, combine 2/3 cup of the olive oil with 1 tablespoon of the curry powder and cook over moderately low heat for 3 minutes. Transfer to a bowl and let cool.

2. Using a turkey injector, inject the bird with the curry oil as follows: 2 tablespoons into each thigh, 1 tablespoon into each drumstick and 2 1/2

tablespoons into each breast half. Let the turkey stand at room temperature for 2 hours. Alternatively, refrigerate the bird overnight and bring to room temperature before roasting.

3. Preheat the oven to 350°. Set the turkey in a roasting pan. In a medium saucepan, melt 12 tablespoons of the butter. Add 2 tablespoons of the curry powder, 1 tablespoon of salt and the remaining 2 tablespoons of olive oil. Brush some of the curry butter all over the turkey.

4. Roast the turkey for 2 hours, basting every 30 minutes with the curry butter and turning the roasting pan for even browning. Increase the oven temperature to 400° and roast for 30 minutes longer, or until the skin is golden brown and an instant-read thermometer inserted in an inner thigh registers 170°. If the turkey browns too quickly, cover it loosely with foil. Transfer the turkey to a carving board and let rest for at least 30 minutes or for up to 1 hour.

5. Pour the pan juices into a bowl; skim off the fat. Place the roasting pan over 2 burners. Add the wine and shallots and cook over moderate heat, scraping up any browned bits from the bottom of the pan, until the wine is almost evaporated, about 8 minutes. Add the reserved pan juices and the Rich Turkey Stock and bring to a simmer.

6. Meanwhile, in a medium saucepan, melt the remaining 3 tablespoons of butter. Add the remaining 1 tablespoon of curry powder and cook over moderately low heat, stirring occasionally, for 3 minutes. Stir in the flour, then gradually whisk in the stock mixture and bring to a simmer. Cook over moderately low heat, whisking, until the gravy is thickened, 5 minutes. Stir in the lime juice. Season with salt. Strain the gravy, transfer to a warmed gravy boat and add the chopped cilantro. Carve the turkey and serve with the gravy.
—*Mory Thomas*
WINE Full-bodied, fragrant Viognier.

Turkey and Tomatillo Chimichangas

4 SERVINGS ●

The turkey filling for these pan-fried burritos, or chimichangas, is a healthy alternative to more traditional, heavier fillings like refried beans and shredded pork or beef.

- 2 medium Hass avocados
- 1/4 cup sour cream
- 1 tablespoon fresh lime juice
- Salt
- 1/2 pound fresh tomatillos—husked, rinsed and coarsely chopped
- 1/4 cup coarsely chopped white onion
- 3 garlic cloves, coarsely chopped
- 3 tablespoons coarsely chopped cilantro
- 2 jalapeños, seeded and minced
- 1/2 teaspoon ground cumin
- 2 tablespoons extra-virgin olive oil
- 1 pound ground turkey
- Four 8-inch flour tortillas
- 1/4 pound thickly sliced smoked provolone cheese, cut into 1/2-inch strips
- Vegetable oil
- Salsa, for serving

1. In a medium bowl, mash the avocados with the sour cream and lime juice and season with salt.

2. In a blender, combine the tomatillos with the onion, garlic, cilantro, jalapeños and cumin. Puree until smooth and season with salt.

3. Heat the olive oil in a large skillet. Add the turkey and cook over moderate heat, stirring, until no longer pink, about 4 minutes. Add the tomatillo sauce and cook over moderately high heat, stirring, until thickened, 5 minutes.

4. Wrap the tortillas in a kitchen towel and heat in a microwave oven, about 30 seconds. Lay the tortillas on a work surface. Spoon the filling just below the center of each tortilla, top with a few strips of cheese and roll up as tightly as possible; secure with toothpicks. Brush the tortillas with vegetable oil.

---

equipment tip

easy carving

IF YOU DON'T OWN A CARVING BOARD with a built-in gutter for catching juices, then set your carving board in a rimmed baking sheet. When you slice your turkey, the juices will flow into the baking sheet, where they can be easily retrieved for gravy and sauces. Another bonus: less mess.

IMPERIAL TURKEY WITH CURRY GRAVY

5. In a large skillet, heat 1 teaspoon of vegetable oil until shimmering. Add the chimichangas and cook over moderate heat, turning a few times, until golden all over, about 7 minutes. Transfer the chimichangas to plates, top with the mashed avocados and salsa and serve.
—*Jim Peyton*

Curried Turkey Skewers with Cucumber Raita

6 SERVINGS ●

The turkey needs to marinate overnight, so plan accordingly.

SKEWERS

- 1 cup plain low-fat yogurt
- ½ cup grated cucumber
- 2 tablespoons Madras curry powder
- 1 tablespoon minced garlic
- 2 pounds skinless, boneless turkey breast, cut into 2-inch cubes
- 3 large bell peppers, cut into thirty-six 2-inch pieces
- 1 large pineapple—peeled, cored and cut into thirty-six 2-inch pieces
- Salt and freshly ground pepper

history

world of curry

OUR CURRIED TURKEY SKEWERS ARE SIMPLE TO MAKE, but curry itself has a complicated history. When South Asians took their curry blends around the world, the ingredients changed to suit local tastes. Sri Lankan cooks who moved to the French West Indies added the local mace and nutmeg. Cooks from northern India introduced sweet spices like cinnamon and cardamom to the Southeast Asian mix of ginger, garlic and lemongrass for Massaman (Muslim) curry. Today Japanese curry is sold in blocks made of curry spices, animal fats and fruit paste.

RAITA

- 2 cups plain low-fat yogurt
- 2 cups peeled, seeded and finely diced cucumbers
- 2 teaspoons Madras curry powder
- 2 small garlic cloves, minced
- Salt and freshly ground pepper

1. PREPARE THE SKEWERS: In a bowl, mix the yogurt, cucumber, curry powder and garlic. Add the turkey; stir to coat. Cover and refrigerate overnight.

2. MAKE THE RAITA: In a large bowl, mix the yogurt with the cucumbers, curry powder and garlic and season with salt and pepper. Refrigerate the raita until chilled and the flavors are blended, 2 to 3 hours.

3. ASSEMBLE THE SKEWERS: Light a grill. On each of twelve 8-inch bamboo skewers, thread 3 pieces each of turkey, bell pepper and pineapple. Season with salt and pepper and grill over a moderately hot fire until the turkey is just cooked through, about 4 minutes per side. Serve the skewers, passing the raita at the table. —*Tony Hill*

Orange-Glazed Duck Breast Brochettes with Asparagus Salad

6 SERVINGS

The duck breasts need to marinate overnight, so plan accordingly.

- Six 6-ounce boneless Pekin duck breast halves
- 2 navel oranges
- 2 large shallots, minced (½ cup)
- ½ cup dry white wine
- 2 teaspoons finely grated orange zest
- Freshly ground pepper
- 1 cup Grand Marnier or other orange liqueur
- 1 cup fresh orange juice
- 2 tablespoons unseasoned rice vinegar
- Salt
- Six 12-inch rosemary branches
- 2 pounds thick asparagus, trimmed
- Olive oil

1. Trim back the skin on the duck breasts so it barely covers the meat. Score the fat in a diamond pattern.

2. Peel the navel oranges with a small, sharp knife, removing all of the bitter white pith. Working over a bowl, cut in between the membranes to release the sections into the bowl.

3. In a medium, shallow baking dish, combine the shallots, wine, orange zest and ½ teaspoon of pepper. Add the duck breasts and turn to coat. Cover and marinate the duck breasts overnight in the refrigerator.

4. In a small saucepan, boil the Grand Marnier with the orange juice over moderately high heat and cook until syrupy and reduced by half, about 12 minutes. In a small bowl, mix 3 tablespoons of the orange syrup with the rice vinegar. Season the vinaigrette with salt and pepper.

5. Light a grill. Slice each duck breast half crosswise into 1½-inch-thick pieces. Strip two-thirds of the leaves from each rosemary branch, leaving a tassel at the top. Scatter the rosemary leaves over the hot coals or on the gas grill heat bars. Thread the pieces of duck onto the rosemary branches, leaving ½ inch between them.

6. Brush the asparagus with olive oil and season with salt and pepper. Grill the asparagus over a medium-hot fire, turning once, until crisp-tender, about 5 minutes. Let cool slightly and cut into 2-inch lengths. In a large bowl, toss the asparagus with the orange sections and the vinaigrette.

7. Season the duck brochettes with salt. Grill, skin side down, over a moderately low fire, brushing with some of the remaining orange syrup, until the skin is deeply browned and crisp, about 5 minutes. Turn the brochettes and grill, brushing frequently with the syrup, until the duck is medium rare. Transfer the brochettes to plates and serve with the asparagus and orange salad.
—*Marcia Kiesel*

Seared Duck Breasts with Honey-Raisin Compote

6 SERVINGS

- ¾ cup dark raisins
- ¼ cup red wine vinegar
- 1 cup rich chicken or duck stock, preferably homemade
- 1 tablespoon unsalted butter
- 1 medium shallot, minced
- 2 tablespoons honey
- 1 teaspoon finely chopped rosemary
- 1 teaspoon finely chopped thyme

Six 10-ounce Pekin duck breast halves

- 2 tablespoons extra-virgin olive oil

Salt and freshly ground pepper

1. In a small bowl, cover the raisins with the vinegar and ½ cup of the chicken stock and let stand at room temperature for 10 minutes.

2. Melt the butter in a medium saucepan. Add the shallot and cook over moderate heat until softened, about 4 minutes. Add the raisin mixture along with the honey, rosemary and thyme and simmer until syrupy, about 5 minutes. Let cool, then transfer to a blender and coarsely puree.

3. Using a sharp paring knife, score the duck skin in a shallow crosshatch pattern, spacing the cuts about ¾ inch apart. Heat the olive oil in 2 medium skillets until shimmering. Add the duck breasts, skin side down, and cook over moderate heat until the skin is deep golden, about 15 minutes; spoon off the rendered fat as it accumulates in the skillets. Season the duck breasts with salt and pepper, turn and cook until browned on the bottom and an instant-read thermometer inserted in the thickest part of one of the breasts registers 135°, about 12 minutes longer. Transfer the duck breasts to a cutting board and let rest for 5 minutes.

4. Meanwhile, wipe out the skillets. Add the remaining ½ cup of chicken stock to 1 of the skillets and cook over moderate heat, scraping up any browned bits from the bottom of the pan. Scrape the pan sauce into the second skillet and cook over moderate heat, scraping up any browned bits from the bottom of the pan. Stir in the raisin puree and cook over moderate heat just until thickened, about 1 minute. Season the sauce with salt and pepper and transfer to a small bowl.

5. Thickly slice the duck breasts on the diagonal and arrange on plates. Spoon the raisin compote alongside and serve. —*Jan Birnbaum*

WINE Full-bodied, fragrant Viognier.

Seared Spiced Duck Breasts

4 SERVINGS

In Gascony, the *magret* is the boned breast, complete with its outside layer of skin and fat, from a duck that has been fattened for foie gras. The *quatre épices,* or four spices—cloves, nutmeg, cinnamon and ginger—are a signature seasoning in this region of Southwest France. In this recipe, freshly ground black pepper is a fifth aromatic.

- 1 whole boneless duck breast (1½ pounds), breast halves separated and patted dry
- 2 teaspoons juniper berries
- ¼ teaspoon freshly grated nutmeg
- ¼ teaspoon ground cinnamon
- ¼ teaspoon ground ginger

Pinch of freshly ground cloves
Pinch of freshly ground pepper
Salt

- 1 tablespoon Armagnac
- 2 teaspoons Dijon mustard
- ¼ cup robust red wine, such as a Cahors or a California Cabernet Sauvignon
- 2 tablespoons red wine vinegar
- 2½ tablespoons unsalted butter

1. Using a sharp paring knife, score the skin side of the duck breasts in a diamond pattern.

2. In a dry skillet, toast the juniper berries over moderately high heat until they are shiny, about 1½ minutes, being careful not to burn them. Immediately transfer the juniper berries to a mortar or spice grinder and let cool completely. Add the nutmeg, cinnamon, ginger, cloves, pepper and ½ teaspoon of salt to the mortar and grind to a fine powder. Transfer the spices to a small bowl and stir in the Armagnac and mustard to make a paste.

3. Rub the spice paste all over the duck breast halves. Set the duck breasts in a glass or ceramic dish, cover with plastic wrap and refrigerate for at least 6 and up to 24 hours. Remove the duck breasts from the refrigerator at least 30 minutes before cooking.

4. Preheat the oven to 325°. Set a heavy medium skillet over moderately high heat until very hot. Set the duck breasts in the pan, skin side down, and cook until the skin is browned and the fat begins to melt, about 3 minutes. Adjust the heat as necessary if the skin is browning too fast. Remove the skillet from the heat and transfer the breasts to a plate. Drain the fat and carefully wipe out the pan with paper towels. Return the duck breasts to the skillet, meat side down, and cook over moderately high heat for 5 minutes longer. Transfer the duck to a small baking dish and keep warm in the oven while you prepare the sauce.

5. Add the red wine and the vinegar to the skillet and bring to a simmer, stirring with a wooden spoon to release all of the browned bits from the bottom of the pan. Cook the sauce until reduced to 3 tablespoons. Remove from the heat and swirl in the butter. Season the sauce with salt and pepper.

6. Slice the duck breasts on the diagonal and fan them out on warmed plates or a warmed serving platter. Spoon the sauce over the duck breats and serve immediately. —*Kate Hill*

WINE Rich, velvety Merlot.

CRUSTY PAN-SEARED RIB-EYE STEAK, P. 124

beef, lamb + game

PAN-ROASTED BEEF FILET WITH RÖSTI POTATOES

CHIPOTLE STEAK WITH TURKISH WHEAT BERRIES

Crusty Pan-Seared Rib-Eye Steak

2 SERVINGS

This recipe makes two very generous portions, but it could easily serve at least one more person. The steak needs to marinate for four hours, so plan accordingly.

One 2-pound bone-in rib-eye steak

  1 teaspoon extra-virgin olive oil
  1 teaspoon kosher salt
  ½ teaspoon freshly ground pepper
  2 tablespoons unsalted butter
  2 medium garlic cloves,
    lightly smashed
  1 rosemary sprig

I. Rub the steak all over with the olive oil and season with the salt and pepper. Wrap in plastic and refrigerate for 3 hours, then let stand at room temperature for 1 hour.

2. Preheat the oven to 500°. Preheat a cast-iron skillet over moderate heat. When the skillet is very hot, add the rib-eye steak, fat side down, and cook until golden, about 5 minutes. Pour off all but 1 teaspoon of fat from the skillet. Turn the steak and brown it on both flat sides, about 4 minutes. Remove the skillet from the heat and add the butter, garlic and rosemary.

3. Transfer the skillet to the oven and roast the steak for about 20 minutes, turning and basting it twice; the meat will be medium rare when an instant-read thermometer inserted horizontally near the bone registers 125°. Transfer the steak to a cutting board and let rest for 10 minutes. Cut the steak off the bone and serve in large pieces or sliced.
—*Traci Des Jardins*

SERVE WITH Buttery Mashed Potatoes (p. 224) and Grilled Red Onion, Celery and Parsley Salad (p. 46).

WINE Tannic, complex Cabernet.

Rib-Eye Steak au Poivre

2 SERVINGS

When making steak au poivre, Maria Guarnaschelli has always stirred a few capers into the sauce, an addition her daughter, Alexandra, did not appreciate as a young girl. Today, however, Alexandra's steak au poivre—with capers—is a favorite at Nick & Stef's Steakhouse in New York City.

  2 tablespoons black peppercorns,
    coarsely crushed
  1 tablespoon minced garlic
  2 teaspoons ground cumin
  2 tablespoons extra-virgin olive oil
  2 rib-eye steaks, cut
    1¾ inches thick
Sea salt
  ¼ cup dry red wine
  1 tablespoon grainy mustard
  1 teaspoon brined green
    peppercorns, drained

1 teaspoon capers in 1 teaspoon
of their brine
1 tablespoon unsalted butter
1 teaspoon chopped parsley

1. In a small bowl, combine the black peppercorns with the garlic, cumin and 1 tablespoon of the olive oil. Rub this mixture all over the steaks and let stand at room temperature for 2 hours.

2. In a large skillet, heat the remaining 1 tablespoon of olive oil until shimmering. Season the steaks with salt, add them to the skillet and cook over moderate heat until browned, about 4 minutes per side for medium rare. Transfer the steaks to a warmed platter and season again with salt.

3. Discard the fat from the skillet. Add the red wine and simmer over low heat until reduced to a syrup, about 2 minutes. Add the mustard, green peppercorns and capers in brine and stir once or twice. Remove the skillet from the heat and stir in the butter. Return the peppered steaks to the skillet and turn to glaze with the sauce. Transfer the steaks to plates, sprinkle with the parsley and serve at once.

—*Alexandra Guarnaschelli*

WINE Rich, smoky-plummy Shiraz.

Pan-Roasted Beef Filet with Rösti Potatoes

4 SERVINGS

At Indigo in London, chef Richard O'Connell serves this dish with spinach, parsnips and country bread croûtes spread with chicken liver pâté.

2¾ pounds baking potatoes, peeled
and coarsely shredded
2 tablespoons chopped chives
2 tablespoons chopped parsley
Salt and freshly ground pepper
6 tablespoons unsalted butter
¼ cup extra-virgin olive oil
Four 1½-inch-thick filet steaks
cut from the wide end
(6 ounces each)
½ cup demiglace
½ teaspoon thyme leaves

1. Squeeze as much liquid from the potatoes as possible. Put the potatoes in a large bowl and stir in the chives and parsley; season with salt and pepper.

2. In a large nonstick skillet, melt 4 tablespoons of the butter in the oil. Stir in the potatoes and spread in an even layer. Cook over moderate heat, turning once, until the potato cake is golden and crisp, 35 minutes; keep warm.

3. Preheat the oven to 400°. Season the meat with salt and pepper. In a large ovenproof skillet, sear the meat over high heat, turning once, until it is well browned, about 8 minutes. Transfer the skillet to the oven and roast the meat for 15 minutes for medium rare. Transfer the steaks to a plate.

4. Set the skillet over high heat. Add the demiglace and thyme and cook, stirring, until reduced to ¼ cup. Swirl in the remaining 2 tablespoons of butter and season with salt and pepper.

5. Cut the potato cake into 4 wedges and transfer to warmed plates. Set the steaks on the wedges. Drizzle the sauce around the steaks and serve at once.

—*Richard O'Connell*

WINE Rich, velvety Merlot.

Chipotle Steak with Turkish Wheat Berries

4 SERVINGS

The steak and wheat berries are refrigerated overnight in a marinade made with spicy chipotle chiles in adobo, so plan accordingly.

1 cup whole wheat berries
(7 ounces)
3 cups water
1 large tomato—peeled, seeded
and chopped
3 chipotle chiles in adobo sauce,
seeded and chopped, plus
1 tablespoon of the sauce
½ cup tomato paste
2 tablespoons fresh lemon juice
2 teaspoons honey
1 large garlic clove, minced
½ teaspoon cinnamon
¼ teaspoon ground cumin
3 tablespoons plus 1 teaspoon
extra-virgin olive oil
Salt and freshly ground pepper
One 2-pound sirloin steak
2 teaspoons white wine vinegar
16 cherry tomatoes, halved
(½ pound)
1 medium cucumber, seeded and
cut into 1-inch dice
2 tablespoons coarsely chopped
flat-leaf parsley

1. In a medium saucepan, combine the wheat berries with the water and bring to a boil. Cover and simmer over low heat until the wheat berries are tender but still chewy, about 2 hours. Drain and let cool to room temperature.

2. Meanwhile, in a mini food processor, puree the chopped tomato with the chipotles and adobo sauce. Transfer to a medium bowl. Stir in the tomato paste, lemon juice, honey, garlic, cinnamon and cumin. Add 3 tablespoons of the olive oil; season with salt and pepper.

3. Put the steak in a shallow dish and coat with ¼ cup of the tomato-chipotle sauce. Stir the wheat berries into the remaining sauce and season with salt. Cover and refrigerate the steak and wheat berries overnight.

4. Light a grill or preheat a grill pan. Bring the steak and wheat berries to room temperature. Oil the grill and cook the steak over a medium-hot fire for about 4 minutes per side, or until lightly charred on both sides and medium rare within. Transfer the steak to a cutting board and let rest for 5 minutes.

5. In a bowl, mix the vinegar with the remaining 1 teaspoon of olive oil. Add the cherry tomatoes, cucumber and parsley, season with salt and pepper and toss well. Slice the steak ¼ inch thick and serve with the wheat berries and the tomato salad. —*Marcia Kiesel*

MAKE AHEAD The tomato-chipotle sauce and the wheat berry salad can be refrigerated for up to 3 days.

WINE Round, supple, fruity Syrah.

Bacon-Cured Skirt Steak with Chanterelles and Shallots

4 SERVINGS

The skirt steaks need to cure overnight, so plan accordingly.

- ¾ **pound double-smoked bacon, sliced ⅛ inch thick**
- Four **½-pound skirt steaks**
- 3 **tablespoons unsalted butter**
- 4 **large shallots, thinly sliced**
- ¾ **pound white mushrooms, thickly sliced**
- ¼ **pound small chanterelle mushrooms, thickly sliced if large**
- **Salt and freshly ground pepper**
- 1 **tablespoon vegetable oil**
- 1 **tablespoon chopped parsley**

1. Lay half of the bacon on a large sheet of plastic. Set the steaks on top; cover with the remaining bacon. Wrap and refrigerate overnight, or for 24 hours.

2. Melt 2 tablespoons of the butter in a skillet. Add the shallots and cook over low heat, stirring, until softened, about 5 minutes. Add all of the mushrooms, season with salt and pepper, cover and cook until they have released their liquid, about 4 minutes. Uncover and cook over moderate heat until browned on the bottom, about 3 minutes. Stir and cook for 4 minutes longer. Add the remaining 1 tablespoon of butter and cook, stirring, for 1 minute. Season the mushrooms with salt and pepper and transfer to a saucepan; keep warm.

3. Remove the bacon from the steak and save for another use. Heat ½ tablespoon of the oil in each of 2 large skillets. Add 2 steaks to each skillet and cook over moderately high heat until browned on the bottom, about 3 minutes. Turn and cook until medium rare, about 3 minutes longer. Transfer to a carving board; let rest for 5 minutes.

4. Stir the parsley into the mushrooms. Thinly slice the steaks across the grain and arrange on plates. Top with the mushrooms and serve. —*Marcia Kiesel*

WINE Intense, berry-flavored Zinfandel.

Grilled Korean-Style Skirt Steak

6 SERVINGS

This recipe is a twist on a traditional Korean short-rib dish called *kalbi kui.* Using skirt steak is much easier than butterflying short ribs. The sweet Korean chili paste called *kochujang* is available at Asian markets.

- ¼ **cup soy sauce**
- 3 **tablespoons Asian sesame oil**
- 3 **tablespoons sugar**
- 3 **tablespoons sake or dry sherry**
- 3 **medium garlic cloves, minced**
- 2 **scallions, chopped**
- ½ **teaspoon freshly ground pepper**
- 2½ **pounds skirt steak, cut into 4-inch pieces**
- **Vegetable oil, for the grill**
- 1 **head romaine lettuce, separated into leaves, and** *kochujang,* **for serving**

1. In a glass baking dish, mix the soy sauce, sesame oil, sugar, sake, garlic, scallions and pepper. Add the skirt steak and turn to coat. Cover with plastic wrap and refrigerate for 2 hours.

2. Light a grill. Lightly oil the grate. Grill the steak over a medium-hot fire for about 6 minutes for medium-rare meat, turning. Let rest for 10 minutes.

3. Slice the steak across the grain. Serve with lettuce and chili paste so diners can wrap their own beef rolls. —*Steven Raichlen*

WINE Intense, berry-flavored Zinfandel.

Glazed Beef with Bourbon-Roquefort Sauce

4 SERVINGS ●

- ½ **cup bourbon**
- Four **1½-inch-thick beef tenderloin steaks (6 ounces each)**
- 1 **cup heavy cream**
- 3 **tablespoons unsalted butter, softened**
- **Salt and freshly ground pepper**
- 2 **ounces Roquefort cheese, crumbled (½ cup)**

1. In a large shallow dish, pour ¼ cup of the bourbon all over the tenderloin steaks and cover. Let stand at room temperature while you start the sauce.

2. In a small saucepan, bring the remaining ¼ cup of bourbon to a boil over moderately high heat. Cook until reduced to 1 tablespoon, about 3 minutes. Add the heavy cream and simmer until reduced by half, about 8 minutes; keep warm.

3. Drain the steaks and pat dry with paper towels; reserve the marinade. In a large, heavy skillet, melt 1 tablespoon of the butter. Season the steaks generously with salt and pepper and cook over high heat, turning once, until browned, about 4 minutes. Lower the heat to moderately high and continue to cook the steaks, turning once and basting occasionally with the bourbon marinade, until the steaks are medium rare, about 12 minutes.

4. Meanwhile, in a small bowl, mix the Roquefort with the remaining 2 tablespoons of butter until smooth. Slowly whisk the Roquefort butter into the bourbon cream over low heat until smooth. Remove the bourbon-Roquefort sauce from the heat and season with salt and pepper.

5. Transfer the steaks to a cutting board and slice across the grain ¼ inch thick. Arrange the slices on plates, spoon some of the Roquefort sauce on top and pass the rest at the table. —*Damon Lee Fowler*

WINE Tannic, complex Cabernet.

---

cooking tip

tender treatment

SKIRT STEAK IS A LONG, FLAT STEAK with muscle fiber that can make it tough. Slicing it across the grain yields a much more tender steak. When cooking steak or chicken, cutting across the grain prevents curling.

Upside-Down Tomato-Beef Pie

6 SERVINGS ●

Adapted from a recipe in the *Hunger is the Best Sauce* cookbook, published in 1944 by the Service League of St. Luke's Episcopal Church of Sea Cliff, New York, this one-dish meal is a clever twist on the Sloppy Joe. The tender biscuit crust that tops the skillet pie is perfect for soaking up the delicious tomatoey ground beef filling.

1 tablespoon vegetable oil
3 large celery ribs, peeled and very thinly sliced
1 small onion, finely chopped
1½ pounds lean ground beef
1 tablespoon plus 1 teaspoon hot paprika
One 10¾-ounce can of condensed tomato soup
¼ cup water
1 tablespoon tomato paste
Salt and freshly ground pepper
1½ cups all-purpose flour
1 tablespoon baking powder
¼ teaspoon celery seeds
5 tablespoons solid vegetable shortening
¾ cup milk

1. Preheat the oven to 450°. Heat the oil in a 9- to 10-inch cast-iron skillet. Add the sliced celery and chopped onion and cook over low heat, stirring occasionally, until softened, about 8 minutes. Raise the heat to moderately high, add the ground beef and cook, breaking it up with a wooden spoon, until no pink remains, about 5 minutes. Add the paprika and cook, stirring, until fragrant, about 1 minute. Stir in the tomato soup, water and tomato paste until thoroughly blended. Season with salt and pepper and remove the skillet from the heat.

2. In a large bowl, mix the flour with the baking powder, 1 teaspoon of salt and the celery seeds. Using a fork, cut in the shortening until the mixture resembles small peas. Gently stir in the milk just until a soft dough forms.

GRILLED KOREAN-STYLE SKIRT STEAK

UPSIDE-DOWN TOMATO-BEEF PIE

3. Using 2 spoons, arrange tablespoon-size dollops of the dough all over the beef filling to within 1 inch of the edge of the skillet. Bake the beef pie for 20 minutes, or until the crust is browned and cooked through and the filling is bubbling. Let the pie stand for 10 minutes before serving. Invert onto a large, flat plate or serve straight out of the skillet. —*Marcia Kiesel*

MAKE AHEAD The beef filling can be refrigerated overnight. Bring to room temperature, then reheat in the cast-iron skillet before proceeding.

WINE Powerful, spicy Syrah.

Grilled Beef Tenderloin with Tuscan Kale and Shallot Confit

8 SERVINGS

Tuscan, or black, kale—*cavolo nero* in Italian—has elongated deep green crinkly leaves. If you can't find it at specialty produce markets, ordinary curly kale makes a fine substitute. This simple marinade is also delicious with pork tenderloin or pork chops. The beef tenderloin is marinated overnight, so plan accordingly.

> 5 tablespoons extra-virgin olive oil
> 1 packed cup thyme sprigs
> Kosher salt and freshly ground pepper
> One 3½-pound trimmed beef tenderloin
> Vegetable oil, for the grill
> 6 garlic cloves, thinly sliced
> 2 pounds Tuscan kale, coarsely chopped
> 1 cup water
> Shallot Confit (recipe follows), for serving

1. In a large glass or ceramic baking dish, combine 3 tablespoons of the olive oil with the thyme sprigs and season with salt and pepper. Add the beef tenderloin and turn to coat with the marinade. Cover the tenderloin with plastic wrap and refrigerate overnight. Let the tenderloin stand at room temperature for 1 hour before grilling. Scrape off the thyme sprigs.

2. Light a grill. Lightly oil the grate. Season the beef tenderloin with salt and grill it over a medium-hot fire, turning occasionally, until the beef is browned all over and an instant-read thermometer inserted in the thickest part of the tenderloin registers 125° for medium-rare meat, 20 to 25 minutes. Transfer the tenderloin to a cutting board and let rest for 10 minutes.

3. Meanwhile, in a large, deep skillet, heat the remaining 2 tablespoons of olive oil until shimmering. Add the sliced garlic and cook over moderate heat, stirring, until golden, about 2 minutes. Add the Tuscan kale and water and cook over moderately high heat, stirring, until the kale is tender, about 10 minutes. Season with salt and pepper and transfer to a bowl.

4. Carve the beef tenderloin into ⅓-inch-thick slices and arrange on plates. Serve the tenderloin with the kale and Shallot Confit. —*Ben Ford*

WINE Powerful, spicy Syrah.

SHALLOT CONFIT

MAKES 1⅓ CUPS ● ●

This rich and subtly sweet condiment is also delicious with grilled chicken and pork or simply spread on toast. To save time, use a food processor to pulse the shallots just until finely chopped. You'll have plenty of fragrant shallot oil left over once the confit is done; use it in dressings.

> 2½ pounds large shallots, peeled and finely chopped
> 1 cup extra-virgin olive oil
> Kosher salt and freshly ground pepper

1. In a medium saucepan, cook the shallots in the olive oil over moderate heat, stirring occasionally, until very soft, about 30 minutes. Reduce the heat to low and continue to cook, stirring often, until dark golden, about 15 minutes.

2. Season the confit with salt and pepper; transfer to a bowl to cool. —*B.F.*

MAKE AHEAD The Shallot Confit can be refrigerated for up to 1 week.

Beef Braciole in Umido

6 SERVINGS ● ●

In umido means "braised" in Italian, and braciole are pounded-thin pieces of beef that are invariably stuffed and rolled.

> Six 4-ounce slices of trimmed beef tenderloin, pounded ⅛ inch thick
> 2 teaspoons minced sage
> 2 teaspoons minced rosemary
> 1 large garlic clove, minced
> 6 thin slices of prosciutto, trimmed (2 ounces)
> Salt and freshly ground pepper
> 1 tablespoon extra-virgin olive oil
> 1 cup dry red wine
> 1 cup water
> 2 tablespoons tomato paste

1. Preheat the oven to 375°. Lay the tenderloin slices on a work surface. In a small bowl, mix the sage with the rosemary and garlic and rub the mixture over the top of each slice. Cover with a slice of prosciutto and roll up the beef, tucking in the sides as you go. Tie the beef braciole with kitchen string and season with salt and pepper.

2. In a large ovenproof skillet, heat the olive oil. Brown the beef braciole over moderately high heat, about 4 minutes. Discard the olive oil. Add the wine to the skillet and simmer for 2 minutes, scraping up the browned bits from the bottom of the pan. Whisk in the water and tomato paste and bring to a simmer. Transfer the skillet to the oven and braise the braciole for 15 minutes.

3. Transfer the braciole to a plate and cover with foil to keep warm. Simmer the braising liquid over moderately high heat until thickened and flavorful, about 12 minutes. Season the sauce with salt and pepper. Return the beef braciole and any accumulated juices to the skillet and simmer briefly until heated through. Transfer the braciole to plates and discard the strings. Pour the red wine sauce on top and serve.

—*Anna Teresa Callen*

WINE Complex, savory Chianti Classico.

During the course of a Web chat on foodandwine.com, Alexandra Guarnaschelli, the talented chef who's responsible for the succulent strip, rib-eye and porterhouse steaks at Manhattan's Nick & Stef's Steakhouse, divulged some of her coveted secrets for excellent steak, steak sauce, meatballs—and even potato salad.

FW: How should I cook a T-bone?
AG: Add some grapeseed oil (or any kind of vegetable oil) to a large stainless steel pan and heat it until it begins to smoke. Meanwhile, season the T-bone on both sides—liberally—with salt and pepper; I prefer coarse sea salt and freshly cracked black pepper. Then, using a pair of kitchen tongs, pick up the steak by the bone and carefully slide it into the smoking pan. Lower the heat and cook the meat undisturbed for three minutes. Then pick up the steak, again by the bone, turn it over and raise the heat. Cook it on the second side for three to five minutes. A 24-ounce one-and-a-half-inch-thick steak treated this way will end up between rare and medium rare. For a more well-done steak, cook for an additional three to five minutes on each side.

FW: Do you have any good tips for side dishes—french fries, corn on the cob and potato salad?
AG: You can make your french fries a lot less greasy and much more crisp if, before frying the cut potatoes, you drop them in boiling salted water for two minutes, drain them and refresh them in ice water. I fry them only one time, as opposed to twice. To jazz up corn on the cob, I brush mine with a mixture of melted butter and brown sugar. As for potato salad, I use red potatoes, celery, red wine vinegar, mayonnaise, lemon and cayenne pepper. Make sure to mix everything while the potatoes are still warm; they're like sponges that way, absorbing the flavors of the other ingredients.

FW: Do you like a steak sauce?
AG: Green-peppercorn sauce is one of my favorites. I make a great one by cooking onions on the grill, then sautéing them in a pan with olive oil, brined green peppercorns (the brining is optional) and sherry.

FW: Is there a way to make inexpensive cuts of meat more tender?
AG: It depends on the cut, and on whether you're grilling or braising. For grilling, I find that pounding the meat with either a mallet or the flat side of a cleaver and marinating it overnight in Dijon mustard with a dash of sherry helps give it a deep flavor and a pleasant texture. For other cuts of meat that are suitable for braising, such as short ribs or osso buco, I simply cook the meat for a long period of time—say, three hours for my short ribs. Then I let them rest for a few additional hours, which allows all the flavors to really mingle and take over.

FW: Any suggestions about what to do with leftover steak?
AG: I make a mint and black pepper vinaigrette with apple cider vinegar, extra-virgin olive oil, chopped fresh mint and mayonnaise, finished off with some cracked black pepper. Warm the steak, slice it, layer it on a platter and drizzle the vinaigrette over it. Then top the steak with a mixture of peppery greens.

FW: When you're making Italian meatballs, do you prefer using bread crumbs or bread?
AG: Out of respect for my loving grandmother, I will tell you that there is only one way to go: Mix one part dry bread crumbs to one part grated Parmesan cheese—usually about a cup of the mixture per pound of meat. The cheese will add moisture and flavor to the meatballs.

FW: Can you suggest accompaniments for grilled lamb?
AG: The most obvious answer is anything with mint or anything that resembles a chutney. Though I serve both things, I personally don't care for either of them! My favorite complement to lamb is orange marmalade: Whisk the marmalade into some of the pan juices from the lamb chops or lamb roast in the still-warm pan. Alternatively, I love to spread a mixture of chopped fresh marjoram and grainy mustard over lamb.

beef, lamb + game

Standing Rib Roast of Beef

8 SERVINGS

Chef Michael Romano's slow-cooking method yields an incredibly juicy, succulent rib roast.

- 3 tablespoons sea salt
- 3 tablespoons very coarsely ground black pepper
- 2 tablespoons Worcestershire sauce
- 1 tablespoon sweet paprika
- ½ teaspoon garlic powder

One 8-pound standing rib roast of beef, chine bone removed

1. Preheat the oven to 550°. In a small bowl, combine the salt with the black pepper, Worcestershire, paprika and garlic powder. Rub the mixture all over the roast, rubbing especially well into the top layer of fat.

2. Set the roast on a rack in a roasting pan, fat side up, then transfer the pan to the center of the oven. Reduce the oven temperature to 325° and roast for about 1 hour and 15 minutes, or until an instant-read thermometer inserted in the center of the roast registers 110°. Transfer the roast to a carving board, cover loosely with foil and let stand for 30 minutes, or until the thermometer registers 120° for medium rare. Carve the roast between the ribs, transfer to plates and serve. —*Michael Romano*

WINE Tannic, complex Cabernet.

---

dictionary
short ribs

SHORT RIBS ARE RECTANGULAR SANDWICHES OF FAT, MEAT, AND BONE that are often cut into 3-inch sections. They are cut from any part along the length of the cow's ribs. They're very flavorful, but tough and fatty, so they're best if slowly braised. Short ribs are sold boneless or bone-in; look for lean ones when purchasing.

London Broil with Red Wine, Fennel and Olives

6 SERVINGS ●

- 2 tablespoons extra-virgin olive oil

One 1½-pound piece of London broil (about 1¼ inches thick), cut in half

Salt and freshly ground pepper

- 1 medium onion, thinly sliced
- 1 small fennel bulb—halved, cored and very thinly sliced crosswise
- ½ pound pitted Calamata olives, coarsely chopped
- 2 large garlic cloves, minced
- 1 cup dry red wine
- 1 cup water
- ¼ cup fresh orange juice
- 2 teaspoons finely chopped sage, plus sage leaves for garnish

1. In a large, deep skillet, heat the olive oil until shimmering. Season the meat with salt and pepper, add to the skillet and cook over moderate heat until lightly browned on both sides, about 4 minutes; transfer to a plate.

2. Add the onion, fennel, olives and garlic to the skillet and cook over moderate heat, stirring occasionally, until very tender, about 8 minutes. Add the wine, water, orange juice and chopped sage and bring to a simmer. Cook over moderate heat for 5 minutes.

3. Add the London broil to the vegetables in the skillet. Cover and cook the meat over moderately low heat until an instant-read thermometer inserted into the thickest part of the meat registers 145° for medium rare, about 12 minutes. Transfer the meat to a cutting board and cover loosely with foil; let stand for 5 minutes.

4. Transfer the onion and fennel mixture to a large platter and keep warm. Thinly slice the London broil and arrange it over the vegetables. Pour the accumulated pan juices over the meat, garnish with the sage leaves and serve immediately. —*Melissa Clark*

WINE Rich, velvety Merlot.

Red Wine Braised Short Ribs

4 SERVINGS, PLUS LEFTOVERS ●

These braised ribs are even better the next day—on their own or in Short Rib Sandwiches with Horseradish Mayonnaise (p. 250).

- ¼ cup pure olive oil
- 6 pounds meaty beef short ribs on the bone

Salt and freshly ground pepper

- 2 celery ribs, coarsely chopped
- 1 carrot, coarsely chopped
- 1 large onion, coarsely chopped
- ½ cup tomato paste
- 5 thyme sprigs
- 3 anchovy fillets, chopped
- 1 bay leaf
- 1 head garlic, halved crosswise
- 1 quart chicken stock or canned low-sodium broth
- 2 cups dry red wine
- ⅓ cup white vinegar

1. Preheat the oven to 325°. Heat 2 tablespoons of the oil in an enameled cast-iron casserole. Season the short ribs with salt and pepper. Add half of the ribs to the casserole and cook over moderately high heat until browned, about 6 minutes. Transfer to a plate. Repeat with the remaining oil and ribs.

2. Add the celery, carrot and onion to the casserole and cook over moderate heat until softened, about 7 minutes. Add the tomato paste and cook, stirring, until glossy, about 2 minutes. Add the thyme sprigs, anchovies, bay leaf and garlic and cook, stirring, for 2 minutes. Add the stock, wine and vinegar and bring to a boil. Return the short ribs to the casserole, then cover them and braise in the oven until the meat is very tender, about 3 hours.

3. Transfer the ribs to a platter. Strain the braising liquid, pressing hard on the solids; skim the fat. Season with salt and pepper. Serve the ribs with the sauce. —*Tom Valenti*

MAKE AHEAD The short ribs can be refrigerated in their sauce for 3 days.

WINE Rich, smoky-plummy Shiraz.

Braised Short Ribs with Redeye Gravy

6 SERVINGS ●

- 3 cups basil leaves and small sprigs
- 15 garlic cloves, halved
- ½ cup extra-virgin olive oil
- 8 pounds meaty beef short ribs, cut crosswise across the bone
- 1 tablespoon cumin seeds
- ¼ cup pure olive oil
- 2 tablespoons Jan's Spice Mix (p. 328)
- 4 large onions, coarsely chopped
- 4 jalapeños, seeded and thinly sliced
- 1 pound plum tomatoes, coarsely chopped
- 2 cups dry red wine
- 1 quart strong brewed coffee
- 3 cups chicken stock or canned low-sodium broth
- 3 bay leaves
- ¼ cup red wine vinegar
- 3 tablespoons tomato paste
- Salt and freshly ground pepper

1. In a food processor, puree the basil leaves and sprigs and the garlic. With the machine on, gradually add the extra-virgin olive oil until blended. Arrange the short ribs in a large roasting pan and pour the basil marinade over them. Turn the ribs to coat, then cover and refrigerate overnight. Bring to room temperature before cooking.

2. In a small skillet, toast the cumin seeds over moderate heat, stirring occasionally, until fragrant, about 1 minute. Transfer to a spice grinder and let cool completely, then grind the seeds to a powder.

3. Scrape most of the marinade off the ribs and reserve. In a large enameled cast-iron casserole, heat 2 tablespoons of the pure olive oil. Season the ribs with the Jan's Spice Mix. Add half of the ribs to the casserole and cook over moderate heat until browned, turning once, about 4 minutes per side. Transfer to a platter. Repeat with the remaining pure olive oil and ribs.

4. Add the onions to the casserole; cook over low heat until softened, about 15 minutes. Increase the heat to moderate and cook, stirring occasionally, until browned, about 10 minutes longer. Add the jalapeños, cumin and the reserved marinade; cook, stirring occasionally, until softened, about 5 minutes. Add the tomatoes and cook over moderately high heat, stirring, until almost dry, 5 minutes. Add the red wine and simmer for 3 minutes.

5. Add the coffee, stock and bay leaves and return the ribs and any accumulated juices to the casserole. Bring to a boil, cover and simmer over low heat until very tender, skimming the fat from the surface occasionally, about 2 hours.

6. Transfer the ribs to a platter and discard the bay leaves. Discard the bones and trim the ribs of excess fat, keeping the meat intact. Boil the gravy over high heat, stirring, until reduced to 6 cups, 12 minutes. Whisk in the vinegar and tomato paste; season with salt and pepper. Add the meat to the gravy, cover and simmer for 5 minutes before serving. —*Jan Birnbaum*

MAKE AHEAD The short rib recipe can be prepared through Step 5 and refrigerated for up to 3 days. Reheat before proceeding.

WINE Rich, smoky-plummy Shiraz.

Boeuf Bourguignon

4 SERVINGS ●

In this homey version of the classic long-simmered stew, the beef needs to marinate overnight in the refrigerator, so plan accordingly.

- 2 pounds trimmed beef chuck, cut into 1½-inch pieces
- 1 bottle (750 ml) of Pinot Noir
- 2 large onions, thinly sliced
- 2 carrots, finely chopped
- 4 thyme sprigs
- 2 bay leaves
- 1½ teaspoons herbes de Provence (see Note)
- 2 tablespoons vegetable oil
- 2 strips bacon, cut into ¼-inch pieces
- 2 tablespoons all-purpose flour
- Salt and freshly ground pepper
- 2 tablespoons unsalted butter
- ½ pound white mushrooms, quartered

1. In a large bowl, cover the beef with the wine. Add the onions, carrots, thyme, bay leaves and herbes de Provence, cover and refrigerate overnight.

2. The next day, drain the meat, vegetables and herbs, reserving the marinade. Pat the meat dry with paper towels. In a medium, enameled cast-iron casserole, heat the oil. Add the bacon and cook over low heat until the bacon is browned and has rendered some fat, about 5 minutes; transfer to a plate.

3. Add the meat to the casserole in 3 batches and brown it well over moderate heat, about 5 minutes per batch. Transfer the meat to a platter.

4. Add the onions and carrots to the casserole and cook, stirring, until browned, about 8 minutes. Stir in the flour, then gradually stir in the reserved marinade. Add the thyme and bay leaves and a pinch of salt and pepper. Return the bacon and meat to the casserole along with any accumulated juices and bring to a boil. Reduce the heat to low and simmer, stirring, until the meat is very tender, about 2½ hours.

5. Heat the butter in a skillet. Add the mushrooms and season with salt and pepper. Cover and cook over moderately low heat until the liquid from the mushrooms has evaporated and they have started to brown, about 5 minutes. Uncover and cook over moderate heat until nicely browned, about 5 minutes. Stir the mushrooms into the stew, season with salt and pepper and serve. —*Chantal Leroux*

NOTE Herbes de Provence is a blend of dried thyme, rosemary, summer savory and bay leaves used in stews and on grilled foods. If you can't find it at the store, substitute dried thyme.

SMOKY BEEF AND LEEK STEW

STEAK AND MOZZARELLA PIRATAS

MAKE AHEAD The stew can be refrigerated for up to 3 days. Reheat gently.
SERVE WITH Noodles or boiled potatoes.
WINE Complex, silky red Burgundy.

Smoky Beef and Leek Stew

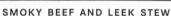

4 SERVINGS ●

- 1 small red bell pepper, chopped
- ½ lemon
- 2 medium artichokes
- 1½ pounds trimmed beef chuck, cut into 1½-inch pieces
- Salt and freshly ground pepper
- All-purpose flour, for dredging
- ¼ cup pure olive oil
- 6 medium leeks, white and tender green parts, halved lengthwise and thinly sliced crosswise
- 2 bay leaves
- 4 garlic cloves, thinly sliced
- 1 tablespoon sweet pimentón (see Note)
- 1 cup finely chopped flat-leaf parsley
- 20 peppercorns, coarsely crushed
- 1 cup dry red wine, preferably Rioja
- 1 quart beef stock or canned low-sodium broth

1. In a mini food processor, puree the red pepper; scrape into a small bowl.
2. Squeeze most of the lemon half into a small bowl of cold water. Working with 1 artichoke at a time, snap off the tough outer leaves. Using a sharp knife, cut off the top half of the artichoke and peel the base and stem. Cut off the stem and drop it into the bowl. Using a melon baller or a spoon, scoop out the furry choke. Rub the artichoke bottom all over with the lemon half, then quarter the artichoke and drop it into the bowl. Repeat the process with the remaining artichoke.

3. Season the beef with salt and pepper and lightly dredge the pieces in flour. In a medium enameled cast-iron casserole, heat 2 tablespoons of the olive oil. Add half of the meat and brown over moderately high heat, about 3 minutes per side. Transfer to a plate and brown the remaining meat in the same oil.
4. Drain the artichokes and pat dry. Pour off the fat from the casserole and add the remaining 2 tablespoons of olive oil. Add the leeks and bay leaves and cook over low heat, stirring occasionally, until the leeks are softened, about 8 minutes. Add the garlic and pimentón and cook, stirring, until fragrant, about 2 minutes. Add the parsley, peppercorns and wine and simmer over moderately high heat for 5 minutes. Add the seared meat, beef stock, pepper puree and the artichokes and bring to a simmer; add a pinch of salt.

Cook the stew over low heat, stirring occasionally, until the meat is tender, about 1½ hours. Season with salt and pepper and serve.

—*Joseph Jiménez de Jiménez*

NOTE Pimentón is available at specialty markets in sweet and hot varieties.

MAKE AHEAD The beef stew can be refrigerated for up to 3 days. Rewarm over moderate heat before serving.

SERVE WITH Quartered new potatoes fried in olive oil and garlic.

WINE Soft, earthy Rioja.

Steak and Mozzarella Piratas

4 SERVINGS ●

Piratas, or pirates, are a type of flour-tortilla taco from Monterrey, Mexico, that is brushed with melted butter or oil, folded over any one of a number of fillings and cooked on a hot griddle until crisp and golden.

1½ tablespoons ancho chile powder
Heaping ¼ teaspoon freshly
　　ground pepper
⅛ teaspoon allspice
⅛ teaspoon cloves
Salt
¾ pound top sirloin, cut into
　　⅓-inch cubes
1 tablespoon plus 1 teaspoon
　　fresh lime juice
Vegetable oil
½ cup coarsely chopped
　　white onion
1 poblano chile, seeded and
　　finely chopped
¼ cup chopped cilantro
2 medium Hass avocados,
　　thinly sliced
Four 8- or 9-inch flour tortillas
½ pound mozzarella cheese,
　　shredded (2 cups)
Salsa, for serving

1. In a medium bowl, combine the ancho chile powder with the ground pepper, allspice, cloves and a heaping ¼ teaspoon of salt. Add the top sirloin and 2 teaspoons of the lime juice and toss to coat the meat.

2. Preheat the oven to 300°. In a large skillet, heat 1½ tablespoons of oil. Add the onion and poblano and cook over moderately high heat until the onion begins to brown. Add the meat and stir until just barely cooked through, about 2½ minutes. Add the cilantro and season with salt.

3. In a bowl, toss the avocados with the remaining 2 teaspoons of lime juice.

4. Heat a large skillet or griddle. Lightly brush a tortilla on both sides with oil and lay it in the skillet. Cook over moderate heat for 45 seconds, then flip the tortilla and sprinkle ¼ cup of the mozzarella over half of it. Top the cheese with a quarter of the sirloin cubes and avocado slices. Sprinkle with another ¼ cup of cheese. Fold the tortilla over the filling and press down with a spatula to form a taco. Cook for 30 seconds, then turn and cook until the underside is golden, 1 minute longer. Keep the pirata warm in the oven while you repeat with the remaining tortillas and fillings. Serve warm, with salsa. —*Jim Peyton*

Skirt Steak Fajitas

6 SERVINGS ●

¼ cup dry red wine
2 tablespoons extra-virgin olive oil
2 tablespoons finely chopped garlic
2 pounds skirt steak, cut
　　into 4-inch pieces
6 large plum tomatoes, seeded
　　and coarsely chopped
3 jalapeños, seeded and
　　finely chopped
½ large white onion,
　　finely chopped
3 tablespoons finely
　　chopped cilantro
3 tablespoons fresh
　　lime juice
Salt and freshly ground pepper
1 Hass avocado, thinly sliced
6 ounces Monterey Jack cheese,
　　shredded (1 cup)
1 cup sour cream
Twelve 9-inch flour tortillas, warmed

1. In a bowl, mix the wine and olive oil with 1 tablespoon and 2 teaspoons of the garlic. Add the skirt steak and toss to coat, then let stand for 15 minutes.

2. Meanwhile, in another bowl, toss the tomatoes with the jalapeños, onion, cilantro, lime juice and the remaining 1 teaspoon of garlic. Season the salsa with salt and pepper.

3. Light a grill or heat a grill pan. Remove the steak from the marinade; season with salt and pepper. Grill over moderately high heat, turning once, until medium rare, about 4 minutes. Transfer to a cutting board; let stand for 3 minutes.

4. Thinly slice the steak across the grain and arrange on a platter. Serve with the salsa, avocado slices, shredded cheese, sour cream and warm tortillas.

—*Ann Chantal Altman*

Italian Baked Stuffed Tomatoes

6 SERVINGS ● ● ●

18 ripe plum tomatoes (about
　　3 pounds)
⅓ cup medium-grain white rice,
　　such as arborio
½ pound lean ground beef
5 large garlic cloves, very
　　finely chopped
½ cup finely chopped
　　flat-leaf parsley
¼ cup thinly sliced basil
Kosher salt and freshly ground pepper
5 tablespoons extra-virgin olive oil

1. Preheat the oven to 325°. Cut across the tomatoes horizontally, leaving the top half slighter smaller than the bottom to create a lid. Set a strainer over a medium bowl. Using your fingers, scoop the tomato seeds into the strainer; press on the seeds to extract the juice. Using a small spoon or melon baller, scoop out the center of the tomatoes and coarsely chop them. Add the chopped centers to the juice in the bowl. Add the rice, beef, garlic, parsley, basil, 2 teaspoons of kosher salt, ¼ teaspoon of pepper and 2½ tablespoons of the olive oil and knead to combine.

2. Set the tomatoes in a baking dish and season with salt. Spoon the filling into the tomatoes, cover with the lids and drizzle with the remaining 2½ tablespoons of oil. Bake for about 1½ hours, basting, until the tomatoes are soft and the rice is cooked. Let stand for 15 minutes before serving warm or at room temperature. —*Benedetta Vitali*

MAKE AHEAD The tomatoes can be kept at room temperature for 2 hours.

WINE Complex, savory Chianti Classico.

Lemongrass Beef Rolls with Rice Noodles

6 SERVINGS

As with much Southeast Asian cooking, this dish, *bo bun* in Vietnamese, mixes a salad, noodles and meat.

- 1½ pounds sirloin steak (1 inch thick), sliced across the grain ⅛ inch thick
- 2 stalks fresh lemongrass, tender white inner bulbs only, chopped
- 2 large shallots, chopped
- 5 garlic cloves, minced
- 6 tablespoons sugar
- 2 teaspoons ground coriander
- ½ teaspoon freshly ground pepper
- ½ cup Asian fish sauce

Vegetable oil

- 1 medium carrot, sliced lengthwise with a vegetable peeler and cut into slivers
- ⅓ cup fresh lemon juice
- 3 tablespoons rice vinegar
- ½ cup water
- 5 jalapeños, thinly sliced
- ¼ pound rice vermicelli
- 3 tablespoons chopped unsalted roasted peanuts
- 1 large handful each of basil, mint and cilantro
- 1½ cups mung bean sprouts
- 1 large head Boston lettuce, separated into leaves

I. Soak 2 dozen 8-inch bamboo skewers in warm water for 30 minutes. Thread the steak onto the skewers and place on a large baking sheet.

2. In a food processor, combine the lemongrass, shallots, two-thirds of the garlic, 3 tablespoons of the sugar and the coriander and pepper. Pulse the mixture until a smooth paste forms. With the machine on, add 3 tablespoons of the fish sauce and 2 tablespoons of oil. Brush the beef with the marinade and let stand for 30 minutes.

3. Meanwhile, on a cutting board, use the side of a large knife to mash the remaining garlic and 3 tablespoons of sugar to a paste. In a small bowl, toss the garlic paste with the carrot slivers and let stand for 15 minutes. Stir in the remaining 5 tablespoons of fish sauce, the lemon juice, rice vinegar, water and one-third of the jalapeños.

4. In a pot of boiling salted water, cook the rice noodles until just wilted, about 1 minute. Drain and rinse under cold water. Drain well; transfer to a platter.

5. Light a grill. Lightly oil the grate. Grill the beef skewers over a medium-hot fire for 1 to 2 minutes per side for medium-rare meat. Arrange the skewers over the noodles and sprinkle with the peanuts. Serve with the dipping sauce, fresh herbs, bean sprouts, lettuce and the remaining two-thirds of the jalapeños so your guests can make their own bundles. —*Steven Raichlen*

WINE Bright, fruity rosé.

Shaking Beef with Pea Shoot Salad

4 SERVINGS ●

- 1 pound beef sirloin, cut into ¾-inch dice
- 2½ tablespoons vegetable oil
- 2 tablespoons minced garlic
- 2½ teaspoons sugar
- 1 tablespoon Asian fish sauce

Freshly ground pepper

- ½ medium onion, very thinly sliced
- 2 teaspoons white wine vinegar
- 2 teaspoons soy sauce
- 2 teaspoons extra-virgin olive oil

Salt

- 6 ounces baby pea shoots

I. In a medium bowl, toss the beef with ½ tablespoon of vegetable oil, 1 tablespoon of garlic, 2 teaspoons of sugar and the fish sauce; season with pepper. Let stand.

2. In a small bowl, toss the onion with the vinegar. In another small bowl, mix the soy sauce with the olive oil and remaining ½ teaspoon of sugar. Season with salt and pepper.

3. In a wok, heat the remaining 2 tablespoons of vegetable oil over high heat until smoking. Add the remaining 1 tablespoon of garlic and ¼ teaspoon of salt; cook until golden, about 30 seconds. Add half of the marinated beef and cook for 3 minutes without stirring; turn and cook 1 minute longer. Transfer to a plate and cook the second batch of beef. Return all the meat to the wok and stir-fry for 30 seconds.

4. On a large platter, toss the pea shoots with the onion and the soy dressing. Spoon the beef on top and serve. —*Joyce Jue*

WINE Light, fruity Pinot Noir.

Spicy Thai Beef Salad

4 SERVINGS ● ●

- 6 tablespoons fresh lime juice
- 5 tablespoons Asian fish sauce
- 2 Thai chiles, minced
- 1 teaspoon sugar
- ½ pound thinly sliced rare roast beef
- 5 small scallions, cut into 1-inch lengths
- 3 medium shallots, thinly sliced
- 1 medium tomato, halved and sliced
- 1 cup thinly sliced peeled cucumber
- ½ cup chopped celery leaves

In a large bowl, mix the lime juice with the fish sauce, chiles and sugar; stir until the sugar is dissolved. Add the beef, scallions, shallots, tomato, cucumber and celery leaves. Toss the salad gently and serve.

—*Sompon and Elizabeth Nabnian*

SPICY THAI BEEF SALAD

HERB-CRUSTED LEG OF LAMB, WITH CUMIN POTATO CAKES (P. 226)

Grilled Flank Steak Salad

4 SERVINGS ●

¼ cup plus 1 tablespoon
extra-virgin olive oil

2 tablespoons fresh lime juice

1 tablespoon molasses

1 tablespoon honey

1 tablespoon coarsely cracked
black peppercorns

½ teaspoon cayenne pepper

2 garlic cloves, minced

1 teaspoon Worcestershire sauce

1 teaspoon Dijon mustard

Salt and freshly ground pepper

2 pounds flank steak

½ cup coarse, dry bread crumbs

¼ cup freshly grated Parmigiano-
Reggiano cheese

2 medium hearts of romaine,
quartered lengthwise

1 handful of red leaf lettuce

1. In a small bowl, mix 1 tablespoon of the olive oil with 1 tablespoon of the lime juice. Stir in the molasses, honey, cracked peppercorns and cayenne.

2. In another small bowl, mix the remaining 1 tablespoon of lime juice with the garlic, Worcestershire sauce and mustard. Gradually whisk in the remaining ¼ cup of olive oil, whisking until incorporated. Season the vinaigrette with salt and pepper.

3. Light a grill or heat a grill pan. Season the flank steak with salt and pepper and grill over high heat for 13 minutes, turning once. Brush the molasses mixture all over the steak and grill for 2 minutes longer for medium-rare meat. Transfer the steak to a cutting board and let stand.

4. In a small bowl, toss the bread crumbs with the Parmigiano and season with salt and pepper. Thinly slice the flank steak across the grain. Arrange the romaine and red leaf lettuce on a platter and drizzle with the vinaigrette. Scatter the bread crumbs over the salad, top with the steak and serve. —*Scott Ehrlich*

WINE Rich, velvety Merlot.

Herb-Crusted Leg of Lamb

8 SERVINGS

¼ cup flat-leaf parsley,
finely chopped

3 garlic cloves, minced

2 teaspoons rosemary,
finely chopped

1 teaspoon thyme, finely chopped

¾ teaspoon dried lavender
(optional)

One 4-pound boneless leg of lamb,
trimmed of all fat

Salt and freshly ground pepper

4 cups chicken stock or canned
low-sodium broth

1 teaspoon fennel seeds,
lightly crushed

1. In a small bowl, combine the parsley with the garlic, rosemary, thyme and lavender. Spread the leg of lamb open on a work surface, boned side up, and season generously with salt and pepper. Spread half of the herb mixture over the lamb and roll it into a roast. Tie the lamb with kitchen string at 1-inch intervals. Spread the remaining herb mixture all over the outside of the roast and season with salt and pepper. Let the leg of lamb stand at room temperature for 1 hour.

2. Meanwhile, in a large skillet, boil the stock over moderately high heat until reduced to 1 cup, about 30 minutes.

3. Preheat the oven to 450°. Set the lamb in a roasting pan and roast in the oven for 10 minutes. Reduce the oven temperature to 350°. Cook the lamb for 45 minutes longer, or until an instant-read thermometer inserted in the thickest part registers 125° for medium rare or 140° for medium.

4. Transfer the lamb to a carving board, cover loosely with foil and let stand for 10 minutes. Add the fennel seeds to the roasting pan and cook over moderate heat until fragrant, about 1 minute. Increase the heat to high, add the reduced stock and cook, scraping up any browned bits on the bottom of the pan; season with salt and pepper.

5. Discard the string. Carve the lamb into thick slices and arrange on a platter. Pour any carving juices into the sauce, spoon it over the lamb and serve.
—*Gary Danko*

MAKE AHEAD The recipe can be prepared through Step 1 and refrigerated overnight. Bring the lamb to room temperature before roasting.

WINE Rich, velvety Merlot.

Lemon-and-Mint Roast Leg of Lamb with Flageolets

8 TO 10 SERVINGS

6 tablespoons extra-virgin olive oil

¼ pound double-smoked slab
bacon, sliced ¼ inch thick and
cut crosswise into matchsticks

1 medium onion, finely chopped

10 garlic cloves—4 whole, 4 thinly
sliced and 2 minced

1 pound flageolet beans, picked
over and rinsed

1 bunch flat-leaf parsley stems,
tied with kitchen string

1 bay leaf

4 thyme sprigs

4 cups chicken stock or canned
low-sodium broth

4 cups water, plus more for
roasting pan

Kosher salt and freshly ground
pepper

One 6½-pound leg of lamb, haitch
bone and thigh bone removed,
tied with kitchen string at
1½-inch intervals

¼ cup fresh lemon juice

1½ loosely packed cups mint leaves,
torn into pieces

½ pound pitted Calamata olives,
coarsely chopped

Oven-Dried Tomatoes (p. 329)

1. Heat 1 tablespoon of the oil in a large enameled cast-iron casserole. Add the bacon and cook over moderately high heat, stirring occasionally, until golden and crisp, about 5 minutes. Add the chopped onion and the 4 whole garlic cloves and cook until softened and just golden, about 5 minutes longer. Add the flageolets, parsley stems, bay leaf and thyme sprigs to the casserole and toss to coat. Add the chicken stock, 3 cups of the water and 3 tablespoons of the olive oil.

2. Preheat the oven to 350°. Top the flageolet beans with crumpled, moistened parchment paper, then cover the casserole with a lid and bake for about 2½ hours, stirring gently 2 or 3 times; the beans are done when they are tender but not mushy. Season the beans with salt and pepper. Drain the beans, reserving their cooking liquid, and discard the parsley bundle, thyme sprigs, garlic cloves and bay leaf.

3. Using a sharp paring knife, make 1-inch incisions about 1 inch apart all over the lamb. Insert the garlic slices into the slits. Increase the oven temperature to 375°.

4. Set the lamb in a large roasting pan and drizzle with the lemon juice. Rub the lamb with the remaining 2 tablespoons of olive oil, the minced garlic and half of the mint. Season the lamb with salt and pepper. Roast for about 1 hour and 45 minutes, or until an instant-read thermometer inserted in the thickest part of the meat registers 130° for medium rare. Add water to the roasting pan occasionally if necessary to prevent the pan juices from burning. Transfer the lamb to a cutting board and cover loosely with aluminum foil. Leave the oven on.

5. Set the roasting pan over 2 burners, add the remaining 1 cup of water and bring to a boil over high heat, scraping up any browned bits from the bottom of the pan. Stir in the olives and the remaining half of the mint and pour the pan sauce into a bowl.

6. Rewarm the flageolet beans over moderate heat; add some of the reserved bean cooking liquid if they seem dry. Season the beans with salt and pepper.

7. Spread the Oven-Dried Tomatoes out on a small baking sheet and heat in the oven until warmed through. Spoon the beans onto a large platter and arrange the dried tomatoes around them. Thickly slice the roast leg of lamb and arrange the slices over the beans. Ladle the olive pan sauce over the lamb slices and beans and serve at once.

—*Carrie Nahabedian*

MAKE AHEAD The lamb and flageolet beans can be prepared through Step 3; refrigerate separately overnight. Let both the lamb and the beans return to room temperature before proceeding with the dish.

WINE Intense, berry-flavored Zinfandel.

grilling international style guide

COUNTRY	TYPICAL DISH	TECHNIQUE	KEY INGREDIENTS
India	Tandoori lamb, chicken, vegetables or fish; ground-lamb (seekh) kebabs.	Grilling over high heat or in a tandoor; using skewers; marinating.	Butter, cardamom, cumin, ginger, lemon, mace, turmeric, yogurt.
Japan	Yakitori; tofu, fish, chicken or beef teriyaki; grilled clams and scallops.	Grilling on hibachis, or without a grate; basting; glazing.	Garlic, ginger, mirin, miso, sake, soy sauce, sesame oil and seeds.
Thailand	Grilled whole fish, squid-on-a-stick, peanut-sauce satays, grilled fruit.	Grilling fish whole; using skewers; using creamy, peanut-based sauces.	Basil, chiles, cilantro, fish sauce, lime, mint, peanuts, tamarind.
Korea	Bulgogi (marinated rib eye), grilled sweet potatoes, sesame mushrooms.	Wrapping grilled meat in lettuce; using spicy sauces or pastes.	Chiles, garlic, scallions, sesame oil, soy sauce, sugar.
Malaysia	Chicken, beef, rabbit or shrimp satays; sweet-and-sour seafood.	Grilling in or on banana leaves; using skewers; grilling fish whole.	Chiles, coconut milk, curry, fried shallots, ginger, peanuts.
Vietnam	Basil-wrapped or lemongrass beef rolls; shrimp mousse on sugarcane.	Grilling on sugarcane; wrapping grilled foods in lettuce and herbs.	Basil, chiles, cilantro, fish sauce, garlic, lemongrass, lime, mint.

Lamb Chops with Vegetable Ragout

4 SERVINGS

- 2 tablespoons coarsely chopped basil leaves
- 2 tablespoons chopped flat-leaf parsley
- 2 teaspoons chopped tarragon
- 5 tablespoons extra-virgin olive oil
- 3 garlic cloves, minced
- 4 double lamb loin chops (8 to 10 ounces each)

Salt and freshly ground pepper

- 2 cups water
- 2 medium carrots, cut into 2-inch matchsticks
- 1 large turnip, peeled and cut into 2-inch matchsticks
- ½ pound shiitake mushrooms, stems discarded, caps quartered
- ¼ pound small chanterelles, trimmed
- 3 tablespoons very finely chopped shallots
- ½ cup dry French vermouth
- 1 cup chicken stock or canned low-sodium broth
- 8 cherry tomatoes, halved

Freshly grated Parmesan cheese, for serving

I. In a large shallow dish, mix together 1 tablespoon each of the basil and parsley, 1 teaspoon of the tarragon, 1 tablespoon of the olive oil and 1 minced garlic clove. Add the lamb chops and rub them all over with the herb mixture. Season the lamb chops generously with salt and pepper, cover with plastic and let them stand at room temperature for at least 30 minutes and for up to 2 hours.

2. Meanwhile, preheat the oven to 425°. In a large skillet, bring the water to a boil. Add the carrots and a pinch of salt and cover. Simmer over low heat for 4 minutes. Add the turnip, cover and cook until both vegetables are tender, about 8 minutes. Drain them and transfer to a plate.

3. Return the skillet to low heat. When hot, add 2 tablespoons of the olive oil and the shiitake and season generously with salt and pepper. Cover and cook the shiitake, stirring occasionally, until lightly browned, about 4 minutes. Add the chanterelles, cover and cook, stirring, until tender, about 3 minutes. Add the shallots and the remaining 2 garlic cloves and cook, stirring occasionally, until fragrant, about 3 minutes longer. Add the cooked carrots and turnip, cover and remove the vegetables from the heat.

4. In a large ovenproof skillet, heat the remaining 2 tablespoons of olive oil until shimmering. Add the marinated lamb chops and cook them over moderately high heat until browned on the bottom, about 3 minutes. Turn the lamb chops over, transfer the skillet to the oven and roast the chops for about 8 minutes for medium rare. Transfer the lamb chops to a plate, cover with foil and keep warm.

5. Discard the fat from the skillet and set the pan over moderately high heat. Add the vermouth and cook until almost evaporated, about 3 minutes. Add the chicken stock and boil until reduced to ¾ cup, about 3 minutes. Add any accumulated lamb juices and pour the liquid over the reserved vegetables. Stir in the cherry tomatoes and simmer until heated through. Stir in the remaining 1 tablespoon each of chopped basil and parsley and 1 teaspoon of chopped tarragon. Season the vegetable ragout with salt and pepper.

6. Spoon the vegetable ragout into shallow bowls and sprinkle with grated Parmesan cheese. Top each plate with a lamb chop and serve at once.

—*Marcia Kiesel*

MAKE AHEAD The lamb can marinate overnight in the refrigerator. Bring to room temperature before proceeding. The vegetable ragout can be prepared through Step 3; refrigerate overnight.

WINE Rich, smoky-plummy Shiraz.

Lamb Chops with Hot Fennel-Coriander Vinaigrette

4 SERVINGS ●

- 1 tablespoon coarsely ground coriander
- 1½ teaspoons ground fennel seeds
- ¼ cup plus 1 tablespoon extra-virgin olive oil
- 2 tablespoons cider vinegar
- 1 tablespoon honey

Salt and freshly ground pepper

- 1 trimmed 8-bone rack of lamb, cut into 4 double chops
- 1 tablespoon unsalted butter
- 1 medium fennel bulb, cored and very thinly sliced
- 2 garlic cloves, slivered
- 1 head escarole (about 1 pound), leaves torn
- ¼ cup coarsely chopped cilantro

I. Light a grill or heat a grill pan over moderately high heat. In a medium saucepan, toast the ground coriander and fennel seeds over moderate heat until fragrant, about 1 minute. Stir in ¼ cup of the olive oil and cook until the oil is warm. Stir in the cider vinegar and honey, season with salt and pepper and keep warm.

2. Season the lamb chops with salt and pepper. Grill the chops for about 8 minutes for medium-rare meat, turning once, until nicely browned. Remove the lamb from heat and keep warm.

3. In a large skillet, melt the butter in the remaining 1 tablespoon of olive oil. Add the sliced fennel and cook over moderate heat, stirring occasionally, until translucent, about 3 minutes. Add the garlic and cook until fragrant, about 2 minutes. Add the escarole leaves and cook, stirring, just until wilted, about 4 minutes. Stir in the cilantro and season with salt and pepper.

4. Spoon the vegetables onto a platter; top with the chops. Spoon the warm vinaigrette over the chops and serve.

—*Scott Ehrlich*

WINE Intense, berry-flavored Zinfandel.

beef, lamb + game

Grilled Lamb Chops with Green and Black Olive Salsa

6 SERVINGS ●

½ cup chopped flat-leaf parsley, plus leaves for garnish

⅓ cup cured green olives, such as Sicilian, pitted and chopped

⅓ cup cured black olives, such as Calamata, pitted and chopped

⅓ cup green olives stuffed with pimientos, chopped

3 tablespoons fresh lemon juice

2 anchovy fillets, rinsed and minced

1 garlic clove, minced

6 tablespoons extra-virgin olive oil

Salt and freshly ground pepper

Twelve 4-ounce lamb rib chops

Lemon wedges, for serving

1. In a small bowl, combine the parsley, olives, lemon juice, anchovies, garlic and 5 tablespoons of the olive oil; season with salt and pepper.

2. Light a grill or preheat a grill pan. Brush the lamb chops with the remaining 1 tablespoon of olive oil and season generously with salt and pepper. Grill the chops over a medium-hot fire, turning once, until browned outside and medium rare within, 5 to 6 minutes per side. Set 2 lamb chops on each plate and spoon the olive salsa on top. Garnish with lemon wedges and parsley leaves and serve. —*Joanne Weir*
WINE Tannic, complex Cabernet.

Grilled Lamb Steaks with Chile-Mint Salsa

4 SERVINGS

3 tablespoons fresh lime juice, plus 1 teaspoon finely grated lime zest

1 tablespoon sugar

2 tablespoons Asian fish sauce

2 jalapeños, seeded and minced

2 tablespoons canola oil, plus more for the grill

½ cup packed mint leaves, plus 2 tablespoons finely chopped mint

1 scallion, finely chopped

2 large garlic cloves, minced

1 teaspoon mild honey

Four 8-ounce lamb leg steaks, cut ½ to ¾ inch thick

Salt and freshly ground pepper

1. In a small bowl, mix the lime juice and lime zest with the sugar, 1 table-spoon of the fish sauce and one-half of the minced jalapeños. Stir until the sugar is dissolved, then stir the canola oil into the chile salsa.

2. In a small saucepan of boiling water, blanch the mint leaves just until wilted. Drain, refresh under cold water and drain again. Squeeze dry, mince and stir into the salsa with the scallion.

3. In another small bowl, mix the remaining 1 tablespoon of fish sauce, 2 tablespoons of chopped mint and half of the jalapeños with the garlic and honey. Spread over the lamb steaks and refrigerate for 1 hour.

4. Light a grill; lightly oil the grate. Season the lamb with salt and pepper. Grill the steaks over a medium-hot fire, turning once, until browned, about 8 minutes for medium. Serve with the salsa.
—*Annabel Langbein*
WINE Tannic, complex Cabernet.

Coriander Lamb with Yogurt and Endives

4 SERVINGS ●

3 tablespoons plain full-fat yogurt

2 garlic cloves, minced

1 tablespoon ground coriander

1½ teaspoons finely grated fresh ginger

1 teaspoon ground cumin

½ teaspoon cayenne pepper

¼ teaspoon ground cinnamon

¼ teaspoon ground cloves

Kosher salt

1½ pounds boneless, trimmed leg of lamb, cut into 1½-inch cubes

3 tablespoons extra-virgin olive oil

3 Belgian endives, quartered lengthwise through the cores

Cucumber Raita, for serving (p. 325)

1. In a large bowl, combine the yogurt, garlic, coriander, ginger, cumin, cayenne, cinnamon, cloves and 1 teaspoon of salt. Add the lamb and toss to coat thoroughly. Cover and let stand at room temperature for 30 minutes.

2. Preheat the broiler. In a large skillet, heat 1 tablespoon of the olive oil. Add the endive quarters and cook over moderately high heat, tossing a few times, until wilted and browned in spots, about 5 minutes. Season with salt and tent with foil to keep warm.

3. Spread the lamb cubes on a broiler pan and brush with 1 tablespoon of the olive oil. Broil, rotating the pan, until the lamb is browned, about 4 minutes. Turn the cubes over, brush with the remaining 1 tablespoon of oil and broil until browned but still pink in the center, about 3 minutes. Transfer the lamb and endives to plates and serve with the Cucumber Raita. —*Madhur Jaffrey*
WINE Complex, savory Chianti Classico.

Lamb Satay with Tamarind Barbecue Sauce

6 SERVINGS

Tamarind concentrate and tamarind puree are available at Latin markets.

1½ pounds boneless leg of lamb, cut into 1-inch cubes

1½ tablespoons ground coriander

1½ teaspoons salt

2¼ teaspoons freshly ground pepper

Vegetable oil

1 cup tamarind concentrate or 1¼ cups tamarind puree

⅓ cup light brown sugar

3 tablespoons sweet soy sauce (kecap manis) or 1½ tablespoons soy sauce mixed with 1½ tablespoons molasses

2 small garlic cloves, minced

6 large shallots, thinly sliced

1. Soak six 10-inch bamboo skewers in warm water for 30 minutes. Meanwhile, in a medium shallow glass baking dish, sprinkle the lamb cubes with 1 table-spoon of the coriander, the salt and

STIR-FRIED PEKING LAMB WITH PEPPERS AND GREEN BEANS

GRILLED LAMB CHOPS WITH PROVENÇAL DRESSING

1½ teaspoons of the pepper. Add 1½ tablespoons of vegetable oil and toss to coat. Let marinate for 30 minutes.

2. In a medium saucepan, combine the tamarind, sugar, sweet soy sauce, garlic and the remaining ½ tablespoon of coriander and ¾ teaspoon of pepper. Bring to a boil, then simmer over moderate heat for 5 minutes. Let cool.

3. In a deep skillet, heat 1 cup of oil until shimmering. Add the shallots and fry over moderate heat, stirring, until golden and crisp, 4 minutes. With a slotted spoon, transfer to paper towels.

4. Light a grill. Lightly oil the grate. Thread the lamb onto the skewers. Set aside half of the barbecue sauce for serving. Grill the lamb over a medium-hot fire for 8 minutes, turning once and basting often with the tamarind sauce for medium-rare meat. Transfer the lamb skewers to plates, sprinkle with the shallots and serve at once with the remaining sauce. —*Steven Raichlen*
WINE Soft, earthy Rioja.

Lamb Marinated in Jasmine Tea with Sweet Pea Sauce
4 SERVINGS
- ½ cup plus 2 tablespoons (about ½ ounce) jasmine tea leaves
- ¼ cup hot water
- Four 6- to 7-ounce pieces of lamb tenderloin
- ¼ cup blanched whole almonds
- ¾ cup crustless fresh brioche crumbs
- 2 tablespoons unsalted butter, softened
- 1 teaspoon finely grated lemon zest (preferably from a Meyer lemon)
- Pinch of cayenne pepper
- Salt and freshly ground pepper
- 2 tablespoons extra-virgin olive oil
- 2 cups shelled fresh or frozen petite peas (10 ounces)
- ¾ cup chicken stock or canned low-sodium broth

1. In a small heatproof bowl, cover ½ cup of the jasmine tea leaves with the hot water and let stand for 5 minutes, or until the tea has absorbed the water. Spread the tea between two layers of dampened cheesecloth. Wrap the lamb loins in the cheesecloth and refrigerate for 2 to 4 hours.

2. In a mini processor, grind the remaining 2 tablespoons of tea to a powder and transfer to a medium bowl. Grind the blanched almonds until fine and add to the bowl. Add the brioche crumbs, butter, lemon zest and cayenne, season with salt and pepper and stir to form a dough-like mass. Working on a sheet of plastic wrap, pat the mixture into a 6-inch square about ¼ inch thick. Wrap with plastic and refrigerate until firm.

3. Preheat the oven to 450°. In a saucepan, heat 1 tablespoon of oil. Add the peas and cook over moderate heat for 1 minute. Pour in the stock; bring to a boil. Cover and simmer the peas until tender, about 5 minutes. In a blender, puree the peas and stock. Strain the puree through a fine sieve into a saucepan; season with salt and pepper.

4. Remove the tea-crumb mixture from the refrigerator and cut into 4 squares. Unwrap the lamb and rub off any bits of tea. Season with salt and pepper. In a large ovenproof skillet, heat the remaining 1 tablespoon of olive oil. Add the lamb and cook over moderately high heat until browned all over, about 6 minutes. Press a tea-crumb square onto each piece of lamb and roast in the oven for 8 to 10 minutes, until the crumbs are crisp and browned and the lamb is medium rare. Transfer to a carving board and let stand for 5 minutes.

5. Reheat the pea sauce and spoon onto 4 plates. Slice the lamb, arrange on the sauce and serve. —*Laurent Gras*
MAKE AHEAD The tea-crumb mixture and the sweet pea sauce can be refrigerated overnight.
SERVE WITH Sautéed vegetables.
WINE Soft, earthy Rioja.

Stir-Fried Peking Lamb with Peppers and Green Beans
4 SERVINGS ● ○

- 1 tablespoon dry sherry or rice wine
- 5 teaspoons soy sauce
- 1½ teaspoons cornstarch
- ½ pound boneless leg of lamb, cut into thin strips
- 3 tablespoons hoisin sauce
- 1½ tablespoons rice vinegar
- 1 teaspoon chile-garlic paste
- ½ teaspoon sugar
- 2½ tablespoons vegetable oil
- 2 large garlic cloves, minced
- 6 ounces green beans, cut into 1½-inch pieces (1½ cups)
- ½ medium onion, thinly sliced
- 1 small red bell pepper, thinly sliced
- 1 medium leek, white part only, cut into 2-inch lengths and thinly sliced lengthwise

1. In a medium bowl, mix the sherry with 2 teaspoons of the soy sauce and the cornstarch. Add the lamb strips and stir to coat.

2. In a bowl, combine the hoisin sauce, vinegar, chile-garlic paste, sugar and the remaining tablespoon of soy sauce.

3. In a wok, heat 2 tablespoons of oil over high heat until smoking. Add the garlic; stir-fry until fragrant, 15 seconds. Add the lamb strips and cook, stirring, until lightly browned, 3 minutes; transfer to a plate.

4. Add the remaining ½ tablespoon of oil to the wok. Add the beans and stir-fry until crisp-tender, about 4 minutes. Add the onion and cook until softened, 2 minutes. Add the pepper and leek and cook, stirring occasionally, until the leek is lightly browned, about 3 minutes. Add the hoisin-vinegar sauce to the wok and cook just until bubbling. Return the lamb to the wok and stir-fry until heated through. Transfer to a platter and serve. —*Joyce Jue*
SERVE WITH White rice.
WINE Light, fruity Pinot Noir.

Grilled Lamb Chops with Provençal Dressing
4 SERVINGS ●

- 2 large anchovy fillets
- 1 small garlic clove, smashed
- 1 tablespoon fresh lemon juice
- ¼ cup extra-virgin olive oil
- 6 Calamata or Niçoise olives, pitted and coarsely chopped
- ½ teaspoon very finely chopped thyme
- ¼ teaspoon very finely chopped rosemary
- Salt and freshly ground pepper
- Twelve 4-ounce baby lamb rib chops

1. In a mini food processor, pulse the anchovy fillets with the smashed garlic and the lemon juice until finely minced. Add the olive oil and process the anchovy mixture until smooth. Add the chopped olives, thyme and rosemary and pulse to blend. Season the Provençal dressing lightly with salt and pepper and reserve.

2. Light a grill or preheat a cast-iron grill pan. Season the lamb chops generously with salt and pepper. Grill the lamb chops over high heat, turning them once, until browned all over, about 7 minutes for medium-rare meat. Transfer the lamb chops to a large serving platter, spoon the Provençal dressing on top and serve. —*Terrance Brennan*
WINE Round, supple, fruity Syrah.

Autumn Lamb and Vegetable Stew
4 SERVINGS ●

- 1 lemon, halved
- 4 medium artichokes
- ¼ cup extra-virgin olive oil
- 4 garlic cloves, halved
- 2 leeks, white and tender green parts only, halved lengthwise and cut crosswise into 2-inch lengths
- 2 celery ribs, cut into 2-inch lengths
- 2 small fennel bulbs, quartered
- 1 quart water

Salt

¼ pound green beans, cut into
2-inch lengths

1½ pounds boneless leg of lamb,
cut into 1½-inch pieces

Freshly ground pepper

2 teaspoons sweet pimentón

2 tablespoons all-purpose flour

½ cup dry white wine,
preferably Rioja

1. Squeeze the juice of 1 lemon half into a bowl of cold water and drop the half into the bowl. Working with 1 artichoke at a time, snap off the tough outer leaves. Using a sharp knife, cut off the top half of the artichoke and peel the base and stem. Cut off the stem and drop it into the bowl. Using a melon baller or a spoon, scoop out the furry choke. Rub the artichoke bottom all over with the other lemon half, then quarter the artichoke and drop the artichoke into the lemon water. Repeat with the remaining artichokes.

2. Drain the artichokes and pat them dry. Heat 2 tablespoons of the olive oil in a large saucepan. Add the artichokes, garlic, leeks, celery and fennel and cook over moderate heat for 2 minutes, stirring occasionally. Add the water and a pinch of salt and bring to a boil. Cover the saucepan and simmer for 15 minutes. Add the green beans and simmer until all of the vegetables are tender, about 10 minutes.

---

cooking tip

searing meat

CONTRARY TO POPULAR BELIEF, SEARING MEAT DOESN'T SEAL IN THE JUICES. Instead, searing creates a sweet brown crust that adds flavor. The best way to sear meat is in a very hot pan, which not only prevents the meat from sticking but allows that amazing crust to develop.

---

3. Drain the vegetables and reserve their cooking liquid. Return the cooking liquid to the saucepan and boil over high heat until reduced to 2 cups, about 10 minutes. Remove from the heat.

4. Season the lamb with salt and pepper and dust with the pimentón. In a large, deep skillet, heat the remaining 2 tablespoons of olive oil until shimmering. Add the lamb and cook over moderate heat until lightly browned, about 3 minutes per side. Transfer to a plate. Add the flour to the skillet and cook over low heat, stirring, for 1 minute. Gradually whisk in the wine and reduced vegetable cooking liquid and simmer for 5 minutes, whisking frequently. Stir in the vegetables and lamb and simmer until heated through, 4 minutes; the lamb should still be pink in the center. Season with salt and pepper and serve. —*Joseph Jiménez de Jiménez*

MAKE AHEAD The stew can be refrigerated overnight.

WINE Soft, earthy Rioja.

Slow-Cooked Lamb Shanks with Verjus

6 SERVINGS ●

Verjus is the tart, unfermented juice of unripe grapes.

2 tablespoons extra-virgin olive oil

6 meaty lamb shanks (about
1 pound each)

Sea salt and freshly ground pepper

10 rosemary sprigs

1 large head garlic, cloves peeled
and 3 minced

1 whole preserved lemon, rinsed
(see Note)

2 cups (500 ml) verjus

1 cup chicken stock or canned
low-sodium broth

6 bay leaves, preferably imported

1 teaspoon whole black
peppercorns, cracked

1. Preheat the oven to 325°. Heat the oil in a large enameled cast-iron casserole. Season the lamb shanks with salt and pepper; add 3 shanks to the casserole.

Cook over moderate heat until browned all over, about 8 minutes, then transfer to a plate. Add the remaining 3 shanks and the rosemary to the casserole and cook until browned. Add the minced garlic and cook for 1 minute. Remove from the heat and return the first 3 shanks to the casserole.

2. Using a sharp knife, remove the pulp from the lemon; discard the pulp. Cut the lemon rind into 8 pieces and add to the lamb along with the verjus, stock, garlic cloves, bay leaves, cracked peppercorns and 1 teaspoon of salt; bring to a boil. Cover tightly and braise in the oven for 3 hours, or until the meat is tender; turn the shanks occasionally.

3. Transfer the lamb to a platter; let cool slightly. Pull the meat off the bones and trim any fat. Discard the rosemary stems and bay leaves and skim as much fat as possible from the sauce in the casserole. Return the meat to the sauce and cook over moderate heat until warm. Spoon the lamb into bowls and serve. —*Maggie Beer*

MAKE AHEAD The cooked lamb shanks can be refrigerated for up to 2 days.

NOTE Preserved lemons are available at Middle Eastern markets and specialty food shops.

WINE Rich, smoky-plummy Shiraz.

Lamb and Kale Moussaka

8 SERVINGS ●

In this unusual Balkan version of moussaka, lightly battered, crisp kale leaves replace the traditional eggplant.

FILLING

1 large egg

1¼ cups low-fat milk

1 cup all-purpose flour

1 teaspoon baking powder

8 packed cups small kale leaves
(from 1½ pounds of kale)

1 tablespoon olive oil

1¼ pounds ground lamb or beef

½ teaspoon salt

½ teaspoon cinnamon

¼ teaspoon freshly ground pepper

Hot Hungarian paprika
- 1 medium onion, finely chopped
- 1 cup chopped flat-leaf parsley
- 1 tablespoon minced garlic
- 1 tablespoon tomato paste mixed with ¾ cup water

Vegetable oil, for frying
- ⅓ cup fine dry bread crumbs
- 1 cup freshly grated Parmesan or Asiago cheese (4 ounces)

CUSTARD TOPPING
- 4 large eggs
- 2 cups low-fat milk
- 1 cup plain whole-milk yogurt

Hot Hungarian paprika

1. MAKE THE FILLING: In a large bowl, whisk the egg with the milk, then lightly whisk in the flour and baking powder just until blended; a few lumps are fine. Cover the batter and let stand at room temperature for 30 minutes.

2. In a pot of boiling water, cook the kale until tender, about 8 minutes. Drain and refresh, then pat thoroughly dry.

3. Heat the olive oil in a large skillet. Add the lamb, salt, cinnamon, pepper and a large pinch of paprika. Cook over moderate heat, breaking up the meat, until lightly browned, about 5 minutes. Stir in the onion, parsley and garlic. Cover and cook over low heat, stirring occasionally, until the onion softens, about 10 minutes. Add the diluted tomato paste, bring to a boil and remove from the heat.

4. Preheat the oven to 375°. In a large, deep skillet, heat 1½ inches of vegetable oil to 375°. Stir half of the kale into the batter. Lift out the leaves, let the excess batter drip off and fry them until browned. Drain on a rack; season with salt. Repeat with the remaining kale.

5. Oil a shallow 3-quart baking dish. Dust the bottom with 3 tablespoons of the bread crumbs and top with half of the fried kale leaves. Spoon the meat filling evenly over the kale and sprinkle with the Parmesan. Top with the remaining fried kale and bread crumbs. Lightly dust with paprika.

6. MAKE THE CUSTARD TOPPING: Beat the eggs with the milk, yogurt and a large pinch of paprika. Pour most of the custard around the edge of the filling and a little on top; let settle for 10 minutes. Bake for about 25 minutes, or until the custard is set and lightly browned. Let stand for at least 5 minutes, then cut into squares and serve.
—*Paula Wolfert*

WINE Round, supple, fruity Syrah.

Rack of Lamb with Soy-Balsamic Marinade

8 SERVINGS

Ask the butcher to french the bones and trim the fat for you.
- ¼ cup soy sauce
- ¼ cup balsamic vinegar
- 1 tablespoon finely grated lemon zest

Four 8-chop racks of lamb, bones frenched, fat trimmed and scored
Salt and freshly ground pepper
- ¼ cup vegetable oil

1. In a glass or ceramic dish, combine the soy sauce, balsamic vinegar and lemon zest. Add the lamb racks, fat side down, and marinate at room temperature for 2 hours, turning once.

2. Preheat the oven to 450°. Remove the lamb racks from the marinade and pat dry. Season the lamb racks generously with salt and pepper. In each of 2 large skillets, heat 2 tablespoons of the vegetable oil until shimmering. Add the lamb racks, fat side down, and cook over moderately high heat until nicely browned, about 3 minutes; turn and sear the meaty side of the racks, about 2 minutes longer.

3. Transfer the lamb racks to a rimmed baking sheet, fat side up. Roast in the upper third of the oven for 15 minutes, or until an instant-read thermometer inserted in the thickest part of each rack registers 120° to 125° (for medium rare). Let the lamb rest for 10 minutes before carving. —*Marcia Kiesel*

WINE Rich, velvety Merlot.

Fettuccine with Wild Boar Ragù

6 SERVINGS ●
- 3 tablespoons extra-virgin olive oil
- 3½ pounds trimmed wild boar or pork shoulder, cut into 1-inch pieces

Salt and freshly ground pepper
- 4 garlic cloves, coarsely chopped
- 1 medium onion, coarsely chopped
- 1 medium carrot, finely chopped
- 2 large rosemary sprigs and 2 large thyme sprigs, tied with string
- 3 cups Chianti or Beaujolais
- 3 cups pork or chicken stock
- 1 pound fettuccine or pappardelle
- ½ cup freshly grated Parmesan cheese, plus more for serving

1. Heat 2 tablespoons of the olive oil in a medium enameled cast-iron casserole. Season the boar pieces with salt and pepper. Add one-third of the meat to the hot oil and cook over moderately high heat, turning occasionally, until browned all over, about 6 minutes. Transfer to a plate. Repeat the process 2 more times, cooking the remaining meat in the hot oil.

2. Add the garlic, onion, carrot and the remaining 1 tablespoon of oil to the casserole; cook over low heat for 5 minutes. Add the herb bundle and cook until the vegetables soften, about 5 minutes longer. Add the browned meat along with any accumulated juices. Add the red wine and stock and bring to a boil. Reduce the heat to low and simmer the ragù, skimming occasionally, until the meat is fork-tender and the sauce is thick, 2½ to 3 hours. Season with salt and pepper.

3. In a large pot of boiling salted water, cook the fettuccine until al dente. Drain and return to the pot. Add the wild boar ragù and toss with the fettuccine. Add ½ cup of the Parmesan, season with salt and pepper and toss again. Transfer the pasta and ragù to bowls and serve with additional Parmesan.
—*Bill Buford*

WINE Soft, earthy Rioja.

PANKO-BREADED PORK CHOPS, P. 149

pork + veal

SKILLET PORK CHOP

GUAVA-GLAZED PORK TENDERLOIN

Hazelnut-Crusted Pork Chops with Morel Sauce

4 SERVINGS

There's something about a morel's woodsy-smoky flavor and unique texture—springy to the bite, with tiny honeycomb-like pockets that are perfect for soaking up delicate cream sauces—that make it irresistible. Fresh morels have a maddeningly short season and can be inconsistent in quality; dried morels are more readily available and happen to be even more intensely flavored—especially small ones. Just avoid packages with a lot of broken pieces or powdery residue, a clear sign of age.

1½ ounces small dried morels (1½ cups)
2 cups boiling water
1 cup hazelnuts (about 5 ounces)
½ cup all-purpose flour
2 large eggs

Four 6- to 8-ounce pork rib chops, pounded ⅓ inch thick
Salt and freshly ground pepper
¼ cup vegetable oil
2 tablespoons unsalted butter
2 large shallots, thinly sliced
2 large garlic cloves, thinly sliced
2 tablespoons Cognac or other brandy
¾ cup heavy cream

1. In a medium heatproof bowl, soak the morels in the boiling water until softened, about 30 minutes. Rub the morels to dislodge any grit, then lift them out of the soaking liquid and coarsely chop any large ones. Reserve the soaking liquid.

2. Preheat the oven to 350°. Put the hazelnuts on a rimmed baking sheet and bake for about 12 minutes, or until richly browned. Transfer the nuts to a kitchen towel and let cool completely.

Rub the nuts together in the towel to remove the skins, then coarsely chop them. In a food processor, pulse the hazelnuts until they become a coarse powder. Leave the oven on.

3. Spread the ground hazelnuts and the flour in 2 shallow bowls. In a third shallow bowl, beat the eggs with a fork.

4. Season the pork chops with salt and pepper. Dredge a pork chop first in the flour, shake off any excess and then dip it in the egg. Coat the pork chop with the ground hazelnuts and transfer it to a platter. Repeat with the remaining pork chops and coatings.

5. In a large skillet, heat the oil until shimmering. Working in 2 batches, cook the pork chops over moderate heat until browned, about 3 minutes per side. Transfer the chops to a rimmed baking sheet and bake for about 4 minutes, or until barely pink in the center.

6. Meanwhile, wipe out the skillet with a paper towel. Add the butter and melt over moderate heat. Reduce the heat to low. Add the shallots and cook, stirring, until softened, about 4 minutes. Add the garlic and cook until golden, about 3 minutes. Add the brandy and carefully light with a long match. When the flames die down, add the morels. Slowly pour in the reserved morel soaking liquid, stopping when you reach the grit. Simmer over moderately low heat until reduced to about ½ cup, about 5 minutes. Add the cream and simmer until thickened slightly, about 5 minutes. Season the sauce with salt and pepper.

7. Set the pork chops on plates, spoon the morel sauce around them and serve. —*Marcia Kiesel*

WINE Subtle, complex white Burgundy.

Skillet Pork Chops

4 SERVINGS

- 2 quarts water
- ½ cup kosher salt
- 1½ cups brown sugar
- ½ cup honey
- 1 lemon, cut into 8 rounds
- 1 small onion, chopped
- 4 thyme sprigs
- 3 garlic cloves, crushed
- 3 allspice berries, crushed
- 1 bay leaf
- 1 teaspoon peppercorns, cracked

Four ¾-pound bone-in pork chops

- 1 tablespoon extra-virgin olive oil

1. In a large pot, bring 1 quart of the water with the salt and sugar to a simmer, stirring. Off the heat, add the remaining 1 quart of water, the honey, lemon, onion, thyme, garlic, allspice, bay leaf and peppercorns; let cool completely. Add the pork chops to the brine and cover with a plate to keep them submerged. Refrigerate for 4 hours.

2. Preheat the oven to 500°. Remove the chops from the brine and pat dry. Heat the olive oil in a large ovenproof skillet. Add the chops and brown over moderately high heat, turning once.

Roast the chops in the oven for about 7 minutes, or until just pink throughout. Let stand for 5 minutes before serving. —*Traci Des Jardins*

WINE Light, fruity Beaujolais.

Glazed Pork Chops with Cinnamon

4 SERVINGS ●

Look for pork chops with a little bit of fat for a more succulent dish.

- 2 tablespoons vegetable oil

Three 2½-inch-long cinnamon sticks

- 2 bay leaves

Eight 5- to 6-ounce thin-cut pork chops

Salt and freshly ground pepper

- 2 medium carrots, cut crosswise into ¼-inch-thick slices
- 1 medium onion, coarsely chopped
- 1 medium celery rib, finely chopped
- 1 cup water
- ½ cup tamari
- 3 tablespoons sugar
- ⅛ teaspoon cayenne pepper

Basmati rice, for serving

1. In a large skillet, heat the oil. Add the cinnamon sticks and bay leaves and cook over high heat for 10 seconds. Lightly season the pork chops with salt and pepper. Add 4 chops to the skillet and cook until browned, about 1 minute per side; transfer to a plate. Repeat with the remaining chops.

2. Add the carrots, onion and celery to the skillet and cook over moderately high heat, stirring a few times, until lightly browned, about 3 minutes. Add the water, tamari, sugar and cayenne. Return the pork chops and their juices to the skillet, overlapping the chops as necessary. Cover and simmer over moderate heat, turning the chops once, until the chops are tender and the sauce is syrupy, about 30 minutes. Discard the cinnamon sticks and bay leaves. Arrange the chops on plates, pour the sauce and vegetables on top and serve with basmati rice.

—*Madhur Jaffrey*

Panko-Breaded Pork Chops

4 SERVINGS ●

Japanese bread crumbs, called *panko,* are bright white, and their large flakes result in a rough, crunchy texture. Look for them in large supermarkets, specialty shops and Asian groceries.

- 1 large egg
- 1 cup Japanese bread crumbs (*panko*)
- 2 tablespoons freshly grated Parmesan cheese
- 1 teaspoon minced sage

Salt and freshly ground pepper

Four ¾-inch-thick pork chops (about ½ pound each)

- ¼ cup extra-virgin olive oil

1. Lightly beat the egg in a shallow bowl. On a large plate, toss the *panko* with the Parmesan cheese, sage, ½ teaspoon of salt and ⅛ teaspoon of pepper. Season the pork chops with salt and pepper. Dip the chops in the egg and then press them into the seasoned crumbs to coat.

2. In a large nonstick skillet, heat the olive oil until shimmering. Add the coated pork chops and fry over moderate heat, turning occasionally, until the crust is golden brown and the chops are cooked through, about 10 minutes. Transfer the chops to plates and serve.

—*Gale Gand*

WINE Rich, velvety Merlot.

Guava-Glazed Pork Tenderloin with Cilantro-Jalapeño Salsa

4 SERVINGS ●

GLAZED PORK

- 1 tablespoon vegetable oil
- 1 tablespoon minced onion
- 1 garlic clove, minced
- 7 ounces guava paste (see Note), chopped (¾ cup)
- ½ cup water
- 1 tablespoon soy sauce
- 1 tablespoon ketchup
- 1 teaspoon cayenne pepper

Salt

Two ¾-pound pork tenderloins

SALSA

½ cup chopped cilantro, plus
cilantro sprigs, for garnish

⅓ cup vegetable oil

¼ cup white wine vinegar

¼ cup minced onion

2 tablespoons chopped chives

2 jalapeños, minced

1 garlic clove, minced

Salt

I. MAKE THE GLAZED PORK: Heat the oil in a small saucepan. Add the onion and garlic and cook over moderate heat, stirring, until softened, about 1 minute. Reduce the heat to low. Add the guava paste and water and cook, stirring, until the paste has dissolved, about 5 minutes. Stir in the soy sauce, ketchup and cayenne. Season with salt.

2. Set the pork in a 9-by-13-inch baking dish; brush with half of the glaze.

3. Light a fire or heat a grill pan over moderate heat. Grill the pork, turning and brushing with the remaining glaze, until browned on all sides and cooked through, about 15 minutes. Transfer the pork to a cutting board, cover loosely with foil and let stand for 10 minutes.

4. MAKE THE SALSA: In a bowl, mix the chopped cilantro, oil, vinegar, onion, chives, jalapeños and garlic. Season with salt.

5. Thinly slice the pork. Garnish with cilantro sprigs and serve with the salsa.
—*Ruth Van Waerebeek*

---

cooking tip
great basting

TAKE CARE WHEN GRILLING MEAT with a sweet glaze, as sugar has a tendency to burn. It's best to baste the meat with a sweet glaze in the last 15 to 20 minutes of grilling. If you're using a meat marinade as a glaze, be certain to boil the marinade first to kill any harmful bacteria.

NOTE Guava paste is available in the Latin section of most supermarkets.
SERVE WITH Fresh fava bean puree.
WINE Intense, berry-flavored Zinfandel.

Pork Tenderloin with Rosemary and Applesauce
6 SERVINGS ●

3 large Granny Smith apples—
peeled, cored and thinly sliced

½ cup dry white wine

¼ cup water

1 tablespoon sugar

One 1-inch piece fresh ginger—
peeled, thickly sliced and
lightly smashed

1 cinnamon stick, broken in half

3 tablespoons unsalted butter

1 tablespoon exta-virgin olive oil

Two ¾-pound pork tenderloins, cut
into 1½-inch medallions and
flattened slightly

Salt and freshly ground pepper

1 rosemary sprig, broken into
1-inch pieces

I. In a saucepan, combine the apples, wine, water, sugar, ginger, cinnamon and 1 tablespoon of the butter and bring to a simmer. Cover and cook over moderately low heat, stirring, until the apples are tender, about 12 minutes. Uncover and cook, stirring, until the liquid is nearly evaporated, about 5 minutes. Discard the ginger and cinnamon.

2. In a skillet, heat the oil until shimmering. Season the pork medallions with salt and pepper. Add them to the skillet and cook over high heat, turning once, until browned, about 10 minutes. Transfer to a plate and keep warm.

3. Return the skillet to high heat and add the remaining 2 tablespoons of butter and the rosemary. Cook, stirring, until the rosemary browns and the butter is fragrant, about 2 minutes. Discard the rosemary sprig. Spoon the applesauce onto plates and top with the pork. Spoon the rosemary butter over the top and serve. —*Melissa Clark*
WINE Dry, full-flavored Alsace Riesling.

Farmer-Style Pork Tenderloin with Pimentón Sauce
4 SERVINGS ● ●

This classic pork dish is often referred to as a farmer's recipe because it is prepared with only the most basic ingredients. Unlike many braised meats, which get their richness from being cooked for hours, this pork tenderloin needs to simmer for only 20 minutes in a wine sauce spiked with smoky pimentón. Made from dried red peppers that have been smoked over oak, then ground, pimentón is produced in La Vera, in the Cáceres region of Spain.

Two ¾-pound pork tenderloins

Salt and freshly ground pepper

2 tablespoons extra-virgin olive oil

2 tablespoons chopped
flat-leaf parsley

1 tablespoon sweet pimentón

2 bay leaves

1 green bell pepper, finely chopped

¼ cup finely chopped onion

2½ tablespoons all-purpose flour

1 cup dry red wine, preferably Rioja

1 cup beef or chicken stock or
canned low-sodium broth

1 teaspoon tomato paste

4 piquillo peppers from a jar,
cut lengthwise into ½-inch-
wide strips

I. Season the pork with salt and pepper. In a large shallow baking dish, mix 1 tablespoon of the olive oil with the parsley and pimentón. Add the tenderloins and turn to coat. Let stand at room temperature for 20 minutes or refrigerate for at least 1 hour or up to 2 hours.

2. In a deep skillet, heat the remaining 1 tablespoon of oil. Add the pork and cook over moderate heat until browned, 3 minutes per side. Transfer to a plate.

3. Add the bay leaves, bell pepper and onion to the skillet. Cook over moderate heat until softened, 4 minutes. Add the flour; stir until a smooth paste forms. Whisk in the wine and simmer, whisking, for 2 minutes. Whisk in the stock and tomato paste and return to a simmer.

4. Return the pork tenderloin and any accumulated juices to the skillet and simmer over low heat for 10 minutes. Turn and simmer for about 10 minutes longer, or just until the pork is pink in the center. Transfer the pork to a cutting board and let stand for 5 minutes.

5. Meanwhile, remove the bay leaves from the pan sauce and pour into a food processor or blender and puree. Return the sauce to the skillet, add the piquillo peppers and bring to a simmer over moderately low heat. Season with salt and pepper. Thickly slice the pork and serve with the pan sauce.

—*Joseph Jiménez de Jiménez*

MAKE AHEAD The recipe can be prepared earlier in the day. Reheat gently.

WINE Soft, earthy Rioja.

Port-Marinated Pork with Prunes and Anchovies

6 SERVINGS ●

12 pitted prunes (5 ounces)
1 cup ruby port
6 garlic cloves, smashed
¼ cup fresh lemon juice
2 tablespoons finely grated lemon zest
Salt and freshly ground pepper
One 2½-pound boneless pork loin roast
12 anchovy fillets
1 tablespoon olive oil
1 tablespoon all-purpose flour

1. In a saucepan, cover the prunes with the port and bring to a simmer. Remove the pan from the heat and let stand until the prunes soften, about 25 minutes. Pour the prunes and port into a shallow dish. Add the garlic, lemon juice and zest and a large pinch each of salt and pepper. Add the pork and turn to coat. Let marinate at room temperature for 4 hours, turning often.

2. Preheat the oven to 400°. Remove and reserve the prunes from the marinade. Strain the marinade into a saucepan and reserve. Roll up the anchovy fillets and stuff each one into a prune.

Make a deep lengthwise slit in the pork, leaving about 1 inch of meat attached. Open the roast like a book and season with salt and pepper. Arrange the stuffed prunes in a row along the slit; close the roast and tie it at 2-inch intervals with kitchen string. Season the roast all over with salt and pepper.

3. In a skillet, heat the oil until shimmering. Add the pork roast, fat side down, and brown over moderate heat on 4 sides, about 1 minute per side. Set the roast in a roasting pan, fat side up. Roast the pork for about 55 minutes; if the pan juices begin to look very dark, add 2 tablespoons of water. The roast is done when an instant-read thermometer inserted in the center registers 145°. Transfer the pork roast to a carving board, cover with foil and let rest for 10 minutes.

4. Scrape out any blackened bits in the roasting pan. Set the pan over moderately low heat and stir in the flour to make a smooth paste. Slowly whisk in the reserved marinade and simmer, whisking, until the sauce is smooth and thickened, about 3 minutes. Pour the sauce into a clean saucepan and season with salt and pepper.

5. Untie the roast and cut it into ½-inch-thick slices. Pour any juices into the sauce and reheat before serving it with the pork roast. —*Taylor Fladgate*

WINE Soft, earthy Rioja.

Roasted Pork Loin Stuffed with Spinach and Prosciutto

12 SERVINGS

To butterfly pork loins, slice them in half lengthwise almost all the way through, leaving a hinge of uncut meat. Or have your butcher do it for you.

Two 10-ounce packages of frozen chopped spinach, thawed
⅔ cup freshly grated Parmesan cheese (about 3 ounces)
2 garlic cloves, minced
3 tablespoons extra-virgin olive oil
Salt and freshly ground pepper

Two 3-pound boneless pork loins, butterflied
¼ pound thinly sliced prosciutto
1½ cups chicken stock or canned low-sodium broth
½ cup dry white wine
1 teaspoon all-purpose flour mixed with 1 tablespoon of water

1. Squeeze any excess water from the chopped spinach. In a medium bowl, mix the spinach with the Parmesan cheese, minced garlic and 2 tablespoons of the extra-virgin olive oil. Season with salt and pepper.

2. Preheat the oven to 400°. Set the pork loins on a work surface, opening them like a book, with the cut side up. Season the inside of the pork loins generously with salt and pepper. Cover the pork loins with a single layer of overlapping prosciutto slices; spoon the spinach filling into the center of the pork loins. Shape the filling into a thin log that runs along the center of each loin. Roll up the pork loins and tie them with kitchen twine at 1½-inch intervals. Season the pork loins generously with salt and freshly ground pepper.

3. Heat the remaining 1 tablespoon of oil in a very large ovenproof skillet until shimmering. Add the pork and cook over moderately high heat until they are browned all over, about 10 minutes. Transfer the pork loins to a large platter.

4. Pour off any fat from the skillet and return it to high heat. Add half of the chicken stock and bring to a boil, scraping up any browned bits from the bottom of the pan. Return the pork loins to the skillet and roast them in the oven for 40 to 45 minutes, or until an instant-read thermometer inserted in the thickest part of the meat registers 145°. Transfer the pork loins to a large cutting board, cover loosely with foil and let stand for 15 minutes.

5. Pour the juices from the skillet into a small saucepan and skim off the fat. Add the remaining ¾ cup of chicken stock to the skillet and set it over high heat.

FAMILY-STYLE PORK TACOS

Add the wine, scraping up any browned bits from the skillet; boil until reduced to a few tablespoons. Add the juices and bring to a boil. Whisk in the flour slurry and simmer until slightly thickened. Season with salt and pepper.

6. Untie the pork loins and slice the meat ½ inch thick. Arrange the slices on plates, drizzle with the pan sauce and serve. —*Giada De Laurentiis*

MAKE AHEAD The recipe can be prepared through Step 2 and refrigerated overnight. Return to room temperature before cooking.

SERVE WITH Sautéed broccoli rabe and roasted red and yellow bell peppers marinated in olive oil and garlic.

WINE Tart, low-tannin Barbera.

Brown Sugar–Glazed Pork Roast

6 SERVINGS ●

This recipe showcases boneless pork shoulder roast—essentially, a butterflied cut that has been rolled and tied neatly. Have your butcher trim off as much fat as possible.

2 garlic cloves, very finely chopped

Salt

One 4½- to 5-pound boneless pork
    shoulder roast, fat trimmed

Freshly ground pepper

¼ cup light brown sugar

2 large onions, quartered and
    very thinly sliced

One 28-ounce can whole peeled
    tomatoes, chopped and juices
    reserved

½ cup ketchup

¼ cup water

2 tablespoons Tabasco

I. Preheat the oven to 350°. On a work surface, using the flat side of a large knife, mash the garlic with 1 teaspoon of salt to a paste. Spread open the pork roast and rub the inside with the garlic paste. Season the pork with pepper and roll up to form a neat roast; tie at 1-inch intervals. Season the outside of the roast with salt and pepper, then rub with the brown sugar.

2. In a large roasting pan, combine the sliced onions with the tomatoes and their juices, the ketchup, water and Tabasco. Set the pork roast on top of the sauce, cover with aluminum foil and bake for 2 hours. Increase the oven temperature to 450°, remove the foil and bake for 45 minutes longer, basting occasionally, until the roast is nicely glazed. Transfer the roast to a carving board, cover loosely with foil and let rest for 10 minutes.

3. Meanwhile, pour the sauce into a large saucepan and simmer over moderately high heat, stirring occasionally, until thickened, about 12 minutes. Season with salt.

4. Untie the roast and carve it into 1-inch-thick slices. Serve with the sauce. —*Marcia Kiesel*

MAKE AHEAD The baked roast can be refrigerated overnight. Slice it and bring to room temperature, then cover with foil and reheat in the tomato sauce.

SERVE WITH Mashed potatoes, rice or lightly buttered pasta.

WINE Intense, berry-flavored Zinfandel.

Pork Rib Roast with Orange-Whisky Glaze

12 SERVINGS

Ask your butcher to remove the chine bones from the rib roasts. The meat needs to brine for two days.

4 quarts warm water

¾ cup kosher salt

¾ cup sugar

Two 6-pound bone-in pork loin rib
    roasts, cut from the loin end,
    chine bones removed

1 tablespoon finely grated
    orange zest

2 cups fresh orange juice

2 large shallots, minced

1 tablespoon grated fresh ginger

¼ cup English dry mustard

¼ cup tomato paste

¼ cup whisky

Salt and freshly ground pepper

¼ cup vegetable oil

I. In a very large pot, combine the water, salt and sugar; stir to dissolve the salt and sugar. Totally submerge the roasts in the brine and refrigerate for 2 days.

2. In a saucepan, combine the orange zest and juice, the shallots and ginger. Boil over moderate heat until almost syrupy, about 20 minutes. Whisk in the mustard, tomato paste and 2 tablespoons of the whisky and simmer for 5 minutes. Off the heat, stir in the remaining 2 tablespoons of whisky. Season with salt and pepper and let cool.

3. Preheat the oven to 375°. Remove the roasts from the brine and pat dry. In each of 2 very large skillets, heat 2 tablespoons of the oil until shimmering. Add the roasts, meaty side down; brown on all sides over moderately high heat, about 15 minutes. Set the roasts in a roasting pan, meaty side down.

4. Spread ¼ cup of the glaze on the rib side of each roast. Roast in the center of the oven for 30 minutes. Turn the roasts and spread the remaining glaze over them. Roast for 1 hour longer, or until the pork is deeply browned and an instant-read thermometer inserted in the thickest part registers 150°. Transfer to a carving board; let rest for 15 minutes. Carve the roasts between the ribs and serve. —*Mory Thomas*

MAKE AHEAD The glaze can be refrigerated for up to 5 days.

WINE Spicy Alsace Gewürztraminer.

Family-Style Pork Tacos

4 SERVINGS ●

1½ tablespoons ancho chile powder

1 teaspoon salt

½ teaspoon dried oregano

¼ teaspoon ground cumin

⅛ teaspoon freshly ground pepper

Pinch of cinnamon

Pinch of allspice

1½ pounds pork tenderloin,
    cut into ⅓-inch cubes

1 medium white onion, chopped

2 tablespoons cider vinegar

5 tablespoons minced cilantro

3 tablespoons extra-virgin olive oil

1 cup shredded mozzarella cheese

16 warmed 6- or 8-inch flour or corn tortillas, mashed avocado, shredded or leaf lettuce, salsa and lime wedges, for serving

1. In a bowl, mix the ancho powder, salt, oregano, cumin, pepper, cinnamon and allspice. Mix in the pork, onion, vinegar and ¼ cup of the cilantro. **2.** Heat the oil in a skillet. Add the pork and stir-fry over moderately high heat until browned outside and just cooked through. Transfer the pork to a colander to drain; sprinkle with the cheese and the remaining 1 tablespoon of cilantro. Transfer the pork to a serving bowl and serve with the tortillas, avocado, lettuce, salsa and lime. —*Jim Peyton*

Jamaican-Style Jerk Spareribs

6 SERVINGS

The spareribs need to marinate overnight, so plan accordingly.

7 pounds pork spareribs, trimmed of excess fat

8 scallions, coarsely chopped

8 large garlic cloves, coarsely chopped

3 Scotch bonnet chiles with some of their seeds, coarsely chopped

1 small onion, coarsely chopped

⅓ cup vegetable oil

¼ cup soy sauce

---

cooking tip

tenderloin

WHEN COOKED PROPERLY, LOW-FAT PORK TENDERLOIN is succulent, juicy and tender. High heat is optimal for cooking the tenderloin quickly and evenly, making it a great choice for fast weeknight meals. For the best results, aim for an internal temperature of 145° to 155°.

1½ tablespoons Chinese five-spice powder

1½ tablespoons freshly ground allspice

1 tablespoon fresh lime juice

1 tablespoon kosher salt

2 teaspoons freshly ground pepper

1. In a large pot of boiling water, cook the spareribs over moderate heat for 25 minutes. Drain and let cool. **2.** In a food processor, combine the chopped scallions with the garlic, chiles, onion, vegetable oil, soy sauce, Chinese five-spice powder, ground allspice, lime juice, salt and pepper and process the mixture to a paste. **3.** Set the spareribs on 2 large rimmed baking sheets and spread the jerk paste all over them. Cover and refrigerate overnight. Bring to room temperature before grilling. **4.** Light a grill. Grill the pork spareribs over a medium-hot fire, turning them frequently if they are browning too fast, until lightly charred and crisp, about 25 minutes. Transfer the ribs to a cutting board and let rest for 10 minutes. Cut in between the ribs, arrange on a platter and serve. —*Marcia Kiesel*

WINE Intense, berry-flavored Zinfandel.

Asian-Style Baby Back Ribs

6 SERVINGS ●

The ribs need to marinate overnight, so plan accordingly.

6 garlic cloves, coarsely chopped

One 4-inch piece of fresh ginger, peeled and coarsely chopped

¾ cup red pepper jelly (see Note)

½ cup hoisin sauce

½ cup soy sauce

½ cup coarsely chopped cilantro

¼ cup rice vinegar

6 tablespoons fresh lime juice

2 tablespoons Asian sesame oil

2 tablespoons Chinese chili-garlic sauce

Six 1½-pound racks of pork baby back ribs

1. In a food processor, combine the garlic, ginger, red pepper jelly, hoisin sauce, soy sauce, cilantro, rice vinegar, lime juice, sesame oil and chili-garlic sauce. Pulse until smooth. **2.** Set the racks in a large baking dish and slather with the marinade. Cover and refrigerate overnight. Bring to room temperature before proceeding. **3.** Preheat the oven to 400°. Line 3 large rimmed baking sheets with foil. Remove the ribs from the marinade; reserve the marinade. Halve each rack so that each piece has 4 to 5 ribs. Set the ribs on the baking sheets, meaty side down, and roast in batches for 30 minutes. Baste with the reserved marinade twice during baking and turn after 15 minutes. **4.** Preheat the broiler. Baste the ribs again and broil 3 inches from the heat for 3 minutes, or until nicely glazed. Let the ribs rest for 10 minutes. Cut between them and serve. —*Kate Heddings*

NOTE Sweet-and-hot red pepper jelly is available at specialty shops or by mail order from Stonewall Kitchen (800-207-JAMS; www.stonewallkitchen.com).

MAKE AHEAD The cooked ribs can be refrigerated overnight. Wrap in foil and reheat before serving.

Chilean Mixed Grill

12 SERVINGS

The *adobo,* or marinade, adds a tangy, garlicky flavor to the grilled steaks and pork chops and also tenderizes them.

Three 750-ml bottles full-bodied red wine, preferably Chilean Merlot

½ cup extra-virgin olive oil

½ cup apple cider vinegar

8 garlic cloves, coarsely chopped

3 tablespoons cracked coriander seeds

12 cracked black peppercorns

1 tablespoon dried oregano

5 to 6 pounds skirt steak, or three 2-pound sirloin steaks, cut 1½ inches thick

12 pork loin chops (¾ pound each), cut ¾ inch thick

CHILEAN MIXED GRILL

1. In a large bowl, combine the red wine with the olive oil, vinegar, garlic, coriander, peppercorns and oregano. Put the skirt steaks and pork chops in 2 large, deep dishes and add half of the red wine marinade to each. Cover both dishes and let the meats marinate in the refrigerator for at least 4 or up to 8 hours, turning occasionally.

2. Light a grill. When it is moderately hot, drain the marinade and add the steaks and chops in batches. Grill the chops until just cooked through, 7 to 8 minutes per side. Grill the steaks until medium rare, 2½ minutes per side for skirt or 12 minutes per side for sirloin. —*Bernardita Del Campo Correa*
WINE Rich, velvety Merlot.

Pork with Sage and Madeira

4 SERVINGS ● ●

- ¾ pound pork tenderloin, cut into 8 slices
- 2 tablespoons chopped sage

Salt and freshly ground pepper

- ¼ cup all-purpose flour
- 2 tablespoons unsalted butter
- 1 tablespoon extra-virgin olive oil
- ¼ cup minced shallots
- 1 cup Madeira

1. On a work surface, lightly pound the pork slices to a ¼-inch thickness. Rub with the sage and season with salt and pepper. Dredge the pork in the flour, shaking off any excess.

2. In a large skillet, melt 1 tablespoon of the butter in the olive oil. Add the pork and cook over moderately high heat, turning once, until lightly browned, about 5 minutes. Transfer to a platter and keep warm.

3. Add the shallots to the skillet and cook, stirring often, until golden, about 2 minutes. Gradually add the Madeira and bring to a boil, stirring; boil until reduced to ¾ cup. Return the pork to the skillet and simmer, turning twice, until cooked and the sauce is slightly thickened, about 3 minutes. Arrange the pork on plates. Swirl the remaining 1 tablespoon of butter into the sauce and season with salt and pepper. Spoon the sauce over the pork and serve. —*Damon Lee Fowler*

SERVE WITH Any steamed green.
WINE Complex, silky red Burgundy.

Pan-Seared Pork Medallions with Riesling and Apples

6 SERVINGS ● ●

- 2 tablespoons unsalted butter
- 4 teaspoons dark brown sugar
- 3 Golden Delicious apples— peeled, halved, cored and cut into eighths
- 1 tablespoon canola oil

Two 1¼- to 1½-pound pork tenderloins, each cut into 6 medallions

Salt and freshly ground pepper

- 1 cup Late Harvest Riesling
- 2½ cups chicken stock or canned low-sodium broth

1. In a large skillet, melt the butter over moderately high heat. Stir in the brown sugar, then add the apples in a single layer and cook until golden brown and tender, 3 to 4 minutes per side.

2. In another large skillet, heat the canola oil over moderately high heat. Season the pork medallions generously with salt and pepper and cook until golden brown all over, about 15 minutes. Transfer the pork to a serving platter and keep warm.

3. Add the wine to the second skillet. Cook over high heat until reduced to ¼ cup, about 3 minutes. Add the stock and simmer until the sauce reduces slightly, about 12 minutes; season with salt and pepper. Add the apples; cook over moderately low heat until warmed through. Pour the apples and sauce over the pork and serve. —*Joanne Weir*
WINE Dry, full-flavored Alsace Riesling.

Spicy Tofu Casserole with Pork

4 SERVINGS ● ● ●

- 1 tablespoon vegetable oil
- ¼ pound boneless pork shoulder, cut into ¼-inch-thick slices across the grain
- 2 garlic cloves, minced
- 1 small onion, thinly sliced

Salt and freshly ground pepper

- 3 tablespoons Korean sweet-spicy red chili paste (kochujang)
- 4 cups beef stock or canned low-sodium broth
- 3 medium zucchini, cut crosswise into ⅓-inch-thick slices
- 15 ounces soft tofu, cut into 1-inch dice
- 2 scallions, thinly sliced
- 1 long red or green fresh hot chile (preferably Korean), thinly sliced

Steamed white rice, for serving

1. Heat the oil in a saucepan. Add the pork, garlic and onion and season with salt and pepper. Cook over high heat, stirring, until the pork is no longer pink, about 4 minutes. Add the chili paste and cook, stirring, for 2 minutes. Add the stock and bring to a boil. Cover and cook over low heat for 15 minutes.

2. Add the zucchini to the saucepan. Cook over moderate heat until almost tender, about 2 minutes. Add the tofu and simmer for 2 minutes. Add the scallions and fresh chile and simmer for 1 minute. Ladle into bowls and serve with white rice on the side. —*Susan Choung*
WINE Bright, fruity rosé.

Firm Tofu with Chili-Meat Sauce and Peas

4 SERVINGS ● ●

¼ cup small tree ear mushrooms

2 tablespoons soy sauce

1 tablespoon dry sherry or rice wine

1 teaspoon Asian sesame oil

1 tablespoon plus 1 teaspoon cornstarch

½ pound ground pork

1½ tablespoons water

1½ tablespoons vegetable oil

1 tablespoon chili-bean sauce

2 garlic cloves, minced

2 teaspoons minced fresh ginger

6 water chestnuts, chopped

4 scallions, white and light green parts only, chopped

½ teaspoon sugar

¼ teaspoon freshly ground white pepper

1 pound firm tofu, drained and cut into ½-inch dice

¾ cup chicken broth

½ cup frozen baby peas, thawed

1. In a small bowl, cover the tree ears with water and let soak for 15 minutes; drain and coarsely chop.

2. In a medium bowl, mix 1 tablespoon of the soy sauce with the sherry, sesame oil and 1 teaspoon of the cornstarch. Stir in the pork. In a small bowl, mix the remaining cornstarch with the water.

3. In a wok, heat the oil until smoking. Add the chili-bean sauce, garlic and ginger and cook over high heat, stirring, until fragrant, about 20 seconds. Add the water chestnuts and chopped tree ears and stir-fry for 15 seconds. Add the pork and stir-fry for 2 more minutes, breaking up any large clumps. Stir in the scallions, sugar and white pepper. Gently stir in the tofu, broth, peas and the remaining 1 tablespoon of soy sauce and bring to a boil. Add the cornstarch mixture and stir until the sauce thickens, about 15 seconds. Transfer the tofu and sauce to a platter and serve. —Joyce Jue

Szechuan Eggplant and Pork

4 SERVINGS ●

½ pound ground pork

2 tablespoons soy sauce

1 tablespoon dry sherry or rice wine

2 tablespoons vegetable oil

1 tablespoon chili-bean sauce

2 garlic cloves, chopped

1 teaspoon minced fresh ginger

½ teaspoon salt

1¼ pounds Asian eggplants, cut into ¾-inch dice

1 tablespoon sugar

½ cup chicken broth

1 tablespoon balsamic vinegar

2 teaspoons cornstarch mixed with 2 tablespoons water

1 teaspoon Asian sesame oil

2 teaspoons sesame seeds, toasted

2 scallions, white and light green parts only, finely chopped

1. In a bowl, mix the pork with 1 tablespoon of the soy sauce and the sherry.

2. In a wok, heat the vegetable oil until smoking. Add the chili sauce, garlic, ginger and salt and cook over high heat until fragrant, 20 seconds. Add the pork and stir-fry until browned, 2 to 3 minutes. Add the eggplant and stir-fry until just softened, 3 minutes. Add the sugar and remaining 1 tablespoon of soy sauce and stir-fry for 30 seconds.

3. Stir in the broth, cover and cook over moderate heat until the eggplant is tender, about 10 minutes. Add the vinegar and cornstarch mixture and stir until the sauce thickens, about 15 seconds. Drizzle the sesame oil over; transfer to a platter. Top with the sesame seeds and scallions and serve. —Joyce Jue

WINE Soft, off-dry Riesling.

Almost Dirty Pork Rice

6 SERVINGS ● ● ●

This variation on the New Orleans classic, dirty rice, substitutes ground pork for chicken giblets and sausage. It's a great accompaniment to chicken and pork dishes as well as duck.

1 tablespoon extra-virgin olive oil

½ pound lean ground pork

1 large onion, finely chopped

1 teaspoon minced garlic

1 large jalapeño, seeded and minced

1 teaspoon ground coriander

1 teaspoon ground cumin

1 teaspoon cayenne pepper

2 cups basmati rice

3 cups chicken stock

1 tablespoon kosher salt

2 bay leaves

4 scallions, thinly sliced

In a saucepan, heat the oil until shimmering. Add the pork and cook over high heat, breaking up the meat with a wooden spoon, until no longer pink, about 5 minutes. Add the onion, garlic and jalapeño; cook, stirring, until softened, about 5 minutes. Add the coriander, cumin and cayenne and stir until fragrant, 30 seconds. Add the rice and cook until chalky white, about 3 minutes. Add the stock, salt and bay leaves; bring to a boil. Reduce the heat to low, cover and simmer until the rice is tender, 15 to 20 minutes. Fluff the rice and stir in the scallions. —Jan Birnbaum

MAKE AHEAD The cooked rice can be refrigerated for up to 2 days. Reheat in a covered baking dish in a 325° oven.

Olive and Feta Meatballs

6 SERVINGS ● ●

These meatballs, rich with the flavor of feta and olives, are well worth the effort.

SAUCE

½ cup navy or Great Northern beans, soaked overnight and drained

¼ cup extra-virgin olive oil

3 garlic cloves, very finely chopped

1 small onion, thinly sliced

1 teaspoon Tabil (p. 328)

1 teaspoon sweet paprika

One 14-ounce can whole tomatoes, drained and chopped

Salt and freshly ground pepper

1 cup hot water

½ preserved lemon, thinly sliced
(see Note)

1 tablespoon capers, drained and
coarsely chopped

MEATBALLS

¼ cup extra-virgin olive oil,
plus more for frying

2 cups packed chopped
flat-leaf parsley

1 medium onion, finely chopped

½ pound ground veal or turkey

½ pound feta cheese, crumbled
(1½ cups)

1 cup fine dry bread crumbs

6 ounces green olives
(1 cup), pitted and cut into
½-inch pieces

2 tablespoons shredded
Gruyère cheese

2 tablespoons Tabil (p. 328)

4 large eggs

All-purpose flour, for dredging

1 poblano chile or green
bell pepper

---

pairing tip

wine and spice

When pairing wine with spicy food
(like the *Hot Mustard-Pickled Peaches*),
follow these rules:

**CHOOSE LOW-ALCOHOL, FRUITY
WINES** like Sauvignon Blanc and rosé.
Fiery foods make high-alcohol wines
taste hotter, tannic reds more bitter
and oak-aged whites more oaky.

**TAME SPICES WITH WINES THAT
HAVE SOME SWEETNESS.** The residual
sugar in many dry and off-dry wines,
such as Riesling and Chenin Blanc, and
in many rosés will balance heat.

MATCH SPICE WITH SPICE. The spice
of a Zinfandel will enhance the heat in
red-meat dishes; Pinot Gris's bitterness
and bite will complement spicy greens.

PICK A WINE WITH BUBBLES. The
fruit and tangy acidity will cool spices.

I. MAKE THE SAUCE: In a small
saucepan, cover the beans with 1 inch
of water and bring to a boil. Cover partially and simmer over low heat, stirring occasionally, until tender, about
40 minutes. Drain and keep covered.

2. Heat the olive oil in a large saucepan.
Add the garlic, onion, Tabil and paprika
and cook over low heat until the onion
softens, about 7 minutes. Add the tomatoes and a pinch each of salt and pepper and bring to a simmer. Add the hot
water, then cover and simmer until very
thick, about 20 minutes. Stir in the
cooked beans, cover and simmer for
about 10 minutes longer. Add the preserved lemon and capers, season the
tomato mixture with salt and pepper
and remove from the heat.

3. MAKE THE MEATBALLS: In a
medium skillet, heat ¼ cup of the olive
oil. Add the parsley and onion and cook
over moderately low heat until the
onion softens, about 8 minutes. Transfer the parsley and onion to a large
bowl and let cool completely. Add the
ground veal, feta, bread crumbs, olives,
Gruyère, Tabil and 2 of the eggs and
mix thoroughly with your hands. Form
the meat mixture into 3 dozen tablespoon-size meatballs.

4. In a large skillet, heat ¼ inch of olive
oil until shimmering. In a medium shallow bowl, beat the 2 remaining eggs.
Working in batches, dredge the meatballs lightly in flour, then dip them in
the beaten eggs, letting any excess egg
drip back into the bowl. Fry the meatballs over moderate heat until browned
all over; reduce the heat if they start
browning too quickly. Transfer the meatballs to a rack to drain.

5. Roast the poblano chile over a gas
flame or under the broiler until charred
all over, about 10 minutes. Transfer the
chile to a bowl, cover with plastic wrap
and let steam for 5 minutes. Peel the
chile and discard the stem, core and
seeds. Cut the poblano chile pepper
into thin strips.

6. Bring the sauce to a simmer. Add the
meatballs, cover and cook over low
heat until heated through, about 10 minutes. Arrange the meatballs and sauce
in a large bowl, garnish with the strips
of chile and serve.

—*Nancy Harmon Jenkins*

NOTE Preserved lemons are available
at Middle Eastern and specialty food
markets.

MAKE AHEAD The meatballs can be
refrigerated overnight in the sauce.
Reheat gently before serving.

WINE Tart, low-tannin Barbera.

Hot Mustard-Pickled Peaches with Baked Ham

4 SERVINGS ●

1 cup water

½ cup white wine vinegar

2 tablespoons sugar

2 whole cloves

Salt

2½ tablespoons dry
English mustard

1 teaspoon ground ginger

1 pound firm, ripe peaches—
peeled, pitted, sliced ¼ inch thick
and slices halved

½ cup pecan halves

2 tablespoons mayonnaise

Freshly ground pepper

10 cups baby mustard and kale
leaves or mesclun (6 ounces)

6 ounces glazed baked ham, cut
into matchsticks

I. In a medium saucepan, combine the
water, vinegar, sugar and cloves and
bring to a boil. Cover and simmer over
low heat for 5 minutes. Remove from
the heat, add a pinch of salt and whisk
in the dry mustard and ginger.

2. Add the peaches to the hot pickling
liquid and let cool completely. Cover
and refrigerate for at least 2 hours and
for up to 5 days.

3. Preheat the oven to 350°. Put the
pecans in a metal pie plate and bake
for about 8 minutes, or until toasted.
Let cool, then coarsely chop.

4. In a bowl, mix ¼ cup of the pickling liquid and the mayonnaise; season with salt and pepper. Add the mustard and kale and toss. Transfer to plates, scatter the peaches, ham and pecans on top and serve. —*Marcia Kiesel*
WINE Bright, fruity rosé.

Polenta with Sausage, Tomato and Olive Ragout

6 SERVINGS

- 2 tablespoons extra-virgin olive oil
- 1 medium onion, chopped

One 28-ounce can peeled Italian tomatoes, seeded and chopped
- ½ cup red wine, such as Cabernet Sauvignon or Merlot
- 2 tablespoons balsamic vinegar
- 2 tablespoons tomato paste
- 1 teaspoon sugar
- ½ teaspoon dried oregano

Pinch of crushed red pepper
Salt and freshly ground pepper
- 6 fresh sweet pork sausages (about 2 pounds)
- 7 cups water
- ¾ cup Calamata olives, pitted
- 1½ cups instant polenta
- 4 tablespoons unsalted butter
- 1 tablespoon chopped rosemary
- ¾ cup freshly grated Parmigiano-Reggiano cheese

Flat-leaf parsley leaves, for garnish

1. Heat the oil in a large skillet. Add the onion and cook over moderately low heat until translucent, about 8 minutes. Add the tomatoes, red wine, balsamic vinegar, tomato paste, sugar, oregano and crushed pepper; season with salt and pepper. Simmer the ragout until it thickens slightly, about 10 minutes.
2. In a skillet, cook the sausages in 1 cup of the water over moderately high heat, turning, until cooked through, about 12 minutes. Thickly slice crosswise on the diagonal, then stir into the ragout with the olives; keep warm.
3. In a saucepan, bring the remaining 6 cups of water to a boil with 2 teaspoons of salt. Add the polenta.

Cook, stirring, until thick, 1 to 2 minutes. Remove from the heat and stir in the butter, rosemary and ½ cup of the cheese; season with salt and pepper. Transfer the polenta to a large platter and make a well in the center. Ladle the sausage ragout into the well, garnish with the remaining ¼ cup of cheese and parsley and serve. —*Joanne Weir*
WINE Intense, berry-flavored Zinfandel.

Goulash with Sausage and Sauerkraut

8 TO 10 SERVINGS ●

- ¾ pound Hungarian sausage, such as kolbász (smoked with paprika), sliced crosswise ½ inch thick
- 1½ pounds boneless beef chuck, cut into 1½-inch cubes
- 1½ pounds boneless pork shoulder, cut into 1½-inch cubes
- ⅓ cup bacon fat or vegetable oil
- 4 large onions (4 pounds), finely chopped
- ⅓ cup sweet Hungarian paprika
- 1 pound sauerkraut, drained
- 3 cups chicken stock or canned low-sodium broth, plus more if needed
- 4 bay leaves
- ½ teaspoon dried thyme

Salt and freshly ground pepper
- 1 cup sour cream, plus more for serving

Snipped chives, for sprinkling

1. In a skillet, fry the sausage over moderately high heat, turning, until lightly browned. Drain on paper towels. Add half of the beef and pork to the skillet and cook until browned all over, about 4 minutes per side. Transfer to a plate and repeat with the remaining meat.
2. Heat the bacon fat in an enameled cast-iron casserole. Add the onions and cook over moderate heat until softened, about 12 minutes. Add the paprika and cook for 5 minutes. Stir in the beef, pork, sauerkraut, stock, bay leaves and thyme. If necessary, add more stock to just cover the meat and sauerkraut.

3. Bring the stew to a boil. Cover and simmer over low heat for 1 hour. Add the sausage and cook until the beef and pork are very tender, about 1 hour. Season with salt and pepper. Let cool, then cover and refrigerate overnight.
4. Reheat the goulash over moderate heat until piping hot. Discard the bay leaves. Stir in the 1 cup of sour cream and cook until warmed through. Sprinkle with chives and serve with sour cream on the side. —*Tina Ujlaki*
MAKE AHEAD The goulash can be prepared through Step 3 and refrigerated for 2 days or frozen for 1 month. Reheat gently before proceeding.
WINE Round, supple, fruity Syrah.

Braised Veal Breast with Butternut Squash Stew

6 SERVINGS

One 3½- to 4-pound boneless veal breast, excess fat trimmed
Salt and freshly ground pepper
- 10 garlic cloves
- 3 large carrots, coarsely chopped
- 3 thyme sprigs
- 2 large Spanish onions, chopped
- 1 quart chicken stock or canned low-sodium broth
- 1 cup canned peeled Italian plum tomatoes, drained and chopped

One 2-pound butternut squash—halved, peeled, seeded and cut into ½-inch dice
- 2 tablespoons vegetable oil

One 15-ounce can chickpeas, drained
- 1 pound kale, tough stems and ribs removed, leaves chopped

1. Preheat the broiler. Set the veal on a baking sheet; season with salt and pepper. Broil 4 inches from the heat for 4 minutes per side, until well browned. Reduce the oven temperature to 300°.
2. Transfer the veal to a large enameled cast-iron casserole. Add the garlic, carrots, thyme, onions, chicken stock and tomatoes and season with salt and pepper. Cover and braise for 3 hours, or until the veal breast is very tender.

BAROLO-BRAISED VEAL

VEAL SCALLOPINE WITH LENTIL SALAD

Transfer the veal breast to a large shallow baking dish and cover with foil; reserve the braising liquid. Raise the oven temperature to 450°.

3. Spread the squash on a large rimmed baking sheet, drizzle with oil and season with salt and pepper. Roast the squash for 15 minutes, or until lightly browned and just tender.

4. Add the chickpeas to the braising liquid and bring to a boil. Simmer, covered, over low heat for 5 minutes. Add the kale and simmer until crisp-tender, about 3 minutes. Stir in the squash and simmer for about 1 minute. Remove the thyme; season with salt and pepper.

5. Reheat the veal in the oven if necessary and transfer to a cutting board, then carve across the grain into ½-inch-thick slices. Arrange the veal on a large, deep platter, top with the vegetable stew and serve. —*Anne Rosenzweig*

MAKE AHEAD The recipe can be prepared through Step 2 and refrigerated for up to 3 days.

WINE Bright, fruity Beaujolais.

Barolo-Braised Veal

8 SERVINGS

The veal marinates overnight in Barolo, so plan accordingly. Alternatively, try a Nebbiolo d'Alba; like Barolo, it's made from the Nebbiolo grape.

- 1½ **bottles Barolo (4½ cups)**
- 3 **celery ribs, coarsely chopped**
- 3 **bay leaves**
- 2 **medium onions, coarsely chopped**
- 2 **carrots, coarsely chopped**
- 2 **whole cloves**

One 4-pound boneless veal shoulder roast, tied

Salt and freshly ground pepper

- 2 **tablespoons extra-virgin olive oil**
- 1 **cup veal or beef stock or low-sodium broth**

I. In a bowl, combine the wine, celery, bay leaves, onions, carrots and cloves. Add the veal and marinate overnight in the refrigerator, turning a few times.

2. The next day, remove the veal from the marinade and pat dry; reserve the marinade. Season the veal with salt and pepper. Heat the olive oil in a large enameled cast-iron casserole. Add the veal and cook over moderately high heat until browned, about 4 minutes per side. Add the reserved marinade and the veal stock and bring to a boil. Reduce the heat to low and simmer the veal, skimming as necessary and turning the meat halfway through, until it's tender and an instant-read thermometer inserted in the center registers 140°, about 2½ hours.

3. Transfer the veal to a carving board and cover loosely with foil. Strain the cooking liquid into a medium saucepan and boil until reduced to 2 cups, about 8 minutes. Season with salt and pepper. Discard the strings from the roast and carve it into ¼-inch-thick slices. Serve with the braising liquid.

—*Giorgio Rivetti*

SERVE WITH Cooked carrots and creamy polenta.

Veal Scallopine with Lentil Salad

4 SERVINGS

- 4 tablespoons unsalted butter
- 1¼ cups Puy lentils (7½ ounces), rinsed
- Salt and freshly ground pepper
- 3½ cups chicken stock or canned low-sodium broth
- 1 bay leaf
- ½ cup finely diced carrot
- ½ cup finely diced zucchini
- ½ cup finely diced onion
- ½ cup finely diced celery
- ¼ cup all-purpose flour
- ¼ cup freshly grated Parmesan cheese
- 3 large eggs
- Eight 2-ounce slices of veal scallopine, pounded thin
- ½ cup plus 1 tablespoon extra-virgin olive oil
- 2 tablespoons balsamic vinegar
- 2 tablespoons chopped parsley

1. In a medium saucepan, melt 2 tablespoons of the butter. Stir in the Puy lentils; season lightly with salt and pepper. Add the chicken stock and bay leaf and bring to a boil. Simmer over low heat until the lentils are al dente, about 30 minutes.

2. Meanwhile, in a medium skillet, melt the remaining 2 tablespoons of butter. Add the diced carrot, zucchini, onion and celery. Season the vegetables with salt and pepper and cook over low heat, stirring, until just tender but not browned, about 10 minutes.

3. When the lentils are done, drain them over a medium bowl, reserving the cooking liquid. Discard the bay leaf. Return the lentils to the saucepan and pour in ½ cup of the reserved cooking liquid. Stir in the vegetables and season with salt and pepper.

4. Preheat the oven to 300°. Mix the flour and Parmesan cheese in a shallow bowl. Put the eggs in another shallow bowl and beat well. Season 4 of the veal slices with salt and pepper and dredge them in the Parmesan flour. Heat ½ cup of the olive oil in a large skillet. Quickly dip the floured veal into the egg mixture, then add the slices to the skillet and fry over moderately high heat until golden brown, about 2 minutes per side. Reduce the heat to moderate if the veal browns too quickly. Transfer the veal to a large rimmed baking sheet and keep warm in the oven. Repeat with the remaining 4 veal slices and keep warm in the oven while you finish the lentils.

5. Bring the lentils to a simmer. Remove from the heat and stir in the balsamic vinegar and the remaining 1 tablespoon of olive oil. Spoon the lentils onto plates, top with the veal, then sprinkle with the parsley and serve.

—*Michael Romano*

MAKE AHEAD The recipe can be prepared through Step 3 up to 6 hours ahead.

WINE Rich, earthy Pinot Noir.

Veal Chops with Tomato and Green Mango Salad

4 SERVINGS

- Four 10- to 12-ounce veal rib chops
- Salt and freshly ground pepper
- ¾ cup extra-virgin olive oil
- ½ cup flat-leaf parsley leaves, plus ¼ cup chopped flat-leaf parsley
- 2 garlic cloves, smashed
- 1 teaspoon thyme leaves
- 4 medium heirloom tomatoes, cut into ½-inch-thick slices
- 2 medium sweet onions, such as Maui, cut into ½-inch-thick slices and separated into rings
- 1 cup basil leaves
- ¼ cup cider vinegar
- ¼ teaspoon sugar
- 1 large green (underripe) organic mango, skin on, finely shredded (about 2 cups)

1. Season the veal chops lightly with salt and pepper. In a large, shallow dish, combine ½ cup of the olive oil with the chopped parsley, garlic and thyme. Add the veal chops and coat well. Let stand at room temperature for 4 hours.

2. In a large shallow dish, arrange the tomatoes and onions in overlapping rows. Tuck the basil and parsley leaves between the tomatoes and onions and season with salt and pepper. Drizzle with 2 tablespoons of the oil; let stand at room temperature for 2 to 4 hours.

ingredient tip
best bacon

DAKIN FARM COB-SMOKED BACON At Dakin Farm in northwestern Vermont's Champlain Valley, the Cutting family uses time-honored methods, slowly smoking bacon over smoldering corncobs. The result is worth the time: Their bacon has a fine, distinctively assertive flavor (800-993-2546; www.dakinfarm.com).

3. Light a grill or preheat a grill pan. Scrape most of the marinade off the chops. Grill over a medium-hot fire until browned and still pink in the center, about 6 minutes per side. Transfer to a platter; let stand for 5 minutes.

4. In a small bowl, mix the vinegar, sugar and the remaining 2 tablespoons of olive oil; season with salt and pepper. In a medium bowl, toss the mango with 3 tablespoons of the vinaigrette. Set a chop on each plate. Spoon the tomato-onion salad alongside and drizzle with the remaining vinaigrette. Sprinkle with the mango and serve. —*Suzanne Tracht*

Pan-Fried Veal Chops with Lemon and Rosemary

6 SERVINGS ●

Six 12-ounce veal rib chops, cut 1 inch thick

  2 tablespoons extra-virgin olive oil

  1 tablespoon minced rosemary

  ¼ teaspoon freshly ground pepper

---

pairing tip

wine + grilling

When pairing wine with grilled food, such as the *Veal Chops* on p. 161, follow these guidelines:

MAKE IT FLAVORFUL Whether full-bodied or light, a wine to partner grilled food should be concentrated. Wimpy wines will disappear.

MAKE IT FRUITY Fruity and even off-dry wines will taste drier with smoky grilled dishes like barbecue. Just be sure that the wine is sweeter than any added flavors (glazes, salsas).

MAKE IT RED When in doubt, reach for a red or rosé. The red- or black-fruit character gives punch to smoky dishes, and even the modest tannins of a rosé can counteract the mild bitterness that comes from charring.

---

  4 tablespoons unsalted butter

Salt

  2 tablespoons fresh lemon juice

  2 tablespoons water

1. Rub the veal chops all over with the olive oil, chopped rosemary and black pepper. Let the chops stand at room temperature for 10 minutes.

2. In a very large skillet, cook the butter over moderately high heat until it starts to brown, about 1 minute. Season the chops with salt. Add them to the skillet and pan-fry over moderately high heat, turning occasionally, until golden and an instant-read thermometer inserted in the thickest part of one of the chops registers 125°, about 15 minutes. Transfer the chops to a platter.

3. Add the lemon juice and water to the skillet and cook for 1 minute, scraping up any browned bits with a wooden spoon. Pour the pan sauce over the veal chops and serve. —*Maggie Beer*

WINE Round, supple, fruity Syrah.

Veal-and-Mushroom Meat Loaf with Bacon

8 TO 10 SERVINGS

The original recipe called for a mixture of ground boiled ham and ground veal. We substituted bacon for the ham to add a nice touch of smokiness.

  4 tablespoons unsalted butter

  ½ pound white mushrooms, cut into ½-inch dice

Salt and freshly ground pepper

  1 medium onion, minced

  1 medium green bell pepper, minced

  ½ pound lean thick-cut bacon, trimmed of fat and coarsely chopped, plus 4 thick-cut slices, halved crosswise

2½ pounds ground veal (not too lean)

  1 cup oyster crackers, crumbled

  ¼ cup ketchup

  ¼ cup drained prepared horseradish

  1 large egg, lightly beaten

  1 tablespoon all-purpose flour

  1 cup sour cream

1. Preheat the oven to 350°. Melt 2 tablespoons of the butter in a large skillet. Add the mushrooms, season with salt and pepper and cook over moderate heat until they release their liquid, about 4 minutes. Increase the heat to moderately high and cook, stirring, until browned, about 4 minutes longer. Add the onion, bell pepper and 1 tablespoon of the butter. Cook over low heat, stirring, until the onion and bell pepper soften, about 10 minutes. Let cool.

2. Mince the chopped bacon in a food processor. In a large bowl, combine the minced bacon with the veal, cracker crumbs, ketchup, horseradish, egg and the cooled mushroom mixture. Season with salt and pepper and mix thoroughly with your hands. Sauté a small piece of the meat-loaf mixture in the skillet over moderate heat and taste for seasoning. Add more salt and pepper to the meat-loaf mixture, if necessary. Pack the meat into a 2-quart loaf pan and arrange the halved bacon strips on top.

3. Bake the meat loaf for 1¼ hours, or until an instant-read thermometer inserted in the center registers 140°. Drain the pan juices into a heatproof bowl and skim off the fat; you should have ⅔ cup of juices.

4. Preheat the broiler. Broil the meat loaf 5 inches from the heat for 1 minute, or until the bacon is browned. Let the meat loaf rest in the pan for at least 10 or for up to 30 minutes.

5. In a small saucepan, melt the remaining 1 tablespoon of butter over low heat. Whisk in the flour until smooth, then whisk in the reserved pan juices. Bring the sauce to a simmer, whisking constantly, until thickened. Add the sour cream and cook, stirring, until hot, about 2 minutes; do not let the sauce boil. Season with salt and pepper. Thickly slice the meat loaf and serve with the sour cream sauce. —*Marcia Kiesel*

MAKE AHEAD The dish can be prepared through Step 2; refrigerate overnight.

WINE Rich, velvety Merlot.

VEAL-AND-MUSHROOM MEAT LOAF WITH BACON

SALMON WITH BABY ARTICHOKES AND SUNCHOKES, P. 167

fish

POACHED SALMON FILLET WITH RAVIGOTE SAUCE

SOY-AND-GINGER-GLAZED SALMON

Poached Salmon Fillets with Ravigote Sauce

4 SERVINGS ● ●

⅓   cup finely chopped onion
⅓   cup coarsely chopped parsley
2   scallions, finely chopped
2   plum tomatoes—halved, seeded and cut into ¼-inch dice
1   tablespoon drained capers
1   large garlic clove, minced
¼   cup extra-virgin olive oil
2   tablespoons fresh lemon juice
Salt and freshly ground pepper
Four 6-ounce skinless salmon fillets

1. In a small bowl, combine the onion, parsley, scallions, tomatoes, capers, garlic, olive oil and lemon juice. Season with salt and pepper.

2. In a large saucepan, bring 3 cups of water to a boil. Add the salmon and return to a boil. Remove from the heat, cover and let stand for 5 to 8 minutes, until the salmon is cooked to your liking. Using a spatula, transfer the salmon to plates, spoon the ravigote sauce on top and serve. —*Jacques Pépin*
SERVE WITH Couscous flavored with fresh herbs.

Soy-and-Ginger-Glazed Salmon with Udon Noodles

4 SERVINGS ●

¼   cup soy sauce
¼   cup sake
3   tablespoons fresh lime juice
2   tablespoons grated fresh ginger
1   tablespoon sugar
Four 6-ounce center-cut salmon fillets, with skin
½   pound fresh udon noodles
1   tablespoon extra-virgin olive oil
1   pound spinach, stems discarded
1   tablespoon sesame seeds, lightly toasted

1. In a small saucepan, combine the soy sauce, sake, lime juice, ginger and sugar and bring to a boil, stirring to dissolve the sugar. Pour the marinade into a glass baking dish and let cool completely. Add the salmon, turn to coat and marinate for 1 to 4 hours, turning occasionally.

2. Preheat the broiler. Remove the salmon fillets from the marinade and arrange on a broiler pan, skin side down. Broil the salmon 5 inches from the heat until golden, about 3 minutes. Turn the fillets and broil for about 4 more minutes, or until the skin is crisp and the fish is not quite cooked through. Transfer to a plate.

3. Meanwhile, bring a medium saucepan of water to a boil. Add the udon noodles and cook until heated through, about 1 minute. Drain the noodles and transfer to soup bowls.

4. Heat the olive oil in a large skillet. Add the spinach by handfuls and cook over high heat, tossing, until wilted. Mound the spinach on the udon and top with the salmon. Spoon the cooking juices in the baking dish over the fish, sprinkle with the sesame seeds and serve. —*Annabel Langbein*
WINE Rich, earthy Pinot Noir.

Salmon with Spiced Tomato Sauce

4 SERVINGS ●

Four 6-ounce skinless salmon fillets
Cayenne pepper
Kosher salt and freshly
    ground pepper
¼ teaspoon turmeric
1 cup crushed tomatoes
1 cup heavy cream
1 tablespoon fresh lemon juice
1 teaspoon ground cumin
¼ teaspoon ground cloves
¼ teaspoon cinnamon
¼ teaspoon freshly grated nutmeg
2 tablespoons unsalted butter
2 tablespoons finely
    chopped cilantro
Steamed rice, for serving

1. Dust the salmon fillets lightly with cayenne, salt, pepper and the turmeric. Cover and refrigerate for 20 minutes.
2. In a medium bowl, combine the crushed tomatoes with the cream, lemon juice, cumin, cloves, cinnamon, nutmeg and ¼ teaspoon of cayenne. Season with salt and pepper.
3. In a large skillet, melt the butter. Add the salmon and cook over moderately high heat until browned, about 3 minutes per side. Pour off the butter. Add the tomato sauce and bring to a simmer. Reduce the heat to low and cook, turning the salmon halfway through and occasionally basting with the sauce, until the fish is just cooked, about 8 minutes. Transfer to 4 plates and spoon the sauce on top. Sprinkle with the cilantro and serve at once with steamed rice. —*Madhur Jaffrey*

Salmon with Lemon-Shallot Relish and Prosciutto Chips

6 SERVINGS ● ●

Baking thin slices of prosciutto results in salty, crispy chips that are delicious as a garnish on salmon or salads.

4 **thin slices of prosciutto (about 2 ounces), cut crosswise into ½-inch strips**
5 **tablespoons extra-virgin olive oil**
Six 6-ounce skinless salmon fillets
Salt and freshly ground pepper
2 tablespoons fresh lemon juice
2 tablespoons snipped chives
2 small shallots, very finely chopped
2 teaspoons finely grated lemon zest
Lemon wedges, for serving

1. Preheat the oven to 400°. Lay the prosciutto strips on a rimmed baking sheet in a single layer and bake for 8 minutes, or until crisp. Transfer the prosciutto to a plate.
2. Brush the baking sheet with 1 tablespoon of the olive oil and arrange the salmon fillets, skinned side down, on the sheet; season with salt and pepper. Roast the salmon for about 10 minutes, or until just cooked through.
3. Meanwhile, in a small bowl, combine the lemon juice with the chives, shallots and lemon zest. Slowly whisk in the remaining 4 tablespoons of olive oil and season with salt and pepper. When the salmon is done, transfer the fillets to plates, top with the lemon-shallot relish and crisp prosciutto and serve at once with lemon wedges.
—*Joanne Weir*
WINE Fruity, low-oak Chardonnay.

Sautéed Salmon with Rhubarb Marmalade

4 SERVINGS ● ●

¾ **cup water**
¼ **cup sugar**
1 teaspoon grated peeled ginger
¼ teaspoon ground allspice

½ vanilla bean, split lengthwise and seeds scraped
1 pound rhubarb, stalks only, cut into 1-inch pieces
Salt and freshly ground pepper
1 tablespoon canola oil
Four 6-ounce salmon fillets, with skin
4 ounces pea shoots or watercress

1. In a medium saucepan, combine the water, sugar, ginger, allspice and vanilla bean and seeds. Add the rhubarb pieces and bring to a boil. Cook over moderate heat, stirring occasionally, until the rhubarb starts breaking down and the sauce is jamlike, about 20 minutes. Season with salt and pepper. Discard the vanilla bean.
2. In a nonstick skillet, heat the oil over moderately high heat. Season the salmon fillets with salt and pepper. Cook, turning once, until lightly browned, 8 minutes. Spoon the sauce onto plates, top with the salmon and pea shoots and serve. —*Terrance Brennan*

Salmon with Baby Artichokes and Sunchokes

8 FIRST-COURSE SERVINGS ●

Sunchokes, or Jerusalem artichokes, aren't artichokes at all. They're actually a tuber related to the sunflower with a sweet, nutty flavor and crisp texture.

½ **lemon plus 1 tablespoon fresh lemon juice**
10 **baby artichokes**
¼ **cup plus 3 tablespoons extra-virgin olive oil**
1¼ **pounds sunchokes, peeled and cut crosswise into ¼-inch-thick slices**
Salt and freshly ground pepper
1 cup chicken stock or canned low-sodium broth
1 small garlic clove, minced
1 thyme sprig
¼ pound baby spinach
Eight 3-ounce skinless center-cut salmon fillets
Warm Fennel Vinaigrette (recipe follows)

1. Squeeze the lemon half into a bowl of cold water and add the lemon half to the water. Working with 1 baby artichoke at a time, cut off the top one-third of the leaves; trim the stem to ½ inch. Pull off the tough outer leaves until you reach the core of tender yellow ones. Quarter the artichoke lengthwise and drop the artichoke quarters into the lemon water.

2. In a large skillet, heat 3 tablespoons of the olive oil until shimmering. Add the sunchoke slices, season with salt and pepper and cook over moderately high heat, stirring frequently, until tender and browned, about 12 minutes. Add ½ cup of the chicken stock and cook, stirring and scraping up any browned bits from the bottom of the skillet, until the stock is reduced to a syrupy glaze, about 2 minutes. Season with salt and pepper and transfer the sunchokes to a plate.

3. Drain the baby artichokes and pat them dry. Wipe out the skillet; add 3 tablespoons of the olive oil and heat until shimmering. Add the baby artichokes and cook over moderate heat, turning occasionally, until crisp-tender and browned, about 5 minutes. Add the garlic and thyme sprig and cook until fragrant, about 30 seconds. Add the remaining ½ cup of chicken stock and the 1 tablespoon of lemon juice and simmer until the artichokes are tender

and glazed, about 5 minutes. Stir in the sunchokes and the baby spinach and cook over high heat just until the spinach wilts, about 1 minute longer. Discard the thyme sprig and keep the vegetables warm.

4. Light a grill or preheat a grill pan. Rub the salmon fillets with the remaining 1 tablespoon of olive oil and season with salt and pepper. Grill the salmon over a medium-hot fire until golden and cooked through, about 2 minutes per side. Spoon the baby artichoke mixture onto plates and top each serving with a salmon fillet. Drizzle the salad with the Warm Fennel Vinaigrette and serve.
—*Ben Ford*

MAKE AHEAD The recipe can be prepared through Step 3 earlier in the day. Gently reheat the artichoke and sunchoke mixture before proceeding.

WINE Lively, assertive Sauvignon Blanc.

WARM FENNEL VINAIGRETTE
MAKES ABOUT 1½ CUPS ● ● ●

- ⅓ cup extra-virgin olive oil
- 2 medium fennel bulbs—halved, cored and finely chopped, plus 2 tablespoons coarsely chopped fennel fronds
- 2 tablespoons sweet wine vinegar, such as Late Harvest Riesling, or seasoned rice vinegar
- 2 tablespoons fresh lemon juice

Salt and freshly ground pepper

1. In a large skillet, heat the olive oil until shimmering. Add the chopped fennel bulbs and cook over moderately high heat, stirring frequently, until golden and tender, 8 to 10 minutes. Let the chopped fennel cool in the skillet for 10 minutes.

2. Stir the vinegar and lemon juice into the fennel and season with salt and pepper. Reheat and stir in the fennel fronds just before serving. —*B.F.*

MAKE AHEAD The vinaigrette can be refrigerated overnight.

Grilled Salmon Salad with Miso Vinaigrette
4 SERVINGS ● ●

Four 8-ounce salmon fillets, with skin

- 1½ tablespoons white miso
- 5½ tablespoons fresh lemon juice
- 2½ tablespoons grated fresh ginger
- ½ teaspoon Asian sesame oil
- 1½ teaspoons soy sauce
- ½ cup plus 1 tablespoon extra-virgin olive oil
- 2 tablespoons snipped chives

Freshly ground pepper

- ½ pound baby spinach

1. Rub the salmon with ½ tablespoon of miso. In a medium bowl, mix 1½ tablespoons of lemon juice, 1½ tablespoons of ginger and the sesame oil. Add the salmon and turn to coat; let stand for 10 minutes.

2. In a bowl, mix the remaining 1 tablespoon of miso with the remaining 1 tablespoon of ginger. Whisk in the remaining ¼ cup of lemon juice and the soy, then whisk in the olive oil. Add the chives and season with pepper.

3. Light a grill or preheat a grill pan. Add the salmon, skin side down. Cover the grill and cook the salmon over a medium-hot fire for 4 to 6 minutes. Flip the salmon and grill for 2 to 4 minutes, or until just cooked through. Transfer to a plate and keep warm.

4. Arrange the spinach on a platter and top with the fillets. Drizzle with half of the vinaigrette and serve with the remaining vinaigrette. —*Kathy Gunst*

Riesling-Poached Salmon
6 SERVINGS ● ●

- 2 teaspoons whole coriander seeds
- 2 cups Riesling

One 2-inch-long cinnamon stick

- 6 skinless center-cut salmon fillets (about ½ pound each)
- ¼ cup water

Coarse sea salt and freshly ground white pepper

- 2 tablespoons extra-virgin olive oil
- 2 tablespoons minced cilantro

---

cooking tip

quick salmon

HERE'S A DELICIOUS WAY TO MAKE SALMON: Place two 6-ounce salmon fillets in a buttered microwave-safe glass dish. Add 2 tablespoons of white wine, season with salt and pepper and cover. Microwave on high for 3 to 5 minutes, then let stand for 5 minutes. Sprinkle with parsley and serve.

---

1. In a large skillet, toast the coriander over moderately high heat until fragrant, about 2 minutes. Add the Riesling and cinnamon stick and bring to a boil. Reduce the heat; simmer for 5 minutes. **2.** Add the salmon and water. Cover and cook over low heat until opaque throughout, about 12 minutes. Transfer the salmon to 6 plates; season with salt and white pepper. Season the poaching liquid with salt and white pepper, then spoon about 1 tablespoon of it over each fillet along with 1 teaspoon of the olive oil. Sprinkle with cilantro and serve. —*Melissa Clark*

Grilled Salmon with Roasted Fennel and Tomatoes

4 SERVINGS ●

- 2 small fennel bulbs (about ½ pound each), quartered and cored
- ¼ cup plus 1 tablespoon extra-virgin olive oil

Salt and freshly ground pepper

- 4 thyme sprigs
- 4 large plum tomatoes, halved lengthwise
- 2 tablespoons fresh lemon juice
- ⅛ teaspoon ground coriander

Four 6-ounce salmon fillets (about 1 inch thick)

1. Preheat the oven to 375°. On a rimmed baking sheet, toss the fennel with 2 tablespoons of the olive oil and season with salt and pepper. Scatter the thyme sprigs over the fennel, cover with foil and bake for 15 minutes. Uncover and bake for about 15 minutes longer, until almost tender. Season the tomatoes with salt and pepper and add them to the baking sheet, cut side down. Bake for 15 minutes, or until the tomatoes are soft and the fennel is golden. Transfer the fennel and tomatoes to a platter and pour the roasting juices on top; discard the thyme sprigs. **2.** Light a grill or preheat a grill pan. In a small bowl, combine the lemon juice, 2 tablespoons of the olive oil and the coriander; season with salt and pepper.

3. Coat the salmon with the remaining 1 tablespoon of olive oil and season with salt and pepper. Grill the salmon over a medium-hot fire until lightly charred and just cooked, about 4 minutes per side. Serve the salmon with the roasted vegetables; pass the lemon dressing at the table. —*Marcia Kiesel*

Seared Tuna with Radish Salad and Wasabi Dressing

4 SERVINGS ● ○

- 3 tablespoons wasabi powder
- 3 tablespoons silken tofu
- 1 tablespoon rice vinegar
- ¼ cup fresh lemon juice or yuzu juice (see Note)
- ¼ cup mirin
- ½ pound radishes, sliced paper-thin
- 3 tablespoons mint leaves, torn in half
- ¼ cup cilantro leaves
- ¼ cup daikon sprouts or other peppery sprouts

Four 6-ounce top-quality tuna steaks, about ¾ inch thick

- 1 tablespoon pure olive oil

Sea salt and freshly ground pepper

1. In a small bowl, whisk the wasabi powder with the tofu, rice vinegar and 1 tablespoon each of the lemon juice and mirin. In a large bowl, toss the radishes with the mint, cilantro and sprouts. **2.** Heat a cast-iron grill pan. Brush the tuna steaks with the olive oil and season generously with salt and pepper. Grill the tuna over high heat until seared outside and medium rare within, 2 to 3 minutes per side. Transfer to a platter. **3.** Add the remaining 3 tablespoons each of lemon juice and mirin to the radishes and toss to mix. Slice the tuna steaks ¼ inch thick and serve with the radish salad and wasabi dressing. —*Michel Nischan*

NOTE Yuzu is a yellow citrus fruit available in Japanese food stores. Both the juice and the zest are used as flavorings.

taste test smoked salmon

PRODUCT	F&W COMMENT	INTERESTING BITE
Perona Farms Smoked Atlantic Salmon 800-750-6190; $22 per pound	"Buttery, fatty and lush."	Perona Farms gets its fish from Canada's Bay of Fundy, where the enormous tides act as a natural water purifier.
Durham's Tracklements Classic Highland Style Salmon 800-844-7853; $45 per 1¼-pound piece	"Creamy texture and full, rounded taste."	The word "tracklements" is a regional British colloquialism that refers to festive side dishes and condiments.
Acme Nova Pacific King Salmon 800-221-0795; $16 per pound	"Sweet, salty and not too fishy."	Acme is one of the last remaining companies to offer wild Pacific King Salmon caught with hooks and lines instead of nets.

Seared Tuna Puttanesca with Fennel Fritters

4 SERVINGS

PUTTANESCA SAUCE

- 1 large tomato—peeled, seeded and chopped
- 2 tablespoons red wine vinegar
- 1 tablespoon Dijon mustard
- 1 garlic clove, quartered
- ½ cup extra-virgin olive oil
- 2 marinated white anchovies (see Note), finely chopped
- 4 Calamata olives, pitted and finely chopped
- 1 teaspoon drained capers, chopped

Salt and freshly ground pepper

SUGAR SNAP PEAS

- ½ pound sugar snap peas
- 1 tablespoon extra-virgin olive oil
- 2 garlic cloves, minced
- 1 small shallot, minced
- 1 medium tomato, cut into ½-inch dice
- ½ teaspoon chopped thyme
- ½ teaspoon chopped capers

Salt and freshly ground pepper

FENNEL FRITTERS

- 2 medium fennel bulbs, trimmed and quartered
- 2 cups all-purpose flour

Salt and freshly ground pepper

- 2 large eggs
- ¼ cup milk

Vegetable oil, for frying

---

cooking tip

grilling fish

THICK, MEATY FISH, SUCH AS SWORDFISH, HALIBUT, TUNA AND SALMON, stand up best on the grill. Trout and tilapia, which are very firm and gelatinous, also grill nicely. Use a grill basket to keep flakier, more delicate fish, such as snapper, flounder, cod and sole, from falling apart.

TUNA

Four 6-ounce tuna steaks, cut about 1¼ inches thick

- 1 tablespoon extra-virgin olive oil

Salt and freshly ground pepper

- 8 marinated white anchovies, for garnish

I. MAKE THE PUTTANESCA SAUCE: In a blender, puree the tomato with the vinegar, mustard and garlic. With the blender on, slowly pour in the olive oil until smooth. Scrape the sauce into a bowl. Stir in the chopped anchovies, olives and capers and season the puttanesca with salt and pepper.

2. MAKE THE SUGAR SNAP PEAS: In a medium saucepan of boiling salted water, blanch the sugar snaps until crisp-tender, about 2 minutes. Drain and refresh in cold water. Reserve the blanching water.

3. Heat the olive oil in a large skillet. Add the garlic and shallot and cook over low heat until softened, about 2 minutes. Add the tomato and sugar snaps and cook, stirring, for 3 minutes. Add the thyme and capers and season with salt and pepper. Remove from the heat.

4. MAKE THE FENNEL FRITTERS: Preheat the oven to 300°. Bring the sugar snap blanching water back to a boil. Add the fennel quarters and cook until tender, about 8 minutes. Drain and let cool. Pat dry with paper towels.

5. Put the flour in a shallow bowl and season generously with salt and pepper. Crack the eggs into another shallow bowl and beat them with the milk. In a medium saucepan, heat 1 inch of vegetable oil to 350°. Dredge the fennel in the flour, then dip the wedges in the beaten eggs and dredge again in the flour. Working in 2 batches, fry the fennel, turning once, until golden brown, about 3 minutes. Transfer the fennel to a rack set over a rimmed baking sheet and keep warm in the oven.

6. MAKE THE TUNA: Light a grill or preheat a grill pan. Rub the tuna with oil and season with salt and pepper.

Grill over high heat until deeply browned outside and rare in the center, about 3 minutes per side. Transfer the tuna to a cutting board and cut each steak into ⅓-inch-thick slices.

7. Reheat the sugar snaps and spoon them onto plates. Lay the sliced tuna on the plates and drizzle the puttanesca sauce around the fish. Set 2 fennel fritters on each plate, garnish with the whole anchovies and serve at once.

—John Harris

NOTE Marinated white anchovies, called _alici,_ are available at specialty food shops.

Grilled Tuna Steaks with Citrus-Ginger Sauce

6 SERVINGS ●

Steamed jasmine rice or couscous would make a nice accompaniment to the tangy citrus sauce on the tuna.

- ¾ cup plus 1 tablespoon safflower oil, plus more for brushing
- ½ cup thinly sliced fresh ginger
- 3 medium shallots, thinly sliced
- 3 large garlic cloves, thinly sliced
- 1 cup fresh red grapefruit juice
- 1 cup fresh orange juice
- ⅓ cup fresh lemon juice
- ¾ cup dry white wine
- 3 tablespoons light soy sauce
- 2 cups chicken stock or canned low-sodium broth

Six 1-inch-thick tuna steaks (about 2¼ pounds total)

Salt and freshly ground pepper

- ¼ cup wasabi paste

I. In a large skillet, heat 1 tablespoon of the safflower oil until shimmering. Add the sliced ginger, shallots and garlic and cook them over moderate heat until softened, about 3 minutes. Add the red grapefruit, orange and lemon juices along with the wine, light soy sauce and stock and bring to a boil over high heat. Cook until the sauce is reduced to ½ cup and is slightly syrupy, about 40 minutes.

2. Set a fine sieve over the jar of a blender. Strain the ginger sauce, pressing down on the solids to extract as much liquid as possible. With the blender on, slowly pour in the remaining ¾ cup of oil until combined.

3. Light a grill or heat 2 grill pans. Lightly brush the tuna steaks with oil and season with salt and pepper. Grill the steaks over moderately high heat, turning once, until medium rare, about 6 minutes. Transfer the steaks to plates, spoon the sauce on top and serve with the wasabi on the side.

—Ann Chantal Altman

Roasted Halibut with Miso-Glazed Sweet Potatoes

10 SERVINGS ●

Ten 8-ounce halibut steaks,
    cut about ¾ inch thick
¼ cup olive oil
2 teaspoons thyme leaves
2 tablespoons unsalted
    butter, melted
2 tablespoons sake
1 tablespoon mirin
2 teaspoons soy sauce
1½ teaspoons yellow miso
3 pounds sweet potatoes, peeled
    and cut into ½-inch dice
Salt and freshly ground pepper
1½ tablespoons fresh lime juice
½ cup loosely packed flat-leaf
    parsley leaves
Five-Vegetable Slaw (p. 220),
    for serving

1. Preheat the oven to 425°. Put the halibut in a large shallow dish and rub the steaks all over with the olive oil and thyme. Let stand at room temperature for 30 minutes.

2. In a large bowl, whisk the melted butter with the sake, mirin, soy sauce and miso until combined. Add the sweet potatoes and toss to coat. Spread the sweet potatoes on a large rimmed non-stick baking sheet and roast them for 35 minutes, turning once, until tender and lightly browned.

SEARED TUNA PUTTANESCA WITH FENNEL FRITTERS

GRILLED TUNA STEAK WITH CITRUS-GINGER SAUCE

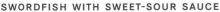

SWORDFISH WITH SWEET-SOUR SAUCE

GRILLED WILD STRIPED BASS WITH HERBS

3. Shortly before serving, heat a cast-iron grill pan until almost smoking. Season the halibut steaks with salt and pepper and grill, turning once, until they are just cooked through, about 7 minutes. Toss the sweet potatoes with the lime juice and parsley. Set the halibut on plates and top with the Five-Vegetable Slaw. Spoon the sweet potatoes alongside and serve.
—Peter Gordon

Swordfish with Sweet-Sour Sauce

6 SERVINGS ● ○

Vitali's Zibibbo restaurant is set on the outskirts of Florence, but she serves her swordfish Sicilian-style, marked by complex Arab and Roman flavors.

⅓ cup golden raisins
¼ cup plus 2 tablespoons extra-virgin olive oil
1 small white onion, thinly sliced
2 large garlic cloves, very thinly sliced
2 tablespoons pine nuts
2 tablespoons small capers, rinsed
2 bay leaves
Pinch of dried oregano
Pinch of crushed red pepper
1 pound ripe tomatoes, coarsely chopped
Salt
1 tablespoon white wine vinegar
1 teaspoon sugar
Six 8-ounce swordfish steaks, without skin, cut ½- to ¾-inch thick
Freshly ground pepper

1. In a small bowl, soak the raisins in warm water for 10 minutes; drain.
2. In a large skillet, heat ¼ cup of the olive oil until shimmering. Add the onion, garlic, pine nuts, capers, bay leaves, oregano and crushed pepper and cook over high heat, stirring occasionally, until the onion is softened and lightly browned, about 5 minutes. Add the tomatoes, season with salt and cook until the tomatoes are slightly broken down, about 3 minutes. Add the raisins, vinegar and sugar and cook, stirring, until the sauce thickens, about 5 minutes longer. Discard the bay leaves.
3. In each of 2 medium skillets, heat 1 tablespoon of the olive oil until shimmering. Season the swordfish steaks with salt and pepper and cook over high heat, turning occasionally, until browned outside and just cooked through, about 6 minutes. Transfer the swordfish to plates, spoon the sweet-sour sauce on top and serve.
—Benedetta Vitali

MAKE AHEAD The sweet-sour sauce can be refrigerated for up to 2 days.
WINE Fruity, low-oak Chardonnay.

Sicilian Stuffed Swordfish with Cherry Tomato Sauce

4 SERVINGS ● ●

1½ pounds skinless swordfish steak, cut 2 inches thick
3 tablespoons raisins
3 tablespoons pine nuts
½ pound coarse Italian bread, crusts removed, cut into 1-inch dice
½ cup dry white wine
½ cup fish stock or bottled clam juice
¼ cup coarsely chopped fennel fronds
3 anchovy fillets, mashed
1 tablespoon plus 1 teaspoon drained capers
1 tablespoon freshly grated Parmesan cheese
Pinch of cinnamon
Pinch of freshly grated nutmeg
Salt and freshly ground pepper
2 tablespoons extra-virgin olive oil, plus more for frying
All-purpose flour, for dredging
¼ teaspoon crushed red pepper
¾ pound cherry tomatoes, quartered
1 cup canned crushed tomatoes
2 ounces Gaeta olives, pitted and coarsely chopped (¼ cup)

1. On a work surface, cut the swordfish steak in half crosswise, then cut each half horizontally into four 5-by-3-inch slices. Gently pound the slices ⅛ inch thick. Cover and refrigerate.
2. In a heatproof bowl, soak the raisins in hot water until softened, about 10 minutes, then drain. In a small skillet, toast the pine nuts over moderate heat, shaking the pan, until lightly browned, about 2 minutes.
3. In a shallow dish, soak the bread in the wine and fish stock for 10 minutes. Gently squeeze the bread almost dry. Finely chop the bread and transfer to a bowl. Gently stir in 2 tablespoons each of the raisins and pine nuts, 2 tablespoons of the fennel fronds, 2 of the anchovies, 1 tablespoon of the capers, the Parmesan, cinnamon and nutmeg. Season with salt and pepper.
4. Lay the swordfish slices out on a work surface and season with salt and pepper. Spoon about ¼ cup of the filling in the center of each slice and roll up like a cigar, folding in the sides as you go. Secure the rolls with toothpicks.
5. In a large skillet, heat ¼ inch of olive oil. Lightly dredge the swordfish rolls in flour, shaking off the excess. Fry 4 of the rolls over moderately high heat until golden brown, about 2 minutes per side; transfer to a plate. Repeat with the remaining rolls. Wipe out the skillet.
6. In the same skillet, heat the 2 tablespoons of olive oil. Add the crushed red pepper, the remaining anchovy fillet and 1 teaspoon of capers and cook for 30 seconds. Add the cherry tomatoes and crushed tomatoes and cook over low heat until thickened, about 15 minutes. Stir in the olives, 1 tablespoon of the fennel fronds and the remaining 1 tablespoon each of pine nuts and raisins. Season with salt and pepper.
7. Add the swordfish rolls to the sauce. Cover and simmer over low heat, turning the rolls a few times, until heated through, about 3 minutes. Set 2 rolls on each plate, remove the toothpicks and spoon some sauce on top. Garnish with the remaining 1 tablespoon of fennel fronds and serve. —Maria Paolillo

MAKE AHEAD The sauce can be refrigerated overnight.

WINE Bright, fruity rosé.

Grilled Wild Striped Bass with Herbs and Sparkling Wine

12 SERVINGS ●

Twelve 6-ounce (1-inch-thick) wild striped bass or red snapper fillets
1½ cups extra-virgin olive oil
1 cup sparkling wine
2 medium shallots, minced
3 tablespoons minced chives
2 tablespoons minced flat-leaf parsley
1 tablespoon minced thyme
1 tablespoon minced lemon zest
Kosher salt and freshly ground pepper
Vegetable oil, for the grill

1. Lay the fish fillets in a large shallow glass baking dish. In a bowl, combine the oil, wine, shallots, chives, parsley, thyme and lemon zest. Pour two-thirds of the marinade over the fish and turn to coat. Cover and refrigerate for 30 minutes.
2. Light a grill. Let the fish stand at room temperature for 10 minutes, then season with salt and pepper. Oil the grate. Grill the fish over a medium-hot fire for 4 minutes per side, or until cooked through. Transfer to plates and serve with the remaining reserved marinade. —David Page and Barbara Shinn

WINE Flinty, high-acid Chablis.

Sea Bass all'Acqua Pazza

6 SERVINGS ●

Acqua pazza means "crazy water"— water flavored with wine and herbs.

2 cups water
1 celery rib, cut into 4 pieces
1 onion, quartered
1 carrot, cut into 4 pieces
3 parsley sprigs
1 teaspoon kosher salt
¼ teaspoon freshly ground pepper
One 4-pound sea bass, cleaned and scaled
5 garlic cloves, smashed
½ cup dry white wine
3 bay leaves
2 tablespoons extra-virgin olive oil

1. Preheat the oven to 375°. In a medium saucepan, combine the water, celery, onion, carrot, 1 parsley sprig and the salt and pepper and bring to a boil. Simmer over low heat for 20 minutes.
2. Set the fish in an oval baking dish and make 3 crosswise slashes on each side. Stuff the fish with the garlic and the remaining 2 parsley sprigs. Strain the vegetable broth over the fish. Add the wine, bay leaves and oil and bake for about 45 minutes. Serve the fish with the "crazy water." —Anna Teresa Callen

fish

Whole Roasted Sea Bass with Artichokes and Tomatoes

4 SERVINGS ● ●

 4 artichokes, stems cut off
 1 pint cherry tomatoes, halved
 2 leeks, white and tender green
 parts only, thinly sliced crosswise
 1 cup dry white wine
 ¼ cup coarsely chopped basil
 ¼ cup extra-virgin olive oil
 1 tablespoon small
 marjoram leaves
Salt and freshly ground pepper
One 4-pound sea bass, cleaned,
 scaled and tail cut off
 1 rosemary sprig

1. Preheat the oven to 450°. Line a large rimmed baking sheet with 2 overlapping 3-foot-long sheets of heavy-duty aluminum foil (half of each sheet should overlap in the middle of the pan). Top the foil with two 3-foot-long sheets of parchment paper, overlapping them in the same way.

2. On a rack in a large saucepan, steam the artichokes over moderately low heat, covered, until the bottoms are tender when pierced, about 50 minutes. Transfer the artichokes to a plate to cool. When the artichokes are cool enough to handle, remove all of the leaves and reserve them for another use. With a teaspoon, scoop out the hairy chokes. Cut the artichoke bottoms into ⅓-inch wedges.

3. In a large bowl, toss the artichokes with the cherry tomatoes, leeks, wine, basil, olive oil and marjoram. Season generously with salt and pepper.

4. Season the outside of the sea bass with salt and pepper and set the fish in the center of the parchment-lined foil. Season the cavity with salt and pepper and add the rosemary sprig; scatter the vegetable mixture all around the sea bass. Fold the parchment neatly over the fish, then close the foil by folding the overhanging ends into the center and crimping the sides tightly. Bake the fish on the bottom shelf of the oven for 1 hour and 10 minutes, then let stand at room temperature for 5 minutes.

5. Carefully open the package. Using 2 forks, gently lift the fish from the bones onto plates. Spoon the vegetables and juices around the fish and serve. —*Pino Luongo*

MAKE AHEAD The recipe can be prepared through Step 3 up to 1 day in advance, but refrigerate the artichokes and the vegetable mixture separately.
WINE Dry, light, refreshing Soave.

Grilled Sea Bass with Rosemary

4 SERVINGS ● ●

One 4-pound sea bass, filleted
Extra-virgin olive oil
 ½ teaspoon chopped rosemary
Salt and freshly ground pepper

1. Light a grill. Rub the skinless side of the fillets with 1 tablespoon of olive oil. Sprinkle with the rosemary and season with salt and pepper. Sandwich the fillets together to re-form the fish. Rub the skin with another tablespoon of olive oil and season with salt and pepper. Loosely tie the fillets together with cotton string.

2. Generously oil the grill. Grill the fish over a moderately low fire until just cooked through and the skin is browned and crisp, about 10 minutes per side. Transfer the fish to a platter and remove the strings. Cut the fish into 4 pieces and serve at once. —*Paolo Fanciulli*

Baked Flounder with Parmesan Crumbs

4 SERVINGS ●

 4 flounder fillets (about
 2 pounds total)
Salt and freshly ground pepper
 ¾ cup freshly grated
 Parmesan cheese
 ½ cup coarse fresh bread crumbs
 4 tablespoons unsalted
 butter, melted
 2 tablespoons extra-virgin olive oil

Preheat the oven to 425°. In a large baking dish, season the flounder fillets with salt and pepper. Mix the Parmesan cheese with the bread crumbs, melted butter and olive oil and sprinkle over the fillets. Bake for about 15 minutes, or until the fish is just cooked through and the Parmesan topping is golden. Let stand for 5 minutes, then transfer to plates and serve.
—*Nigel Slater*

Japanese Steamed Cod with Daikon

4 SERVINGS ● ●

 1½ cups Dashi (recipe follows)
 1 tablespoon mirin
 1 tablespoon soy sauce
 1 teaspoon cornstarch mixed with
 2 teaspoons water
Four 5-ounce cod fillets, skinned
Salt
 ½ cup finely grated daikon
Thin strips of lemon zest, for garnish

1. In a medium saucepan, mix the Dashi with the mirin and soy sauce. Whisk in the diluted cornstarch and simmer over low heat until reduced to ½ cup, about 30 minutes.

2. Season the cod with salt. Top each fillet with 2 tablespoons of the grated daikon. Place the fillets in a steamer set over simmering water and steam over moderate heat until the fish is just cooked through, about 5 minutes.

3. Transfer the cod to plates. Spoon the sauce around the fillets, garnish with lemon zest and serve. —*Kazuo Yoshida*

---

dictionary

daikon defined

DAIKON (used in the cod recipe on this page) is a large Asian radish that is crisp, sweet and juicy. Its skin is generally creamy white, pale green or black and its length averages 10 inches (though some daikon can grow much longer). If it's unavailable, sweet red radishes can be substituted.

BAKED FLOUNDER WITH PARMESAN CRUMBS

fish

DASHI

MAKES 5 CUPS ● ● ●

Dashi is essentially a stock made from water, flakes of dried bonito (a type of tuna) and kombu (dried seaweed). It is the cornerstone of many Japanese recipes. Premade dashi is available at Asian markets; it's often called bonito soup stock.

- **6 cups water**
- **1 ounce bonito flakes (2 cups)**
- **½ ounce kombu (optional)**

Combine all of the ingredients in a medium saucepan and bring to a boil. Strain the dashi into a bowl. —*K.Y.*

Cod with Braised Endives in Blood Orange Glaze

6 SERVINGS

- **1 tablespoon finely grated blood orange zest**
- **10 cilantro stems**
- **1 bay leaf**
- **1 stick (4 ounces) unsalted butter**
- **6 medium Belgian endives, halved lengthwise**
- **Salt and freshly ground pepper**
- **1 cup fresh blood orange juice**
- **15 coriander seeds, coarsely crushed**
- **1 teaspoon sugar**
- **3 tablespoons olive oil**
- **Six 6-ounce skinless cod fillets**
- **Cayenne pepper**

I. Preheat the oven to 400°. In a small saucepan of boiling water, blanch the blood orange zest for 1 minute; drain. Tie the cilantro stems and bay leaf into a bundle with kitchen string.

2. Melt 4 tablespoons of the butter in a large ovenproof skillet. Add the endives, cut side down, and season with salt and pepper. Add the blood orange juice and zest, the cilantro bundle, coriander seeds and sugar and bring to a boil. Press a round of parchment on top of the endives, cover the skillet with a lid and transfer to the oven. Braise for about 30 minutes, or until the endives are very tender.

3. Transfer the endives to a platter. Strain the braising liquid into a glass measuring cup. In the same skillet, melt 1 tablespoon of the butter. Add the endives, cut side down, and cook over moderately high heat until browned, about 4 minutes. Turn the endives over, add ½ cup of the braising liquid and cook, shaking the pan, until the liquid is reduced to a glaze, about 1 minute. Season with salt and pepper.

4. In each of 2 large skillets, melt 1½ tablespoons of butter in 1½ tablespoons of olive oil. Season the cod fillets with salt and cayenne pepper. Add 3 of the cod fillets to each skillet and cook over moderately high heat, turning once, until browned and cooked through, 3 to 4 minutes per side. Set a piece of the cod on each plate and arrange 2 endive halves alongside. Drizzle the remaining blood orange glaze over the fish and serve.

—*Jean-Georges Vongerichten*

WINE Medium-bodied, round Pinot Blanc.

Pompano with Ginger Sauce

4 SERVINGS ● ●

- **2 tablespoons sugar**
- **2 tablespoons fresh lime juice**
- **1½ tablespoons finely grated fresh ginger**
- **1 tablespoon Asian fish sauce or soy sauce**
- **1 garlic clove, minced**
- **Four 6-ounce pompano fillets**
- **Salt and freshly ground pepper**
- **¼ cup cilantro sprigs**

Light a grill or preheat a grill pan. In a small bowl, mix the sugar with the lime juice, ginger, fish sauce and garlic. Season the pompano fillets with salt and pepper and grill over a hot fire, turning once, for about 3 minutes per side, or until just cooked through. Transfer the grilled pompano to a platter or plates. Stir the ginger sauce and spoon over the pompano. Garnish with the cilantro sprigs and serve at once.

—*Marcia Kiesel*

Sautéed Skate with Brown Butter

6 SERVINGS

- **5 tablespoons vegetable oil**
- **2 slices of firm-textured white bread, cut into ½-inch dice**
- **1 small lemon**
- **Six 7-ounce skinless skate fillets**
- **Salt and freshly ground pepper**
- **3 tablespoons unsalted butter**
- **3 tablespoons drained capers**
- **2 tablespoons red wine vinegar**
- **3 large radishes, cut into ½-inch dice**
- **3 tablespoons chopped parsley**

I. In a large skillet, heat 2 tablespoons of the oil over high heat. Add the bread dice and cook over moderately low heat, stirring a few times, until browned, about 4 minutes. Drain the croutons on paper towels. Wipe out the skillet.

2. Peel the lemon with a small, sharp knife, removing all of the bitter white pith. Cut in between the membranes to release the lemon sections; cut the sections into ½-inch dice.

3. Add 1½ tablespoons of the oil to the skillet and heat until shimmering. Season the skate with salt and pepper. Add 3 of the skate fillets to the skillet and sauté over moderately high heat until browned on the bottom, about 4 minutes. Turn and cook until opaque throughout, about 2 minutes longer. Using a spatula, transfer the skate to a platter and keep warm; repeat with the remaining 1½ tablespoons of oil and 3 skate fillets.

4. Add the butter to the skillet and cook over moderate heat until browned, about 2 minutes. Add the capers and diced lemon sections and cook, stirring once or twice, for 30 seconds, then add the red wine vinegar. Stir in any accumulated juices from the skate and pour the pan sauce over the fish. Scatter the croutons, radishes and parsley over the skate and serve at once.

—*Jacques Pépin*

WINE Dry, medium-bodied Pinot Gris.

Red Snapper with Sweet-and-Sour Eggplant

4 SERVINGS ● ○

- 1 cup water
- 1 cup red wine vinegar
- ⅓ cup plus 1 tablespoon sugar
- 1 bay leaf
- ½ medium eggplant, peeled and cut into ¾-inch cubes
- ¼ cup finely chopped onion
- 1 tablespoon unsalted butter, softened

Salt and freshly ground pepper

- ¼ cup plus 2 tablespoons extra-virgin olive oil
- 6 plum tomatoes (1¼ pounds), cut into large chunks
- 3 garlic cloves, crushed
- 3 thyme sprigs
- 1 teaspoon fresh lemon juice

Four 6-ounce red snapper fillets

1. In a saucepan, combine the water, red wine vinegar, sugar and bay leaf; bring to a boil. Add the eggplant and onion and cook over moderately low heat, stirring occasionally, until the eggplant is tender but not falling apart, 20 minutes. Drain the eggplant and return it to the saucepan. Stir in the butter to coat and season with salt and pepper. Discard the bay leaf.

2. Meanwhile, in another saucepan, heat ¼ cup of the olive oil. Add the tomatoes, garlic, thyme and lemon juice and season with salt and pepper. Cook over moderate heat until thickened, about 20 minutes. Discard the thyme.

3. Preheat the broiler. Season the red snapper with salt and pepper. In a large nonstick ovenproof skillet, heat the remaining 2 tablespoons of olive oil until shimmering. Add the snapper fillets, skin side down, and cook over moderately high heat until browned, about 5 minutes. Transfer the skillet to the broiler and broil the fish until just cooked through, about 5 minutes longer. Spoon the eggplant onto plates, top with the snapper and serve with the tomato sauce. —*Terrance Brennan*

POMPANO WITH GINGER SAUCE

SAUTÉED SKATE WITH BROWN BUTTER

fish

Grilled Red Snapper with Sweet Garlic Barbecue Sauce

6 SERVINGS ●

In Thailand, variations on this simple but spectacular whole grilled fish turn up at beachfront grill shacks and upscale restaurants alike.

- 4 whole red snappers or black bass (about 1¾ pounds each), cleaned
- 8 medium garlic cloves, coarsely chopped
- ½ cup coarsely chopped cilantro
- 1 tablespoon salt
- 2 teaspoons ground coriander
- 2 teaspoons freshly ground white pepper

Vegetable oil
- 3 tablespoons Asian fish sauce
- 3 tablespoons fresh lime juice
- 1½ tablespoons sugar

Sweet Garlic Barbecue Sauce (recipe follows) and lime slices, for serving

1. Make 3 crosswise slashes down to the bone on both sides of each fish. Place the fish in 2 large shallow glass baking dishes.

2. In a mini food processor, pulse the garlic with the cilantro, salt, coriander and white pepper until finely chopped. With the machine on, slowly add 2 tablespoons of vegetable oil and process to a paste.

3. Slather the garlic-cilantro paste in the fish cavities and slashes and spread any extra paste over the skin; refrigerate for 1 hour.

4. In a small bowl, whisk the fish sauce with the lime juice, sugar and 3 tablespoons of vegetable oil. Set the mixture aside for basting.

5. Light a grill. Lightly oil the grate. Grill the prepared snapper, covered, over a medium-low fire for about 25 minutes, basting twice with the lime mixture and turning once, until cooked through. Transfer the snapper to a platter and fillet before serving with the Sweet Garlic Barbecue Sauce and lime slices.

—*Steven Raichlen*

SWEET GARLIC BARBEQUE SAUCE

MAKES ABOUT 1¼ CUPS ● ● ●

- ½ cup fresh lemon juice
- ½ cup Asian fish sauce
- ¼ cup honey
- 4 serrano or Thai chiles, chopped
- 3 tablespoons chopped cilantro
- 2 tablespoons chopped garlic
- ½ teaspoon freshly ground pepper

In a medium bowl, combine the lemon juice, fish sauce, honey, chiles, cilantro, garlic and pepper. Stir well and serve.

—*S.R.*

Fillet of Sole with Capers, Almonds and Lemon

4 SERVINGS ● ●

- 1 cup all-purpose flour

Salt and freshly ground pepper

Eight 3-ounce sole fillets
- 3½ tablespoons unsalted butter
- 2 tablespoons canola oil
- ¼ cup slivered almonds
- ¼ cup drained capers
- 1 small lemon, sliced crosswise paper-thin

1. Spread the flour in a pie plate and season with salt and pepper. Lightly dredge the sole fillets in the seasoned flour, tapping off the excess; transfer to a plate.

2. In a large skillet, melt 1 tablespoon of the butter in 1 tablespoon of the canola oil. Add half of the coated sole fillets and cook over high heat, turning once, until golden and crisp, 3 to 4 minutes. Transfer the sole to a platter, cover with foil and keep warm. Repeat the process with another 1 tablespoon each of butter and oil and the remaining sole fillets.

3. Add the remaining 1½ tablespoons of butter and the slivered almonds to the skillet. Cook over high heat, stirring frequently, until golden, about 2 minutes. Add the capers and lemon slices and cook until heated through, 1 minute longer. Spoon the sauce over the sole fillets and serve at once.

—*Kathy Gunst*

Lemon Sole with Tomato-Olive Risotto

4 SERVINGS ●

Four 6-ounce lemon sole fillets
- 1 teaspoon thyme leaves

Salt and freshly ground pepper
- ¼ cup balsamic vinegar
- 6½ cups chicken stock
- 1 teaspoon tomato paste
- 3 tablespoons extra-virgin olive oil
- 1 small onion, finely chopped
- 1 cup arborio rice
- ½ cup dry white wine
- 3 tablespoons unsalted butter
- ¼ cup chopped Gaeta olives
- ¼ cup chopped sun-dried tomatoes
- ¼ cup freshly grated Parmesan cheese
- 1 ounce baby arugula leaves

1. Sprinkle the fillets with the thyme and season with salt and pepper. Fold each fillet into thirds and refrigerate.

2. In a small saucepan, simmer the vinegar until reduced to 1 tablespoon. In a medium saucepan, bring the stock to a simmer. Stir in the tomato paste; cover and keep warm over low heat.

3. Heat 2 tablespoons of the olive oil in a large saucepan. Add the onion and cook over low heat, stirring, until softened. Stir in the rice until evenly coated. Add the wine; simmer over moderate heat, stirring, until fully absorbed. Add 1 cup of the hot stock and cook, stirring constantly, until almost absorbed. Add 5 more cups of stock, 1 cup at a time, stirring until absorbed between additions. The risotto is done when it is creamy and the rice is al dente, about 20 minutes total cooking time. Cover and keep warm.

4. In a medium skillet, heat the remaining 1 tablespoon of olive oil until shimmering. Add 2 tablespoons of the butter and then the sole, folded side down. Cook over moderate heat, basting often with the butter, until the sole is browned on the bottom, about 3 minutes. Reduce the heat to low, turn the fish over and baste again.

Cover and cook until the fish is white throughout, about 4 minutes longer.

5. Rewarm the risotto over moderate heat, then stir in the remaining ½ cup of stock. Add the olives, sun-dried tomatoes, Parmesan and the remaining 1 tablespoon of butter to the risotto and season with salt and pepper. Spoon the risotto into shallow bowls; set the fish on top and drizzle the reduced balsamic vinegar around it. Top the fish with the arugula and serve. —*Richard O'Connell*

Bacon-Wrapped Trout with Lemon Relish

4 SERVINGS ● ● ●

- 1 tablespoon extra-virgin olive oil
- 1 large garlic clove, thinly sliced
- 1 large lemon—peeled, pith removed, seeded and finely chopped

Salt and freshly ground pepper

- 12 strips of thick-cut smokehouse bacon

Four 6-ounce trout or fresh herring fillets, skinned

1. Heat the olive oil in a small skillet. Add the sliced garlic and cook over low heat until golden, about 1 minute. Add the chopped lemon and cook over moderate heat until slightly softened, about 2 minutes. Scrape the lemon relish into a small glass or stainless steel bowl and season with salt and pepper.

2. Wrap 3 slices of bacon around each trout or herring fillet. Secure the bacon with toothpicks.

3. Heat a large skillet over moderately high heat. Add the bacon-wrapped trout fillets and cook until the bacon is browned and crisp and the fish is just cooked through, 3 to 4 minutes per side. Transfer to plates, spoon the relish on top and serve. —*Marcia Kiesel*

MAKE AHEAD The lemon relish can be refrigerated overnight. Reheat gently before serving.

WINE Bright, citrusy Riesling.

Pan-Fried Trout with Peanuts and Lime

4 SERVINGS ●

- ¼ cup plus 1 tablespoon extra-virgin olive oil

Four 8-ounce trout fillets

Salt

Cayenne pepper

- 1 small head Bibb lettuce, finely shredded

Freshly ground black pepper

- 1 tablespoon unsalted butter
- ¾ cup dry-roasted peanuts
- ½ cup fresh lime juice
- 3 tablespoons plus 1 teaspoon mustard seeds

1. In a large skillet, heat ¼ cup of the olive oil until shimmering. Season the trout fillets with salt and a dash of cayenne. Add the fillets to the skillet, skin side down, and cook over moderate heat for 6 minutes. Cover the skillet and continue cooking the fillets for about 6 minutes longer, or until just opaque throughout. Transfer the fish to a platter and keep warm.

2. Add the lettuce to the skillet and stir-fry over high heat until wilted, about 30 seconds. Season with salt and black pepper. Spoon the lettuce over the trout and keep warm.

3. Add the butter and the remaining 1 tablespoon of olive oil to the skillet. Add the peanuts and cook over moderately high heat, stirring constantly, until golden, about 3 minutes. Add the lime juice and mustard seeds, season with salt and black pepper and cook, stirring constantly, for 15 seconds. Spoon the peanut mixture over the trout fillets and serve at once. —*Scott Ehrlich*

Lake Trout with Fingerling Potatoes and Bacon

4 SERVINGS

Unless you can catch the lake trout yourself, you will probably have to make the recipe with salmon fillets, which will work just as well.

- 20 fingerling potatoes (1½ pounds)
- ¼ pound thickly sliced bacon, cut crosswise into ½-inch strips
- 4 tablespoons unsalted butter
- 2 leeks, white and light green parts only, halved lengthwise and thinly sliced crosswise

Salt and freshly ground pepper

Four 5-ounce skinless lake trout fillets

- 1 teaspoon canola oil
- 1½ cups dry white wine
- 1 tablespoon chopped thyme

1. In a large saucepan of boiling salted water, cook the potatoes until tender, about 15 minutes. Drain.

2. In a medium skillet, cook the bacon over moderate heat until crisp, about 4 minutes. Drain on paper towels and wipe out the pan. Melt 1 tablespoon of the butter in the skillet, add the leeks and cook over low heat, stirring, until softened, about 6 minutes. Season with salt and pepper.

3. Heat a 12-inch cast-iron skillet. Season the trout with salt and pepper. Heat the oil in the skillet. Add the trout and cook over high heat until browned, about 3 minutes. Turn the trout. Add the wine, potatoes, leeks and the remaining 3 tablespoons of butter. Simmer over low heat until the trout is barely done, about 4 minutes. Transfer the fish to shallow bowls. Simmer the vegetables until the wine taste mellows, about 4 minutes. Add the bacon and thyme and season with salt and pepper. Spoon the vegetables and sauce around the trout and serve. —*Paul Kahan*

MAKE AHEAD The recipe can be prepared through Step 2 and refrigerated overnight. Bring to room temperature before proceeding.

Catfish with Pecan Brown Butter

4 SERVINGS ●

- 6 tablespoons unsalted butter

Four 6-ounce catfish fillets

Salt and freshly ground pepper

Pinch of cayenne pepper

- ⅓ cup all-purpose flour

fish

½ cup pecans, halved lengthwise

Finely grated zest of 1 lemon

2 teaspoons fresh lemon juice

Lemon wedges, for serving

1. Melt 2 tablespoons of the butter in a large skillet. Season the catfish fillets with salt and pepper and the cayenne. Coat the catfish lightly with flour, then add them to the skillet and cook over moderately high heat, turning once, until golden on both sides and cooked through, about 10 minutes. Transfer the catfish fillets to a platter; tent with foil and keep warm. Wipe out the skillet.

2. Melt the remaining 4 tablespoons of butter in the skillet. Add the pecans and cook over moderately high heat, until the pecans and butter are browned and fragrant, about 3 minutes. Stir in the lemon zest and juice and season with salt. Spoon the pecan butter over the catfish fillets and serve immediately with lemon wedges. —*Damon Lee Fowler*

WINE Dry, medium-bodied Pinot Gris.

Tuscan Fish Stew

4 SERVINGS ● ○

Four ¾-inch-thick slices of
   Tuscan bread

5 garlic cloves, 4 minced, 1 peeled

6 tablespoons extra-virgin olive oil

1 medium red onion,
   finely chopped

1 pound mussels, scrubbed
   and debearded

1 pound cockles or Manila
   clams, scrubbed

1 cup dry white wine

1 cup drained canned Italian
   peeled tomatoes, chopped

¼ cup finely chopped
   flat-leaf parsley

¾ pound thick, firm white-fleshed
   fish fillets, such as snapper,
   halibut or sea bass, cut into
   2-inch pieces

½ pound large shrimp, peeled
   and deveined

Salt and freshly ground pepper

1 cup water

1. Preheat the oven to 350°. Toast the bread on the oven rack for 8 minutes, turning once, until golden and crisp. Rub the toast with the peeled garlic and drizzle with 2 tablespoons of the olive oil. Turn off the heat and keep the toast warm in the oven with the door ajar.

2. In a large saucepan, heat the remaining ¼ cup of olive oil until shimmering. Add the onion and the minced garlic and cook over moderate heat, stirring, until golden, about 4 minutes. Add the mussels, cockles and wine and cook over high heat, stirring frequently, until most of the shellfish shells have opened and the liquid has reduced by half, 4 minutes. Add the chopped tomatoes and 3 tablespoons of the parsley, cover and bring to a boil.

3. Add the fish and shrimp and season with salt and pepper; bring to a boil. Add the water to slow the cooking. Simmer over moderately low heat until cooked through, 7 minutes. With a slotted spoon, transfer the seafood to a large, deep platter, cover and keep warm.

4. Boil the broth until reduced by one-fourth, 5 minutes, then pour it over the fish stew. Season the stew with salt and pepper, spoon into bowls and sprinkle with the remaining 1 tablespoon of parsley. Serve hot, with the garlicky toast. —*Pino Luongo*

Penne with Fish Sauce

4 SERVINGS ● ○

Any white-fleshed fish fillets can be used in this simple pasta.

¾ pound penne

¼ cup extra-virgin olive oil

1½ pounds swordfish, cut into
   2-by-½-inch strips

Salt and freshly ground pepper

1 medium onion, finely chopped

2 garlic cloves, minced

½ cup dry white wine

1 teaspoon finely grated lemon zest

1½ tablespoons fresh lemon juice

¼ cup coarsely chopped
   flat-leaf parsley

1. In a large pot of boiling salted water, cook the penne until al dente. Drain, reserving ½ cup of the pasta water.

2. Meanwhile, in a large, deep skillet, heat 2 tablespoons of the olive oil until shimmering. Season the swordfish with salt and pepper, add half to the skillet and cook over high heat until lightly browned on both sides and barely cooked through, about 2 minutes. Transfer to a large plate; repeat with 1 tablespoon of the olive oil and the remaining swordfish.

3. Add the remaining 1 tablespoon of olive oil to the skillet. Add the onion and garlic and cook over low heat, stirring occasionally, until softened, about 5 minutes. Add the wine and simmer over moderately high heat until almost evaporated, about 3 minutes. Stir in the lemon zest and juice, penne and the reserved pasta water. Fold in the swordfish and the parsley, season with salt and pepper and serve.

—*Paolo Fanciulli*

Provençal-Style Calamari Salad with Gremolata

4 SERVINGS ● ○

1 medium red bell pepper

1 medium yellow bell pepper

1 pound cleaned small calamari,
   preferably bodies only, cut into
   ⅓-inch rings

2 tablespoons red wine vinegar

½ teaspoon anchovy paste

Sea salt and freshly ground pepper

¼ cup plus 2 tablespoons
   extra-virgin olive oil

1 cup flat-leaf parsley leaves

1 tablespoon minced
   lemon zest

1 medium garlic clove, minced

¼ pound arugula

¼ cup chopped oil-packed sun-dried
   tomatoes, drained

¼ cup Niçoise olives, pitted
   and chopped

3 tablespoons chopped capers

1 small shallot, minced

PROVENÇAL-STYLE CALAMARI SALAD WITH GREMOLATA

1. Roast the red and yellow bell peppers directly over a gas flame or under the broiler until they are charred all over. Transfer the peppers to a bowl, cover with plastic wrap and let cool. Peel, core and seed the peppers, then cut them into ½-inch dice.

2. Prepare an ice-water bath. In a large saucepan of boiling salted water, cook the calamari over high heat until white and firm, about 1 minute. Drain and chill in the ice bath. Drain and pat dry.

3. In a small bowl, whisk the red wine vinegar with the anchovy paste and a generous pinch each of salt and pepper. Gradually whisk in the olive oil until the vinaigrette is emulsified.

4. On a work surface, mince the parsley leaves with the minced lemon zest and garlic. Transfer the gremolata to a small bowl.

5. In a large bowl, toss the arugula with 1 tablespoon of the vinaigrette. Season with salt and pepper and arrange on a large platter. Add the remaining vinaigrette to the bowl and toss with the roasted peppers, calamari, sundried tomatoes, olives, capers, shallot and 3 tablespoons of the gremolata. Season the salad with salt and pepper and spoon over the arugula. Sprinkle with the remaining gremolata and serve.
—*Michael Leviton*

WINE Aromatic, zesty Albariño.

---

cooking tip

cooking squid

THERE'S AN ART TO COOKING SQUID PROPERLY. When undercooked, squid has a rubbery texture, but when it's overcooked it can become as tough as shoe leather. A good rule of thumb is to cook squid very quickly over high heat (no more than a few minutes) or braise it slowly until it's tender. Just don't braise it too long or it dries out.

Spicy Squid Salad with Watercress and Lima Beans
4 SERVINGS
The large lima beans need to soak overnight, so plan accordingly.

- ¼ cup extra-virgin olive oil
- 4 garlic cloves, very finely chopped
- 1 jalapeño, seeded and finely chopped
- ½ habanero chile, seeded and minced
- ½ teaspoon finely grated lemon zest
- 1¼ pounds cleaned squid, bodies cut into ¼-inch-thick rings and large tentacles halved
- ½ pound dried large lima beans, soaked overnight and drained
- 1 bay leaf
- 4 thin strips of lean bacon, cut crosswise into ½-inch pieces
- 2 teaspoons Jan's Spice Mix (p. 328)
- ½ cup Calamata olives, pitted and halved

Lemon-Shallot Vinaigrette (p. 326)
- 1 pound watercress, large stems discarded (12 packed cups)

1. In a large glass baking dish, combine 3 tablespoons of the olive oil with the garlic, jalapeño, habanero and lemon zest. Add the squid and toss to coat. Cover and refrigerate for 1 hour.

2. Meanwhile, in a medium saucepan, cover the lima beans with 2 inches of water. Add the bay leaf and bring to a boil. Cover partially and simmer over low heat until the beans are tender, 40 to 50 minutes. Remove from the heat and let the beans stand in their cooking liquid. Drain just before using and discard the bay leaf.

3. In a large, deep skillet, heat the remaining 1 tablespoon of olive oil. Add the bacon pieces and cook over moderate heat until crisp, about 4 minutes. Using a slotted spoon, transfer the bacon to a paper towel–lined plate. Increase the heat to high and cook the bacon fat until sizzling. Add the squid

and its marinade in an even layer and cook, without stirring, until the squid begins to turn white, about 1 minute. Sprinkle the spice mix over the squid and cook, stirring, until just tender, about 1 minute. Gently fold in the bacon, lima beans and olives and cook just until warmed through. Stir in half of the Lemon-Shallot Vinaigrette and remove from the heat.

4. In a large bowl, toss the watercress with the remaining Lemon-Shallot Vinaigrette and transfer to individual plates. Top the watercress with the warm squid salad and serve at once.
—*Jan Birnbaum*

MAKE AHEAD The lima beans can be refrigerated overnight in their cooking liquid. Bring them to room temperature before draining and proceeding. Cook the marinated squid and finish the dish just before serving.

Calamari with Potatoes and Piment d'Espelette
6 FIRST-COURSE SERVINGS ●
- ½ pound fingerling potatoes, cut into ⅓-inch dice

Salt
- 6 ounces pancetta, sliced ¼ inch thick and cut into matchsticks
- 1 pound small cleaned calamari, bodies thinly sliced into rings
- 1 teaspoon piment d'Espelette (see Note)
- ¼ cup clam juice

1. In a small saucepan, cover the diced potatoes with 1 inch of cold water and bring to a boil. Lightly salt the potatoes and cook them until tender, about 8 minutes, then drain.

2. In a large skillet, cook the pancetta over moderately high heat, turning the slices occasionally, until browned and almost crisp, about 7 minutes. Add the boiled potatoes to the skillet. Cook, stirring occasionally, until lightly browned, about 5 more minutes. Add the calamari and cook until it turns

milky white, 1 to 2 minutes. Stir in the piment d'Espelette and clam juice and cook for 30 seconds longer. Season with salt and serve at once.
—*Pascal Rigo*

NOTE Piment d'Espelette is a sweet, mildly spicy ground pepper native to the Basque country. It is available at specialty food shops, spice shops and at Williams-Sonoma stores across the country (877-812-6235).

WINE Aromatic, zesty Albariño.

Octopus and Potato Salad

6 SERVINGS ● ●

- 1 medium onion, chopped
- 1 carrot, chopped
- 1 celery rib, chopped
- 4 quarts water

Kosher salt

- 1½ pounds octopus tentacles
- 1½ pounds large Yukon Gold potatoes
- 6 tablespoons finely chopped flat-leaf parsley
- 6 tablespoons extra-virgin olive oil

Freshly ground pepper

- 2 garlic cloves, very finely chopped
- 1 jalapeño, seeded and very finely chopped

I. In a large pot, combine the chopped onion, carrot, celery and water. Add a small handful of salt and bring to a boil. Add the octopus tentacles and simmer them over moderate heat until tender, about 45 minutes. Remove from the heat and let the octopus cool in the broth for 30 minutes. Drain the octopus tentacles.

2. Meanwhile, put the potatoes in a large saucepan, cover with cold water and bring to a boil. Cook until tender, about 30 minutes. Drain and let cool slightly. Peel the potatoes and cut them into ¾-inch pieces.

3. In a medium bowl, toss the potatoes with 3 tablespoons of the parsley and 3 tablespoons of the olive oil; season with salt and pepper.

4. Cut the octopus into ¾-inch pieces and transfer to a large bowl. Add the remaining 3 tablespoons of chopped parsley, 3 tablespoons of olive oil and the garlic and jalapeño. Season the octopus with salt and pepper and toss well to combine. Transfer the potato salad to a large platter. Spoon the octopus and dressing on top and serve warm or at room temperature.
—*Benedetta Vitali*

MAKE AHEAD The Octopus and Potato Salad can be refrigerated for up to 4 hours. Bring to room temperature before serving.

Potato and Smoked Mackerel Dauphinoise

4 SERVINGS

This is a seafood-spiked variation on the classic French gratin, pommes dauphinoise. You might need an accompanying bowl of salad leaves, perhaps arugula or baby spinach, to wipe up any mustardy, smoky cream that remains on your plate.

- 1 pound large new potatoes, peeled and cut into ⅛-inch-thick slices
- ½ pound smoked mackerel or smoked trout fillets, skin discarded, flesh broken into large pieces
- 2 bay leaves
- 2 cups heavy cream
- 1 tablespoon grainy mustard

Salt and freshly ground pepper

Preheat the oven to 375°. In an 8-by-10-inch oval gratin dish, gently toss the sliced potatoes with the smoked mackerel and the bay leaves. In a medium bowl, mix the heavy cream with the mustard and season with salt and pepper. Pour the cream mixture over the potatoes and fish and bake for about 1 hour, or until the cream has thickened and the potatoes are tender and golden on top. Discard the bay leaves and serve the gratin hot or warm.
—*Nigel Slater*

WINE Medium-bodied, round Pinot Blanc.

Golden Asian Fish Cakes with Spicy Slaw

4 FIRST-COURSE SERVINGS ●

Monkfish works well here, but any firm white fish can be used.

SLAW

- 2 medium carrots
- 1 medium sweet apple, such as Gala or Red Delicious
- 2 heads baby bok choy (1 pound), very thinly sliced crosswise
- ¼ cup fresh lime juice
- 2 tablespoons chopped basil
- 1 tablespoon very finely chopped shallots
- 1 tablespoon sugar
- 1 teaspoon hot chili sauce

Salt

FISH CAKES

- ½ pound monkfish fillet, cut into 1-inch pieces
- ¼ cup cilantro leaves
- 1 egg, lightly beaten
- 1 tablespoon cornstarch
- 1 stalk fresh lemongrass, tender inner bulb only, chopped
- 2 teaspoons Asian fish sauce

Salt and freshly ground pepper

- 3 tablespoons vegetable oil

I. MAKE THE SLAW: In a food processor, julienne the carrots and apple; transfer to a bowl. Stir in the bok choy, lime juice, basil, shallots, sugar and chili sauce and season with salt.

2. MAKE THE FISH CAKES: In a food processor, pulse the monkfish with the cilantro, egg, cornstarch, lemongrass and fish sauce until smooth; season with salt and pepper. Using moist hands, pat the mixture into 8 cakes.

3. In a medium nonstick skillet, heat the oil until shimmering. Add the fish cakes and cook over moderately high heat until golden brown, about 7 minutes per side; transfer to paper towels to drain.

4. Set 2 fish cakes on each plate; serve the slaw alongside. —*Wendy Kalen*

MAKE AHEAD The formed fish cakes can be refrigerated for 1 day.

WINE Lively, assertive Sauvignon Blanc.

GRILLED SEAFOOD PAELLA, P. 193

shellfish

GRILLED JUMBO SHRIMP WITH GARLIC-HERB BUTTER

PAN-SEARED SHRIMP WITH HOT CHORIZO BUTTER

Grilled Shrimp with Shallots and Fresh Thyme

6 SERVINGS ● ●

1¼ cups extra-virgin olive oil

½ cup fresh lemon juice

½ cup light soy sauce

6 small shallots, finely chopped (about ⅔ cup)

⅓ cup thyme leaves, chopped

1 teaspoon Tabasco sauce

Salt and freshly ground pepper

2 pounds peeled and deveined medium shrimp

Mesclun and crusty bread, for serving

1. In a large glass or ceramic baking dish, combine the olive oil with the lemon juice, soy sauce, shallots, thyme and Tabasco. Season the marinade with salt and pepper. Thread the shrimp onto skewers, then arrange them in the marinade and let the skewered shrimp stand for 15 minutes.

2. Light a grill or preheat a grill pan. Cook the shrimp over moderately high heat, turning once, until just cooked through, about 3 minutes.

3. Transfer the shrimp marinade to a small saucepan and bring to a boil over moderately high heat. Remove the shrimp from their skewers and brush them lightly with the marinade. Arrange the mesclun on a serving platter and top with the shrimp. Spoon some of the marinade over the shrimp and serve at once with bread. —*Ann Chantal Altman*

Grilled Jumbo Shrimp with Garlic-Herb Butter

4 FIRST-COURSE SERVINGS ● ●

The best way to eat these shrimp in the shell is to peel them at the table and lick the garlicky butter off your fingers.

1 stick (4 ounces) unsalted butter

¼ cup finely chopped parsley

¼ cup finely chopped basil

3 garlic cloves, finely chopped

1 shallot, finely chopped

16 jumbo shrimp in the shell, preferably with heads left on

Salt and freshly ground pepper

White rum, for sprinkling (optional)

1. In a small saucepan, combine the butter with the parsley, basil, garlic and shallot and melt over low heat.

2. Light a grill or preheat a grill pan. Halve the shrimp lengthwise, leaving them attached 1 inch below the head. Devein the shrimp and spread them open. Season with salt and pepper, then brush liberally with the melted herb butter.

3. Grill the shrimp over a medium-hot fire, shell side down, until lightly charred, about 1 minute. Turn and grill the other side until lightly browned, about 40 seconds. Turn the shrimp once again. Brush them liberally with more herb butter, sprinkle with rum and grill until barely cooked through and bubbling, about 1 minute longer. Serve at once. —*Eric Ripert*

MAKE AHEAD The garlic-herb butter can be refrigerated overnight. Melt the butter before using.

WINE Dry, light, refreshing Soave.

Grilled Shrimp with Lemon-Basil Pesto

6 SERVINGS ● ●

This lemony pesto is also good with chicken, fish or scallops.

- 2 tablespoons pine nuts
- 3 cups packed basil leaves
- 2 garlic cloves, very finely chopped
- 2 tablespoons fresh lemon juice
- 4 teaspoons finely grated lemon zest
- ½ cup extra-virgin olive oil
- ⅓ cup freshly grated Parmigiano-Reggiano cheese

Salt and freshly ground pepper

1½ pounds jumbo shrimp, shelled and deveined

Lemon wedges, for serving

1. In a small skillet, toast the pine nuts over moderate heat, shaking the pan occasionally, until golden brown, about 2 minutes; let cool.

2. In a food processor, pulse the pine nuts with the basil leaves, garlic, lemon juice, lemon zest and 6 tablespoons of the olive oil until combined. Add the Parmigiano-Reggiano cheese and pulse until smooth. Scrape the pesto into a bowl and season with salt and pepper.

3. Light a grill or preheat a cast-iron grill pan. Thread 2 or 3 shrimp on each of 6 skewers; brush with the remaining 2 tablespoons of oil. Season the shrimp with salt and pepper and grill over a medium-hot fire until opaque and cooked through, about 2 minutes per side. Serve the shrimp hot, with the pesto and lemon wedges. —*Joanne Weir*

WINE Lively, assertive Sauvignon Blanc.

Black Pepper Shrimp

4 SERVINGS ●

- 2 tablespoons extra-virgin olive oil
- 1 tablespoon finely ground black pepper
- 1 tablespoon ground coriander
- 1 pound large shrimp, shelled and deveined
- 1 tablespoon fresh lime juice

Sea salt

1. In a large shallow dish, combine the olive oil, pepper and coriander. Add the shrimp and turn to coat well. Cover and refrigerate overnight.

2. Light a grill or heat a grill pan over high heat. Stir the lime juice into the shrimp and season with salt. Grill the shrimp until just cooked through, about 3 minutes per side. Serve hot. —*Floyd Cardoz*

Spicy Shrimp with Citrus Avocado Sauce

4 SERVINGS ● ●

- 1 Hass avocado, peeled
- 1 garlic clove, minced
- 2 tablespoons fresh orange juice
- 1 tablespoon plus 1 teaspoon fresh lime juice

Cayenne pepper

Salt

- ¼ cup extra-virgin olive oil
- 1 tablespoon grated orange zest
- 1 tablespoon ground allspice
- 1 tablespoon molasses
- 2 teaspoons finely grated lime zest
- 2 pounds shelled and deveined large shrimp

1. In a blender, puree the avocado with the garlic, orange juice and lime juice. Season with cayenne and salt. With the machine on, gradually blend in 2 tablespoons of the olive oil.

2. Light a grill or heat a grill pan. In a medium bowl, mix the remaining 2 tablespoons of olive oil with the orange zest, allspice, molasses and lime zest. Season with cayenne and salt. Add the shrimp and toss to coat.

3. Grill the shrimp over moderately high heat until just cooked through, about 3 minutes per side. Transfer the shrimp to a platter and serve the avocado sauce on the side. —*Scott Ehrlich*

Pan-Seared Shrimp with Hot Chorizo Butter

4 SERVINGS ● ●

Chorizo makes this shrimp smoky and moderately hot. The spectacular Spanish paprika called pimentón picante adds another layer of smoke and spice.

- 2 hot chorizo sausages (5 ounces)
- 1 stick (4 ounces) unsalted butter, softened
- 2 scallions, coarsely chopped
- ¾ teaspoon pimentón picante (see Note) or hot paprika

Salt

1¾ pounds medium shrimp, shelled and deveined

- 3 tablespoons brandy
- 2 tablespoons water

Lemon wedges and crusty bread, for serving

1. In a small saucepan, cover the chorizo with water and bring to a boil. Simmer over moderate heat for 5 minutes, then drain. Thinly slice 1 of the sausages and finely chop the other.

2. In a medium bowl, blend the butter with the scallions, pimentón and chopped chorizo and season with salt.

3. In a large skillet, cook the sliced chorizo over very low heat until the fat is rendered, about 4 minutes. Add the shrimp and cook over moderate heat until barely pink, about 2 minutes per side. Add the brandy, tip the skillet and, using a long match, carefully ignite the brandy. When the flames die down, add the chorizo butter and cook, stirring, until just melted, about 2 minutes. Remove the skillet from the heat and stir in the water to make a creamy sauce.

4. Transfer the shrimp and sauce to a shallow serving dish and garnish with the lemon wedges. Serve at once with crusty bread. —*Marcia Kiesel*

shellfish

NOTE Pimentón picante can be mail-ordered from the Spanish Table (206-682-2827; www.spanishtable.com).
MAKE AHEAD The chorizo butter can be frozen for up to 1 month.
WINE Bright, fruity rosé.

Shrimp in Black Bean Sauce

4 SERVINGS ● ●

1½ pounds shelled and deveined
    medium shrimp
1 tablespoon cornstarch
2 tablespoons peanut oil
One 2-inch piece of ginger, peeled and
    julienned, plus 1½ tablespoons
    minced ginger
8 scallions, white and light
    green parts only, cut into
    1½-inch lengths
¼ teaspoon hot chili oil
2½ tablespoons Chinese black beans,
    rinsed and coarsely chopped
¼ cup soy sauce
⅓ cup water
1 tablespoon rice vinegar
White rice, for serving

1. In a medium bowl, toss the shrimp with the cornstarch.
2. In a wok, heat the peanut oil until shimmering. Add the minced ginger, half of the scallions and the chili oil and stir-fry over high heat for 30 seconds. Add the shrimp and julienned ginger; stir-fry for 1 minute. Add the remaining scallions and the black beans.

---

cooking tip

shrimp stock

TO MAKE SHRIMP STOCK FOR USE IN SOUPS, STEWS AND RISOTTOS, place shrimp shells in a saucepan and cover with cold water. Add 1 bay leaf and a dollop of tomato paste. Simmer over moderately low heat for 20 minutes. Strain the stock into a bowl and use at once or refrigerate for up to 2 days.

Stir in the soy, water and vinegar. Simmer until the sauce is slightly thickened, about 2 minutes. Serve with white rice. —*Kathy Gunst*

Kung Pao Shrimp with Cashews

4 SERVINGS ● ●

¼ cup fresh orange juice
3 tablespoons red wine vinegar
1½ tablespoons soy sauce
1 tablespoon sugar
1½ teaspoons cornstarch
2 tablespoons vegetable oil
8 small dried red chiles, 4 halved
½ teaspoon salt
1 onion, cut into 1-inch pieces
1½ teaspoons minced fresh ginger
2 large garlic cloves, minced
½ red bell pepper, cut into
    1-inch pieces
½ green bell pepper, cut into
    1-inch pieces
1 pound shelled and deveined
    large shrimp
1 cup roasted cashews
½ teaspoon Asian sesame oil

1. In a bowl, mix the orange juice, vinegar, soy sauce, sugar and cornstarch.
2. In a wok, heat the oil over high heat until smoking. Add the chiles and salt; stir-fry until browned, 45 seconds. Add the onion, ginger and garlic; stir-fry until fragrant, 15 seconds. Add the peppers and cook until crisp-tender, 30 seconds. Add the shrimp and stir-fry until nearly cooked through, about 5 minutes. Stir the sauce, add to the wok and cook until thickened slightly, 30 seconds. Stir in the cashews and sesame oil; serve. —*Joyce Jue*

Nyonya Grilled Shrimp with Coconut Sauce

6 SERVINGS

To the Chinese immigrants who moved to Malaysia and Singapore in the nineteenth century, *nyonya* meant grandmother. Now it usually refers to a cooking style that combines common ingredients from Malaysia and China.

SHRIMP

2¼ pounds large shrimp, shelled
    and deveined
3 medium garlic cloves, chopped
One ¾-inch piece of peeled fresh
    ginger, chopped
2 tablespoons Worcestershire
    sauce
1 tablespoon ground coriander
1½ teaspoons curry powder
¼ teaspoon ground cloves
1 large jalapeño, seeded
    and chopped
Vegetable oil
Salt and freshly ground pepper

COCONUT SAUCE

6 medium shallots, chopped
6 jalapeños, seeded and chopped
3 stalks fresh lemongrass, tender
    white inner bulbs only, chopped
6 medium garlic cloves, chopped
4 teaspoons chopped fresh ginger
¾ teaspoon turmeric
¾ teaspoon freshly ground pepper
3 tablespoons vegetable oil
¾ cup unsweetened coconut milk
¼ cup fresh lime juice
4 teaspoons light brown sugar
1 tablespoon soy sauce
Salt

1. MARINATE THE SHRIMP: Soak twelve 12-inch bamboo skewers in warm water for 30 minutes. Thread the shrimp ½ inch apart on pairs of parallel skewers and place in a shallow baking dish.
2. In a blender or food processor, puree the garlic, ginger, Worcestershire sauce, coriander, curry powder, cloves, jalapeño and ½ cup of oil. Season with salt and pepper. Pour the marinade over the shrimp and turn to coat. Cover and refrigerate for 30 minutes, turning once.
3. MAKE THE COCONUT SAUCE: In a food processor, combine the shallots, jalapeños, lemongrass, garlic, ginger, turmeric and pepper; pulse until minced. In a medium skillet, heat the oil until shimmering. Add the shallot mixture and cook over moderate heat until fragrant and light golden, about 3

minutes. Add the coconut milk, lime juice, brown sugar, soy sauce and a pinch of salt and simmer for 4 minutes. If the sauce separates, return to the food processor and process until it comes together. Scrape into a bowl.

4. Light a grill. Lightly oil the grate. Grill the shrimp over a medium-hot fire until just cooked through, about 2 minutes per side. Transfer to plates and serve with the sauce. —*Steven Raichlen*

Garlicky Shrimp Tacos

4 SERVINGS ●

¼ cup sun-dried tomatoes

Heaping ¼ teaspoon dried thyme

Heaping ¼ teaspoon dried marjoram

Heaping ¼ teaspoon dried tarragon

Heaping ¼ teaspoon cayenne pepper

Salt

1 tablespoon unsalted butter

2½ tablespoons extra-virgin olive oil

8 garlic cloves, minced

3 plum tomatoes, diced

1 pound cooked and peeled small bay shrimp

¼ cup finely chopped cilantro

8 taco shells or warmed 6-inch corn tortillas

2 Hass avocados, cut into ⅓-inch dice

Salsa and lime wedges, for serving

1. In a bowl, cover the sun-dried tomatoes with hot water and let stand for 5 minutes. Drain, pat dry and finely chop.

2. In a small bowl, combine the thyme, marjoram, tarragon, cayenne and ¼ teaspoon of salt.

3. In a large skillet, melt the butter in the olive oil over moderate heat. Add the garlic and cook until fragrant, about 30 seconds. Add the fresh and sun-dried tomatoes and the herb mixture and cook for 2 minutes, stirring. Add the shrimp and cilantro and cook until the shrimp are just heated through.

4. Fill the taco shells or tortillas with the shrimp mixture and top with the diced avocados. Serve the tacos with salsa and lime wedges. —*Jim Peyton*

Low-Country Shrimp and Rice

4 SERVINGS ●

1 cup long-grain rice

2 cups water

Salt

5 tablespoons unsalted butter

1 medium onion, finely chopped

1 garlic clove, minced

1 pound medium shrimp, shelled and deveined

Cayenne pepper

1 tablespoon finely chopped flat-leaf parsley

1. Place the rice in a colander and rinse in cold water; drain. In a medium saucepan, bring the water to a boil and season lightly with salt. Stir in the rice and bring to a boil over high heat. Reduce heat to low, cover and simmer for 15 minutes. Remove the saucepan from the heat and let stand, covered, for 5 minutes, then fluff the rice with a fork.

2. Meanwhile, melt the butter in a large skillet. Add the onion and cook over moderately high heat, stirring frequently, until golden brown, about 7 minutes. Add the garlic and cook for 30 seconds. Add the shrimp and a pinch of cayenne and cook, stirring, until the shrimp are opaque, about 3 minutes; season with salt. Remove the skillet from the heat and stir in the rice. Transfer the shrimp and rice to a platter, sprinkle with the parsley and serve. —*Damon Lee Fowler*

WINE Light, soft Chenin Blanc.

Frogmore Stew with Shrimp and Andouille

4 SERVINGS

1 tablespoon plus 1 teaspoon unsalted butter

1 tablespoon extra-virgin olive oil

1 large leek, white and tender green part only, finely diced

1 celery rib, peeled and finely diced

1 garlic clove, minced

4 plum tomatoes, coarsely chopped

1 teaspoon finely grated lemon zest

1 tablespoon thyme leaves

1 tablespoon chopped flat-leaf parsley

2 ears of corn, shucked, each cut crosswise into 4 rounds

16 small new potatoes, scrubbed

3 cups fish or shrimp stock or 1½ cups bottled clam juice mixed with 1½ cups water

1 cup tomato juice

½ tablespoon Old Bay seasoning

1½ pounds large shrimp, shelled and deveined

¾ pound andouille sausage, cut on the diagonal into ½-inch rounds

1 small lemon, thinly sliced

Salt and freshly ground pepper

½ bunch watercress, stemmed

4 thick slices of grilled country bread, for serving

In a large enameled cast-iron casserole, melt 1 teaspoon of the butter in the olive oil. Add the leek, celery and garlic and cook over low heat until softened, about 5 minutes. Add the tomatoes, lemon zest, thyme, parsley, corn, potatoes, fish stock, tomato juice and Old Bay seasoning and bring to a boil. Cover and simmer until the corn and potatoes are almost tender, about 5 minutes. Add the shrimp, sausage and lemon slices, cover and simmer until the shrimp are just cooked through, about 5 minutes. Remove from the heat, stir in the remaining 1 tablespoon of butter and season with salt and pepper. Ladle the stew into bowls, garnish with the watercress and serve with the grilled bread. —*Hugh Acheson*

Watermelon Salad with Grilled Shrimp

4 SERVINGS ●

CUCUMBER WATER

2 large cucumbers (about 1¼ pounds)—peeled, seeded and coarsely chopped

2 tablespoons sugar

2 tablespoons rice vinegar

1 tablespoon kosher salt

SANTORINI SALAD WITH GRILLED SHRIMP

ASIAN SHRIMP SALAD

SALAD

2	cups diced (½ inch) seedless red watermelon
2	cups diced (½ inch) seedless yellow watermelon
1½	pounds red tomatoes, seeded and cut into ½-inch dice
1	large cucumber—peeled, seeded and cut into ½-inch dice
½	cup minced shallots
¼	cup extra-virgin olive oil
3½	tablespoons fresh lemon juice
2	tablespoons chopped tarragon
1	pound large shrimp, shelled and deveined
¼	cup pure olive oil

Salt and freshly ground pepper

2 cups baby salad greens

1. MAKE THE CUCUMBER WATER: In a blender, puree the cucumbers with the sugar, rice vinegar and salt. Strain the puree through a fine sieve set over a medium bowl. Refrigerate the cucumber water until chilled.

2. MAKE THE SALAD: In a large bowl, toss the red and yellow watermelon with the tomatoes, cucumber, shallots, extra-virgin olive oil, lemon juice and tarragon. Cover and refrigerate for at least 2 hours and for up to 6 hours.

3. Shortly before serving, light a grill or heat a grill pan. In a large bowl, toss the shrimp with the pure olive oil and season with salt and pepper. Grill the shrimp over high heat until browned and just cooked, about 3 minutes per side.

4. Spoon the watermelon salad into 4 shallow bowls. Arrange the grilled shrimp on top. Ladle the cucumber water into each bowl, top with the baby salad greens and serve. —*Grant Achatz*

MAKE AHEAD The cucumber water can be made up to 1 day ahead. Stir before adding to the salad.

Shrimp Salad with Red Grapes

4 FIRST-COURSE SERVINGS ● ● ●

1½	tablespoons fresh lemon juice
¾	teaspoon sugar
¼	teaspoon cayenne pepper

Salt

3 tablespoons pure olive oil

1 large shallot, thinly sliced

¼ teaspoon mustard seeds

1 garlic clove, minced

1 pound medium shrimp, shelled and deveined

Freshly ground pepper

1 cup (6 ounces) red seedless grapes, halved

1 tablespoon chopped cilantro

I. In a small bowl, combine the lemon juice with the sugar, cayenne and ½ teaspoon of salt.

2. In a large skillet, heat the olive oil. Add the thinly sliced shallot and cook over moderately low heat, stirring a few times, until browned and crisp, about 4 minutes. With a slotted spoon, transfer the shallot to a plate.

3. Add the mustard seeds to the skillet and cook over moderate heat until they just begin to pop, about 10 seconds. Add the garlic and shrimp, season with salt and pepper and cook, stirring, until opaque, about 3 minutes. Transfer the shrimp to a bowl and stir in the grapes, cilantro, lemon dressing and half of the fried shallot. Sprinkle the remaining fried shallot on top of the salad and serve at once. —*Madhur Jaffrey*

Santorini Salad with Grilled Shrimp

4 SERVINGS ●

In parts of Greece, the traditional feta and vegetable salad is prepared without any vinegar; it simply gets a drizzle of fruity olive oil.

2 tablespoons fresh lemon juice

1 tablespoon chopped shallots

¼ cup plus 1 tablespoon extra-virgin olive oil

1 tablespoon plus 1 teaspoon chopped oregano

Salt and freshly ground pepper

1 pound large shrimp, shelled and deveined

1 cucumber—halved, seeded and cut into ½-inch dice

¾ pound cherry or grape tomatoes, halved

1 small green bell pepper, cut into ½-inch dice

1 small yellow bell pepper, cut into ½-inch dice

12 Calamata olives, pitted

2 teaspoons finely grated lemon zest

½ pound Greek or French feta cheese, cut horizontally into 4 slabs

I. In a medium bowl, combine the lemon juice with the shallots, 1 tablespoon of the olive oil and 1 teaspoon of the oregano; season with salt and pepper. Add the shrimp, toss well and let stand at room temperature for 10 minutes.

2. In a bowl, combine the cucumber with the tomatoes, bell peppers, olives, lemon zest and the remaining 1 tablespoon of oregano. Season the salad with salt and pepper and toss well.

3. Light a grill or preheat a grill pan. Thread the shrimp onto 4 skewers and grill over moderate heat, turning once, until cooked through, about 3 minutes.

4. Mound the salad on plates and top with the feta. Drizzle each salad with 1 tablespoon of the olive oil and sprinkle with salt. Remove the shrimp from the skewers, arrange alongside the salad and serve. —*Wendy Kalen*

WINE Lively, assertive Sauvignon Blanc.

Asian Shrimp Salad with Snow Peas, Jicama and Bell Peppers

6 SERVINGS ● ●

½ cup vegetable oil

1½ pounds shelled rock shrimp or medium shrimp (split lengthwise)

3 tablespoons oyster sauce

2 tablespoons red wine vinegar

1½ teaspoons Dijon mustard

1 tablespoon chopped fresh ginger

1 garlic clove, coarsely chopped

½ pound snow peas

1 medium jicama (¾ pound), peeled and cut into matchsticks

1 red bell pepper, thinly sliced

1 yellow bell pepper, thinly sliced

½ red onion, halved and thinly sliced

Salt and freshly ground pepper

¼ cup chopped cilantro

Lemon wedges, for serving

I. In a large nonstick skillet, heat 1 tablespoon of the oil over high heat. Add half of the shrimp and sauté until opaque and just cooked through, about 3 minutes; transfer to a large plate. Repeat with another 1 tablespoon of oil and the remaining shrimp; let cool.

2. In a blender, puree the oyster sauce with the vinegar, mustard, ginger and garlic. With the blender on, add the remaining 6 tablespoons of oil.

3. Bring a medium saucepan of salted water to a boil. Add the snow peas and cook until bright green, about 1½ minutes. Drain the snow peas, refresh under cold water and pat dry.

4. In a serving bowl, combine the snow peas, jicama, peppers, onion and shrimp. Add the dressing, toss well and season with salt and pepper. Sprinkle on the cilantro and serve with lemon wedges. —*Ann Chantal Altman*

Grilled Seafood Paella

6 SERVINGS ●

You can substitute fish stock or three parts bottled clam juice diluted with one part water for the shrimp stock. After adding the broth, don't stir the paella again; that way a deliciously crisp crust can form on the bottom. It's important to have all the ingredients and two heavy-duty oven mitts ready grillside before you start.

BROTH

2 tablespoons vegetable oil

Shells reserved from the 1½ pounds medium shrimp

1 medium onion, thinly sliced

1 small carrot, thinly sliced

3 tablespoons tomato paste

¼ cup dry sherry

2 quarts water

6 large garlic cloves, chopped

4 thyme sprigs

2 bay leaves

1 large chipotle chile in adobo

Large pinch of saffron

Salt

PAELLA

2 tablespoons extra-virgin olive oil

4 scallions, cut into 1-inch lengths

1 small onion, finely chopped

1 large poblano chile—stemmed, seeded and cut into ½-inch dice

1¾ cups short-grain Spanish rice, such as Valencia or Bomba

2 medium tomatoes, chopped

1 cup corn kernels

½ pound green beans, preferably flat Romano, cut into 1-inch lengths

1 teaspoon kosher salt

Large handful of woody herb sprigs, such as rosemary or thyme

1½ pounds medium shrimp, shelled and deveined

1½ pounds small mussels, scrubbed and debearded

1. MAKE THE BROTH: In a large saucepan, heat the oil. Add the shrimp shells; cook over moderate heat, stirring, until browned, 5 minutes. Add the onion and carrot and cook until the onion begins to brown, 5 minutes longer. Stir in the tomato paste and cook for 2 minutes, stirring. Add the sherry, boil for 1 minute, then add the water and return to a boil. Stir in the garlic, thyme, bay leaves, chipotle and saffron; simmer over low heat for 25 minutes.

2. Strain the broth into a saucepan, pressing on the solids to extract liquid. You should have 6 cups. Season with salt. Cover and keep warm over low heat.

3. MAKE THE PAELLA: Light a grill. If using charcoal, build a large fire that will last at least 30 minutes. Start more coals in a chimney starter in case the fire isn't sufficient to finish cooking the paella. If using a gas grill, set the center burner on high heat and the side or front and back burners on low.

4. Place a large paella pan or a 14-inch stainless steel roasting pan over a medium-hot fire. Add the oil and heat until sizzling. Add the scallions, onion and poblano and cook over a low fire, stirring, until the vegetables soften, about 5 minutes. Add the rice and cook, stirring, for 2 minutes. Add the tomatoes, corn, beans and salt and stir.

5. Add the hot broth to the rice; shake the pan to smooth the surface. If using charcoal, scatter the herbs over the coals. If using a gas grill, place the herbs in a smoker box or scatter over the heat bars; reduce the heat to moderately low. Cover the grill and simmer the paella, shaking the pan once or twice, until the broth is absorbed and the rice is al dente, about 20 minutes. Add hot coals to the fire if it starts to fade.

6. Scatter the shrimp over the rice and nestle the mussels in it, hinge side down. Cover the grill; cook until the shrimp are pink and the mussels open, about 5 minutes. Discard any mussels that do not open. Transfer the paella to bowls, scraping up the crusty rice from the pan, and serve. —*Marcia Kiesel*

WINE Aromatic, zesty Albariño.

Mussels in Tomato Sauce with Sausage

6 SERVINGS

10 ounces pork sausage, casings removed

2 tablespoons extra-virgin olive oil

½ medium white onion, minced

1 medium red bell pepper, cut into ½-inch dice

1 medium fennel bulb (about 1 pound)—halved, cored and cut into ½-inch dice

1 garlic clove, minced

2¼ cups tomato sauce

¼ cup clam juice or fish stock

Salt and freshly ground pepper

2 pounds mussels, scrubbed and debearded

2 dill sprigs, coarsely chopped

Grilled country bread, for serving

1. In a skillet, cook the sausage over moderately high heat, breaking it up, until crisp, about 15 minutes. Transfer to a plate. Wipe out the skillet.

2. Heat the oil in the skillet until shimmering. Add the onion and cook over moderately high heat until translucent, about 3 minutes. Add the red pepper and fennel and cook over low heat until just tender, about 15 minutes.

3. Add the garlic, tomato sauce and clam juice and season with salt and pepper. Bring to a simmer, then add the mussels and the reserved sausage. Cover and cook over moderately high heat until the mussels open, about 10 minutes. Discard any unopened mussels. Season with dill and serve at once with grilled bread. —*Pascal Rigo*

WINE Tangy, crisp Vernaccia.

Wok-Seared Scallops with Tangerine Sauce

4 SERVINGS ● ●

1 teaspoon cornstarch

Salt

1 pound sea scallops

3 tablespoons tangerine juice, plus 1 tablespoon minced tangerine zest

1 tablespoon hoisin sauce

1 tablespoon red wine vinegar

1 tablespoon soy sauce

1 teaspoon dark brown sugar

1 teaspoon chile-garlic paste

1 large garlic clove, minced

1 teaspoon minced fresh ginger

3 tablespoons vegetable oil

1 medium zucchini, halved lengthwise and thinly sliced crosswise on the diagonal

1 medium yellow squash, halved lengthwise and thinly sliced crosswise on the diagonal

1 small carrot, thinly sliced on the diagonal

4 water chestnuts, finely chopped (optional)

MUSSELS IN TOMATO SAUCE WITH SAUSAGE

shellfish

1. In a large bowl, mix the cornstarch with ½ teaspoon of salt. Add the scallops and toss to coat.

2. In a small bowl, mix the tangerine juice with the hoisin sauce, vinegar, soy sauce, brown sugar and chile-garlic paste. In another small bowl, combine the tangerine zest with the minced garlic and ginger.

3. In a wok, heat 1½ tablespoons of the vegetable oil over high heat until smoking. Add the coated scallops in a single layer and cook without stirring until they are golden on the bottom, about 3 minutes. Turn and cook until the scallops are firm and nicely browned, about 1½ minutes longer. Transfer the scallops to a plate.

4. Add the remaining 1½ tablespoons of vegetable oil to the wok along with the tangerine zest mixture and cook until fragrant, about 30 seconds. Add the sliced zucchini, squash and carrot and the water chestnuts and cook, stirring frequently, until the vegetables are crisp-tender, about 4 minutes. Stir the tangerine sauce and add it to the wok. Cook the sauce until slightly thickened, about 30 seconds longer. Return the scallops to the wok, stirring just until heated through, and serve at once.
—*Joyce Jue*

Scallops with Shiitake in Lapsang Souchong Broth

4 SERVINGS ● ●

Lapsang souchong, a variety of black tea, gives this dish a smoky aroma—the broth smells like bacon as it cooks.

- 1 cup brewed Lapsang souchong tea, at room temperature
- 1 tablespoon soy sauce
- 1 teaspoon sugar
- 1 teaspoon cornstarch
- 3 tablespoons peanut oil
- 1 pound large sea scallops
- Salt
- 2 teaspoons minced garlic
- 1 teaspoon minced peeled ginger

- ½ pound shiitake mushrooms, stems discarded and caps thinly sliced
- 12 scallions, white and tender green parts, cut into 1½-inch lengths

1. In a medium bowl, stir together the tea with the soy sauce and sugar. Pour ¼ cup of this broth into a small bowl and whisk in the cornstarch until no lumps remain.

2. In a large, heavy skillet, heat 1 tablespoon of the oil until shimmering. Season the scallops with salt. Add them to the skillet in a single layer and cook over high heat until golden on the bottom, about 4 minutes. Turn the scallops and cook for 1 minute longer. Transfer the scallops to the medium bowl with the lapsang souchong broth.

3. Return the skillet to high heat. Add the remaining 2 tablespoons of oil and the garlic and ginger and cook, stirring, for 5 seconds. Add the shiitake and scallions and cook, stirring frequently, until lightly browned, about 2 minutes. Add the scallops and their broth and bring to a simmer, scraping up any bits from the bottom of the skillet. Whisk the cornstarch mixture, add it to the scallops and cook until the broth thickens slightly, about 2 minutes. Serve the scallops in shallow bowls. —*Suki Hertz*
SERVE WITH Brown rice.

Scallop and Corn Bacon Burgers with Spicy Mayo

6 SERVINGS ● ●

Scallops make incredibly juicy burgers despite their low fat content. To keep the burgers moist, don't overcook them; there should be a thin layer of barely cooked scallop at the center.

- ½ cup mayonnaise
- 3 tablespoons ketchup
- Tabasco sauce
- Kosher salt and freshly ground pepper
- 3 ears of corn, shucked
- 1½ pounds sea scallops, coarsely chopped

- Vegetable oil
- 6 soft hamburger buns, split
- 6 lettuce leaves
- 6 thick tomato slices
- 12 slices of cooked thick-cut bacon

1. In a small bowl, blend the mayonnaise with the ketchup. Season with Tabasco, salt and pepper. Refrigerate until ready to serve.

2. In a medium saucepan of boiling water, cook the corn until tender, about 4 minutes. Transfer to a plate and let cool slightly. Working over the plate, cut the kernels from the cobs; you'll need 1½ cups of corn kernels.

3. In a food processor, process ¾ cup of the corn kernels to a paste. Add one-third of the scallops, 1½ teaspoons of salt and ½ teaspoon of pepper and process to a paste. Add the remaining scallops and process until just blended; there should be small lumps of scallop in the mixture. Scrape the mixture into a medium bowl and stir in the remaining ¾ cup of corn kernels. With oiled hands, pat the mixture into burgers, then cover and refrigerate them until ready to grill.

4. Light a grill. Toast the hamburger buns over a medium-hot fire, about 10 seconds. Brush the scallop burgers with vegetable oil and grill them over a medium-hot fire until they are nicely charred and barely cooked in the center, about 4 minutes per side.

5. Spread a thin layer of spicy mayonnaise on both halves of the toasted buns. Place the lettuce and tomato slices on the bottom halves and top with the scallop burgers. Top each burger with 2 slices of bacon. Close the sandwiches and serve at once with the remaining spicy mayonnaise on the side. —*Marcia Kiesel*
MAKE AHEAD The recipe can be prepared through Step 3 and the spicy mayo and uncooked burgers refrigerated separately overnight.
WINE Fruity, low-oak Chardonnay.

There's a reason that Le Bernardin is known as the most phenomenal seafood restaurant in Manhattan: its brilliant chef, Eric Ripert. During a Web chat on foodandwine.com, Ripert offered advice on everything from buying the freshest tuna steaks and preparing tartare to salt-baking whole fish, roasting lobsters and serving crabmeat.

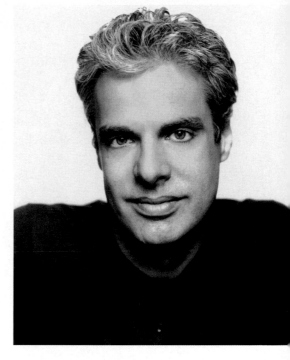

FW: What should I look for when buying tuna steaks? Any tips?
ER: The tuna should be bright pink, moist and completely odorless. If it looks like a piece of chocolate, it is too old. If it is very red, it doesn't have enough fat, which means it won't have any flavor.

FW: What is the best way to make tuna tartare at home?
ER: Cut very cold sushi-quality tuna into ⅛-inch dice. In a separate bowl, mix salt, pepper, vegetable oil, chopped scallions, chopped capers, chives, a bit of fresh lemon juice and a bit of Dijon mustard. Then fold the tuna into the dressing. Don't fold in the tuna until you've mixed all the ingredients (mixing everything from the beginning will cause the tuna to darken). Serve the tartare immediately, making sure that it is very cold.

FW: Do you have any simple and delicious recipes for baked fish?
ER: Spread some thinly sliced potatoes in the bottom of a baking dish; on top, layer thinly sliced onions, tomatoes and a little chopped garlic and parsley. Pour in equal parts water and white wine, up to a quarter of an inch from the bottom; add salt and pepper and place the fish—preferably grouper—on top. For a fillet, bake at 400 degrees for about 12 minutes, until the liquid evaporates.

FW: What about salt-baked fish?
ER: One technique is to put kosher salt on the bottom of an ovenproof platter, place a cleaned whole fish on top (I like red snapper) and cover it with more salt. I'd bake a four-pound fish at 400 degrees for approximately 20 minutes, then let it rest at room temperature for 15 minutes. It's cooked when the upper crust is totally hard. To test for doneness, stick a skewer through the crust and into the fish and leave it there for 30 seconds; when you remove it, it should be warm—not cold, not hot.

FW: What's the best method for cooking a whole lobster?
ER: Rub it with canola oil, some butter, salt, pepper and rosemary and roast it in a 400-degree oven. As a guide, I'd cook a two-pound lobster for approximately 15 minutes.

FW: Can you suggest some simple seafood appetizers?
ER: Toss some shrimp with salt, pepper, chopped cilantro and a little vegetable oil and bake for a few minutes, then serve in a bowl with a sauce made with chicken stock, unsweetened coconut milk, fresh lime juice, diced avocado and diced tomatoes.

FW: Any ideas for crabmeat?
ER: I like to mix crabmeat with mayonnaise, chives, lemon juice, curry powder and diced tomatoes; then I shape it using a ramekin and serve it with a sauce made of tomato juice, olive oil and sherry vinegar.

FW: Do you fish?
ER: Yes, mostly in rivers and lakes. My favorite places to fish are lakes that are covered with ice, when I have to make a hole.

FW: I heard you once say that you cook for the food, not with the food. Can you elaborate?
ER: It's an important distinction. For example, if I'm cooking halibut and I add broccoli, potatoes, asparagus and tomatoes and then I serve it with two kinds of sauce—maybe a red one and a green one to add color appeal—I won't really have done anything to elevate the halibut's flavors. To do that, I'd add fewer ingredients, but the right ones. I always compare chefs to jewelers: The fish is a diamond, and my job is to find the right cut and the right setting for it. If I were making a piece of jewelry with diamonds, gold, sapphires and rubies, in the end I'd lose the diamonds.

FW: What do you like to eat when you're not at the restaurant?
ER: My only day off is Sunday, and I try to eat a T-bone steak.

GRILLED SEA SCALLOPS WITH CORN SALAD

OATMEAL-CRUSTED SOFT-SHELL CRABS

Tequila-Mint Scallop Tostadas

4 SERVINGS ●

2 tablespoons extra-virgin olive oil
2 large tomatoes, chopped
1 small red onion, chopped
2 Serrano chiles, seeded
    and minced
1½ pounds sea scallops, quartered
2 tablespoons dry white wine
2 tablespoons tequila
½ cup shredded Monterey
    Jack cheese
¼ cup finely chopped mint, plus
    12 mint leaves for garnish
Salt and freshly ground pepper
12 small outer leaves of Bibb lettuce
2 ripe Hass avocados, mashed with
    1 tablespoon fresh lime juice
12 large tortilla chips
¼ cup grated cotija cheese
    or crumbled feta
Lime wedges, for serving

1. Heat the oil in a skillet. Add the tomatoes, onion and chiles and cook over moderate heat, stirring, until the onion is softened, 8 minutes. Add the scallops, wine and tequila. Cook until the scallops are opaque, 3 to 4 minutes. Turn off the heat, add the Jack cheese and chopped mint and season with salt and pepper.

2. Arrange 3 lettuce leaves on each plate and fill with the avocado. Spoon the scallops on top. Garnish with the tortilla chips, cotija cheese and mint. Serve with lime wedges. —*Jim Peyton*

Grilled Sea Scallops with Corn Salad

6 SERVINGS ● ●

6 ears of corn, shucked
1 pint grape tomatoes, halved
3 scallions, white and light green
    parts only, thinly sliced
⅓ cup basil leaves, finely shredded
Salt and freshly ground pepper
1 small shallot, minced
2 tablespoons balsamic vinegar
2 tablespoons hot water
1 teaspoon Dijon mustard
¼ cup plus 3 tablespoons
    safflower oil
1½ pounds sea scallops (about 30)

1. In a large pot of boiling salted water, cook the corn until tender, about 5 minutes. Drain and cool. Stand the corn in a large bowl and slice off the kernels. Add the tomatoes, scallions and basil and season with salt and pepper.

2. In a blender, puree the shallot with the balsamic vinegar, hot water and mustard. With the blender on, slowly add 6 tablespoons of the safflower oil until combined. Season the vinaigrette with salt and pepper, then toss with the corn salad.

3. In a large bowl, toss the remaining 1 tablespoon of oil with the scallops; season with salt and pepper. Heat a large grill pan. Add half of the scallops at a time to the pan and grill over moderately high heat, turning once, until browned, about 4 minutes per batch. Mound the corn salad on plates, top with the scallops and serve.
—*Ann Chantal Altman*

Curried Scallop Salad with Mango Dressing

4 FIRST-COURSE SERVINGS ●

Seeds from 2 cardamom pods
½ teaspoon cumin seeds
¼ teaspoon fennel seeds
Pinch of crushed red pepper
¼ cup extra-virgin olive oil
2 tablespoons red
   wine vinegar
1 small shallot, minced
1 garlic clove, minced
Salt and freshly ground pepper
1 small ripe mango—peeled,
   pitted and cut into ¼-inch dice
1 pound sea scallops
2 tablespoons vegetable oil
6 cups packed arugula leaves
   (3 ounces)
4 plum tomatoes, quartered
½ cup peeled and julienned
   jicama

1. In a small skillet, toast the cardamom, cumin and fennel seeds with the crushed red pepper over moderate heat until the spices are fragrant, about 1 minute. Transfer to a spice grinder and let cool. Grind to a powder.

2. In a small bowl, mix the ground spices with the olive oil, vinegar, shallot and garlic and season with salt and pepper. Stir in the mango.

3. Season the scallops with salt and pepper. In a large skillet, heat the vegetable oil until shimmering. Add the scallops and cook over high heat, turning once, until browned, about 2 minutes per side. Transfer the seared scallops to a large plate.

4. In a large bowl, combine the arugula, tomatoes and jicama. Add half of the mango dressing and toss well. Mound the arugula salad on plates and arrange the seared scallops on top. Drizzle the scallops with the remaining mango dressing and serve at once.
—*Thomas John*

MAKE AHEAD The recipe can be prepared through Step 2 and refrigerated overnight. Stir in the diced mango just before serving.

Lobster and Green Bean Salad with Lemon-Tarragon Dressing

4 SERVINGS ● ●

Salt
½ pound green beans, cut into
   2-inch lengths
½ cup crème fraîche or sour cream
1 teaspoon finely grated lemon zest
1 tablespoon fresh lemon juice
1½ teaspoons seasoned rice vinegar
1 tablespoon chopped tarragon
Freshly ground pepper
1¼ pounds cooked lobster meat
   (from three 1½-pound lobsters),
   cut into 1-inch pieces

1. In a large pot of boiling salted water, cook the beans until crisp-tender, about 5 minutes. Drain the beans in a colander and refresh under cold water. Drain and pat dry.

2. In a large bowl, mix the crème fraîche with the lemon zest, lemon juice, vinegar and tarragon. Season with salt and pepper. Add the lobster and green beans and toss to coat. —*Michael Leviton*
MAKE AHEAD The salad can be refrigerated for 3 hours.
WINE Fruity, low-oak Chardonnay.

Oatmeal-Crusted Soft-Shell Crabs with Brown Butter

4 SERVINGS ●

1 cup quick-cooking oatmeal
1 cup Wondra flour
Salt and freshly ground pepper
1 large egg
½ cup buttermilk
8 medium soft-shell crabs, cleaned
1 stick plus 2 tablespoons
   salted butter
½ cup vegetable oil
2 tablespoons drained capers
1 tablespoon fresh lemon juice
1 tablespoon coarsely chopped
   flat-leaf parsley

1. In a spice mill or clean coffee grinder, grind the oatmeal to a fine powder. Transfer the oatmeal to a large shallow bowl and whisk in the flour. Season the mixture generously with salt and pepper. In another large shallow bowl, beat the egg with the buttermilk.

2. Line a baking sheet with wax paper. Dip 1 crab at a time in the buttermilk mixture and shake off any excess, then dredge it thoroughly in the oatmeal flour to make a thin coating. Transfer the crab to the prepared baking sheet. Repeat with the remaining crabs.

3. In each of 2 large skillets, melt 2 tablespoons of the butter in 4 tablespoons of the oil over moderately high heat. Fry 4 crabs in each skillet until browned and crisp on the bottom, about 3 minutes. Turn the crabs and fry until just cooked through, 1 to 2 minutes longer. Using a slotted spatula, transfer 2 crabs to each plate.

4. Wipe out 1 of the skillets. Add the remaining 6 tablespoons of butter and cook over moderately high heat until it starts to brown, about 3 minutes.

---

cooking tip
cleaning crabs

TO CLEAN A SOFT-SHELL CRAB, use a pair of kitchen shears to remove the pointy tips along the sides of the shell. Flip open the sides, brush back the gills with the shears and cut them off. Remove the tail at the base, then the eyes, taking care not to take off too much of the edible flesh around them.

Add the capers and cook until they start sizzling and open into flowers, about 1 minute. Add the lemon juice and swirl to blend with the butter. Drizzle the brown butter sauce over the crabs and around the plates. Sprinkle the parsley over the crabs and serve at once.

—*Charlie Palmer*

SERVE WITH Shaved fennel and pea shoot salad with lemon vinaigrette.

WINE Dry, mineral-flavored Chenin Blanc.

Crabby Carolina Rice

4 SERVINGS ● ●

This dish was inspired by the crab boils of the mid- and southern-Atlantic coast. Here, the requisite Old Bay Seasoning is lightly toasted to bring out its warm nuances. Although Maryland crabmeat might seem a natural choice, F&W's Marcia Kiesel favors the sweeter, more reliably flavorful crabmeat from Maine.

1½ cups Carolina or other long-grain white rice
1 tablespoon Old Bay Seasoning
2½ tablespoons unsalted butter
14 ounces crabmeat, preferably Maine crab claw meat
1 tablespoon vegetable oil
1 medium onion, finely chopped
2 garlic cloves, minced
½ cup chopped canned tomatoes, drained
1 teaspoon fresh lemon juice
Salt
2 scallions, thinly sliced

I. In a large saucepan of boiling water, cook the rice over moderately high heat, stirring occasionally, until tender, about 12 minutes. Drain and spread on a baking sheet to cool.

2. In a large skillet, toast the Old Bay Seasoning over low heat until fragrant, about 40 seconds. Scrape the spice mixture into a small bowl and let cool. Melt the butter in the skillet. Add the crabmeat and 1 teaspoon of the Old Bay Seasoning and cook over moderately high heat for 1½ minutes, tossing gently with a spatula. Transfer to a plate.

3. Heat the oil in the skillet. Add the onion and cook over moderately low heat until softened, about 4 minutes. Add the garlic and the remaining 2 teaspoons of Old Bay and cook, stirring, until fragrant, about 2 minutes. Add the tomatoes and cook until dry, about 4 minutes. Add the rice and cook over moderate heat, stirring, until heated through, about 3 minutes. Add the crabmeat and lemon juice and cook, stirring, until hot. Season with salt and transfer to warmed bowls. Sprinkle the scallions over the rice and serve.

—*Marcia Kiesel*

MAKE AHEAD The recipe can be prepared through Step 1 and refrigerated overnight.

WINE Bright, citrusy Riesling.

Steamed King Crab with Gewürztraminer Sauce

4 SERVINGS ● ●

1 cup Gewürztraminer
4 tablespoons unsalted butter
2½ pounds frozen King crab legs, cut crosswise between the joints
2 tablespoons minced chives
1 tablespoon minced lemon balm or ¼ teaspoon finely grated lemon zest
1 tablespoon minced spearmint

I. In a saucepan, boil the Gewürztraminer over moderately high heat until reduced by half, about 10 minutes. Whisk in the butter and remove from the heat.

2. Using kitchen shears, cut along the length of the crab leg shells. Arrange the legs in a single layer in a large steamer basket or bamboo steamer; steam the crab legs until heated through, about 4 minutes. Transfer the crab to a serving platter.

3. Gently rewarm the sauce over low heat and stir in the chives, lemon balm and spearmint. Pour the sauce into warmed dipping bowls and serve at once with the crab. —*Marcia Kiesel*

WINE Spicy Alsace Gewürztraminer.

Roasted Shrimp and Scallop Papillotes

30 SERVINGS ●

The seafood is wrapped in parchment paper and then these "papillotes" are inserted in white paper bags for a dramatic presentation. Each bag will serve six people. You will need five 8-by-14-inch #420-size bags (the number is on the bottom). Look for the bags in delis or takeout shops; omit them if they are unavailable.

4 pounds large sea scallops, cut in half horizontally
4 pounds large shrimp, shelled and deveined
½ cup extra-virgin olive oil, plus more for drizzling
Salt and freshly ground pepper
½ cup chervil leaves or ¼ cup tarragon leaves
10 thin lemon slices, plus lemon wedges, for serving
Miami Tartar Sauce (p. 325)

I. Preheat the oven to 425°. In a bowl, toss the seafood with ½ cup of the olive oil and season with salt and pepper.

2. Cut five 18-inch-long sheets of parchment paper and lay them on a work surface. Arrange the scallops and shrimp on one half of each parchment square in slightly overlapping rows, leaving a 3-inch border at the edges. Drizzle with olive oil, scatter the chervil on the seafood and lay the lemon slices on top.

3. Fold the parchment over the seafood and fold the 3 open edges of each package up to seal in the juices. Carefully slide each package, seam side up, into the bottom of a paper bag. Tightly roll down the top of each bag; staple shut.

4. Set the bags upright on 2 large baking sheets. Bake for 25 minutes, shifting the pans halfway through. Transfer to trays. With scissors, cut the top off each bag to reveal the packet. Unfold the packets. Drizzle with olive oil. Serve with lemon and Miami Tartar Sauce. —*Jennifer Rubell*

WINE Lively, assertive Sauvignon Blanc.

ROASTED SHRIMP AND SCALLOP PAPILLOTE

SUMMER SUCCOTASH SALAD, P. 219

vegetables

ROASTED BROCCOLI WITH ANCHO BUTTER

MACEDONIAN CHEESE-STUFFED PEPPERS

Roasted Broccoli with Ancho Butter

12 SERVINGS ●

- 3 ancho chiles (about 1½ ounces)
- Boiling water
- ¼ cup extra-virgin olive oil
- ¼ cup pine nuts
- 4 large garlic cloves, thinly sliced
- ½ teaspoon ground cumin
- ½ teaspoon ground coriander
- 1½ sticks (6 ounces) unsalted butter, softened
- Salt
- Three 1½-pound heads of broccoli, cut lengthwise into large spears, stalks peeled

1. Preheat the oven to 450°. In a heat-proof medium bowl, cover the anchos with boiling water and let stand until softened, about 20 minutes. Drain the chiles and pat dry. Discard the stems and seeds, then coarsely chop.

2. Meanwhile, in a small skillet, heat 2 tablespoons of the olive oil until shimmering. Add the pine nuts and cook over moderately high heat, stirring constantly, until lightly browned, about 3 minutes. Add the garlic, cumin and coriander and continue cooking, stirring, until the garlic is softened and the pine nuts are deep golden, about 1 minute longer. Let cool.

3. In a food processor, puree the pine nut mixture with the anchos and butter. Season the ancho butter with salt and scrape into a bowl.

4. In a large bowl, toss the broccoli with the remaining 2 tablespoons of olive oil, then spread on 2 large rimmed baking sheets. Roast the broccoli in the upper and lower thirds of the oven for 15 minutes, or until crisp-tender, shifting the pans from top to bottom and back to front halfway through.

Add the ancho butter to the broccoli and toss to coat. Season with salt and roast for 10 minutes longer, or until the broccoli is tender. Transfer to a platter and serve the broccoli warm or at room temperature. —*Grace Parisi*

MAKE AHEAD The recipe can be prepared through Step 3 and refrigerated for up to 3 days.

Roasted Cauliflower and Broccoli with Curried Croutons

6 SERVINGS ●

- One 2-pound head of cauliflower, cut into florets
- One 1½-pound head of broccoli, cut into florets, thick stems peeled and cut crosswise into ⅓-inch-thick slices
- 1 tablespoon plus 2 teaspoons olive oil
- Salt

2 teaspoons unsalted butter
1 tablespoon Madras
curry powder
Three ¼-inch-thick slices of crusty
country bread, cut into
¼-inch dice
2 teaspoons fresh lemon juice
1 tablespoon chopped mint

1. Preheat the oven to 425°. On a large rimmed baking sheet, toss the cauliflower with the broccoli and 1 tablespoon of the olive oil. Season with salt. Roast for 45 minutes, turning occasionally, until the vegetables are tender and lightly browned.

2. Meanwhile, in a large skillet, melt the butter in 2 teaspoons of olive oil. Add the curry powder and stir over moderate heat until fragrant, about 45 seconds. Add the diced bread and cook, stirring occasionally, until toasted, about 20 minutes.

3. Toss the vegetables with the lemon juice and mint, sprinkle with the curried croutons and serve. —*Wendy Kalen*

Champagne-Roasted Cauliflower with Gruyère
12 SERVINGS ● ●

2 heads of cauliflower
(6½ pounds total), cored
2 cups dry Champagne
2 cups chicken stock or
low-sodium broth
3 garlic cloves, lightly smashed
2 large thyme sprigs
Salt and freshly ground white pepper
2 tablespoons unsalted butter
¼ cup all-purpose flour
1 cup whole milk
½ pound Gruyère cheese, shredded

1. Preheat the oven to 400°. Set the heads of cauliflower in a 10-by-16-inch glass or ceramic baking dish. Add the Champagne, stock, garlic and thyme to the baking dish and season the cauliflower with salt and white pepper. Cover with foil and roast for 1 hour and 40 minutes, or until tender, basting with the pan juices every 30 minutes.

2. Preheat the broiler. Broil the cauliflower for 5 minutes, or until golden brown, shifting the dish as necessary. Strain the pan juices and reserve 2 cups. Keep the cauliflower warm.

3. Melt the butter in a large saucepan. Add the flour and whisk over moderate heat for 1 minute. Whisk in the 2 cups of pan juices and the milk; whisk until smooth. Add the cheese and cook, whisking frequently, until the sauce is thickened, 5 minutes. Season with salt and white pepper. Pour the sauce over the warm cauliflower and serve.

—*Mory Thomas*

MAKE AHEAD The cauliflower and the cheese sauce can be refrigerated separately overnight. Reheat before serving.

Wasabi-Pickled Cauliflower
MAKES ABOUT 1½ QUARTS ● ● ●
These spicy pickles go nicely with grilled beef, lamb, pork or duck.

3 cups water
½ cup white wine vinegar
½ cup wasabi powder (2 ounces)
1 tablespoon kosher salt
1 tablespoon sugar
One 2¼-pound head of cauliflower,
cut into 1-inch florets

1. In a medium saucepan, combine the water with the vinegar, wasabi, salt and sugar and bring to a boil.

2. In a heatproof bowl, pour the pickling liquid over the cauliflower; cool to room temperature. Refrigerate overnight.
—*Jean-Georges Vongerichten*

MAKE AHEAD The cauliflower can be refrigerated for 2 weeks.

Macedonian Cheese-Stuffed Peppers
8 SERVINGS
This is a popular restaurant dish from the Greek town of Salonika; it's traditionally made with long green frying peppers.

8 green frying peppers or colored
bell peppers (3 to 4 ounces each)
3 tablespoons extra-virgin olive oil
1 jalapeño, seeded and minced

3 tablespoons grated onion
Salt and freshly ground pepper
7 ounces Manouri cheese
6 ounces Greek feta cheese,
drained
1 large egg, lightly beaten
1½ tablespoons fresh lemon juice
½ teaspoon dried Greek oregano
2 tablespoons coarsely grated
Pecorino cheese

1. Make a slit halfway around each pepper about ½ inch below the stem. In a large pot of boiling salted water, cook the peppers until just tender, about 5 minutes. Drain and let cool. Gently fold back the tops of the peppers and cut out the cores with scissors. Remove any remaining seeds. Pat the peppers dry with paper towels.

2. In a small skillet, heat 2 tablespoons of the olive oil. Add the jalapeño and onion, season with salt and pepper and cook over moderate heat, stirring, until softened, about 3 minutes. Let cool.

3. Preheat the broiler. In a medium bowl, finely crumble the Manouri and feta cheeses. Add the jalapeño and onion mixture and the egg, lemon juice and oregano and beat briefly with a fork until light and well blended. Season the filling with salt and pepper. Gently fold back the tops of the peppers and stuff them with the cheese filling, using a small spoon. Close the peppers and lay them on a baking sheet. Brush with the remaining 1 tablespoon of olive oil.

4. Broil the peppers 8 inches from the heat for about 6 minutes, or until lightly charred. Turn the peppers, brush with any oil on the sheet and broil for 4 to 5 minutes longer, or until the filling is hot. Sprinkle with the Pecorino and serve hot or warm. —*Paula Wolfert*

Cauliflower Tagine
6 SERVINGS
¾ cup extra-virgin olive oil
1 large onion, thinly sliced
10 garlic cloves, finely chopped
1 green bell pepper, thinly sliced

2 tablespoons sweet paprika

2 tablespoons Tabil (p. 328)

1 tablespoon tomato paste

Salt and freshly ground pepper

¼ cup thinly sliced oil-packed
    sun-dried tomatoes, drained

½ cup water

One 2½-pound head of cauliflower,
    cored and cut into 2-inch florets

1 cup fine dry bread crumbs

3 ounces Gruyère cheese,
    shredded (1 cup)

5 large eggs, beaten

1. Preheat the oven to 400°. Lightly grease a 9-by-13-inch glass or ceramic baking dish. In a large skillet, heat the olive oil. Add the onion and cook over low heat, stirring occasionally, until softened, about 8 minutes. Add the garlic, bell pepper, paprika, Tabil, tomato paste and a pinch each of salt and pepper. Cover and cook, stirring occasionally, until the pepper softens, about 7 minutes. Add the sun-dried tomatoes and water and simmer for 1 minute. Season with salt and pepper and transfer to the prepared baking dish.

2. In a large pot of boiling salted water, cook the cauliflower until just tender, 5 minutes. Drain and pat dry. Spread the cauliflower in the baking dish.

3. In a medium bowl, toss the bread crumbs and Gruyère; season with salt and pepper. Stir in the beaten eggs and pour the mixture over the cauliflower.

---

kitchen tip

grilling veggies

TO OIL A LARGE QUANTITY OF VEGETABLES for grilling or roasting without making a mess, place the vegetables you are preparing in a plastic bag and drizzle the oil over them. Using your hands, massage the oil into the vegetables. You can also season the vegetables in the bag.

Cover the baking dish with foil and bake in the upper third of the oven for about 15 minutes, or until bubbling around the edges. Uncover and bake for about 15 minutes longer, until browned and crisp on top. Let the tagine stand for 10 minutes before serving.

—*Nancy Harmon Jenkins*

MAKE AHEAD The recipe can be prepared ahead through Step 2 and refrigerated separately. Bring to room temperature before proceeding.

Provençal Stuffed Zucchini

8 FIRST-COURSE OR

4 MAIN-COURSE SERVINGS ●

8 round zucchini (½ pound each)

Salt and freshly ground pepper

1 tablespoon extra-virgin olive oil

3 meaty slices of bacon,
    finely chopped

1 large onion, finely chopped

1 large red bell pepper, cut into
    ¼-inch dice

3 garlic cloves, minced

1 pound ground pork

One 1-pound eggplant, cut into
    ¼-inch dice

½ cup fine dry bread crumbs

½ cup chopped Calamata olives
    (3 ounces)

½ cup chopped basil

½ cup freshly grated
    Parmesan cheese

¼ cup chopped sun-dried tomatoes

2 teaspoons finely chopped thyme

1. Preheat the oven to 375°. Cut a thin slice off the tops of the zucchini and reserve. Using a small spoon, scoop out the flesh and finely chop it. Season the zucchini cups with salt and pepper and turn upside down to drain on paper towels for 15 minutes. Set the cups right side up on a baking sheet and bake for 20 minutes.

2. Heat the oil in a skillet. Add the bacon and cook over low heat until the fat is rendered, about 4 minutes. Add the onion, red pepper and garlic, cover and cook until softened, about 8 minutes.

Add the ground pork, season with salt and pepper and cook over moderately low heat, breaking up the meat, until it is mostly white. Add the eggplant and cook, stirring occasionally, for 5 minutes. Add the chopped zucchini and cook for 10 minutes longer. Remove the skillet from the heat and stir in the bread crumbs, olives, basil, Parmesan, sun-dried tomatoes and thyme. Season the stuffing with salt and pepper.

3. Mound the stuffing in the zucchini cups, top with the lids and bake in the oven for 50 minutes. Serve hot, warm or at room temperature.

—*Daniel Johnnes*

NOTE If using long zucchini, halve them lengthwise and scoop out the flesh, but don't prebake. Stuff them and bake in the oven for 15 minutes.

MAKE AHEAD The zucchini can be kept at room temperature for 4 hours.

WINE Powerful, spicy Syrah.

Honey-Roasted Root Vegetable Salad

4 SERVINGS ● ●

ROASTED VEGETABLES

1 pound medium beets, with 1 inch
    of the stem attached

1 pound carrots, peeled and cut
    into 1½-inch pieces

1 pound parsnips, peeled and cut
    into 1½-inch pieces

1 pound turnips, peeled and cut
    into 1½-inch pieces

3 tablespoons vegetable oil

3 small white onions (about
    ¾ pound), cut into 2-inch wedges

Salt and freshly ground pepper

3 tablespoons honey, warmed

1 tablespoon chopped
    sage leaves

4 ounces fresh goat cheese, at
    room temperature

¼ cup minced fresh herbs,
    such as chives, tarragon and
    flat-leaf parsley

2 tablespoons
    extra-virgin olive oil

PROVENÇAL STUFFED ZUCCHINI

SALAD

¼ cup extra-virgin olive oil

2 tablespoons sherry vinegar

1 large garlic clove, minced

1 tablespoon minced herbs, such as chives, tarragon and flat-leaf parsley

Salt and freshly ground pepper

4 cups packed arugula leaves (from two 4-ounce bunches)

1. ROAST THE VEGETABLES: Preheat the oven to 400°. Tightly wrap the beets in a double layer of aluminum foil and roast on the bottom shelf of the oven for 1½ hours, or until tender when pierced with a knife. When the beets are cool enough to handle, peel and cut them into 1-inch pieces.

2. Meanwhile, divide the carrots, parsnips and turnips between 2 large rimmed baking sheets. Toss the vegetables in each pan with 1 tablespoon of the vegetable oil. Arrange the onion wedges on the baking sheets, keeping them intact. Brush the onion wedges all over with the remaining 1 tablespoon of vegetable oil. Generously season the vegetables with salt and pepper. Roast the vegetables for 40 minutes. Brush the vegetables with the warm honey and sprinkle with the sage. Continue to roast the vegetables for 25 minutes longer, or until they are tender and glazed. Loosen the vegetables with a spatula and let them cool to room temperature in the pans.

3. In a small bowl, mix the goat cheese with the herbs and olive oil and season with salt and pepper.

4. MAKE THE SALAD: In a small bowl, combine the oil with the vinegar, garlic and herbs; season with salt and pepper. In a large bowl, toss the arugula with 1 tablespoon of the vinaigrette and arrange on plates. Add the roasted vegetables to the large bowl, toss with the remaining vinaigrette and arrange on the arugula. Dot each plate with small spoonfuls of the herbed goat cheese and serve. —Michael Romano

MAKE AHEAD The herbed goat cheese and the vinaigrette can be refrigerated separately overnight. Bring the goat cheese to room temperature before serving the salad. The vegetables can be roasted earlier in the day and kept at room temperature.

Roasted Butternut Squash and Fried Apples

10 SERVINGS ●

Pumpkin and sweet potatoes are fine substitutes for the squash here.

One 3-pound butternut squash, peeled and cut into ¾-inch chunks

10 tablespoons (5 ounces) unsalted butter, 6 tablespoons melted

2 tablespoons finely chopped dill

Salt and freshly ground pepper

2½ pounds tart, firm apples— peeled, halved, cored and cut into ¾-inch chunks

3 tablespoons light brown sugar

¼ teaspoon cinnamon

1. Preheat the oven to 425°. In a large bowl, toss the squash with the melted butter and the dill. Season with salt and pepper and spread on a large rimmed baking sheet. Roast the squash for 30 minutes, turning once, or until browned and just tender.

2. Meanwhile, melt 2 tablespoons of the butter in a large nonstick skillet. Add half of the apples in a single layer and cook over high heat, turning once, until golden and crisp-tender, about 5 minutes. Add half each of the brown sugar and cinnamon and cook, stirring gently, until the apples are lightly caramelized, about 2 minutes. Transfer the apples to a plate. Wipe out the skillet and repeat the cooking process with the remaining butter, apples, brown sugar and cinnamon.

3. Toss the roasted squash with the caramelized apples and serve warm or at room temperature. —Robert Stehling

MAKE AHEAD The squash and caramelized apples can be refrigerated overnight and heated in a 350° oven.

Butternut Squash Gratin with Creamed Spinach

8 SERVINGS ●

These individual gratins will be neatest if you use squash with long, even necks.

Two 2-pound butternut squash, necks only, peeled and each cut crosswise into sixteen ¼-inch-thick rounds

1 tablespoon extra-virgin olive oil

Salt and freshly ground pepper

One 10-ounce bag cleaned spinach, stemmed and rinsed

1¼ cups heavy cream

2 tablespoons crème fraîche

¼ cup freshly grated Parmesan

1. Preheat the oven to 425°. Arrange the squash rounds on 2 rimmed baking sheets and brush with the olive oil. Season with salt and pepper and bake for 20 minutes, or until barely tender. Increase the oven temperature to 475°.

2. Meanwhile, set a medium saucepan over moderately high heat. Add the spinach, 1 handful at a time, and cook, stirring frequently, until wilted. Drain the spinach, squeeze dry and coarsely chop.

3. In the same saucepan, bring the heavy cream to a boil, then simmer over low heat until slightly thickened, about 3 minutes. Add the spinach and simmer, stirring occasionally, until creamy but not runny. Season with salt and pepper, transfer to a plate and let cool.

4. Lightly oil a large shallow baking dish. In a small bowl, stir the crème fraîche into the Parmesan. Spread the Parmesan cream on 8 squash rounds. Arrange 8 of the remaining rounds in the baking dish. Spoon a scant tablespoon of the creamed spinach over each round. Repeat this layering 2 more times and top with the Parmesan cream rounds.

5. Cover the gratins with foil and bake until heated through, about 10 minutes. Preheat the broiler. Uncover and broil for 2 minutes, or until browned. Transfer to plates and serve. —Daniel Boulud

MAKE AHEAD The gratins can be refrigerated for 1 day. Reheat before serving.

vegetables

Eggplant and Butternut Squash Tagine

6 SERVINGS ●

The great virtue of this delicious tagine is that it can be made ahead and served at room temperature.

- 2 pounds eggplant, cut crosswise into ½-inch-thick slices

Salt

- 2 pounds butternut squash, peeled and cut crosswise into ½-inch-thick slices
- 2 tablespoons extra-virgin olive oil, plus more for brushing

Freshly ground pepper

- ¾ pound skinless, boneless chicken breast, cut into ½-inch pieces
- 8 large scallions, finely chopped
- ¼ cup drained capers
- 1 large green bell pepper
- ½ cup shredded Gruyère cheese
- 6 large eggs, beaten

1. Arrange the eggplant slices on a work surface and sprinkle with salt. Transfer the eggplant to a colander, top with a plate and weigh it down with heavy cans. Set the colander in the sink and let the eggplant drain for 1 hour.
2. Meanwhile, preheat the oven to 425°. Brush the squash slices on both sides with olive oil and arrange them on 2 large baking sheets. Season with salt and pepper and bake for about 25 minutes, or until tender and golden brown.
3. Pat the eggplant slices dry. Brush them on both sides with olive oil and arrange on 2 large baking sheets. Bake for about 25 minutes, or until tender and golden brown. Transfer the roasted eggplant to a plate. Turn the oven down to 350°.
4. In a medium skillet, heat 1 tablespoon of the olive oil. Add the chicken and scallions and cook over moderately low heat, stirring, until the chicken is white throughout, about 5 minutes. Transfer to a food processor. Add the capers and the remaining 1 tablespoon of olive oil and season with salt and pepper; process to a coarse paste.

5. Roast the bell pepper directly over a gas flame or under the broiler until charred all over. Transfer the pepper to a bowl, cover with plastic wrap and let steam for 5 minutes. Peel the pepper and discard the core, seeds and stem. Cut lengthwise into ¼-inch-wide strips.
6. Lightly grease a large baking dish. Line the dish with half of the eggplant slices. Spread half of the pureed chicken over the eggplant and sprinkle with half of the Gruyère. Top with the squash slices and drizzle with 3 tablespoons of the beaten eggs. Top with the remaining chicken, Gruyère and eggplant slices. Arrange the bell pepper strips over the eggplant in a lattice pattern. Pour the remaining beaten eggs evenly over the filling, tilting the dish as necessary.
7. Cover the tagine with foil and bake for 20 minutes. Uncover and bake for about 20 minutes longer, or until the tagine is bubbling hot and the eggs are set. Let stand for at least 20 minutes and for up to 2 hours before serving.
—*Nancy Harmon Jenkins*

MAKE AHEAD The eggplant and squash tagine can be prepared through Step 5 and refrigerated overnight.

Crispy Artichoke Meatballs

6 SERVINGS ● ●

The small amount of beef in these artichoke meatballs helps hold them together. If artichokes are unavailable, substitute plain mashed potatoes.

- 8 large artichokes
- 1 lemon, halved
- ½ pound ground beef
- 8 large scallions, minced
- 2 cups finely chopped flat-leaf parsley (½ pound)
- 2 cups coarse fresh bread crumbs
- ½ cup shredded Gruyère cheese

One 3-ounce jar capers, drained and coarsely chopped

- 3 tablespoons Tabil (p. 328)
- 1 teaspoon freshly ground pepper
- ½ teaspoon cinnamon

Kosher salt

- 3 tablespoons plus 1 teaspoon sweet paprika
- 4 large eggs, beaten

All-purpose flour, for dredging

Vegetable oil, for frying

- ¼ cup extra-virgin olive oil

One 14-ounce can whole tomatoes, tomatoes chopped and liquid reserved

1. Using a serrated knife, cut the top third and the stem off each artichoke. Snap off the outer leaves, and with a small, sharp knife, trim the tough green skin from around each artichoke. Rub the artichokes all over with the lemon.
2. In a saucepan of boiling salted water, simmer the artichokes until tender when pierced through the bottom, about 15 minutes. Drain and let cool. With a spoon, scoop out the hairy chokes. Roughly chop the artichokes. In a food processor, coarsely chop the artichokes. You should have about 3 cups.
3. In a large bowl, mix the artichokes with the beef, scallions, parsley, bread crumbs, Gruyère, capers, Tabil, pepper, cinnamon and 2 teaspoons of salt. Add 3 tablespoons of the paprika and the eggs and mix with your hands until thoroughly combined.
4. Form the meat mixture into 3 dozen tablespoon-size meatballs. Form each into a football shape; dredge in flour.
5. In a large skillet, heat ½ inch of vegetable oil until shimmering. Working in 2 batches, fry the meatballs over moderately high heat, turning occasionally, until deep brown, about 12 minutes; reduce the heat if the meatballs brown too quickly. Transfer to paper towels to drain; keep warm.
6. Heat the olive oil in a large skillet. Add the remaining 1 teaspoon of paprika and cook over low heat until fragrant, about 10 seconds. Add the tomatoes and their liquid; simmer over low heat until the sauce thickens, about 10 minutes. Season with salt. Spoon the sauce onto a platter. Set the meatballs on top and serve. —*Nancy Harmon Jenkins*

CRISPY ARTICHOKE MEATBALLS

vegetables

MAKE AHEAD The meatballs can be fried up to 6 hours ahead and kept at room temperature. Reheat in a 350° oven for 10 minutes. The sauce can be refrigerated for up to 2 days.

Pickled Jerusalem Artichokes

MAKES ABOUT 1½ QUARTS ● ● ●

These artichokes would pair well with grilled pork, lamb, beef, duck, tuna, shrimp or salmon.

- 2½ cups Champagne vinegar
- 1 cup water
- 3 tablespoons sugar
- 1 tablespoon kosher salt
- 1 tablespoon coriander seeds
- 1 tablespoon black peppercorns
- 6 cardamom pods
- 6 whole cloves
- 1 bay leaf
- 1 star anise pod
- 2 pounds Jerusalem artichokes, sliced ¹⁄₁₆ inch thick on a mandoline

1. In a large saucepan, combine all of the ingredients except for the Jerusalem artichokes and bring to a boil over moderately high heat.

2. In a heatproof bowl, pour the pickling liquid over the artichokes. Cover with a plate and let cool to room temperature. Refrigerate overnight.

—*Jean-Georges Vongerichten*

MAKE AHEAD The artichoke pickles can be refrigerated for 2 weeks.

---

kitchen tip

leftover herbs

MANY RECIPES CALL FOR USING A SMALL AMOUNT OF FRESH HERBS, leaving a lot left over. One way to use up extra herbs is to make compound butters. Chop the herbs and mix them into softened butter, then freeze for up to 2 months. Use the butter on potatoes, pasta, fish or meat.

Haricots Verts and Goat Cheese Gratin with Hazelnuts

8 SERVINGS ●

- ½ cup hazelnuts
- 2 pounds haricots verts
- One 11-ounce log of fresh goat cheese, softened
- 1 cup crème fraîche, at room temperature (8 ounces)
- 2 large egg yolks
- 2 tablespoons toasted hazelnut oil
- Salt and freshly ground pepper
- 2 tablespoons unsalted butter, softened
- 2 tablespoons chopped flat-leaf parsley

1. Preheat the oven to 350°. Butter a large shallow baking dish. In a pie plate, toast the hazelnuts until browned, about 8 minutes. Let cool, then rub them against each other in a kitchen towel to remove the skins. Coarsely chop the nuts; leave the oven on.

2. In a large pot of boiling salted water, cook the haricots verts until just tender, about 8 minutes. Drain, rinse under cold water and pat dry with paper towels. Transfer the haricots verts to the prepared baking dish.

3. In a large bowl, beat the goat cheese with the crème fraîche, egg yolks and hazelnut oil. Season the mixture with salt and pepper.

4. Cover the haricots verts with foil and bake for about 15 minutes, or until heated through. Preheat the broiler. Toss the hot haricots verts with the softened butter. Spread the goat cheese topping over the beans and sprinkle with the hazelnuts. Broil 6 inches from the heat for about 4 minutes, rotating the dish as necessary, until browned all over. Sprinkle with the parsley and serve.

—*Pascal Chaupitre*

NOTE For a more elegant presentation, in Step 3, beat the crème fraîche with the egg yolks and hazelnut oil and pour this mixture over the haricots verts. Arrange overlapping slices of goat cheese on top before broiling.

Spicy Green Beans with Bacon and Tomatoes

12 SERVINGS ● ●

- ¼ cup extra-virgin olive oil
- ½ pound smoky slab bacon, sliced ⅓ inch thick and cut into 1-inch matchsticks
- 1 large white onion, cut into ½-inch dice
- 4 large garlic cloves, minced
- 3 pounds green beans, trimmed
- ½ teaspoon crushed red pepper
- One 35-ounce can peeled Italian tomatoes, drained and coarsely chopped
- 2 cups chicken stock or canned low-sodium broth
- 2 bay leaves
- Salt

1. In a large enameled cast-iron casserole, heat the olive oil until shimmering. Add the bacon and cook over moderate heat, stirring, until crisp, about 8 minutes. Using a slotted spoon, transfer the bacon to a plate. Add the onion and garlic to the casserole and cook, stirring, until softened, about 8 minutes. Add the green beans and crushed red pepper and cook, tossing, until the beans are coated with fat and just beginning to soften, about 3 minutes. Add the tomatoes, chicken stock, bay leaves and crisp bacon, season with salt and bring to a boil. Reduce the heat to moderately low, cover partially and cook, stirring occasionally, until the beans are tender, about 20 minutes.

2. Using a slotted spoon, transfer the green beans to a large bowl. Bring the cooking liquid to a boil and cook over high heat until reduced by half, about 15 minutes. Return the beans to the casserole and heat through. Transfer to a bowl; discard the bay leaves. Serve warm or at room temperature.

—*Grace Parisi*

MAKE AHEAD The green beans can be refrigerated in the reduced cooking liquid for up to 2 days. Rewarm over moderate heat before serving.

Chinese Long Beans with Cracked Black Pepper

4 SERVINGS ● ●

- 1 tablespoon vegetable oil
- ½ small onion, thinly sliced
- 1 pound Chinese long beans or green beans, cut into 3-inch lengths
- ½ medium red bell pepper, peeled with a vegetable peeler and cut into ⅓-inch dice
- ½ teaspoon sugar
- ¼ cup water
- 2 tablespoons soy sauce
- 1 teaspoon cracked black pepper

Heat the oil in a large skillet. Add the onion and cook over moderately high heat, stirring occasionally, until lightly browned, about 3 minutes. Add the long beans and red pepper and stir-fry until the beans are slightly softened and browned in spots, about 5 minutes. Add the sugar and stir to coat. Add the water, cover and cook over moderately low heat until the water has evaporated and the beans are tender, about 5 minutes. Add the soy sauce and cracked pepper and cook for 1 minute. Transfer to a platter and serve.
—*Jean-Georges Vongerichten*

Hot and Sour Vegetables

4 SERVINGS ● ●

- 2 cups small broccoli florets
- 10 Brussels sprouts, quartered
- 2 small carrots, cut into ⅛-inch-thick slices on the diagonal
- 2 small zucchini, cut into ½-inch-thick slices on the diagonal
- 3 tablespoons vegetable oil
- 4 dried red chiles, broken in half
- 1 tablespoon fermented black beans, rinsed and chopped
- 2 teaspoons minced fresh ginger
- 1 teaspoon minced garlic
- 1 medium onion, sliced lengthwise
- ¼ pound shiitake mushrooms, stemmed and thickly sliced
- 2 tablespoons soy sauce
- 1½ tablespoons white wine vinegar
- 1 teaspoon sugar
- ¼ cup chicken broth
- 2 teaspoons cornstarch mixed with 1 tablespoon water
- 1 teaspoon Asian sesame oil

1. Fill a wok two-thirds full with water and bring to a boil. Add the broccoli, Brussels sprouts, carrots and zucchini and blanch until crisp-tender, about 3 minutes. Drain well and shake dry.

2. Wipe out the wok. Add the oil, and when it begins to smoke, add the dried chiles, fermented black beans, ginger and garlic and stir fry until fragrant, about 20 seconds. Add the onion and mushrooms and stir-fry until just beginning to brown, about 2 minutes. Add the blanched vegetables and cook for 1 minute, then add the soy sauce, vinegar and sugar and stir-fry for 30 seconds. Add the broth and bring to a boil. Add the cornstarch mixture and cook, stirring, until the sauce thickens, about 15 seconds. Swirl the sesame oil over the vegetables and serve. —*Joyce Jue*

Rice-and-Cremini-Stuffed Cabbage Rolls

4 SERVINGS ●

The mixture of brown and wild rices in the filling stands up well to the assertive Savoy cabbage.

- 1 cup brown rice
- ¼ cup wild rice
- One 2-pound head of Savoy cabbage, cored
- 2 cups whole-milk yogurt
- 3 garlic cloves, minced
- Salt and freshly ground pepper
- 2 tablespoons unsalted butter
- ½ pound cremini or white mushrooms, thickly sliced
- 1 tablespoon fresh lemon juice
- 2 shallots, minced
- 2 tablespoons chopped dill
- 3 cups chopped canned tomatoes, drained
- 2 tablespoons tomato paste
- ½ cup walnuts, toasted and coarsely chopped

1. In a saucepan of boiling water, cook the brown and wild rices, covered, over low heat, stirring, until tender, about 45 minutes. Drain; transfer to a bowl.

2. In a large saucepan of boiling water, cook the cabbage, cored side down, over moderately high heat until the outer leaves begin to loosen, about 10 minutes. Using tongs, carefully peel 8 outer leaves from the head as they become loose. Reserve the remaining cabbage for another use. Cut each of the 8 leaves in half; discard the center rib.

3. In a medium bowl, blend the yogurt and garlic; season with salt and pepper.

4. Melt the butter in a skillet. Add the mushrooms and lemon juice; season with salt. Cook over moderate heat until tender and their liquid has evaporated, about 6 minutes. Add the shallots and cook, stirring, until softened, about 4 minutes. Add the mushrooms and shallots to the rice. Stir in 1 tablespoon of the dill and ½ cup of the yogurt sauce; season with salt and pepper.

5. Add the tomatoes to the skillet and cook over moderately high heat until their liquid has evaporated, about 5 minutes. Stir in the tomato paste and season with salt and pepper.

6. Preheat the oven to 375°. Spread a cabbage leaf on a work surface, cut side facing you. Place ¼ cup of the rice filling within ½ inch of the edge. Roll the leaf over the filling, tucking in the sides as you roll. Repeat with the remaining leaves and filling.

7. Spoon half of the tomato sauce into a shallow 10-by-14-inch glass baking dish. Add ¼ cup of water; arrange the cabbage rolls in the dish, seam side down. Spoon the remaining tomato sauce over the rolls and cover with foil.

8. Bake the rolls for 45 minutes, until heated through and the sauce is bubbling. Transfer to plates. Spoon the remaining 1½ cups of yogurt sauce on top. Sprinkle with the walnuts and the remaining 1 tablespoon of dill and serve. —*Marcia Kiesel*

vegetables

MAKE AHEAD The cabbage rolls and yogurt sauce can be prepared through Step 7, covered with plastic wrap (not foil) and refrigerated separately for up to 3 days. Bring to room temperature before baking.

WINE Bright, fruity rosé.

Leek-and-Cheese Sprinkle Pie

8 SERVINGS ● ●

Paula Wolfert learned to make this homey vegetable "pie," with its sprinkling of cornmeal on the top and bottom, from a woman in the Greek town of Metsovo. Serve this rustic pie like the locals do, cut into squares, with a glass of cold buttermilk on the side.

- **5 leeks (2 pounds), white and tender green parts, quartered lengthwise and cut into ½-inch pieces**
- **Kosher salt**
- **1¾ pounds spinach, large stems discarded, leaves shredded**
- **3 tablespoons plus 1 teaspoon olive oil**
- **Freshly ground pepper**
- **⅓ cup fine stone-ground cornmeal**
- **6 ounces Greek feta cheese**
- **6 ounces freshly grated Parmesan cheese**
- **2 tablespoons chopped dill (optional)**

1. In a large colander, toss the leeks with 1 teaspoon of salt. In another colander, toss the spinach with 1 teaspoon of salt. Set the colanders in the sink and let the vegetables soften for 1 hour. Rinse the leeks and spinach thoroughly under cold running water to wash off all the salt. Wrap the leeks in cheesecloth; twist the cheesecloth and squeeze until the leeks are as dry as possible. Repeat with the spinach.

2. Preheat the oven to 400°. In a large skillet, heat 1½ tablespoons of the olive oil. Add the leeks and season with pepper. Cover partially and cook over moderate heat for about 2 minutes, or until the leeks have absorbed the oil.

Transfer the leeks to a large plate to cool. In the same skillet, cook the spinach in 1½ tablespoons of the olive oil until softened, about 2 minutes.

3. Grease a 9-by-1-inch glass pie plate with the remaining 1 teaspoon of oil. Sprinkle ¼ cup of the cornmeal in the plate and rotate to coat. Sprinkle the cornmeal with water until it is barely damp and spread it in an even layer.

4. In a medium bowl, mix the leeks with the spinach, feta and Parmesan cheeses and dill; season with salt and pepper. Spread the vegetables in the plate and smooth the surface with moistened palms. Sprinkle the remaining 1 tablespoon plus 1 teaspoon of cornmeal over the top. Lightly press the cornmeal into the leeks. Sprinkle the top 3 times with hot water.

5. Bake the pie for about 1 hour, or until a crust forms on the surface. Transfer to a wire rack, sprinkle with a few drops of water and let cool for at least 20 minutes before cutting into wedges.

—*Paula Wolfert*

MAKE AHEAD The pie can be kept at room temperature for up to 6 hours. Rewarm before serving.

WINE High-acid, savory Vermentino.

Teriyaki Tofu with Lemon

6 SERVINGS ● ●

- **¾ cup soy sauce**
- **¾ cup sake or dry sherry**
- **¾ cup mirin**
- **2 tablespoons sugar**
- **1½ teaspoons finely grated lemon zest**
- **1½ teaspoons cornstarch**
- **1½ tablespoons fresh lemon juice**
- **Vegetable oil, for the grill**
- **Three 15-ounce blocks of extra-firm or firm tofu, drained and halved horizontally to form 6 slabs**
- **3 tablespoons Asian sesame oil**
- **3 tablespoons chopped scallion greens**
- **1½ tablespoons lightly toasted sesame seeds**

1. In a small saucepan, combine the soy sauce with the sake, mirin, sugar and lemon zest and bring to a boil. Simmer the mixture over low heat until fragrant, about 5 minutes.

2. In a small bowl, mix the cornstarch into the lemon juice, stirring to dissolve. Whisk into the soy sauce mixture and bring to a boil, then cook over low heat for 1 minute, stirring constantly. Let the teriyaki sauce cool.

3. Light a grill. Lightly oil the grate. Pat the tofu dry with paper towels. Place in a shallow baking dish and brush with the sesame oil. Grill the tofu over a medium-hot fire for about 6 minutes, basting frequently with the teriyaki sauce, just until heated through and browned. Transfer the tofu to a platter. Drizzle with the remaining sauce, sprinkle with the scallion greens and sesame seeds and serve at once.

—*Steven Raichlen*

Soy-Glazed Tofu with Spinach

6 SERVINGS ● ●

- **¼ cup plus 2 tablespoons soy sauce**
- **1½ tablespoons honey**
- **1½ tablespoons sherry or dry white wine**
- **1½ teaspoons grated fresh ginger**
- **2 small garlic cloves, minced**
- **½ teaspoon Asian sesame oil**
- **Three 15-ounce packages of firm tofu, drained and halved horizontally**
- **4 scallions, white and light green parts only, thinly sliced**
- **Two 10-ounce bags spinach, washed**
- **1 teaspoon cornstarch mixed with 1 tablespoon water**

1. In a small bowl, whisk the soy sauce with the honey, sherry, ginger, garlic and sesame oil. Place 3 of the tofu halves in a glass pie plate and spoon half of the soy mixture on top. Sprinkle with half of the scallions and top with the remaining tofu halves. Pour the remaining soy mixture over the tofu and scatter the remaining scallions on top.

During a summer Web chat, Amanda Hesser, the *New York Times* food columnist and author of *The Cook and the Gardener,* answered a wide range of questions—about summer soups and fruits, good potluck dishes, favorite hors d'oeuvres and beloved cookbooks—and shared her fresh, unfussy attitude toward food.

FW: What's your very favorite summer fruit?

AH: Very ripe, small plums. I prefer them raw; there's something about plums that makes them turn sour when they're cooked. It almost seems like some act of defiance on the fruit's part, because they're lovely when eaten fresh and ripe. I like the tension of the thin skin holding in all of this sweet, juicy nectar. And the only time they're like that is the summer.

FW: Do you have a suggestion for a summer potluck dish—something fun that travels well?

AH: I like to make chicken salad using both light and dark meat; it really changes the flavor and texture of it. I make my own mayonnaise, with a touch of sour cream or crème fraîche to give it a little tang. Oh! And some chopped tarragon. Chicken and tarragon are incredible together.

FW: What's an obscure summer ingredient that I should try?

AH: Summer savory is a wonderful herb. It has a deep fragrance, kind of spicy and piney, like thyme, but more powerful. It's excellent with grilled pork or chicken.

FW: Any ideas for fruit salads?

AH: Slice fresh, ripe plums and peaches, then toss in a couple of blueberries and raspberries. Add a tiny sprinkle of sugar, a drizzle of honey and a dozen or so whole mint leaves. Gently fold it all together, then sprinkle a little plum eau-de-vie over

it and fold it all together once more. Let it sit for about 30 minutes, so that the flavors have time to fully blend.

FW: Do you have any tips for preparing great summer soups?

AH: In Europe, summer soups are often served at room temperature. Serving soup first is a nice way to add a contrast of temperatures to an otherwise grilled meal. One of my favorite summer soups is a creamy white gazpacho, made with almonds and, sometimes, cucumbers. I went to a wedding where they served this soup in shot glasses with a little surprise at the bottom: caviar.

FW: Can you suggest some new uses for watermelon?

AH: Tomato and watermelon go very well together. You can cube tomatoes and watermelon and dress them just like a salad with oil, a mild vinegar, salt and pepper. Some chefs mix in herbs, goat cheese or even onions.

FW: Got any breakfast tips?

AH: Last year I visited Spain and fell in love with a dish called revueltos, which means, essentially, scrambled eggs. They're much simpler than omelettes—truly a one-pan meal. You begin by sautéing mushrooms or onions or a little thickly cut bacon in a nonstick pan. Then crack eggs into the pan and very quickly swish them around over moderately high heat until the eggs are just barely cooked (they continue to cook on the way to the table), and that's it. It sounds

ordinary, but there's something about the speed of the cooking that keeps the eggs incredibly fluffy and creamy, and the flavors that you add at the beginning remain distinct.

FW: Can you suggest an alternative to crudités and dip?

AH: A favorite hors d'oeuvres of mine is leeks and tarragon on toast. Sauté the leeks in a little butter or olive oil; when they're almost cooked, add some cream, goat cheese and a pinch of chopped tarragon. Then spoon it onto toasts.

FW: What cookbooks do you love?

AH: Marcella Hazan's *Essentials of Classic Italian Cooking,* Carol Field's *The Italian Baker,* Richard Olney's *Lulu's Provençal Table,* Patricia Wells's *Bistro Cooking* and Elizabeth David's *French Provincial Cooking.*

FW: And which ingredients do you think are underexposed?

AH: Meyer lemons! Meyer lemons should replace regular lemons.

GOLDEN TOFU WITH PEAS

2. Pour 1 inch of water into a wide, deep skillet and bring to a boil. Place the spinach in a steamer basket and put the basket in the skillet. Cover and steam the spinach just until wilted, about 3 minutes. Drain the spinach very well, then transfer it to a large plate; cover with foil and keep warm.

3. Place a ramekin or biscuit cutter in the center of the skillet. Set the pie plate with the tofu on the ramekin, cover and steam until the tofu is hot, about 10 minutes. Arrange the tofu around the spinach, cover and keep warm. Pour the tofu sauce into a saucepan and bring to a simmer. Stir in the cornstarch mixture and cook over moderate heat, stirring occasionally, until thickened, about 3 minutes. Pour the sauce over the tofu and serve. —*Melissa Clark*

Golden Tofu with Peas

4 SERVINGS ● ○

- 2 tablespoons vegetable oil
- 1 pound firm tofu—drained, patted dry and cut into ¾-inch cubes
- ¼ teaspoon cumin seeds
- 2 medium shallots, minced
- 2 teaspoons finely grated fresh ginger
- 1 garlic clove, minced
- 1 teaspoon ground coriander
- 1 teaspoon seeded and minced jalapeño
- 1 cup coarsely grated plum tomato
- 1 cup water
- 1 teaspoon kosher salt
- ½ teaspoon sugar

Freshly ground pepper

- 2 cups fresh or thawed frozen peas

Steamed rice, for serving

I. In a large nonstick skillet, heat the oil until shimmering. Add the tofu and cook over moderately high heat until browned on the bottom, about 2 minutes. With a spatula, carefully turn the tofu and cook until browned on the other side, about 2 minutes. With a slotted spoon, transfer the tofu to a plate.

2. Add the cumin seeds to the skillet and cook over moderately high heat for 10 seconds. Add the shallots and cook, stirring occasionally, until beginning to brown, about 2 minutes. Add the ginger and garlic and stir-fry until fragrant, about 1 minute. Add the coriander and jalapeño to the skillet and stir-fry for 30 seconds longer.

3. Add the tomato and cook over moderately high heat until thickened, about 1 minute. Add the water, salt and sugar, season with pepper and bring to a simmer. Cover and cook over low heat for 5 minutes. Add the tofu and peas, cover and simmer until the peas are just heated through, about 5 minutes. Transfer to a serving bowl and serve with steamed rice alongside. —*Madhur Jaffrey*

Sautéed Spinach with Almonds and Red Grapes

4 SERVINGS ●

- ¼ cup extra-virgin olive oil
- ¼ cup blanched whole almonds, coarsely chopped
- ¼ cup finely chopped onion
- ½ cup seedless red grapes
- 2 garlic cloves, thinly sliced

Two 10-ounce packages of spinach, large stems discarded, leaves washed

- 2 tablespoons dry white wine, preferably Rioja
- 1 tablespoon unsalted butter

Salt and freshly ground white pepper

Heat the olive oil in a large skillet. Add the chopped almonds and onion and cook over moderate heat, stirring, until the almonds are golden, about 4 minutes. Add the grapes and garlic and cook for 2 minutes. Stir in the spinach in handfuls, adding more as the leaves wilt. When all of the spinach has been added, stir in the white wine and butter, letting it melt. Season with salt and white pepper and serve at once. —*Joseph Jiménez de Jiménez*

Chilled Moorish Spinach and Almond Salad

8 SERVINGS ● ●

- ¼ cup dried currants
- ¼ cup extra-virgin olive oil

Scant ½ teaspoon ground cumin

Scant ½ teaspoon ground cinnamon

Scant ¼ teaspoon ground allspice

Scant ⅛ teaspoon ground nutmeg

Pinch of ground cloves

- 2 tablespoons sherry vinegar
- 1 tablespoon fresh lemon juice
- 1 teaspoon mild honey
- 2 small shallots, thinly sliced

Salt and freshly ground pepper

- ½ tablespoon vegetable oil
- 1 cup blanched slivered almonds
- 1 pound baby spinach

I. In a small bowl, cover the currants with water. Let soak for 5 minutes, then drain and return to the bowl.

2. Heat the olive oil in a medium skillet. Add the cumin, cinnamon, allspice, nutmeg and cloves and cook over low heat, stirring frequently, until fragrant, about 30 seconds. Scrape the spice oil into a medium bowl and let cool. Whisk in the vinegar, lemon juice and honey. Add the shallots and the reconstituted currants. Season the dressing with salt and pepper. Wipe out the skillet.

3. Heat the vegetable oil in the skillet. Add the slivered almonds and cook over moderate heat, stirring constantly, until golden, about 5 minutes. Transfer the almonds to paper towels to drain and then let cool.

4. Prepare an ice-water bath. In a large pot of boiling salted water, blanch the spinach for 10 seconds. Drain and cool in the ice-water bath. Drain again and squeeze dry. Gently separate the spinach leaves and add them to the dressing. Add the almonds and toss. —*Ana Sortun*

MAKE AHEAD The spinach salad can be refrigerated overnight. Keep the toasted almonds at room temperature and add them just before serving.

vegetables

Cider-Braised Collards with Ham

12 SERVINGS ● ● ●

¼ cup extra-virgin olive oil

2 medium onions, finely chopped

3 large garlic cloves, minced

1½ tablespoons pure chile powder

½ teaspoon cayenne pepper

1 tablespoon light brown sugar

Two 1-pound meaty ham hocks

3 cups chicken stock or
low-sodium broth

One 750-ml bottle sparkling
apple cider

2 bay leaves

Salt and freshly ground pepper

6 pounds collard greens, stems
and tough inner ribs discarded,
leaves cut crosswise into
1-inch ribbons

---

cooking tips

vegetarian menu planning

SPICE THINGS UP Add complexity with bold spices or exotic spice blends.
FOCUS ON TEXTURE Crisp nuts and chewy dried fruit make grain dishes and salads more satisfying, while olive and nut oils and creamy sauces add a richness that elevates humble foods like beans. Roasting or braising vegetables gives them a luscious texture, not to mention a deep flavor.
OFFER GRAINS AND GREENS Hearty grain or bean dishes should be offset by something light, raw and refreshing—like a spinach salad.
GO FOR VARIETY A buffet of small dishes in a wide range of flavors makes a vegetarian meal exciting.
DON'T BE AFRAID TO SERVE WINE WITH VEGETABLES Avoid oaky and tannic wines, which pair best with red meat and other fatty foods; instead, opt for fruity wines with soft textures.

1. In a large pot, heat the oil until shimmering. Add the onions and garlic and cook over moderate heat, stirring occasionally, until softened, about 6 minutes. Add the chile powder and cayenne and cook just until fragrant, about 1 minute. Add the brown sugar and cook, stirring, until dissolved, about 1 minute longer. Add the ham hocks, chicken stock, sparkling cider and bay leaves. Season lightly with salt and pepper and bring to a boil. Reduce the heat to low, cover and simmer until the ham hocks are tender, about 2 hours.

2. Remove the ham hocks from the broth and let them cool slightly. Skim the fat from the broth. Remove the meat from the ham hocks and cut it into 1-inch pieces.

3. Bring the broth to a boil. Add the collard greens in large handfuls, stirring and allowing the greens to wilt before adding more. When all of the greens have been added, return the meat to the pot, cover and simmer until the collards are tender, about 30 minutes. Season the collards with salt and pepper and transfer to a large bowl. Discard the bay leaves and serve.

—*Grace Parisi*

MAKE AHEAD The braised collard greens can be covered with plastic wrap and refrigerated for up to 2 days. Rewarm over moderate heat before serving.

Tomato Gratin with Orange Zest

4 SERVINGS ● ●

Grapeseed oil

2 navel oranges, zest peeled
with a vegetable peeler

1 cup water

¼ cup sugar

2 tablespoons unsalted butter

2 medium shallots, minced

5 medium tomatoes—4 peeled,
seeded and cut into ½-inch dice,
1 peeled and thinly sliced

Salt and freshly ground pepper

2 tablespoons freshly
grated Parmesan cheese

1. Preheat the oven to 275°. Line a baking sheet with foil and lightly oil the foil. In a small saucepan, combine the orange zest with the water and sugar and bring to a boil. Simmer over moderate heat until syrupy, about 10 minutes. Drain the zest. Spread the strips out on the baking sheet and bake for about 45 minutes, or until dry but not browned. Let cool completely, then grind to a powder in a spice grinder.

2. In a medium saucepan, melt the butter. Add the shallots and cook over moderately low heat until softened, about 4 minutes. Add the diced tomatoes and season with salt and pepper. Cover and cook over moderately low heat until the the tomato mixture is thick, 10 minutes.

3. Preheat the broiler. Spread the tomato mixture in a small, shallow baking dish. Layer the tomato slices on top, overlapping them slightly. Season with salt and pepper.

4. Toss the Parmesan with ½ teaspoon of the orange-zest powder and sprinkle all over the tomatoes. Broil for about 2 minutes, or until bubbling and golden on top. Serve the gratin hot.

—*Jean-Georges Vongerichten*

MAKE AHEAD The orange-zest powder can be stored in an airtight container for up to 2 months.

Onion-Fennel Gratin

4 SERVINGS

Look for small, young, tender organic fennel bulbs.

2 tablespoons unsalted butter, cut
into small pieces, plus more for
buttering the dish

4 small to medium fennel
bulbs, trimmed

Kosher salt

2 tablespoons extra-virgin olive oil

4 medium onions, thinly sliced

Freshly ground pepper

1 cup freshly grated Pecorino
Romano cheese

¼ cup fresh bread crumbs

1. Preheat the oven to 350°. Butter a 9-by-13-inch glass or ceramic baking dish. Put the fennel bulbs in a large saucepan of water and add 1 teaspoon of salt. Bring the water to a simmer over moderate heat and cook the fennel for 1 minute. Drain the fennel and let cool completely; pat dry with paper towels. Cut the fennel lengthwise through the core into ¼-inch-thick slices.

2. In a large skillet, heat the olive oil. Add the onions and cook over moderately high heat, stirring occasionally, until golden and softened, about 10 minutes. Season with salt and pepper.

3. Spread one-third of the onions in the baking dish and arrange half of the fennel slices on top. Season with salt and pepper and sprinkle with ½ cup of the Pecorino. Top with half of the onions, the remaining fennel and then the remaining onions. Sprinkle the remaining ½ cup of Pecorino and the bread crumbs on top and dot with the butter. Cover with foil and bake for 1 hour, or until the fennel is tender.

4. Preheat the broiler. Uncover the fennel and broil for 2 minutes, rotating the dish, until evenly browned. Let the fennel stand for 5 minutes before serving.
—*Michael Romano*
WINE Fruity, low-oak Chardonnay.

Spiced Corn on the Cob
4 SERVINGS

- 2 tablespoons canola oil
- 1 tablespoon coriander seeds
- ½ cinnamon stick
- ½ tablespoon allspice berries
- ½ teaspoon turmeric
- ½ teaspoon cracked black pepper
- ½ dried red chile
- 1 medium shallot, coarsely chopped
- 2 teaspoons finely chopped fresh ginger
- 1 gallon water
- 4 ears of corn, shucked
- 1 teaspoon ground cumin

- 1 teaspoon chaat masala (see Note)
- 1 teaspoon kosher or coarse sea salt
- ½ teaspoon cayenne pepper
- 3 tablespoons melted unsalted butter
- 2 tablespoons fresh lime juice

1. In a large saucepan, heat the oil. Add the coriander, cinnamon, allspice, turmeric, black pepper and dried chile and cook over moderate heat until fragrant, about 1 minute. Add the shallot and ginger and cook, stirring, until softened, about 2 minutes. Add the water and bring to a boil over moderate heat. Cover and simmer for 20 minutes. Add the corn and simmer, uncovered, until tender, about 5 minutes.

2. Meanwhile, in a small skillet, toast the ground cumin over moderate heat until fragrant, about 10 seconds. Scrape the cumin into a small bowl and let cool. Stir in the chaat masala, salt and cayenne.

3. Brush the corn with melted butter and drizzle with the lime juice. Sprinkle the spiced salt over the corn and serve at once. —*Floyd Cardoz*

NOTE Chaat masala is a spice blend that can be found at Indian and Middle Eastern markets.

MAKE AHEAD The aromatic cooking liquid can be refrigerated overnight. The spice mixture can be stored in a jar for up to 2 days.

Steamed Corn with Peppery Tomato-Basil Butter
12 SERVINGS ● ●

- 2 tablespoons extra-virgin olive oil
- 2 large tomatoes (1 pound total)— peeled, seeded and chopped
- 2 teaspoons minced garlic
- 1½ sticks (6 ounces) unsalted butter, softened
- 2 teaspoons coarsely ground pepper
- 1 teaspoon kosher salt
- 1 tablespoon minced basil
- 12 ears of corn, shucked

1. Heat the olive oil in a small saucepan. Add the chopped tomatoes and garlic and cook over moderate heat, stirring occasionally, until reduced to ⅓ cup, about 20 minutes. Transfer the reduced tomatoes to a bowl and let cool to room temperature.

2. In a food processor, combine the reduced tomatoes with the butter, pepper and salt and pulse until blended. Scrape the tomato butter into a bowl and stir in the minced basil.

3. In a large pot of boiling water, steam the corn until just tender, about 3 minutes. Drain and transfer to a large platter and serve accompanied by the tomato-basil butter.
—*David Page and Barbara Shinn*

MAKE AHEAD The tomato-basil butter can be wrapped in plastic and refrigerated for up to 2 days.

Summer Succotash Salad
12 SERVINGS ● ● ●
DRESSING

- ¼ cup red wine vinegar
- 2 tablespoons whole-grain mustard
- 2 tablespoons minced shallot
- ¼ cup extra-virgin olive oil
- ¼ cup vegetable oil
- 1 tablespoon finely chopped thyme
- 1 tablespoon finely chopped tarragon

Kosher salt and freshly ground pepper
VEGETABLES

- 1 pound yellow wax beans, cut into 1½-inch lengths
- 1 pound green beans, cut into 1½-inch lengths
- 1 cup shelled fresh or frozen lima beans or edamame (about 1 pound unshelled)
- 2 tablespoons extra-virgin olive oil
- 4 ears of corn, shucked and kernels cut from the cobs
- 2 pints cherry tomatoes, halved (4 cups)
- 3 scallions, minced

Salt and freshly ground pepper

vegetables

1. MAKE THE DRESSING: In a food processor, combine the vinegar, mustard and shallot and process until smooth. With the machine on, slowly add the olive and vegetable oils and process until emulsified. Add the thyme and tarragon and pulse just until combined. Transfer to a bowl and season with salt and pepper.

2. PREPARE THE VEGETABLES: In a large pot of boiling salted water, cook the yellow wax and green beans until crisp-tender, about 7 minutes. Using a slotted spoon, transfer the beans to a colander and refresh under cold water. Drain and pat dry. Add the limas to the pot and boil until tender, about 4 minutes. Drain and refresh under cold water. Drain well and pat dry.

3. In large skillet, heat the olive oil until shimmering. Add the corn and cook over moderate heat, stirring often, until crisp-tender, about 3 minutes. Transfer the corn to a plate to cool.

4. In a very large bowl, combine the yellow wax and green beans with the lima beans, corn, tomatoes and scallions. Add the dressing and toss to coat. Season with salt and pepper and serve.
—*David Page and Barbara Shinn*

MAKE AHEAD The herb dressing can be refrigerated for up to 3 days. The dressed salad can be refrigerated for up to 4 hours. Let the salad return to room temperature before serving.

---

kitchen tip

cabbage

FOR EXTRA-CRISP CABBAGE, soak it first in a large bowl of lightly salted ice water for 10 minutes. Drain and rinse the cabbage and proceed with the recipe. Another tip: When boiling cabbage or cauliflower, add a little white vinegar to the cooking water to reduce the unpleasant odor.

Five-Vegetable Slaw

6 SERVINGS ● ○

You will need a mandoline to thinly slice the vegetables.

- 3 tablespoons fresh lemon juice
- 1 teaspoon honey
- 1 teaspoon minced fresh ginger
- ½ teaspoon minced garlic
- Salt and freshly ground pepper
- ¼ cup plus 2 tablespoons extra-virgin olive oil
- ½ seedless cucumber, peeled and cut into 2-inch lengths
- 1 small kohlrabi or 2 thick broccoli stalks, peeled
- 1 small beet, peeled
- 2 cups finely shredded Savoy cabbage
- 1 cup mung bean sprouts

1. In a small bowl, whisk the lemon juice with the honey, ginger and garlic and season with salt and pepper. Whisk in the olive oil.

2. Using a mandoline on a very thin setting, slice the cucumber, kohlrabi and beet. Stack the slices and cut them into matchsticks.

3. Toss the kohlrabi and cucumber with the cabbage and bean sprouts, then with the dressing; season with salt and pepper. Toss in the beet and serve.
—*Peter Gordon*

Asian Vegetable Slaw

4 SERVINGS ● ○

You will need a mandoline to thinly slice the vegetables.

- ¼ cup mayonnaise
- 1 tablespoon mirin
- 1 tablespoon rice vinegar
- ½ tablespoon soy sauce
- ½ tablespoon fresh lemon juice
- 1 small jalapeño, seeded and minced
- 1 cup finely shredded red cabbage
- 1 cup finely shredded napa cabbage
- 1 cup julienned carrot
- 1 cup julienned jicama
- 1 cup julienned daikon

- ½ small seedless cucumber, peeled and sliced paper-thin
- 2 scallions, thinly sliced
- 1 cup mung bean sprouts
- Salt

In a large bowl, mix the mayonnaise, mirin, rice vinegar, soy sauce, lemon juice and jalapeño. Add the red and napa cabbages, carrot, jicama, daikon, cucumber, scallions and bean sprouts, season with salt and toss well; serve.
—*Jean-Georges Vongerichten*

Braised Savoy Cabbage with Cinnamon and Orange

8 SERVINGS ● ●

Orange zest and a hint of cinnamon add complexity to this simple cabbage dish.

- One 2½-pound Savoy cabbage, halved and cored, leaves separated
- 2 tablespoons unsalted butter
- 2 tablespoons extra-virgin olive oil
- 1 medium onion, thinly sliced
- 1 garlic clove, minced
- Salt and freshly ground pepper
- 1 cup Chardonnay
- 2 cups beef stock or low-sodium broth
- 1 teaspoon finely grated orange zest
- Large pinch of cinnamon

1. Bring a large pot of water to a boil. Add the cabbage leaves and blanch for 1 minute. Drain and cut into thin shreds.

2. In a large enameled cast-iron casserole, melt the butter in the olive oil. Add the onion and garlic and cook over low heat until softened, about 7 minutes. Add the cabbage and season with salt and pepper. Cover and cook over low heat for 10 minutes, stirring a few times. Add the wine and simmer until almost evaporated. Add the stock, cover and simmer, stirring occasionally, until tender, 40 minutes. Stir in the orange zest and cinnamon, season with salt and pepper and serve. —*Giorgio Rivetti*

MAKE AHEAD The cabbage can be prepared up to 4 hours ahead. Add the orange and cinnamon before reheating.

ASIAN VEGETABLE SLAW

TOMATILLO-QUINOA SALAD, P. 233

potatoes, grains + more

FAST RECIPES

CRUNCHY BAKED POTATOES WITH MALDON SALT

WARM NEW POTATO SALAD WITH TALEGGIO

Crunchy Baked Potatoes with Maldon Salt

4 SERVINGS ● ●

Harvested by hand from the waters off Essex, England, Maldon sea salt has a great crunch and a remarkably subtle, briny flavor. It doesn't seem so expensive when you consider that it's half the price of its less mellow-tasting French cousin, fleur de sel. Uncomplicated foods, such as baked potatoes, sautéed vegetables and poached fish, show it off to its best advantage.

2 pounds small red or Yukon Gold potatoes (about 2 inches in diameter), scrubbed
Extra-virgin olive oil
Maldon sea salt

I. Preheat the oven to 450°. Pierce the potatoes all over with a fork. Arrange them on the oven rack and bake for 1¾ to 2 hours, or until hard and crisp.

2. Using a serrated knife, split the baked potatoes without cutting them all the way through. Drizzle with olive oil, sprinkle with Maldon salt and serve. —Bob Bowe

Warm New Potato Salad with Taleggio and Arugula

4 SERVINGS ● ●

This dish displays a wonderful contrast of textures—the waxy potatoes, spiky arugula leaves and soft, melting cheese come together in each bite.

2 pounds small new potatoes, wiped clean
Salt
¾ pound arugula
2 tablespoons extra-virgin olive oil
½ pound Taleggio or other mild semisoft cheese, thinly sliced
Freshly ground pepper

I. In a large saucepan, cover the potatoes with cold water, set a lid on top and bring to a boil. Add salt, reduce the heat to low and simmer until the potatoes are tender, 12 to 15 minutes; drain.

2. Preheat the broiler. In a bowl, toss the arugula with the oil. Transfer to a large ovenproof platter. Cut the potatoes in half and arrange on the arugula in a single layer. Top with the sliced Taleggio cheese and season with salt and pepper. Broil for about 1 minute, or until the cheese melts, and serve. —Nigel Slater

Buttery Mashed Potatoes

4 GENEROUS SERVINGS ● ●

2 pounds baby Yukon Gold potatoes, scrubbed
1 stick (4 ounces) unsalted butter, at room temperature
¼ cup milk or half-and-half
Salt and freshly ground white pepper

1. In a large saucepan, cover the potatoes with cold water, bring to a boil and cook until tender, 20 minutes; drain.

2. Pass the potatoes through a ricer or food mill set over the saucepan; discard the skins. Using a wooden spoon, beat in the butter a little bit at a time. Beat in the milk and season with salt and pepper. —*Traci Des Jardins*

MAKE AHEAD The potatoes can be refrigerated for 3 hours and reheated in a covered baking dish in a 325° oven.

Creamy Potato-Corn Mash

6 SERVINGS

> 3 ears of corn, kernels cut off and cobs cut into 2-inch lengths
> 1½ cups heavy cream
> 2 pounds Yukon Gold potatoes, peeled and cut into 2-inch chunks
> 2 garlic cloves, smashed
> Salt
> 3 tablespoons unsalted butter
> ¼ cup sour cream
> Freshly ground pepper

1. In a medium saucepan, bring the corn cobs and cream to a simmer. Remove from the heat, cover and let steep for 30 minutes; discard the cobs.

2. Meanwhile, in a saucepan, cover the potatoes with water. Add the garlic and a large pinch of salt. Bring to a boil; cook over moderately high heat until the potatoes are tender, 20 minutes.

3. Melt 1 tablespoon of the butter in a skillet. Add the corn kernels and 2 tablespoons of water, cover and cook over moderate heat until tender, about 5 minutes. Uncover and cook, without stirring, until browned on the bottom, about 4 minutes. In a blender, puree the corn and corn cream until smooth.

4. Drain the potatoes and garlic and return to the saucepan. Shake the potatoes over moderately high heat for 1 minute to dry them; remove from the heat and mash. Stir in the corn cream, sour cream and the remaining 2 tablespoons of butter. Season with salt and pepper and serve. —*Jan Birnbaum*

Potato Sformato with Mortadella and Buffalo Mozzarella

6 SERVINGS ●

> 1½ pounds Yukon Gold potatoes, peeled and cut into 2-inch chunks
> Salt
> ¾ cup warmed milk
> Freshly ground pepper
> 3 ounces mortadella, cut into ¼-inch dice
> 5 ounces fresh mozzarella, preferably buffalo, cut into ½-inch dice
> 1 tablespoon unsalted butter, cut into small pieces

1. Preheat the oven to 425°. Butter a 7-by-11-inch baking dish. In a saucepan, cover the potatoes with water and bring to a boil over moderately high heat. Salt the water and cook the potatoes until tender, about 12 minutes; drain. Shake the potatoes over moderately high heat until very dry. Remove from the heat.

2. Mash the potatoes with a potato masher, stirring in the milk. Season with salt and pepper. Fold in the mortadella and mozzarella, then spread the potatoes in the prepared baking dish. Dot the top with the butter and bake in the upper third of the oven for about 12 minutes, or until bubbling. Turn on the broiler and broil for about 2 minutes, or until crusty and browned on top. Let rest for 5 minutes before serving. —*Anacleto and Tina Bleve*

MAKE AHEAD The *sformato* can be assembled in the baking dish and refrigerated overnight. Bring to room temperature before baking.

WINE Light, zesty, fruity Dolcetto.

Chantilly Potatoes with a Parmesan Crust

6 SERVINGS ●

> 2 pounds Yukon Gold potatoes, peeled and cut into 2-inch chunks
> Salt
> ½ cup cold milk
> 7 tablespoons unsalted butter, softened

> Freshly ground pepper
> 1 cup heavy cream
> ½ cup freshly grated Parmesan cheese

1. Preheat the oven to 400°. Butter a 9-by-13-inch baking dish. Put the potatoes in a large saucepan and cover with water. Salt the water and bring to a boil, then simmer the potatoes over moderate heat until tender, about 12 minutes. Drain the potatoes, return to the saucepan and shake over high heat for 1 minute to dry. Pass the potatoes through a ricer into a large bowl. Beat in the milk and 6 tablespoons of the butter and season with salt and pepper.

2. In a large stainless steel bowl, whip the cream to soft peaks. Beat one-third of the cream into the potatoes, then fold in the remaining cream. Scrape the potatoes into the prepared dish. Dot with the remaining 1 tablespoon of butter and sprinkle the Parmesan over the top. Bake the potatoes for 25 minutes. Preheat the broiler and broil the potatoes for 2 minutes, or until browned. Let stand for 10 minutes before serving. —*Maria Guarnaschelli*

Creamy Potato and Onion Gratin

6 SERVINGS ●

Slicing the potatoes thinly is essential to this dish. You can buy an inexpensive plastic mandoline at most housewares stores.

> 6 medium Yukon Gold potatoes (2 pounds), peeled and thinly sliced on a mandoline
> Salt and freshly ground pepper
> 1 tablespoon minced rosemary
> 1 tablespoon minced thyme
> 1 large onion, thinly sliced on a mandoline
> 3 tablespoons unsalted butter, cut into ¼-inch pieces
> 1 cup heavy cream
> 1 cup milk

1. Preheat the oven to 400°. Butter a 9-by-13-inch baking dish. Layer one-fourth of the potatoes in the dish.

potatoes, grains + more

Season the potatoes generously with salt and pepper and sprinkle with some of the rosemary and thyme. Layer one-third of the onion over the potatoes and dot with some of the butter. Continue layering the remaining potatoes and onion, seasoning them with salt, pepper, rosemary and thyme and dotting with butter; end with a layer of potatoes. Combine the heavy cream and milk and pour over the potatoes. Dot the top with any remaining butter.

2. Bake the potato gratin in the oven for about 1 hour, or until it is bubbling and browned on top and the potatoes are tender when pierced with a knife. Let the gratin rest for 10 minutes, then divide among plates and serve.

—*Taylor Fladgate*

MAKE AHEAD The baked gratin can stand at room temperature for 4 hours. Reheat briefly before serving.

Grilled Smashed Potatoes

6 SERVINGS ● ●

12 small red potatoes (3 pounds), scrubbed
⅓ cup extra-virgin olive oil
2 tablespoons fresh lemon juice
2 garlic cloves, minced
Salt and freshly ground pepper

1. In a large saucepan of boiling salted water, cook the potatoes until just tender, about 12 minutes. Drain and let cool. Using the heel of your hand, slightly flatten each potato; be careful to keep the potatoes intact.

2. Light a grill. In a small bowl, whisk the olive oil with the lemon juice and garlic. Season with salt and pepper. Brush the potatoes generously with the dressing and sprinkle with salt.

3. Grill the potatoes over a medium-hot fire until crisp and browned, about 3 minutes per side. Serve at once.

—*Marcia Kiesel*

MAKE AHEAD The smashed boiled potatoes can be refrigerated for up to 3 days. Bring the potatoes to room temperature before grilling.

Cumin Potato Cakes

8 SERVINGS ●

For a more luxurious dish, the potato cakes can be paired with roasted quail and topped with a poached quail egg.

4 pounds baking potatoes
2 teaspoons cumin seeds
4 large eggs, lightly beaten
2 bunches chives, snipped (½ cup)
¼ cup cornstarch
2 teaspoons baking powder
2 teaspoons ground cumin
1 tablespoon plus 1 teaspoon kosher salt
2 tablespoons unsalted butter
2 tablespoons extra-virgin olive oil

1. Preheat the oven to 375°. Prick the potatoes and bake for 50 minutes, or until tender. When cool enough to handle, scoop the flesh into a bowl and coarsely mash; let cool slightly. Lower the oven temperature to 250°.

2. In a small skillet, toast the cumin seeds over moderate heat, shaking the pan occasionally, until fragrant, about 2 minutes. Transfer the cumin seeds to a plate to cool.

3. In a large bowl, mix the eggs with the chives, cornstarch, baking powder, ground cumin, toasted cumin seeds and salt. Add the potatoes and coarsely mash just until chunky and incorporated. Divide the potato mixture into 16 equal portions, then form each portion into a 2½-inch patty.

4. In a large nonstick skillet, melt 1 tablespoon of the butter in 1 tablespoon of the olive oil. Add 8 potato patties to the skillet and cook over moderate heat, turning once, until crisp and golden, about 5 minutes per side. Transfer the skillet to the oven and keep warm. Repeat with the remaining patties. Transfer the hot potato cakes to a platter and serve at once. —*Gary Danko*

MAKE AHEAD The potato cake recipe can be prepared through Step 3 and refrigerated overnight. Bring to room temperature before frying.

Skillet-Roasted New Potatoes

12 SERVINGS ●

4½ pounds medium red or white new potatoes, scrubbed
24 unpeeled garlic cloves
½ cup extra-virgin olive oil
12 small thyme or rosemary sprigs
Kosher salt and freshly ground pepper

Preheat the oven to 400°. In a large bowl, toss the potatoes with the garlic, olive oil and thyme. Season with salt and pepper; transfer to a very large cast-iron skillet. Roast the potatoes for 1 hour and 15 minutes, or until tender, shaking the skillet occasionally. Transfer to a platter and serve.

—*David Page and Barbara Shinn*

Sweet Potato Spoon Bread

10 TO 12 SERVINGS ● ●

Spoon bread, a cross between corn bread and soufflé, is a Southern classic.

1 pound sweet potatoes
2¼ cups stone-ground yellow cornmeal, plus more for dusting
1½ tablespoons sugar
1½ teaspoons salt
1½ teaspoons baking soda
1½ tablespoons unsalted butter, at room temperature
3 cups boiling water
1½ cups buttermilk
1½ tablespoons mild honey
¼ teaspoon ground cumin
¼ teaspoon freshly ground white pepper
Scant ⅛ teaspoon ground cloves
⅛ teaspoon cayenne pepper
5 large egg whites, at room temperature

1. Preheat the oven to 375°. With a fork, pierce the sweet potatoes all over and set them directly on the oven rack. Bake the sweet potatoes for about 1 hour, or until they are tender; let cool slightly. Slit the skins and scoop the flesh into a large bowl. Mash until smooth. You should have 1¼ cups of mashed sweet potatoes. Increase the oven temperature to 425°.

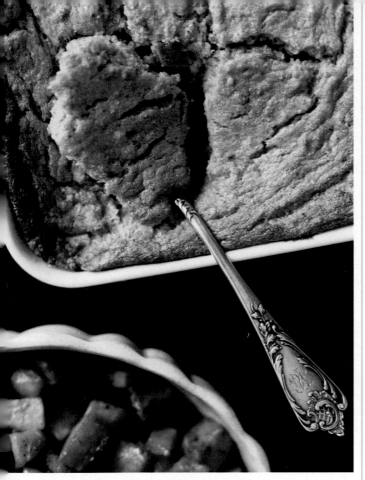

SWEET POTATO SPOON BREAD

POTATO SALAD WITH HONEY-BUTTERMILK DRESSING

2. Meanwhile, lightly butter a shallow 2-quart glass or ceramic baking dish and dust it with cornmeal, tapping out any excess. In another large bowl, whisk the 2¼ cups of cornmeal with the sugar, salt and baking soda. Stir the butter into the boiling water until it is melted, then stir the butter-and-water mixture into the dry ingredients until incorporated. Let cool slightly.

3. Using an electric mixer, beat the buttermilk, honey, cumin, white pepper, cloves and cayenne into the mashed sweet potatoes until combined. At medium speed, beat in the cornmeal mixture.

4. In a clean stainless steel bowl, using clean beaters, beat the egg whites until stiff but not dry. Fold the beaten egg whites into the sweet-potato mixture until no white streaks remain. Pour the batter into the prepared baking dish.

Bake for about 40 minutes, or until golden and risen and a toothpick inserted in the center comes out clean. Serve the spoon bread warm or at room temperature. —*Robert Stehling*

MAKE AHEAD The spoon bread can be made early in the day, wrapped in foil and reheated in a 350° oven.

Potato Salad with Honey-Buttermilk Dressing

4 SERVINGS ● ●

6 medium red potatoes (about 1 pound), scrubbed

Salt

½ pound green beans, cut into 1½-inch lengths

½ cup low-fat buttermilk

1 tablespoon mild honey, such as clover or acacia

1 tablespoon chopped flat-leaf parsley

1 tablespoon chopped chives

1 tablespoon minced shallots

1 tablespoon cider vinegar

1 teaspoon Dijon mustard

1 teaspoon chopped tarragon

1 scallion, white part only, thinly sliced

½ teaspoon finely grated lemon zest

Freshly ground pepper

8 medium radishes, thinly sliced

1. In a saucepan, cover the potatoes with cold water and bring to a boil. Reduce the heat to moderately low and simmer until the potatoes are tender, about 20 minutes. Drain and let cool slightly, then cut into ½-inch dice.

2. Meanwhile, in another medium saucepan of boiling salted water, cook the green beans until crisp-tender, about 6 minutes. Drain the beans in a colander and refresh under cold water. Drain well and pat dry.

potatoes, grains + more

3. In a large bowl, mix the buttermilk with the honey, parsley, chives, shallots, vinegar, mustard, tarragon, scallion and lemon zest. Season with salt and pepper. Add the radishes and beans; toss to coat. Add the potatoes, season with salt and pepper and toss the salad gently. Transfer the salad to plates and serve at room temperature.

—Gene Opton

Barossa Potato Salad with Maple-Cured Bacon
6 SERVINGS
The key ingredient in this salad is a good-quality maple-cured bacon.

- 2¼ **pounds medium red potatoes, scrubbed**
- **Sea salt**
- 3 **tablespoons unsalted butter, melted**
- 3 **thick slices maple-cured bacon (2 ounces)**
- ½ **cup heavy cream**
- 2 **tablespoons red wine vinegar**
- 1 **medium red onion, very finely chopped**
- ¼ **cup snipped chives**
- **Freshly ground pepper**

1. In a large saucepan, cover the potatoes with water, season generously with salt and bring to a boil. Simmer over moderate heat until the potatoes are tender, about 25 minutes. Drain and let cool slightly, then peel the potatoes and cut them into ½-inch pieces. Transfer the potatoes to a large bowl and toss with the melted butter.

2. Meanwhile, in a small skillet, cook the bacon over moderate heat until browned and crisp, about 6 minutes. Drain on paper towels and crumble into small pieces. Wipe out the skillet.

3. Add the cream to the skillet and bring to a boil. Remove from the heat and stir in the vinegar. Pour the cream over the potatoes, add the onion, chives and bacon and fold together gently. Season the potato salad with salt and pepper and serve warm. *—Maggie Beer*

MAKE AHEAD The potato salad can be prepared through Step 2 up to 4 hours ahead. Let the cooked potatoes and bacon stand at room temperature.
WINE Bright, citrusy Riesling.

Warm Potatoes with Onions, Bacon and Cheese
8 SERVINGS
In the French Alps, cooks garnish this hearty side dish, known as tartiflette, with thin slices of the local Reblochon cheese. Any leftovers make a great omelet filling.

- 4 **pounds Yukon Gold potatoes, peeled and cut into 1-inch dice**
- **Salt**
- ¼ **pound thickly sliced bacon, cut crosswise into strips**
- 2 **large onions, finely chopped**
- **Freshly ground pepper**
- 1 chilled 5-ounce whole Reblochon or Pont-l'Évêque cheese, rind removed, cheese halved horizontally
- ½ **cup dry white wine**

1. Preheat the oven to 425°. In a large saucepan, cover the diced potatoes with water and bring to a boil. Add salt to the water and cook until the potatoes are tender, about 12 minutes. Drain the potatoes well.

2. In a large skillet, cook the bacon strips over low heat, stirring occasionally, until crisp, about 7 minutes. Add the onions to the skillet and cook, stirring occasionally, until softened, about 12 minutes longer. Add the cooked potatoes, season with salt and pepper and toss to coat.

3. Place the 2 cheese halves on the bottom of a small roasting pan and spoon the potatoes and bacon and onions on top. Pour the white wine into the pan and bake for about 12 minutes, or until the cheese has melted. Using 2 metal spatulas, gently stir the potatoes to coat with melted cheese, sprinkle with pepper and serve at once.

—Claudine Peltot

Maple-Cider Baked Beans
6 SERVINGS ● ●
The dried beans need to be soaked overnight, so plan accordingly.

- 1 **pound dried beans, such as Jacob's cattle, pinto or flageolet—picked over, rinsed and soaked overnight in cold water**
- 2 **quarts vegetable stock or water**
- 2 **tablespoons extra-virgin olive oil**
- 2 **medium onions, thinly sliced**
- 1 **garlic clove, smashed**
- ½ **cup canned tomatoes, chopped**
- ⅓ **cup amber maple syrup**
- 2 **tablespoons cider vinegar**
- 1 **tablespoon chopped flat-leaf parsley**
- 1 **teaspoon chopped sage**
- 1 **bay leaf**
- **Salt and freshly ground pepper**

1. Drain and rinse the beans. In a large saucepan, cover the beans with the stock; bring to a boil. Cover and simmer over moderately high heat until the bean skins begin to split, 20 minutes.

2. Preheat the oven to 350°. Heat the oil in a large enameled cast-iron casserole. Add the onions and garlic, cover and cook over low heat until the onions soften, about 5 minutes. Uncover and cook over moderate heat, stirring, until browned, about 4 minutes. Add the tomatoes, maple syrup, vinegar, parsley, sage, bay leaf and ¾ teaspoon of salt; bring to a boil. Add the beans and their cooking liquid and bring to a boil.

3. Cover and bake for about 4 hours, stirring, until the beans are very tender and the sauce is thick. Remove the bay leaf, season the beans with salt and pepper and serve. *—Sam Hayward*
MAKE AHEAD The baked beans can be refrigerated for 5 days. Reheat gently.

New Orleans Red Beans
8 SERVINGS ●

- 1 **tablespoon plus 1 teaspoon minced garlic**
- **Kosher salt**
- 1 **teaspoon dried oregano**

½ teaspoon dried thyme

¼ teaspoon ground cumin

¼ teaspoon freshly ground
   black pepper

⅛ teaspoon cayenne

⅛ teaspoon ground white pepper

1 tablespoon olive oil

10 ounces smoked ham, cut into
   ½-inch dice (2 cups)

Two 5-ounce andouille sausages,
   halved lengthwise and cut
   crosswise into ¼-inch-thick
   slices (2 cups)

1 large Spanish onion,
   finely chopped

5 large celery ribs,
   finely chopped

1 large green bell pepper—
   cored, seeded and
   finely chopped

2 bay leaves

4 cups chicken stock or canned
   low-sodium broth

4 cups water

1 pound dried kidney beans,
   picked over and rinsed

¼ cup finely chopped
   flat-leaf parsley

Steamed white rice or garlic bread,
   for serving

1. In a small bowl, combine the minced garlic with 4 teaspoons of the kosher salt. Crumble in the oregano and add the thyme, cumin, black pepper, cayenne and white pepper.

2. In a large enameled cast-iron casserole, heat the olive oil until shimmering but not smoking. Add the smoked ham and cook over moderate heat, stirring occasionally, until lightly browned, about 4 minutes. Add the andouille sausage slices and cook, stirring from time to time, until they are lightly browned, 5 to 6 minutes. Add the Spanish onion, chopped celery, green bell pepper and bay leaves and cook, stirring, until the vegetables soften, about 10 minutes. Add the spice-and-salt mixture and cook, stirring, until fragrant, about 3 minutes.

3. Add the chicken stock and water to the casserole. Stir in the kidney beans and bring to a boil. Cover and cook the beans over low heat for 1 hour. Stir in half of the chopped parsley and cook uncovered over moderately low heat until the beans are tender and the liquid is thick, about 1 hour longer. Stir in the remaining chopped parsley and season with salt and black pepper. Remove the bay leaves. Ladle the beans into bowls and serve with white rice or garlic bread. —*Frank Brigtsen*

MAKE AHEAD The beans can be refrigerated for up to 2 days.

Southwestern Bean Gratin

8 TO 10 SERVINGS ●

The beans need to soak overnight, so plan accordingly.

1 cup dried kidney beans, picked
   over and rinsed

1 cup dried pinto or rattlesnake
   beans, picked over and rinsed

1 cup dried black beans, picked
   over and rinsed

Two 1-pound smoked ham hocks
   or ½ pound lean double-smoked
   slab bacon cut into 2 pieces

3 quarts water

6 cups chicken stock or canned
   low-sodium broth

3 medium ancho chiles, stemmed
   and seeded

2 tablespoons vegetable oil

2 large onions, chopped

4 large jalapeños, seeded
   and chopped

2 tablespoons minced garlic

½ cup barbecue sauce

2 tablespoons tomato paste

Salt and freshly ground pepper

1 cup butter cracker crumbs

¼ pound extra-sharp Cheddar
   cheese, shredded

Lime wedges, for serving

1. In a large bowl, soak the kidney and pinto beans in cold water overnight. Soak the black beans overnight in another bowl.

2. Drain the two bowls of beans separately and transfer each batch to a large saucepan. Add 1 ham hock or piece of bacon to each saucepan. Add 2 quarts of the water and 4 cups of the stock to the pinto and kidney beans. Add the remaining 1 quart of water and 2 cups of stock to the black beans.

3. Bring the beans in the saucepans to a boil, then cover partially and cook over low heat until they are almost tender, about 1 hour for the kidney and pinto beans and 35 minutes for the black beans. Drain the beans; reserve the kidney and pinto bean cooking liquid. Discard the black bean cooking liquid.

4. Remove the meat from the ham hocks and shred; reserve the ham hock fat and 1 bone. If using bacon, trim the fat and cut the meat into medium pieces. Reserve the bacon fat.

5. In a heated cast-iron skillet, toast the anchos, pressing with a spatula, until fragrant and blistered, about 30 seconds. Transfer to a bowl, cover with boiling water and soak until softened, about 15 minutes. Drain and finely chop.

6. In a large enameled cast-iron casserole, cook the ham hock fat or bacon fat in the oil over moderately high heat until the fat is crisp, about 5 minutes. Discard the fat. Add the chopped onions, jalapeños, garlic and anchos and cook over moderate heat, stirring occasionally, until softened, about 8 minutes.

---

cooking tip

soaking beans

IF TIME DOESN'T PERMIT AN OVERNIGHT SOAKING OF DRIED BEANS, use this method for a quick soak. Rinse the beans, then place them in a saucepan and cover with water. Boil for 2 minutes, then remove from the heat, cover and let stand for 1 hour. Drain and proceed with the recipe.

PIGEON PEA AND CALABAZA STEW

Add the reserved ham or bacon meat and cook, stirring, until golden, about 3 minutes. Add the barbecue sauce, tomato paste, the reserved ham hock bone and all of the drained beans. Stir in 4 cups of the reserved bean cooking liquid and season with salt and pepper. Cover and cook over moderately low heat until the beans are tender and the gravy is thick, about 1½ hours longer; add more of the bean cooking liquid if the beans seem dry. Discard the ham hock bone and transfer the beans to a large shallow baking dish or individual crocks.

7. Preheat the oven to 425°. In a bowl, toss the cracker crumbs with the cheese. Sprinkle the mixture over the beans. Bake the gratin for about 25 minutes, or until bubbling and golden. Serve with lime. —*Robert McGrath*

MAKE AHEAD The gratin can be prepared through Step 6 and refrigerated overnight. Let return to room temperature before baking.

Pigeon Pea and Calabaza Stew
4 SERVINGS ●
Dried pigeon peas can take up to two days of soaking, but you can substitute ½ pound of brown lentils, which can be cooked right out of the bag in only 45 minutes.

- ½ pound dried pigeon peas (1½ cups), soaked for 2 days and drained (see Note)
- 2 cups chicken stock or canned low-sodium broth
- 1 cup water
- ¼ cup Classic Sofrito (p. 328)
- 4 large cilantro sprigs
- One 2-ounce piece of smoked ham
- 1 pound calabaza or butternut squash—peeled, seeded and cut into 1-by-¼-inch matchsticks
- Salt and freshly ground pepper

In a medium saucepan, combine the soaked and drained pigeon peas with the chicken stock, water, Classic Sofrito, cilantro and ham and bring to a boil.

Reduce the heat to low and simmer, skimming occasionally, until the peas are tender, about 2 hours. Add the squash and simmer until it is tender, about 10 minutes longer. Season with salt and pepper. Remove the ham, cut it into ½-inch pieces and return to the stew. Discard the cilantro and serve. —*Eric Ripert*

NOTE Dried pigeon peas are available at every Latin market or by mail order from Earthy Delights (800-367-4709; www.earthy.com).

MAKE AHEAD The stew can be refrigerated for up to 3 days.

SERVE WITH Steamed rice.

Chorizo and Pinto Bean Stew
4 SERVINGS ●
- ½ pound dried pinto beans, soaked overnight and drained (1½ cups)
- 3 cups chicken stock or low-sodium broth
- ¼ pound sweet chorizo
- ¼ pound hot chorizo
- ¼ cup Classic Sofrito (p. 328)
- One 2-ounce piece of smoked ham
- 1 medium tomato, seeded and coarsely chopped
- 1 small carrot, halved
- 1 small celery rib, halved
- 1 small onion, quartered
- 1 parsley sprig
- 1 oregano sprig
- Salt and freshly ground pepper
- Lime wedges, for serving

1. In a medium saucepan, combine the pinto beans with the stock, chorizos, Classic Sofrito, ham, tomato, carrot, celery, onion, parsley and oregano and bring to a boil. Simmer over low heat, skimming occasionally, until the beans are tender, about 1½ hours.

2. Remove the chorizos; slice them ¼ inch thick and return to the stew. Remove the carrot, coarsely chop it and return to the stew. Discard the parsley and oregano and season the stew with salt and pepper. Serve the bean stew with the lime wedges. —*Eric Ripert*

MAKE AHEAD The chorizo and bean stew can be refrigerated for up to 3 days. Reheat gently.

SERVE WITH Steamed rice.

WINE Intense, berry-flavored Zinfandel.

Creamy Lima Bean Gratin
10 SERVINGS ● ●
- 4 tablespoons unsalted butter, 2 tablespoons melted
- 2 large leeks, white and tender green parts, thinly sliced crosswise
- ¾ pound shiitake or cremini mushrooms, stems discarded and caps thinly sliced
- 3 cups chicken stock or low-sodium broth
- 3 cups heavy cream
- 2 bay leaves
- 1 tablespoon finely chopped tarragon
- Salt and freshly ground pepper

dictionary
basic beans

CANNELLINI Versatile, mild and creamy, these beans take on the flavors of foods they're cooked with.

FLAGEOLET This small, pale green variety—white beans that have been harvested early—is often used in French cuisine, usually in stews or accompanying roast meats.

GARBANZO Also widely known as chickpeas, these firm, nutty legumes are ideal for salads, dips and soups.

GIGANDE These huge, white, slightly flattened beans are a bit sweet, with a dry texture; they do well in soups and are delicious dressed with olive oil.

RATTLESNAKE So named because it's speckled like snakeskin, this new brown-bean hybrid is related to the pinto. Rattlesnakes add an earthy, winy flavor to stews and casseroles.

Four 10-ounce boxes of frozen baby lima beans

½ cup fine, dry bread crumbs

¼ cup freshly grated Parmesan cheese

1. Preheat the oven to 400°. In a large skillet, melt 2 tablespoons of the butter. Add the sliced leeks and cook over low heat, stirring, until they are softened, about 3 minutes. Add the mushrooms, cover and cook over low heat, stirring occasionally, until they are tender, 15 minutes. Add the stock, cream, bay leaves and tarragon and bring to a boil. Season with salt and pepper and remove from the heat. Discard the bay leaves.

2. Put the frozen lima beans in the bottom of a 12- to 14-cup glass or ceramic baking dish. Pour the hot cream mixture over the limas. Bake for 1¼ hours, or until the cream sauce is thickened.

3. Preheat the broiler. In a small bowl, toss the bread crumbs with the Parmesan and melted butter. Sprinkle the crumbs over the lima beans and broil for about 1 minute, rotating the dish for even browning. Let the gratin stand for 15 minutes before serving.
—*Robert Stehling*

MAKE AHEAD The gratin can be baked for 50 minutes, then cooled and refrigerated overnight. Bring to room temperature and bake in a 400° oven for 15 minutes, until the limas are tender, before adding the crumb topping and broiling.

---

cooking tip

seed secrets

TO GET THE MOST OUT OF SEEDS LIKE CUMIN AND FENNEL, toast them. Place the seeds in a small, dry skillet over moderate heat and toast, shaking the pan, until they are fragrant. Another tip: A handy trick for cleaning out a spice grinder is to run a piece of soft bread through the grinder.

Spicy Asparagus and Lentil Salad with Fennel

4 SERVINGS ●

1 cup green lentils, rinsed and picked over

1 small onion, halved

Salt and freshly ground pepper

¾ pound medium asparagus, tips cut to 1 inch, stems chopped

1 medium fennel bulb—quartered, cored and thinly sliced

1 celery rib, finely chopped

2 small tomatoes (6 ounces each), finely chopped

2 jalapeño or serrano chiles, seeded and minced

2 tablespoons coarsely chopped cilantro

2 tablespoons coarsely chopped flat-leaf parsley

3 tablespoons fresh lemon juice

1½ tablespoons extra-virgin olive oil

1½ tablespoons soy sauce

1 medium Belgian endive, spears separated

4 cups loosely packed mixed baby lettuces (3 ounces)

1. Bring a medium saucepan of water to a boil. Add the lentils and onion halves and season with salt and pepper. Reduce the heat to low, cover and simmer until the lentils are tender, about 15 minutes. Drain; discard the onion. Transfer the lentils to a medium bowl and let cool.

2. Cook the asparagus tips and stems in a medium saucepan of boiling salted water until barely tender, about 4 minutes. Drain and rinse in cold water, then drain again and pat dry. Add the asparagus to the lentils. Add the fennel, celery, tomatoes, jalapeños, cilantro, parsley, lemon juice, olive oil and soy sauce to the salad, season with salt and pepper and toss to mix.

3. Arrange the endive spears on plates. Mound the lettuce in the center, top with the asparagus-lentil salad and serve. —*Hubert Keller*

Rice and Lentil Stew with Olive Gremolata

4 SERVINGS ●

Similar to *risi e bisi*, the porridgelike Venetian dish of rice and peas, this satisfying vegetarian stew is a great way to use arborio or other medium-grain Italian rice, and it's easier than risotto.

2 quarts water

½ cup French or Italian green lentils

Salt

1 tablespoon extra-virgin olive oil

1 medium onion, finely chopped

1 shallot, minced

¾ cup chopped flat-leaf parsley

2 thyme sprigs

1 bay leaf

1½ cups frozen peas

1 cup Italian medium-grain rice (6½ ounces), such as arborio

16 Gaeta or Calamata olives (1 ounce), pitted and chopped

2 garlic cloves, minced

1 tablespoon plus 1 teaspoon finely grated lemon zest

4 cups coarsely chopped romaine lettuce (about ½ head)

½ teaspoon crushed red pepper

1. In a medium saucepan, bring 2 cups of the water to a boil. Add the lentils, cover and cook over low heat, stirring occasionally, until almost tender, about 30 minutes. Add a large pinch of salt and simmer until tender, about 3 minutes longer. Drain the lentils and spread them on a plate to cool.

2. Heat the olive oil in a medium enameled cast-iron casserole. Add the onion and shallot and cook over low heat, stirring occasionally, until softened, about 5 minutes. Add 2 cups of the water, ¼ cup of the parsley, the thyme sprigs, bay leaf and a pinch of salt and bring to a boil. Reduce the heat to moderately low, then cover and simmer for 15 minutes. Add the peas, rice and the remaining 1 quart of water. Cover and cook over moderately low heat, stirring occasionally, until the rice is tender, about 20 minutes.

3. Meanwhile, in a small bowl, toss the olives with the garlic, lemon zest and the remaining ½ cup of parsley. Season the gremolata with salt.

4. Gently stir the lentils into the stew. Add the romaine and crushed red pepper, cover and cook over low heat until the lettuce is wilted, about 3 minutes. Season with salt. Discard the thyme sprigs and bay leaf. Ladle the stew into bowls, top with the olive gremolata and serve. —*Marcia Kiesel*

WINE Light, zesty, fruity Dolcetto.

Tabbouleh with Marinated Artichokes and Baby Spinach

4 SERVINGS ●

MARINATED ARTICHOKES

- 4 large artichokes
- ½ teaspoon cumin seeds
- 3 tablespoons extra-virgin olive oil
- 2 tablespoons sherry vinegar
- 2 teaspoons finely chopped oregano

Salt and freshly ground pepper

TABBOULEH AND SPINACH

- 1 cup boiling water
- 1 cup coarse bulgur (6 ounces)
- 3 tablespoons extra-virgin olive oil
- 3 tablespoons fresh lemon juice
- 2 scallions, finely chopped
- 1 bunch curly-leaf parsley (4 ounces), coarsely chopped
- 1 plum tomato, finely diced
- 1 tablespoon chopped mint

Salt and freshly ground pepper

- 10 cherry tomatoes, halved
- 2 packed cups baby spinach leaves (3 ounces)
- ¼ cup crumbled feta cheese (2 ounces)
- 2 tablespoons toasted pine nuts

I. MAKE THE MARINATED ARTICHOKES: Cut the stems off the artichokes. Place the stems and artichokes in a steamer basket set over 1 inch of simmering water. Cover and steam over moderate heat until the artichoke bottoms are tender when pierced with a knife, about 40 minutes.

When cool enough to handle, pull the leaves off the artichokes and trim off any fibrous outer skin. Using a spoon, scrape out the hairy chokes. Quarter the artichoke bottoms. Peel the stems and cut them into ½-inch rounds.

2. In a skillet, toast the cumin over moderate heat until fragrant, about 40 seconds. Transfer to a spice grinder and let cool. Grind the cumin to a powder and transfer to a large shallow dish. Stir in the olive oil, vinegar and oregano and season with salt and pepper. Add the artichokes and coat well with the cumin marinade. Let stand at room temperature for 1 hour or refrigerate overnight.

3. MAKE THE TABBOULEH AND SPINACH: In a large heatproof bowl, pour the boiling water over the bulgur. Cover and let stand until the water is absorbed and the bulgur is tender, about 40 minutes. Fluff with a fork. Stir in the olive oil, lemon juice, scallions, parsley, plum tomato and mint; season with salt and pepper. Cover and refrigerate for 1 hour, or until chilled.

4. In a bowl, toss the cherry tomatoes with the spinach, feta and pine nuts. Spoon 2 tablespoons of the marinade from the artichokes over the salad and toss well; season with salt and pepper.

5. Spoon the tabbouleh onto plates and surround with the artichokes. Top with the salad and serve. —*Deborah Knight*

MAKE AHEAD The recipe can be prepared through Step 3 up to 1 day ahead.

Tomatillo-Quinoa Salad

6 SERVINGS ●

- 2 cups quinoa (¾ pound)
- 3 cups water
- 8 tomatillos (½ pound), husked
- 1 medium yellow onion, chopped
- ½ cup chopped cilantro
- 7 tablespoons fresh lime juice
- ⅓ cup chopped flat-leaf parsley
- ⅓ cup extra-virgin olive oil
- 2 tablespoons Champagne vinegar
- 1 serrano chile, seeded and minced
- 1 garlic clove, minced

Salt and freshly ground pepper

- ½ large cucumber, thinly sliced
- 1 bunch radishes (¾ pound), thinly sliced
- 1 red onion, thinly sliced
- 1 red bell pepper, thinly sliced
- 10 ounces cooked corn (2 cups)
- 4 ounces queso añejo or ricotta salata, quartered and thinly sliced
- 1 tablespoon finely grated lime zest

I. Preheat the oven to 350°. Toast the quinoa on a baking sheet for 8 minutes. Bring the water to a boil in a saucepan. Add the quinoa, cover and simmer until the water is absorbed, 15 minutes; cool.

2. In a medium saucepan of boiling water, blanch the tomatillos for 3 minutes. Drain and rinse under cold water.

3. In a blender, puree the tomatillos, yellow onion, cilantro, lime juice, parsley, oil, vinegar, chile and garlic. Transfer to a large bowl and stir in the quinoa. Season with salt and pepper. Garnish with the cucumber, radishes, red onion, bell pepper, corn, queso añejo and lime zest; serve. —*Paula Disbrowe*

Warm Chickpea, Fennel and Parsley Salad

6 SERVINGS ●

Soaked dried chickpeas have a much deeper flavor than canned, which can be substituted if you're in a hurry.

- 1½ cups dried chickpeas (¾ pound), soaked overnight and drained
- 1 large onion, quartered
- 12 thyme sprigs

Salt

- 2 garlic cloves, very finely chopped
- 2 tablespoons red wine vinegar
- ½ cup extra-virgin olive oil
- 2 celery ribs, finely chopped
- 1 small fennel bulb (¾ pound)— halved, cored and finely chopped
- ¾ cup loosely packed flat-leaf parsley leaves
- ½ cup finely chopped red onion

CHICKEN AND BULGUR SALAD WITH AVOCADO

MEYER LEMON RISOTTO WITH BASIL

1. In a large pot, cover the chickpeas with water. Add the quartered onion and the thyme sprigs. Bring the chickpeas to a boil, then simmer them over moderate heat for 1 hour. Stir in 1 teaspoon of salt and simmer the chickpeas until they are tender, about 10 minutes longer. Discard the onion quarters and thyme sprigs.

2. Meanwhile, in a medium bowl, mash the garlic to a puree with 1 teaspoon of salt. Stir in the red wine vinegar, then gradually whisk in the olive oil.

3. Drain the chickpeas and add them to the bowl. Toss with the chopped celery, fennel, parsley and onion. Season the salad with salt and serve warm.
—*Maggie Beer*

MAKE AHEAD The recipe can be prepared through Step 1 and refrigerated overnight. Rewarm before continuing.
WINE Fruity, low-oak Chardonnay.

Warm Wheat Berry and Quinoa Salad

8 SERVINGS ● ●

1½ cups wheat berries (about ¾ pound), rinsed
1 large onion, finely chopped
5½ to 6 cups beef stock or canned low-sodium broth
Kosher salt
1 cup quinoa (6 ounces), rinsed
⅓ cup finely chopped flat-leaf parsley
Freshly ground pepper

1. In a large saucepan, combine the wheat berries and chopped onion with 3½ cups of the beef stock and 1 teaspoon of salt. Bring to a boil, then cover and simmer over moderately low heat until the wheat berries are tender but still chewy, about 1 hour. Remove the wheat berries from the heat.

2. In a medium saucepan, combine the quinoa with 2 cups of the beef stock and ½ teaspoon of salt and bring to a boil. Cover and simmer over low heat until the quinoa is tender and most of the liquid has been absorbed, about 12 minutes. Remove the quinoa from the heat and stir. Cover and let stand for 5 minutes, then add the quinoa to the wheat berries.

3. Stir the remaining ½ cup of beef stock into the grain mixture if it seems dry. Cover and cook the grains over moderate heat, stirring occasionally, until warmed through, about 5 minutes. Stir the chopped parsley into the grain salad, season with salt and pepper and serve. —*Ben Ford*

MAKE AHEAD The recipe can be prepared through Step 2 and refrigerated overnight. Bring the salad to room temperature before proceeding.

Chicken and Bulgur Salad with Avocado

4 SERVINGS ●

- 1 cup bulgur
- 1 cup boiling water
- Two 6-ounce boneless chicken breasts, with skin
- 5 tablespoons grapeseed oil
- Salt and freshly ground pepper
- ½ cup fresh orange juice
- ½ cup coarsely chopped basil leaves
- 5 tablespoons fresh lemon juice
- 2 large scallions, thinly sliced
- 2 Hass avocados, cut into 1-inch chunks
- 1 medium fennel bulb (¾ pound), cored and cut into ½-inch pieces
- 1 cup cherry tomatoes, halved

I. Preheat the oven to 500°. In a heat-proof bowl, cover the bulgur with the boiling water. Cover the bowl with a plate and let stand until the water has been absorbed and the bulgur is tender, about 30 minutes.

2. On a rimmed baking sheet, coat the chicken with 1 tablespoon of the oil and season with salt and pepper. Roast the chicken on the top shelf for 15 minutes, or until golden brown and just cooked through; let cool. Slice the breasts diagonally about ¼ inch thick.

3. In a small bowl, whisk the orange juice with the basil, lemon juice, scallions and the remaining ¼ cup of grapeseed oil; season the vinaigrette with salt and pepper.

4. In a large bowl, toss the bulgur, chicken, avocados, fennel and tomatoes with the vinaigrette; season with salt and pepper. Mound the salad onto plates and serve. —*Marcia Kiesel*

MAKE AHEAD The salad can be refrigerated for up to 2 hours.

WINE Ripe, creamy-textured Chardonnay.

Meyer Lemon Risotto with Basil

6 FIRST-COURSE SERVINGS ●

If you can't find any Meyer lemons, use regular (Eureka) lemons.

- 6 cups chicken stock or canned low-sodium broth
- 2 tablespoons unsalted butter
- 1 medium red onion, finely chopped
- 1 tender inner celery rib, finely chopped, plus ¼ cup chopped leaves
- ½ Thai chile, minced
- Salt and freshly ground pepper
- 1 garlic clove, minced
- 1½ cups arborio rice (10 ounces)
- ½ cup white vermouth
- ½ cup freshly grated Parmesan cheese, plus more for serving
- ⅓ cup mascarpone cheese
- 1 tablespoon finely grated Meyer lemon zest
- 1 tablespoon finely grated Eureka lemon zest
- 1 tablespoon fresh Meyer lemon juice
- 1 tablespoon fresh Eureka lemon juice
- ¼ cup plus 2 tablespoons julienned basil leaves

I. Bring the stock to a boil in a saucepan; cover and keep hot. Melt the butter in a large saucepan. Add the onion, celery rib and chile, season with salt and pepper and cook over low heat, stirring, until softened, about 7 minutes. Add the celery leaves and garlic and cook for 1 minute. Add the rice and stir until glossy, about 1 minute.

2. Add the vermouth to the rice and simmer over moderate heat until almost absorbed, about 3 minutes. Add the hot stock, 1 cup at a time, and cook, stirring constantly between additions, until most of the stock has been absorbed before adding more. The rice is done when it's tender and most of the liquid is absorbed, about 20 minutes total. Stir in the ½ cup of Parmesan, the mascarpone, the lemon zests and juices and the basil. Season with salt and pepper. Spoon the risotto into bowls and serve with the additional Parmesan. —*Jean-Georges Vongerichten*

WINE Dry, light, refreshing Soave.

Shrimp and Goat Cheese Risotto

4 SERVINGS ●

- 1 quart chicken stock or canned low-sodium broth
- ¾ pound medium shrimp, shelled and deveined
- 1 tablespoon unsalted butter
- 2 tablespoons extra-virgin olive oil
- 2 garlic cloves, minced
- 1 small onion, finely chopped
- 1 cup arborio rice (8½ ounces)
- ½ cup dry white wine
- ½ cup chopped basil leaves
- ¼ cup soft fresh goat cheese (1½ ounces)
- 2 tablespoons freshly grated Parmesan cheese
- ¼ teaspoon finely grated fresh ginger
- ¼ teaspoon finely grated lemon zest
- Salt and freshly ground pepper

I. In a medium saucepan, bring the stock to a simmer. Add the shrimp, cover and simmer over moderate heat until just cooked, about 2 minutes. With a slotted spoon, transfer the shrimp to a plate to cool. Cover the stock and keep it at barely a simmer.

2. In a medium saucepan, melt the butter in the olive oil. Add the garlic and onion and cook over low heat, stirring, until softened, about 4 minutes. Add the rice and cook over moderate heat, stirring, until it is coated with oil, about 1 minute. Add the wine and simmer until almost evaporated, about 3 minutes. Add 1 scant cup of the simmering stock and cook, stirring constantly, until it is absorbed. Continue to add the stock, 1 cup at a time, stirring constantly until it is absorbed. The risotto is done when the rice is tender but still slightly firm and creamy, about 25 minutes total. Stir in the shrimp. Remove the risotto from the heat and stir in the basil, goat cheese, Parmesan, ginger and lemon zest. Season the risotto with salt and pepper and serve.
—*Marcia Kiesel*

WINE Lively, assertive Sauvignon Blanc.

Porcini Mushroom Risotto

8 SERVINGS

Simmer the mushroom trimmings and a few chopped tomatoes in the vegetable stock to enhance the flavor.

- ½ ounce dried porcini mushrooms (½ cup)
- 1 cup boiling water
- 6½ cups vegetable stock or low-sodium broth
- 4 tablespoons unsalted butter
- 2 tablespoons extra-virgin olive oil
- 1 small onion, minced
- 1 garlic clove, minced
- ½ pound cremini or shiitake mushrooms, stems trimmed and caps cut into ½-inch dice
- 2 cups arborio rice (14 ounces)
- 1½ cups dry white wine
- ½ cup freshly grated Parmesan cheese, plus Parmesan shavings for garnish
- Salt and freshly ground pepper

1. In a heatproof bowl, soak the dried porcinis in the boiling water until softened, about 20 minutes. Rub the mushrooms in the water to remove any grit.

cooking tip

leftover rice

SOUP A handful of rice can turn a bowl of soup into a main course; tomato soup is a classic candidate.

SALAD Toss long-grain rice with chicken, tuna or vegetables, then dress with a seasoned vinaigrette.

SAUCES A quick way to thicken pan juices from roasts or braises is by pureeing them with some cooked rice.

FRIED Stir-fry rice with leftover vegetables or meat, then season with sesame oil and soy sauce.

RICE PUDDING Simmer cooked rice with sweetened milk, dried fruits and cinnamon for a homey dessert.

Lift the porcini mushrooms out of the soaking liquid and coarsely chop. Reserve the mushroom soaking liquid.

2. In a medium saucepan, bring the vegetable stock to a boil. Cover and keep the stock at a bare simmer over low heat. In a large saucepan or medium enameled cast-iron casserole, melt 2 tablespoons of the butter in the olive oil. Add the onion and garlic and cook over moderate heat until softened but not browned, about 4 minutes. Add the cremini mushrooms and cook, stirring, until they are softened, about 4 minutes. Add the rice to the pan and cook, stirring, until coated, about 1 minute.

3. Add the white wine to the rice and simmer until almost evaporated. Add the chopped porcinis and the reserved mushroom soaking liquid, stopping before you reach the grit at the bottom. Add enough hot stock to just cover the rice and cook, stirring constantly, until the stock has been absorbed. Add more stock. Continue cooking and stirring, adding more stock as it is absorbed, until the rice is just tender and a creamy sauce forms, about 30 minutes.

4. Remove the risotto from the heat; stir in the remaining 2 tablespoons of butter and the grated Parmesan. Season the risotto with salt and pepper and ladle into bowls. Top with Parmesan shavings and serve. —*Giorgio Rivetti*

Vegetable Risotto Dressing

8 SERVINGS ●

- 2 tablespoons extra-virgin olive oil
- ½ pound shiitake mushrooms, stems discarded, caps thinly sliced
- 3 carrots, cut into ⅓-inch dice
- Salt and freshly ground pepper
- ¾ pound Broccolini or broccoli, peeled and cut into ½-inch pieces
- 1 roasted red bell pepper, peeled and cut into ½-inch dice
- 2 tablespoons unsalted butter
- 1 small shallot, minced
- ½ cup arborio rice

- 2 cups chicken stock or canned low-sodium broth
- ¼ cup freshly grated Parmesan cheese
- 1 cup *panko* (Japanese bread crumbs)

1. Heat the olive oil in a large skillet. Add the mushrooms and carrots, season with salt and pepper and cook over moderately high heat for 5 minutes. Add the Broccolini and cook for 2 minutes. Stir in the red pepper.

2. Preheat the oven to 350°. Melt the butter in a medium saucepan. Add the shallot and cook over moderate heat until softened but not browned, about 4 minutes. Add the rice and cook for 1 minute. Add the stock and bring to a boil. Add the Parmesan, cover and cook for about 17 minutes. Stir the rice and *panko* into the vegetables and season with salt and pepper.

3. Butter a 6-cup baking dish and spread the rice mixture in it. Bake for about 45 minutes, or until lightly browned. Let rest for 10 minutes before serving. —*Jean-Georges Vongerichten*

Vegetable Pilaf with Pancetta

8 SERVINGS ●

- 2 tablespoons unsalted butter
- 2 ounces meaty pancetta, finely diced
- 1 medium onion, finely diced
- 1 large celery rib, peeled and finely diced
- 1 medium carrot, finely diced
- 2 cups basmati rice (1 pound)
- ½ teaspoon kosher salt
- 3 cups chicken stock or canned low-sodium broth
- 1 bay leaf

Preheat the oven to 350°. In a 4- to 4½-quart roasting pan, melt the butter over low heat. Add the pancetta and cook, stirring, until lightly browned, about 5 minutes. Add the onion and cook, stirring, until softened, about 4 minutes. Add the celery and carrot and cook until softened, about 4 minutes.

Stir in the rice, then add the salt, stock and bay leaf and bring to a boil. Cover with foil and bake for 25 minutes. Uncover, fluff the rice and cover again until ready to serve. —*Pascal Chaupitre*
MAKE AHEAD The pilaf can stand, covered, for 1 hour. Serve at room temperature or reheat in a 350° oven.

Dirty Turkey-Rice Purloo
10 SERVINGS ●

¼ cup plus 1 tablespoon peanut oil
1 large onion, finely chopped
1 red bell pepper, finely chopped
1 green bell pepper, finely chopped
3 large celery ribs, finely chopped
1 tablespoon minced garlic
1 cup finely diced peeled eggplant
Reserved giblets (including the liver) from a 16- to 18-pound turkey, trimmed and cut into ¼-inch dice
½ pound smoked sausage, such as kielbasa or andouille, cut into ½-inch dice
Salt and freshly ground pepper
½ cup dry red wine
1 quart Rich Turkey Stock (recipe follows), chicken stock or low-sodium broth
2 bay leaves
1 teaspoon crushed red pepper
½ teaspoon dried thyme
½ pound fresh or thawed frozen okra, cut crosswise into ½-inch-thick slices
1 cup canned crushed tomatoes
1 pound long-grain rice, preferably Carolina

1. Preheat the oven to 375°. In a large, deep skillet, heat 2 tablespoons of the oil. Add the onion and cook over low heat until golden, 7 minutes. Add the bell peppers and celery and cook until softened, 8 minutes. Add the garlic and eggplant; cook, stirring, until the eggplant softens, 5 minutes. Scrape into a large enameled cast-iron casserole.
2. Heat 1 tablespoon of the oil in the skillet. Add the giblets and the sausage and season with salt and pepper.

Cook over high heat until browned, 5 minutes. Stir in the wine and cook until reduced to a syrup, 1 minute. Add the stock and bring to a boil; transfer to the casserole. Add the bay leaves, crushed pepper and thyme.
3. In the skillet, heat 1 tablespoon of the oil until shimmering. Add the okra and cook over moderately high heat, stirring, until browned, 4 minutes. Stir in the tomatoes and cook until heated through. Add to the casserole.
4. Heat the remaining 1 tablespoon of oil in the skillet. Add the rice and stir over moderate heat just until golden, about 3 minutes; scrape into the casserole. Cover and bake for 45 minutes, or until the rice is tender and the stock is absorbed. Discard the bay leaves. Fluff the rice and serve. —*Robert Stehling*
MAKE AHEAD The purloo can be made through Step 3; refrigerate overnight.

RICH TURKEY STOCK
MAKES ABOUT 3 QUARTS ● ●

7 pounds turkey parts, such as wings, thighs and drumsticks
16 cups water
1 large onion, thickly sliced
1 large carrot, thickly sliced
1 large celery rib, thickly sliced
2 garlic cloves, sliced
1 teaspoon kosher salt
Freshly ground pepper

1. Preheat the oven to 400°. In a roasting pan, roast the turkey parts for 1½ hours, or until browned; transfer to a pot.
2. Set the roasting pan over 2 burners. Add 3 cups of the water and boil, scraping up the browned bits from the bottom of the pan. Add the liquid to the pot.
3. Add the onion, carrot, celery, garlic, salt, several pinches of pepper and the remaining 13 cups of water to the pot. Bring to a boil. Reduce the heat to moderately low, cover partially and simmer for about 2½ hours. Strain the stock and skim the fat before using. —*R.S.*
MAKE AHEAD The stock can be refrigerated for 3 days or frozen for 1 month.

Winter Vegetable—Chicken Paella
6 SERVINGS

1 large leek, white and tender green parts only, halved lengthwise
¼ cup extra-virgin olive oil
1 pound butternut squash, peeled and cut into 1-inch dice
Kosher salt and freshly ground pepper
12 boneless chicken thighs, with skin
1 large onion, finely chopped
10 ounces chorizo or other spicy cured sausage, cut into ¼-inch-thick slices
¼ teaspoon saffron threads, crumbled
¼ teaspoon cayenne pepper
2 cups Spanish Valencia rice
3½ cups hot chicken stock
One 14½-ounce can whole tomatoes, drained and chopped
½ pound Swiss chard, stems discarded, leaves coarsely chopped

1. Preheat the oven to 425°. Brush the leek with 1 teaspoon of the olive oil and arrange on one side of a baking sheet, cut side down. On the other side, toss the squash with 2 teaspoons of the oil. Season with salt and pepper and roast for 20 minutes, or until golden and just tender. Cut the leek into 1-inch lengths. Reduce the oven temperature to 350°.
2. Heat 1 tablespoon of the oil in a 14- to 16-inch paella pan or skillet. Season the chicken with salt and pepper; cook over moderate heat until golden, 10 minutes. Transfer to a plate. Add the onion and the remaining 2 tablespoons of oil to the pan; cook over low heat until softened. Add the chorizo, saffron and cayenne; cook over moderately high heat, stirring, for 2 minutes. Add the rice and 1½ teaspoons of salt; cook, stirring, for 2 minutes. Stir in the stock, tomatoes, chard, leek and squash.
3. Nestle the chicken into the rice, skin side up. Simmer over low heat for 5 minutes. Transfer to the 350° oven.

potatoes, grains + more

Bake the paella for about 30 minutes, or until the stock is absorbed, the rice is tender and the chicken is cooked through. Remove from the oven and cover with a towel; let stand for 10 minutes. Serve at once. —*David Tanis*

Red Lentil Köfte with Tomato-Cucumber Salad

8 SERVINGS ●

The köfte here are fried, but they can also be served grilled, baked or "raw."

 - 2 tablespoons unsalted butter
 - 1 medium white onion, minced
 - 1 carrot, finely chopped
 - 1 tablespoon tomato paste
 - 2 teaspoons hot paprika
 - 1 teaspoon ground cumin
 - 1 cup red lentils, picked over and rinsed
 - 4 cups water
 - 1 cup medium-ground bulgur
 - Salt and freshly ground pepper
 - All-purpose flour, for dusting
 - Vegetable oil, for frying
 - 1 small red onion, finely chopped
 - 1 European cucumber—peeled, halved, seeded and finely diced
 - 1 small green bell pepper, minced
 - 1 pound tomatoes, seeded and cut into ½-inch dice
 - 6 tablespoons extra-virgin olive oil
 - 1½ tablespoons fresh lemon juice
 - 1 tablespoon pomegranate molasses (optional)
 - ¼ cup minced flat-leaf parsley
 - 8 romaine lettuce leaves, torn into large pieces

1. Melt the butter in a saucepan. Add the white onion and carrot and cook over moderate heat until softened, about 5 minutes. Stir in tomato paste, paprika and cumin; add the lentils and water and bring to a boil. Simmer over moderate heat until the lentils are tender and have absorbed about three-fourths of the liquid, about 8 minutes. Stir in the bulgur and remove from the heat. Let stand until the liquid is absorbed and the bulgur is softened, 20 minutes.

Season the bulgur with salt and pepper. Transfer to a rimmed baking sheet and spread out in an even layer to cool.
2. Put ½ cup of flour in a plate. Divide the lentil mixture into 16 portions; form into ¾-inch-thick patties. Dredge the patties in the flour, shake off any excess and set on a floured baking sheet. In a large skillet, heat ¼ inch of vegetable oil until shimmering. Working in batches, fry the patties over moderately high heat, turning once, until golden, about 5 minutes. Drain on paper towels. Add more oil to the skillet as necessary.
3. In a bowl, toss the red onion, cucumber, bell pepper and tomatoes. In a small bowl, whisk the olive oil, lemon juice and molasses. Pour all but 2 tablespoons of the dressing over the salad, season with salt and pepper and toss. Stir in 2 tablespoons of the parsley.
4. In a bowl, toss the romaine with the remaining 2 tablespoons of dressing and arrange on a platter. Set the lentil cakes on the lettuce. Spoon the salad on top and sprinkle with the remaining parsley and serve. —*Ana Sortun*

MAKE AHEAD The cooked lentil patties can be refrigerated overnight. Reheat in a 350° oven before serving.

Quick, Soft, Sexy Grits

6 SERVINGS ● ●

 - 6 cups chicken stock or canned low-sodium broth
 - 2 cups heavy cream
 - 4 tablespoons unsalted butter
 - 2 large garlic cloves, minced
 - Kosher salt and freshly ground pepper
 - 2 cups quick grits
 - Tabasco

In a large saucepan, combine the chicken stock, cream, butter and garlic. Add 2 teaspoons of salt and ¼ teaspoon of pepper and bring to a boil. Slowly whisk in the grits and cook over low heat, whisking often, until thick and completely smooth, about 10 minutes. Season with salt, pepper and Tabasco and serve. —*Jan Birnbaum*

Arepas with Cheese

MAKES FOUR 6-INCH AREPAS

 - 3 cups white masa harina (see Note)
 - 6 ounces finely grated feta cheese or mozzarella cheese, plus more for topping
 - 1 teaspoon salt
 - 1¾ cups warm water
 - 3 tablespoons softened unsalted butter, plus more for spreading

1. In a large bowl, mix the masa harina with 6 ounces of the feta and the salt. Slowly add the water while stirring with a wooden spoon. Add 3 tablespoons of the butter and stir until smooth. Turn the dough out onto a work surface and knead for 1 to 2 minutes, or until it comes together in a smooth mass.
2. Set a cast-iron griddle over moderate heat. Divide the arepa dough into 4 equal pieces and roll each piece into a ball. On a clean work surface, flatten the balls of arepa dough and pat them into 5-inch rounds with smooth edges.
3. Spread 1 teaspoon of softened butter on one side of an arepa. Set the arepa on the griddle, buttered side down. Using a flat spatula, press the arepa into a 6-inch round about ⅓ inch thick; carefully smooth the edges if necessary. Cook the arepa over moderately low heat without turning until browned on the bottom, about 6 minutes; reduce the heat to low if the arepa browns too quickly. Spread the top of the arepa with 1 teaspoon of butter, flip and cook for 6 minutes longer, or until browned. Transfer the arepa to a plate, sprinkle with cheese and serve. Repeat with the remaining arepas. —*Claudia Marulanda*

NOTE Masa harina is a type of corn flour that is made from ground, precooked dehydrated yellow or white corn with lime. It is available at Latin American markets, some supermarkets and at many health food stores. It can also be mail-ordered from the Kitchen Market (888-HOT-4433).

RED LENTIL KÖFTE WITH TOMATO-CUCUMBER SALAD

STEAK SANDWICHES, P. 249

breads, pizzas + sandwiches

ROASTED VEGETABLE GALETTE

ANDOUILLE PIZZA WITH ONION CONFIT

Roasted Vegetable Galette

4 SERVINGS

One 9-ounce sheet of puff
    pastry, chilled
  4 plum tomatoes, halved
    lengthwise
Salt and freshly ground pepper
2½ tablespoons extra-virgin olive oil
  3 leeks, white and tender green
    parts only, halved lengthwise
    and thinly sliced crosswise
Six 1-ounce fingerling potatoes,
    halved lengthwise
1½ teaspoons chopped thyme
  8 oil-cured olives, pitted and
    chopped

1. Preheat the oven to 325°. Line a cookie sheet with parchment paper. On a lightly floured surface, roll out the puff pastry ¹⁄₁₆ inch thick. Cut out a 12-inch round; transfer to the cookie sheet. Refrigerate for at least 20 minutes.

2. Arrange the tomatoes on a rimmed baking sheet, season with salt and pepper and bake for 1 hour.

3. Meanwhile, in a large skillet, heat 2 tablespoons of the olive oil. Add the leeks, season with salt and pepper and cook over low heat, stirring occasionally, until tender, about 10 minutes. Let cool to room temperature.

4. In a bowl, toss the potatoes with the remaining ½ tablespoon of oil and season with salt and pepper. When the tomatoes are done, slide them to one side of the baking sheet and scatter the potatoes on the other. Bake at 350° for 20 minutes, or until the potatoes are tender and golden and the tomatoes are lightly browned. Let cool.

5. Turn the oven up to 400°. Spread the leeks on the puff pastry round to within 1 inch of the edge. Top with the tomatoes, potatoes and thyme.

Bake for about 30 minutes, or until the edge is puffed and golden. Scatter the olives over the galette, cut into wedges and serve. —*Rori Trovato*

MAKE AHEAD The recipe can be prepared ahead through Step 4; refrigerate overnight. Bring the toppings to room temperature before assembling.

WINE Medium-bodied, round Pinot Blanc.

Andouille Pizza with Onion Confit and Fontina Cheese

MAKES TWO 14-INCH PIZZAS

For a crisp and chewy crust, be sure to bake the pizza on a stone that has been preheated for at least 30 minutes. It's also best to bake one pizza at a time to allow for maximum air circulation.

 ¼ cup extra-virgin olive oil, plus
    more for brushing
  2 pounds onions, thinly sliced
 ⅓ cup white wine vinegar

2 tablespoons dry white wine
Pinch of sugar
Kosher salt
Two 1-pound balls of frozen pizza
dough, thawed
Cornmeal, for dusting
½ cup oil-packed sun-dried
tomatoes, drained and
thinly sliced
¼ pound imported Fontina
cheese, shredded
¼ pound mozzarella, shredded
6 ounces andouille sausage,
sliced ¼ inch thick
1 tablespoon minced
flat-leaf parsley

1. In a large saucepan, heat ¼ cup of the oil until shimmering. Add the onions and cook over moderate heat, stirring, until softened, about 5 minutes. Add the vinegar, wine, sugar and a pinch of salt. Cover partially and cook over low heat, stirring, until the onions are very soft, about 20 minutes. Uncover and cook over moderate heat, stirring, until browned, about 30 minutes longer; add water if the onions seem dry. Transfer the onion confit to a bowl and let cool.

2. Meanwhile, set a pizza stone on the bottom shelf of the oven. Preheat the oven to 500° for 30 minutes.

3. On a floured surface, roll out 1 ball of dough to a 14-inch round. Transfer to a pizza peel or cookie sheet dusted with cornmeal. Spread half of the onion confit over the dough to within 1 inch of the edge. Top with half of the tomatoes, Fontina, mozzarella, andouille and parsley. Lightly brush the edge with olive oil.

4. Slide the pizza onto the stone and bake for about 10 minutes, or until the crust is browned and the top is bubbling. Let cool for 5 minutes, then cut into wedges and serve. Meanwhile, repeat with the remaining dough and toppings. If you don't have a pizza stone, assemble the pizzas on lightly oiled baking sheets coated with cornmeal. Let rise for 30 minutes before baking on the sheet. —Jan Birnbaum

Grilled Pizzas Stuffed with Cheese and Radicchio Salad
6 SERVINGS ● ●
The key to these pizzas is to have your rolled-out dough ready on baking sheets and all of your fillings set out grillside before you start.

2 cups fresh ricotta cheese
(1 pound)
¾ cup shredded mozzarella
(3 ounces)
Salt and freshly ground pepper
6 anchovy fillets, minced
3 tablespoons extra-virgin olive oil,
plus more for brushing
2½ tablespoons fresh lemon juice
2 small garlic cloves, minced
1½ pounds pizza dough, thawed
if frozen
1 pint yellow or orange cherry
tomatoes, halved
4 cups thinly sliced radicchio

1. In a bowl, mix the ricotta and mozzarella. Season with salt and pepper.

2. In a bowl, mix the anchovies with the 3 tablespoons of oil, lemon juice and garlic. Season with salt and pepper.

3. Oil 3 large baking sheets. Cut the pizza dough into 6 equal pieces and pat into disks. On a lightly floured surface, roll each disk into an 8-inch round and dust with flour. Place 2 rounds on each baking sheet and let stand in a draft-free place until they begin to rise, about 20 minutes.

4. Light a grill. If using a gas grill, set the center burner on high heat and the front and back or side burners on low. Brush the dough generously with olive oil. Using your hands, stretch each piece out into a 9-inch round, lifting the dough as necessary.

5. Working with 1 piece of dough at a time, quickly lift it off the baking sheet and drape it over the center of the grill; use long-handled tongs to straighten out any folds. Grill the dough over a hot fire for 10 seconds, then slide it over to a low fire and grill until lightly charred on the bottom, about 10 seconds longer.

Flip the pizza and spread a scant ½ cup of the cheeses over half of it. Rotate the pizza over the hot and cooler areas of the grill to finish cooking the dough and heat the cheese, about 40 seconds. Transfer the pizza to a plate.

6. Add the tomatoes and radicchio to the anchovy dressing and toss. Spoon a rounded ½ cup of the radicchio salad over the cheese and fold the other half of the crust over the filling, cut in half and serve at once. Repeat with the remaining dough and fillings. —Marcia Kiesel
WINE Tart, low-tannin Barbera.

Tomato Mozzarella Pizza
MAKES TWO 10-INCH PIZZAS
As an easy way to add variety to her hors d'oeuvre course, Giada De Laurentiis uses at least two other pizza toppings besides the classic one here.

Two ½-pound balls of Pizza Dough
(p. 244) or thawed frozen
pizza or bread dough
Flour, for dusting and rolling
One 14-ounce can peeled Italian plum
tomatoes, drained
2 tablespoons coarsely
chopped basil leaves
1 large garlic clove, very finely
chopped
1 tablespoon extra-virgin olive oil
Salt and freshly ground pepper
1½ cups coarsely shredded
mozzarella (6 ounces)

1. Set a pizza stone or heavy baking sheet in the bottom third of the oven. Preheat the oven to 550°, allowing at least 30 minutes for the stone to heat.

2. On a lightly floured work surface, roll 1 ball of dough into a 6-inch round. Turn the edges of the dough up slightly to form a lip, then stretch the dough out to a 10-inch round. Transfer the dough to a lightly floured pizza peel or upside-down baking sheet.

3. In a food processor, pulse the tomatoes with the basil, garlic and olive oil until finely chopped. Season the sauce with salt and pepper.

4. Spread half of the tomato sauce on the pizza dough to within ½ inch of the rim. Slide the pizza onto the hot stone and bake for 5 minutes, or until the sauce is slightly dry and the crust is lightly golden. Remove the pizza from the oven, scatter half of the mozzarella on top and bake for 4 minutes longer, or until the cheese is bubbling and the crust is golden and crisp. Let rest for 5 minutes before cutting into wedges or squares. Repeat with the remaining dough, sauce and cheese to make the second pizza. —*Giada De Laurentiis*
WINE Dry, crisp sparkling wine.

VARIATION 1:
Rosemary and Sea Salt Pizza

1. Prepare the Tomato Mozzarella Pizza through Step 2 (p. 243).
2. In a small bowl, toss 1 tablespoon of finely chopped rosemary with 1½ teaspoons of coarse sea salt.
3. Brush the dough with 2 tablespoons of olive oil. Slide the pizza onto the stone and bake for 5 minutes, or until the crust is lightly golden; deflate any bubbles while baking. Transfer the pizza to the peel; sprinkle with half of the rosemary mixture. Bake for 2 minutes longer, or until the crust is golden. Let rest for 5 minutes; cut into wedges or squares. Repeat with the remaining pizza dough and topping. —*G.L.*
WINE High-acid, savory Vermentino.

VARIATION 2:
Mixed-Olive Tapenade Pizza

1. Prepare the Tomato Mozzarella Pizza through Step 2 (p. 243).
2. In a large bowl, combine ¾ pound of black and green olives, pitted and coarsely chopped, with 2 mashed anchovy fillets, 1 large minced garlic clove, ½ teaspoon of finely chopped rosemary and 2 tablespoons of extra-virgin olive oil. Season the tapenade with kosher salt and crushed red pepper.
3. Brush the pizza dough with 1 tablespoon of extra-virgin olive oil and carefully slide it onto the hot stone. Bake for about 5 minutes, or until the crust is lightly golden and crisp; poke the dough to deflate any bubbles while baking. Remove the pizza from the oven and spread half of the tapenade over it to within ½ inch of the rim. Bake the pizza for 2 minutes longer, until the crust is golden and crisp. Let the pizza stand for 5 minutes, then cut into wedges or squares. Repeat with the remaining dough and tapenade. —*G.L.*
WINE High-acid, savory Vermentino.

PIZZA DOUGH

MAKES SIX ½-POUND BALLS OF PIZZA DOUGH ●

- 2 envelopes active dry yeast
- 2 cups warm water
- ½ teaspoon sugar
- 5 cups all-purpose flour, plus more for kneading
- 2 teaspoons kosher salt
- Olive oil, for brushing

1. In a glass measuring cup, sprinkle the yeast over the warm water. Stir in the sugar, then let the yeast mixture stand until foamy, 5 minutes.
2. In a large bowl, mix 2 cups of the all-purpose flour with the kosher salt. Add the yeast mixture and stir until smooth and incorporated. Add the remaining 3 cups of flour and continue stirring until a stiff dough forms. Turn the pizza dough out onto a lightly floured surface. Knead the pizza dough until

smooth and elastic, about 5 minutes, then transfer to a large bowl lightly brushed with olive oil.
3. Cover the bowl of pizza dough with plastic wrap and let rise in a warm, draft-free spot until doubled in volume, about 1 hour.
4. Punch down the dough and knead it 3 times. Divide the dough into 6 pieces and roll into balls. Transfer to a lightly floured baking sheet and cover loosely with plastic wrap. —*G.L.*
MAKE AHEAD The recipe can be prepared through Step 2, covered with plastic and refrigerated overnight. Alternatively, the dough balls can be frozen for up to 1 month.

Alsatian Pizza

4 SERVINGS ●

Alsatian pizza, also known as tarte flambée, is invariably thin-crusted, topped with onions, bacon and a creamy cheese like fromage blanc and baked in a hot wood oven until crisp.

- ½ pound frozen pizza or bread dough, thawed
- 1 tablespoon plus 2 teaspoons extra-virgin olive oil
- ½ cup fromage blanc or fresh ricotta
- 1 tablespoon all-purpose flour
- ½ cup crème fraîche or sour cream
- Salt and freshly ground pepper
- ¼ pound thickly sliced smoky bacon, cut crosswise into ¼-inch strips
- 1 medium onion, thinly sliced

1. Divide the dough into 4 pieces. On a lightly floured work surface, roll out each piece to a 4-inch round; let rest for 10 minutes. Roll each round out to an 8-inch round ⅛ inch thick.
2. Lightly oil 2 large baking sheets with 2 teaspoons of the olive oil. Transfer 2 dough rounds to each baking sheet. Fold each edge over onto itself to form a thin lip. Refrigerate the dough rounds until chilled, about ½ hour.

3. In a food processor, pulse the fromage blanc until smooth. Add the flour, crème fraîche and the remaining 1 tablespoon of olive oil and season with salt and pepper. Process again, until the mixture is smooth.

4. In a medium skillet, cook the bacon over moderate heat until the fat is rendered, about 4 minutes. Add the onion and cook just until softened, about 2 minutes. Remove the pan from the heat and let cool.

5. Preheat the oven to 425°. Spread the fromage blanc mixture over the dough rounds to within ¼ inch of the edge. Sprinkle with the cooked bacon and onion. Bake the pizza on the bottom shelf of the oven for about 12 minutes, or until the crust is golden brown. Cut the pizza into wedges and serve at once. —*André Soltner*

WINE Dry, medium-bodied Pinot Gris.

Spinach, Mushroom and Cheese Quesadillas

4 SERVINGS ● ○

- 6 tablespoons unsalted butter
- 6 ounces mushrooms, thinly sliced
- Salt and freshly ground pepper
- 1 large zucchini, coarsely chopped
- One 10-ounce package frozen chopped spinach, thawed and squeezed dry
- 1 tablespoon extra-virgin olive oil
- 1 medium white onion, finely chopped
- 1 garlic clove, minced
- 2 medium jalapeños, seeded and finely chopped
- 1 teaspoon dried oregano
- ¼ cup finely chopped black olives
- ½ cup grated cotija cheese or crumbled feta
- 3 ounces mozzarella cheese, shredded (¾ cup)
- Eight 8-inch flour tortillas
- Sour cream, for serving

1. In a large skillet, melt 1 tablespoon of the butter over moderately high heat. Add the sliced mushrooms and season with salt and pepper. Cook, stirring occasionally, until the mushrooms begin to brown, 6 to 7 minutes.

2. In a food processor, pulse the zucchini until minced. Add the spinach and process until minced.

3. In a saucepan, melt 1 tablespoon of the butter in the oil over moderate heat. Add the onion, garlic, jalapeños and oregano and cook, stirring, until the onion is softened but not browned, about 8 minutes. Add the spinach mixture and the olives and cook, stirring, until the mixture is hot and any liquid has evaporated, about 5 minutes. Season with salt. Remove from the heat and let cool for 5 minutes, then stir in the cotija and mozzarella cheeses.

4. Lay 4 of the tortillas on a work surface and top them with the vegetable filling and the cooked mushrooms. Top with the remaining tortillas and press together lightly with your hands to form the quesadillas.

5. Set a large skillet over moderately high heat. Add ½ tablespoon of the butter and 1 of the quesadillas and cook, without turning, until golden brown, about 2 minutes. Flip the quesadilla over, adding another ½ tablespoon of the butter to the skillet. Continue cooking until golden, another 1 to 2 minutes. Repeat the process with the remaining butter and quesadillas. Quarter the quesadillas and serve with sour cream. —*Jim Peyton*

taste test frozen pizza

PRODUCT	F&W COMMENT	INTERESTING BITE
Wolfgang Puck Wood-Fired Italian Sausage & Pepperoni	"For frozen pizza, this is impressive."	This new line of pizza gets its smoky flavor from two kinds of wood: maple and aspen.
Freschetta Supreme	"The crust has a great crunch and a nice, soft interior."	Robert McGrath and Bradley Ogden were among five chefs who helped on the recipe after a research trip to Tuscany.
DiGiorno Rising Crust Pepperoni	"The pepperoni tastes really fresh."	DiGiorno invented "rising-crust technology" (in which uncooked crusts rise and bake in the oven) in 1995.
Amy's Tomato & Spinach	"If you like garlic, you'll enjoy this pizza."	The pies are made with honey, organic cane juice and organic feta.

breads, pizzas + sandwiches

Turkish Flat Bread Stuffed with Cheese

MAKES ONE 15-INCH ROUND

To turn this into an Italian hors d'oeuvre, drizzle it with truffle oil. The quick-to-make dough needs to rest overnight, so plan accordingly.

1½ cups bread flour

½ teaspoon salt

3 tablespoons extra-virgin olive oil, plus more for brushing

2 teaspoons fresh lemon juice

6 tablespoons tepid water

7 ounces Teleme or Crescenza cheese, chilled and cut into 1-inch pieces

Coarse sea salt, for sprinkling

1. In a food processor, pulse the flour and salt. Add the 3 tablespoons of oil and lemon juice. With the machine on, pour in the water and process until the dough resembles wet sand. Transfer to a lightly floured work surface and knead until smooth. Divide the dough in half and pat into 2 disks. Brush lightly with olive oil. Wrap the disks in plastic and refrigerate overnight. Bring the dough to room temperature before proceeding.

2. Set a baking stone on the top rack of the oven and preheat the oven to 500°. On a lightly floured work surface, roll out each disk of dough to a 10-inch round. Cover with plastic wrap and let rest for 10 minutes.

3. Working with 1 dough round at a time, stretch the dough: Pull the dough from the center out toward the edge, rotating as necessary, until you have pulled it to a thin 15-inch round. Trim off any thick edges. If there are any cracks or tears in the dough, pinch them together. Transfer the dough to a floured 15-inch pizza pan. Stretch the second round of dough in the same way.

4. Scatter the cheese over the dough in the pan to within 1 inch of the rim; lightly moisten the rim. Cover with the second round of dough and press the edges to seal. Trim the edges if necessary. Generously brush the top with oil and sprinkle with salt. Make four or five 1-inch slits in the top, near the center.

5. Bake the flat bread for about 10 minutes, until golden brown and the topping is bubbling. Slide the flat bread onto a work surface and cut it into squares or wedges. Serve at once.

—*Paula Wolfert*

VARIATION 1:

Flat Bread with Feta, Parsley and Sesame Seeds

Prepare the Turkish Flat Bread dough through Step 3. Blanch 1 bunch of parsley in boiling water for 10 seconds, then drain, squeeze dry and finely chop. Crumble 7 ounces of feta and the chopped parsley over the dough as in Step 4 of the Turkish Flat Bread and top with the second round of dough. Brush with olive oil and sprinkle with sesame seeds and coarse sea salt before baking as directed above. —*P.W.*

VARIATION 2:

Flat Bread with Mixed Greens, Winter Squash and Cheese

This savory stuffed Ligurian flat bread is traditionally made with a wide variety of greens ranging in flavor from peppery to sweet. Paula Wolfert salts the greens, leeks and grated squash to draw out moisture, concentrate flavor and eliminate any inherent bitterness.

½ pound mixed greens for braising

Kosher salt

½ cup chopped leek white

½ cup grated winter squash

1 tablespoon olive oil, plus more for brushing

¼ cup freshly grated Parmigiano-Reggiano cheese

¼ cup ricotta cheese

½ cup shredded mozzarella cheese

Freshly grated nutmeg

Freshly ground pepper

1. Prepare the Turkish Flat Bread dough through Step 3.

2. In a nonreactive bowl or colander, rub the greens with ½ tablespoon of salt. Let stand for 1 hour. In another bowl, toss the leek and squash with ¼ teaspoon of salt; let stand for 1 hour.

3. Rinse the greens and squeeze dry. Shred them coarsely. Rinse the leek and squash and squeeze dry.

4. In a skillet, heat 1 tablespoon of oil. Add the leek and squash and cook over moderately high heat until tender, about 3 minutes. Add the greens and cook until wilted, about 3 minutes. Transfer to a bowl to cool. Add the cheeses and season with salt, nutmeg and pepper.

5. Spread the filling on the dough as in Step 4 of the Turkish Flat Bread. Cover with the second round of dough. Brush with oil and bake as directed for 10 minutes, until browned. —*P.W.*

Grilled Smithfield Ham and Swiss Sandwiches

4 SERVINGS ●

1 tablespoon caraway seeds

¼ cup Dijon mustard

2 tablespoons honey

8 slices of white sandwich bread, crust removed

½ pound thinly sliced Swiss cheese

¼ pound Smithfield ham, very thinly sliced

⅓ cup drained sauerkraut

10 pepperoncini (pickled peppers), thinly sliced

4 tablespoons unsalted butter

---

1. In a small skillet, toast the caraway seeds over moderate heat, shaking the pan occasionally, until fragrant, about 2 minutes; let cool. In a small bowl, mix the mustard with the honey and toasted caraway seeds.

2. Spread some of the caraway mustard on 4 slices of the bread. Top with the Swiss cheese, Smithfield ham, sauerkraut and sliced pepperoncini. Top with the remaining 4 slices of bread, closing the sandwiches.

3. In a skillet, melt the butter over moderate heat. Add the sandwiches, cover and cook, turning once, until golden and the cheese is melted, about 6 minutes. Cut each sandwich in half, transfer to plates and serve hot with the remaining caraway mustard on the side. —*Scott Ehrlich*

The Perfect Ham Sandwich

4 SERVINGS ●

This is one of sandwich expert Dan Segall's signature creations, a fresh execution of a classic. Butter is his first fundamental because it keeps the bread from getting soggy.

- 4 soft ciabatta rolls, split
- 2 tablespoons unsalted butter
- 2 teaspoons whole-grain mustard
- 2 teaspoons Dijon mustard
- 1 large plum tomato, thinly sliced
- ½ small red onion, thinly sliced

Kosher salt and freshly ground pepper

- ½ pound Pavé d'Affinois cheese, with rind, cut into eight ¼-inch-thick slices
- ¾ pound glazed smoked ham, hand-sliced ¼ inch thick

Lay open the ciabatta rolls on a work surface. Spread both sides of the rolls with the butter and whole-grain and Dijon mustards. Lay the tomato and onion slices on the bottom half of each roll and season with salt and pepper. Top with the cheese and ham slices. Close the sandwiches, cut in half and serve. —*Dan Segall*

TURKISH FLAT BREAD STUFFED WITH CHEESE

GRILLED SMITHFIELD HAM AND SWISS SANDWICH

BARBECUED BRISKET SANDWICHES

PROSCIUTTO, BRIE AND APPLE PANINI

Prosciutto, Brie and Apple Panini with Scallion Butter

4 SERVINGS ●

Olga's Cup & Saucer in Providence, Rhode Island, offers terrific panini, like this twist on ham and cheese.

- **4** tablespoons plus 2 teaspoons unsalted butter, softened
- **1** scallion, finely chopped
- **½** teaspoon fresh lemon juice
- **¼** teaspoon Dijon mustard
- **4** soft hero or ciabatta rolls, halved lengthwise, or eight ½-inch-thick slices of peasant bread
- **¾** pound thinly sliced prosciutto
- **½** pound Brie, rind removed, cheese cut into 4 pieces
- **1** large Granny Smith apple— peeled, cored and thinly sliced

1. In a bowl, beat 4 tablespoons of the butter until creamy. Stir in the scallion, lemon juice and mustard until smooth.

2. Preheat a griddle over low heat. Spread the scallion butter on the cut sides of the rolls. Lay the prosciutto on the bottom halves; top with the Brie and the apple slices and close the sandwiches. Lightly spread the remaining 2 teaspoons of butter on the outside of the rolls (it will be a very thin layer).

3. Put the sandwiches on the griddle. Cover with a heavy skillet and cook over low heat, turning occasionally, until toasted and the Brie is melted, 10 minutes. Cut the panini in half and serve.
—*Olga Bravo*

Asparagus Sandwiches

4 SERVINGS ● ●

- **1** red bell pepper
- **3** tablespoons mayonnaise
- **1** tablespoon grainy mustard
- **1½** teaspoons red miso
- **1** teaspoon fresh lemon juice
- **1** small garlic clove, minced
- **⅛** teaspoon cayenne pepper

Salt and freshly ground pepper

- **16** thick asparagus (1½ pounds)
- **1** medium red onion, thickly sliced
- **1** tablespoon extra-virgin olive oil

Eight ½-inch-thick slices of peasant bread
- **¼** cup chopped basil

1. Light a grill or preheat a grill pan. Grill the bell pepper until charred all over. Transfer to a bowl, cover with plastic wrap and let steam for 5 minutes. Peel the pepper and discard the skin, core and seeds, then slice ½ inch thick.

2. In a bowl, mix the mayonnaise, mustard, miso, lemon juice, garlic and cayenne. Season with salt and pepper.

3. Brush the asparagus and onion slices with the olive oil and season with salt and pepper. Grill over a moderately hot fire until the asparagus are crisp-tender and the onion slices are tender, about 5 minutes per side for each. Transfer the vegetables to a platter. Toast the bread slices on the grill.

4. Spread the mayonnaise on 4 slices of toast and sprinkle with the basil. Top with the asparagus, onion and strips of red pepper. Close the sandwiches, cut them in half and serve. —*Hubert Keller*

Avocado and Jack Cheese Sandwiches

4 SERVINGS ●

½ pound tomatillos, husked
1 tablespoon vegetable oil
¼ teaspoon ground cumin
¼ teaspoon ground coriander
¼ teaspoon ground cayenne pepper
2 scallions, white and tender green parts only, finely chopped
1 garlic clove, minced
1 large jalapeño, seeded and minced
2 tablespoons minced cilantro
1 teaspoon fresh lime juice
Salt and freshly ground pepper
2 tablespoons sour cream
2 tablespoons mayonnaise
Eight ½-inch-thick slices of sourdough bread
4 ounces arugula
2 Hass avocados, cut into thick slices
4 ounces sliced Monterey Jack cheese, at room temperature

1. Heat a medium skillet until hot to the touch. Add the tomatillos and cook over high heat, turning, until blackened in spots but not mushy, about 5 minutes. Transfer the tomatillos to a plate. Add the vegetable oil to the skillet along with the cumin, coriander and cayenne and cook over moderate heat just until the spices are fragrant, about 30 seconds; let cool.

2. Coarsely chop the tomatillos and transfer to a medium bowl. Add the scallions, garlic, jalapeño, cilantro, lime juice and spiced oil. Season the salsa with salt and pepper.

3. In a bowl, stir the sour cream and mayonnaise with ½ cup of the salsa.

4. Lightly toast the bread. Spread the creamy salsa on each slice of toast and top half of the slices with the arugula, avocados and Jack cheese. Close the sandwiches, cut them in half and serve with the remaining salsa on the side. —*Grace Parisi*

Barbecued Brisket Sandwiches with Firecracker Sauce

12 SERVINGS ● ●

You can serve this brisket right out of the oven, but finishing it on the grill gives it a delightful smoky flavor that perfectly complements the spicy barbecue sauce.

2 tablespoons coarsely ground coriander seeds
2 tablespoons coarsely ground cumin seeds
2 tablespoons coarsely ground mustard seeds
2 tablespoons hot paprika
1 tablespoon ancho chile powder
Kosher salt and freshly ground pepper
1 teaspoon ground ginger
One 6-pound beef brisket
3 tablespoons extra-virgin olive oil
2 medium onions, chopped (about 2 cups)
2 tablespoons minced garlic
2 tablespoons apple cider vinegar
2 tablespoons dark brown sugar
2 tablespoons Worcestershire sauce
2 tablespoons soy sauce
4 cups canned peeled tomatoes, seeded and chopped
1 cup hickory wood chips
Vegetable oil, for the grill
2 dozen potato rolls
Lettuce leaves, sliced tomatoes and red onions, for serving

1. Preheat the oven to 300°. In a bowl, combine the coriander, cumin and mustard seeds, paprika, chile powder, 1 tablespoon each of salt and pepper and the ginger. Set the brisket in a large enameled cast-iron casserole and rub the spices all over the meat.

2. Heat the oil in a saucepan. Add the onions and garlic; cook over moderate heat until softened, about 5 minutes. Add the vinegar, sugar, Worcestershire and soy sauce; simmer for 5 minutes. Add the tomatoes and bring to a simmer.

3. Pour the sauce over the brisket. Cover with foil or a tight-fitting lid and bake for 4 hours, turning twice, until the meat is very tender and the sauce is thickened. Transfer to a platter. Pour the sauce into a saucepan and let stand for 10 minutes, then skim off the fat.

4. Light a grill. If using charcoal, scatter the hickory chips over the coals. If using a gas grill, place the chips in the smoker box or scatter them on the heat bars. Lightly oil the grate. Grill the brisket, covered, over a medium-low fire for 45 minutes, turning once, until nicely charred. Transfer to a cutting board.

5. Boil the sauce over moderately high heat until reduced to 4 cups, about 20 minutes. In a blender or food processor, puree until smooth. Pour into a bowl. Season with salt and pepper.

6. Thinly slice the brisket diagonally across the grain; arrange on the rolls. Top with the lettuce, tomatoes and red onions, drizzle with barbecue sauce and serve. —*David Page and Barbara Shinn*

MAKE AHEAD The brisket can be refrigerated in its sauce for up to 5 days or frozen for up to 1 month. Bring to room temperature before grilling.

WINE Light, fruity Pinot Noir.

Steak Sandwiches

4 SERVINGS ●

2 garlic cloves
Sea salt
1 stick (4 ounces) unsalted butter, at room temperature
1 cup coarsely chopped flat-leaf parsley
2 tablespoons fresh lemon juice
2 teaspoons Dijon mustard
Freshly ground pepper
Four 6-ounce strip steaks
2 baguettes or 4 ciabatta rolls

1. Crush the garlic cloves and coarsely chop them; sprinkle with 1 teaspoon of salt. Using the tip of a chef's knife, mash the garlic with the salt in small circular motions until pasty. Transfer to a small bowl and mash in the butter, parsley, lemon juice and mustard. Season with salt and pepper.

2. Preheat a grill pan. Season the steaks with salt and pepper. Grill them over moderately high heat for about 2 minutes per side for medium rare. Transfer to a cutting board and let rest for about 5 minutes. Halve the baguettes lengthwise and cut them in half. Warm the bread in the grill pan. Spread the baguettes with 4 tablespoons of the butter. Thinly slice the meat and lay the slices on the baguettes. Brush the meat with the remaining 4 tablespoons of butter and serve. —*Nigel Slater*

Short Rib Sandwiches with Horseradish Mayonnaise

4 SERVINGS ●

3 pounds Red Wine Braised Short Ribs (p. 130)
Vegetable oil, for brushing
1 large Spanish onion, cut into 8 thick slices
4 kaiser rolls, split
½ cup mayonnaise
2 tablespoons drained horseradish
Salt and freshly ground pepper

---

cooking tip

mussels

TO PREPARE MUSSELS for the *Warm Seafood Sandwiches* on this page, pull off the beards (the dark threads protruding from the shell) by grasping them between your thumb and a small knife. But don't do this until you're ready to cook: Mussels die and spoil as soon as they lose their beards.

---

1. In a medium saucepan, reheat the short ribs in their sauce until warmed through. Transfer the ribs to a plate and bring the sauce to a boil. Remove from the heat and keep warm.

2. Light a grill or preheat a grill pan. Lightly brush the grate or grill pan with oil. Grill the onion over the cooler part of the fire until lightly charred, about 5 minutes per side. Transfer to a plate. Grill the short ribs over a hot fire until browned, about 45 seconds per side. Transfer to a work surface and cut into thick slices; discard the bones. Cover with foil. Toast the rolls on the grill or in the grill pan.

3. In a bowl, combine the mayonnaise and horseradish; season with salt and pepper. Spread the rolls with the mayonnaise, top with the onion and short ribs and drizzle with sauce. Serve with the remaining sauce on the side. —*Tom Valenti*

Warm Seafood Sandwiches

4 SERVINGS ● ● ●

¼ cup plus 2 tablespoons extra-virgin olive oil
¼ teaspoon crushed red pepper
½ pound cleaned small squid, cut into ½-inch rings
1 pound mussels, scrubbed and debearded
1½ pounds littleneck clams, scrubbed
½ cup water
One 24-inch baguette (10 ounces), ends trimmed
2 tablespoons fresh lemon juice
1 tablespoon chopped flat-leaf parsley
Salt and freshly ground pepper

1. In a large, deep skillet, heat 3 tablespoons of the olive oil until shimmering. Add the crushed red pepper and cook over high heat for 20 seconds to season the oil. Add the squid and cook, stirring, until opaque, about 1 minute. Using a slotted spoon, transfer the squid to a plate.

2. Add the mussels, clams and water to the skillet, cover and cook over high heat, stirring occasionally, until the shells open, 2 to 3 minutes for the mussels and 5 to 8 minutes for the clams. Transfer the mussels and clams to a large bowl as they open. Remove the mussels and clams from their shells and rinse briefly to remove any grit. On a work surface, coarsely chop the mussels, clams and squid.

3. Using a serrated knife, cut the baguette almost in half lengthwise, leaving one side attached. Scoop out the soft white bread from the center of the baguette and tear it into ½-inch pieces.

4. Wipe out the skillet, add 1 tablespoon of olive oil and heat until shimmering. Add the bread pieces and cook over moderate heat, stirring constantly, until golden and crisp, about 5 minutes. Add the seafood, lemon juice, parsley and the remaining 2 tablespoons of olive oil; season with salt and pepper. Spoon the filling onto the baguette, cut it crosswise into 4 pieces and serve. —*Pino Luongo*

WINE Dry, light, refreshing Soave.

Shrimp BLT

4 SERVINGS ●

Paulie's in Houston makes a classic BLT even better by adding grilled shrimp in a creamy sauce.

12 slices of smoked bacon
2 tablespoons extra-virgin olive oil
3 scallions, finely chopped
¼ cup dry white wine
1 tablespoon Champagne or white wine vinegar
¼ cup heavy cream
2 tablespoons unsalted butter
Salt and freshly ground pepper
1 pound large shrimp, shelled and deveined
4 kaiser rolls, split
¼ cup mayonnaise
2 teaspoons Dijon mustard
4 thick slices of tomato
4 lettuce leaves

WARM SEAFOOD SANDWICHES

1. In a large skillet, cook the bacon until crisp and brown, about 5 minutes; drain.
2. In a large, deep skillet, heat 1 tablespoon of the olive oil until shimmering. Add the scallions and cook over moderate heat, stirring, until softened, about 3 minutes. Add the wine and vinegar and boil over high heat until reduced to 2 tablespoons, about 3 minutes. Add the cream and cook until reduced by half, about 2 minutes. Stir in the butter; season the sauce with salt and pepper.
3. Preheat a cast-iron grill pan. In a bowl, toss the shrimp with the remaining 1 tablespoon of olive oil; season with salt and pepper. Grill the shrimp, turning once, until just cooked through, about 4 minutes. Add the shrimp to the sauce; simmer just until the sauce is thick enough to coat the shrimp, 3 minutes.
4. Toast the kaiser rolls. In a bowl, whisk the mayonnaise with the mustard and spread it on the top half of each roll. Arrange the bacon on the bottom half of each roll and top with the shrimp and sauce, sliced tomato and the lettuce leaves. Cover with the tops of the rolls, cut in half and serve. —*Kathy Petronella*

Parmesan Garlic Bread

4 SERVINGS ●

- 6 tablespoons unsalted butter, at room temperature
- 1 cup coarsely chopped flat-leaf parsley

---

cooking tip

buttermilk

IF YOU DON'T HAVE BUTTERMILK ON HAND for the *Onion-Buttermilk Pinwheels* on the opposite page, make your own using pantry staples. Stir 1 cup of whole milk with 1 tablespoon of white vinegar or lemon juice; let the buttermilk mixture stand for 5 minutes. That's it!

- ½ cup freshly grated Parmesan cheese
- 3 garlic cloves, minced

Salt and freshly ground pepper

- 1 baguette

1. Preheat the oven to 425°. In a small bowl, mash the butter until creamy. Mix in the parsley, Parmesan cheese and garlic and season with salt and pepper.
2. Cut the baguette crosswise into ¾-inch-thick slices without cutting all the way through the loaf. Spread some of the butter inside each cut and wrap the bread loosely in foil. Bake in the middle of the oven for 20 minutes. Uncover the top of the baguette and bake for about 5 minutes longer, or until the top is golden and crisp. Serve hot.
—*Nigel Slater*

Multigrain Molasses Bread

MAKES TWO 8½-BY-4½-INCH LOAVES ● ●

This recipe requires a standing mixer for the best results.

- 2 envelopes active dry yeast

Warm water

- 3 tablespoons molasses
- 5 tablespoons unsalted butter
- 2 cups buttermilk
- 1 cup whole wheat flour
- 1 cup stone-ground yellow cornmeal
- ½ cup quick-cooking oats
- 1 tablespoon fine sea salt
- 1 cup cooked brown rice
- 2 tablespoons instant mashed potato flakes
- 4½ cups bread flour
- 1 tablespoon sesame seeds

1. In a medium bowl, mix the yeast with ½ cup of warm water and 1 teaspoon of the molasses; let stand until foamy, about 5 minutes.
2. Melt the butter in a medium saucepan; pour out and reserve 2 tablespoons, leaving 3 tablespoons in the pan. Add the buttermilk to the pan and cook over low heat just until warm to the touch, about 2 minutes.

3. In the bowl of a standing electric mixer fitted with a paddle, combine the whole wheat flour, cornmeal, oats and salt. Add the buttermilk mixture and the remaining molasses; beat at low speed for 2 minutes. Add the yeast and the rice; beat for 1 minute. Beat in the potato flakes and 1 cup of the bread flour. Beat in 3 cups of the remaining bread flour, ½ cup at a time, until a soft, slightly sticky dough forms, about 5 minutes.
4. Cover the dough with plastic wrap and let rest for 10 minutes. Using a dough hook, knead the dough at low speed for 6 minutes. Scrape onto a lightly floured surface and knead until smooth and no longer sticky, adding up to ½ cup of the remaining bread flour.
5. Lightly oil a large bowl, add the dough and turn to coat; cover with plastic wrap. Let stand in a warm, draft-free spot until doubled in bulk, 1½ hours.
6. Brush two 8½-by-4½-inch loaf pans with some of the reserved melted butter and sprinkle with sesame seeds. Turn the dough out onto a lightly floured surface and cut in half. Shape into loaves and ease into the prepared pans. For braided loaves, quarter the dough and roll each piece into a 12-inch-long rope. Loosely twist 2 ropes together and ease the loaves into the pans; tuck the ends underneath. Brush with more of the butter and cover with plastic; let stand until risen 1 inch above the pan rims, about 1 hour.
7. Preheat the oven to 375°. Bake the loaves in the center of the oven for 50 minutes, or until risen and golden and an instant-read thermometer inserted in the centers registers 190°. Brush with the remaining butter and turn out onto wire racks to cool. —*Beth Hensperger*

MAKE AHEAD The recipe can be prepared through Step 6; let the dough rise in the refrigerator overnight, or freeze it for up to 1 week. Thaw completely and let rise. The baked bread can be frozen for up to 1 month or stored at room temperature for up to 2 days.

Pumpkin Seed Bread

MAKES 2 SMALL LOAVES ● ●

1⅛ teaspoons active dry yeast

1½ cups water, at room temperature

1¾ cups plus 1⅓ cups unbleached
all-purpose flour

1 cup cornmeal, plus more
for sprinkling

1 tablespoon kosher salt

1⅓ cups toasted pumpkin
seeds (6 ounces)

1. Dissolve ⅛ teaspoon of the yeast in
1 cup of the water. Stir in 1¾ cups of the
flour. Cover with plastic wrap and let
stand overnight in a warm spot.

2. Dissolve the remaining 1 teaspoon
of yeast in ¼ cup of the water. Put 1
cup of the cornmeal in a large heatproof bowl. Bring the remaining ¼ cup
of water to a boil, then stir it into the
cornmeal and let cool. Stir in the salt,
both yeast mixtures and the remaining
1⅓ cups of flour to make a soft dough.
Transfer to a floured surface and knead
until smooth and elastic, about 15 minutes. Knead in the pumpkin seeds.
Return the dough to the bowl, cover
with plastic wrap and let rise for 1 hour.

3. Turn the dough out onto a work
surface and gently fold 4 times. Return
the dough to the bowl, cover and let
rise until doubled in bulk, about 1 hour.

4. Sprinkle a baking sheet with cornmeal. Turn the dough out onto a work
surface and divide in half. Shape each
half into a round loaf. Set the loaves on
the baking sheet and let rise until doubled in bulk, about 1½ hours.

5. Set a pizza stone on the middle rack
of the oven and preheat the oven to
500°. Fill a roasting pan with water and
set it on the bottom rack. Make 3 slashes in the tops of the loaves; transfer to
the stone and bake for 10 minutes.
Reduce the oven temperature to 450°
and bake for 20 minutes. Let the loaves
cool on a rack for 45 minutes before
slicing into eighths. —*David Norman*

MAKE AHEAD The bread can be made
up to 2 days ahead.

Jim Lahey's Pane Casareccio

MAKES 3 MEDIUM LOAVES OR
1 LARGE FOCACCIA ●

About 6 cups bread flour

1½ teaspoons salt

1 teaspoon active dry yeast

3 cups warm water

FOR FOCACCIA

Extra-virgin olive oil

Coarse salt

Water

Fresh rosemary leaves

1. TO MAKE THE DOUGH: In the
bowl of a standing mixer, whisk 6 cups
of flour with the salt and yeast. Add the
water and mix with the paddle at medium speed for 5 minutes. (The dough
will climb the paddle—that's fine. It
will also be quite soft and tacky; if it
seems too sticky, however, add up to
another ¼ cup of flour.) Switch to the
dough hook and knead at medium
speed until the dough pulls away from
the bowl and makes a slapping sound,
about 8 minutes.

2. Transfer the dough to a large, lightly
oiled bowl and cover with plastic wrap.
Let rise in a warm, draft-free place until
doubled in bulk, about 2 hours, depending on the temperature of your kitchen.

3. TO MAKE EACH 10-INCH LOAF:
Scrape the dough out onto a floured
surface; it will be tacky. Dust the top
of the dough lightly with flour. Roll one-
third of the dough into a ball and set
it on a wheat bran–dusted or lightly
floured baking sheet. Dust the loaf with
wheat bran and cover with a cloth. Let
rise until doubled, about 1 hour.

4. Preheat the oven to 450°. Preheat a
3-quart enameled cast-iron casserole.
Transfer the dough to the casserole,
cover with the lid and bake for 40 minutes. Uncover and bake the loaf for 5 to
10 minutes longer, until browned. Transfer the loaf to a rack and let cool.

5. TO MAKE FOCACCIA: Pat the
dough out about 1 inch thick on a
lightly oiled 12-by-18-inch baking
sheet. In the center of the dough, mix

2 tablespoons of olive oil with ½ teaspoon of salt and ½ tablespoon of water
until blended, then rub the mixture all
over the dough. Using your fingertips,
dimple the dough all over. Let rise,
uncovered, for 1 hour, or until doubled.

6. Sprinkle the focaccia with rosemary
and salt and bake for 20 to 25 minutes,
until risen and browned. —*Jim Lahey*

Onion-Buttermilk Pinwheels

MAKES 2 DOZEN ROLLS ●

2 envelopes active dry yeast

2 tablespoons sugar

¼ cup warm water

1½ cups buttermilk

2 large eggs, lightly beaten

5¾ cups flour, plus more for rolling

Salt

2 sticks plus 2 tablespoons
unsalted butter, 1½ sticks
softened

3 pounds sweet onions, chopped

Pinch of freshly grated nutmeg

Pinch of ground cloves

1 large egg white, lightly beaten

1. In a medium bowl, mix the yeast,
sugar and water; let stand for 5 minutes.
Mix in the buttermilk and eggs. In a
large bowl, whisk 5 cups of the flour
with 2 teaspoons of salt. Make a well in
the center of the flour; add the buttermilk mixture. Stir with a wooden spoon
until nearly blended; beat in the 1½
sticks of softened butter until a soft
dough forms.

2. Scrape the dough onto a work surface sprinkled with the remaining ¾ cup
of flour. Knead until smooth, 3 minutes.
Transfer the dough to a lightly oiled bowl,
cover and let rise in a warm, draft-free
spot until doubled in bulk, about 1 hour.

3. Melt 3 tablespoons of the butter in a
saucepan. Add the onions and cook
over high heat until softened, 7 minutes. Reduce the heat to moderate and
cook, stirring, until golden, 20 minutes;
add a bit of water if the onions stick.
Stir in the nutmeg and cloves. Season
with salt. Transfer to a bowl to cool.

RED PEPPER CORN BREAD

BAY LEAF–SCENTED SPOON ROLLS

4. Butter two 9-inch round cake pans. Melt the remaining 3 tablespoons of butter. Turn the dough out onto a lightly floured surface, punch it down and divide in half. Roll 1 piece of the dough out to an 8-by-16-inch rectangle; a long side of the rectangle should be facing you. Keep the other piece covered. Spread half of the onions all over the dough to within 1 inch of the top. Starting at the bottom edge, roll as tightly as possible into a cylinder. Pinch the edge to seal, then brush with half of the melted butter. Cut crosswise into 12 slices, wiping the knife after each slice. Arrange the rolls, cut side up, in 1 of the pans, 9 around the outside and 3 in the center. Wipe the work surface and repeat with the remaining dough, onions and melted butter. Cover the rolls with plastic; let rise until almost touching the rims of the pan, about 1 hour.

5. Preheat the oven to 425°. Brush the rolls with the egg white. Bake for 35 minutes, or until risen and golden. Let cool in the pans for 5 minutes, then turn out onto a wire rack. Serve hot or at room temperature. —*Grace Parisi*

MAKE AHEAD The baked rolls can be wrapped in foil and stored at room temperature for up to 2 days. Reheat in a 350° oven, then unwrap and bake until slightly crusty. Alternatively, freeze for up to 1 month. Thaw before reheating.

Red Pepper Corn Bread

12 SERVINGS ●

Farmer cheese, which is available at most supermarkets, is a sweet and creamy fresh cheese that dairy farmers originally made for their families. Any fresh cheese, such as ricotta or goat cheese, will give this savory corn bread the same moist texture.

2 tablespoons extra-virgin olive oil
½ cup chopped red bell pepper
1 small onion, minced (about ½ cup)
2 garlic cloves, minced
2 cups yellow cornmeal
2 cups all-purpose flour
¼ cup sugar
2 tablespoons baking powder
1 teaspoon salt
2 cups farmer cheese
(15 ounces), softened
2 large eggs, lightly beaten
2 cups whole milk
1 stick (4 ounces) unsalted butter, melted and cooled slightly, plus 3 tablespoons chilled butter
2 tablespoons minced rosemary

1. Preheat the oven to 375°. In a skillet, heat the oil until shimmering. Add the red pepper, onion and garlic and cook over moderate heat until softened, about 5 minutes. Transfer to a plate.

2. Preheat a 9-inch cast-iron skillet in the oven for 5 minutes. Meanwhile, in a large bowl, whisk the cornmeal with the flour, sugar, baking powder and salt. In a food processor, puree the farmer cheese until smooth. Add the eggs, 1 at a time, and process until blended. Add the milk and the melted butter and process until smooth. Transfer to a bowl and stir in the pepper and onion mixture and the rosemary. Add the cheese mixture to the dry ingredients and beat with a wooden spoon until the batter is just moistened.

3. Add the 3 tablespoons of chilled butter to the cast-iron skillet and swirl to coat. Pour the batter into the hot skillet, smooth the surface and bake for about 50 minutes, or until the corn bread is golden and a cake tester inserted in the center comes out clean. Cut the corn bread into wedges and serve.
—*David Page and Barbara Shinn*

MAKE AHEAD The corn bread can be wrapped in foil and refrigerated for up to 2 days. Rewarm in a 325° oven.

Bay Leaf–Scented Spoon Rolls
MAKES 2 DOZEN ROLLS ●

- 2 cups warm water
- ½ cup sugar
- 2 envelopes active dry yeast
- 4 cups self-rising cake flour
- 4 cups all-purpose flour
- 1 teaspoon salt
- 2 sticks cold unsalted butter, diced, plus 4 tablespoons melted
- 3 cups sour cream
- 24 bay leaves

I. Butter 2 standard-size 12-cup muffin pans. In a small bowl, mix the water, sugar and yeast and let stand until foamy, about 5 minutes.

2. In a large bowl, whisk the cake and all-purpose flours with the salt. Using a pastry blender or 2 knives, cut in the cold butter until the mixture resembles small peas. Stir in the yeast mixture with a wooden spoon until blended. Stir in the sour cream until combined.

3. Spoon the dough into the prepared muffin pans and let stand at room temperature for 1 hour.

4. Preheat the oven to 400°. Spike each roll with a bay leaf and bake for 10 minutes. Lightly brush the tops of the rolls with the butter and bake for 15 minutes, or until golden. Pull out the bay leaves and serve warm. —*Mory Thomas*

MAKE AHEAD The rolls can be stored overnight at room temperature in an airtight container. Reheat in a 350° oven. The unbaked rolls can be refrigerated overnight in the pans. Let stand in a warm spot for 2 hours before baking.

Buttermilk Biscuits
MAKES 2 DOZEN BISCUITS ● ●
These biscuits get their incredibly flaky texture from a combination of vegetable shortening and butter.

- 6 cups all-purpose flour
- 3 tablespoons baking powder
- 1 tablespoon sugar
- 2¼ teaspoons salt
- ¾ teaspoon baking soda
- ¾ cup cold solid vegetable shortening
- 6 tablespoons cold unsalted butter, cut into ½-inch dice
- 2½ cups plus 2 tablespoons buttermilk

I. Preheat the oven to 450°. In a bowl, whisk the flour with the baking powder, sugar, salt and baking soda. Using a pastry blender or 2 knives, cut in the shortening and the butter until the mixture resembles coarse meal. Make a well in the center and add the buttermilk. Stir just until a dough forms. Turn the dough out onto a lightly floured surface and knead 3 or 4 times.

2. Pat or roll the dough out to a ½-inch-thick round. Using a lightly floured 2½-inch round biscuit cutter, stamp out 24 biscuits as close together as possible. Transfer the biscuits to an ungreased baking sheet and bake for 15 to 20 minutes, or until the biscuits are risen and golden. Serve warm. —*Robert Stehling*

MAKE AHEAD The biscuits can be baked early in the day and reheated in a 350° oven. Alternatively, the unbaked biscuits can be refrigerated overnight on the baking sheet or frozen for up to 1 month.

Florida Grapefruit Biscuits
MAKES ABOUT 14 BISCUITS ● ●

- 3 cups all-purpose flour
- 1 tablespoon baking powder
- 1 teaspoon salt
- ½ teaspoon baking soda
- 6 tablespoons cold unsalted butter, cut into small pieces
- 1 tablespoon sugar, plus more for sprinkling
- 1 teaspoon finely grated pink grapefruit zest
- 1 cup fresh pink grapefruit juice
- Milk, for brushing

I. Preheat the oven to 425°. Sift the flour, baking powder, salt and baking soda into a large bowl. Using a pastry blender or 2 knives, cut the butter into the dry ingredients until the mixture resembles coarse meal.

2. In a small bowl, rub 1 tablespoon of the sugar with the grapefruit zest until the sugar is a deep pink color. Add the grapefruit juice and stir until the sugar is dissolved. Pour the grapefruit juice into the mixture in the large bowl and stir just until the dough comes together.

3. Scrape the biscuit dough out onto a lightly floured work surface and knead 2 or 3 times until smooth. Roll out the dough to a ½-inch-thick square. Cut the dough into 2-inch squares and transfer to a large baking sheet. Lightly brush the tops of the biscuits with milk and sprinkle with sugar. Bake the grapefruit biscuits for 15 minutes, or until they have risen and are browned on the bottom. Let the grapefruit biscuits cool slightly before serving.
—*Marcia Kiesel*

MAKE AHEAD The biscuits can be baked early in the day and stored at room temperature. Reheat in a 350° oven before serving.

breads, pizzas + sandwiches

Sesame-Cornmeal Crackers

MAKES ABOUT 200 ONE-INCH
CRACKERS ● ●

These sesame crackers are a savory version of the traditional sweet benne (sesame) wafers that are popular throughout the South.

- ½ cup sesame seeds
- 3 cups all-purpose flour
- 1 cup stone-ground white cornmeal
- 1 tablespoon kosher salt
- ¾ cup peanut oil
- ¾ cup plus 2 tablespoons water

1. In a spice mill, grind ¼ cup of the sesame seeds to a fine powder. In a food processor, pulse the ground sesame seeds with the flour, cornmeal and salt. Add the peanut oil and process until the mixture resembles moist sand. Add the water all at once and pulse just until incorporated. Turn the cracker dough out onto an unfloured work surface and knead just until smooth. Wrap the dough in plastic and let rest at room temperature for 15 minutes.

2. Preheat the oven to 375°. Divide the dough into 4 pieces. On a lightly floured surface, roll out 1 piece of dough ⅛ inch thick; keep the rest wrapped. Sprinkle 1 tablespoon of the sesame seeds over the dough and press them into the pastry with a rolling pin. Cut the pastry into 1-inch squares and transfer to ungreased baking sheets. Repeat with the remaining dough and sesame seeds.

3. Bake the sesame crackers in the upper and lower thirds of the oven for about 20 minutes, or until golden and crisp, shifting the pans from top to bottom and front to back halfway through. Let the crackers cool completely on the baking sheets before serving.

—*Robert Stehling*

MAKE AHEAD The Sesame-Cornmeal Crackers can be stored in an airtight container at room temperature for up to 5 days or frozen for up to 1 month.
WINE Dry, fruity sparkling wine.

Foie Gras French Toast

8 SERVINGS ●

- ¼ pound foie gras terrine, cut into ¼-inch dice
- 4 chicken livers, finely chopped
- 2 small black truffles, peeled and minced

Salt and freshly ground pepper

- 3 large eggs
- ½ cup milk
- 8 slices white sandwich bread
- 2 tablespoons unsalted butter

1. In a medium bowl, mix the foie gras with the chicken livers and truffles and season with salt and pepper.

2. In a pie plate, beat the eggs with the milk and season with salt and pepper. Soak the bread in the custard until saturated, then transfer to a large baking sheet. Spread 2 tablespoons of the foie gras mixture on each slice.

3. Melt 1 tablespoon of the butter in a large nonstick skillet. Add 4 slices of soaked bread to the skillet, liver side up, and cook until golden, about 2 minutes. Carefully flip the bread and cook until browned and the chicken livers are just cooked through, about 2 minutes longer. Transfer to a plate, cover and keep warm while you cook the remaining bread in the remaining butter. Serve hot.

—*Jean-Georges Vongerichten*

Spinach-Shiitake Bread Puddings

8 SERVINGS

- 3 tablespoons unsalted butter, plus more for brushing
- 2 medium shallots, minced
- 1 leek, white and tender green, cut into 2-inch julienne strips
- ½ pound shiitake mushrooms, stemmed, caps coarsely chopped

Salt and freshly ground pepper
One 5-ounce bag baby spinach
One 1-pound round loaf of sourdough bread, crusts removed, bread cut into 1-inch cubes

- 2 cups shredded Swiss cheese
- 1 cup grated Parmesan cheese

- 2 large eggs
- 1½ cups milk
- 1½ cups heavy cream

1. In a medium skillet, melt 2 tablespoons of the butter. Add the shallots and leek and cook over moderate heat, stirring, until softened, about 4 minutes. Add the mushrooms, season with salt and pepper and cook over moderately high heat until lightly browned, about 7 minutes; transfer to a large bowl.

2. Melt the remaining 1 tablespoon of butter in the skillet. Add the spinach and cook, tossing, until wilted, about 1 minute. Add the spinach to the mushrooms with the bread, Swiss cheese and ½ cup of the Parmesan and toss.

3. Beat the eggs in a small bowl. In a saucepan, bring the milk and cream to a boil, then gradually whisk into the eggs. Stir the custard into the bread and let stand, stirring occasionally, until absorbed, about 15 minutes.

4. Preheat the oven to 400°. Butter eight ¾-cup ramekins and set them on a baking sheet. Spoon the pudding into the ramekins and bake for 20 minutes, or until browned. Let cool for 15 minutes.

5. Preheat the broiler. Turn the bread puddings out onto an ovenproof platter. Sprinkle with the remaining ½ cup of Parmesan and broil for about 30 seconds, or until golden. Serve hot.

—*Jean-Georges Vongerichten*

Soft Pretzels

MAKES 20 PRETZELS ●

Boiling the formed pretzels before baking gives them a chewy interior, like a bagel. The baking soda in the water makes the baked pretzels shine.

- 1⅓ cups plus 2 tablespoons warm water
- 1 envelope active dry yeast
- ⅓ cup light brown sugar
- 4 cups all-purpose flour
- 2 quarts cold water
- ½ cup baking soda

Kosher salt or pretzel salt
Mustard, for serving

1. In the bowl of a standing electric mixer fitted with a dough hook, mix 2 tablespoons of the warm water with the yeast and let stand until foamy. Add the remaining 1⅓ cups of warm water along with the sugar and swirl to dissolve the sugar. Add the flour and mix at medium-low speed until a firm, pliable dough forms.

2. Turn the pretzel dough out onto a lightly floured work surface and knead for 2 minutes. Roll the dough into a 2-foot-long sausage. Cut the dough into 20 pieces, then cover with plastic wrap and a damp cloth and let rest for 10 minutes.

3. Roll each piece of dough into a 12-inch-long rope. To form pretzels, shape each rope into a U; cross the two sides of the U over each other, twist and press the ends down on the pretzel. Arrange the pretzels on a lightly floured surface about 1 inch apart and cover with lightly oiled plastic wrap. Let the pretzels rest for 30 minutes.

4. Preheat the oven to 425°. In a large stockpot, bring the cold water to a boil. Add the baking soda. Carefully slide 5 of the pretzels into the boiling water and boil for 30 seconds, turning once. Using a slotted spoon, transfer the pretzels right side up to a rack to drain; sprinkle lightly with salt. Repeat with the remaining pretzels, in 3 batches.

5. Lightly oil 2 large baking sheets. Arrange the pretzels on the baking sheets and bake on the upper and middle racks of the oven for about 10 minutes, or until browned all over; shift the pans from top to bottom and back to front halfway through if necessary, for even baking. Let the pretzels cool on the baking sheets for about 5 minutes, then transfer them to a wire rack. Serve the pretzels warm or at room temperature, with mustard. —*Gale Gand*

MAKE AHEAD The pretzels can be frozen for up to 1 month. Let return to room temperature, then reheat in a 350° oven before serving.

FOIE GRAS FRENCH TOAST

SOFT PRETZELS

BUTTERMILK WAFFLES WITH FRESH STRAWBERRIES, P. 268

breakfast + brunch

GARDEN FRITTATA

WILD MUSHROOM TOASTS WITH HAM AND EGGS

Garden Frittata

4 TO 6 SERVINGS ● ●

- ½ **pound fava beans, shelled (about ½ cup)**
- 3 **tablespoons extra-virgin olive oil**
- 2 **garlic cloves, minced**
- 3 **baby pattypan squash, cut into ½-inch pieces**
- 3 **baby zucchini with blossoms, squash cut into ½-inch pieces, blossoms quartered lengthwise**

Salt and freshly ground pepper

- 8 **large eggs**
- ¼ **cup milk**
- 6 **ounces sorrel, stems discarded and leaves chopped**
- ¼ **cup fresh or thawed frozen petite peas**
- 4 **scallions, white and light green parts only, thinly sliced**
- 2 **teaspoons snipped chives**

ɪ. Blanch the favas in boiling water for 1 minute. Drain, rinse in cold water and drain again. Pinch the skins off.

2. Preheat the oven to 350°. In an ovenproof skillet, heat 2 tablespoons of the olive oil over moderate heat. Add the favas, garlic, squash and zucchini; season with salt and pepper. Cook until just softened, 3 minutes. Transfer to a plate.

3. In a bowl, beat the eggs and milk; season with salt and pepper. In the same skillet, heat the remaining 1 tablespoon of oil over moderately high heat. Pour in the eggs, then stir in the cooked vegetables, sorrel, peas, scallions and chives; season with salt and pepper. Cook over moderate heat until the edge is set, 2 minutes. Transfer the skillet to the oven and cook for 25 minutes, or until the frittata is set in the center and browned on top. Serve hot or at room temperature. —*Peggy Knickerbocker*

MAKE AHEAD The frittata can be refrigerated overnight. Bring to room temperature before serving.

Mushroom and Ham Quiche

MAKES ONE 10½-INCH QUICHE ● ●

TART SHELL

- 1½ **cups all-purpose flour**
- 1 **stick (4 ounces) cold unsalted butter, cut into small pieces**

Pinch of salt

- ¼ **cup ice water**

FILLING

- 2 **tablespoons unsalted butter**
- ½ **pound white mushrooms, sliced ¼ inch thick**

Salt and freshly ground pepper

- 4 **large eggs**
- ¾ **cup heavy cream**
- ½ **cup milk**
- 3 **ounces ham, sliced ¼ inch thick and cut into ¾-inch matchsticks**

1 **cup shredded Gruyère**
   or other Swiss-type cheese
   (3 ounces)

1. MAKE THE TART SHELL: In a food processor, pulse the flour with the butter and salt until the mixture resembles coarse meal. Add the water and pulse a few times until a crumbly dough forms. Turn the dough out onto a work surface and knead 3 times, until it just comes together. Pat into a disk, wrap in plastic and refrigerate for at least 1 hour.

2. Preheat the oven to 350°. On a lightly floured work surface, roll the dough out to a 12-inch round. Transfer the round to a 10½-inch tart pan with a removable bottom; fit into the bottom and sides. Roll the rolling pin across the top of the pan to remove the excess dough. Line the dough with foil and fill it with rice or pie weights. Bake the tart shell for about 1 hour, or until golden around the edge. Remove the foil and rice and bake the shell for about 18 minutes longer, or until golden on the bottom. Transfer the tart shell to a wire rack and let it cool completely. Increase the oven temperature to 375°.

3. MAKE THE FILLING: In a large skillet, melt the butter. Add the mushrooms, season with salt and pepper and cook over moderate heat, stirring occasionally, until tender and browned, about 8 minutes. Let cool.

4. In a medium bowl, whisk the eggs with the cream, milk, ¾ teaspoon of salt and ¼ teaspoon of pepper. Scatter the mushrooms, ham and cheese in the tart shell and pour the custard on top. Bake the quiche for about 30 minutes, or until it is lightly browned on top and the custard is just set. Transfer to a rack to cool for 15 to 20 minutes. Unmold the quiche, cut into wedges and serve. —*Chantal Leroux*

MAKE AHEAD The dough and unbaked tart shell can be refrigerated up to 2 days or frozen for up to 1 month. The quiche can be made up to 4 hours ahead.
WINE Light, fruity Beaujolais.

Ham and Sausage Strata
12 SERVINGS ●

The strata needs to be refrigerated for at least 4 hours or overnight before baking, so plan accordingly.

Two ½-**pound baguettes, cut into**
   ½-inch dice
2 **tablespoons unsalted butter**
2 **tablespoons extra-virgin olive oil**
1 **large onion, finely chopped**
3 **celery ribs, peeled and cut into**
   ½-inch pieces
1 **jalapeño, seeded and minced**
¾ **pound sweet Italian sausages**
   (about 4), casings removed
1 **pound smoked baked ham,**
   cut into ⅓-inch pieces
1 **andouille sausage (about**
   4 ounces), finely diced
1 **tablespoon thyme leaves**
1 **tablespoon kosher salt**
½ **teaspoon freshly ground pepper**
½ **pound Gruyère cheese,**
   cut into ⅓-inch pieces
½ **cup freshly grated**
   Parmesan cheese
2 **large eggs, lightly beaten**
4 **cups chicken stock**
1½ **cups half-and-half or whole milk**

1. Preheat the oven to 375°. Spread the bread on 2 large baking sheets and bake in the upper and lower thirds of the oven for 10 minutes, or until golden and crisp; shift the pans from top to bottom and front to back halfway through.

2. In a large enameled cast-iron casserole, melt the butter in the olive oil. Add the onion, celery and jalapeño and cook over moderate heat, stirring, until softened, 6 minutes. Add the Italian sausages and cook, breaking up any large pieces, until no longer pink, 8 minutes. Stir in the ham, andouille, thyme and salt and pepper. Transfer to a large bowl to cool.

3. Add the Gruyère, Parmesan and toasted bread to the meat. In another bowl, whisk together the eggs, stock and half-and-half and add to the meat and bread mixture; toss until evenly mixed and moistened. Cover the strata with plastic wrap and refrigerate for at least 4 hours or overnight.

4. Preheat the oven to 350°. Butter a 4-quart glass or ceramic baking dish. Transfer the strata to the prepared baking dish and smooth the surface. Butter a large sheet of foil and cover the baking dish with it. Bake the strata in the center of the oven for 30 minutes, or until barely set. Remove the foil and bake for 45 minutes longer, or until the strata is bubbling and the top is golden and crusty. Let cool for 15 minutes before serving. —*Grace Parisi*

MAKE AHEAD The baked strata can be kept at room temperature for up to 4 hours. Reheat before serving.

Wild Mushroom Toasts with Ham and Fried Eggs
4 SERVINGS ● ○

Four ½-**inch-thick slices cut from an**
   oval loaf of crusty bread
3 **tablespoons extra-virgin olive oil,**
   plus more for brushing
¾ **pound oyster mushrooms,**
   stems discarded and large
   mushrooms halved
Salt and freshly ground pepper
2 **garlic cloves, minced**
4 **thin slices Serrano ham**
   (about 2 ounces)
4 **large eggs**
2 **tablespoons chopped**
   flat-leaf parsley

1. Preheat a grill pan. Lightly brush both sides of the bread with olive oil. Grill the bread over high heat, turning once, until lightly charred and crisp, about 30 seconds per side. Transfer to plates.

2. In a large skillet, heat the 3 tablespoons of olive oil. Add the mushrooms, season with salt and pepper and cook over moderately high heat, stirring, until softened and browned, about 5 minutes. Add the garlic and cook, stirring, until fragrant, about 2 minutes. Using a slotted spoon, spread the mushrooms on the toasts.

3. Add the Serrano ham to the skillet and cook over moderately high heat until warmed through and slightly crisp, about 5 seconds per side. Set the ham over the mushrooms. Crack the eggs into the skillet and fry them over easy. Top each toast with an egg, sprinkle with the parsley and serve at once.
—*Joseph Jiménez de Jiménez*
WINE Bright, fruity rosé.

Spanish-Style Beet, Carrot and Egg Sandwich
4 SERVINGS ●

¼ cup mayonnaise
1½ tablespoons ketchup
½ teaspoon fresh lemon juice
½ teaspoon Worcestershire sauce
Tabasco
Salt and freshly ground pepper
¼ cup vegetable oil
1 small onion, thinly sliced
1 small beet, peeled and thinly sliced
2 medium carrots, thinly sliced
1 medium Yukon Gold potato, peeled and thinly sliced
3 large eggs, lightly beaten
4 bialys or bagels, split

1. In a small bowl, mix the mayonnaise with the ketchup, lemon juice and Worcestershire sauce. Season the sauce with Tabasco and salt and pepper.
2. In a large nonstick skillet, heat the oil until almost smoking. Add the sliced onion and cook over moderate heat until softened, about 3 minutes. Add the beet slices and cook until almost tender, about 5 minutes. Stir in the carrots and cook for 5 minutes. Add the potato, season with salt and cook until all of the vegetables are tender, about 7 more minutes.
3. In a medium bowl, beat the eggs with a dash of Tabasco and season with salt and pepper. Gently stir the eggs into the vegetables in the skilllet, then cover and cook over moderate heat until the eggs are just barely set on top, about 5 minutes. Using a metal spatula, flip the vegetable omelet over and cook for 1 minute longer. Transfer the omelet to a work surface, cover loosely with foil and keep warm.
4. Meanwhile, lightly toast the bialys. Spread the sauce on the bialys. Cut the vegetable omelet into 4 wedges, set a wedge on each bialy, close the sandwiches and serve. —*Scott Ehrlich*

Bacon, Egg and Cucumber Salad
6 SERVINGS ●

This chopped salad can also be mounded on toasts and served as crostini.

3 medium cucumbers—peeled, halved, seeded and cut into ½-inch dice
3 tablespoons white wine vinegar
3 tablespoons water
2 tablespoons unsalted butter
1 tablespoon sugar
Salt and freshly ground pepper
1 tablespoon olive oil
6 ounces sliced bacon
6 large eggs
2 tablespoons chopped parsley
Toasted country bread, for serving

1. In a medium saucepan, combine the cucumbers with the vinegar, water, butter and sugar and bring to a boil. Cover and simmer over moderately low heat for 5 minutes. Uncover and cook over moderate heat until the sauce thickens slightly and the cucumbers are crisp-tender, about 10 minutes. Season with salt and pepper and keep warm.
2. Heat the olive oil in a large skillet. Add the bacon and cook over moderate heat until crisp, about 8 minutes. Drain the bacon on paper towels. Fry the eggs in the same skillet until the yolks are soft but not runny. Transfer the eggs to a cutting board and coarsely chop them.
3. Gently stir the eggs into the cucumbers. Coarsely crumble in the bacon and toss gently. Spoon the salad onto plates, sprinkle with parsley and serve with the toast. —*Taylor Fladgate*
WINE Medium-bodied, round Pinot Blanc.

Indian-Spiced Creamy Scrambled Eggs
4 SERVINGS ● ●

8 large eggs
¼ cup heavy cream
Salt and freshly ground pepper
2 tablespoons extra-virgin olive oil
½ teaspoon cumin seeds
2 scallions, thinly sliced crosswise
1 jalapeño, seeded and minced
1 teaspoon finely grated fresh ginger
½ teaspoon curry powder
¼ cup chopped seeded plum tomato

1. In a medium bowl, beat the eggs lightly with a fork. Add the heavy cream to the eggs, season with salt and pepper and beat again.
2. In a large nonstick skillet, heat the olive oil. Add the cumin seeds and cook over moderately high heat for 10 seconds. Add the scallions, jalapeño, ginger, curry powder and a generous pinch of salt and cook, stirring, until fragrant, about 1 minute. Add the tomato and cook for 20 seconds. Pour in the eggs, and as they cook, use a spatula to draw them into the center, forming large curds. When the eggs are almost set, remove the pan from the heat. Continue to draw the eggs into the center until cooked through. Transfer the scrambled eggs to plates and serve.
—*Madhur Jaffrey*

Shirred Eggs with Sorrel
4 SERVINGS ● ●

This rich and tangy dish is lovely for breakfast, lunch or supper.

4 tablespoons unsalted butter
2 packed cups thickly sliced sorrel leaves (2 ounces)
8 large eggs
¼ cup heavy cream
Salt and freshly ground pepper

Preheat the oven to 375°. Add 1 tablespoon of the butter to each of four 4-inch shallow baking dishes and top

with ½ cup of sorrel. Bake for about 3 minutes, or until the sorrel has wilted. Remove the dishes from the oven and add 2 eggs to each. Top with 1 tablespoon of the heavy cream and bake for about 10 minutes, or until the whites are firm and the yolks are runny. Season with salt and pepper and serve.
—*Chantal Leroux*

SERVE WITH Fried potatoes.
WINE Medium-bodied, round Pinot Blanc.

Cornmeal and Corn Pancakes with Poached Eggs

4 SERVINGS

- ½ cup all-purpose flour
- ½ cup coarse yellow cornmeal
- Salt and freshly ground pepper
- ¼ teaspoon baking powder
- 1½ cups corn kernels (6 ounces)
- 7 large eggs
- 1 egg yolk
- 4 tablespoons unsalted butter, melted
- ¼ cup chopped basil
- 2 scallions, minced
- 1 tablespoon minced red onion
- ½ cup crème fraîche
- 1 teaspoon fresh lemon juice
- 1 tablespoon vinegar
- Canola oil, for frying
- ¼ cup snipped chives

1. In a small bowl, whisk the flour with the cornmeal, ½ teaspoon salt, ¼ teaspoon pepper and the baking powder. In a food processor, chop the corn kernels. Add 3 of the eggs and the egg yolk, 1 at a time, and process until incorporated. Add the melted butter, basil, scallions and the flour mixture and process just until combined; scrape into a bowl.

2. Put the onion in a small strainer and rinse under cold water. Pat dry and transfer to a small bowl. Stir in the crème fraîche and lemon juice and season with salt and pepper.

3. Bring a medium saucepan of water to a boil. Add the vinegar. Carefully crack the 4 remaining eggs into the water and poach until the whites are firm and the yolks are runny, about 4 minutes. Using a slotted spoon, gently remove the eggs and keep warm in a large bowl of hot water.

4. In a cast-iron skillet, heat a thin film of oil. Drop heaping tablespoons of the batter in the skillet and cook over moderate heat until bubbles form on the surface. Flip the pancakes and cook for about 1 more minute; transfer to a baking sheet and keep warm in a low oven. Repeat the process with the remaining batter.

5. Arrange 3 pancakes on each plate. Top with a poached egg and a dollop of the crème fraîche. Sprinkle with the chives and serve at once. —*Paul Kahan*

Smoked Salmon–Stuffed Tomatoes

8 SERVINGS ● ●

- 8 medium tomatoes (6 ounces each)
- 3 tablespoons extra-virgin olive oil
- 3 large celery ribs, peeled and cut into ⅓-inch dice
- 2 large carrots, cut into ⅓-inch dice
- Salt and freshly ground pepper
- ½ pound fromage blanc
- 3 ounces thinly sliced smoked salmon, half cut into ⅓-inch dice
- 2 tablespoons chopped basil
- 1 tablespoon chopped chervil
- 1 tablespoon chopped chives
- 1 tablespoon fresh lemon juice

1. Using a small, sharp knife, cut off the top of each tomato and reserve. Scoop out the seeds and pulp.

2. In a large skillet, heat 2 tablespoons of the olive oil. Add the celery and carrots and cook over moderately low heat until crisp-tender, about 6 minutes. Season with salt and pepper and transfer to a large bowl to cool. Add the fromage blanc, diced smoked salmon, basil, chervil, chives, lemon juice and the remaining 1 tablespoon of olive oil and mix. Season the filling with salt and pepper.

3. Stuff the tomatoes with the filling, replace the tops and set each one on a plate. Twirl the remaining slices of smoked salmon into roses and set beside the tomatoes. Serve at room temperature or chilled.
—*Pascal Chaupitre*

MAKE AHEAD The stuffed tomatoes can be refrigerated for 4 hours.

Salmon Potpies

6 SERVINGS

- 14 ounces chilled all-butter puff pastry
- 1½ cups plus 2 tablespoons heavy cream
- Two 8-ounce bottles of clam juice
- 2 cups water
- ½ pound tiny new potatoes, scrubbed
- 1½ pounds skinless salmon fillet, cut into 1-inch dice
- 3 tablespoons all-purpose flour
- 2 tablespoons unsalted butter, softened
- ¼ pound thickly sliced bacon, cut into ¼-inch dice
- 1 medium onion, finely chopped
- 1 pound celery root, peeled and cut into ¼-inch dice
- 3 tablespoons chopped dill
- 2 tablespoons chopped parsley
- 1½ tablespoons fresh lemon juice
- 1 teaspoon finely grated lemon zest
- Salt and freshly ground pepper

---

cooking tip
boiling eggs

FOR PERFECT HARD-COOKED EGGS, place the eggs in a saucepan and cover with 1½ inches of cold water. Bring to a rolling boil, remove the pan from the heat, cover and let sit for 15 minutes. Rinse the eggs under cold running water for 5 minutes. One other tip: Older eggs are best for hard-boiling.

SALMON POTPIE, P. 263

I. Preheat the oven to 375°. Line a baking sheet with parchment. On a floured surface, roll out the puff pastry to a 13-by-16-inch rectangle. Using a 5-inch plate, cut out 6 rounds. Transfer to the baking sheet and brush with 2 tablespoons of the heavy cream. Bake for 15 minutes.

2. In a large saucepan, boil the clam juice and water. Add the potatoes and cook until tender; transfer to a plate. Add the salmon and simmer gently for 4 minutes; transfer to a plate. Add the remaining 1½ cups of heavy cream and simmer over low heat, stirring occasionally, until reduced to 3 cups, about 20 minutes.

3. Blend the flour and butter; gradually whisk into the simmering sauce until smooth. Cook, stirring, for 3 minutes.

4. In a large skillet, cook the bacon over low heat until crisp; transfer to a plate. Pour off all but 3 tablespoons of the fat. Add the onion and cook until softened. Add the celery root, cover and cook, stirring occasionally, for 15 minutes.

5. Stir the celery root, potatoes, bacon, dill, parsley, lemon juice and zest into the sauce; season with salt and pepper. Fold in the salmon and heat through. Spoon the stew into 1¼-cup bowls or ramekins, top with the pastry puffs and serve. —*John Snell*

WINE Ripe, creamy-textured Chardonnay.

Chicken-Vegetable Shortcakes

4 SERVINGS ●

BISCUITS

- 2 cups all-purpose flour
- 1 tablespoon baking powder
- 1 teaspoon salt
- 2 tablespoons vegetable shortening, chilled
- ¾ cup grated sharp Cheddar cheese (2 ounces)
- 1 cup buttermilk

CHICKEN

- 2 tablespoons unsalted butter
- 1 pound skinless, boneless chicken thighs, cut into 1-inch pieces

Salt and freshly ground pepper
- ¼ cup julienned country ham or prosciutto (1 ounce)
- 4 scallions, white and light green parts only, cut into 1-inch lengths
- 2 cups small broccoli florets
- 1 medium carrot, halved lengthwise and thinly sliced crosswise
- 1 tablespoon chopped thyme leaves

Pinch of cayenne pepper
- ¼ cup dry sherry
- 1 cup heavy cream

I. MAKE THE BISCUITS: Preheat the oven to 450°. In a bowl, whisk the flour, baking powder and salt. With a pastry blender, cut in the shortening until the mixture resembles coarse meal. Add the Cheddar cheese and toss to coat. Stir in the buttermilk until the dough comes together.

2. Turn the dough out onto a lightly floured work surface and pat it into a ½-inch thickness. Dip a 3-inch round biscuit cutter in flour and cut out 8 biscuits. Transfer the biscuits to a baking sheet and bake for 10 to 12 minutes, or until golden brown.

3. MAKE THE CHICKEN: In a large, deep skillet, melt the butter. Add the chicken, season with salt and pepper and cook over moderately high heat until golden brown, about 8 minutes; transfer to a plate. Add the ham to the skillet and cook, stirring, for 1 minute. Add the scallions, broccoli and carrot, cover and cook over low heat until the broccoli is bright green, 3 minutes.

4. Return the chicken to the skillet. Add the thyme, cayenne and a pinch each of salt and pepper. Cook over moderate heat for 1 minute. Add the sherry and simmer until almost evaporated, about 2 minutes. Add the cream and simmer until thickened slightly, about 5 minutes; season with salt and pepper.

5. Split the biscuits and set 2 bottoms on each plate. Spoon the chicken and sauce over the biscuit bottoms, add the tops and serve. —*Damon Lee Fowler*

WINE Subtle, complex white Burgundy.

Fig and Blue Cheese Tarts

4 SERVINGS ●

- 6 ounces all-butter puff pastry
- 2 ounces blue cheese, preferably Fourme d'Ambert, crumbled
- 4 fresh black Mission figs, each cut crosswise into 6 slices

I. Preheat the oven to 350°. Line a baking sheet with parchment paper. On a lightly floured surface, roll the pastry out to a scant ¼-inch thickness. Cut out four 4-inch rounds. Place the rounds on the sheet; freeze for 5 minutes.

2. Using a fork, prick the dough all over. Cover the rounds with parchment and another baking sheet. Bake for about 20 minutes, until the pastry is golden and crisp. Remove the baking sheet and the top layer of parchment. Scatter the cheese over the pastry and arrange the figs on top. Bake for 5 minutes, until the cheese is melted and the figs are warm. —*Terrance Brennan*

Smoked Ham and Walnut Salad

8 SERVINGS ● ● ●

- ½ cup coarsely chopped walnuts (2 ounces)
- 2 tablespoons dried currants
- ¼ cup plus 1 tablespoon heavy cream
- 3 tablespoons Dijon mustard
- 1½ tablespoons Pernod or other French anise liqueur
- 1½ tablespoons red wine vinegar
- 1 large garlic clove, minced

Salt and freshly ground pepper
- 6 packed cups frisée (about 6 ounces)
- ½ small onion, thinly sliced
- 1 pound smoked ham, cut into ¼-inch-thick slices, then cut into ⅓-inch-thick matchsticks

I. Preheat the oven to 350°. Toast the walnuts in a pie plate for 7 minutes, or until lightly browned. Let the walnuts cool and coarsely chop them.

2. In a small bowl, cover the currants with hot water and let soak until softened, about 10 minutes; drain.

GOLDEN SAUSAGES AND SHALLOTS IN WHITE WINE

LEMON-RICOTTA PANCAKES DRIZZLED WITH HONEY

3. In another small bowl, whisk the heavy cream with the mustard, Pernod, red wine vinegar and garlic and season with salt and pepper.

4. In a medium bowl, toss the frisée with the onion and currants. Add ¼ cup of the creamy dressing and toss to coat. Transfer the salad to a platter. Add the ham to the bowl, toss with the remaining dressing and arrange on the salad. Garnish with the walnuts and serve. —*Marcia Kiesel*

MAKE AHEAD The recipe can be prepared 1 day ahead through Step 3. The walnuts and currants can stand, covered, at room temperature. The dressing can be refrigerated.

Golden Sausages and Shallots in White Wine

8 SERVINGS ● ●

Diots, a French regional specialty rarely seen outside the Savoie, are the traditional basis for this dish, but any good, small fresh pork sausage can be used in its place. French-style pork sausages can be mail-ordered from The French Butcher (212-725-4165).

- 3 pounds breakfast sausages or other fresh pork sausages
- 2 tablespoons unsalted butter
- 2 pounds medium shallots, peeled
- 1½ cups dry white wine

Salt and freshly ground pepper

Prick the sausages all over with a fork. Melt the butter in a large skillet. Add the sausages and cook over moderately low heat, turning occasionally, until lightly browned all over, about 8 minutes. Pour off all but 2 tablespoons of the fat. Add the shallots and white wine and bring to a boil. Cover and cook over low heat, stirring occasionally, until the shallots are tender and the wine has reduced slightly, about 20 minutes. Season the sausages with salt and pepper, transfer to plates and serve. —*Marcia Kiesel*

WINE Full-bodied, fragrant Viognier.

Griddled Sausages with Potato and Carrot Salad

4 SERVINGS

- 16 baby carrots
- ¾ pound small red potatoes, cut into ⅛-inch-thick slices
- ¼ cup plus 3 tablespoons extra-virgin olive oil
- 3 tablespoons fresh lemon juice
- 2 tablespoons chopped capers
- 1 tablespoon chopped dill
- 1 tablespoon chopped chives

Salt and freshly ground pepper

Four 6-ounce fresh rabbit or poultry sausages

- 2 tablespoons grainy mustard
- 1 tablespoon sherry vinegar
- 1 tablespoon minced shallots
- 1 teaspoon chopped thyme
- 1 tablespoon unsalted butter

1. In a medium saucepan of boiling salted water, cook the carrots until just tender, about 4 minutes. Using a slotted spoon, transfer the carrots to a colander, refresh under cold water and slice in half lengthwise. Add the potato slices to the boiling water and cook until just tender, about 4 minutes. Using a slotted spoon, transfer the potatoes to a large plate. Reserve the cooking water.
2. In a large bowl, combine ¼ cup of the olive oil with the lemon juice, capers, chopped dill and chives. Add the carrots and potatoes, toss to combine and season with salt and pepper. Let the potato and carrot salad stand at room temperature for 1 hour.
3. Bring the cooking water back to a boil. Add the sausages and simmer over moderate heat until they are cooked through, about 5 minutes. Transfer the sausages to a plate.
4. In a small bowl, combine the remaining 3 tablespoons of olive oil with the mustard, sherry vinegar, shallots and thyme and season with salt and pepper.
5. Melt the butter in a medium cast-iron skillet. Add the sausages and cook over moderately low heat until browned all over, about 8 minutes.

6. Slice the sausages. Mound the sausages and potato and carrot salad on plates. Drizzle 2 teaspoons of the mustard dressing over each plate and serve. —*Paul Kahan*

Sausage Patties with Caramelized Onions

4 SERVINGS

- 1½ tablespoons extra-virgin olive oil
- 1 small onion, finely chopped, plus 2 large onions, thinly sliced
- 1 pound ground pork
- 1 large Granny Smith apple, peeled and cut into ¼-inch dice
- 1 large egg, lightly beaten
- ½ cup fine cracker crumbs
- 1 tablespoon light brown sugar
- 1 tablespoon finely chopped sage
- ½ teaspoon freshly grated nutmeg
- ¼ teaspoon cayenne pepper

Finely grated zest of 1 lemon

Salt and freshly ground pepper

- 2 tablespoons unsalted butter
- ½ cup Madeira

1. In a large skillet, heat ½ tablespoon of the olive oil until shimmering. Add the chopped onion and cook over moderate heat, stirring occasionally, until softened, about 4 minutes. Transfer the onion to a bowl. Add the ground pork, diced apple, egg, cracker crumbs, sugar, sage, nutmeg, cayenne and grated lemon zest to the onion in the bowl. Season the ground pork mixture with salt and pepper. Mix well with your hands, then shape into 8 patties about ½ inch thick.
2. In the same skillet, melt 1 tablespoon of the butter in the remaining 1 tablespoon of olive oil. Add the sliced onions and cook over moderate heat, stirring occasionally, until golden brown, about 20 minutes. Season the onions with salt and pepper. Add the Madeira to the skillet and continue cooking until almost completely evaporated, about 3 minutes; keep warm.

3. In another skillet, melt the remaining 1 tablespoon of butter. Add the patties and cook over moderately high heat, turning once, until browned, about 8 minutes. Lower the heat to moderate and cook, turning once, until no trace of pink remains, about 8 minutes longer. Spoon the onions onto a platter, top with the sausage and serve.
—*Damon Lee Fowler*

WINE Spicy Alsace Gewürztraminer.

Lemon-Ricotta Pancakes Drizzled with Honey

4 SERVINGS ● ○

- 1 cup part-skim ricotta
- 2 large eggs
- 2 large egg whites
- ½ cup all-purpose flour
- 1 tablespoon vegetable oil
- 1 teaspoon finely grated lemon zest
- ¼ teaspoon salt
- 2 tablespoons mild honey, such as clover, sage or star thistle

1. In a blender, mix the ricotta with the eggs, egg whites, flour, oil, grated lemon zest, salt and 2 teaspoons of the honey until smooth.

---

health note

honey habit

IS HONEY A HEALTH FOOD? Gram for gram, honey contains as many antioxidants as apples and melons, says Nicki Engeseth, Ph.D., a food chemist at the University of Illinois. Since a cantaloupe-size portion of honey is probably more than you want, Engeseth suggests working it into your diet the way health-foodniks have been doing for years: by using it as a sugar substitute in tea, with fruit and in cereal. Her research has also shown that honey helps keep meat fresher—so basting Easter ham with honey is sensible as well as tasty.

2. Meanwhile, heat a nonstick griddle over moderately low heat. Working in batches if necessary, pour 2 rounded tablespoons of the batter onto the griddle for each pancake, allowing enough room for them to spread slightly. Cook the pancakes until the bottoms are golden, the tops are slightly set and small bubbles appear on the surface, 2 to 3 minutes. Flip the pancakes over and cook until golden, about 1 minute longer. Transfer the pancakes to individual plates, drizzle with the remaining 4 teaspoons of honey and serve at once. —*Gene Opton*

Buttermilk Waffles with Fresh Strawberries

4 SERVINGS ●

 1 cup all-purpose flour
 ¾ teaspoon baking powder
 1 tablespoon plus 2 teaspoons granulated sugar
 ¼ teaspoon salt
 1 large egg
 1 cup buttermilk
 4 tablespoons unsalted butter, melted and cooled
 1 pint strawberries, hulled and sliced
 1 cup sour cream
 3 tablespoons light brown sugar
 ½ teaspoon ground ginger (optional)
 Pure maple syrup, for serving

---

baking tip
flakier scones

MAKE SURE THE PASTRY CUTTER, BOWL AND BUTTER are all well chilled. Work quickly to incorporate the butter into the dry ingredients, aiming for pea-size clumps. Alternatively, rub the butter into the dry ingredients with your fingers, creating large flakes. Be careful not to overmix the dough.

---

1. Preheat an 8-inch-square nonstick waffle iron. Preheat the oven to 200°. In a large bowl, whisk the flour with the baking powder, 1 tablespoon of granulated sugar and the salt. In a medium bowl, whisk the egg with the buttermilk and butter. Using a wooden spoon, gradually stir the wet ingredients into the flour mixture just until incorporated; the batter will be lumpy.

2. Pour half of the batter into the waffle iron. Bake until browned, about 5 minutes. Keep the waffle warm on a baking sheet in the oven. Repeat the process with the remaining batter.

3. In a bowl, toss the strawberries with the remaining 2 teaspoons of granulated sugar. In a small bowl, whisk the sour cream with the brown sugar and ginger. Cut the waffles into 4 squares. Set 2 squares on each plate and spoon the sour cream mixture on top. Garnish with the strawberries and serve with maple syrup. —*Wendy Kalen*

Flaky Currant Scones

MAKES 1 DOZEN SCONES ● ●

 2 cups all-purpose flour
 2 tablespoons sugar
 2 teaspoons baking powder
 ¼ teaspoon salt
 4 tablespoons cold unsalted butter, cut into small pieces
 ½ cup dried currants
 1 large egg, lightly beaten
 ½ cup milk, plus more for brushing

1. Preheat the oven to 425°. In a large bowl, mix the flour with the sugar, baking powder and salt. Using a pastry blender or 2 knives, cut in the butter until the mixture resembles coarse meal. Stir in the currants. Add the egg and ½ cup of milk and stir with a fork just until the dough comes together. Do not overmix.

2. Turn the dough out onto a lightly floured surface. Gently pat the dough into a ¾-inch-thick slab. Using a 2-inch fluted biscuit cutter, cut out 12 rounds, rerolling the dough as needed.

3. Lightly dust a baking sheet with flour. Transfer the scones to the baking sheet and lightly brush the tops with milk. Bake the scones for about 15 minutes, or until golden. Transfer to a rack to cool slightly. Serve the scones warm or at room temperature. —*Wendy Kalen*

MAKE AHEAD The baked currant scones can be stored in an airtight container for up to 1 day.

Irish Soda Bread

MAKES ONE 9-INCH ROUND LOAF ●
This dense and hearty soda bread is perfect used in a sandwich with fromage blanc, smoked salmon, watercress and thinly sliced red onion.

 2½ cups all-purpose flour
 2¼ cups whole wheat flour
 ¾ cup rolled oats
 1 tablespoon plus 1½ teaspoons baking powder
 2 teaspoons sugar
 2 teaspoons salt
 ¾ teaspoon baking soda
 1¾ cups buttermilk
 6 tablespoons unsalted butter, melted and cooled

1. Preheat the oven to 350°. In a medium bowl, whisk the all-purpose flour with the whole wheat flour, rolled oats, baking powder, sugar, salt and baking soda. Add the buttermilk and cooled butter and stir with a wooden spoon until the dough is well combined.

2. Turn the bread dough out onto a lightly floured surface and knead it 10 times. Shape the dough into a 9-inch round loaf and transfer to a baking sheet. Using a small, sharp knife, slash an X about ¼ inch deep in the top of the bread. Bake for about 1 hour, or until the bread is golden and the bottom sounds hollow when lightly tapped. Transfer the soda bread to a wire rack and let cool completely before slicing. —*Wendy Kalen*

MAKE AHEAD The bread can be made up to 1 day ahead.

IRISH SODA BREAD

OATMEAL WITH PINEAPPLE AND GOLDEN RAISINS

Banana-Walnut Bran Muffins

MAKES 1 DOZEN MUFFINS ● ●

- 1¼ cups all-purpose flour
- 1¼ cups oat bran
- ⅓ cup brown sugar
- ⅓ cup granulated sugar
- 1 tablespoon baking powder
- 1 teaspoon baking soda
- ½ teaspoon salt
- ½ teaspoon cinnamon
- ⅓ cup part-skim ricotta
- ⅓ cup buttermilk
- ⅔ cup skim milk
- 2 tablespoons unsalted butter, melted
- 1 tablespoon pure vanilla extract
- 1 large egg, lightly beaten
- 1 large egg white
- 2 large ripe bananas, coarsely mashed
- 1 cup walnuts, coarsely chopped (4 ounces)

1. Preheat the oven to 400°. Spray a 12-cup nonstick muffin pan with oil. In a large bowl, whisk the flour with the oat bran, brown and granulated sugars, baking powder, baking soda, salt and cinnamon. In a food processor, puree the ricotta with the buttermilk. Add the milk, melted butter, vanilla, egg and egg white and pulse until smooth. Add the bananas and pulse just until blended.

2. Using a rubber spatula, fold the banana mixture and ½ cup of the walnuts into the dry ingredients. Spoon the batter into the muffin cups and sprinkle the remaining ½ cup of walnuts on top. Bake the muffins for about 18 minutes, or until a toothpick inserted in the center of one comes out clean. Turn the muffins out onto a wire rack to cool. —*Suki Hertz*

MAKE AHEAD The muffins can be made up to 2 days ahead.

Oatmeal with Pineapple and Golden Raisins

6 SERVINGS ●

- 5 cups water
- 1¼ cups steel-cut oats (½ pound)
- 1 cup finely diced fresh pineapple (7 ounces)
- ½ cup golden raisins
- 1 tablespoon unsalted butter
- ½ cup brown sugar
- ¼ cup buttermilk

1. Bring the water to a boil in a large, heavy saucepan. Stir in the oats and remove from the heat. Cover and let stand at room temperature until softened, at least 4 hours or overnight.

2. Add the pineapple, raisins and butter to the oats and cook over moderate heat, stirring, until thick and the oats are tender, about 12 minutes. Remove the pan from the heat. Stir in the sugar and buttermilk and serve. —*Suki Hertz*

breakfast + brunch

Muesli

8 SERVINGS ●

This al dente version of the classic Swiss cereal was developed by writer David Colman. He recommends soaking the oats in hot water rather than cooking them; cooking, he finds, will destroy their firm, nutty texture.

½ cup pecan halves
2 cups steel-cut oats
3 cups boiling water
1 cup raisins, dried cherries and dried cranberries
2 tablespoons light brown sugar
4 cups whole milk

1. Preheat the oven to 350°. Spread the pecans in a pie plate and toast for about 7 minutes, or until fragrant. Let cool slightly, then coarsely chop.

2. In a heatproof bowl, mix the oats with the boiling water. Cover and let stand for 1 hour. Stir in the raisins, dried cherries and cranberries and refrigerate overnight or up to a week.

3. To serve, stir the pecans and sugar into the muesli. Spoon ½ cup of muesli into 8 serving bowls, stir ½ cup of milk into each bowl and serve at once. —David Colman

---

health note

good oats

AS A HEALTH FOOD, OATS ARE POTENT MEDICINE: One study has shown that adding a half cup of oat bran (the amount in about 3½ cups of cooked oatmeal—rolled, steel-cut or quick-cooking) to your daily diet may reduce LDLs (bad cholesterol) by as much as a quarter. Oats also help reduce the risk of certain cancers and are a good source of B vitamins and iron. High in complex carbohydrates, they're a feel-good ingredient too, raising mood-lifting serotonin levels in the brain and decreasing food cravings.

Apple-Cranberry Oatmeal

2 SERVINGS ● ●

For additional crunch, Michael Romano sometimes adds chopped toasted hazelnuts to this oatmeal.

2 tablespoons shelled pumpkin seeds
2 cups apple cider
⅓ cup fresh or frozen cranberries
1¼ cups old-fashioned rolled oats
1 Granny Smith apple, peeled and cut into ⅓-inch pieces
⅛ teaspoon cinnamon
Plain yogurt and maple syrup, for serving

1. Preheat the oven to 400°. Spread the pumpkin seeds in a pie plate. Toast the seeds for about 4 minutes, or until lightly browned.

2. In a saucepan, bring the cider and cranberries to a boil. Cover and simmer over moderate heat until the cranberries burst, about 2 minutes. Stir in the oats, apple and cinnamon and simmer over moderate heat, stirring occasionally, until the oats are cooked, about 7 minutes. Stir in the pumpkin seeds and turn off the heat. Let the oatmeal stand for 10 minutes, or until thick. Serve with the yogurt and maple syrup. —Michael Romano

---

Baked Apple Tartines with Walnuts and Armagnac

MAKES 2 TARTINES ●

1 medium apple—peeled, halved, cored and cut into ¼-inch-thick slices
1 tablespoon fresh lemon juice
2 tablespoons brown sugar
1 tablespoon Armagnac
Pinch of freshly grated nutmeg
Two ½-inch-thick slices of country bread, cut from a 6-inch-wide loaf
3 tablespoons unsalted butter
3 tablespoons coarsely chopped walnuts
Confectioners' sugar, for sifting

1. Preheat the oven to 425°. In a bowl, toss the apples slices with the lemon juice. Add the brown sugar, Armagnac and nutmeg and toss gently to coat. Let stand for 10 minutes.

2. Spread each slice of the bread with 1 tablespoon of the butter and set on a nonstick baking sheet, buttered side up. Fan the apple slices in an overlapping pattern over the bread; drizzle with any remaining juices. Dot with the remaining 1 tablespoon of butter and top with the walnuts. Bake the tartines on the bottom shelf of the oven for 15 minutes, or until the apples are tender and the bread is toasted on the bottom. Sift confectioners' sugar over the tartines and serve. —Kate Hill

---

Apple Tea Cake

8 SERVINGS ●

3 Golden Delicious apples (about 1½ pounds)—peeled, halved, cored and cut into eighths
1¾ cups plus 2 teaspoons sugar
2 cups (500 ml) verjus
2 cups all-purpose flour
1 teaspoon baking soda
1 teaspoon cream of tartar
¼ teaspoon salt
1 stick (4 ounces) unsalted butter, softened
1 teaspoon pure vanilla extract
2 large eggs
¾ cup milk
¼ teaspoon ground cinnamon
Crème fraîche, for serving

1. In a saucepan, combine the apples, ¼ cup of the sugar and 1 cup of the verjus and bring to a boil, stirring, just until the sugar dissolves. Simmer, stirring, until the apples are softened but not broken down, about 8 minutes. Let the apples cool in the syrup for 15 minutes. Set a strainer over a bowl and drain the apples, reserving the syrup.

2. Preheat the oven to 350°. Butter and flour a 9-inch springform pan. In a bowl, sift the flour, baking soda, cream of tartar and salt. In a large bowl, using an

electric mixer, beat the butter with ½ cup of the sugar at medium speed until fluffy. Add the vanilla, then the eggs, 1 at a time; beat well between additions. At low speed, beat in the dry ingredients in 3 batches, alternating with the milk.

3. Scrape the batter into the prepared pan and smooth the surface. Arrange the apple slices on the batter in concentric circles and press them in halfway. In a bowl, mix 2 teaspoons of the sugar with the cinnamon; sprinkle evenly over the apples. Bake the cake in the middle of the oven for 1 hour, or until golden and risen and a toothpick inserted in the center comes out clean.

4. Meanwhile, in a medium saucepan, simmer the remaining 1 cup of sugar with the remaining 1 cup of verjus over moderate heat until a deep amber caramel forms, about 12 minutes. Remove from the heat. Immediately whisk in the reserved apple syrup. Brush ½ cup of the syrup all over the cake and let cool. Remove the springform ring and transfer the apple cake to a serving plate. Cut into wedges and serve warm, with the remaining syrup and crème fraîche. —*Maggie Beer*

MAKE AHEAD The cake can be covered and refrigerated overnight; rewarm before serving.

Autumn Apple Buckle

10 TO 12 SERVINGS ●

Buckles, simple streusel-topped cakes studded with fruit, are traditionally made with summer berries. This recipe substitutes tart apples, for a denser, more coffee-cake-like dessert.

CRUMB TOPPING

1½ cups all-purpose flour
¾ cup dark brown sugar
1 teaspoon cinnamon
¾ teaspoon finely grated lemon zest
Pinch of salt
1 stick (4 ounces) plus 1 tablespoon unsalted butter, softened
½ cup coarsely chopped walnuts

BATTER

2 cups all-purpose flour
2 teaspoons baking powder
¼ teaspoon ground ginger
¼ teaspoon salt
1½ sticks (6 ounces) unsalted butter, softened
½ cup sugar
¼ cup honey
1 teaspoon finely grated lemon zest
1 teaspoon pure vanilla extract
2 large eggs
½ cup half-and-half
2 pounds Granny Smith apples— peeled, cored and cut into ½-inch dice
Sweetened sour cream, for serving

1. Preheat the oven to 350°. Butter and flour a 10-inch springform pan.

2. MAKE THE CRUMB TOPPING: In a food processor, pulse the flour with the brown sugar, cinnamon, lemon zest and salt. Add the butter and process until the mixture resembles moist sand. Add the chopped walnuts and pulse 3 times. Transfer the mixture to a bowl and press into large crumbs.

3. MAKE THE BATTER: In a medium bowl, whisk the flour with the baking powder, ginger and salt. In a large bowl, using a handheld electric mixer, beat the butter until creamy. Add the sugar and beat until light and fluffy, about 3 minutes. Beat in the honey. Add the lemon zest, vanilla and eggs and beat until smooth. Add the dry ingredients in 2 batches, alternating with the half-and-half, and beat at low speed until smooth. Fold in the apples.

4. Scrape the batter into the prepared pan and smooth the top. Sprinkle with the crumb topping. Bake the buckle in the center of the oven for 1 hour and 15 minutes, or until the topping is golden and a toothpick inserted in the center comes out clean. Let cool for at least 1 hour before unhinging the springform and removing the ring. Cut the buckle into wedges and serve with sweetened sour cream. —*Jan Birnbaum*

MAKE AHEAD The buckle can be refrigerated for up to 2 days. Bring to room temperature before serving.

Blackberry—Cream Cheese Tortilla Blintzes

4 SERVINGS ●

½ cup dried currants
1 tablespoon plus 1 teaspoon dark rum or brandy
5 ounces cream cheese, at room temperature
2 tablespoons blackberry preserves
½ teaspoon cinnamon
Salt
½ cup chopped walnuts, plus more for serving
Four 7- or 8-inch thin flour tortillas
2 tablespoons unsalted butter, melted
Confectioners' sugar, for sprinkling

1. Preheat the oven to 425°. In a small bowl, cover the currants with the rum and let stand for 5 minutes, stirring twice. Meanwhile, in a food processor, puree the cream cheese with the blackberry preserves, cinnamon and a pinch of salt. Scrape the cream cheese mixture into a medium bowl and stir in ½ cup of the walnuts and the currants with their soaking liquid.

2. Line a baking sheet with foil and oil it lightly. Wrap the tortillas in a kitchen towel and heat in a microwave oven until warm and pliable, about 30 seconds.

3. Place the tortillas on the prepared baking sheet and spoon one-fourth of the cream cheese filling just below the center of each one. Fold the left and right sides of the tortillas partially over the filling. Roll up the tortillas to form small burritos. Brush with the melted butter and bake for 5 minutes. Brush again with butter and bake for 5 minutes longer, until golden. Remove from the oven, brush once more with butter and sprinkle with confectioners' sugar; let cool for 5 minutes. Transfer the blintzes to plates, sprinkle with chopped walnuts and serve at once. —*Jim Peyton*

LEMON-COCONUT TART WITH PASSION FRUIT CREAM, P. 279

tarts, pies + fruit desserts

OLD-FASHIONED BLUEBERRY PIE

FRIED APPLE PIES

Old-Fashioned Blueberry Pie

MAKES ONE 9-INCH PIE ●

To serve 12 people, you will need to make two pies.

Flaky Pie Pastry (recipe follows)
- 4 cups blueberries
- ¾ cup sugar
- ¼ cup all-purpose flour
- 1 tablespoon fresh lemon juice
- ½ teaspoon ground cinnamon

1. On a lightly floured surface, roll out the Flaky Pie Pastry into two 12-inch rounds ⅛ inch thick. Fit 1 round into a 9-inch glass pie plate. Transfer the other round to a baking sheet lined with wax paper. Refrigerate until ready to use.

2. Preheat the oven to 375°. In a bowl, toss the berries with the sugar, flour, lemon juice and cinnamon. Pour the filling into the lined pie plate. Brush the rim of the bottom crust with water; drape the top crust over the filling.

Press the dough edges together and trim the overhang to ½ inch; fold the overhang under the edge and crimp decoratively.

3. Using a sharp knife, make a 1-inch slash in the center of the top crust. Bake the pie for 1 hour, or until the filling is bubbling and the crust is golden. Transfer to a wire rack to cool before serving. —*David Page and Barbara Shinn*

MAKE AHEAD The pie can be refrigerated for up to 2 days.

FLAKY PIE PASTRY

MAKES ENOUGH FOR ONE 9-INCH DOUBLE-CRUST PIE ●

- 2 cups all-purpose flour
- 2 tablespoons sugar
- 1 teaspoon salt
- 1½ sticks (6 ounces) cold unsalted butter, cut into small pieces
- 5 to 6 tablespoons ice water

1. In a large bowl, mix the flour, sugar and salt. Using a pastry blender, cut in the butter until the mixture resembles coarse meal. Stir in 5 tablespoons of the water, until just moistened. If the dough seems dry, stir in the remaining 1 tablespoon of water.

2. Turn the dough out onto a lightly floured surface and knead 3 times. Divide the dough into 2 pieces, pat into 6-inch disks, wrap in plastic and refrigerate until chilled, at least 1 hour. —*D.P. and B.S.*

MAKE AHEAD The dough can be refrigerated for 1 day or frozen for 1 month.

Perfect Apple Pie

MAKES ONE 9-INCH PIE ●

- 2½ cups plus 1½ tablespoons all-purpose flour
- 1 teaspoon salt
- 2 teaspoons granulated sugar

2 sticks (8 ounces) cold unsalted butter, cut into tablespoons

½ cup cold solid vegetable shortening

Ice water

4½ pounds Golden Delicious apples

Juice of 1 large lemon

1 cup packed dark brown sugar

¼ teaspoon cinnamon

2 teaspoons milk

1. MAKE THE DOUGH: In a food processor, pulse 2½ cups of the flour with the salt and 1 teaspoon of sugar. Add 8 tablespoons of the butter and the shortening; pulse until the mixture resembles small peas. Add ⅓ cup of ice water and pulse until evenly moistened. Squeeze some of the mixture with your hand; it should come together. If it crumbles, add another 1 tablespoon of ice water and pulse again to incorporate.

2. Turn the dough out onto a work surface and gently press with the heel of your hand, then gather into a ball with a few quick strokes. Divide in half and form into disks. Cover with plastic wrap and refrigerate for at least 30 minutes or up to 2 days.

3. On a lightly floured surface, roll 1 disk of dough into a 13-inch round ⅛ inch thick. Fit the round into a 9-inch glass pie plate and trim the overhang to ½ inch. Refrigerate the pie shell. Roll out the second disk into a 12-inch round ⅛ inch thick; transfer to a parchment-lined baking sheet. Cover with plastic wrap and refrigerate.

4. MEANWHILE, MAKE THE FILLING: Peel, halve and core the apples, then cut into ¾-inch wedges and toss with the lemon juice in a large bowl. In a 12-inch skillet, melt the remaining 8 tablespoons of butter over low heat. Stir in the brown sugar, then add the apples and turn to coat. Increase the heat to high and cook, turning occasionally, until most of the apple wedges are tender but not mushy, 15 minutes. Do not overcook.

5. Immediately scoop the apples and their juices onto a rimmed baking sheet. Sprinkle the remaining 1½ tablespoons of flour and the cinnamon over them and toss until the flour disappears. Place the baking sheet on a wire rack and let the apples cool to room temperature, 40 minutes.

6. Preheat the oven to 450°. Arrange the apples in the pie shell; drizzle the juices over them. Moisten the pie rim with a wet pastry brush. Center the top crust over the apples and press the rim to seal. Using scissors, trim the top crust to a ½-inch overhang, then fold it under and crimp decoratively. Dissolve the remaining 1 teaspoon of sugar in the milk and lightly brush the top of the pie. Pierce several holes in the top of the pie with a fork.

7. Bake the apple pie for 25 minutes, or until the crust is golden brown. If the crust begins to brown too quickly, cover the rim with foil. Reduce the heat to 375° and bake for 20 minutes longer, or until you can hear the apple pie filling bubbling.

8. Transfer the apple pie to a wire rack and let cool for at least 1 hour before cutting into wedges and serving.

—*Peggy Cullen*

MAKE AHEAD The pie can be stored at room temperature for up to 2 days.

WINE Light, sweet late-harvest Riesling.

Fried Apple Pies

12 SERVINGS ●

2¼ cups all-purpose flour, plus more for dusting

1 teaspoon kosher salt

½ teaspoon baking powder

¾ cup hot skim milk

½ cup solid vegetable shortening, chilled and cut up

2 cups unsulphured dried apple slices (7 ounces)

2½ cups water

½ cup light brown sugar

¼ cup raisins (optional)

Vegetable oil, for frying

1. In a medium bowl, mix the flour with the salt and baking powder. In a large bowl, combine the hot milk with the shortening and stir just until nearly melted; there should be a few pea-size pieces of shortening left. Add the flour and stir with a fork just until a dough forms. Gather the dough and knead until smooth. Roll the dough into a 6-inch log, wrap in plastic and refrigerate until chilled, at least 2 hours.

2. In a medium saucepan, combine the apples with the water and bring to a boil. Cover and cook over low heat, stirring occasionally, until the apples are very soft and the liquid has been absorbed, about 45 minutes. Add the brown sugar and mash with a fork or potato masher until blended. Stir in the raisins and let cool.

3. Cut the log of dough into 12 even pieces and roll each piece into a ball. Working with half of the balls at a time, on a very lightly floured surface, roll out each ball to a 6-inch round. Brush the edges with water. Mound 2 heaping tablespoons of the apple filling on the lower half of each round. Fold the dough over the filling to make a half-moon, leaving a ½-inch border; press the edges to seal. Using a lightly floured fork, crimp the edges decoratively. Transfer the pies to a large, lightly floured baking sheet and repeat with the remaining balls of dough and filling.

4. In a large skillet, heat ½ inch of vegetable oil over moderately high heat until shimmering. Cut a tiny piece of dough from one of the pies and add it to the oil. When the dough browns, add as many pies as will fit comfortably and fry over moderate heat, turning once, until golden brown all over, 3 to 4 minutes. Drain the pies on paper towels and fry the rest. Serve the fried apple pies immediately. —*Ronni Lundy*

MAKE AHEAD The apple pies can be prepared through Step 3 and refrigerated overnight.

WINE Rich, sweet Sauternes.

tarts, pies + fruit desserts

Roasted Peach Pies with Cream

4 SERVINGS

PASTRY

- 1 cup all-purpose flour
- 1½ teaspoons sugar

Pinch of kosher salt

- 1 stick (4 ounces) cold unsalted butter, cut into small pieces
- 2 tablespoons ice water

FILLING

- 4 large peaches (about 6 ounces each), cut into ½-inch-thick slices
- ¼ cup granulated sugar
- 1 cup heavy cream
- 1 tablespoon confectioners' sugar, plus more for sprinkling

1. MAKE THE PASTRY: In a food processor, pulse the flour, sugar and salt. Add the butter; pulse until the mixture resembles coarse meal. Drizzle the water over and pulse just until a dough forms. Turn out onto a lightly floured surface and pat into a disk. Wrap in plastic; refrigerate for at least 30 minutes.

2. Preheat the oven to 425°. Cut the dough into 8 equal pieces. Working with 1 piece at a time and keeping the rest refrigerated, roll the dough between 2 sheets of wax paper into a 4-inch round. Refrigerate the pastry round and repeat with the remaining dough.

3. Arrange the rounds on a baking sheet. Bake about 15 minutes, or until golden. Transfer to a rack and let cool.

4. MAKE THE FILLING: Butter a large rimmed baking sheet. Spread the peaches on the sheet and sprinkle with the granulated sugar. Roast for 15 minutes, or until the peaches are soft and slightly browned at the edges; let cool.

5. In a bowl, beat the cream with the 1 tablespoon of confectioners' sugar until soft peaks form. Place 4 of the pastry rounds on plates. Top with half each of the peaches and whipped cream. Lay a second pastry round on the cream and top with the remaining peaches and whipped cream. Sprinkle with confectioners' sugar and serve. —*Eric Moshier*

WINE Rich, sweet Sauternes.

Bourbon Pumpkin Pie with Pecan Streusel

MAKES ONE 10-INCH PIE ●

- 1½ sticks (6 ounces) unsalted butter, at room temperature
- 1 cup packed dark brown sugar
- ½ cup all-purpose flour
- ½ cup pecan halves
- 1¼ cups canned pumpkin puree
- 3 large eggs, separated
- 1½ tablespoons cornstarch
- ½ teaspoon cinnamon
- ¼ teaspoon freshly grated nutmeg
- ¼ teaspoon ground cloves
- ¼ teaspoon salt
- ½ cup milk
- ¼ cup bourbon
- 1 Flaky Pie Shell (recipe follows)

1. Preheat the oven to 350°. In a medium bowl, combine 4 tablespoons of the butter and ¼ cup of the brown sugar with the flour and pinch into moist crumbs. Stir in the pecans.

2. In a large bowl, using an electric mixer, beat the remaining stick of butter and ¾ cup of brown sugar at medium speed until light and fluffy, about 1 minute. Beat in the pumpkin puree, egg yolks, cornstarch, cinnamon, nutmeg, cloves and salt, then beat in the milk and bourbon.

3. In a stainless steel bowl, using clean beaters, beat the egg whites until stiff but not dry peaks form. Gently fold the beaten whites into the pumpkin mixture until no white streaks remain.

4. Pour the pumpkin custard into the baked Flaky Pie Shell. Sprinkle the pecan streusel on top. Bake the pie in the middle of the oven for about 1 hour, or until risen and golden and a toothpick inserted in the center comes out with only a few moist crumbs attached. Let cool completely and serve. —*Robert Stehling*

MAKE AHEAD The pie can be refrigerated overnight.

SERVE WITH Sweetened whipped cream.

WINE Sweet, fragrant Muscat ice wine.

Tangy Buttermilk Pie

MAKES ONE 10-INCH PIE ●

Chef Stehling updates his mom's version of a Southern favorite, chess pie, by cutting the sweetness with a heavy hit of lemon juice and by folding egg whites into the custard.

- 1 stick unsalted butter, softened
- 1½ cups sugar
- 3 large eggs, separated
- ¼ cup all-purpose flour
- 2 cups buttermilk
- 1 tablespoon fresh lemon juice
- ¼ teaspoon freshly grated nutmeg
- 1 Flaky Pie Shell (recipe follows)

1. Preheat the oven to 350°. In a large bowl, using an electric mixer, beat the butter with the sugar at medium speed until light and fluffy. Beat in the egg yolks and flour, then beat in the buttermilk, lemon juice and nutmeg until incorporated.

2. In a medium stainless steel bowl, using clean beaters, beat the egg whites until stiff but not dry peaks form. Fold the beaten whites into the buttermilk mixture until no white streaks remain. Pour the buttermilk custard into the baked Flaky Pie Shell and bake in the center of the oven for about 45 minutes, until the custard is golden and risen or a toothpick inserted in the center comes out clean. Let cool and serve. —*Robert Stehling*

MAKE AHEAD The pie can be refrigerated overnight and served at room temperature or lightly chilled.

WINE Sweet, fragrant Muscat ice wine.

FLAKY PIE SHELLS

MAKES 2 PIE SHELLS ●

- 3 cups all-purpose flour
- 2 teaspoons sugar
- 1 teaspoon salt
- ½ cup cold solid vegetable shortening
- 6 tablespoons cold unsalted butter, cut into ½-inch dice
- ½ cup ice water

ROASTED PEACH PIE WITH CREAM

tarts, pies + fruit desserts

1. In a food processor, pulse the flour, sugar and salt until combined. Add the shortening and butter and pulse until the mixture resembles small peas. Sprinkle the water on top and pulse just until the dough comes together.

2. Turn the dough out onto a lightly floured surface and knead 2 or 3 times. Divide the dough in half and pat into disks. Wrap in plastic and refrigerate until firm, at least 30 minutes.

3. Preheat the oven to 350°. Let the dough stand at room temperature for 10 minutes. On a lightly floured surface, roll out 1 disk to a 14-inch round ⅛ inch thick. Wrap the pastry around the rolling pin and carefully fit it into a 10-inch glass pie plate. Trim the overhang to ½ inch. Fold the overhang under and crimp the edges. Refrigerate the uncooked pie shell for 10 minutes. Repeat with the remaining pie dough.

4. Line the pie shells with foil and fill with pie weights or dried beans. Bake in the center of the oven for 20 minutes, or until just set. Carefully remove the foil and weights and bake the pie shells for 10 minutes longer, or until lightly browned and cooked through. Let cool completely before filling. —*R.S.*

MAKE AHEAD The baked pie shells can be kept wrapped in plastic at room temperature for up to 2 days. Alternatively, the dough disks can be wrapped well and frozen for up to 1 month.

---

baking tip
phyllo dough

ALWAYS THAW PHYLLO DOUGH OVERNIGHT IN THE REFRIGERATOR. Because phyllo is so thin, it needs to thaw slowly. It also needs to be kept moist while you're working with it. To prevent drying out, cover sheets of phyllo with waxed paper topped by a slightly damp kitchen towel.

Cherry Phyllo Pie
8 SERVINGS ● ●

- ½ cup hazelnuts
- ½ cup light brown sugar
- ¾ teaspoon cinnamon
- 9 sheets of phyllo dough (½ pound)
- 3 tablespoons cornstarch
- ¼ teaspoon ground cardamom
- ¼ teaspoon salt
- 2 pounds sweet cherries, pitted
- 1 tablespoon fresh lemon juice
- ¼ teaspoon pure almond extract
- 1 tablespoon unsalted butter

1. Preheat the oven to 375°. Toast the hazelnuts in a pie plate for 10 minutes. Transfer to a kitchen towel and let cool. Rub the nuts together in the towel to remove the skins. In a food processor, finely grind the hazelnuts with 2 tablespoons of the brown sugar and ¼ teaspoon of the cinnamon.

2. Coat a 9-inch glass pie plate with nonstick canola spray. Lay a sheet of phyllo in the pie plate, coat with nonstick spray and sprinkle with 2 tablespoons of the hazelnut mixture; repeat 5 more times, overlapping the sheets to cover the plate. Fold the phyllo overhang under itself to make a rim.

3. In a medium bowl, mix the cornstarch with the cardamom, salt and the remaining 6 tablespoons of brown sugar and ½ teaspoon of cinnamon. Add the cherries, lemon juice and almond extract and toss to combine. Pile the filling in the phyllo shell and dot with the butter. Bake the pie for 1 hour, or until bubbling.

4. Meanwhile, lay 1 sheet of phyllo on a baking sheet, coat lightly with nonstick spray and sprinkle with 1 tablespoon of the hazelnut mixture. Repeat 2 more times, stacking the sheets. Using a cookie cutter, stamp out shapes from the phyllo sheets and bake for 30 minutes. Let the shapes and pie cool on a rack. Decorate the pie with the shapes and serve at room temperature. —*Wendy Kalen*

Tangy Key Lime Pie
MAKES ONE 9-INCH PIE ●

Based on a recipe from the *Florida Keys Cooking* pamphlet, published in 1946 by Patricia's Notebook newsletter, this pie is not the ordinarily dense and cloyingly sweet version. Folding in beaten egg whites gives it a light, mousselike texture. The pie needs to chill overnight, so plan accordingly.

CRUST
- 1½ cups graham cracker crumbs
- 4 tablespoons unsalted butter, melted

FILLING
- 3 large eggs, separated
- 1 large egg, lightly beaten
- One 14-ounce can sweetened condensed milk
- ⅓ cup fresh lime juice, preferably made from Key limes
- ½ teaspoon finely grated lime zest, plus more for garnish
- Sweetened whipped cream, for serving

1. MAKE THE CRUST: Preheat the oven to 325°. In a medium bowl, mix the graham cracker crumbs and melted butter. Press the crumbs evenly over the bottom and up the sides of a 9-inch glass pie plate. Bake the crust for about 15 minutes, or until firm. Let cool.

2. MAKE THE FILLING: In a large bowl, whisk the 3 egg yolks with the lightly beaten whole egg until thickened. Beat in the condensed milk, then beat in the lime juice and zest.

3. In a large stainless steel bowl, beat the egg whites until firm peaks form. Fold one-third of the beaten whites into the key lime custard, then fold in the remaining whites just until incorporated. Pour the custard into the pie crust and bake for 15 minutes, or until barely set. Transfer to a rack and let cool completely, then refrigerate overnight. Serve with sweetened whipped cream and garnish with lime zest. —*Marcia Kiesel*

WINE Light, sweet late-harvest Riesling.

Caramelized Almond Tart

MAKES ONE 9-INCH TART ●

This cookielike tart has a crust that resembles chewy shortbread.

PASTRY

- ¾ cup all-purpose flour
- 1 tablespoon baking powder

Pinch of salt

- 6 tablespoons unsalted butter, at room temperature
- ½ cup sugar
- 1 large egg, beaten

TOPPING

- ⅔ cup sliced almonds (2½ ounces)
- ¼ cup sugar
- 2 tablespoons unsalted butter
- 2 tablespoons milk

I. **MAKE THE PASTRY:** Preheat the oven to 350°. In a medium bowl, whisk the flour with the baking powder and salt. In a large bowl, using a handheld electric mixer, beat the butter with the sugar until light and fluffy. Add the egg and beat well. Gradually add the flour mixture and beat until incorporated, then stir by hand to blend thoroughly.

2. Scrape the dough into a 9-inch tart pan with a removable bottom. Using a piece of plastic wrap, pat the dough into the pan in an even layer. Bake for about 20 minutes, or until the pastry is firm and golden brown. Transfer the pastry to a rack to cool completely. Leave the oven on.

3. MAKE THE TOPPING: Spread the sliced almonds on a baking sheet and toast in the oven for about 4 minutes, or until golden brown.

4. In a small saucepan, cook the sugar and butter over low heat, stirring, until the mixture turns light brown, about 3 minutes. Slowly add the milk and cook, stirring, until the mixture is smooth. Remove the pan from the heat and stir in the sliced almonds. Spread the topping over the tart base and bake for 10 minutes, or until sizzling and set. Let cool slightly. Cut the almond tart into wedges and serve warm or at room temperature. —*Taylor Fladgate*

MAKE AHEAD The dough can be made through Step 1, scraped out onto a work surface and patted into a flat disk, then wrapped in plastic and refrigerated for 1 week or frozen for 2 weeks. Let the dough soften slightly before patting it into the tart pan. The tart base can be made through Step 2 and allowed to cool, then stored overnight at room temperature in an airtight container. The finished tart can be kept at room temperature for 6 hours.

WINE Complex tawny port.

Creamy Ricotta Tart with Pine Nuts

MAKES ONE 11-INCH TART ●

This tart was inspired by a recipe from Viana La Place and Evan Kleiman's *Cucina Rustica*.

- ½ cup pine nuts (about 3 ounces)
- 1½ cups plus 2 tablespoons all-purpose flour
- 1 cup sugar

Pinch of salt

- 1 stick (4 ounces) unsalted butter, melted and cooled slightly
- ½ cup water
- 6 ounces cream cheese, softened
- 1 cup ricotta cheese
- 3 large egg yolks
- 2 large eggs

I. Preheat the oven to 350°. In a small skillet, toast the pine nuts over moderate heat, stirring frequently, until golden, about 4 minutes. Transfer to a plate and let cool.

2. In a food processor, combine ¼ cup of the pine nuts, the flour, 2 tablespoons of the sugar and the salt; process until the mixture is finely ground. Add the butter and pulse until crumbly. Press the pine nut dough evenly into an 11-inch fluted tart pan with a removable bottom. Refrigerate for at least 30 minutes.

3. Line the tart shell with aluminum foil and fill with pie weights or dried beans. Bake in the lower third of the oven for about 25 minutes, or until just set.

Carefully remove the foil and the pie weights, then bake for about 10 minutes longer, or until golden. Let the tart shell cool completely.

4. In a small saucepan, combine the remaining sugar with the water; bring to a boil, stirring. Let cool slightly.

5. In a clean food processor, pulse the cream cheese with the ricotta until smooth. Add the egg yolks and whole eggs, 1 at a time; process until smooth. With the machine on, slowly add the sugar syrup; process until smooth.

6. Pour the custard into the tart shell and bake for 20 minutes, or until almost set. Scatter the remaining ¼ cup of toasted pine nuts on top and bake for about 10 minutes longer, or until the custard is set. Let cool and serve. —*Giada De Laurentiis*

MAKE AHEAD The tart can be refrigerated for up to 3 days.

WINE Sweet, luscious Italian vin santo.

Lemon-Coconut Tart with Passion Fruit Cream

MAKES TWO 10-INCH TARTS ●

This tart is extremely easy to make and superdelicious. The passion fruit cream finishes it off perfectly.

- 4 large eggs, at room temperature
- 2½ cups granulated sugar
- 1 tablespoon finely grated lemon zest
- ½ cup fresh lemon juice
- 3 cups heavy cream
- 3 cups shredded unsweetened coconut

Sweet Tart Shells (recipe follows)

- ½ pound mascarpone (1 cup), at room temperature
- ½ cup superfine sugar
- ⅔ cup fresh passion fruit pulp (from about 10 passion fruits), plus more for garnish (see Note)

I. Preheat the oven to 325°. In a large bowl, whisk the eggs with the granulated sugar and lemon zest until combined. Whisk in the lemon juice and 2 cups of the cream, then stir in the coconut.

HAZELNUT AND RASPBERRY JAM LINZER TART

WARM NECTARINE AND BLUEBERRY SHORTCAKE

Pour the filling into the tart shells. Bake the tarts for about 50 minutes, or until the filling is just set and the tops are deep golden around the edges. Transfer to racks and let cool.

2. In a bowl, combine the mascarpone with the remaining 1 cup of cream and the superfine sugar. Beat at medium speed just until the cream begins to thicken. Add the passion fruit pulp and beat until the cream is thick. Refrigerate until firm, at least 1 hour or overnight.

3. Cut the tarts into wedges and top with a dollop of the passion fruit cream. Spoon some passion fruit pulp over the cream and serve. —*Peter Gordon*

NOTE Passion fruit is available year-round at supermarkets. Look for heavy fruit with dimpled, deep purple skin.

MAKE AHEAD The tarts can be kept at room temperature for 2 days. Refrigerate the passion fruit cream.

SWEET TART SHELLS

MAKES 2 TART SHELLS ●

- 3 **cups all-purpose flour**
- ¼ **cup plus 2 tablespoons confectioners' sugar**
- ½ **teaspoon salt**
- 2 **sticks (½ pound) unsalted butter, cut into ½-inch pieces and chilled**
- 1 **large egg yolk**
- 6 **tablespoons ice water**

1. In a food processor, pulse the flour, sugar and salt. Add the butter and pulse until the mixture resembles coarse meal. In a small bowl, whisk the egg yolk with the ice water. With the machine on, slowly add the egg yolk mixture. Process just until the dough comes together. Turn out onto a work surface and gently knead it 3 times. Divide the dough in half and pat it into 2 disks. Wrap the disks in plastic and refrigerate until chilled, at least 30 minutes or overnight.

2. Preheat the oven to 375°. Let the dough stand at room temperature for 10 minutes to warm slightly. On a lightly floured work surface, roll out each disk of dough to a 12-inch round about ⅜ inch thick. Fit the dough into two 10-inch fluted tart pans with removable bottoms. Trim off any excess dough. Line each shell with foil and fill with pie weights or dried beans.

3. Bake the tart shells in the oven for about 25 minutes, or until they are just set and slightly dry. Remove the foil and weights and continue baking the tart shells for 5 to 10 minutes longer, or until they are dry and lightly golden. Transfer the tart shells to wire racks and let cool completely. —*P.G.*

MAKE AHEAD The baked Sweet Tart Shells can be kept wrapped in plastic wrap and stored at room temperature for up to 2 days.

Hazelnut and Raspberry Jam Linzer Tart

MAKES ONE 10-INCH TART ●

- ½ cup hazelnuts (3 ounces)
- 2 sticks (½ pound) unsalted butter, softened
- 1 cup confectioners' sugar
- 2 cups all-purpose flour
- ½ teaspoon baking powder
- ⅛ teaspoon ground cloves

Pinch of salt

- 2 large eggs, lightly beaten
- 2 tablespoons brandy
- 1 teaspoon pure vanilla extract
- 1 cup seedless raspberry jam
- 1½ tablespoons cornstarch
- 1 large egg white, lightly beaten

1. Preheat the oven to 350°. Spread the hazelnuts in a pie plate and toast until fragrant and the skins blister, about 12 minutes. Transfer the nuts to a kitchen towel and let cool slightly, then vigorously rub the nuts together to remove the skins. When the hazelnuts are completely cool, pulse them in a food processor until finely ground. Transfer the ground nuts to a bowl.

2. Add the butter and confectioners' sugar to the food processor and process until light and fluffy. Add the ground hazelnuts, flour, baking powder, cloves and salt and pulse until combined. Add the eggs, brandy and vanilla and process just until a soft dough forms.

3. Scrape the dough onto a large sheet of plastic wrap. Transfer one-third of the dough to a separate sheet of plastic and roll it into a 6-inch log. Pat the remaining dough into a 6-inch disk. Wrap and refrigerate the dough until firm, at least 2 hours or overnight.

4. Preheat the oven to 350°. Let the 6-inch disk of dough stand at room temperature for 10 minutes, then set it in a 10-inch fluted tart pan with a removable bottom. Press the dough evenly over the bottom and up the side of the tart pan. In a bowl, mix the jam and cornstarch; spread the jam on the bottom of the tart. Refrigerate until chilled.

5. Cut the log of dough into 6 slices. On a lightly floured surface, roll each slice into a ½-inch-thick strip. Halve 1 strip crosswise. Transfer the strips of dough to a baking sheet and refrigerate until chilled. Lay the strips diagonally across the tart, trimming them to fit; press the ends into the crust rim.

6. Brush the dough strips with the beaten egg white. Bake the tart for about 40 minutes, or until the crust is lightly browned and the jam is bubbling slightly. Let cool completely, then unmold the tart. Slide onto a plate, cut into wedges and serve.

—*Grace Parisi*

MAKE AHEAD The tart can be stored at room temperature overnight in an airtight container.

SERVE WITH Sweetened whipped cream or vanilla ice cream.

WINE Sweet, fortified, fragrant Muscat.

Warm Nectarine and Blueberry Shortcakes

8 SERVINGS

- 2 cups all-purpose flour
- 1 tablespoon baking powder
- 2 tablespoons granulated sugar
- ½ teaspoon kosher salt
- 1 stick plus 2 tablespoons cold unsalted butter, 1 stick diced
- 2¾ cups heavy cream, plus more for brushing
- ½ cup turbinado sugar
- ⅓ cup confectioners' sugar, plus more for dusting
- 1 tablespoon pure vanilla extract
- 1¾ pounds small nectarines or peaches, pitted and thinly sliced
- 2 pints blueberries
- 1½ tablespoons fresh lemon juice

1. Preheat the oven to 425°. In a food processor, pulse the flour with the baking powder, granulated sugar and salt. Add the diced butter and pulse until the mixture resembles coarse meal. Add ¾ cup of the heavy cream and continue processing until the dough just comes together.

2. Turn the dough out onto a lightly floured surface; knead 3 times. Roll out the dough ½ inch thick. Using a floured 2¾-inch round biscuit cutter, stamp out 8 shortcakes as close together as possible; transfer to a large baking sheet. Brush the tops of the shortcakes with cream and sprinkle with 2 heaping tablespoons of the turbinado sugar. Bake the shortcakes for 15 minutes, or until golden brown. Transfer to a wire rack to cool.

3. In a bowl, beat the remaining 2 cups of cream, ⅓ cup of confectioners' sugar and vanilla until soft peaks form.

4. Melt the remaining 2 tablespoons of butter in a large skillet. In a bowl, toss the nectarines with the berries, the remaining ⅓ cup of turbinado sugar and the lemon juice. Add to the skillet and cook over high heat, stirring, until the fruit begins to release its juices, about 2 minutes. Remove from the heat.

5. Cut the shortcakes in half. Set the bottoms on plates; top with the fruit. Add a dollop of whipped cream, close the shortcakes, dust with confectioners' sugar and serve. —*Ben Ford*

Warm Chocolate Soufflé Tarts

8 SERVINGS ●

Claudia Fleming created these soufflé tarts at Gramercy Tavern. The tarts fall slightly, but they're still airy, beautiful and spectacularly delicious.

baking tip

pie basics

COLD INGREDIENTS YIELD THE BEST PIE CRUST. Even the flour should be chilled. The best flour is all-purpose or pastry flour. Lard and shortening produce a more tender crust than butter or vegetable oil; the best results come from using half lard, half butter. And *always* avoid overmixing dough.

tarts, pies + fruit desserts

SOUFFLÉ FILLING

- 5 tablespoons unsalted butter
- 2½ ounces bittersweet chocolate, chopped
- 2 large eggs, at room temperature
- ¼ cup plus 3 tablespoons sugar
- 1½ tablespoons all-purpose flour

DOUGH

- 1 stick (4 ounces) unsalted butter, at room temperature
- ½ cup confectioners' sugar
- 1 large egg yolk
- ¾ teaspoon pure vanilla extract
- 1¼ cups sifted all-purpose flour
- ¼ cup Dutch process cocoa powder
- ¼ teaspoon salt

I. MAKE THE SOUFFLÉ FILLING: In a medium saucepan, stir the butter and chocolate over low heat until nearly melted; remove from the heat and stir until thoroughly melted.

2. In a bowl, using an electric mixer, beat the eggs with the sugar until pale and thick, about 5 minutes. Stir one-third of the beaten egg mixture into the melted chocolate to lighten it, then fold that into the remaining egg mixture. Sift the flour over the batter and fold it in. Refrigerate until chilled.

3. MAKE THE DOUGH: In a standing electric mixer fitted with a paddle, beat the butter and confectioners' sugar until light and fluffy. Beat in the egg yolk and vanilla. Sift the flour, cocoa and salt; add to the bowl and beat at low speed just until blended. Form the dough into a 4-inch log, wrap in plastic and refrigerate until firm, at least 30 minutes.

4. Preheat the oven to 325°. Line a baking sheet with parchment. Cut the log of dough into eight ½-inch slices. On a lightly floured work surface, with a lightly floured rolling pin, roll each piece of dough out to a 4½-inch round. Set eight 3¼-by-¾-inch flan rings on a heavy baking sheet. Ease the dough rounds into the rings. With a sharp knife, trim the overhanging dough flush with the rims of the rings. Prick the dough twice with a fork and freeze until firm.

5. Cut out eight 4-inch squares of foil and line the tart shells with them; fill the shells with pie weights or dried beans. Bake the tart shells for 15 minutes, or until dry and just set. Remove the foil and weights and bake the tart shells for about 5 minutes longer, or until cooked through. Transfer the shells to a rack and let cool before filling.

6. Remove the flan rings. Fill the tart shells with the chilled soufflé filling and bake for about 20 minutes, or until the tops are shiny, puffed and cracked. Serve the tarts warm. —*Claudia Fleming*

WINE Rich, sweet Banyuls.

Chocolate-Crusted Plum Galette

8 SERVINGS ●

PASTRY

- 1¼ cups sifted all-purpose flour
- 2 tablespoons plus 1 teaspoon sugar
- 2 tablespoons unsweetened cocoa powder
- ¼ teaspoon salt
- 1 stick (4 ounces) unsalted butter, cut into ½-inch pieces and chilled
- ¼ teaspoon pure vanilla extract
- 3 to 4 tablespoons ice water
- 1 egg white, lightly beaten

FILLING

- 1 orange, preferably organic, washed and patted dry
- 2 tablespoons unsalted butter
- ¼ cup sugar
- 1 teaspoon minced rosemary
- ½ teaspoon pure vanilla extract
- 1½ pounds red or black plums— halved, pitted and cut into 8 wedges each
- 2 tablespoons water

Whipped cream, for serving

I. MAKE THE PASTRY: In a food processor, pulse the flour with 2 tablespoons of the sugar, the cocoa and the salt until combined . Add the butter and pulse until the crumbs are the size of small peas. In a small cup, stir the vanilla into 3 tablespoons of ice water, then sprinkle over the mixture.

Pulse just until the crumbs are moistened; if the crumbs seem very dry, pulse in the remaining 1 tablespoon of ice water. Turn the crumbs out onto a work surface and gather them together; pat the pastry into a disk. Wrap the pastry in plastic and refrigerate until chilled, about 30 minutes.

2. Preheat the oven to 400°. On a lightly floured surface, roll out the pastry to a 14-inch round (see Note). Transfer the round to a baking sheet lined with parchment paper. Fold 1 inch of the pastry over onto itself to form a pleated rim and prick the rest of the pastry with a fork. Brush the rim with egg white and sprinkle with the remaining 1 teaspoon of sugar. Freeze until firm.

3. Bake the pastry for 20 minutes, or until it's nearly cooked through and dry to the touch.

4. MAKE THE FILLING: Using a peeler, remove two 3-by-1-inch strips of zest from the orange. Cut the strips into fine julienne with a sharp knife.

5. In a large nonstick skillet, melt the butter over high heat. Stir in the sugar, orange zest, rosemary and vanilla. Add the plums and water and cook, stirring occasionally, until the sugar dissolves and the plums are barely softened, about 5 minutes.

6. Spread the cooked plums and their juices over the pastry and bake for 35 minutes, or until the fruit is tender and the crust is cooked through. Cut the galette into wedges and serve warm or at room temperature, with whipped cream. —*Serena Bass*

NOTE For a different look, roll out the pastry into a square or rectangle.

MAKE AHEAD The pastry dough can be prepared through Step 1 and refrigerated for up to 2 days, or it can be frozen, well wrapped in plastic and foil, for up to 2 months. Thaw the pastry dough before rolling it out. The baked galette can stand at room temperature for up to 6 hours.

WINE Rich, sweet Banyuls.

Lemon Pudding Cakes with Apricot Sauce

8 SERVINGS ●

The unusual thing about these lemony cakes is that while they are baking, the batter splits, creating a creamy, puddinglike top and soufflé-like bottom.

CAKES

1¼ cups whole milk
Zest of 2 lemons
5 tablespoons unsalted butter, at room temperature
1 cup plus 2 tablespoons sugar
5 large eggs, separated
¼ cup plus 2 tablespoons all-purpose flour
⅔ cup fresh lemon juice (2 lemons)

SAUCE

One 8½-ounce jar apricot halves in syrup, drained
½ cup apricot preserves
3 tablespoons water
2 teaspoons fresh lemon juice
Salt

I. MAKE THE CAKES: Preheat the oven to 325°. Lightly spray eight 6-ounce ramekins with vegetable cooking spray and arrange them in a small roasting pan.

2. In a small saucepan, combine the milk with the lemon zest and bring just to a simmer. Strain the milk through a sieve into a medium bowl and let cool to room temperature.

3. In a medium bowl, using an electric mixer, beat the butter with 6 tablespoons of the sugar at moderately high speed until light and fluffy, about 5 minutes. At medium speed, beat in the egg yolks, 1 at a time, until incorporated. Using a spoon, stir in the flour, lemon juice and infused milk until combined.

4. In a large bowl, using clean beaters, beat the egg whites until soft peaks form. Add the remaining ¾ cup of sugar, 1 tablespoon at a time, beating until the egg whites are firm and glossy; do not overbeat. Working in batches, gently fold the meringue into the batter just until combined.

5. Spoon the batter into the prepared ramekins. Pour enough hot water into the roasting pan to reach halfway up the sides of the ramekins. Bake for 30 to 35 minutes, or until small cracks appear on top of each cake. Using tongs, transfer the ramekins to a rack to cool.

6. MAKE THE SAUCE: In a food processor or blender, puree the apricots with the preserves, water, lemon juice and salt until smooth.

7. Run a blunt knife around each cake and invert onto a dessert plate. Spoon the apricot sauce around the cakes and serve. —Gary Danko

MAKE AHEAD The recipe can be prepared through Step 6 up to 2 days ahead. Refrigerate the cakes and the apricot sauce separately. Serve cold or at room temperature.

WINE Light, sweet late-harvest Riesling.

Banana Brioche Bread Pudding

12 SERVINGS ●

1 cup plus 3 tablespoons sugar, plus more for the baking dish
2 cups milk
2 cups heavy cream
1 pound brioche, crusts trimmed, bread cut into 3-inch chunks
2 sticks (½ pound) unsalted butter, softened
8 large egg yolks, at room temperature
3 very ripe large bananas, mashed
4 large egg whites, at room temperature
1 cup best-quality store-bought fudge sauce, plus more for serving
Butterscotch sauce, for serving

I. Preheat the oven to 350°. Butter a 4-quart glass or ceramic baking dish and coat with sugar, tapping out any excess.

2. In a saucepan, combine the milk and cream and bring just to a simmer. Put the brioche in a large bowl, pour the milk evenly over it and let stand until nearly absorbed, stirring once or twice.

3. In a medium bowl, beat the butter until creamy. Add 1 cup of the sugar and beat until fluffy. Beat in the egg yolks, 1 at a time. Fold the mixture into the soaked brioche, then stir in the mashed bananas.

4. In a clean bowl, whip the egg whites to soft peaks. Gradually add 2 tablespoons of the sugar and beat until the whites are stiff and glossy, about 2 minutes. Fold the whites into the pudding.

5. Transfer the pudding to the prepared baking dish; smooth the surface. Dollop spoonfuls of the fudge sauce on top and swirl it into the pudding. Sprinkle the top with the remaining 1 tablespoon of sugar. Set the baking dish in a roasting pan and add enough hot water to reach two-thirds of the way up the side. Bake for 1 hour, or until the pudding is set and the top is brown.

6. Cool the pudding slightly in the water. Transfer to a rack to cool for 15 minutes. Serve with fudge and butterscotch sauce. —Mindy Segal

MAKE AHEAD The bread pudding can be refrigerated for up to 2 days. Reheat before serving.

health note

lemon aid

LEMONS ARE A SOURCE OF VITAMIN C (the juice of one lemon provides about half the recommended daily requirement), and they promote the absorption of calcium and iron from other foods. (Now there's an incentive to squeeze lemon on your spinach and broccoli.) Like many fruits and vegetables, lemons contain powerful antioxidants that help prevent heart disease and cancer. Researchers believe that the pectin in whole lemons may help lower cholesterol, too—a good reason to spread lemon marmalade on your morning toast.

tarts, pies + fruit desserts

Pear and Apple Oat Crisp

8 SERVINGS ● ●

- ¾ cup rolled oats
- ½ cup plus 1 tablespoon all-purpose flour
- ½ cup brown sugar
- ¼ cup sliced almonds, chopped
- ¼ teaspoon salt
- 4 tablespoons cold unsalted butter, cut into ¼-inch pieces
- 2 tablespoons canola oil
- 3 large ripe Bosc pears—peeled, cored and thinly sliced
- 2 large Golden Delicious apples—peeled, cored and thinly sliced
- ⅓ cup dried cranberries
- 2 tablespoons fresh lemon juice

1. Preheat the oven to 375°. Spray an 8-by-11-inch baking dish with oil. In a bowl, mix the oats with ½ cup of the flour, the brown sugar, almonds and salt. Using your fingertips, rub in the butter. Stir in the oil.

2. In a large bowl, toss the pears, apples and dried cranberries with the lemon juice and the remaining 1 tablespoon of flour. Spread the fruit in the prepared baking dish and sprinkle the oat crumbs on top. Bake for 45 minutes, or until the fruit is tender and the topping is golden. *—Suki Hertz*

MAKE AHEAD The pear and apple crisp can be kept at room temperature for up to 6 hours.

WINE Rich, sweet Sauternes.

Banana Soufflés

4 SERVINGS ● ○

These simple, airy soufflés are the perfect marriage of Puerto Rican ingredients and French technique.

- 1 tablespoon unsalted butter, melted
- 5 tablespoons sugar
- 2 firm, ripe bananas, mashed (1¼ cups)
- 1 tablespoon fresh lime juice
- 1 large egg yolk
- 3 large egg whites
- Salt

1. Preheat the oven to 400°. Brush four 1-cup ramekins with melted butter. Add 2 tablespoons of the sugar to 1 of the ramekins and rotate it to coat with sugar. Tap the excess sugar into another ramekin and repeat until all the ramekins are coated with sugar.

2. In a food processor, puree the bananas with the lime juice, egg yolk and 2 tablespoons of the sugar until smooth. Scrape the banana mixture into a large bowl.

3. In a stainless steel bowl, beat the egg whites with a pinch of salt until soft peaks form. Add the remaining 1 tablespoon of sugar and beat until firm and glossy. Using a rubber spatula, beat one-fourth of the beaten whites into the banana mixture, then gently fold in the remaining whites. Spoon the soufflé mixture into the prepared ramekins and tap lightly on a countertop. Transfer the soufflés to a baking sheet and bake in the center of the oven for about 15 minutes, or until golden brown and risen. Serve at once. *—Eric Ripert*

WINE Sweet, fortified, fragrant Muscat.

Honey-Roasted Plums with Mascarpone and Pistachios

8 SERVINGS ● ●

- 1 cup mild honey, such as clover
- 2 tablespoons unsalted butter, at room temperature
- 1 tablespoon fresh lemon juice
- 1 teaspoon orange flower water (optional)
- 8 large firm, ripe red or black plums, halved and pitted
- ½ cup mascarpone, at room temperature
- ¼ cup roasted unsalted pistachios, finely chopped

1. Preheat the oven to 400°. In a small saucepan, melt the honey and butter with the lemon juice over moderately low heat. Stir in the orange flower water, if using. Scrape the honey syrup into a medium bowl, add the halved plums and toss to coat thoroughly.

Arrange the plums, cut side down, in a large baking dish and spoon half of the honey syrup evenly over them.

2. Roast the plums for 15 minutes, or until barely tender and beginning to brown on the bottom. Turn the plums and spoon the remaining honey syrup over them. Roast the plums for 10 minutes longer, or until tender but not falling apart. Transfer the plums to plates and drizzle with the honey syrup. Top with a dollop of mascarpone, sprinkle with the pistachios and serve. *—Ana Sortun*

MAKE AHEAD The roasted plums can be refrigerated in their syrup overnight. Reheat the plums in a 325° oven until warmed through before serving.

Curried Fruit Compote

MAKES ABOUT 2½ CUPS ● ●

- 2 cups water
- ¼ cup dried cranberries
- ¼ pound dried pear halves
- ½ cup light brown sugar
- 1 tablespoon Madras curry powder
- 1 Granny Smith apple—peeled, cored and cut into 1-inch dice

1. Bring the water to a boil in a medium saucepan. Pour ¼ cup of the water into a glass measuring cup, add the cranberries and let soak until softened, about 10 minutes; drain. Meanwhile, add the dried pear halves to the saucepan, cover and let soak until softened, about 20 minutes.

2. Remove the pear halves and cut them into 1-inch pieces. Add the brown sugar and curry powder to the saucepan and simmer over moderate heat until the sugar has dissolved. Add the apple and simmer over moderate heat until tender, about 4 minutes.

3. In a food processor, puree ¼ cup of the pears with 1 cup of the cooking liquid. Stir the pear puree back into the saucepan. Add the cranberries and the remaining pears and serve warm or at room temperature. *—Tony Hill*

CURRIED FRUIT COMPOTE

MAKE AHEAD The fruit compote can be refrigerated for 2 days.

SERVE WITH Roast pork, turkey or angel food cake.

WINE Light, sweet late-harvest Riesling.

Breton Prune Flan

8 SERVINGS ● ●

Far Breton, a pudding made with raisins and prunes, is found at practically every pastry shop and farmers' market in Brittany, but this recipe, enriched with butter and Armagnac-soaked prunes, is the best you're ever likely to taste.

18   large pitted prunes
¼   cup Armagnac or dark rum
1   cup all-purpose flour
½   cup plus 2 tablespoons sugar
Pinch of salt
3   large eggs
2   cups milk
4   tablespoons unsalted butter, melted and cooled

I. In a bowl, soak the prunes in the Armagnac, stirring, until most of the liquid is absorbed, 2 hours or overnight.

2. Preheat the oven to 400°. Lightly butter a shallow 6-cup baking dish. In a large bowl, whisk the flour with the sugar and salt, then make a well in the center. Crack the eggs into the well and add ½ cup of the milk. Using a whisk, beat the eggs with the milk, working in some of the flour. Gradually add the remaining 1½ cups of milk and the melted butter while whisking in more of the dry ingredients. Continue whisking until smooth.

3. Using a wooden spoon, work the batter through a fine sieve into the prepared baking dish. Scatter the prunes in the dish and bake for about 35 minutes, or until risen and deep golden. Let cool slightly before cutting into rectangles. The flan can also be served at room temperature or rewarmed.
—*Jane Sigal*

MAKE AHEAD The flan can be kept at room temperature for up to 4 hours.

WINE Complex tawny port.

Tapioca and Rhubarb Parfait

4 SERVINGS ● ● ●

COMPOTE

1   pound medium rhubarb stalks without leaves, peeled and cut into ½-inch pieces
½   cup sugar
2   tablespoons fresh lemon juice
¼   teaspoon cinnamon
¼   teaspoon ground ginger

TAPIOCA

3   tablespoons quick-cooking tapioca
2   cups whole milk
2   large eggs, lightly beaten
5   tablespoons sugar
¼   teaspoon salt
1   teaspoon pure vanilla extract
½   cup crème fraîche
8   thin slices crystallized ginger, for garnish

I. MAKE THE COMPOTE: In a medium saucepan, mix the rhubarb with the sugar, lemon juice, cinnamon and ground ginger and bring to a boil.

Reduce the heat to low and simmer, stirring frequently, until the rhubarb is tender but not falling apart, about 8 minutes. Transfer the rhubarb to a bowl and let cool. Cover and refrigerate until thick, at least 1 hour and up to 1 day.

2. MAKE THE TAPIOCA: In a saucepan, whisk the tapioca, milk, eggs, sugar and salt. Let stand for 5 minutes, or until the tapioca begins to swell.

3. Bring the tapioca to a boil over moderately high heat, whisking constantly. Reduce the heat to moderately low and cook, stirring constantly, until slightly thickened, about 1 minute. Remove from the heat and stir in the vanilla. Set the saucepan in a bowl of ice water and stir often until cool and thick, about 5 minutes. Stir in the crème fraîche.

4. Spoon ¼ cup of the rhubarb compote into 4 parfait glasses and top with half of the tapioca. Repeat with the remaining compote and tapioca. Garnish each parfait with 2 slices of crystallized ginger and serve. —*Lauren Chattman*

MAKE AHEAD The recipe can be prepared through Step 3 and the 2 parts refrigerated separately overnight.

WINE Rich, sweet Sauternes.

Berry Parfaits with Vanilla Cream and Ginger

4 SERVINGS ●

1   cup heavy cream, chilled
1½   tablespoons sugar
½   teaspoon pure vanilla extract
3   cups mixed berries, such as raspberries, blueberries, blackberries and sliced strawberries
¼   cup finely diced crystallized ginger
Mint sprigs, for garnish

In a large bowl, whip the cream until soft peaks form. Add the sugar and vanilla and beat until firm. Spoon half of the berries into 4 wineglasses and top with the whipped cream. Add the remaining berries, garnish with the ginger and mint and serve. —*Kathy Gunst*

Sweet Wine Sabayon with Berries

4 SERVINGS ● ○

- 4 large eggs yolks, at room temperature
- ¼ cup plus 2 tablespoons sugar
- ¾ cup sweet wine, such as Muscat de Beaumes-de-Venise, at room temperature
- 1 teaspoon grated orange zest
- 2 cups mixed fresh berries

Mint sprigs, for garnish

I. Pour 2 inches of water into a saucepan and bring to a boil. Prepare an ice-water bath in a medium bowl. Place 4 large wineglasses in the freezer to chill.

2. Place the egg yolks in a stainless steel bowl. Whisk in the sugar until pale and slightly thickened, about 2 minutes. Add the wine and orange zest. Set the bowl over the boiling water and whisk constantly over moderately low heat until the sabayon is thick and has doubled in volume, about 8 minutes. Set the bowl in the ice-water bath and let cool, stirring, about 15 minutes.

3. Spoon the sabayon into the wineglasses. Garnish with the berries and mint and serve. —*Terrance Brennan*

WINE Sweet, fortified, fragrant Muscat.

Creamy Strawberry Sorbet

6 SERVINGS ● ○

- 1 pint strawberries, hulled and finely diced
- 1½ cups sugar
- 1 cup water

Zest and juice of 2 navel oranges

Zest and juice of 2 lemons

I. In a bowl, toss the berries with ½ cup of the sugar. Cover with plastic wrap and let stand at room temperature for 4 hours or refrigerate overnight; stir occasionally until the sugar is dissolved and the strawberries are very juicy.

2. In a saucepan, combine the remaining 1 cup of sugar with the water and citrus zests. Bring to a boil over moderate heat and cook just until the sugar dissolves, stirring; let the syrup cool.

3. Strain the syrup into a glass bowl. Strain the strawberry juice into the syrup; add the orange and lemon juices.

4. In a food processor, puree one-third of the strawberries with ½ cup of the syrup until smooth. Stir into the syrup and freeze for 30 minutes. Using a fork, stir the ice crystals around the edges into the liquidy center and return to the freezer. Continue to stir and freeze until the mixture resembles soft snow, about 40 minutes. Stir in the remaining strawberries, freeze until just firm but not solid and serve. —*Benedetta Vitali*

MAKE AHEAD The sorbet can be frozen for 2 days. Thaw in the refrigerator until soft and slushy before serving.

Ginger-Poached Pink Grapefruit

6 SERVINGS ● ○

- 3 large pink grapefruits
- 2 cups water
- 2 cups sugar

One 4-inch piece of fresh ginger, thinly sliced and gently smashed

- 1 whole star anise pod
- 1 whole clove
- ½ vanilla bean, split lengthwise
- 3 tablespoons finely diced crystallized ginger (optional)

Plain whole-milk yogurt, for serving

I. Using a sharp knife, peel the grapefruits, removing all of the bitter white pith. Working over a bowl, cut in between the membranes, releasing the sections into the bowl. Squeeze the juice from the membranes into the bowl.

2. In a skillet, combine the water, sugar, ginger, star anise, clove and vanilla bean and bring to a boil, stirring, until the sugar is dissolved. Simmer over moderate heat until the syrup is slightly reduced, about 10 minutes. Remove the ginger, star anise, clove and vanilla.

3. Add the grapefruit and juice to the skillet and cook over moderate heat for 1 minute. Using a slotted spoon, transfer the grapefruit to a serving bowl. Simmer the syrup over moderate heat until reduced to 2 cups, about 5 minutes.

Pour the syrup over the grapefruit and garnish with the crystallized ginger. Serve warm or at room temperature, with yogurt. —*Melissa Clark*

Fresh Cherry Soup with Lemon Sorbet

4 SERVINGS ● ○

- 1½ pounds sweet cherries, rinsed and pitted
- 1 cup dry red wine
- 1 cup water
- 1 tablespoon light brown sugar
- ¼ cup plus 2 tablespoons reduced-fat sour cream
- 3 tablespoons fresh lemon juice
- ¼ teaspoon pure almond extract
- 4 rounded tablespoons lemon sorbet
- 4 mint sprigs, for garnish

I. In a saucepan, bring the cherries, wine, water and sugar to a boil; simmer over low heat for 10 minutes. Let cool for 15 minutes, then pass the cherries through a food mill fitted with a fine disk into a glass bowl or puree in a food processor. Cover and refrigerate until cold, at least 2 hours or overnight.

2. Whisk the sour cream, lemon juice and almond extract into the cherry soup. Ladle the soup into bowls and top with the lemon sorbet. Garnish each bowl with mint and serve. —*Suki Hertz*

Sliced Fresh Guava with Shaved Coconut

30 SERVINGS ● ○

Two 1½-pound coconuts

Thirty 5-ounce guavas, cut crosswise into ¼-inch-thick slices

I. To crack the coconuts, lay them sideways in the sink. Using a hammer, crack a coconut in the middle. Rotate the coconut slightly and crack again; keep rotating until the shell breaks. Using the tip of a paring knife, pry the coconut flesh from the shell. Thinly shave the coconut with a sharp vegetable peeler.

2. Arrange the guava on plates, top with the coconut and serve. —*Jennifer Rubell*

VANILLA SUNDAE WITH CRISPED RICE-AND-PEANUT CRUNCH, P. 316

cakes, cookies + other desserts

ALMOND CORNMEAL CAKE

VIENNESE DOBOS TORTE

Almond Cornmeal Cake

MAKES ONE 8-INCH CAKE ●

For a slightly moister texture, sour cream is added to this traditionally all-butter cake.

- ½ cup fine yellow cornmeal
- ½ cup cake flour
- 1 teaspoon baking powder
- 1 stick (4 ounces) unsalted butter, softened
- ¼ cup almond paste, softened
- 1¼ cups confectioners' sugar, plus more for dusting
- ½ teaspoon pure vanilla extract
- 4 large egg yolks
- 2 large eggs
- ¼ cup sour cream

1. Preheat the oven to 350°. Butter and flour an 8-inch round cake pan. In a medium bowl, whisk the yellow cornmeal with the cake flour and baking powder until combined.

2. In a food processor, combine the softened butter and almond paste and process until very smooth. Add the 1¼ cups of confectioners' sugar and the vanilla; process until light and fluffy. With the machine on, add the egg yolks and whole eggs, 1 at a time, processing between additions, until smooth. Add the sour cream and process until fully blended. Scrape the batter into a bowl and stir in the dry ingredients.

3. Scrape the batter into the prepared cake pan and smooth the surface. Bake in the lower third of the oven for about 35 minutes, or until the cake is golden, puffy and pulls away from the side of the pan. Transfer to a wire rack and let cool in the pan for about 10 minutes. Invert the cake onto the rack and let cool completely. Turn the cake right side up, sift confectioners' sugar on the top and serve. —*Giada De Laurentiis*

MAKE AHEAD The Almond Cornmeal Cake can be stored in an airtight container at room temperature for up to 4 days, or kept covered in the refrigerator for up to 1 week.

SERVE WITH Raspberry coulis.

WINE Sweet, luscious Italian vin santo.

Gâteau Basque

8 SERVINGS ●

Plan to use a 9-by-1-inch flan ring.

PASTRY

- ½ cup sugar
- 1 stick (4 ounces) unsalted butter, at room temperature
- Finely grated zest of 1 lemon
- ⅛ teaspoon salt
- 1 large egg
- 1 large egg yolk
- 1½ cups plus 2 tablespoons all-purpose flour
- 1 teaspoon baking powder

FILLING

1¾ **cups whole milk**

½ **vanilla bean, split lengthwise, seeds scraped**

¼ **cup plus 2 tablespoons sugar**

4 **large egg yolks**

¼ **cup all-purpose flour**

1 **tablespoon light rum**

½ **teaspoon pure almond extract**

¾ **cup black-cherry preserves**

Egg wash made with 1 large egg yolk mixed with 1 tablespoon milk

I. MAKE THE PASTRY: In a food processor, pulse the sugar with the butter, lemon zest and salt until smooth. Add the egg and egg yolk and pulse to blend. In a small bowl, whisk the flour with the baking powder. Add the dry ingredients to the processor and pulse until a soft dough forms. Turn the dough out onto a work surface and divide it into 2 pieces, 1 just slightly larger than the other. Pat the dough into disks, wrap in plastic and refrigerate until firm, at least 30 minutes.

2. MAKE THE FILLING: In a medium saucepan, heat the milk with the vanilla seeds and bean until steaming. In a medium bowl, whisk the sugar with the egg yolks until pale. Add the flour and whisk until smooth. Gradually add ½ cup of the hot milk, whisking vigorously. Pour the mixture back into the saucepan and cook over moderate heat, whisking constantly, until boiling and thick, about 4 minutes. Strain the pastry cream into a bowl through a fine sieve; discard the vanilla bean. Stir in the rum and the almond extract. Cover and refrigerate until firm.

3. Preheat the oven to 325°. Butter a 9-by-1-inch flan ring and set it on a cookie sheet lined with parchment paper. Working between 2 pieces of plastic wrap, roll out the larger disk of dough to an 11-inch round. Ease the dough into the flan ring, pressing it into the corners and leaving a slight overhang. Spread the cherry preserves evenly over the bottom of the tart shell.

Add the pastry cream in dollops, then carefully spread it over the preserves. Working between 2 more pieces of plastic wrap, roll out the second disk of dough to a 10-inch round and lay it over the pastry cream. Pinch the edges of the top and bottom crusts together and roll the overhang onto the top crust. Using a knife, make shallow slash marks along the edge.

4. Using the tines of a fork, deeply score the top crust in a crosshatch pattern. Brush with the egg wash. Bake in the center of the oven for 55 minutes, or until the top is golden brown. Transfer the baking sheet to a wire rack and let the tart cool completely.

5. To unmold, place a second cookie sheet over the tart and invert. Remove the ring and carefully invert the tart onto a cake plate. Cut the tart into wedges and serve. —*Pascal Rigo*

MAKE AHEAD The tart can be refrigerated for 2 days. Serve cold or at room temperature.

WINE Sweet, fortified, fragrant Muscat.

Viennese Dobos Torte

12 SERVINGS ●

CAKE

10 **large eggs, separated, at room temperature**

1 **cup granulated sugar**

2½ **sticks (10 ounces) unsalted butter, softened**

½ **cup confectioners' sugar**

1 **teaspoon finely grated lemon zest**

1 **teaspoon pure vanilla extract**

⅛ **teaspoon salt**

1½ **cups all-purpose flour**

FILLING

4 **large eggs, at room temperature**

⅔ **cup granulated sugar**

¼ **teaspoon pure vanilla extract**

4 **ounces bittersweet chocolate, coarsely chopped**

3 **tablespoons water**

1½ **sticks (6 ounces) unsalted butter, at room temperature**

Confectioners' sugar, for sifting

CARAMEL

½ **cup granulated sugar**

2 **tablespoons water**

I. MAKE THE CAKE: Preheat the oven to 350°. Lightly coat two 12-by-17-inch jelly-roll pans with vegetable oil spray; line them with parchment or wax paper.

2. In a standing electric mixer fitted with a whisk, beat the egg whites until soft peaks form. At high speed, gradually add the granulated sugar and beat until the whites are glossy and firm, about 1 minute. Transfer the whites to a large bowl; rinse and dry the mixing bowl.

3. Add the egg yolks, butter, confectioners' sugar, lemon zest, vanilla and salt to the mixing bowl and beat at moderate speed until creamy. Beat in one-fourth of the beaten whites. Transfer the batter to a large bowl. Fold in one-third of the flour, followed by one-third of the remaining whites; repeat with the remaining flour and whites until no streaks of white remain. Divide the batter between the prepared pans and spread evenly with an offset spatula. Bake the cakes for about 12 minutes, or until firm, shifting the pans halfway through baking. Let cool.

4. MAKE THE FILLING: In a large heatproof bowl set over a saucepan of simmering water, beat the eggs with the sugar until tripled in volume and an instant-read thermometer inserted in the mixture registers 165°, about 6 minutes. Whisk in the vanilla. Remove the bowl from the pan and pour out the water. Add the chocolate and water to the pan and cook over moderate heat, stirring, until the chocolate is melted. Scrape the chocolate into a medium bowl. Whisk in one-fourth of the egg mixture, then gradually whisk in the rest. Let cool.

5. In a bowl, using a handheld mixer, beat the butter until fluffy. Beat in the chocolate mixture. Refrigerate until firm.

6. Sift confectioners' sugar over the cakes. Top each jelly-roll pan with a baking sheet; invert to release the cakes

Remove the parchment and dust the cakes with confectioners' sugar. Cut each cake crosswise into three 5-by-12-inch rectangles. Place 1 cake layer on a platter. Beat the filling until thick and fluffy, about 2 minutes; spread ½ cup evenly over the layer. Repeat to make a total of 5 layers, reserving the last cake rectangle and ¼ cup of filling. Thinly frost the sides with the remaining ¼ cup of filling. Refrigerate until very firm.

7. MAKE THE CARAMEL: Spray a large sheet of wax paper with vegetable oil spray. Center the remaining cake layer on the sheet. In a medium saucepan, cook the sugar and water over moderately high heat, stirring, until an amber caramel forms, 5 minutes. Carefully pour the caramel over the cake layer and spread it thinly with a small offset spatula. (About one-fourth of the caramel will end up on the paper.) Working quickly, cut the cake in half crosswise with a buttered sharp knife, then cut it in half crosswise again to form 4 rectangles. Cut each rectangle into 3 strips to make 12 equal strips. Trim any excess caramel from the sides. Let the caramel harden completely.

8. Arrange the caramel cake strips side by side on the top of the cake. Cut into slices and serve. —*Kurt Gutenbrunner*
MAKE AHEAD The finished cake can be refrigerated, uncovered, for 2 days.
WINE Complex tawny port.

Vanilla Bean Cake
MAKES ONE 10-INCH CAKE ●
This is a version of pastry chef Bill Yosses's signature dessert at Citarella Restaurant, in New York City. The batter needs to chill for at least 8 hours before baking, so plan accordingly.

s white chocolate,
d, plus a block of white
te for shaving
ons unsalted butter
ans, split lengthwise,
aped
, separated

⅓ cup bread flour, sifted
Pinch of cream of tartar
⅓ cup sugar

1. Butter a 10-inch springform pan. Line the bottom with parchment paper and butter the paper.
2. In a large bowl set over a pot of barely simmering water, stir the chopped white chocolate with the butter until almost melted. Remove the bowl from the heat, add the vanilla seeds and stir until smooth. Stir in the egg yolks. Sift the bread flour over the batter and stir it in.
3. In a large bowl, beat the egg whites with the cream of tartar to soft peaks. Gradually add the sugar and beat until the whites are stiff and glossy. Beat one-fourth of the egg whites into the batter, then fold in the remaining whites until no streaks remain. Pour the batter into the prepared pan and smooth the top. Cover with plastic wrap and refrigerate for 8 hours or overnight.
4. Preheat the oven to 375°. Bake the cake in the middle of the oven for about 30 minutes, until puffed and golden and a toothpick inserted in the center comes out clean. Let the cake cool completely in the pan; it will fall dramatically.
5. Run a thin knife around the edge of the cake, then remove the side of the pan. Slide the cake onto a plate. Using a vegetable peeler, shave white chocolate curls over the cake. —*Bill Yosses*
MAKE AHEAD The baked cake can be refrigerated for up to 2 days. Serve at room temperature.

Orange Tea Cake
MAKES ONE 9-INCH CAKE ●
This moist, citrusy olive-oil cake is traditionally made with a blood orange called *maltaise de Tunisie,* which adds a beautiful red blush. It's best to use organic oranges; if they are unavailable, wash the oranges well before using.
One ¾-pound blood orange or other thin-skinned orange
1½ cups sugar
⅓ cup extra-virgin olive oil

2 cups all-purpose flour
1 tablespoon baking powder
4 large eggs, beaten
2 teaspoons pure vanilla extract

1. Preheat the oven to 375°. Butter and flour a 9-inch springform pan. Cut the top and bottom off the orange and discard. Thinly slice the orange and discard any seeds. Transfer the orange slices to a food processor and puree. Add ½ cup of the sugar and the olive oil and pulse just until combined.
2. In a medium bowl, whisk the flour with the baking powder. In another medium bowl, using a handheld electric mixer, beat the eggs with the remaining 1 cup of sugar at moderate speed until thick, about 8 minutes. Fold in half of the flour mixture, then fold in the orange puree and vanilla. Fold in the remaining flour mixture.
3. Scrape the batter into the prepared pan and bake for 20 minutes. Lower the oven temperature to 325° and bake the cake for 30 minutes, or until golden on top and a toothpick inserted in the center comes out clean. Transfer the cake to a rack to cool, then unmold and serve. —*Nancy Harmon Jenkins*
MAKE AHEAD The cake can be stored overnight in an airtight container.

Lemon Meringue Cake
MAKES ONE 9-INCH LAYER CAKE ●
For an even more dramatic effect, a small kitchen torch can be used to brown the meringue.
CAKE
3 cups cake flour
1 tablespoon baking powder
½ teaspoon salt
2 sticks (½ pound) unsalted butter, softened
2 cups sugar
4 large eggs, at room temperature
4 large egg yolks, at room temperature
1 teaspoon pure vanilla extract
1 cup milk, at room temperature

LEMON MERINGUE CAKE

LEMON CURD

- 9 large egg yolks
- 1 cup sugar
- ½ cup fresh lemon juice
- ¼ teaspoon salt
- 1 stick (4 ounces) unsalted butter, cut into 8 tablespoons

MERINGUE

- 2¼ cups sugar
- 1½ cups egg whites (from about 1 dozen extra-large eggs)
- ¾ teaspoon fresh lemon juice

1. MAKE THE CAKE: Preheat the oven to 350°. Butter two 9-inch round cake pans and line the bottoms with parchment paper. Butter the paper and dust the pans lightly with flour, tapping out any excess.

2. In a medium bowl, sift together the cake flour, baking powder and salt.

3. In the bowl of a standing mixer, beat the butter with the sugar at high speed until fluffy, about 5 minutes. Add the eggs and egg yolks, 1 at a time, beating well after each addition. Beat in the vanilla. Beat in the flour mixture at low speed in 3 batches, alternating with the milk; beat just until smooth.

4. Scrape the batter into the prepared pans and smooth the surfaces. Bake for 35 to 40 minutes, or until a toothpick inserted in the center of each cake comes out clean. Let the cakes cool on racks for 10 minutes, then unmold them onto racks; let cool completely.

---

baking tip

slicing secret

SLICING LAYER CAKE CAN BE A CHALLENGE. Use a sharp knife to trace a line all the way around the circumference where you intend to separate the cake into layers. Then, with a taut piece of dental floss, slice the cake horizontally, gently sawing the floss back and forth to cut.

---

5. MAKE THE LEMON CURD: Fill a large bowl with ice water. In a heavy, medium saucepan, whisk the egg yolks with the sugar, lemon juice and salt until combined. Add the butter and cook over moderate heat, stirring constantly, until the lemon curd is thickened and just beginning to simmer, about 5 minutes; scrape the bottom of the bowl constantly so the mixture doesn't curdle. Set the saucepan in the ice-water bath and chill the curd, whisking occasionally.

6. MAKE THE MERINGUE: In a medium saucepan, bring 1 inch of water to a boil. In the clean bowl of a standing mixer, whisk the sugar, egg whites and lemon juice until combined. Set the bowl over the saucepan and cook, whisking constantly, until the sugar dissolves, about 6 minutes.

7. Return the bowl to the mixer and beat the meringue at medium speed for about 10 minutes, or until cooled to room temperature. Continue beating at high speed until the meringue is thick, shiny and billowy, about 15 minutes longer.

8. ASSEMBLE THE CAKE: Using a serrated knife, trim the cake tops to make them level. With the serrated knife, halve each cake horizontally. Set 1 layer on a cake plate, cut side up, and spread it with one-third of the lemon curd. Set another layer on top and spread with another third of the curd. Repeat once more and then top with the final cake layer. With a large offset spatula, frost the side of the cake with a thin layer of the meringue. Top the cake with the remaining meringue and swirl decoratively, then serve.

—*Scott Bieber*

MAKE AHEAD The cake layers can be wrapped in plastic and refrigerated for 2 days or frozen for up to 1 month. The curd can be refrigerated for 3 days. The assembled cake can be refrigerated for up to 2 days.

WINE Light, sweet late-harvest Riesling.

Lemony Yogurt Cake

MAKES ONE 9-INCH CAKE ●

- 2½ cups all-purpose flour
- ½ teaspoon baking soda
- ¼ teaspoon salt
- 1 stick (4 ounces) unsalted butter, at room temperature
- 2 cups sugar
- 1 cup plain whole-milk yogurt
- 3 large eggs, lightly beaten
- 1 tablespoon finely grated lemon zest
- 1 tablespoon fresh lemon juice
- ½ teaspoon pure vanilla extract

Confectioners' sugar, for dusting

1. Preheat the oven to 350°. Butter and flour a 9-inch-square cake pan. In a medium bowl, whisk the flour with the baking soda and salt. In a large bowl, beat the butter with the sugar until smooth. Beat in the yogurt, followed by the eggs, lemon zest, lemon juice and vanilla. Gradually beat in the dry ingredients until blended.

2. Scrape the batter into the prepared pan and bake for about 45 minutes, or until golden brown and a cake tester inserted in the center of the cake comes out clean. Transfer the cake to a rack to cool for 10 minutes, then invert the cake onto the rack and let cool completely. Dust with confectioners' sugar before serving.

—*Maria Guarnaschelli*

SERVE WITH Sliced pears tossed in a little lemon juice.

WINE Light, sweet late-harvest Riesling.

Citrusy Angel Food Cake

10 SERVINGS ● ●

- 1½ cups granulated sugar
- 3 tablespoons finely grated lemon zest
- 1 cup cake flour
- ½ teaspoon salt
- 1½ cups large egg whites (11 or 12), at room temperature
- 1 tablespoon water
- 1 teaspoon cream of tartar
- ½ teaspoon pure vanilla extract

1½ tablespoons plus 2 teaspoons
   fresh lemon juice
1 cup confectioners' sugar, sifted
2 tablespoons heavy cream

I. Preheat the oven to 325°. In a small bowl, stir 1 cup of the granulated sugar with the lemon zest. In a medium bowl, sift the flour with the salt and the remaining ½ cup of granulated sugar.

2. In a large bowl, beat the egg whites until foamy. Add the water, cream of tartar, vanilla and 2 teaspoons of the lemon juice and beat at medium-high speed until soft peaks form. Gradually add the lemon sugar and beat until the whites are stiff and glossy. Fold in the flour mixture in 3 batches.

3. Spoon the batter into an angel food cake pan with a removable bottom and smooth the top. Using a knife, cut through the batter several times to release any air bubbles. Bake the cake for about 45 minutes, or until the top is golden brown and feels springy when lightly pressed. Invert the cake pan onto the neck of a wine bottle and let the cake cool completely.

4. In a small bowl, whisk the confectioners' sugar with the cream until smooth. Whisk in the remaining 1½ tablespoons of lemon juice. Run a thin knife around the side and tube to unmold the cake. Transfer to a platter and drizzle with the lemon glaze.
—*Tasha Prysi*

WINE Light, sweet late-harvest Riesling.

Orange Cream Cheese Pound Cake with Passion Fruit Icing

MAKES TWO 8½-INCH LOAVES ● ●
If passion fruits aren't available, substitute 1 tablespoon of fresh lemon juice or orange juice. You can also omit the icing altogether.

2½ cups all-purpose flour
2 teaspoons baking powder
¼ teaspoon salt
2½ sticks (10 ounces) unsalted
   butter, softened
½ pound cream cheese, softened

1½ cups sugar
Finely grated zest of 2 oranges
4 large eggs
2 teaspoons pure vanilla extract
2 tablespoons sour cream
2 ripe passion fruits (see Note)
1¼ cups confectioners' sugar

I. Preheat the oven to 350°. Butter and flour two 8½-by-4½-inch loaf pans. In a medium bowl, whisk the flour with the baking powder and salt.

2. In a large bowl, using a handheld electric mixer, cream 2 sticks of the butter with the cream cheese at moderate speed. Add the sugar and orange zest and beat until light and fluffy, about 2 minutes. Add the eggs, 1 at a time, beating well between additions. Beat in the vanilla. Add the dry ingredients and beat at low speed until blended. Add the sour cream and beat until smooth. Divide the batter between the prepared pans and smooth the tops.

3. Bake the pound cakes for about 1 hour, or until the tops are golden brown and cracked and a toothpick inserted in the centers comes out clean. Let cool in the pans for 15 minutes, then turn the pound cakes out onto a rack and set them right side up to cool completely.

4. Cut the passion fruits in half and scrape the seedy fruit into a strainer set over a medium bowl. Press the fruit with the back of a spoon to release the juices; discard the seeds. Melt the remaining ½ stick of butter in a small saucepan. Add the confectioners' sugar and passion fruit juice; cook over very low heat, stirring, until smooth. Drizzle the icing over the cakes, letting it drip down the sides. Let the icing set, then slice the cakes and serve.
—*Maggie Beer*

NOTE Passion fruits should be deep purple and heavy, with dimpled skin.

MAKE AHEAD The cakes can be stored at room temperature in an airtight container for up to 5 days or frozen for up to 1 month.

Orange Cupcakes with Macadamia Nut Crackle

MAKES 24 CUPCAKES ●
If you want to make more than 24 cupcakes, prepare the batter in two separate batches.

6 tablespoons unsalted butter
1 cup cake flour
⅔ cup sifted cornstarch
¾ cup plus 2 tablespoons sugar
6 large eggs, at room
   temperature, beaten
2 teaspoons pure vanilla extract
1 tablespoon finely grated
   orange zest
Pinch of salt
Orange–Cream Cheese Icing
   (recipe follows)
Macadamia Nut Crackle
   (recipe follows)

I. Preheat the oven to 350°. Line 24 muffin cups with paper liners. Melt the butter in a small saucepan; keep warm.

2. In a small bowl, whisk the flour with the cornstarch. In a large stainless steel bowl, whisk the sugar, eggs, vanilla, orange zest and salt. Set the bowl over a pot of barely simmering water and whisk the mixture constantly until warm to the touch. Remove from the heat.

3. Using a handheld electric mixer, beat the mixture at high speed until pale, thick and tripled in volume, about 5 minutes. Sprinkle the dry ingredients on top and fold them into the batter.

4. Pour the warm butter down the side of the bowl, letting it sink to the bottom. Working quickly, fold the butter into the batter until blended. Immediately spoon the batter into the muffin cups until three-quarters full. Bake the cupcakes for about 12 minutes, until light golden and springy to the touch. Let cool slightly in the pans, then transfer the cupcakes to racks to cool.

5. Frost each cupcake with a scant 1½ tablespoons of the Orange–Cream Cheese Icing and sprinkle with 1 tablespoon of the Macadamia Nut Crackle.
—*Jennifer Rubell*

CHOCOLATE CUPCAKE WITH CREAM FILLING

JAPANESE FRUIT CAKE

MAKE AHEAD The frosted cupcakes can be refrigerated for 2 days. Bring to room temperature and sprinkle with the crackle just before serving.

ORANGE–CREAM CHEESE ICING
MAKES ABOUT 2 CUPS ● ●

- 6 tablespoons unsalted butter, softened
- 4½ ounces cream cheese, softened
- 1½ cups confectioners' sugar, sifted
- 1½ teaspoons finely grated orange zest

In a large bowl, using a handheld electric mixer, beat the butter with the cream cheese until smooth. Add the confectioners' sugar and orange zest and continue beating until the icing is light and fluffy. —*J.R.*

MAKE AHEAD The orange icing can be refrigerated for up to 3 days. Let return to room temperature and then rewhip before using.

MACADAMIA NUT CRACKLE
MAKES ABOUT 2 CUPS ● ●

- 1 cup sugar
- 1 tablespoon light corn syrup
- 2 tablespoons water
- 1 tablespoon unsalted butter
- ½ cup roasted, salted macadamia nuts (3 ounces), finely chopped
- ⅛ teaspoon baking soda

Lightly oil a large baking sheet. In a medium saucepan, bring the sugar, corn syrup and water to a boil, stirring just until the sugar dissolves. Stop stirring and cook over moderately high heat until the syrup turns an amber caramel, about 5 minutes. Stir in the butter and nuts. Add the baking soda and stir just until foamy. Immediately pour the caramel onto the prepared baking sheet. Let cool, then crack into ½-inch bits. —*J.R.*

MAKE AHEAD Store the crackle in an airtight container at room temperature for up to 2 days.

Chocolate Cupcakes with Cream Filling

MAKES 12 CUPCAKES ●

CUPCAKES

- ½ cup plus 2 tablespoons cake flour
- ⅓ cup unsweetened Dutch-process cocoa
- ½ teaspoon baking powder
- ¼ teaspoon baking soda
- Pinch of salt
- 2 large eggs, separated
- ⅓ cup canola oil
- ½ cup plus 2 tablespoons sugar
- 2 tablespoons water

FILLING

- 6 tablespoons unsalted butter, softened
- 1½ cups confectioners' sugar
- ¾ cup Marshmallow Fluff
- 1½ tablespoons plus 1 teaspoon heavy cream

FROSTING

- ¼ cup heavy cream
- 4 ounces bittersweet chocolate, finely chopped
- 1 tablespoon unsalted butter, softened

I. MAKE THE CUPCAKES: Preheat the oven to 350°. Spray a 12-cup non-stick muffin pan with vegetable oil spray. In a medium bowl, sift the flour and cocoa with the baking powder, baking soda and salt. In another bowl, using an electric mixer, beat the egg yolks with the canola oil, ½ cup of the sugar and the water. Beat in the dry ingredients at low speed until smooth.

2. In a clean bowl, using clean beaters, beat the egg whites at high speed until soft peaks form. Add the remaining 2 tablespoons of sugar and beat until stiff and glossy. Beat one-fourth of the whites into the batter, then fold in the remaining whites until no streaks remain. Spoon the batter into the muffin cups, filling them halfway. Bake for 15 minutes, or until the cupcakes are springy when touched. Let cool for 5 minutes, then turn them out onto a wire rack to cool completely.

3. MAKE THE FILLING: In a medium bowl, beat the butter with the confectioners' sugar, Marshmallow Fluff and 1½ tablespoons of the cream at medium speed until fluffy. Transfer all but ½ cup of the filling to a pastry bag fitted with a ¼-inch plain round tip. Beat the remaining 1 teaspoon of cream into the remaining ½ cup of filling and reserve.

4. Line a large baking sheet with wax paper. Insert the tip of the pastry bag about ½ inch deep into the bottom of each cupcake; squeeze lightly to press the filling into the cupcakes. Set the cupcakes on the sheet.

5. MAKE THE FROSTING: Heat the cream in a small saucepan until steaming. Add the chocolate and let stand for 5 minutes. Add the butter and stir until smooth. Spread the top of each cupcake with the frosting. Spoon the reserved filling into a pastry bag fitted with a very small plain tip and pipe decorative swirls on each cupcake. Refrigerate the cupcakes for at least 10 minutes to set the frosting. —*Nicole Kaplan*

MAKE AHEAD The chocolate cupcakes can be stored in an airtight container for up to 2 days.

WINE Rich, sweet Banyuls.

Japanese Fruit Cake

MAKES ONE 9-INCH CAKE ●

This recipe, adapted from *Dolphin Dishes: The Submarine Cook Book,* published in 1952 by the New London Navy Relief Society of New London, Connecticut, has a somewhat puzzling title. Perhaps this cake was considered Japanese because it contained coconut, an exotic ingredient at the time.

CAKE

- 3 cups cake flour (not self-rising)
- 1½ teaspoons baking powder
- ½ teaspoon baking soda
- ¼ teaspoon salt
- 2 sticks (½ pound) unsalted butter, softened
- 1½ cups granulated sugar
- 4 large eggs
- 1 teaspoon pure vanilla extract
- 1 cup buttermilk
- ½ cup finely chopped walnuts
- 3 tablespoons dried currants
- 1½ teaspoons cinnamon
- 1 teaspoon ground allspice
- ½ teaspoon ground cloves

COCONUT FROSTING

- 2 cups shredded unsweetened coconut
- 3 large egg whites, lightly beaten
- 2¼ cups confectioners' sugar
- ½ cup water
- ½ teaspoon cream of tartar
- 1½ teaspoons pure vanilla extract
- ¾ teaspoon finely grated lemon zest

I. MAKE THE CAKE: Preheat the oven to 350°. Butter and flour two 9-inch round cake pans. In a medium bowl, sift the cake flour with the baking powder, baking soda and salt. In a large bowl, using an electric mixer, beat the butter with the granulated sugar at high speed until light and fluffy, about 5 minutes. Beat in the eggs, 1 at a time, beating well after each addition.

2. In a small bowl, stir the vanilla into the buttermilk. Using a rubber spatula, stir the dry ingredients into the batter in 2 batches, alternating with the buttermilk. Scrape half of the batter into 1 of the prepared cake pans and smooth the surface.

3. Fold the walnuts, currants, cinnamon, allspice and cloves into the remaining cake batter. Scrape the spice batter into the second cake pan and smooth the surface. Bake the cakes in the middle of the oven for about 35 minutes, or until a toothpick inserted in the center of each comes out clean. Transfer the cakes in their pans to wire racks and let cool for 15 minutes, then turn them out onto the racks and let cool completely. Leave the oven on.

4. MEANWHILE, MAKE THE COCONUT FROSTING: Spread the coconut on a rimmed baking sheet and bake for about 8 minutes, stirring, until golden. Transfer to a plate and let cool.

cakes, cookies + other desserts

5. In a medium saucepan, bring 1 inch of water to a simmer over moderate heat. In a medium stainless steel bowl, combine the egg whites with the confectioners' sugar, water and cream of tartar. Using clean beaters, beat at medium speed until blended. Set the bowl over the pan of simmering water and continue beating at high speed until the frosting is thick and fluffy, about 7 minutes. Remove the bowl from the pan and beat the vanilla and lemon zest into the frosting.

6. Using a serrated knife, cut each cake layer in half horizontally. Set 1 plain cake layer on a cake plate and spread with 1 cup of the frosting. Sprinkle ½ cup of the toasted coconut over the frosting, then spoon ½ cup of the frosting around the edge and in the center of the cake. Top with a spice cake layer. Continue frosting and sprinkling with the toasted coconut, using the remaining cake layers and alternating the plain and spice cakes. Spread the top of the cake with the remaining frosting and sprinkle with the remaining coconut. Cut into wedges and serve. —*Marcia Kiesel*

MAKE AHEAD The uncut plain and spice cake layers can be wrapped tightly in plastic and stored overnight at room temperature. The frosted cake can be stored at room temperature for up to 4 hours before serving.

---

baking tip
chopping nuts

A QUICK, NEAT WAY TO CHOP NUTS is to place them in a plastic zip-top bag and then pound them with a meat mallet a few times until they're broken. Another tip: When a recipe calls for chopping nuts in a food processor, add some of the sugar from the recipe to prevent clumping.

Vanilla Bean Cheesecake with Walnut Crust
MAKES 1 CHEESECAKE ● ●

- 1½ cups walnut pieces
- 1¾ cups sugar
- 4 tablespoons unsalted butter, melted
- 2 cups sour cream
- 1 tablespoon pure vanilla extract
- 2 pounds cream cheese, softened
- 1 vanilla bean, split lengthwise, seeds scraped
- 4 large eggs, at room temperature
- ¼ teaspoon pure almond extract
- ½ cup heavy cream

1. Preheat the oven to 350°. Butter a 10-inch springform pan. In a food processor, pulse the walnuts and ¼ cup of the sugar until finely ground. Add the butter; pulse until the mixture resembles moist sand. Press the crumbs into the bottom of the pan. Bake for 12 minutes, until browned around the edges.

2. In a small bowl, mix the sour cream with ¼ cup of the sugar and 1 teaspoon of the vanilla.

3. Reduce the oven temperature to 300°. In a standing electric mixer fitted with a paddle or using a handheld electric mixer, beat the cream cheese at low speed with the remaining 1¼ cups of sugar and the vanilla seeds just until combined. Beat in the eggs, 1 at a time. Add the remaining 2 teaspoons of vanilla and the almond extract. Slowly beat in the cream. Pour the batter into the pan and bake for 65 to 70 minutes, until lightly golden and slightly jiggly in the center.

4. Pour the sour cream topping over the cheesecake and smooth the surface. Return the cheesecake to the oven and bake for 5 minutes longer. Transfer to a rack and let cool. Run a sharp, thin-bladed knife around the cake and remove the ring. Refrigerate the cake for 3 hours, then cover loosely with plastic wrap and refrigerate overnight before serving. —*Peggy Cullen*
WINE Rich, sweet Sauternes.

Marbled Pumpkin Cheesecake with a Brownie Crust
12 SERVINGS ●
BROWNIE CRUST

- 4 tablespoons unsalted butter
- 2 ounces bittersweet chocolate, coarsely chopped
- ¼ cup sugar
- 1 large egg, lightly beaten
- ¼ cup all-purpose flour
- ½ teaspoon baking powder
- ⅛ teaspoon salt
- ¼ cup finely chopped walnuts

CHEESECAKE

- 4 ounces bittersweet chocolate, coarsely chopped
- 1½ pounds cream cheese, softened
- 1 cup sugar
- 4 large eggs, at room temperature
- 1½ tablespoons cornstarch
- 1 teaspoon pure vanilla extract
- 2 cups canned pumpkin puree (1 pound)
- ½ teaspoon cinnamon
- ½ teaspoon freshly grated nutmeg

Pinch of ground cloves

1. MAKE THE BROWNIE CRUST: Preheat the oven to 325°. Lightly butter a 9-inch springform pan. In a medium saucepan, melt the butter with the coarsely chopped chocolate over low heat, stirring constantly. Remove the melted chocolate mixture from the heat and let it cool slightly, then stir in the sugar and the lightly beaten egg until well blended.

2. In a small bowl, whisk the flour with the baking powder and salt. Add the dry ingredients to the melted chocolate mixture. Stir the chopped walnuts into the brownie batter. Spread the batter in the bottom of the prepared springform pan and smooth the surface with a spatula. Bake for about 10 minutes, or until risen and dry to the touch. Let cool completely. Wrap the outside of the pan in a large sheet of foil. Leave the oven on.

MARBLED PUMPKIN CHEESECAKE WITH A BROWNIE CRUST

cakes, cookies + other desserts

3. MAKE THE CHEESECAKE: In a medium glass bowl, melt the chopped chocolate in a microwave oven on high for about 1 minute, stirring halfway through. In a large bowl, using an electric mixer, beat the cream cheese until smooth. Add the sugar and beat until light and fluffy. Add the eggs, 1 at a time, beating well between additions. Beat in the cornstarch and vanilla. Add 1 cup of the cheesecake batter to the melted chocolate and stir until well blended. Beat the pumpkin puree and the cinnamon, nutmeg and cloves into the remaining cheesecake batter.

4. Pour three-fourths of the pumpkin cheesecake batter over the brownie crust. Pour the chocolate batter on top of the pumpkin cheesecake batter. If the chocolate batter is too thick to pour easily, heat it in a microwave oven on high for 10 seconds. Spoon the remaining pumpkin cheesecake batter on top of the chocolate batter. Use a table knife to make a few decorative swirls. Do not overswirl.

5. Set the springform pan in a medium roasting pan. Add enough hot water to the roasting pan to reach halfway up the side of the springform pan. Bake the pumpkin cheesecake in the hot-water bath in the center of the oven for 1½ hours, or until it is firm around the edges but slightly jiggly in the center. Turn the oven off, prop the door several inches open and let the cheesecake stand in the water bath in the warm oven for 1 hour, or until it is completely set.

6. Remove the marbled pumpkin cheesecake from the water bath and refrigerate it until thoroughly chilled, at least 4 hours or overnight. Remove the foil and springform pan ring from the cheesecake. Carefully transfer the cheesecake to a platter, cut into wedges and serve. —*Grace Parisi*

MAKE AHEAD The baked cheesecake can be refrigerated in the springform pan for up to 4 days.

WINE Sweet, fortified, fragrant Muscat.

Hazelnut-Rum Cake

MAKES ONE 9-INCH CAKE ●

This nutty, dense, not-too-sweet cake gets quite a kick from rum.

- 1⅓ cups hazelnuts (6 ounces)
- 1½ cups all-purpose flour
- ¼ teaspoon baking powder
- Pinch of salt
- 1½ sticks (6 ounces) unsalted butter, softened
- ⅔ cup granulated sugar
- 4 large eggs, lightly beaten
- ½ cup dark rum
- 2 large egg whites
- Confectioners' sugar, for dusting

1. Preheat the oven to 350°. Butter and flour a 9-inch round cake pan. Toast the hazelnuts on a rimmed baking sheet, stirring occasionally, for about 10 minutes, or until lightly browned. Let the toasted hazelnuts cool on the baking sheet, then transfer them to a kitchen towel and rub them together to remove the skins. Transfer the hazelnuts to a food processor and finely chop.

2. In a small bowl, sift the flour with the baking powder and salt. In a large bowl, using a handheld mixer, beat the butter with the granulated sugar until fluffy. Beat in the eggs, 1 at a time, until incorporated. Using a rubber spatula, fold in the flour mixture in 3 batches, alternating with the rum and hazelnuts.

3. In a medium stainless steel bowl, beat the egg whites until stiff. Beat one-third of the egg whites into the batter, then gently fold in the remaining whites. Scrape the batter into the prepared pan and bake for about 35 minutes, or until the cake springs back when lightly pressed. Transfer to a wire rack and let the cake cool in the pan for 15 minutes. Turn the cake out onto the rack and cover loosely with a kitchen towel until cooled to room temperature. Turn the cake right side up and dust the top with confectioners' sugar, then cut into wedges and serve. —*Giorgio Rivetti*

WINE Complex tawny port.

Chocolate Peanut Butter Cookies

MAKES ABOUT 48 COOKIES ●

- 2 ounces unsweetened chocolate, coarsely chopped
- 1 ounce bittersweet chocolate, coarsely chopped
- 1½ cups all-purpose flour
- ¾ teaspoon baking soda
- ½ teaspoon salt
- 1 stick (4 ounces) unsalted butter, softened
- ½ cup packed light brown sugar
- ½ cup granulated sugar
- ½ teaspoon pure vanilla extract
- ½ cup creamy or chunky peanut butter
- 1 large egg, lightly beaten

1. Preheat the oven to 375°. Line several large cookie sheets with parchment paper. In a microwave oven or in a medium heatproof bowl set over a saucepan of simmering water, melt the unsweetened and bittersweet chocolates. Let cool slightly.

2. In a medium bowl, whisk the flour with the baking soda and salt. In a large bowl, using an electric mixer, beat the butter at high speed until it is light and fluffy. Add the brown sugar, granulated sugar and vanilla and beat at medium speed until well combined. Beat in the peanut butter, then beat in the melted chocolate and the egg. At low speed, gradually beat in the dry ingredients until incorporated into the chocolate peanut butter cookie dough.

3. Using your hands, roll the cookie dough into 48 one-inch balls, then arrange the balls 2 inches apart on the prepared baking sheets. Using the tines of a fork, flatten the balls to a ½-inch thickness. Bake 1 sheet of the cookies at a time for about 12 minutes, or until the cookies are semifirm to the touch when lightly pressed. Rotate the cookie sheet halfway through baking for even browning. Slide the parchment paper with the chocolate peanut butter cookies onto a wire rack to cool. —*Maida Heatter*

MAKE AHEAD The chocolate cookies can be stored at room temperature between sheets of wax paper overnight in an airtight container.

Hazelnut—Chocolate Chip Tuiles

MAKES ABOUT 60 COOKIES ●

⅓ cup hazelnuts
⅔ cup all-purpose flour
¼ teaspoon salt
1 stick (4 ounces) unsalted butter, softened
⅓ cup light brown sugar
⅓ cup granulated sugar
1 egg, lightly beaten
1 teaspoon pure vanilla extract
1 ounce bittersweet chocolate, finely chopped

I. Preheat the oven to 350°. Spread the hazelnuts on a rimmed baking sheet and toast for about 7 minutes, or until deeply browned; let cool slightly. Transfer the hazelnuts to a kitchen towel and rub them together to remove the skins. Let the nuts cool completely. In a food processor, pulse the hazelnuts until coarsely ground.

2. Butter 2 large, heavy baking sheets. In a medium bowl, whisk the ground hazelnuts with the flour and salt. In a large bowl, using an electric mixer, beat the butter with the light brown and granulated sugar until light and fluffy. Beat in the egg and vanilla. At low speed, beat in the dry ingredients just until combined. Stir in the chopped chocolate just until incorporated.

3. Drop rounded teaspoons of the tuile batter 3 inches apart on the prepared baking sheets. Using the back of a spoon, spread the batter into 1½-inch rounds. Bake for about 10 minutes, or until the edges are golden. Using a thin metal spatula, immediately transfer the tuiles to a rack; alternatively, drape the tuiles over a rolling pin until cool. Repeat with the remaining batter.
—*Wendy Kalen*

MAKE AHEAD The tuiles can be stored in an airtight container for 3 days.

Chocolate-Hazelnut Sandwiches

MAKES ABOUT 60 COOKIES ●

These hazelnut cookies are filled with a blend of chocolate and Nutella, a hazelnut-chocolate spread.

1 cup plus 2 tablespoons hazelnuts (6 ounces)
1⅓ cups blanched almonds (7 ounces)
2⅓ cups confectioners' sugar
Finely grated zest of 1 orange
¾ cup plus 2 tablespoons milk
1½ sticks (6 ounces) unsalted butter, melted, plus more for brushing
5 large egg whites, at room temperature
2 tablespoons granulated sugar
1 cup all-purpose flour, plus more for dusting
3½ ounces bittersweet chocolate, coarsely chopped
⅔ cup Nutella (hazelnut-chocolate spread)

I. Preheat the oven to 350°. In a pie plate, toast the hazelnuts for about 12 minutes, or until fragrant and the skins blister. Transfer the nuts to a kitchen towel and rub them together to remove the skins. Let cool completely, then transfer them to a food processor and finely grind. Transfer to a bowl. Finely grind the almonds and add them to the hazelnuts. Stir in the confectioners' sugar, then stir in the orange zest, the milk and the melted butter.

2. In a clean bowl, using an electric mixer, beat the egg whites at medium speed until soft peaks form. Gradually add the granulated sugar and beat at high speed until the whites are stiff and glossy. Sift ½ cup of the flour over the nut mixture and stir it in. Fold in half of the whites with a rubber spatula. Sift and fold in ½ cup of the flour, then fold in the rest of the egg whites.

3. Increase the oven temperature to 375°. Brush 2 large cookie sheets with melted butter and dust with flour, tapping off any excess. Drop scant teaspoons of the batter 1½ inches apart on the prepared sheets. Bake the cookies on the upper and middle racks of the oven for 12 to 14 minutes, or until browned at the edges, shifting the sheets halfway through baking. Immediately transfer the cookies to wire racks to cool. Repeat with the remaining batter. Wipe the cookie sheets clean and let them cool completely. Butter and flour the sheets before reusing.

4. Melt the chocolate in a microwave oven, about 1 minute. Stir in the Nutella. Line 2 baking sheets with wax paper. For each sandwich, drop a scant ½ teaspoon of the chocolate filling on the bottom of a cookie; cover with another cookie and press gently so the filling spreads to the edge. Repeat with the remaining cookies and filling. Transfer the cookies to the prepared baking sheets and refrigerate until set, about 10 minutes. —*Pierre Hermé*

MAKE AHEAD The cookies can be stored in an airtight container at room temperature for up to 1 week or frozen for up to 2 months.

WINE Sweet, luscious Italian vin santo.

Chocolate Chocolate Chip Cookies

MAKES ABOUT 50 COOKIES ● ●

The fleur de sel in these slice-and-bake double-chocolate cookies doesn't make them salty; it brings out the chocolate taste and adds a mysterious flavor.

---

baking tip

chocolate

MANY RECIPES CALL FOR MELTING CHOCOLATE in a double boiler, being careful to melt it slowly enough to prevent scorching. You can also melt chocolate in a microwave oven: Place ¼ pound of chopped chocolate in a microwave-safe bowl and melt at 50 percent power for 3 minutes.

LINZER COOKIES

CHOCOLATE-DIPPED FLORENTINE SHORTBREADS

2⅔ cups all-purpose flour

⅔ cup unsweetened
Dutch-process cocoa

2 teaspoons baking soda

2 sticks plus 6 tablespoons (11 ounces) unsalted butter, softened

1 cup light brown sugar

½ cup granulated sugar

2½ teaspoons fleur de sel

1 teaspoon pure vanilla extract

10 ounces bittersweet chocolate, chopped into ¼-inch pieces (2 cups)

I. In a medium bowl, sift the flour with the cocoa and baking soda. In a large bowl, cream the butter. Add the brown sugar, granulated sugar, fleur de sel and vanilla and beat until combined. Beat in the sifted dry ingredients just until blended; the dough will be fairly crumbly but will hold together. Knead in the chopped chocolate until evenly distributed. Divide the dough evenly in half and transfer to 2 large sheets of plastic wrap. Shape each piece of dough into a 1½-inch-wide log and wrap in the plastic. Refrigerate the dough until firm, at least 2 hours.

2. Preheat the oven to 350°. Line 4 cookie sheets with parchment paper. Using a sharp, thin knife, cut the dough logs into ⅜-inch slices and arrange them about 1 inch apart on the prepared cookie sheets. If the slices crumble, re-form the cookies, pressing the dough together. Bake the cookies on the middle and lower racks of the oven for about 17 minutes, or until they are puffed and cracked on top; shift the pans from top to bottom and front to back halfway through. Let the cookies cool on the cookie sheets for 5 minutes, then transfer them to wire racks to cool completely. —*Pierre Hermé*

MAKE AHEAD The cookies can be stored in an airtight container at room temperature for up to 1 week or frozen for up to 2 months.

Chocolate-Dipped Florentine Shortbreads

MAKES ABOUT 48 COOKIES ●

This recipe combines tender shortbread with elegant florentines. Florentines are Italian caramelized almond cookies that are studded with glittering candied fruit and often topped with a layer of chocolate.

PASTRY

1½ sticks (6 ounces) unsalted butter, cut into ½-inch dice and chilled

6 tablespoons sugar

¼ teaspoon salt

1½ cups plus 2 tablespoons all-purpose flour

TOPING

½ cup heavy cream

Finely grated zest of 1 orange

1 cup plus 3 tablespoons sugar

1 tablespoon light corn syrup

⅓ cup water

½ cup chestnut honey

1 stick (4 ounces) unsalted butter

3¼ cups sliced blanched almonds (¾ pound)

⅔ cup finely diced candied orange rind (¼ pound)

¾ pound bittersweet chocolate, coarsely chopped

I. MAKE THE PASTRY: Preheat the oven to 350°. Lightly butter the bottom and sides of an 11-by-17-inch rimmed baking sheet. Line the bottom with parchment paper, leaving about 1 inch overhanging at the short ends. Butter the parchment.

2. In a food processor, pulse the butter, sugar and salt 6 times. Add the flour and process until the mixture resembles coarse meal. Spread the crumbs on the baking sheet and press them into a thin, even layer with floured hands. Prick the dough all over with a fork. Refrigerate for 10 minutes, or until firm. Bake in the middle of the oven for 15 minutes, or until lightly browned. Transfer the baking sheet to a wire rack. Increase the oven temperature to 425°.

3. MEANWHILE, MAKE THE TOPPING: In a small saucepan, heat the cream and orange zest over moderate heat just until bubbles appear around the edge, about 5 minutes. In a heavy medium saucepan, combine the sugar, corn syrup and water and bring to a boil over moderately high heat, stirring just until the sugar dissolves. Cook the syrup over moderately high heat, swirling the pan occasionally, until a medium amber caramel forms, about 5 minutes. Remove the pan from the heat. Add the honey, the infused cream and the butter and stir until the butter melts. Cook the caramel topping over moderately high heat until a candy thermometer

registers 255°, about 4 minutes. Stir in the almonds and candied orange rind and immediately spread the caramel over the pastry with a wooden spoon.

4. Return the baking sheet to the oven and bake the pastry for 10 minutes, or until the topping is bubbling. Transfer the baking sheet to a rack and let cool for 30 minutes.

5. Run a knife around the edge of the baking sheet to loosen the pastry and slide the parchment paper onto a work surface. Using a sharp, heavy knife, cut the pastry into 2½-inch strips. Cut the strips into 2½-by-3-inch rectangles. Cut each rectangle diagonally in half.

6. Line 2 large baking sheets with wax paper. Melt two-thirds of the chocolate in a bowl in a microwave oven for about 1 minute. Add the remaining chocolate and stir until completely melted. Dip 1 corner of each cookie into the chocolate and transfer it to the prepared baking sheets. Refrigerate until the chocolate is just set, about 5 minutes.

—*Pierre Hermé*

MAKE AHEAD The cookies can be stored in an airtight container at room temperature for up to 1 week or frozen for up to 2 months.

Linzer Cookies

MAKES ABOUT 48 COOKIES ●

You could use store-bought seedless raspberry preserves to fill these cookies, but Hermé's method of pureeing the raspberries in a blender to extract all the pectin from the seeds is clever and easy, and it makes a better filling than any you can buy.

3 sticks (¾ pound) unsalted butter, softened

1⅓ cups confectioners' sugar

½ cup finely ground blanched almonds (2½ ounces)

2 tablespoons plus 1 teaspoon cinnamon

Pinch of salt

4 large egg yolks

2 tablespoons aged dark rum

3 cups all-purpose flour, plus more for rolling

¼ teaspoon baking soda

2 cups fresh or flash-frozen raspberries

¾ cup granulated sugar

1½ teaspoons fresh lemon juice

1 large egg, beaten, for glazing (optional)

I. In a large bowl, beat the butter with the confectioners' sugar at medium speed just until blended. Add the ground almonds, cinnamon and salt and beat just until combined. Beat in the egg yolks and the rum, then add the 3 cups of flour and the baking soda and beat at low speed just until evenly combined. Divide the dough in half and scrape it onto 2 sheets of plastic wrap. Wrap the dough, flatten into disks and refrigerate until firm, at least 3 hours.

2. Meanwhile, puree the raspberries in a blender for 5 minutes. Transfer the puree to a medium saucepan. Add the granulated sugar and bring to a boil, stirring until the sugar dissolves. Simmer over moderate heat for 5 minutes. Stir in the lemon juice. Strain the jam into a bowl through a fine sieve and refrigerate until chilled, about 4 hours.

3. Line 2 large baking sheets with parchment paper. Liberally flour a work surface. Roll out 1 disk of the dough ¼ inch thick, flouring the dough and the rolling pin as necessary. Using a 2-inch round cookie cutter dipped in flour, stamp out as many rounds as possible (to be used as the bottoms of the cookies). Using a small spatula, arrange the rounds about ½ inch apart on the prepared baking sheets. Gather the scraps and pat into a disk. Roll out and stamp out as many more rounds as possible. Refrigerate until firm, at least 30 minutes.

4. On a large sheet of floured wax paper, roll out half of the second disk of dough, flouring the dough and rolling pin as necessary. Stamp out as many rounds as possible. Using a 1⅛-inch round cutter, stamp out the centers of the rounds on the wax paper; remove and reserve the centers. (These rings will be used as the tops of the cookies.) Slide the wax paper onto a baking sheet and chill the rings for 30 minutes. Repeat with the last piece of dough. Gather the scraps and pat into a disk; chill if necessary. Roll out and stamp out more tops and bottoms, then refrigerate.

5. Remove 1 sheet of the cookie bottoms from the refrigerator and brush lightly with water. Using a spatula, set the tops on the bottoms; press lightly to help them adhere. Prick the centers of the cookies with a fork. Refrigerate the cookies until chilled. Assemble the remaining cookies.

6. Preheat the oven to 350°. Brush the cookies with the beaten egg and bake in the middle and lower racks of the oven for 18 to 20 minutes, or until browned and the glaze is lightly crackled; shift the pans from top to bottom and front to back halfway through. Transfer the baking sheets to racks to cool.

7. Spoon the jam into the cookies. Let stand at room temperature for at least 2 hours, or until set. —*Pierre Hermé*

NOTE The Linzer dough can be cut into decorative shapes, but the cookies aren't particularly sweet without the raspberry jam, so dust them with confectioners' sugar once they've cooled.

MAKE AHEAD The cookies can be refrigerated in an airtight container for up to 1 week or frozen for up to 2 months.

WINE Sweet, fortified, fragrant Muscat.

Greek Butter Cookies

MAKES 72 COOKIES ●

- 3 sticks (12 ounces) unsalted butter, cut into pieces
- 1⅓ cups all-purpose flour
- ½ cup cake flour
- ¾ cup blanched almond flour (see Note)
- 1¼ teaspoons baking powder
- ¼ teaspoon salt
- 7 tablespoons confectioners' sugar, plus more for sifting

- 1 large egg yolk
- 1 tablespoon ouzo
- ½ teaspoon pure vanilla extract
- ¼ teaspoon pure almond extract

1. In a medium saucepan, melt the butter over low heat without stirring. Skim off the foam and discard. Strain the clear melted butter into a bowl, leaving all of the milky residue behind. (You will need 1 cup plus 2 tablespoons of clarified butter.) Pour the clarified butter onto a rimmed baking sheet and refrigerate until firm, about 30 minutes.

2. Preheat the oven to 350°. In a bowl, whisk the all-purpose, cake and almond flours, baking powder and salt.

3. Scrape the butter into a medium bowl. Using a handheld mixer, beat the butter at medium speed until very light and fluffy, at least 5 minutes. At low speed, gradually add the 7 tablespoons of confectioners' sugar and beat for 2 minutes. Add the egg yolk and beat for 2 minutes longer. Mix in the ouzo and the vanilla and almond extracts.

4. Beat in the dry ingredients in 3 batches; the dough will be quite soft. Wrap the dough in plastic and refrigerate for at least 1 hour.

5. For each cookie, roll 2 teaspoons of dough into a ball; pat the ball into a 1-inch round about ½ inch thick. Arrange the cookies 1 inch apart on ungreased baking sheets and bake for about 15 minutes, or until the cookies are pale but not browned. Generously sift confectioners' sugar over the hot cookies and let cool for 5 minutes. Transfer the butter cookies to wire racks to cool completely. —*Paula Wolfert*

NOTE Almond flour, or almond meal, is nothing more than very finely ground almonds. It is available at specialty food shops and baking supply stores. Buy it at a shop that rotates its stock often, as the meal has a tendency to turn rancid. Store any unused almond meal in a sturdy plastic bag in the freezer.

MAKE AHEAD Store the cookies in an airtight container for up to 1 month.

Leckerli

MAKES ABOUT 60 COOKIES ●

Hermé learned to make these chewy, nutty cookies flavored with spices and candied citrus rind from his father, an Alsatian baker, who picked up the recipe in Switzerland.

- ¾ cup acacia honey
- ½ cup granulated sugar
- ½ teaspoon finely grated lemon zest
- ¼ teaspoon cinnamon
- ¼ teaspoon freshly ground black pepper
- Pinch of freshly grated nutmeg
- Pinch of ground ginger
- Pinch of ground cloves
- Pinch of freshly ground white pepper
- Scant ⅔ cup finely diced candied lemon and orange rind
- 1¼ cups plus 2 tablespoons sliced almonds (4½ ounces)
- ¼ cup kirsch
- 2 cups plus 2 tablespoons all-purpose flour, plus more for dusting
- ½ teaspoon baking soda
- ⅔ cup confectioners' sugar
- 1½ tablespoons water

1. In a medium saucepan, combine the honey with the granulated sugar, lemon zest, cinnamon, black pepper, nutmeg, ginger, cloves and white pepper. Cook over low heat, stirring occasionally, until the honey and sugar are melted, about 3 minutes. Remove the pan from the heat and add the candied citrus rind, 1 cup plus 2 tablespoons of the almonds and 3 tablespoons plus 1 teaspoon of the kirsch. Sift the 2 cups plus 2 tablespoons of flour and the baking soda over the mixture and stir to incorporate. Line a baking sheet with plastic wrap. Scrape the dough onto the plastic and flatten into a disk. Wrap and refrigerate until firm, about 2 hours.

2. Liberally flour a work surface. Roll out the dough to a 12-inch square about ⅜ inch thick. Line a large cookie sheet with parchment paper and slide the dough onto it. Prick all over with a fork. Scatter the remaining ¼ cup of almonds on top. Cover with plastic wrap and refrigerate overnight.

3. Preheat the oven to 400°. In a small bowl, mix the confectioners' sugar with the water and the remaining 2 teaspoons of kirsch. Bake the cookie square for 14 minutes, or until golden. Immediately brush the glaze on top. Slide the parchment onto a rack and let the cookie cool completely. On a work surface, using a large, sharp knife, trim the edges of the square, then cut it into four 3-inch-wide strips. Cut each strip into ¾-inch bars. —*Pierre Hermé*

MAKE AHEAD The cookies can be stored in an airtight container at room temperature for up to 1 week or frozen for up to 2 months.

Sablés

MAKES ABOUT 48 COOKIES ●
Hermé takes the traditional chunky sablé and makes it into a very thin, crisp cookie to emphasize its buttery flavor.

2½ sticks (10 ounces) salted
    butter, softened
1⅓ cups sugar
2 large egg whites
2 cups plus 2 tablespoons
    all-purpose flour

I. In a large bowl, beat the butter until creamy. Add the sugar and beat until combined. Beat in the egg whites, 1 at a time, then beat in the flour. Refrigerate the dough until firm, if necessary. Divide the dough in half and transfer to 2 large sheets of plastic wrap. Shape the dough into 2-inch-thick logs, and wrap in the plastic. Refrigerate until firm, at least 2 hours.

2. Preheat the oven to 350°. Using a sharp, thin knife, cut 1 log of dough into ¼-inch-thick slices. Arrange the cookies 2 inches apart on 2 large cookie sheets. Bake the cookies on the middle and lower racks of the oven for about 17 minutes, or until golden at the edges, shifting the pans from top

to bottom and back to front halfway through. Let the cookies cool on the sheets for 5 minutes, then transfer them to wire racks to cool completely. Wipe the cookie sheets clean and let cool completely, then repeat with the second log of dough. —*Pierre Hermé*

MAKE AHEAD The cookies can be stored in an airtight container at room temperature for up to 1 week or frozen for up to 2 months.

Sparkly Cinnamon Coins

MAKES ABOUT 72 COOKIES ●
These crisp slice-and-bake refrigerator cookies get their sparkle from crystallized sugar. They are so small, you'll be tempted to eat them by the handful, but they are so flavorful that you will be satisfied with just a few.

2 sticks (½ pound) unsalted
    butter, softened
½ cup granulated sugar
2 teaspoons cinnamon
¼ teaspoon fine sea salt
½ teaspoon pure vanilla extract
2½ cups all-purpose flour
Crystallized sugar, for rolling
    (see Note)

I. In a medium bowl, beat the butter until creamy. Beat in the granulated sugar until combined. Beat in the cinnamon, salt and vanilla, then beat in the flour. Divide the dough into thirds; wrap each piece in plastic wrap and shape into a 10-inch log about 1¼ inches thick. Refrigerate until firm, about 1 hour.

2. Preheat the oven to 350°. Line 3 large baking sheets with parchment paper. Unwrap 1 piece of dough. Sprinkle crystallized sugar into a 3-by-10-inch rectangle on a sheet of wax paper. Roll the log in the sugar, pressing lightly. Slice the log ⅜ inch thick. Arrange the coins about 1 inch apart on 1 of the prepared baking sheets. Repeat with the remaining 2 logs of cookie dough. Bake the cookies for about 17 minutes, or until golden. Let cool on the baking sheets. —*Pierre Hermé*

NOTE Crystallized sugar is a coarse decorating sugar that comes in plain white as well as a wide array of colors. It's available at cake-decorating stores, specialty food shops and many supermarkets. It can be mail-ordered from New York Cake and Baking Distributor (212-675-2253; www.nycake.com).

MAKE AHEAD The cookies can be stored in an airtight container at room temperature for up to 1 week or frozen for up to 2 months.

Coconut-Allspice Diamonds

MAKES ABOUT 60 COOKIES ●
These simple cookies have a crisp texture and a delicate allspice flavor. They can be cut into just about any shape.

2 sticks plus 6 tablespoons
    (11 ounces) unsalted butter,
    softened
1⅓ cups confectioners' sugar
½ cup whole blanched almonds,
    finely ground, or ½ cup almond
    flour or meal
1 cup finely grated unsweetened
    coconut (3 ounces)
2 large eggs
2¾ cups all-purpose flour, plus more
    for dusting
1¾ teaspoons ground allspice
½ teaspoon fine sea salt
Pinch of freshly grated nutmeg
1 tablespoon milk
1 teaspoon pure vanilla extract
1 teaspoon instant espresso
    powder

I. In a large bowl, beat the butter until creamy. Beat in the confectioners' sugar, almonds and coconut. Beat in 1 of the eggs. Add the 2¾ cups of flour, the allspice, salt and nutmeg and beat just until combined. Divide the dough in half and flatten into disks, then wrap in plastic and refrigerate until firm, at least 2 hours.

2. Liberally flour a large sheet of wax paper. Transfer 1 of the disks of dough to the paper, dust with flour and cover with another sheet of wax paper. Roll out the dough to a 12-inch square about ¼ inch thick, lifting and repositioning the paper from time to time. Set the dough on a cookie sheet and refrigerate until firm, at least 30 minutes. Repeat with the second disk of dough.

3. Preheat the oven to 350°. Line 3 large baking sheets with parchment paper. Remove the top sheet of wax paper from 1 square of rolled-out dough and set it on a cutting board. Cut the dough into 1½-inch-wide strips. Using a ruler positioned on the diagonal, cut 1½-inch-wide strips, to create diamonds. Using a thin spatula, arrange the cookies ¾ inch apart on the baking sheets. Repeat with the second square of dough. Gather all of the scraps into a disk and refrigerate until firm. Roll out the dough ¼ inch thick, then cut more diamonds.

4. In a small bowl, beat the remaining egg with the milk, vanilla and espresso. Brush the diamonds with the glaze. Bake the cookies on the middle and lower racks of the oven for about 17 minutes, or until browned, shifting the pans from top to bottom and back to front halfway through. Let the cookies cool on the baking sheet.

—*Pierre Hermé*

MAKE AHEAD The cookies can be stored in an airtight container at room temperature for up to 1 week or frozen for up to 2 months.

Carrot Cookies with Orange—Brown Butter Glaze

MAKES ABOUT 24 COOKIES ●

- 3 large carrots, peeled and finely grated (about 1¼ cups)
- ¼ cup water
- 2 cups all-purpose flour
- 2 teaspoons baking powder
- ⅛ teaspoon salt
- 1 cup solid vegetable shortening
- ¾ cup sugar
- 1 large egg
- Finely grated zest of 1 lemon (about 1 tablespoon)

- 1 teaspoon pure vanilla extract
- 3 tablespoons unsalted butter
- 3 tablespoons fresh orange juice
- 1 teaspoon finely grated orange zest
- 1¾ cups sifted confectioners' sugar

1. Preheat the oven to 350°. In a medium saucepan, cook the carrots in the water over moderate heat until tender, about 5 minutes. Drain and pat dry.

2. In a medium bowl, whisk the flour with the baking powder and salt. Using an electric mixer, in another bowl, beat the shortening with the sugar at medium speed until light and fluffy. Beat in the egg, then beat in the carrots, lemon zest and vanilla. Beat in the dry ingredients at low speed just until combined.

3. Spoon 2-tablespoon-size mounds of batter onto 2 ungreased cookie sheets and bake for about 25 minutes on the top and middle racks of the oven, or until golden and risen; shift the sheets from top to bottom and front to back halfway through baking. Transfer the cookies to a wire rack to cool slightly.

4. Meanwhile, in a small saucepan, cook the butter over moderately high heat until golden brown, about 5 minutes. Remove from the heat and let cool slightly. Add the orange juice, orange zest and confectioners' sugar and whisk until a thin glaze forms. Spread the glaze over the warm cookies and let stand until set. —*Mory Thomas*

MAKE AHEAD The cooled cookies can be stored between sheets of wax paper in an airtight container for up to 3 days.

Chocolate-Glazed Hazelnut Meringues

MAKES ABOUT 40 MERINGUES ● ●

- 1 cup hazelnuts (5 ounces)
- 1⅔ cup confectioners' sugar
- 4 teaspoons all-purpose flour
- 4 large egg whites
- ¾ cup granulated sugar
- 4 ounces bittersweet chocolate, coarsely chopped
- ⅓ cup heavy cream

1. Preheat the oven to 350.° Line 2 baking sheets with parchment paper.

2. Spread the hazelnuts in a pie plate and toast in the oven until fragrant and the skins have blistered, about 12 minutes. Let cool slightly. Wrap the nuts in a towel and rub them together to loosen the skins; let cool completely.

3. In a food processor, coarsely grind the hazelnuts with the confectioners' sugar and flour. In a large bowl, using an electric mixer, beat the egg whites at high speed until firm peaks form. Gradually add the granulated sugar and beat until the whites are glossy, about 3 minutes longer. Using a large rubber spatula, fold in the hazelnut mixture until it is fully incorporated.

4. Transfer the meringue to a large pastry bag fitted with a ½-inch round tip. Pipe 1½-inch mounds 1 inch apart on the prepared baking sheets. Bake the meringues on the upper and lower racks of the oven for about 15 minutes, or until the cookies are golden and crisp but still a bit soft inside; shift the pans from top to bottom and front to back halfway through baking. Let the meringues cool on the sheets.

5. Meanwhile, put the chocolate in a bowl. In a small saucepan, bring the cream to a boil. Pour the cream over the chocolate and let stand for 1 minute, then stir until smooth. Drizzle the chocolate glaze over the meringues and let stand until set. —*Gale Gand*

WINE Complex tawny port.

Pecan and Brown Butter Biscotti

MAKES ABOUT 84 BISCOTTI ●

- 2 cups pecans (½ pound), coarsely chopped
- 1 stick (4 ounces) unsalted butter
- 2 cups all-purpose flour
- ½ teaspoon baking powder
- ¾ teaspoon salt
- 1 cup sugar
- 3 large eggs
- 1 teaspoon pure vanilla extract

1. Preheat the oven to 350°. Line 2 baking sheets with parchment paper for the biscotti.

2. Bake the pecans on a rimmed baking sheet for about 10 minutes, or until lightly toasted and fragrant; let cool. In a saucepan, cook the butter over moderate heat until brown and fragrant, about 8 minutes. Pour the butter onto a rimmed baking sheet to firm up.

3. In a medium bowl, whisk the flour, baking powder and salt. In another medium bowl, using an electric mixer, beat the browned butter and sugar until combined. At low speed, beat in the eggs, 1 at a time, until incorporated. Beat in the vanilla. Gradually beat in the dry ingredients; stir in the pecans.

4. Gather the dough into a ball. Divide the dough in half. Shape each piece of dough into a 14-inch-long log on 1 of the baking sheets. Gently flatten the logs until they are 1½ inches thick.

5. Bake the logs for 25 minutes, or until golden and lightly cracked on top. Remove the logs from the oven. Using a serrated knife, cut the warm logs diagonally into ⅜-inch-thick slices. Arrange the slices on their sides on the baking sheets and bake for about 20 minutes, or until golden. Transfer the biscotti to racks to cool. —*Wendy Kalen*

MAKE AHEAD The biscotti can be stored in an airtight container for 2 weeks.

Lemon-Lavender Shortbread

MAKES ABOUT 18 COOKIES ●

⅓ cup sugar

1 teaspoon dried lavender, chopped

1 teaspoon finely grated lemon zest

1 stick (4 ounces) unsalted butter, softened

1 cup all-purpose flour

½ teaspoon salt

1. In a medium bowl, mix the sugar with the chopped lavender and grated lemon zest. Using a handheld electric mixer, beat in the butter at moderate speed. At low speed, beat in the flour and salt

until a soft dough forms. Transfer the dough to a sheet of wax paper and refrigerate for 20 minutes. Form the dough into a 4-inch log and chill for at least 45 minutes longer.

2. Preheat the oven to 350°. Slice the shortbread dough into ¼-inch-thick rounds and place the rounds on ungreased baking sheets. Freeze the rounds for 10 minutes.

3. Bake the shortbread for 20 to 25 minutes, or until the edges are lightly browned. Transfer the baked shortbread to a wire rack to cool completely.
—*Alison Attenborough*

MAKE AHEAD The cookie-dough log can be frozen for up to 1 month. Thaw slightly before slicing. The baked shortbread can be stored in an airtight container for up to 5 days.

Classic Fudge Brownies

MAKES 16 BROWNIES ● ●

This recipe can be doubled and baked in a 9-by-13-inch metal baking pan.

2 ounces unsweetened chocolate, coarsely chopped

1 stick (4 ounces) unsalted butter, cut into tablespoons

1 cup sugar

2 large eggs

1 teaspoon pure vanilla extract

½ cup all-purpose flour

Pinch of salt

½ cup coarsely chopped walnuts

1. Preheat the oven to 375°. Butter an 8-inch-square metal baking pan. In a saucepan, melt the chocolate with the butter over low heat. Let cool slightly.

2. In a bowl, beat the sugar with the eggs and vanilla. Add the melted chocolate and beat until smooth. Stir in the flour and salt, then fold in the nuts.

3. Scrape the batter into the prepared baking pan and bake for 25 minutes, or just until firm. Let cool completely in the pan. Cut into squares and serve.
—*Dana Cowin*

MAKE AHEAD The brownies can be kept in an airtight container for 2 days.

Coconut Macaroon Bars with Chocolate-Covered Chestnuts

12 SERVINGS ●

2¼ cups finely shredded unsweetened coconut (7½ ounces)

½ cup plus 2 tablespoons turbinado sugar

2 large egg whites, lightly beaten

1 teaspoon pure vanilla extract

¼ teaspoon salt

1 cup granulated sugar

1 cup water

36 whole roasted chestnuts (from a 15-ounce vacuum-packed jar)

⅓ cup dark rum or Cognac

4 ounces semisweet chocolate, finely chopped

¼ cup heavy cream

1. Preheat the oven to 350°. Line a large rimmed baking sheet with parchment paper. In a medium bowl, mix the coconut with the turbinado sugar, egg whites, vanilla and salt until combined. Transfer the macaroon mixture to the prepared baking sheet and pat it into a 12-by-4-inch rectangle ½ inch thick. Bake for about 25 minutes, or until golden around the edge. Let cool completely on the baking sheet.

2. Meanwhile, in a medium saucepan, combine the granulated sugar and water and cook over moderately high heat until reduced by a quarter. Add the chestnuts and rum and cook over moderate heat, stirring occasionally,

CHOCOLATE-FROSTED ÉCLAIRS

until the chestnuts are coated in thick syrup, about 15 minutes. Pour the syrup and chestnuts into a bowl and let cool. **3.** In a glass bowl, melt the chocolate and cream in a microwave oven on high for 1 minute, stirring halfway through. **4.** Transfer the macaroon rectangle to a platter and arrange the chestnuts on top in 3 rows of 12. Pour the chocolate over the entire top of the macaroon rectangle. Let stand at room temperature for 30 minutes, or until set. Slice into bars and serve. —*Mory Thomas*

MAKE AHEAD The chocolate-covered macaroon rectangle can be refrigerated for up 2 days. Bring to room temperature before slicing.

Crêpes with Creamy Caramel
12 SERVINGS

- 5 large eggs
- 3¼ cups milk
- 1 teaspoon salt
- 2 cups all-purpose flour
- 6 tablespoons unsalted butter, 4 melted and 2 softened
- 1 jar (1 pound) of dulce de leche

Confectioners' sugar, for dusting

1. In a medium bowl, whisk the eggs with the milk and salt. Gradually whisk in the flour, then the melted butter. Let rest at room temperature for 30 minutes. **2.** Heat the oven to 325°. Brush an 8-inch nonstick skillet with softened butter. Pour in ¼ cup of the batter and tilt to coat. Cook for 45 seconds over moderately high heat. Turn and cook for 10 seconds longer. Transfer to a plate. Repeat with the remaining butter and batter, reducing the heat to moderate when the pan becomes too hot; stack the crêpes. Spread 1 scant tablespoon of dulce de leche on each crêpe and fold in quarters. Arrange the crêpes, overlapping, on 2 baking sheets and bake for about 5 minutes, or until warmed through. Transfer to a platter, dust with confectioners' sugar and serve. —*Bernardita Del Campo Correa*

WINE Rich, sweet Sauternes.

Chocolate-Frosted Éclairs
MAKES 12 ÉCLAIRS ●
CHOUX PASTRY

- 1 cup water
- 1 stick (4 ounces) unsalted butter
- 2 tablespoons sugar
- ¼ teaspoon salt
- 1 cup plus 2 tablespoons all-purpose flour
- 4 large eggs

PASTRY CREAM

- 2 cups whole milk
- ¼ vanilla bean, seeds scraped
- ½ cup plus 2 tablespoons sugar
- 5 tablespoons cake flour

Pinch of salt

- 1 large egg
- 2 large egg yolks
- ¼ cup plus 2 tablespoons heavy cream

CHOCOLATE GLAZE

- 4 ounces bittersweet chocolate
- 4 tablespoons unsalted butter, softened

1. MAKE THE CHOUX PASTRY: Preheat the oven to 400°. In a medium saucepan, bring the water, butter, sugar and salt to a boil over moderate heat. Remove the pan from the heat. Add the flour and stir vigorously with a wooden spoon for about 2 minutes, until the dough comes together and a film forms on the bottom of the pan. Transfer the choux pastry dough to a large bowl and continue beating at medium speed until slightly cooled, about 1 minute. Add the eggs, 1 at a time, beating well after each addition.

2. Transfer the dough to a pastry bag fitted with a 1-inch round tip. Pipe twelve 5-inch-long logs onto an ungreased baking sheet and bake for 10 minutes. Turn the oven down to 325° and bake the shells for about 30 minutes longer, or until golden brown. Transfer to a rack and let cool.

3. MAKE THE PASTRY CREAM: In a medium saucepan, bring the milk, vanilla bean and seeds just to a boil. Meanwhile, in a large bowl, whisk the sugar

with the cake flour and salt. Whisk in the egg and egg yolks. Slowly add the hot milk, whisking constantly. Pour the mixture back into the saucepan and bring to a boil over moderate heat, whisking constantly. Continue to boil the pastry cream, whisking constantly, until thick, about 30 seconds longer. Immediately strain the pastry cream through a fine sieve into a medium bowl. Cover with plastic wrap and refrigerate for at least 30 minutes, or until cool.

4. In a medium bowl, whip the heavy cream until soft peaks form. Whisk the pastry cream, then fold in the whipped cream until blended.

5. MAKE THE CHOCOLATE GLAZE: In a medium glass bowl, melt the chocolate in a microwave oven on high for 1 minute, stirring halfway through. Whisk in the butter until smooth.

6. With a serrated knife, split the éclair shells lengthwise. Spoon a generous amount of the pastry cream into the bottom half of each shell. Dip the top half of each shell into the chocolate glaze, close the éclairs and serve.
—*Joanne Chang*

MAKE AHEAD The shells, pastry cream and chocolate glaze can all be made early in the day. Keep the pastry shells at room temperature and refrigerate the pastry cream and the glaze; melt the glaze if necessary and assemble the éclairs shortly before serving.

---

ingredient tip

dulce de leche

THIS TRADITIONAL ARGENTINEAN DESSERT translates as "sweet milk." It's made from cow's milk simmered with sugar over low heat for many hours, until a thick, brownish milk caramel forms. Although small jars sell for $7 or more, the Argentinean import from Smucker's is half that.

cakes, cookies + other desserts

Spiced Cake Doughnuts

MAKES ABOUT 30 DOUGHNUTS ●

Lauren Groveman often shakes the warm doughnuts in a plastic bag filled with cinnamon sugar or a combination of unsweetened cocoa powder and granulated sugar.

   3 cups sifted all-purpose flour, plus more for dusting
   1 cup unsifted cake flour
   1 tablespoon baking powder
1½ teaspoons salt
   1 teaspoon baking soda
   1 teaspoon cinnamon
   1 teaspoon freshly grated nutmeg
   ¾ cup sugar
   3 extra-large eggs, at room temperature
1½ teaspoons pure vanilla extract
   1 cup sour cream, at room temperature
   ¼ cup plus 1 tablespoon solid vegetable shortening, melted
   ¼ cup milk
Vegetable oil, for deep-frying
Dark Chocolate Glaze (p. 311) or Vanilla Glaze (p. 311)
Chopped nuts, toasted coconut and sprinkles, for decorating (optional)

1. In a bowl, whisk both flours with the baking powder, salt, baking soda, cinnamon and nutmeg. In a large bowl, beat the sugar with the eggs until pale and thick. Beat in the vanilla.

2. In another bowl, whisk the sour cream, shortening and milk. Beat into the eggs in 2 batches, alternating with the dry ingredients. Cover the bowl loosely with plastic and refrigerate until chilled, at least 2 hours or overnight.

3. In a large, heavy skillet, heat 4 inches of vegetable oil to 370°. Line a rack with several paper towels.

4. Meanwhile, turn the dough out onto a floured surface and roll out ½ inch thick. Using a 2½-inch doughnut cutter dipped in flour, cut out as many doughnuts as possible. Reroll the scraps once to cut out more doughnuts.

5. Working in batches, fry the doughnuts over moderate heat until golden brown, turning them once, about 1 minute per side. Check the temperature of the oil to make sure it doesn't get too hot or too cool. Using a slotted spoon, transfer the doughnuts to the paper towel–lined rack to drain. Serve warm or let cool before glazing with the Dark Chocolate Glaze or the Vanilla Glaze and decorating with chopped nuts, toasted coconut and sprinkles.

—Lauren Groveman

MAKE AHEAD The recipe can be prepared through Step 2 and refrigerated overnight. The finished doughnuts can be made up to 4 hours ahead.

Fluffy Yeast Doughnuts

MAKES ABOUT 18 DOUGHNUTS ●

As a make-ahead strategy, prepare separate batches of the dry ingredients in advance and store them in labeled and sealed plastic bags.

   ½ cup milk
   ¼ cup plus 1 tablespoon solid vegetable shortening
   2 packages active dry yeast
   ½ cup warm water
   ½ cup sugar, plus more for sprinkling
   ½ cup sour cream, at room temperature
   2 extra-large eggs, at room temperature
   1 extra-large yolk, at room temperature
   2 teaspoons salt
1½ teaspoons pure vanilla extract
About 5 cups sifted all-purpose flour, plus more sifted flour for dusting
Vegetable oil, for deep-frying
Dark Chocolate Glaze (recipe follows) or Vanilla Glaze (recipe follows)
Chopped nuts, toasted coconut and sprinkles, for decorating (optional)

1. In a small saucepan, warm the milk with the shortening over low heat until the shortening is almost melted. In a

large bowl, stir the yeast into the warm water, sprinkle with a pinch of sugar and let stand until foamy, about 3 minutes. Stir the warm milk mixture into the yeast along with the ½ cup of sugar and the sour cream, the whole eggs, egg yolk, salt and vanilla. Gradually stir in 4¾ cups of the flour until a soft, sticky dough forms. Scrape the dough out onto a floured surface and use a pastry scraper to knead the dough until smooth, adding as much of the remaining flour as necessary. The dough should be soft and slightly sticky, but smooth and elastic.

2. Gather the dough into a ball, transfer it to a lightly oiled bowl and cover with a sheet of oiled plastic wrap. Let the dough rise in a warm, draft-free spot for 2 hours. Punch down the dough and turn it over in the bowl. Cover and refrigerate the dough for 2 hours or overnight.

3. On a lightly floured work surface, roll out the chilled dough ⅓ inch thick. Using a 3½-inch doughnut cutter dipped in flour, cut out as many doughnuts as possible and transfer them to a sheet of floured wax paper. The scraps can be rerolled once to cut out more doughnuts. Loosely cover the doughnuts with wax paper and let rise until soft and billowy, about 20 minutes.

4. In a large, heavy skillet, heat 4 inches of vegetable oil to 365°. Line a rack with several paper towels. Working in batches, fry the doughnuts until golden brown, about 1 minute per side. Check the temperature of the frying oil to make sure it doesn't get too hot or cool. Using a slotted spoon, transfer the doughnuts to the paper towel–lined rack to drain. Serve warm or let cool before glazing with the Dark Chocolate Glaze or the Vanilla Glaze and decorating with chopped nuts, coconut and sprinkles.

—Lauren Groveman

MAKE AHEAD The recipe can be prepared through Step 2 and refrigerated overnight. The finished doughnuts can be made up to 4 hours ahead.

VARIATION To make jelly doughnuts, cut out 2½-inch rounds of dough with a biscuit cutter. Fry as instructed. Use a piping bag to squeeze jelly into the sides of the cooled doughnuts.

DARK CHOCOLATE GLAZE

MAKES 2 CUPS ●

- 2 ounces bittersweet chocolate, chopped
- 2½ ounces unsweetened chocolate, chopped
- ¾ cup heavy cream
- ¾ cup plus 2 tablespoons sugar
- 4 tablespoons unsalted butter, at room temperature
- ¾ teaspoon pure vanilla extract

Salt

Place the chocolates in a bowl. In a small saucepan, combine the cream and sugar and cook over moderate heat, stirring, until the sugar dissolves. Pour the warm cream over the chocolate and let stand until melted, about 5 minutes; whisk until smooth. Whisk in the butter, vanilla and a pinch of salt. Let the chocolate glaze cool until slightly thickened, about 15 minutes. —*L.G.*

VANILLA GLAZE

MAKES 1½ CUPS ●

- 5 cups sifted confectioners' sugar
- ¼ cup milk
- ¼ cup light corn syrup
- 1 teaspoon pure vanilla extract

In a bowl, whisk the confectioners' sugar with the milk and corn syrup until smooth. Stir in the vanilla. —*L.G.*

VARIATION To make a frosting suitable for piping, stir 1½ cups confectioners' sugar into the glaze.

Bittersweet Chocolate Mousse with Cocoa Nib Whipped Cream

8 SERVINGS ● ●

- ½ pound bittersweet chocolate, coarsely chopped
- ½ cup milk
- 2 tablespoons brandy
- 4 large eggs, at room temperature

SPICED CAKE DOUGHNUTS AND FLUFFY YEAST DOUGHNUTS

BITTERSWEET CHOCOLATE MOUSSE

cakes, cookies + other desserts

¼ cup plus 1 tablespoon sugar

¼ cup water

1 cup heavy cream

2 tablespoons coarsely chopped cocoa nibs (see Note), plus more for garnish

1. In a medium stainless steel bowl, combine the chocolate and the milk. Set the bowl in a skillet of barely simmering water and stir until the chocolate is nearly melted. Remove the bowl from the skillet and stir until completely melted. Stir in the brandy. Keep the skillet of water at a bare simmer.

2. In another heatproof bowl, whisk the eggs with ¼ cup of the sugar and the water until blended. Set the bowl in the skillet and stir gently and thoroughly, scraping the bottom frequently, until an instant-read thermometer inserted in the eggs registers 160°. Remove the bowl from the skillet. Beat the eggs at high speed to the consistency of softly whipped cream, about 4 minutes.

3. Fold one-fourth of the egg mixture into the melted chocolate, then fold the 2 mixtures together until no streaks remain. Pour the mousse into eight ½-cup bowls; refrigerate until chilled.

4. Meanwhile, in a small saucepan, boil the heavy cream with 2 tablespoons of the cocoa nibs. Remove from the heat, cover and let stand for 20 minutes. Strain the cream into a bowl and refrigerate until very cold.

---

baking tip

egg whites

TO GET THE MOST VOLUME, beat egg whites at room temperature until they are stiff but not dry. If they become overbeaten, gently stir in another egg white that has been beaten by hand until frothy; once it's incorporated, remove ¼ cup of beaten egg white to achieve the correct quantity.

---

5. Add the remaining 1 tablespoon of sugar to the chocolate-infused cream and beat to soft peaks. Spoon a dollop of the cream on top of each mousse, garnish with cocoa nibs and serve.
—*Alice Medrich*

NOTE Cocoa nibs are roasted, shelled cocoa beans broken into small bits. They are available at specialty food shops.

MAKE AHEAD The mousse can be refrigerated overnight.

WINE Rich, sweet Banyuls.

Chocolate Mousse with Szechuan Pepper Sabayon

8 SERVINGS ●

1¼ pounds bittersweet or semisweet chocolate, coarsely chopped

2½ cups plus ⅓ cup heavy cream

4 large egg yolks

3 tablespoons water

2 tablespoons honey

16 Szechuan peppercorns, crushed

1. Melt the chocolate in a medium saucepan set over a pot of barely simmering water, stirring occasionally, about 5 minutes. Let cool for 5 minutes.

2. In a large bowl, beat 2½ cups of the cream until soft peaks form. Working quickly, fold in the cooled chocolate, using a rubber spatula.

3. In a medium stainless steel bowl set over a pan with 1 inch of simmering water, whisk the egg yolks with the water, honey and peppercorns until doubled in volume, about 5 minutes. Remove the bowl from the heat and, using a handheld mixer, beat the sabayon at high speed until completely cool, about 5 minutes. Beat the remaining ⅓ cup of heavy cream to soft peaks, then gently fold it into the sabayon. Using 2 tablespoons, shape the chocolate mousse into large eggs and carefully set 1 on each plate. Spoon the sabayon around the chocolate mousse and serve. —*Pascal Chaupitre*

SERVE WITH Thin butter cookies.

WINE Rich, sweet Banyuls.

Praline Chocolate Mousse

4 SERVINGS ●

⅓ cup almonds

¼ cup sugar

2 tablespoons water

1½ cups heavy cream

5 ounces bittersweet chocolate, coarsely chopped

1 tablespoon dark rum or Grand Marnier

1 teaspoon confectioners' sugar

1. Preheat the oven to 350°. Oil a cookie sheet. Spread the almonds in a pie plate and bake for about 7 minutes, or until fragrant and richly browned.

2. In a small saucepan, combine the sugar and water and simmer over moderately low heat, swirling the pan a few times, until an amber caramel forms, about 5 minutes. Stir in the almonds. Scrape the almond caramel onto the oiled cookie sheet and spread it out as much as possible. Let cool completely. Break the praline into pieces, then finely chop it with a large, heavy knife.

3. In another small saucepan, bring ½ cup of the heavy cream to a simmer. Add the chopped chocolate, remove from the heat and let stand until melted; whisk until smooth. Stir in the rum and ½ cup of the chopped praline. Transfer the mixture to a medium bowl and let cool just until tepid.

4. In another medium bowl, beat ½ cup of the heavy cream until firm peaks form. Fold the whipped cream into the chocolate mixture. Spoon the chocolate mousse into ramekins and refrigerate until set, at least 2 hours.

5. In the same bowl, beat the remaining ½ cup of cream with the confectioners' sugar to very soft peaks. Spoon the cream into a bowl, sprinkle with the remaining chopped praline and serve with the mousse. —*Jacques Pépin*

MAKE AHEAD The recipe can be prepared through Step 4 up to 2 days ahead. Cover the mousse with plastic wrap. Store the praline at room temperature in an airtight container.

Almond Crème Caramel

6 SERVINGS ●

For additional flavor, cook the caramel as long as possible to add an almost bitter edge to the dessert. The baked custards need to be refrigerated overnight, so plan accordingly.

CARAMEL

1 cup sugar
½ cup water

CUSTARD

1 cup sliced almonds
3 cups half-and-half
3 tablespoons light brown sugar
10 large egg yolks
2 large eggs
½ cup plus 2 tablespoons granulated sugar
1 tablespoon Orzata almond syrup, optional (see Note)

Boiling water

1. MAKE THE CARAMEL: In a small saucepan, combine the sugar and water and bring to a boil, stirring until the sugar dissolves. Cook over moderate heat, without stirring, until a deep-amber caramel forms, about 10 minutes. Immediately pour the caramel into six 1-cup ramekins or custard cups and gently swirl to coat the bottoms and slightly up the sides. Set the ramekins in a small roasting pan.

2. MAKE THE CUSTARD: Preheat the oven to 300°. In a medium skillet, toast the almonds over moderate heat, stirring constantly, until golden and fragrant, about 5 minutes. In a medium saucepan, heat the half-and-half until steaming. Remove from the heat and stir in the toasted almonds and brown sugar and let steep for 30 minutes.

3. In a medium bowl, whisk the egg yolks with the eggs and granulated sugar just until combined. Rewarm the half-and-half mixture over low heat. Gradually whisk ½ cup of the hot half-and-half into the eggs. Whisk the eggs into the half-and-half, then strain the custard into a pitcher. Stir the Orzata into the custard.

4. Pour the custard into the ramekins. Carefully set the roasting pan on the middle rack of the oven and fill the pan with enough boiling water to reach halfway up the sides of the ramekins. Cover the pan with foil. Bake the custards for 30 minutes, or until they are set but still slightly wobbly in the center. Remove the roasting pan from the oven and discard the foil. Let the custards cool in the water bath. Cover the ramekins with plastic wrap and refrigerate overnight.

5. To unmold the custards, run a thin-bladed knife around each ramekin. Cover with dessert plates and invert the custards onto the plates. Scrape any remaining caramel over the custards and serve. —Tim Goodell

NOTE Orzata is a sweet, almond-flavored syrup that is found at liquor stores and gourmet food shops.

MAKE AHEAD The baked almond custards can be refrigerated in the ramekins for up to 2 days.

WINE Rich, sweet Sauternes.

Classic Tiramisu

4 SERVINGS ●

For a more elaborate presentation, line a charlotte mold with the coffee-soaked ladyfingers, then fill it with the mascarpone. Unmold onto a plate to serve.

One 17½-ounce container mascarpone
4 large eggs, separated (see Note)
¼ cup sugar
1 cup strong brewed coffee
24 ladyfingers (from a 7-ounce package)

Sweetened cocoa powder, for dusting

1. In a medium bowl, beat the mascarpone with the egg yolks and 3 tablespoons of the sugar. In a large stainless steel bowl, whip the egg whites until they hold soft peaks. Add the remaining 1 tablespoon of sugar and beat until the peaks are firm and glossy. Fold half of the egg whites into the mascarpone, then fold in the remaining whites.

2. Pour the coffee into a deep dish. Dip both sides of 12 of the ladyfingers into the coffee and arrange them in a single layer in a deep 8-inch-square glass baking dish. Spread half of the mascarpone filling on top. Dip the remaining 12 ladyfingers in the coffee and arrange them in a layer over the filling. Spread the remaining mascarpone over the ladyfingers and dust generously with cocoa. Refrigerate the tiramisu until thoroughly chilled, at least 2 hours or overnight. —Graziella Dionisi

NOTE Please be aware that this recipe uses raw eggs.

WINE Rich, sweet Sauternes.

Hazelnut Semifreddo with Gianduja Sauce

MAKES 1 QUART ● ●

¾ cup hazelnuts (¼ pound)
1 cup sugar
2 tablespoons water
1⅓ cups heavy cream
3 large egg whites
2 ounces gianduja or bittersweet chocolate, coarsely chopped
¼ teaspoon pure vanilla extract

Pinch of salt

1. Oil a baking sheet and line eight ½-cup ramekins or custard cups with plastic wrap, leaving 3 inches of overhang. Preheat the oven to 350°. Toast the hazelnuts on a rimmed baking sheet for 10 minutes, or until richly browned. Transfer to a kitchen towel and let cool. Rub the nuts together in the towel to remove the skins; finely chop them.

2. Put ½ cup of the sugar in a small saucepan. Stir the water into the sugar and bring the mixture to a boil over moderate heat. Simmer this sugar syrup, brushing down the sides of the saucepan with a wet pastry brush, until a deep brown caramel forms, about 5 minutes. Remove the pan from the heat and, using a wooden spoon, stir in the hazelnuts. Immediately scrape the caramel-and-hazelnut mixture onto the oiled baking sheet and let cool until hard.

CREAMY BUTTERSCOTCH PUDDING WITH TOFFEE

3. Break this praline into small pieces and transfer to a food processor. Grind to a coarse powder.

4. In a stainless steel bowl, whip 1 cup of the cream until it holds firm peaks and refrigerate. In a large stainless steel bowl, beat the egg whites until they hold firm and glossy peaks, gradually adding the remaining ½ cup of sugar. Using a rubber spatula, fold in the ground praline, followed by the whipped cream. Spoon the semifreddo into the prepared ramekins, pressing with the spoon to remove any air pockets. Cover with the overhanging plastic and freeze until firm, about 2 hours.

5. In a saucepan, bring the remaining ⅓ cup of cream to a boil over moderate heat. Remove the pan from the heat; stir in the chocolate until melted. Stir in the vanilla and a pinch of salt and let cool slightly. Refrigerate the chocolate sauce until thick, about 1 hour.

6. Unwrap the semifreddo and unmold onto dessert plates. Drizzle the sauce around the plates and serve.
—Maria Paolillo

MAKE AHEAD The semifreddo can be frozen for 3 days. The chocolate sauce can be refrigerated for 3 days.
WINE Sweet, luscious Italian vin santo.

Deep Chocolate Pudding
4 SERVINGS ● ● ●

- 1 cup heavy cream
- 1 cup whole milk
- 1 egg, lightly beaten
- ¼ cup plus 2 tablespoons sugar
- 2 tablespoons unsweetened cocoa powder
- 2 tablespoons cornstarch
- ⅛ teaspoon salt
- 2 tablespoons plus 1 teaspoon unsalted butter
- 3 ounces bittersweet chocolate, finely chopped

Whipped cream, for serving

1. In a saucepan, whisk the cream, milk and egg. In a bowl, whisk the sugar with the cocoa, cornstarch and salt.

Add to the saucepan and bring to a boil over moderately high heat, whisking constantly. Strain the pudding into a medium bowl. Stir in the butter and chocolate until melted.

2. Pour the pudding into a large glass baking dish. Press plastic wrap directly on the surface and refrigerate for 30 minutes, or until chilled. Spoon the pudding into bowls, top with whipped cream and serve. *—Scott Ehrlich*

MAKE AHEAD The pudding can be refrigerated for up to 2 days.

Creamy Butterscotch Pudding with Toffee
6 SERVINGS ●

- 6 tablespoons unsalted butter
- 1 cup plus 2 tablespoons packed light brown sugar
- 2 cups heavy cream, 1¼ cups warmed
- 3 tablespoons cornstarch
- ¼ teaspoon kosher salt
- 2 cups whole milk
- 3 large egg yolks
- 2 teaspoons pure vanilla extract
- ½ tablespoon bourbon
- ½ tablespoon apple-cider vinegar
- ½ cup crunchy toffee pieces, such as broken Heath or Skor bars

1. In a heavy saucepan, melt the butter. Add the sugar; cook over low heat, stirring, until the sugar is dissolved, about 3 minutes. Stir in the warm cream.

2. In a bowl, combine the cornstarch and salt. Add ½ cup of the milk and whisk until smooth. Add to the saucepan with the remaining 1½ cups of milk and cook over moderate heat, stirring constantly, until thickened, about 4 minutes. Off the heat, whisk in the egg yolks, 1½ teaspoons of the vanilla and the bourbon. Return the pudding to the heat and bring to a boil, stirring constantly. Off the heat, whisk in the vinegar. Strain the pudding through a fine sieve set over a bowl. Pour the pudding into six 6- to 8-ounce parfait glasses or dessert bowls. Press a piece

of plastic on the surface of each pudding and refrigerate until chilled, at least 3 hours or overnight.

3. In a bowl, whip the remaining ¾ cup of cream and remaining ½ teaspoon of vanilla to soft peaks. Garnish the puddings with the whipped cream and toffee and serve. *—Natasha MacAller*

MAKE AHEAD The dish can be prepared through Step 2; refrigerate for 2 days.
WINE Sweet, fortified, fragrant Muscat.

Sticky Toffee Pudding
6 SERVINGS ● ●

TOFFEE SAUCE
- 2½ cups heavy cream
- 1 stick (4 ounces) unsalted butter
- ½ cup light corn syrup
- 1 cup granulated sugar

CAKE
- 6 ounces pitted dates, preferably Medjool (about 7 dates)
- ¾ cup water
- ¾ cup plus 2 tablespoons all-purpose flour
- 1 teaspoon baking powder
- ¼ teaspoon baking soda

Pinch of salt
- 4 tablespoons unsalted butter, softened
- ¾ cup packed light brown sugar
- 1 large egg
- ½ teaspoon pure vanilla extract

Vanilla ice cream or lightly sweetened whipped cream, for serving

---

baking tip

brown sugar

TO KEEP BROWN SUGAR FROM HARDENING, put a slice of apple peel in the jar for extra moisture. If the sugar has already hardened, soften it by placing 1 cup of it in a covered dish and microwaving it on high for 30 to 60 seconds, repeating as necessary. Watch to make sure it doesn't melt.

cakes, cookies + other desserts

I. MAKE THE TOFFEE SAUCE: In a saucepan, combine 1¼ cups of the cream, the butter, corn syrup and sugar; bring to a boil. Cook over moderately low heat, stirring, until deep amber, about 40 minutes. Carefully whisk in the remaining 1¼ cups of cream. Strain the sauce into a bowl.

2. MAKE THE CAKE: In a saucepan, simmer the dates in the water over moderately low heat until the water is nearly absorbed and the dates are soft, about 15 minutes. Transfer to a food processor and puree until very smooth.

3. Preheat the oven to 350°. Lightly butter six ½-cup ramekins. In a bowl, whisk the flour, baking powder, baking soda and salt. In a medium bowl, using an electric mixer, beat the butter with the brown sugar at medium speed until light and fluffy. Beat in the egg and vanilla, then beat in the date puree. At low speed, beat in the dry ingredients. Spoon the batter into the ramekins and smooth the tops. Bake for 20 minutes, or until a toothpick inserted into the centers comes out clean; let cool slightly.

4. Using a small serrated knife, trim the cakes level with the ramekin rims. Unmold the cakes and invert them onto a rack. Slice each cake in half horizontally. Wipe out the ramekins and spoon 1 tablespoon of the toffee sauce into each. Return the bottom layers of the cakes to the ramekins, cut side up.

baking tip

caramel

WHEN MAKING CARAMEL, the sugar has to dissolve completely before simmering; otherwise you'll end up with a hard, uncaramelized sugar mess. To dissolve the sugar, cook the mixture over low heat until you see absolutely no more crystals. Then increase the heat to start caramelizing.

Spoon another tablespoon of the toffee sauce into the ramekins and top with the remaining cake layers. Spread another tablespoon of the toffee sauce over the cakes. Place the ramekins on a baking sheet and bake for 10 minutes, or until bubbling around the edges.

5. Let the puddings cool for 5 minutes, then run a thin knife around the insides of the ramekins; invert each pudding onto a plate. Rewarm the remaining toffee sauce and spoon some around the puddings. Serve with vanilla ice cream or whipped cream. —*David Guas*

WINE Sweet, fortified, fragrant Muscat.

Vanilla Sundaes with Crisped Rice-and-Peanut Crunch

4 SERVINGS ● ●

Vegetable oil
- 1 **cup crisped rice cereal**
- ½ **cup dry-roasted peanuts, coarsely chopped**
- 3 **tablespoons light corn syrup**

Salt

Vanilla ice cream and hot chocolate sauce, for serving

I. Preheat the oven to 350°. Oil a rimmed baking sheet. In a bowl, toss the crisped rice and peanuts with the corn syrup to evenly coat; add a pinch of salt. Spread the mixture as thinly as possible on the baking sheet and bake for 10 minutes, until crisp. Transfer the warm crunch to a plate; let cool. Break the crunch into large pieces.

2. Scoop ice cream into sundae glasses and add chocolate sauce. Top with the crunch and serve. —*Marcia Kiesel*

MAKE AHEAD The crunch can be stored overnight in an airtight container.

Cinnamon-Spiced Mocha Floats

4 SERVINGS ●

Cinnamon is known as a sweet spice, but it can have a pungent bite. Vietnamese cinnamon, also known as Saigon cinnamon, is an especially fragrant variety, and its taste is sharper than that of regular cinnamon.

- ¾ **cup boiling water**
- ½ **cup finely ground espresso (1 ounce)**
- ¼ **cup plus 1½ tablespoons granulated sugar**
- 1 **teaspoon cinnamon, preferably Vietnamese (see Note), plus more for sprinkling**
- 2 **ounces bittersweet or semisweet chocolate, coarsely chopped**
- 1 **cup heavy cream**
- ¼ **teaspoon pure vanilla extract**

Chilled club soda

I. In a glass measuring cup, pour the boiling water over the espresso. Cover the measuring cup with a small plate and let steep for 10 minutes. Strain the espresso through a paper filter into a small saucepan.

2. Whisk ¼ cup of the sugar and 1 teaspoon of the cinnamon into the espresso and bring to a boil. Reduce the heat to moderate and simmer for 1 minute. Remove the saucepan from the heat, add the chocolate and, using a wooden spoon, stir until smooth. Using a rubber spatula, scrape the mocha mixture into a small bowl and let cool to room temperature, stirring a few times.

3. Meanwhile, in a large bowl, whip the cream with the remaining 1½ tablespoons of sugar and the vanilla until the cream holds soft peaks. Add the cooled mocha mixture and whip until the cream holds firm peaks. Cover and freeze until set, about 3 hours.

4. Using a medium ice cream scoop, add 3 or 4 small scoops of the frozen cream to tall soda glasses. Add club soda and sprinkle cinnamon over the top. Serve at once with a straw and a long-handled spoon. —*Marcia Kiesel*

NOTE Vietnamese cinnamon is available by mail order from Penzeys Spices (800-741-7787; www.penzeys.com).

MAKE AHEAD The mocha cream can be frozen for up to 2 days. Let it stand at room temperature for about 10 minutes before scooping.

Chocolate Malteds

MAKES 8 MINI MALTEDS

These shakes were inspired by Claudia Fleming's favorite soda-fountain treat when she was growing up.

- ¼ cup water
- 2½ tablespoons sugar
- ½ tablespoon light corn syrup
- 3 tablespoons unsweetened Dutch process cocoa
- 1 cup heavy cream
- 6 ounces bittersweet chocolate, chopped
- ½ cup plus 1½ tablespoons Ovaltine
- ½ cup half-and-half
- 1 pint vanilla ice cream, preferably homemade, softened
- ½ cup milk

1. In a small saucepan, bring the water, sugar and corn syrup to a boil. In a heat-proof bowl, whisk 3 tablespoons of the hot sugar syrup with the cocoa. Whisk the cocoa syrup into the sugar syrup in the saucepan and simmer over low heat for 3 minutes. Return the syrup to the heatproof bowl.

2. In another saucepan, heat ¼ cup of the heavy cream until steaming. Off the heat, stir in the chopped bittersweet chocolate until melted. Whisk the melt-ed chocolate and cream mixture into the cocoa syrup.

3. Put ½ cup of the Ovaltine in another bowl. Very gradually whisk in the half-and-half until smooth. Whisk in ¼ cup of the heavy cream and the chocolate mixture. Strain the mixture through a fine sieve into a bowl and refrigerate until cold, at least 2 hours.

4. In another bowl, whip the remaining ½ cup of heavy cream to soft peaks. Add the remaining 1½ tablespoons of Ovaltine and whip until firm.

5. In a blender, combine the ice cream with the chocolate mixture and the milk and blend until smooth and thick. Pour into 8 small glasses, top with the whipped cream and serve at once.
—*Claudia Fleming*

Caramel Fondue

MAKES 4 CUPS ●

- 2 cups sugar
- ½ cup corn syrup
- ¼ cup water
- 1½ cups heavy cream
- 1 stick (4 ounces) unsalted butter, cut into tablespoons
- 2 teaspoons pure vanilla extract

Pound cake, angel food cake, brownies, bananas, pineapple, pears and apples, for dipping

Shaved chocolate, chopped nuts, grated coconut and minced dried fruit, for sprinkling

1. In a saucepan, combine the sugar, corn syrup and water. Cook over low heat, stirring, until the sugar dissolves, about 10 minutes. Increase the heat to moderately high and simmer, brushing down the sides of the saucepan occa-sionally with a wet brush, until the syrup starts to turn golden. Gently swirl the pan and continue to simmer until a deep amber caramel forms, about 40 minutes total from the time you started.

2. Remove the pan from the heat. Care-fully stir in the cream; stir in the butter until melted. Return the pan to the heat and bring just to a simmer. Remove from the heat and stir in the vanilla.

3. Let the caramel cool for 30 minutes, whisking occasionally. Pour the caramel into a serving bowl or fondue pot set over low heat and serve with the cake, fruit and garnishes. —*Peggy Cullen*

MAKE AHEAD The caramel can be refrig-erated for up to 1 week. Rewarm gent-ly over low heat.

Milk Chocolate Jewels

MAKES ABOUT 2 POUNDS ● ●

Plastic chocolate molds are available from Broadway Panhandler (866-COOKWARE). If you don't want to use molds, pour the melted chocolate onto a parchment-lined baking sheet and sprinkle with the toppings; let set, then break the chocolate into pieces.

- 1½ pounds milk chocolate, tempered (see Note)
- ½ cup dried cranberries, chopped
- ½ cup dried blueberries (optional)
- ¼ cup finely diced candied ginger

Arrange plastic chocolate molds on baking sheets and fill them halfway with the tempered chocolate. Sprinkle on the dried fruit and candied ginger and refrigerate until set, about 15 minutes. Unmold the chocolates and store at room temperature for up to 2 weeks.
—*Michael Recchiuti*

NOTE To temper 1½ pounds of bitter-sweet or milk chocolate, set a large bowl over a pan of simmering water. Add 1 pound of chopped chocolate to the bowl and stir until melted and an instant-read thermometer registers between 112° and 118°. Remove the bowl from the pan. Add the remaining chocolate and stir until melted and the thermometer registers between 88° and 90°. Use immediately.

Dark Chocolate with Cashew-Sesame Brittle

MAKES ABOUT 2 POUNDS ●

- ½ cup sugar
- 2 tablespoons water
- 1 cup roasted cashews
- 3 tablespoons sesame seeds
- 1½ pounds bittersweet chocolate, tempered (see Note for previous recipe)

1. Line a baking sheet with parchment paper. In a saucepan, cook the sugar and water over moderate heat, stirring just until dissolved. Simmer undisturbed until light amber, about 5 minutes. Stir in the cashews and sesame seeds and cook for 1 minute; immediately pour the caramel onto the baking sheet and refrigerate until set, about 15 minutes. Chop the brittle into ½-inch pieces.

2. Fill molds halfway with the choco-late. Top with the brittle and refriger-ate until set, 15 minutes. Unmold the chocolates and store at room temper-ature for 2 weeks. —*Michael Recchiuti*

PORT-CRANBERRY SAUCE, P. 329

sauces + condiments

AROMATIC ANISE BUTTER

GARLIC-HERB BUTTER

Aromatic Anise Butter

MAKES ABOUT ²⁄₃ CUP ● ●

- 1 stick (4 ounces) unsalted butter, softened
- 1 packed tablespoon coarsely chopped flat-leaf parsley
- 1½ teaspoons snipped chives
- 1 teaspoon minced garlic
- ¾ teaspoon Pernod or other anise-flavored liqueur
- ½ teaspoon salt
- Scant ¼ teaspoon freshly ground white pepper
- 2 tablespoons soft fresh bread crumbs
- 1½ teaspoons dry white wine

In a mini-processor, combine the butter, parsley, chives, garlic, Pernod, salt and pepper and process until smooth. Add the bread crumbs and wine and process until blended, scraping down the sides of the bowl. —*Jacques Pépin*

MAKE AHEAD The butter can be frozen for up to 1 month. Let return to room temperature before serving.

SERVE WITH Poached, grilled or sautéed fish and shellfish.

Garlic-Herb Butter

MAKES ABOUT ¾ CUP ● ●

- ⅓ cup chopped flat-leaf parsley leaves
- 2½ tablespoons chopped basil
- 2½ tablespoons chopped chives
- 2 large garlic cloves, coarsely chopped
- 10 pecan halves
- 1 stick (4 ounces) unsalted butter, softened
- 1 tablespoon dry white wine
- ¼ teaspoon salt
- ¼ teaspoon freshly ground pepper
- 2 tablespoons finely chopped shallots

In a mini-processor, combine the chopped parsley, basil and chives with the garlic and pecans and pulse until finely chopped. Add the softened butter, white wine, salt and pepper and process until fairly smooth. Add the shallots and pulse just until incorporated into the butter.

—*Jacques Pépin*

MAKE AHEAD The butter can be frozen for up to 1 month. Let return to room temperature before serving.

SERVE WITH Steamed vegetables, steak, seafood or chicken.

Piquillo-Tuna Butter

MAKES 1½ CUPS ● ● ●

European and European-style butters are made with significantly more butterfat and less water than mass-produced American butters. But it takes more than fat to create fabulous butter. Although color, texture, aroma and flavor vary according to their places of origin, premium butters are satiny-smooth and creamy, with a delicate taste that can range from sweet and nutty to tangy. These butters are best when used most simply—spread on crusty bread, mixed into a creamy spread or dip or added to sauces to lend distinct richness. The foil-wrapped brands tend to stay fresh the longest.

- 4 ounces unsalted European-style butter, softened
- 6 ounces imported jarred tuna fillet packed in olive oil, drained
- 8 medium piquillo peppers
- 2 teaspoons fresh lemon juice

Salt and freshly ground pepper

In a food processor, combine the butter, tuna, piquillo peppers and lemon juice; process until creamy. Season with salt and pepper and serve with toast, spread on sandwiches or use as a dip. —*Marcia Kiesel*

MAKE AHEAD The butter can be refrigerated for up to 1 week.

Lobster Butter

MAKES ABOUT ½ CUP ● ●

This is a wonderful recipe to have on hand for using up cooked lobster roe (eggs) or tomalley (liver). Be sure to ask your fishmonger for a female lobster if you plan to make this butter.

- 1 stick (4 ounces) unsalted butter, softened

Cooked roe (eggs) and tomalley (liver) from two 1-pound lobsters

- ¼ teaspoon salt
- ¼ teaspoon freshly ground pepper
- 1 teaspoon fresh lemon juice
- 1 tablespoon chopped dill
- 1 teaspoon paprika

Combine all of the ingredients in a mini-processor and puree until blended. —*Jacques Pépin*

MAKE AHEAD The butter can be frozen for 1 month.

SERVE WITH Poached or grilled fish and shellfish.

Red Pepper Butter

MAKES ABOUT 1¼ CUPS ● ●

- 2 garlic cloves
- 1 tablespoon finely chopped jalapeño, without seeds
- 1 cup drained roasted sweet peppers or pimientos, from a jar
- 6 tablespoons unsalted butter, softened
- ⅓ cup pecan pieces
- ¼ teaspoon salt

In a mini-processor, puree the garlic and jalapeño. Add the peppers, softened butter, pecan pieces and salt and process until smooth. —*Jacques Pépin*

MAKE AHEAD The butter can be frozen for up to 1 month. Let return to room temperature before serving.

SERVE WITH Seafood, chicken, corn, pasta, bagel chips or toast.

Suzette Butter

MAKES ABOUT ¾ CUP ● ●

- 1 stick (4 ounces) unsalted butter, softened
- 2 tablespoons confectioners' sugar
- 1 tablespoon finely grated orange zest
- ¼ cup fresh orange juice

In a mini-processor, combine the butter with the confectioners' sugar and orange zest and process until smooth. Add the orange juice and process until fully incorporated, scraping down the side of the bowl as necessary. —*Jacques Pépin*

MAKE AHEAD The butter can be frozen for up to 1 month.

SERVE WITH Toast, warm muffins or sweet rolls; cooked fruit (put a pat on before roasting in the oven).

Tarragon Butter

MAKES ABOUT ¾ CUP ● ●

- 1 stick (4 ounces) unsalted butter, softened
- ¼ cup extra-virgin olive oil

One 1-ounce bunch of tarragon, coarsely chopped (½ cup)

- ¼ teaspoon salt

In a mini-processor, combine the softened butter with the olive oil and process until smooth. Add the tarragon and salt and pulse until the tarragon is finely chopped. Season with more salt, as necessary. —*Jacques Pépin*

MAKE AHEAD The butter can be frozen for up to 1 month.

SERVE WITH Chicken, poached fish or shellfish or vegetables.

Green Tomato Marmalade

MAKES 1 CUP ● ●

This marmalade is perfect with white fish, salmon, mackerel and pork.

- 1 pound green tomatoes, chopped
- ½ cup sugar
- 3 tablespoons fresh lemon juice

Salt

1. In a bowl, mix the tomatoes, sugar and lemon juice. Refrigerate overnight.

2. In a medium saucepan, bring the mixture to a boil. Simmer over low heat, stirring often, until reduced to 1 cup, about 1 hour. Season with salt. —*Jean-Georges Vongerichten*

MAKE AHEAD The marmalade can be refrigerated for 2 weeks.

---

cooking tip

compound butters

Compound butters, which combine unsalted butter with flavorings—from tarragon to garlic to roasted peppers to Pernod—can elevate simple cooked food in an instant. It's a good idea to prepare them in a food processor, not only because the machine simplifies the job, but also because the spinning blade aerates them and helps absorb liquids, such as lemon juice or wine. The butters can be refrigerated for two weeks or frozen for a month, so they're ideal make-ahead recipes.

sauces + condiments

Jalapeño-Lemon Relish

MAKES 1 CUP ● ● ●

Match this relish with swordfish, tuna or shrimp.

- 6 jalapeños, seeded and minced
- ½ cup extra-virgin olive oil
- Julienned zest of 1 lemon
- 2 teaspoons kosher salt

Combine the jalapeños, oil, lemon zest and salt in a bowl. Let stand at room temperature for 6 hours. —*Jean-Georges Vongerichten*

MAKE AHEAD The relish can be refrigerated for 2 weeks.

Hot Pepper Jelly

MAKES ABOUT 6 CUPS ● ●

This intensely spicy condiment is also great as a barbecue sauce for grilled pork and chicken.

- 6 large ancho chiles (4 ounces)
- 1 quart boiling water
- 4 large chipotle chiles in adobo, stemmed and seeded, plus ¼ cup adobo sauce from the can
- 6 cups sugar
- 2 cups apple cider vinegar
- One 3-ounce packet liquid fruit pectin

1. In a large heatproof bowl, cover the ancho chiles with the boiling water. Let stand until the chiles are softened, about 30 minutes.

2. Drain the anchos, reserving 1 cup of the soaking liquid. Discard the stems and seeds. In a food processor, puree the anchos with the soaking liquid. Strain through a coarse sieve set over a bowl, pressing with a rubber spatula. You should have 1½ cups of puree.

3. In the food processor, puree the chipotle chiles with the adobo sauce. Strain the chipotle puree into the ancho puree and mix well.

4. In a large stainless steel saucepan, combine the sugar and cider vinegar and bring to a boil over moderately high heat, stirring, until the sugar has completely dissolved. Boil over moderately high heat for 5 minutes. Add the chipotle chile puree and boil for 1 minute.

Add the liquid fruit pectin and boil for 1 minute longer. Pour the hot pepper jelly into heatproof jelly jars and let cool to room temperature, then refrigerate. —*Robert Stehling*

MAKE AHEAD The pepper jelly can be refrigerated for up to 1 year.

SERVE WITH Sesame-Cornmeal Crackers (p. 256) or store-bought sesame water crackers and soft goat cheese.

Jalapeño-Ginger Glaze

MAKES ABOUT ¾ CUP ● ●

Refrigerate this spicy glaze for up to one week.

- 1 scallion, white and tender green parts only, minced
- 1 garlic clove, minced
- ½ teaspoon finely grated peeled fresh ginger
- 1 tablespoon sugar
- Salt
- ½ cup hot pepper jelly, preferably jalapeño pepper jelly (6 ounces)
- 1½ tablespoons distilled white vinegar

On a work surface, using the side of a large knife, mash the scallion, garlic and ginger with the sugar and ½ teaspoon of salt until a coarse paste forms. Transfer the paste to a small saucepan. Stir in the hot pepper jelly and vinegar and bring to a boil. Transfer to a glass jar and let cool. —*Grace Parisi*

APPLICATIONS Brush on chicken, pork chops, spareribs and pork tenderloin during the last few minutes of grilling, broiling or roasting and cook until glossy.

Creamy Mustard Sauce

MAKES 1½ CUPS ●

- 2 cups dry white wine
- 1 medium shallot, thinly sliced
- 1 tablespoon black peppercorns
- 1 bay leaf
- 2 cups chicken or veal stock
- 1 cup heavy cream
- ½ cup grainy mustard
- ¼ cup Dijon mustard
- Salt and freshly ground white pepper

In a medium saucepan, boil the wine, shallot, peppercorns and bay leaf until reduced to 1 cup, about 10 minutes. Add the stock and boil until reduced to 1½ cups, about 40 minutes. Strain into a clean saucepan. Add the cream and mustards and simmer until reduced to 1½ cups, 30 minutes. Season with salt and white pepper. —*Traci Des Jardins*

MAKE AHEAD The sauce can be refrigerated for up to 2 days.

SERVE WITH Steak, pork or chicken.

Red Wine Shallot Sauce

MAKES ABOUT ¾ CUP

- 1 stick (4 ounces) unsalted butter
- 3 medium shallots, minced
- 3 cups dry red wine
- 6 thyme sprigs
- 1 bay leaf
- 1 tablespoon peppercorns
- 2 cups veal or chicken stock
- Salt and freshly ground pepper

Melt 2 tablespoons of the butter in a saucepan. Add the shallots and cook until softened. Add the wine, herbs and peppercorns and boil until reduced to 1 cup, about 20 minutes. Add the stock and boil until reduced to ¾ cup, 30 minutes. Strain into a small saucepan. Over low heat, whisk in the remaining 6 tablespoons of butter. Season with salt and pepper and serve. —*Traci Des Jardins*

SERVE WITH Steak, pork or fish.

Maple-Chipotle Barbecue Sauce

MAKES ABOUT 1 CUP ● ●

Refrigerate this sweet and smoky barbecue sauce for up to two weeks.

- 3 large chipotle chiles in adobo, stems discarded
- ¼ cup ketchup
- ¼ cup pure maple syrup
- 1 cup low-sodium chicken broth
- ⅛ teaspoon ground allspice
- 1 tablespoon vegetable oil
- 1 medium onion, minced
- 2 large garlic cloves, minced
- Salt and freshly ground pepper
- 1 tablespoon fresh lemon juice

HOT PEPPER JELLY, WITH SESAME-CORNMEAL CRACKERS (P. 256)

1. In a blender, combine the chipotles with the ketchup, maple syrup, broth and allspice and puree until smooth.

2. In a medium saucepan, heat the oil until shimmering. Add the onion and garlic and cook over moderately high heat until golden, 5 minutes. Add the chipotle puree. Season with salt and pepper. Cook over moderate heat until thickened, 15 minutes. Stir in the lemon juice. Transfer to a bowl and let cool.

—Grace Parisi

APPLICATIONS Brush on chicken, beef, lamb, pork or ham during the last few minutes of grilling, broiling or roasting. Or, dilute with a little chicken stock and use to deglaze pan drippings.

Chili-Garlic Peanut Sauce

MAKES ABOUT 1½ CUPS ● ● ●

- 1 tablespoon peanut oil
- 1 large shallot, finely chopped
- 1 large garlic clove, finely chopped
- ¼ cup unsweetened coconut milk
- ½ cup chunky peanut butter
- 1 tablespoon dark brown sugar
- 1 teaspoon Asian chili-garlic sauce or Tabasco sauce
- ½ teaspoon finely grated peeled fresh ginger
- 1 cup water
- 2 tablespoons fresh lime juice
- 2 tablespoons unsalted dry-roasted peanuts, coarsely chopped

Salt

---

cooking tip

ginger

GINGER IS EASIER TO GRATE OR CRUSH when it's been frozen, because freezing breaks down the fibers. To mince fresh ginger, place a small peeled chunk in a garlic press and squeeze. Or place small peeled coins of ginger in a plastic bag and pound with a meat mallet until crushed.

In a medium saucepan, heat the peanut oil until shimmering. Add the shallot and garlic and cook over moderate heat, stirring frequently, until golden, about 3 minutes. Remove from the heat and whisk in the coconut milk, peanut butter, brown sugar, chili-garlic sauce and ginger. Gradually whisk in the water. Simmer the sauce over moderately low heat, stirring occasionally, until slightly thickened, about 10 minutes. Let cool slightly, then whisk in the lime juice and peanuts. Season with salt. Transfer the peanut sauce to a small bowl or a glass jar and serve warm, at room temperature or chilled.

—Grace Parisi

MAKE AHEAD The peanut sauce can be refrigerated for up to 5 days.

APPLICATIONS Serve as a condiment with grilled beef, pork, poultry or shrimp. Toss with shredded lettuce, cabbage, cucumbers, carrots and apples or with steamed green beans.

Thai Green Curry Coconut Sauce

MAKES ABOUT 2 CUPS ● ●

Thai green curry paste and fish sauce are available in the Asian section of most large supermarkets and at health food stores.

One 14-ounce can unsweetened coconut milk

- 1½ teaspoons Thai green curry paste, or more to taste
- 1 cup chicken stock or low-sodium broth

Four 1-inch strips of lemon zest (see Alternatives)

One 1-inch piece of fresh ginger— peeled, thinly sliced and lightly smashed

Four 1-inch strips of lime zest (see Alternatives)

- 3 tablespoons Asian fish sauce
- 1½ tablespoons light brown sugar
- 2 tablespoons fresh lime juice
- ¼ cup coarsely chopped cilantro
- 2 tablespoons finely chopped basil

1. In a saucepan, whisk ¼ cup of the coconut milk with the curry paste. Stir in the remaining coconut milk, the stock, lemon zest, ginger, lime zest, 2 tablespoons of the fish sauce and the sugar and bring to a simmer. Cook over moderately high heat until reduced by one-quarter, about 15 minutes.

2. Discard the lemon zest, ginger and lime zest. Stir in the lime juice, cilantro, basil and the remaining 1 tablespoon of fish sauce; transfer to a bowl.

—Grace Parisi

MAKE AHEAD The curry sauce can be refrigerated in a glass jar for up 2 days.

ALTERNATIVES Replace the lemon zest with the bottom 4 inches of 1 stalk of lightly smashed fresh lemongrass, and replace the lime zest with 4 kaffir lime leaves that have been lightly crushed.

APPLICATIONS Use as a stir-fry sauce or as a poaching liquid for chicken, shrimp or vegetables. Or, toss with Asian noodles or serve over rice.

Spicy Ginger Stir-Fry Sauce

MAKES ABOUT 1 CUP ● ● ●

- ½ cup chicken stock or low-sodium broth
- 3 tablespoons low-sodium soy sauce
- 1 tablespoon sherry or Chinese cooking wine
- 1 tablespoon sugar
- 1 teaspoon cornstarch dissolved in 1 tablespoon water
- ½ teaspoon distilled white vinegar
- ½ teaspoon sesame oil
- 1 tablespoon peanut oil
- 3 tablespoons minced peeled fresh ginger
- ½ teaspoon crushed red pepper

1. In a small bowl, combine the stock with the soy sauce, sherry, sugar, cornstarch slurry, vinegar and sesame oil. Stir to dissolve the sugar.

2. In a saucepan, heat the peanut oil until shimmering. Add the ginger and crushed red pepper and stir over high heat until fragrant and golden brown.

Add the stock mixture and boil over high heat until thickened and glossy, about 1 minute. Transfer the ginger sauce to a glass jar and let cool. —*Grace Parisi*

MAKE AHEAD This sauce can be refrigerated for up to 2 weeks.

APPLICATIONS Add while stir-frying pork, chicken, shrimp or beef. Use as a dipping sauce for dumplings, steamed vegetables or rotisserie chicken. Drizzle over grilled meats or fish.

Roasted Pepper–Caper Aioli
MAKES ABOUT 1 CUP ● ●
- 1 red bell pepper
- ½ cup mayonnaise
- 2 tablespoons drained capers
- 2 tablespoons chopped flat-leaf parsley
- 1 teaspoon fresh lemon juice
Salt and freshly ground pepper

I. Roast the pepper under the broiler, until charred all over, about 8 minutes. Transfer to a bowl, cover with plastic wrap and let steam for 5 minutes. Peel and finely chop the pepper. Discard the seeds.

2. In a small bowl, mix the roasted pepper with the mayonnaise, capers, parsley and lemon juice. Season with salt and pepper and serve. —*Andrew DiCataldo*

MAKE AHEAD The aioli can be refrigerated for up to 3 days.

Miami Tartar Sauce
MAKES ABOUT 2 CUPS ● ●
- ¼ cup dry red wine
- 1¼ cups mayonnaise
- 3 tablespoons chopped parsley
- 2 tablespoons chopped sweet gherkins
- 2 tablespoons chopped capers
- 2 tablespoons minced shallot
- 2 tablespoons fresh lemon juice
Salt and freshly ground pepper

I. In a saucepan, simmer the wine over moderately low heat until reduced to 1 tablespoon, about 10 minutes. Let cool.

2. In a bowl, mix the mayonnaise, parsley, gherkins, capers and shallot. Stir in the lemon juice and reduced red wine and season with salt and pepper. —*Jennifer Rubell*

MAKE AHEAD The tartar sauce can be refrigerated for 3 days.

Ancho Chile Pesto with Queso Fresco
MAKES ABOUT ⅔ CUP ● ●
Queso fresco is a mild, soft, crumbly cheese from Mexico; farmer cheese or feta is a fine substitute.
- ¼ cup pine nuts
- 2 ancho chiles, stemmed and seeded
Boiling water
- 4 large garlic cloves, unpeeled
- ⅛ teaspoon dried oregano
- 2 tablespoons peanut or canola oil
- ⅓ cup crumbled queso fresco (2½ ounces)
- 1 tablespoon heavy cream
Salt and freshly ground black pepper
Cayenne pepper

I. Preheat the oven to 375°. Bake the pine nuts in a pie plate for about 2 minutes, or until lightly toasted. Transfer to a plate and let cool completely.

2. In a small heatproof bowl, cover the anchos with boiling water and let soak until softened, about 10 minutes. Drain the chiles, reserving 2 tablespoons of the soaking liquid.

3. Meanwhile, in a small skillet (not nonstick), cook the garlic cloves over moderate heat until softened and blackened in spots, about 10 minutes. Let cool slightly, then peel.

4. In a mini-processor, pulse the garlic cloves, reconstituted anchos, reserved chile soaking liquid, pine nuts and oregano until finely chopped. With the machine on, add the peanut oil and process until a chunky paste forms. Add the queso fresco and the cream, season with salt, pepper and cayenne and pulse to blend. —*Grace Parisi*

MAKE AHEAD The ancho chile pesto can be refrigerated in an airtight container for up to 5 days.

APPLICATIONS Spread on the inside of softened corn tortillas when making enchiladas or fajitas. Toss with steamed or sautéed vegetables. Use as a condiment with grilled steaks, chicken or pork. Add to sour cream or Greek-style yogurt for a quick dip. Mix with ground meat as a seasoning for meatballs.

Cucumber Raita
MAKES ABOUT 2 CUPS ● ● ●
- 1 cup plain full-fat yogurt
- 1 cup peeled and seeded diced (½ inch) cucumber
- 1 small garlic clove, minced
- 3 tablespoons finely chopped mint
Salt and freshly ground pepper

In a medium bowl, combine the yogurt, cucumber, garlic and mint. Season with salt and pepper; refrigerate until serving. —*Madhur Jaffrey*

SERVE WITH Grilled or roast lamb, chicken or salmon.

Three-Herb Salsa Verde
MAKES 1½ CUPS ● ● ●
- ¾ cup minced flat-leaf parsley leaves
- 2 tablespoons minced chervil
- 2 tablespoons minced tarragon
- 2 tablespoons chopped capers
- 2 anchovy fillets, mashed
- 2 small garlic cloves, minced
- 1 small shallot, minced
- ½ cup pure olive oil
- ½ cup extra-virgin olive oil
Salt and freshly ground pepper

In a medium bowl, combine the parsley, chervil, tarragon, capers, anchovies, garlic and shallot. Stir in the pure and extra-virgin olive oils and season with salt and pepper. —*Traci Des Jardins*

MAKE AHEAD The salsa can be refrigerated for up to 6 hours.

SERVE WITH Steak, chicken, fish, lamb or pork.

sauces + condiments

Citrus Salsa with Rosemary

- 12 navel oranges
- 4 lemons
- 4 limes
- 2 cups kumquats (10 ounces)—washed, dried and thinly sliced
- ½ cup extra-virgin olive oil
- ¼ cup snipped chives
- 1 tablespoon rosemary leaves
- 2 teaspoons sugar

Salt and freshly ground pepper

I. Using a small, sharp knife, peel the oranges, lemons and limes, removing all of the bitter white pith. Working over a bowl, cut in between the membranes to release the citrus sections into the bowl; pour off and reserve the citrus juices for another use.

2. Add the kumquats, olive oil, chives, rosemary and sugar to the citrus sections. Season with salt and pepper and serve. —*Jennifer Rubell*

MAKE AHEAD The salsa can be refrigerated for up to 6 hours.

Champagne Vinegar Chimichurri

MAKES 3 CUPS ● ● ●

In South America, chimichurri (which varies by country, but always includes parsley, garlic, olive oil and salt) is usually served with grilled meats.

- 1 cup finely chopped flat-leaf parsley
- ½ cup finely chopped cilantro leaves
- ¼ cup plus 2 tablespoons Champagne vinegar
- 2 teaspoons minced garlic
- 1 teaspoon crumbled dry oregano
- 1 teaspoon ancho chile powder
- 2 cups extra-virgin olive oil

Salt and freshly ground pepper

In a bowl, combine the parsley, cilantro, vinegar, garlic, oregano and ancho powder; let stand for 10 minutes. Stir in the olive oil; season with salt and pepper. —*Jennifer Rubell*

MAKE AHEAD The chimichurri can be refrigerated for 2 days. Bring to room temperature before serving.

Lemon-Shallot Vinaigrette

MAKES ABOUT ½ CUP ● ● ●

This vinaigrette is great drizzled over grilled fish, chicken or vegetables.

- ½ teaspoon finely grated lemon zest plus 2 tablespoons fresh lemon juice
- 2 tablespoons minced shallots
- 1¼ teaspoons Dijon mustard
- 1¼ teaspoons white wine vinegar
- 1 small garlic clove, minced
- ⅓ cup extra-virgin olive oil

Salt and freshly ground pepper

In a blender, combine the lemon zest and juice, shallots, mustard, vinegar and garlic and puree until smooth. With the machine on, slowly add the olive oil until emulsified. Pour the vinaigrette into a bowl and season with salt and pepper. —*Jan Birnbaum*

MAKE AHEAD The vinaigrette can be refrigerated for up to 6 hours.

Creamy French Dressing

MAKES ABOUT 2 CUPS ● ● ● ●

- 2 garlic cloves, halved
- 1 tablespoon Dijon mustard
- 4 large yellow celery ribs from the inner heart, finely chopped (about 1¼ cups)
- ½ small onion, finely chopped
- ¼ cup plus 2 tablespoons extra-virgin olive oil
- ¼ cup plus 2 tablespoons canola oil or other mild vegetable oil
- ¼ cup cider vinegar
- 2 tablespoons minced flat-leaf parsley
- ½ teaspoon dried thyme

Salt and freshly ground pepper

In a blender, combine the garlic with the Dijon mustard, celery, onion, olive oil, canola oil and cider vinegar and blend at high speed until emulsified and creamy. Scrape the French dressing into a glass jar and stir in the parsley and thyme. Season the dressing with salt and pepper and refrigerate until serving. —*Marcia Kiesel*

MAKE AHEAD The dressing can be refrigerated for up to 3 weeks. Shake well before using.

SERVE WITH A lettuce-and-tomato salad or a steamed vegetable, such as asparagus, green beans or carrots, or a roasted vegetable, such as beets.

Tangy Ranch Dressing

MAKES ABOUT 1 CUP ● ●

- 1 large garlic clove, crushed

Salt

- ¼ cup buttermilk
- ¼ cup mayonnaise
- 2 tablespoons whole-milk yogurt or sour cream
- 4 teaspoons cider vinegar
- ¼ cup grapeseed or vegetable oil
- 1 scallion, minced

Freshly ground pepper

Cayenne pepper

In a small bowl, using the back of a spoon, mash the garlic to a paste with a large pinch of salt. Add the buttermilk, mayonnaise, yogurt and vinegar and whisk until smooth. In a thin, steady stream, whisk in the oil. Stir in the scallion. Season the dressing with salt and a generous pinch each of pepper and cayenne. —*Grace Parisi*

MAKE AHEAD The dressing can be refrigerated in a glass jar for up to 5 days.

APPLICATIONS Use as a dipping sauce for fresh vegetables. Use as a marinade for chicken or pork. Toss with steamed vegetables, a green salad or a grape-tomato-and-red-onion salad, or with boiled or roasted potatoes.

Carrot-Miso Dressing

MAKES ABOUT 1 CUP ● ● ●

- ½ cup fresh carrot juice (see Note)
- 1 medium carrot, coarsely chopped

One ¾-inch-thick slice of peeled fresh ginger

- 2 tablespoons fresh lime juice
- 1 tablespoon soy sauce
- 1 teaspoon miso paste
- ½ cup peanut oil

Cayenne pepper

CITRUS SALSA WITH ROSEMARY

CARROT-MISO DRESSING

In a small saucepan, boil the carrot juice over moderately high heat until it is reduced to 3 tablespoons, about 10 minutes. Transfer to a blender and let cool slightly. Add the chopped carrot, ginger, lime juice, soy sauce and miso and blend until the carrot is minced. With the machine on, add the oil in a thin, steady stream. Season the dressing with cayenne and transfer to a glass jar. —*Grace Parisi*

NOTE Fresh carrot juice is available in supermarkets and health food stores.

MAKE AHEAD The dressing can be refrigerated for up to 5 days.

APPLICATIONS Use as a dipping sauce for fresh or steamed vegetables or boiled shrimp. Serve with poached or grilled salmon or tuna. Toss with cold soba noodles, steamed broccoli or snow peas. Drizzle over grilled chicken breasts or pork tenderloin.

Coconut Curry Tomato Sauce
MAKES ABOUT 4 CUPS ● ● ●

- 2 tablespoons peanut or canola oil
- 1 medium onion, thinly sliced
- 1 garlic clove, minced
- 1 jalapeño, seeded and minced
- ½ tablespoon minced fresh ginger
- 1½ tablespoons mild curry powder
- One 28-ounce can peeled tomatoes, chopped and juices reserved
- One 14-ounce can unsweetened coconut milk
- 1 teaspoon sugar
- Salt and freshly ground pepper
- 2 tablespoons chopped cilantro

In a large saucepan, heat the oil until shimmering. Add the onion, garlic, jalapeño and ginger; cook over moderately high heat, stirring, until softened, 5 minutes. Add the curry powder and cook until fragrant, 1 minute. Add the tomatoes and their juices, the coconut milk and sugar; bring to a boil. Season with salt and pepper and simmer over moderate heat, stirring occasionally, until slightly thickened, 20 minutes. Stir in the cilantro and transfer to a bowl. —*Grace Parisi*

MAKE AHEAD The sauce can be refrigerated for up to 5 days.

APPLICATIONS Use as a poaching liquid for chicken, shrimp, lamb, pork or vegetables. Add to a sauté at the last minute. Toss with boiled potatoes or serve over rice. Mix with chicken stock and vegetables or seafood for a quick soup.

Garlic, Rosemary and Black Pepper Marinade
MAKES ABOUT ¾ CUP ● ● ●

- ½ cup fresh lemon juice
- ¼ cup plus 2 tablespoons extra-virgin olive oil
- 4 garlic cloves, minced

sauces + condiments

2 tablespoons minced rosemary

2 tablespoons fleur de sel

2 tablespoons cracked black
peppercorns

Mix all of the ingredients in a bowl.
—*Jean-Georges Vongerichten*

MAKE AHEAD The marinade can be
refrigerated for 5 days.

APPLICATIONS Use this marinade on
pork or veal chops, steaks, or spareribs
(marinate for 1 hour); or on chicken
(marinate for 20 minutes).

Sicilian Lemon Marinade
MAKES ABOUT 1⅓ CUPS ● ● ●

⅔ cup extra-virgin olive oil

Zest of 2 large lemons, removed
in wide strips with a
vegetable peeler

3 bay leaves

3 large rosemary sprigs,
cut into 1-inch lengths

½ teaspoon cracked black
peppercorns

Kosher salt

⅓ cup fresh lemon juice

⅓ cup water

In a saucepan, combine the oil with the
lemon zest, bay leaves, rosemary sprigs
and cracked peppercorns and cook over
moderate heat just until sizzling. Add a
large pinch of salt; remove from the
heat. Let cool slightly, then stir in the
lemon juice and water. —*Grace Parisi*

MAKE AHEAD This marinade can be
refrigerated for up to 1 week.

APPLICATIONS Use as a 1-hour marinade
for swordfish, tuna or shrimp, or to marinate veal, chicken or pork for up to 4
hours before grilling, broiling or sautéing.
Strain and toss with salad greens, olives,
croutons and roasted potatoes or drizzle over poached fish.

Classic Sofrito
MAKES ABOUT 1 CUP ● ● ●

This spicy, garlicky condiment is excellent with all kinds of bean stews as well
as with scrambled eggs, quesadillas or
grilled meats.

3 garlic cloves

Kosher salt

2 tablespoons extra-virgin olive oil

1 medium onion, finely chopped

2 or 3 Scotch bonnet chiles, with
some seeds included, finely
chopped

1 medium tomato—peeled, seeded
and coarsely chopped

¼ cup coarsely chopped cilantro

On a cutting board, mince the garlic,
then, using the back of a spoon, mash
it to a paste with a large pinch of salt.
Heat the olive oil in a medium saucepan. Add the onion and chiles and cook
over low heat, stirring occasionally,
until softened, about 5 minutes. Add
the garlic and cook, stirring, for 1
minute. Add the tomato and cook over
moderately high heat until the juices
have evaporated, about 4 minutes. Stir
in the cilantro and let cool completely.
—*Eric Ripert*

MAKE AHEAD The sofrito can be refrigerated for up to 3 days.

Tamarind Glaze
MAKES 1½ CUPS ● ● ●

Use this sweet, spicy glaze on shrimp,
short ribs, thinly sliced beef, chicken
or pork.

½ cup tamarind pulp with seeds
(6 ounces)

½ cup boiling water

¾ cup honey

¼ cup Asian fish sauce

2 Thai chiles, minced

2 garlic cloves, minced

Salt

In a medium heatproof bowl, blend the
tamarind pulp with the boiling water to
a paste. Pass the paste through a coarse
strainer into another bowl, pressing
down with a firm rubber spatula to
remove the seeds and fibers. Stir in the
honey, fish sauce, chiles and garlic.
Season the glaze with salt.
—*Jean-Georges Vongerichten*

MAKE AHEAD The glaze can be refrigerated for 1 month.

Jan's Spice Mix
MAKES ABOUT 1 CUP ● ●

7 tablespoons kosher salt

2 tablespoons cayenne pepper

2 tablespoons sweet Hungarian
paprika

2 tablespoons freshly ground
black pepper

1 tablespoon ancho chile powder

1 tablespoon dry mustard

2 teaspoons ground cumin

2 teaspoons ground coriander

1 teaspoon freshly ground
white pepper

Mix all of the spices in a small jar.
Cover tightly and store at room tem-
perature for up to 1 month.
—*Jan Birnbaum*

Tabil
MAKES ABOUT ¾ CUPS ● ● ●

The traditional Tunisian spice blend
called *tabil* is made with onions and
garlic dried in the strong Tunisian sun.
Use this fast, simple recipe for a close
approximation.

½ cup coriander seeds

3 tablespoons caraway seeds

3 dried red chiles, seeded

In a large skillet, toast the coriander,
caraway and chiles over low heat until
fragrant, about 2 minutes. Let cool,
then grind the mixture to a powder.
Store the *tabil* in a jar in a cool, dry
place for up to 2 weeks.
—*Nancy Harmon Jenkins*

Spiced Cranberry Ketchup
MAKES 2 CUPS ● ●

This very tart cranberry condiment is a
great contrast to the sweetness in a
typical Thanksgiving menu and is perfect on sandwiches made with leftover
turkey.

1 tablespoon peanut oil

2 tablespoons coarsely
chopped shallots

4 cups cranberries (18 ounces)

1½ cups dry red wine

½ cup red wine vinegar

½ cup packed light brown sugar
¼ teaspoon ground ginger
⅛ teaspoon cinnamon
⅛ teaspoon ground cardamom
⅛ teaspoon ground allspice
Salt

Heat the oil in a medium saucepan. Add the shallots and cook over moderately low heat until softened, about 4 minutes. Add the cranberries, wine, vinegar, brown sugar, ginger, cinnamon, cardamom and allspice and bring to a boil. Simmer over low heat for 30 minutes, or until the mixture is very thick. Let cool slightly, then transfer to a food processor and puree. Season with salt. Transfer the ketchup to a glass jar. —*Robert Stehling*

MAKE AHEAD The ketchup can be refrigerated for up to 2 weeks.

Port-Cranberry Sauce
MAKES ABOUT 2 CUPS ● ● ●

½ cup ruby port
Three 1-by-3-inch strips of orange zest, cut into thin matchsticks
½ cup fresh orange juice
12 ounces fresh cranberries
¾ cup sugar

In a medium saucepan, combine the port with the orange zest and orange juice and bring to a boil. Add the cranberries and sugar and simmer over moderately low heat until the sauce is jamlike, about 25 minutes. Transfer to a bowl and serve warm or at room temperature. —*Grace Parisi*

MAKE AHEAD The cranberry sauce can be refrigerated for up to 2 weeks.

Applesauce with Dried Cranberries
MAKES ABOUT 3 CUPS ● ● ●

2¼ pounds large McIntosh apples— peeled, quartered and cored
2 tablespoons fresh lemon juice
Three 1-by-3-inch strips of lemon zest
½ cup sugar
½ cup sparkling apple cider
½ cup dried cranberries

In a large saucepan, bring the apples, lemon juice and zest, sugar, sparkling cider and cranberries to a boil. Cover and simmer over moderately low heat until the apples soften, about 20 minutes; stir to break up the apples slightly. Transfer the applesauce to a bowl and discard the lemon zest. Serve warm or at room temperature.
—*Grace Parisi*

MAKE AHEAD The applesauce can be refrigerated for up to 1 week.

Pear-Spiked Applesauce
MAKES 4 CUPS ● ● ●

4 McIntosh apples (1½ pounds)— peeled, quartered and cored
2 Bartlett pears—peeled, quartered and cored
1 cup water
1 tablespoon fresh lemon juice
1 teaspoon sugar
¼ teaspoon cinnamon (optional)

In a large, heavy saucepan, bring the apples, pears, water and lemon juice to a boil. Reduce the heat to low and simmer until the fruit breaks down to a thick, chunky puree, about 30 minutes. Remove from the heat and stir in the sugar and cinnamon. Serve the applesauce warm or chilled.
—*Gale Gand*

MAKE AHEAD The applesauce can be refrigerated for up to 1 week.

Oven-Dried Tomatoes
MAKES 24 TOMATO HALVES ● ●

Drying plum tomatoes in the oven dramatically intensifies their flavor and sweetness.

12 large plum tomatoes (about 1¾ pounds), cored and halved lengthwise
2 tablespoons extra-virgin olive oil
2 tablespoons very finely chopped shallots
1 garlic clove, very finely chopped
1 teaspoon minced thyme
Salt and freshly ground pepper

Preheat the oven to 200°. On a large rimmed baking sheet, toss the plum tomatoes with the oil, shallots, garlic and thyme and season generously with salt and pepper. Turn the tomatoes cut side up and roast them for about 3½ hours, or until they are somewhat dry but still plump. —*Tim Goodell*

MAKE AHEAD The tomatoes can be refrigerated in a single layer for 3 days.

Homemade Maraschino Cherries
MAKES 3 CUPS ● ●

1½ cups water
1 cup sugar
½ cup red grape juice
1 star anise pod
Kosher salt
1 pound large, fresh cherries
3 tablespoons fresh lemon juice
1 teaspoon pure almond extract

In a nonreactive saucepan, combine the water, sugar, red grape juice, star anise and a pinch of kosher salt. Bring to a boil, then reduce the heat to low and simmer, stirring occasionally, until the sugar dissolves. Add the cherries (with or without their stems), lemon juice and almond extract and simmer until the cherries are just tender, about 5 minutes. Remove from the heat and let the cherries cool in the syrup. Transfer the cherries and their syrup to a jar, cover and refrigerate overnight or for up to 2 weeks. —*Nick Mautone*

---

dictionary

tamarind

TAMARIND IS THE FRUIT OF A TREE that grows in Asia, Africa and India. The tamarind pod is harvested for its sweet-and-sour pulp, which, once it's dried, is used as a seasoning in different cuisines. It's sold in many forms—from paste to powder—in Asian and Middle Eastern markets.

TABLA'S TART AND FRUITY SANGRIA, P. 333

beverages

TABLATINI

VINHO VERDE PUNCH

Tablatini

MAKES 4 DRINKS ●

2 cups pineapple juice

8 stalks fresh lemongrass,
6 coarsely chopped and
2 halved crosswise

4 small fresh pineapple wedges

Crushed ice

1 cup Absolut Citron vodka

¼ cup fresh lime juice

1. In a medium saucepan, simmer the pineapple juice with the chopped lemongrass over moderate heat for 15 minutes; let cool. Strain the pineapple juice into a jar and chill.

2. Spear the pineapple wedges with the halved lemongrass stalks. Fill a pitcher with ice and add the infused pineapple juice, vodka and lime juice. Strain the Tablatini into chilled martini glasses and garnish with the skewered pineapple. —*Floyd Cardoz*

Golden Ginger Punch

MAKES 30 DRINKS ● ●

Use freshly pressed pineapple juice if it's available; it makes a world of difference in this refreshingly spicy punch.

6 ounces fresh ginger, plus
½ cup fresh ginger matchsticks,
for garnish

4 quarts pineapple juice,
preferably fresh (from about
8 pineapples)

1 bottle (750 ml) vodka

Ice cubes, for serving

1. Puree the 6 ounces of ginger in a food processor. Scrape the ginger into a fine sieve set over a small bowl and press hard to extract the juice. Discard the solids.

2. In a large punch bowl, stir together the pineapple juice, vodka and ginger juice. Add the ginger matchsticks and serve in tall glasses over ice. —*Jennifer Rubell*

Vinho Verde Punch

MAKES 12½ CUPS ●

Vinho Verde is a white or red wine from northwestern Portugal. It means "green wine," referring to its youthfulness.

2 navel oranges

4 bottles (750 ml each) white
Vinho Verde

1 cup Rosemary Syrup
(recipe follows)

1 seedless cucumber, peeled
and thinly sliced

⅓ cup mint leaves

Ice cubes, for serving

1. Using a knife, peel the oranges, removing all of the white pith. Working over a bowl, cut in between the membranes to release the sections into the bowl.

2. In a punch bowl, mix the wine, Rosemary Syrup, oranges and cucumber; let stand for 1 hour. Garnish with mint and serve over ice. —*Eben Klemm*

Rosemary Gin Fizz

MAKES 1 DRINK ● ●

- ¼ cup gin
- 2 tablespoons fresh lemon juice
- 1 tablespoon Rosemary Syrup (recipe follows)
- Ice cubes
- Cold club soda
  - 1 rosemary sprig and fresh red currants, for garnish

In a tall glass, stir together the gin, lemon juice and Rosemary Syrup. Fill the glass halfway with ice; top with club soda. Garnish with the rosemary sprig and red currants and serve.

—Eben Klemm

ROSEMARY SYRUP

MAKES 2 CUPS ● ●

Pungent and sweet rosemary syrup adds unexpected punch to a variety of cocktails; it's best mixed with clear spirits, like vodka, gin and light rum.

- 2 cups water
- ½ cup sugar
- 4 rosemary sprigs, rinsed

Combine all of the ingredients in a saucepan. Bring to a boil, then simmer over moderately low heat for 2 minutes. Remove from the heat and let steep for 10 minutes. Strain the syrup and chill. *—E.K.*

MAKE AHEAD The syrup can be refrigerated for up to 1 week.

Spiced Red Wine Punch

MAKES 12½ CUPS ● ●

- 4 bottles (750 ml each) fruity red wine, such as Beaujolais or Shiraz
- 1¼ cups Holiday Spice Syrup (recipe follows)
- Pomegranate seeds and sliced kumquats, for garnish
- Ice cubes, for serving

Combine the red wine and spice syrup in a very large punch bowl and let stand at room temperature for 1 hour. Garnish with the pomegranate seeds and kumquat slices and serve over ice.

—Eben Klemm

December Stormy

MAKES 1 DRINK

- ¼ cup dark rum
- 2 tablespoons fresh lime juice
- 1 tablespoon Holiday Spice Syrup (recipe follows)
- Ice cubes
- ¾ cup ginger beer or ginger ale
- Lime rounds, for garnish

In a tall glass, stir the rum with the lime juice and spice syrup. Half-fill the glass with ice, top with ginger beer and serve, garnished with lime rounds.

—Eben Klemm

HOLIDAY SPICE SYRUP

MAKES 3 CUPS ●

- 1 quart water
- 1 cup sugar
- 5 star anise pods
- 5 allspice berries
- Three 3-inch cinnamon sticks
- 1 vanilla bean, split lengthwise, seeds scraped

Combine the water, sugar, star anise pods, allspice, cinnamon and vanilla bean and seeds in a large saucepan and simmer over moderately low heat for 30 minutes. Remove from the heat and let steep for 10 minutes. Strain the spice syrup into a bowl and chill. *—E.K.*

MAKE AHEAD The syrup can be refrigerated for up to 1 week.

Tabla's Tart and Fruity Sangria

MAKES ABOUT 2 QUARTS ●

- 1 bottle (750 ml) dry red wine
- ½ cup pineapple juice
- ½ cup fresh orange juice
- ⅓ cup dry white wine
- ¼ cup gin
- ¼ cup light rum
- ¼ cup Cointreau or Triple Sec
- ¼ cup brandy
- 2 tablespoons superfine sugar
- 2 cups assorted sliced fresh fruit, such as apples, oranges, plums, pineapple and grapes, and rhubarb
- Ice cubes, for serving

Combine all of the ingredients, except the ice, in a pitcher. Refrigerate for at least 1 day and for up to 2 days. Serve in tall glasses over ice. *—Floyd Cardoz*

Pink Floyd

MAKES 4 DRINKS ●

- Crushed ice
- 1 cup gin
- ½ cup Cointreau
- ½ cup fresh lime juice
- ½ cup cranberry juice
- 2 tablespoons Pimm's liqueur
- 2 tablespoons superfine sugar
- 4 lemon twists, for garnish

Fill a large cocktail shaker with crushed ice. Add the gin, Cointreau, fresh lime juice, cranberry juice, Pimm's and superfine sugar and shake well. Strain the drink into martini glasses and garnish with the lemon twists.

—Floyd Cardoz

Lime Drop

MAKES 4 DRINKS ●

- 1½ cups plus 2 tablespoons fresh lime juice
- ¼ cup superfine sugar
- 2 tablespoons chopped fresh ginger
- Crushed ice
- 1½ cups gin
- 4 thinly sliced lime rounds

1. In a large cocktail shaker, muddle ¼ cup of the lime juice with 2 tablespoons of the superfine sugar and the ginger.

_ *bar tips* _

mixing drinks

PUT IN THE CHEAPEST INGREDIENTS FIRST so that if you mess up, your mistake won't cost you too much.

ONCE YOU ADD CLUB SODA to a drink, be careful not to overmix. Overmixing will make the soda flat.

A LITTLE WAXED PAPER rubbed on the rim of a bottle prevents dripping.

Fill the shaker with crushed ice, then add 1¼ cups of the lime juice and the gin; shake the drink vigorously.

2. Pour the remaining 2 tablespoons of lime juice and 2 tablespoons of sugar into 2 bowls. Dip the rims of 4 cocktail glasses first in the lime juice and then in the sugar. Strain the cocktail into the glasses; garnish with the lime rounds. —*Floyd Cardoz*

Tamarind Margarita

MAKES 4 DRINKS ● ●

- 1 tablespoon tamarind pulp (see Note)
- 3 tablespoons water
- 1 cup Herradura Silver tequila
- 2 tablespoons superfine sugar

Crushed ice

- ½ cup plus 2 tablespoons fresh lime juice
- ¼ cup Cointreau
- 2 tablespoons fresh orange juice
- 1½ tablespoons kosher salt mixed with 1 teaspoon finely grated orange zest
- 4 lime wedges, for garnish

Ice cubes, for serving

dictionary

tea types

The *Rooibus Chai* on p. 337 is an untraditional tealike drink. Purists may prefer one of the following five types. Moving from delicate to robust: WHITE TEA has a sweet taste and a fragrance reminiscent of chestnuts. GREEN TEA ranges from clear, sweet and flowery to iridescent and bittersweet to nutty and buttery. Complex OOLONG TEA offers a nearly infinite spectrum of colors, aromas and flavors. Almost as varied, BLACK TEA can be full-bodied or light and crisp. Rare PU-ERH TEA has the pungent aroma of wet leaves.

I. In a saucepan, simmer the tamarind and water over low heat, stirring, until the pulp dissolves. Press the mixture into a shaker through a fine-mesh sieve. Add ½ cup of the tequila and the sugar; shake well. Add ice to the shaker, then add ½ cup of lime juice, the Cointreau, the orange juice and the remaining ½ cup of tequila; shake well.

2. Pour the remaining 2 tablespoons of lime juice and the salt mixture into 2 bowls. Dip the rims of 4 old-fashioned glasses first in the lime juice and then in the salt mixture. Fill the glasses with ice. Strain the drink into the glasses and garnish with the lime wedges. —*Floyd Cardoz*

NOTE Tamarind pulp is available at Asian and Middle Eastern markets and specialty food shops.

Watermelon Mojito

MAKES 4 DRINKS ●

- 20 mint leaves, chopped
- 2 tablespoons superfine sugar
- ½ cup fresh lime juice

Crushed ice

- ¾ cup light rum
- 6 ounces seedless watermelon, pureed

In the bottom of a large cocktail shaker, muddle the mint, sugar and ¼ cup of the lime juice. Fill the shaker with ice. Add the rum, pureed watermelon and the remaining ¼ cup of lime juice and shake well. Strain into old-fashioned glasses over ice. —*Floyd Cardoz*

Sereno Cocktails

MAKES 4 DRINKS ● ●

Eric Ripert invented this delicious rum drink on the spot in Puerto Rico.

- 6 large basil leaves
- 2 large limes, quartered
- 2 navel oranges, quartered
- 2 cups fresh orange juice
- ¾ cup sugar
- ¼ teaspoon minced Thai chile, with some seeds

- ¼ teaspoon freshly grated nutmeg, plus more for garnish
- 1½ cups dark rum
- 4 cups crushed ice

I. In a large bowl, combine 2 of the basil leaves with the limes, oranges, orange juice, sugar, chile and ¼ teaspoon of nutmeg. Using a potato masher or a large wooden pestle, pound the limes and oranges until the sugar is dissolved and a rich syrup forms. Squeeze and discard the lime and orange quarters. Stir in the rum.

2. Fill 4 large wineglasses or highball glasses with the crushed ice and bury a basil leaf in each. Fill with the rum drink, garnish each drink with grated nutmeg and serve. —*Eric Ripert*

MAKE AHEAD The recipe can be prepared through Step 1 and refrigerated overnight.

Kir Royale

MAKES 1 DRINK ●

- 1 tablespoon crème de cassis (black currant liqueur)
- 6 ounces dry sparkling wine, such as Crémant de Bourgogne

Pour the crème de cassis into a wineglass or Champagne flute, add the sparkling wine and serve. —*Chantal Leroux*

Blackberry Champagne Cocktail

MAKES 1 DRINK ●

- 1 tablespoon Chambord liqueur

Chilled Champagne

- ½ rounded teaspoon blackberry or passion fruit sorbet

Pour the Chambord into a Champagne flute and top with Champagne. Add the sorbet and serve at once. —*Eben Klemm*

Tamarind and Tonic

MAKES 30 DRINKS ● ● ●

The unusual combination of tamarind syrup and tonic makes this drink both dry and exceptionally refreshing, with a slight bitterness.

TAMARIND AND TONIC

2 cups tamarind syrup
(see Note)
4 quarts chilled tonic
2 lemons, thinly sliced
Ice cubes, for serving

Combine all of the ingredients in a large punch bowl or 2 large pitchers and serve in tall glasses over ice.

—Jennifer Rubell

NOTE Sweetened tamarind syrup (tamarindo) is available at most Asian and Latin markets.

Lemon-Mint Spritzer

MAKES 1 DRINK ●

Ice cubes
6 crushed mint leaves
¼ cup Lemon Syrup (recipe follows)
1 cup sparkling water
1 lemon twist, for garnish

Fill a tall glass with ice cubes and the mint leaves. Pour in the Lemon Syrup and sparkling water, garnish with the lemon twist and serve. *—Tasha Prysi*

Lemon Royal

MAKES 1 DRINK ●

Sparkling wine
1 teaspoon Lemon Syrup
(recipe follows)
1 lemon twist, for ganish

Fill a Champagne flute with sparkling wine. Add the Lemon Syrup, garnish with the lemon twist and serve.

—Tasha Prysi

LEMON SYRUP

MAKES 3 CUPS ● ●

1 cup sugar
1 cup water
1½ cups fresh lemon juice

In a small saucepan, combine the sugar with the water and bring to a boil. Simmer over moderately low heat, stirring, until the sugar dissolves. Pour the syrup into a heatproof bowl and let cool to room temperature, then stir in the lemon juice. *—T.P.*

MAKE AHEAD The Lemon Syrup can be refrigerated for up to 1 month.

Coconut-Lime Frappé

MAKES 2 DRINKS ● ●

1 tablespoon unsweetened shredded coconut
2 medium limes
1 pint coconut sorbet
1 cup plain nonfat yogurt

1. Preheat the oven to 350°. Spread the coconut in a pie plate and toast for about 5 minutes, until golden; let cool. **2.** Using a sharp knife, peel the limes, removing the bitter white pith. Working over a blender, cut in between the membranes to release the sections. Squeeze the juice from the membranes into the blender. Puree the lime sections and juice with the sorbet and yogurt until smooth. Pour the frappé into glasses, garnish with the coconut and serve. *—Patrick Coston*

Strawberry-Mint Frappé

MAKES 2 DRINKS ● ●

1 pint strawberry sorbet
4 medium strawberries, sliced
½ cup plain nonfat yogurt
12 medium mint leaves, plus 4 small sprigs, for garnish

In a blender, puree the sorbet, strawberries, yogurt and mint leaves until smooth, 30 seconds. Pour into tall glasses, garnish with mint and serve. *—Patrick Coston*

Vanilla-Orange Frappé

MAKES 2 DRINKS ● ●

1 medium navel orange, zested
1 vanilla bean, split lengthwise, seeds scraped
1 pint mandarin orange sorbet
½ cup plain nonfat yogurt

Using a sharp knife, peel the orange, removing the bitter white pith. Working over a blender, cut in between the membranes to release the sections. Squeeze the membranes' juice into the blender. Puree the orange sections and juice, vanilla seeds, sorbet and yogurt until smooth. Pour into glasses, garnish with the zest and serve. *—Patrick Coston*

Maraschino Muddle

MAKES 6 DRINKS ● ●

Ice cubes
¼ cup fresh lemon juice
¼ cup fresh lime juice
¼ cup white grape juice
1 tablespoon sugar
1½ teaspoons orange flower water
12 Homemade Maraschino Cherries (p. 329), plus ¾ cup of their syrup
3 orange slices, halved
1 teaspoon Angostura bitters

Club soda

Fill a cocktail shaker with cracked ice. Add the lemon, lime and grape juices, sugar and orange flower water and shake vigorously. In each glass, put 2 Homemade Maraschino Cherries, an orange slice, 2 tablespoons of maraschino syrup and a dash of bitters. Fill with ice, add the juices, top with club soda and serve. *—Nick Mautone*

Rooibus Chai

MAKES 4 DRINKS ● ●

Rooibus leaves, which are grown in South Africa, resemble tea leaves but come from a different plant and aren't tannic. They have recently made an appearance on store shelves here. You can substitute black tea; add it during the last 5 minutes of simmering.

4 cups water
⅔ cup whole milk
2 cinnamon sticks
2 teaspoons cardamom pods, lightly crushed
1 teaspoon whole cloves
2 quarter-size slices of fresh ginger, lightly smashed
¼ teaspoon whole black peppercorns
2 tablespoons sugar
2 tablespoons loose rooibus leaves

Combine all of the ingredients in a medium saucepan and bring to a boil. Simmer over moderately low heat until the drink is a pale rust color, about 20 minutes. Strain the chai and serve hot. *—Suki Hertz*

wine glossary

Elin McCoy, a contributing editor at FOOD & WINE, has created the ultimate user-friendly guide to pairing wine and food. Her glossary here, with descriptions of the key wine varieties and advice on pairing specific bottles with specific recipes, is both flexible and focused. We know you'll find it handy.

champagne + sparkling wine

The most famous sparkling wine is, of course, Champagne, which comes from the region of the same name northeast of Paris. Champagne is usually a blend of Pinot Noir, Chardonnay and sometimes Pinot Meunier grapes, and it's produced in a wide spectrum of styles, ranging from dry (Brut) to sweet (Doux), and from austere and light-bodied to full, toasty and rich.

The very best French Champagnes have both more elegance and more complexity than the sparkling wines produced elsewhere in the world. Nevertheless, California, the Pacific Northwest and Australia all make wonderful New World versions using the same grapes and the same method as French Champagne. Italian Prosecco and Spanish Cava are good, inexpensive alternatives.

The brisk, appetite-stimulating acidity of sparkling wine, whether Champagne or another choice, makes it an ideal aperitif; it also pairs nicely with salty, smoky and spicy dishes.

DRY, LIGHT, CRISP CHAMPAGNE
BOTTLES
- Pommery Brut Royal
- Perrier Jouët Grand Brut
DISH
- Grilled Oysters Casino, 26

DRY, RICH CHAMPAGNE
BOTTLES
- Veuve Clicquot Ponsardin Yellow Label Brut
- Bollinger Special Cuvée
DISHES
- Mushroom Pomponnettes, 11
- Smashed Potatoes with Caviar, 19
- Golden Gratinéed Shellfish, 26

DRY, FRUITY SPARKLING WINE
BOTTLES
- Chandon Blanc de Noirs (California)
- Mumm Brut Prestige Cuvée Napa
DISHES
- Cheese-Fried Piquillo Toasts, 13
- Tostones with Smoked Salmon, 19
- Citrus-Pickled Shrimp, 22
- Tomato Mozzarella Pizza, 243

wine glossary

DRY, CRISP SPARKLING WINE

BOTTLES

- Domaine Ste. Michelle Cuvée Brut (Washington State)
- Mionetto Prosecco di Valdobbiadene (Italy)
- Jaume Serra Cristalino Cava Dry (Spain)

DISHES

- Farmhouse Cheddar and Fig Crackers, 10
- Orange-Glazed Duck Breast Brochettes with Asparagus Salad, 120
- Sesame-Cornmeal Crackers, 256

whites

albariño + vinho verde

Spain's most exciting white wine, and now its most fashionable, is the zesty and aromatic Albariño. Made predominantly in the Rias Baixas region, the wine has seductive aromas of citrus, honey and kiwi and flavors of fresh ginger, lemon and almond. The texture is creamy and at the same time crisp and light, the whole shot through with a lively acidity. All this makes it a perfect partner for scallops and other seafood. The Albariño grape is called Alvarinho in Portugal, where it's used to make the best Vinho Verdes. These slightly fizzy bottlings, light and refreshing, go beautifully with oily fish like sardines.

AROMATIC, ZESTY ALBARIÑO

BOTTLES

- Martín Códax Albariño
- Burgáns Albariño
- Salnesur Condes de Albarei Albariño
- Aveleda Quinta da Aveleda Vinho Verde Alvarinho
- Morgadio da Torre Vinho Verde Alvarinho

DISHES

- Caldo Verde, 68
- Calamari with Potatoes and Piment d'Espelette, 82

- Provençal-Style Calamari Salad with Gremolata, 180
- Grilled Seafood Paella, 193

chardonnay + white burgundy

The world's most popular white wine originally came from the Burgundy region of eastern France, but it's now made successfully in just about every wine-growing country in the world, in an enormous range of styles and flavors. In France, the best white Burgundies are elegant, complex and rich, with flavors of earth, nuts and minerals; the simpler wines from nearby Mâcon and Rully suggest green apples and lemons. California and Australian versions are often higher in alcohol and lush with tropical fruit flavors. Most Chardonnays (Chablis is generally an exception) are aged in oak barrels, which tend to give them a buttery richness and toasty vanilla aromas and flavors. The biggest and oakiest Chardonnays can be tricky to match with food, but they are marvelous partners for sweet corn and for rich fish and poultry dishes made with cream, butter, cheese or coconut.

FRUITY, LOW-OAK CHARDONNAY

BOTTLES

- Maison Louis Jadot Pouilly-Fuissé (France)
- Mâcon-Lugny Les Charmes (France)

DISHES

- Zucchini Soup with Basil, 64
- Spaghetti alla Pirata, 84
- Salmon with Lemon-Shallot Relish and Prosciutto Chips, 167
- Swordfish with Sweet-Sour Sauce, 172
- Scallop and Corn Bacon Burgers with Spicy Mayo, 196
- Lobster and Green Bean Salad with Lemon-Tarragon Dressing, 199
- Onion-Fennel Gratin, 218
- Warm Chickpea, Fennel and Parsley Salad, 233

FLINTY, HIGH-ACID CHABLIS

BOTTLE

- Domaine Robert Vocoret (France)

DISHES

- Pasta with Mussels, 82
- Grilled Wild Striped Bass with Herbs and Sparkling Wine, 173

RIPE, CREAMY-TEXTURED CHARDONNAY

BOTTLES

- Lindemans Bin 65 (Australia)
- Meridian Santa Barbara County (California)
- Sonoma-Cutrer Russian River Ranches (California)

DISHES

- Chicken and Sweet-Potato Chowder, 70
- Sautéed Chicken with Mushroom Dill Cream Sauce, 95
- Coq au Vin with Coconut Milk, 97
- Grilled Texas Chicken, 98
- Lemon-Herb Chicken with Roasted Vegetables and Walnuts, 106
- Chicken and Bulgur Salad with Avocado, 235
- Salmon Potpies, 263

SUBTLE, COMPLEX WHITE BURGUNDY

BOTTLES

- Domaine Olivier Leflaive Puligny-Montrachet (Burgundy)
- Domaine Louis Latour Meursault (Burgundy)

DISHES

- Escargots in Herbed Cream, 27
- Smothered Chicken, 95
- Hazelnut-Crusted Pork Chops with Morel Sauce, 148
- Chicken-Vegetable Shortcakes, 265

chenin blanc

This underappreciated grape is grown widely in the Loire region of France, where it's used to make dry Vouvray and Savennières, as well as delicious sweet wines and a few sparkling ones. But it has also found a home in South

Africa, California and Washington State, which typically turn it into a light dry or semidry white with overtones of green apples and peaches and an acidity that can range from soft to zesty. It's an interesting aperitif and a good partner for light fish dishes. Distinguished dry examples have an underlying mineral chalkiness.

LIGHT, SOFT CHENIN BLANC

BOTTLE
- Hogue Cellars (Washington State)

DISH
- Low-Country Shrimp and Rice, 191

DRY, MINERAL-FLAVORED CHENIN BLANC

BOTTLES
- Mulderbosch (South Africa)
- Chappellet Napa Valley (California)
- Domaine Huët Vouvray Sec (Loire Valley)

DISHES
- Chicken Braised with Lemon and Garlic, 107
- Oatmeal-Crusted Soft-Shell Crabs with Brown Butter, 199

gewürztraminer

The great examples of this flamboyant, fragrant white wine come from Alsace; most of them are bone-dry, but they can range all the way to very sweet (labeled *vendange tardive*—late harvest). Regardless of style, they have an irresistible, heady scent of lychees and cloves; concentrated, spicy (*Gewürz* is the German word for "spice") apricot and ginger flavors; and a rich texture that is at the same time low in acid. They are superb companions for Muenster cheese, chicken liver pâté, smoked fish and baked ham. New World bottlings from California and Washington State are usually lighter, with just a hint of sweetness; they go well with curries and fusion dishes flavored with ginger, coriander, cloves or lemongrass.

SPICY ALSACE GEWÜRZTRAMINER

BOTTLES
- Domaine Trimbach
- Lucien Albrecht

DISHES
- Pork Rib Roast with Orange-Whisky Glaze, 153
- Steamed King Crab with Gewürztraminer Sauce, 200
- Sausage Patties with Caramelized Onions, 267

SPICY NEW WORLD GEWÜRZTRAMINER

BOTTLES
- Columbia Crest Columbia Valley (Washington State)
- Navarro Vineyards Anderson Valley (California)

DISH
- Goan Chicken Curry, 100

pinot blanc

Sometimes called the poor man's Chardonnay, Pinot Blanc is underappreciated and undervalued in its French stronghold, Alsace, and overlooked elsewhere—which is too bad, because this mild wine is dependable, easy to like and reasonably priced. As with most Alsace wines, there's no oak or excessive alcohol screaming for attention. In Austria, Pinot Blanc is called Weissburgunder; it's also produced, on a small scale, in California, Oregon and Italy (where it's dry, light and leafy and known as Pinot Bianco). Pinot Blanc's apple and pear flavors, mineral edge and crisp acidity marry well with vegetables and fish dishes.

MEDIUM-BODIED, ROUND PINOT BLANC

BOTTLES
- Hugel Cuvée Les Amours (Alsace)
- Marcel Deiss Bergheim (Alsace)
- Chalone Vineyard (California)

DISHES
- Chicken Croquettes, 22
- Spring Vegetable Soup, 58
- Skillet Chicken with Summer Succotash, 107
- Cod with Braised Endives in Blood Orange Glaze, 176
- Potato and Smoked Mackerel Dauphinoise, 183
- Roasted Vegetable Galette, 242
- Shirred Eggs with Sorrel, 262
- Bacon, Egg and Cucumber Salad, 262

pinot gris + pinot grigio

The region or country where the Pinot Gris grape grows makes all the difference in the wine's style and flavor. In Alsace, it's a high-impact wine with a musky aroma and bold, concentrated flavors of bitter almonds, spice and honey. It's available in dry and opulently sweet (*vendange tardive)* versions; the dry ones are good with smoky and creamy dishes. In Oregon, where the grape is an emerging star, pear and mango flavors prevail, along with a scent of honeysuckle. The best bottlings here are lighter and less intense than those from Alsace, with a creamy yet slightly crisp character that's versatile with food and ideal with salmon. The Italian version, the popular Pinot Grigio, is light, simple and crisp, with bright, clean, lightly spicy flavors. It works best as an aperitif or with fresh seafood.

DRY, MEDIUM-BODIED PINOT GRIS

BOTTLES
- Domaine Schlumberger Les Princes Abbés (Alsace)
- Pierre Sparr, Sparr Prestige (Alsace)
- King Estate (Oregon)
- Elk Cove (Oregon)

DISHES
- Chicken Liver Crostini with Beet Salsa, 13
- Ten-Minute Smoked Salmon with Avocado-Radish Salad, 28
- Roasted Poussins with Anchovy-Mustard Pan Sauce, 115

wine glossary

- Sautéed Skate with Brown Butter, 176
- Catfish with Pecan Brown Butter, 179
- Alsatian Pizza, 244

LIGHT, SPICY PINOT GRIGIO
BOTTLES
- Santa Margherita Alto Adige (Italy)
- Alois Lageder Alto Adige (Italy)

DISHES
- Lebanese Chicken Salad, 52
- Gumbo-Style Crab Soup with Okra and Tomatoes, 71

riesling

The versatile Riesling grape produces light but striking wines that range from pale, dry and delicate to golden, apricot-scented and honey-sweet; the latter can age for decades. The lighter German ones have a pinpoint balance of fruitiness and mouthwatering acidity. Those from Alsace are weightier and very dry, with steel and mineral flavors. Other regions also make good, if less complex, Rieslings. Austria's are vibrant and powerful; Australia's have zingy lime scents and flavors; Washington State's are soft, with a touch of sweetness. Riesling's fruit, its acidity, its low alcohol and its lack of oak make it one of the most food-friendly of wines, a lovely complement to delicate fish, to spicy Asian and Latin dishes and to all smoked and salty foods.

BRIGHT, CITRUSY RIESLING
BOTTLES
- Selbach-Oster Mosel (Germany)
- Wolf Blass Gold Label (Australia)
- Chateau Ste. Michelle Eroica (Washington State)

DISHES
- Cold Soba Noodle Salad with Cucumber and Shiitake, 91
- Thai Chicken with Mushrooms, Green Beans and Basil, 94
- Bacon-Wrapped Trout with Lemon Relish, 179

- Crabby Carolina Rice, 200
- Barossa Potato Salad with Maple-Cured Bacon, 228

SOFT, OFF-DRY RIESLING
BOTTLES
- Bonny Doon Pacific Rim Dry Riesling (California)
- Hogue Cellars Fruit Forward Johannisberg Riesling (Washington State)

DISHES
- Summer Greens and Herbs with Roasted Beets and Hazelnuts, 41
- Cornish Hen Salad with Scotch Bonnet Vinaigrette, 53
- Vietnamese Lemongrass Chicken with Caramel Sauce, 94
- Honey-Glazed Chicken Drumsticks, 104
- Szechuan Eggplant with Pork, 157

DRY, FULL-FLAVORED ALSACE RIESLING
BOTTLES
- Domaine Trimbach
- Domaine Marcel Deiss

DISHES
- Pork Tenderloin with Rosemary and Applesauce, 150
- Pan-Seared Pork Medallions with Riesling and Apples, 156

sauvignon blanc

Tart acidity, aromas of fresh-cut grass and herbs, green pepper and sometimes citrus flavors give Sauvignon Blancs the world over a character people either love or hate. Sancerre and Pouilly-Fumé from France's Loire Valley have flint and mineral flavors. The lively New Zealand bottlings taste of passion fruit and gooseberries. South Africa's are elegant and bright, California's are lighter, and all are fresh and crisp. When the grape is blended with rounder, heavier Sémillon, as it typically is in Bordeaux, the result is mellow and full-bodied. The riper, oak-aged Sauvignon Blancs hint of melons

and toast. The lighter versions of the wine go beautifully with salads and with almost all fish and green vegetables—even asparagus.

LIVELY, ASSERTIVE SAUVIGNON BLANC
BOTTLES
- Brancott Estate Marlborough (New Zealand)
- Villa María Marlborough (New Zealand)
- Dry Creek Fumé Blanc Sonoma County (California)
- Pascal Jolivet Pouilly-Fumé (France)
- La Poussie Sancerre (France)

DISHES
- Spicy Mussels with Ginger and Lemongrass, 27
- Citrus-Marinated Scallops and Roasted Red Pepper, 28
- Grilled Antipasto with Garlicky Bean Dip, 32
- Open-Face Onion, Goat Cheese and Pine Nut Tart, 35
- Arugula, Fennel and Dried Plum Salad, 41
- Garden Vegetable Panzanella, 48
- Spicy Red Lentil Coconut Soup with Shrimp Dumplings, 71
- Lazy Linguine with Cherry Tomatoes and Herbs, 77
- Handmade Pasta with Tomato and Artichoke Sauce, 81
- Chicken Tonnato with Arugula, Tomatoes and Olives, 96
- Chicken with Cherry Tomato Pesto Sauce, 96
- Coconut Curry Chicken, 99
- Basil Chicken Curry with Coconut Rice, 100
- Chicken Tikka with Cucumber Raita, 103
- Macedonian Lemon Chicken, 107
- Spice-Crusted Chicken Breasts with Lemon-Cucumber Raita, 108
- Salmon with Baby Artichokes and Sunchokes, 167
- Golden Asian Fish Cakes with Spicy Slaw, 183

wine glossary

- Grilled Shrimp with Lemon-Basil Pesto, 187
- Santorini Salad with Grilled Shrimp, 193
- Roasted Shrimp and Scallop Papillotes, 200
- Shrimp and Goat Cheese Risotto, 235

ROUND, RICH SAUVIGNON BLANC
BOTTLES
- Simi California
- Château Carbonnieux Pessac-Léognan Blanc (France)

DISHES
- Sautéed Chicken with Garlic and Parsley, 96
- Chicken in Tarragon Cream Sauce, 97
- Country Chicken and Mushroom Pie, 109

soave

Italy produces many delicious light white wines; three of them are particularly well known and universally loved. Soave, from Veneto, is a wine that is both fruity and inexpensive. Verdicchio, from Marche, has a sharp acidity followed by a tangy finish. Finally, Gavi, from Piedmont, is a delicate wine marked by citrus and mineral notes.

DRY, LIGHT, REFRESHING SOAVE
BOTTLES
- Pieropan Soave Classico
- Monte Schiavo Verdicchio dei Castelli di Jesi Classico San Floriano
- Coppo Gavi La Rocca

DISHES
- Winter Vegetable Salad with Bagna Cauda Dressing, 42
- Penne with Cherry Tomatoes, Olives and Pecorino, 76
- Bucatini with Pecorino and Coarse Pepper, 77
- Linguine with Seafood Sauce, 85
- Whole Roasted Sea Bass with Artichokes and Tomatoes, 174

- Meyer Lemon Risotto with Basil, 235
- Warm Seafood Sandwiches, 250

vermentino

Vermentino is assertive and savory, with a salty, lemony edge and razorlike acidity—all of which makes it a perfect partner for any kind of shellfish. Though the grape grows throughout Italy, the Vermentinos of Tuscany and Sardinia generally have the most character and the most complexity.

HIGH-ACID, SAVORY VERMENTINO
BOTTLES
- Antinori Bolgheri Vermentino (Italy)
- Argiolas Costamolino Vermentino di Sardegna (Italy)

DISHES
- Salad of Potatoes, Beans, Zucchini and Herbs, 50
- Spaghetti with Scallops, Sun-Dried Tomatoes and Olives, 82
- Penne with Tuna and Capers, 87
- Tuna with Pasta and Frisée, 87
- Roast Chicken with Olives and Yogurt, 107
- Leek-and-Cheese Sprinkle Pie, 214
- Rosemary and Sea Salt Pizza, 244
- Mixed-Olive Tapenade Pizza, 244

vernaccia di san gimignano

Vernaccia di San Gimignano is, according to Tuscan tradition, "the wine that kisses, bites and stings." It's also the best known of the many wines made from the Vernaccia grape that flourishes throughout Italy. The grapes for this version—generally considered Tuscany's finest white wine—grow on the hillsides surrounding San Gimignano, the medieval town famous for its picturesque bell towers. The wine is fresh and reliable, with no oak. Its tangy mineral and citrus flavors and its crisp acidity pair beautifully with pasta and with shellfish.

TANGY, CRISP VERNACCIA DI SAN GIMIGNANO
BOTTLES
- Teruzzi & Puthod
- San Quirico
- Melini Lydia

DISHES
- Saffron Shrimp and Stuffed Cherry Peppers, 29
- Linguine Fine with Zucchini, Basil and Dill, 76
- Fettuccine with Shrimp, Zucchini and Basil, 82
- Mussels in Tomato Sauce with Sausage, 194

viognier

Whether it's the classic bottling from the northern Rhône Valley appellation of Condrieu in France or one of the newer versions from California and, now, Australia, the appeal of Viognier is its exotic honeysuckle aroma, its intense ripe-peach and ripe-apricot flavors and, most of all, its fleshy, mouth-filling texture. The aroma leads you to expect sweetness, but in the mouth it's bone-dry. Low in acid and often high in alcohol, Viognier is typically rich and powerful. Opulent dishes with tropical or dried fruit, curry or smoky flavors are good matches.

FULL-BODIED, FRAGRANT VIOGNIER
BOTTLES
- Bonterra Mendocino County (California)
- Pepperwood Grove California
- Calera Mount Harlan (California)
- Yalumba Eden Valley Australia
- Jean-Luc Colombo Côtes-du-Rhône Blanc, Les Figuières (France)

DISHES
- Glazed Cornish Hens with Garlicky Radicchio, 113
- Imperial Turkey with Curry Gravy, 118
- Seared Duck Breasts with Honey-Raisin Compote, 121
- Golden Sausages and Shallots in White Wine, 266

rosés

Rosés are as refreshing as white wines while offering the body and the fruit of light reds. They come from many lands and from many different grapes and range in style from simple summer thirst-quenchers to sophisticated marvels. The best, from Provence and the Tavel appellation of the southern Rhône Valley, are savory, bone-dry bottlings made from Rhône grapes—Syrah, Grenache and Cinsaut. Italy, Spain and California produce their own dry, delectable versions. What they all have in common is zesty fruit and a liveliness and acidity that make them delightful with smoky, sweet and hot spices and thus ideal companions for Chinese, Thai, Middle Eastern, Cajun and Southwestern dishes.

BRIGHT, FRUITY ROSÉ
BOTTLES
• Château Routas Côteau Varois Rosé Rouvière (France)
• Château d'Acqueria Tavel (France)
• Iron Horse Rosato di Sangiovese (California)
• Castello di Ama Rosato (Italy)
• Rosé di Regaleali Tasca d'Almerita (Italy)
• La Palma Rosé Rapel Valley (Chile)
DISHES
• Piquillo Peppers Stuffed with Shrimp and Wild Mushrooms, 30
• Chickpea Soup with Seared Monkfish and Thyme, 67
• Linguine with Fresh Tuna, Tomatoes and Lemon, 87
• Curried Chicken and Red Pepper Kebabs, 104
• Teriyaki-Glazed Turkey with Shallot Gravy, 117
• Lemongrass Beef Rolls with Rice Noodles, 134
• Spicy Tofu Casserole with Pork, 156
• Hot Mustard-Pickled Peaches with Baked Ham, 158

• Sicilian Stuffed Swordfish with Cherry Tomato Sauce, 173
• Pan-Seared Shrimp with Hot Chorizo Butter, 187
• Rice-and-Cremini-Stuffed Cabbage Rolls, 213
• Wild Mushroom Toasts with Ham and Fried Eggs, 261

reds

barbera

The second-most-planted grape in Italy (after Sangiovese), Barbera produces its finest wines—tart, bright and medium-bodied, with very little tannin—in the Piedmont areas of Asti and Alba. (A few California wineries also make Barbera, with mixed results.) Both simple styles (fresh, fruity and without oak) and more serious bottlings (plummy and oaky) have a high acidity that gives them vibrancy and zip. Licorice, berries and cherries are typical flavors; the taste is straightforward, mouth-filling and, for a red, quite refreshing. Barbera's tartness combines superbly with antipasti, tomatosauced pastas and bitter greens.

TART, LOW-TANNIN BARBERA
BOTTLES
• Michele Chiarlo Barbera d'Asti
• Bruno Giacosa Barbera d'Alba
• Coppo Camp du Rouss Barbera d'Asti
DISHES
• Green Olive Gnocchi with Green Olive Sauce, 78
• Rigatoni with Pork Ragù and Fresh Ricotta, 88
• Spicy Chicken and Rice, 110
• Rooster Gumbo with Tomatoes and Okra, 112
• Roasted Pork Loin Stuffed with Spinach and Prosciutto, 151
• Olive and Feta Meatballs, 157
• Grilled Pizzas Stuffed with Cheese and Radicchio Salad, 243

beaujolais

This fruity and famously charming wine is made from the Gamay grape in the Beaujolais region of France. Bottlings range from the simple Beaujolais-Villages, best when it's young, to deeper, more complex *cru* examples from villages with their own appellations, such as Moulin-à-Vent, which age well. What they all share is a smooth texture, an exuberant juiciness and strawberry-cherry flavors. Though Beaujolais isn't as fashionable as it once was, its low tannin, fresh, fruity acidity and lack of oak still enable it to pair well with a variety of foods. It traditionally accompanies roast chicken, and it's also excellent with turkey and most cheeses.

LIGHT, FRUITY BEAUJOLAIS
BOTTLES
• Georges Duboeuf Beaujolais-Villages
• Château de La Chaize Brouilly
• Louis Jadot Château des Jacques Moulin-à-Vent
DISHES
• Kentucky Pan-Fried Chicken, 97
• Roast Chicken with Oven-Dried Tomato Vinaigrette, 103
• Roast Spice-Brined Chicken, 104
• Roasted Capon Stuffed with Veal and Smoked Ham, 113
• Skillet Pork Chops, 149
• Braised Veal Breast with Butternut Squash Stew, 159
• Mushroom and Ham Quiche, 260

cabernet sauvignon + bordeaux

Cabernet Sauvignon is not merely the classic grape of Bordeaux; it is really the king of grapes, producing some of the world's most complex, elegant, powerful and long-lived red wines. In Bordeaux, where it's often blended with Merlot and Cabernet Franc, it dominates the wines of the Médoc and Graves regions, playing a smaller

wine glossary

role in St-Emilion and Pomerol. Those made with a larger proportion of Cabernet Sauvignon typically have black currant and plum aromas and flavors; herbal, olivelike and even minty elements all add complexity. Mouth-puckering tannins, enhanced by aging in oak barrels, give the wines astringency and bite when they're young; aging smoothes out the tannins and brings out aromas and flavors of cedar and cigar boxes. Many California bottlings are also blends. The fruit in New World Cabernets tends to be sweeter and riper than in the classic Bordeaux. Cabernet Sauvignon has a particular affinity for the pungent flavors of lamb; it also pairs well with roasts and steaks.

TANNIC, COMPLEX CABERNET
BOTTLES
- Gallo of Sonoma (California)
- Beringer Knights Valley (California)
- Robert Mondavi Napa Valley (California)
- Casa Lapostolle Cuvée Alexandre (Chile)
- Château Léoville-Barton (France)
- Château Gloria (France)

DISHES
- Crusty Pan-Seared Rib-Eye Steak, 124
- Glazed Beef with Bourbon-Roquefort Sauce, 126
- Standing Rib Roast of Beef, 130
- Grilled Lamb Steaks with Chile-Mint Salsa, 140
- Grilled Lamb Chops with Green and Black Olive Salsa, 140

chianti + sangiovese

Italy's best-known wine—a medium-bodied, brightly flavored, smooth-textured red—is made primarily from the Sangiovese grape in the Chianti region of Tuscany. Wines simply labeled "Chianti" tend to be soft and simple, with cherry flavors and a touch of fresh thyme; those labeled "Chianti

Classico" and "Riserva" are more intense and complex, with deeper licorice, sweet-sour dried cherry and earthy flavors and a considerable hit of tannin. Chianti's acidity and its suggestion of saltiness make it an excellent partner for many foods, especially olives and garlic, tomato-sauced pastas, grilled steaks and Pecorino and other tangy cheeses. A clone of the Sangiovese grape is the base for Brunello di Montalcino, which is deep, rich and marvelously full-bodied. Many producers also make big, rich Sangiovese–Cabernet Sauvignon blends, which are known as Super-Tuscans.

SIMPLE, FRUITY CHIANTI OR SANGIOVESE
BOTTLES
- Castello di Gabbiano Chianti
- Marchese Antinori Santa Christina

DISHES
- Baked Rigatoni with Mushroooms and Prosciutto, 90
- Moroccan Couscous-Stuffed Chicken Breasts, 108

COMPLEX, SAVORY CHIANTI CLASSICO OR SANGIOVESE
BOTTLES
- Ruffino Chianti Classico Riserva Ducale
- Fontodi Chianti Classico
- Foppiano Alexander Valley Sangiovese (California)

DISHES
- Orecchiette with Brussels Sprouts and Bacon, 88
- Beef Braciole in Umido, 128
- Italian Baked Stuffed Tomatoes, 133
- Coriander Lamb with Yogurt and Endives, 140

dolcetto

Italy's answer to Beaujolais: a plummy, grapey, delicious wine from Piedmont (and now from a few wineries in California, too). It's light and spicy, with a juiciness reminiscent of cranberries,

and best when it's young. It's a versatile wine that's lovely with osso buco and most meaty pasta dishes as well as many creamy cheeses.

LIGHT, ZESTY, FRUITY DOLCETTO
BOTTLES
- Renato Ratti Dolcetto d'Alba
- Aldo Conterno Dolcetto d'Alba
- Niebaum-Coppola Dolcetto Napa Valley (California)

DISHES
- Country Captain, 110
- Roast Turkey with Cherry Salsa, 118
- Potato Sformato with Mortadella and Buffalo Mozzarella, 225
- Rice and Lentil Stew with Olive Gremolata, 232

merlot

Merlot, Bordeaux's major red grape after Cabernet Sauvignon, is similar in flavor but less assertive; because of its softer texture, it's often blended with Cabernet to tame that grape's hard tannins. When Merlot is the dominant grape, as in Bordeaux's Pomerol and St-Emilion, or when it's bottled on its own, the result has a rich, velvety texture and a come-hither juiciness, with aromas and flavors of plums and black cherries. The smooth texture and the luscious fruit combine well with medium-weight meats—duck, pork, veal—especially in dishes with a hint of sweetness. Washington State and California's Napa and Sonoma regions also make delightful Merlots.

RICH, VELVETY MERLOT
BOTTLES
- Chateau Souverain Alexander Valley (California)
- Markham Napa Valley (California)
- Canoe Ridge Columbia Valley (Washington State)
- Château La Grave à Pomerol

DISHES
- Pasta with Sausage, Basil and Mustard, 89

wine glossary

- Seared Spiced Duck Breasts, 121
- Pan-Roasted Beef Filet with Rösti Potatoes, 125
- London Broil with Red Wine, Fennel and Olives, 130
- Grilled Flank Steak Salad, 137
- Herb-Crusted Leg of Lamb, 137
- Rack of Lamb with Soy-Balsamic Marinade, 145
- Panko-Breaded Pork Chops, 149
- Chilean Mixed Grill, 154
- Veal-and-Mushroom Meat Loaf with Bacon, 162

pinot noir + red burgundy

The most sensual and beguiling of all red wines, the best Pinot Noirs are from Burgundy, but California, Oregon and New Zealand have all done wonders with this difficult grape. Though Pinot Noir appears in many different styles, its hallmarks are seductive scents and flavors that suggest cherries, strawberries and damp earth or mushrooms, and, above all, a silky texture. Bottlings range from light- to medium-bodied and from simple to complex, but very few are tannic, and almost all can be drunk young. California's Pinot Noirs are beginning to rival Burgundy's for elegance and complexity; Oregon's have delicacy, charm and bright cherry fruit, though a few wineries there are also making bigger wines. The wine's low tannin, tart fruitiness and subtle flavors make it flexible with food. Fruity styles work well with Asian flavors and fish; earthier ones respond beautifully to mushrooms and game.

LIGHT, FRUITY PINOT NOIR
BOTTLES
- Argyle Willamette Valley Oregon
- Erath Oregon
DISHES
- Grilled Chicken Wings and Livers with Balsamic-Mustard Glaze, 19
- Roasted Leek and Potato Salad, 49

- Shaking Beef with Pea Shoot Salad, 134
- Stir-Fried Peking Lamb with Peppers and Green Beans, 143
- Barbecued Brisket Sandwiches with Firecracker Sauce, 249

RICH, EARTHY PINOT NOIR
BOTTLES
- Acacia Carneros (California)
- Sanford Santa Barbara (California)
- Domaine Drouhin Oregon
DISHES
- Roast Chicken with Shallots and Dried Cranberries, 105
- Veal Scallopine with Lentil Salad, 161
- Soy-and-Ginger-Glazed Salmon with Udon Noodles, 166

COMPLEX, SILKY RED BURGUNDY
BOTTLES
- Bouchard Père et Fils Volnay Caillerets Ancien Cuvée Carnot
- Louis Jadot Santenay Clos de Malte
DISHES
- Roasted Cornish Game Hens with Toasted Bread Crumbs, 115
- Boeuf Bourguignon, 131
- Pork with Sage and Madeira, 156

rioja + tempranillo

Tempranillo, which reigns supreme among Spanish grapes, gives the renowned red blends of the Rioja region their herbal scent, earthy flavor and elegant texture. Riojas made in a modern style have forward fruit and just a little oak; the more traditional, more complex ones are mellower and oakier. The newly fashionable Ribera del Duero region produces delicious blends in a bigger, richer, fruitier style. In both places, the younger versions, labeled "Crianza," are spicy, easy-drinking wines; "Reservas" and "Gran Reservas" are more subtle and refined, with flavors of leather and earth. These

are big red wines; hearty bean and spicy sausage stews, grilled meats and earthy dishes (for instance, with wild mushrooms) have flavors and textures that make apt matches.

SOFT, EARTHY RIOJA
BOTTLES
- Martinez Bujanda Conde de Valdemar Crianza
- Marqués de Riscal Reserva
- Cune Imperial Gran Reserva
- Montecillo Reserva
DISHES
- Curried Chicken with Chickpeas and Potatoes, 98
- Roasted Marjoram Chicken, 105
- Sautéed Chicken Livers with Onions and Port, 109
- Smoky Beef and Leek Stew, 132
- Lamb Satay with Tamarind Barbecue Sauce, 140
- Lamb Marinated in Jasmine Tea with Sweet Pea Sauce, 142
- Autumn Lamb and Vegetable Stew, 143
- Fettuccine with Wild Boar Ragù, 145
- Farmer-Style Pork Tenderloin with Pimentón Sauce, 150
- Port-Marinated Pork with Prunes and Anchovies, 151

shiraz + syrah

The intense and concentrated wines that are made from Syrah grapes are packed with blueberry and blackberry fruit and with spicy, peppery, sometimes smoky scents and flavors. Syrah is the star grape in France's northern Rhône Valley, where it goes into dense, powerful wines that take on a chocolaty, leathery character as they age. Elsewhere in the Rhône, it is one of several grapes in softer, rounder, less tannic blends such as the much loved Châteauneuf-du-Pape. In California, where the grape is gaining popularity, it's often blended with other Rhône varietals. It's also one of the most widely planted grapes in

Australia, where it goes by the name Shiraz and yields wines that range from solid all the way to superb (including a sparkling red). Many of the Australian bottlings are thick, chocolaty and jammy, with notes of sweet vanilla from oak aging. Syrah's big, spicy-peppery flavors demand equally robust, flavorful foods. Grilled meat and game are appropriate, and the Rhône blends pair superbly with spicy dishes and barbecue.

RICH, SMOKY-PLUMMY SHIRAZ
BOTTLES
- Greg Norman Limestone Coast Southern Australia
- Rosemount Estate Diamond Label Southeastern Australia

DISHES
- Rib-Eye Steak au Poivre, 124
- Red Wine Braised Short Ribs, 130
- Braised Short Ribs with Redeye Gravy, 131
- Lamb Chops with Vegetable Ragout, 139
- Slow-Cooked Lamb Shanks with Verjus, 144

ROUND, SUPPLE, FRUITY SYRAH
BOTTLES
- E. Guigal Côtes-du-Rhône (France)
- Fetzer Valley Oaks California

DISHES
- Grilled Chorizos with Salsa, 20
- Chipotle Steak with Turkish Wheat Berries, 125
- Grilled Lamb Chops with Provençal Dressing, 143
- Lamb and Kale Moussaka, 144
- Goulash with Sausage and Sauerkraut, 159
- Pan-Fried Veal Chops with Lemon and Rosemary, 162

POWERFUL, SPICY SYRAH
BOTTLES
- Jaboulet Crozes-Hermitage Domaine de Thalabert (France)
- Domaine du Pesquier Gigondas

DISHES
- Upside-Down Tomato-Beef Pie, 127
- Grilled Beef Tenderloin with Tuscan Kale and Shallot Confit, 128
- Provençal Stuffed Zucchini, 206

zinfandel

Though it's generally believed to have first traveled over to the United States from Italy, Zinfandel is really California's own grape. And it's an enormously versatile one that is used to make everything from bland, semi-sweet blush wines to jammy, highly intense reds. The Zinfandels that go best with most foods are the medium-to full-bodied bottlings that emphasize the grape's characteristic raspberry-boysenberry, often spicy fruit. These bright berry flavors and the wine's lively acidity make it a good partner for hearty food. Grilled or barbecued meats are excellent choices; so are spicy, salty dishes.

INTENSE, BERRY-FLAVORED ZINFANDEL
BOTTLES
- Ravenswood Napa Valley
- Ridge Geyserville Sonoma
- Dry Creek Heritage Clone Sonoma County
- Seghesio Sonoma County

DISHES
- Bacon-Cured Skirt Steak with Chanterelles and Shallots, 126
- Grilled Korean-Style Skirt Steak, 126
- Lemon-and-Mint Roast Leg of Lamb with Flageolets, 137
- Lamb Chops with Hot Fennel-Coriander Vinaigrette, 139
- Guava-Glazed Pork Tenderloin with Cilantro-Jalapeño Salsa, 149
- Brown Sugar–Glazed Pork Roast, 153
- Jamaican-Style Jerk Spareribs, 154
- Polenta with Sausage, Tomato and Olive Ragout, 159
- Chorizo and Pinto Bean Stew, 231

dessert wines

The many varieties of grapes that are used to make dessert wines are typically picked long after the other grapes have been harvested, at the point when they are very, very ripe. This late harvesting allows their natural sweetness to further increase, and it also concentrates their flavors.

late-harvest riesling + ice wine

Most late-harvest Rieslings are produced in Germany, California and Australia. These wines have a low alcohol content, intensely sweet lemon and apricot flavors and a sharp acidity—characteristics that make them an obvious match for fresh fruit tarts. Ice wine (*Eiswein* in German) comes from grapes that have been frozen on the vine and then pressed before they thaw out—and it's even sweeter. The classic German bottlings are scarce and quite expensive; New World versions are more affordable.

LIGHT, SWEET LATE-HARVEST RIESLING
BOTTLES
- Joseph Phelps Johannisberg Riesling Special Select Late Harvest (Napa Valley)
- Inniskillin Ice Wine (Canada)
- Mt Horrocks Cordon Cut Riesling (Australia)
- Hogue Columbia Valley Late Harvest White Riesling (Washington State)

DISHES
- Perfect Apple Pie, 274
- Tangy Key Lime Pie, 278
- Lemon Pudding Cakes with Apricot Sauce, 283
- Curried Fruit Compote, 284
- Lemon Meringue Cake, 292
- Lemony Yogurt Cake, 294
- Citrusy Angel Food Cake, 294

wine glossary

sauternes + sweet sémillon

A felicitous blend of Sémillon and Sauvignon Blanc grapes, both of which have been touched with the *Botrytis cinerea* mold—the so-called noble rot—produces the great sweet wines of France's Sauternes region. These gratifying, nectarlike wines, with their rich, complex vanilla and cream flavors, go wonderfully well with creamy desserts. The bottlings from California and from Australia, which are typically made with just the Sémillon grape, tend to be simpler and fruitier than the ones from France.

RICH, SWEET SAUTERNES

BOTTLES
- Château d'Arche Sauternes (France)
- Far Niente Dolce Napa Valley (California)

DISHES
- Fried Apple Pies, 275
- Roasted Peach Pies with Cream, 276
- Pear and Apple Oat Crisp, 284
- Tapioca and Rhubarb Parfait, 286
- Vanilla Bean Cheesecake with Walnut Crust, 298
- Crêpes with Creamy Caramel, 309
- Almond Crème Caramel, 313
- Classic Tiramisu, 313

muscat

The Muscat grape grows all over the world. The fragrant wines that it produces range from peachy-spicy and lightly sweet to unctuous, complex and liqueurlike and on to ice wines with hints of candied orange peel that can stand up to the most sugary desserts. Beaumes-de-Venise, a fortified wine from a picturesque village in France's Rhône Valley, is one of the most popular and versatile examples, with luxurious fruit flavors that make it an excellent partner for a wide array of desserts, most notably ice cream.

SWEET, FRAGRANT MUSCAT ICE WINE

BOTTLE
- Bonny Doon Muscat Vin de Glacière (California)

DISHES
- Bourbon Pumpkin Pie with Pecan Struesel, 276
- Tangy Buttermilk Pie, 276

SWEET, FORTIFIED, FRAGRANT MUSCAT

BOTTLES
- M. Chapoutier Muscat de Beaumes-de-Venise
- Quady Electra Orange Muscat (California)

DISHES
- Hazelnut and Raspberry Jam Linzer Tart, 281
- Banana Soufflés, 284
- Sweet Wine Sabayon with Berries, 287
- Gâteau Basque, 291
- Marbled Pumpkin Cheesecake with a Brownie Crust, 298
- Linzer Cookies, 303
- Creamy Butterscotch Pudding with Toffee, 315
- Sticky Toffee Pudding, 315

tawny port

Acidity, aromas of almonds and apricots and complex flavors of nuts, dried fruit and caramel characterize this Portuguese fortified wine. It pairs best with desserts that have similar flavors.

COMPLEX TAWNY PORT

BOTTLES
- Taylor-Fladgate 20-Year-Old
- Fonseca 10-Year-Old

DISHES
- Caramelized Almond Tart, 279
- Breton Prune Flan, 286
- Viennese Dobos Tort, 291
- Hazelnut-Rum Cake, 300
- Chocolate-Glazed Hazelnut Meringues, 306

vin santo

Tuscany produces the lion's share of vin santo, but the wine is also produced in Alto Adige, Veneto and, especially, Umbria. The grapes for vin santo are dried for several months before they are pressed, a process employed in order to concentrate their flavors. Vin santo can be dry or sweet. The sweet vin santos are thick and luscious and taste of almonds, honey and apricots.

SWEET, LUSCIOUS ITALIAN VIN SANTO

BOTTLE
- Villa Pillo

DISHES
- Creamy Ricotta Tart with Pine Nuts, 279
- Almond Cornmeal Cake, 290
- Chocolate-Hazelnut Sandwiches, 301
- Hazelnut Semifreddo with Gianduja Sauce, 313

banyuls

A rich, sweet red wine is often the perfect partner for a chocolate dessert. Banyuls, from France's Roussillon region, has the right thick texture, along with a higher than usual alcohol content and terrifically concentrated sweet plum and cocoa flavors to go along with it.

RICH, SWEET BANYULS

BOTTLE
- Les Clos de Paulilles

DISHES
- Warm Chocolate Soufflé Tarts, 281
- Chocolate-Crusted Plum Galette, 282
- Chocolate Cupcakes with Cream Filling, 297
- Bittersweet Chocolate Mousse with Cocoa Nib Whipped Cream, 311
- Chocolate Mousse with Szechuan Pepper Sabayon, 312

The ever enthusiastic—and often irreverent—Kevin Zraly, founder of New York City's Windows on the World Wine School, leads a minicourse on red wines: the importance of tannin, the significance of scent and the best food matches.

FW: What is tannin?
KZ: Tannin is a natural preservative that is found in foods like walnuts, tea and grapes. The tannins in wine derive primarily from grape skins but can also come from the oak barrels in which certain wines are aged (which is why even some white wines, which are made without grape skins, have tannins). Tannins, when balanced with fruit, leave a tactile sensation in your mouth that is felt in the middle of your tongue. As a wine gets older, its tannins mellow and become visible in the wine as sediment. Of course, tannins are just one component of a wine's structure; the best wines have a balance of tannins, fruit and acids.

FW: What does it mean when a wine is said to be full-bodied or big?
KZ: A big wine generally has more alcohol, more tannins and more concentrated fruit; big wines are best drunk with food.
FW: Is it okay to chill red wine?
KZ: Of course. Room temperature is probably a bit too high for most reds, and restaurants often serve their reds too warm. Don't be afraid to ask for an ice bucket to bring a wine down to a preferable temperature or, at home, to put a bottle of red in the fridge for an hour before serving it. Your personal preference is what should guide you, and, when you're paying, you should enjoy your wine just as you like it.

FW: Why bother smelling wine?
KZ: It's simple: Your tongue can only detect four main tastes, but your nose can identify more than 2,000 different odors. Studies have shown that women have a keener sense of smell than men, but anyone can tell whether a wine is good or bad based on its smell. Wine should smell, well, like fruit—not gym socks or vinegar or anything unpleasant. That's why the tradition of having restaurant customers take a sip of wine to determine whether it's gone bad is not necessary: It's all in the nose! The first taste of a wine is always a shock to your tastebuds.
FW: What's a safe red wine to bring as a gift to a dinner party?
KZ: It's safe to bring Pinot Noir, Sangiovese and Tempranillo, which are versatile and light in style, with the right balance of fruit and acid. They all pair well with fish, meat, poultry and vegetables.

ZRALY'S CHEAT SHEET

REGION	VARIETAL	FLAVOR/BODY	BEST RECENT VINTAGE	BEST FOOD MATCHES
BURGUNDY	PINOT NOIR	Soft, easy, fruit-driven, fragrant—an inviting wine that says "drink me."	1999	Chicken, salmon, tuna.
RIOJA	TEMPRANILLO	Fresh fruit taste; light to medium in color, body and tannins.	1994 1995 1996 1998	Picnic pick— great with grilled foods.
TUSCANY	SANGIOVESE	Fruity, refreshingly acidic and light; a great complement to food.	1997 1999 2000	Cheese, pasta primavera, risotto.
NAPA	CABERNET SAUVIGNON	Very tannic and medium- to full-bodied; there are no light Cabernets.	1997 1999 2001	Lamb, venison, steak.
BAROSSA	SHIRAZ	Medium- to full-bodied (a light Shiraz is rare), spicy and peppery.	1998 1999 2001	Spicy foods— or your best burger.

cellar notes

pairings we love _____

wines to remember _____

tips for entertaining

This new section of style ideas—culled from stories in FOOD & WINE Magazine—proves that a beautiful table can make a great meal even better. On these pages you'll find inspired suggestions for place settings and floral arrangements that will surprise and delight your guests, whatever the occasion.

STORY An intimate New Year's Eve dinner at the home of New Zealand cinematographer and vintner Michael Seresin.

IDEA Tall single stems add drama to the table. Their green and white colors are echoed in the Champagne flutes and plates (from the Terence Conran Shop; 866-755-9079).

STORY Innovative arrangements from top restaurant floral designers.
IDEA Manhattan designer Karen Bussen (212-643-6880) creates an unexpected arrangement by inserting calla lilies and pincushion proteas into a cluster of geometric resin vases (by Lawrence Essentials, from Bergdorf Goodman; 800-558-1855).

STORY A Trinidadian-inspired party to celebrate Ismail Merchant's film *The Mystic Masseur*.
IDEA F&W's Dana Cowin decorates the table with objects from around her house: a modern orange vase, an antique cream-colored African figure and a nineteenth-century bowl filled with Scotch bonnet peppers.

STORY New York City hostess Rena Sindi throws a party for her book, *Be My Guest: Theme Party Savoir Faire*.
IDEA Olivier Giugni of L'Olivier Floral Atelier (212-774-7676) places trimmed burgundy lady's slipper orchids in a vase instead of the usual terra cotta pot and wraps the base with broad banana leaves.

entertaining tips

STORY A stylish yet inexpensive dinner party hosted by Celia Tejada, the vice president of design and brand direction at Pottery Barn.
IDEA Tejada adds a touch of fantasy to the decor of her Sonoma, California, home with an oversize tea cup holding several dozen yellow tulips—a play on size and scale.

STORY Inspirations from New York City flower pros.
IDEA Floral designers Catherine Guialdo and Kristine Ellis of Color of Magic (212-967-5439) love playing with textures and colors. These scabiosas in a Japanese ceramic tea cup—only inches high—are a perfect way to adorn a simple place setting.

STORY Chef Eric Ripert of New York City's Le Bernardin finds culinary inspiration in Puerto Rico.
IDEA The vibrant green hues of the Caribbean are represented in this tropical centerpiece. The limes, avocado and plaintains keep the arrangement both low and color-coordinated.

STORY A perfect pairing of wine
and food: Rioja and tapas.
IDEA Tapas is all about variety, and
this assortment of flowers reflects
that. Single blooms of different
colors in differently shaped small
bowls and cups are grouped together
on a ceramic tray by Arabia from
Pitt Petri (716-852-7876).

STORY Fresh ideas for flower
arrangements.
IDEA Most flower arrangements
are vertical, but floral designer Jane
Packer (212-754-1731) goes for a
spiral formation instead. She swirls
calla lilies in a spherical vase, then
adds water; finally, she floats a single
rose in the center.

STORY A garden lunch with
forward-thinking French porcelain
maker Philippe Deshoulières.
IDEA Deshoulières sets a stylish
table, matching his cypress-pattern
"Balade en Toscane" plates with
the sylvan arrangement on the table:
miniature topiaries of various
heights placed in tiny terra cotta pots.

entertaining tips

STORY A July 4th winemaker's party at a lighthouse on Long Island's North Fork, an emerging wine region. IDEA A nautical theme plays out on the table with fossilized starfish set on top of navy napkins from ABH Designs (212-688-3764). Playful origami boats with flags flying high add a further patriotic note.

STORY An extravagant theme dinner celebrating signature style. IDEA Instead of using traditional place cards, lettering artist Karen Charatan (201-930-9608) uses a brown fabric marker to trace guests' signatures onto napkins. Next, to make the signatures stand out, she goes over them with paint.

STORY Fashion designer Han Feng sets the scene for a spectacular outdoor wedding. IDEA Feng writes each guest's name in calligraphy on a strip of paper then fastens it to a Bosc pear with a tiny pin. For a touch of romance, she ties the napkins with green satin ribbons that trail to the ground.

STORY A wonderful—and inexpensive—dinner party at the Sonoma home of Pottery Barn design guru Celia Tejada.
IDEA A faux bird's nest decorates each place setting; a plant marker from Smith & Hawken (800-940-1170) becomes a name card; and a message on a tag adorns the cutlery.

STORY A Trinidadian party to celebrate Ismail Merchant's film *The Mystic Masseur*.
IDEA Place mats are cut from silver-patterned orange paper (Print Icon; 212-255-4489). A delicate plastic leaf (also from Print Icon) adds a tropical note to the setting, and a Trinidadian food dictionary tells what's for dinner.

STORY An elegant party in New York with the theme of signatures.
IDEA On one side of a sheet of iridescent brown card stock, the dinner menu; on the other side, a handwriting analysis for each guest at the party from Graphology Consulting Group (212-387-8100)—all strung together with grosgrain ribbon.

menu index

porch supper

seaside lunch

harvest dinner

281

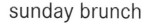

ice-skating party

STARTER
Alsatian Potato and Bacon Tart, 34

MAIN COURSE
Roast Spice-Brined Chicken, 104

Crunchy Baked Potatoes with
Maldon Salt, 224

Eggplant and Butternut Squash
Tagine, 210

Winter Vegetable Salad with Bagna
Cauda Dressing, 42

WINE LIGHT, FRUITY BEAUJOLAIS

DESSERTS
Warm Chocolate Soufflé Tarts, 281

Sparkly Cinnamon Coins, 305

WINE RICH, SWEET BANYULS

vegetarian buffet

BUFFET
Fire-Roasted Tomato Bisque, 64

Roasted Vegetable Galette, 242

Rice-and-Cremini-Stuffed
Cabbage Rolls, 213

Roasted Broccoli with
Ancho Butter, 204

Warm Chickpea, Fennel and
Parsley Salad, 233

WINE MEDIUM-BODIED, ROUND
PINOT BLANC

DESSERTS
Honey-Roasted Plums with
Mascarpone and Pistachios, 284

Vanilla Bean Cheesecake with
Walnut Crust, 298

sunday brunch

STARTER
Fig and Blue Cheese Tarts, 265

MAIN COURSE
Garden Frittata, 260

Golden Sausages and Shallots
in White Wine, 266

Asparagus Sandwiches, 248

WINE ROUND, RICH SAUVIGNON
BLANC

DESSERTS
Orange Cream Cheese Pound Cake
with Passion Fruit Icing, 295

Ginger-Poached Pink Grapefruit, 287

menu index

137

easter

passover

fourth of july

63

115

thanksgiving

STARTERS

Sesame-Cornmeal Crackers, 256
with Hot Pepper Jelly, 322

Fresh Goat Cheese and Crispy
Shallot Dip, 16

MAIN COURSE

Bacon-Roasted Turkey with
Sweet-Onion Gravy, 115

Orecchiette with Brussels Sprouts
and Bacon, 88

Buttery Mashed Potatoes, 224

Cider-Braised Collards with
Ham, 218

Sweet Potato Spoon Bread, 226

Bay Leaf–Scented Spoon
Rolls, 255

Arugula, Fennel and Dried Plum
Salad, 41

Port-Cranberry Sauce, 329

WINE LIGHT, ZESTY, FRUITY DOLCETTO

DESSERTS

Marbled Pumpkin Cheesecake
with a Brownie Crust, 298

Perfect Apple Pie, 274

southern christmas

STARTERS

Port-Glazed Walnuts with Stilton, 19

Tostones with Smoked Salmon, 19

Red Pepper, Garlic and Pecorino
Gougères, 12

MAIN COURSE

Pork Rib Roast with Orange-Whisky
Glaze, 153

Creamy Potato-Corn Mash, 225

Roasted Sweet Potato and Onion
Salad, 50

Maple-Cider Baked Beans, 228

Arugula, Fennel and Dried Plum
Salad, 41

WINE SPICY, ALSACE GEWÜRZTRAMINER

DESSERTS

Sticky Toffee Pudding, 315

Milk Chocolate Jewels, 317

50

new year's eve

COCKTAIL

Blackberry Champagne
Cocktail, 334

STARTERS

Golden Gratinéed Shellfish, 26

Bagna Cauda with Crudités, 17

MAIN COURSE

Standing Rib Roast of Beef, 130

Champagne-Roasted Cauliflower
with Gruyère, 205

Spinach and Orange Salad
with Parmesan Pecans, 41

WINE TANNIC, COMPLEX CABERNET

DESSERTS

Vanilla Bean Cheesecake
with Walnut Crust, 298

Chocolate-Dipped Florentine
Shortbreads, 302

85 staff favorites

The editors at FOOD & WINE test and taste recipes all day long, and when they go home, a few of those recipes—the ones they just can't stop thinking about— go home with them. The 85 listed here are the editors' personal favorites, the dishes they make when they're cooking for family, entertaining friends or simply feeding themselves. These recipes might become your favorites, too.

HORS D'OEUVRES
- Farmhouse Cheddar and Fig Crackers, 10
- Cheese-Fried Piquillo Toasts, 13
- Pierogi Crostini with Two Toppings, 14
- Egyptian Spiced Carrot Puree, 16
- Swedish Meatballs, 20
- Manchurian Pork-and-Zucchini Dumplings, 21

FIRST COURSES
- Steamed Mussels with Smoky Bacon, 27
- Ten-Minute Smoked Salmon with Avocado-Radish Salad, 28
- Grilled Antipasto with Garlicky Bean Dip, 32

SALADS
- "Red Hot" Beet Salad with Goat Cheese Toasts, 45
- Roasted Leek and Potato Salad, 49
- Greek Bean-and-Beet Salad with Skordalia, 50

SOUPS
- Fresh Shell Bean Soup with Pistou, 58
- Butternut Squash Soup with Popcorn and Sage, 60
- Bulgur and Fava Bean Soup, 64
- Lentil and Swiss Chard Soup, 66
- Chickpea Soup with Seared Monkfish and Thyme, 67
- Mexican Black Bean Soup with Sausage, 68

PASTA
- Wagon Wheels with Broccoli and Parmesan Cheese, 77
- Green Olive Gnocchi with Green Olive Sauce, 78
- Handmade Pasta with Tomato and Artichoke Sauce, 81
- Chilled Capellini with Clams and Caviar, 81
- Tuna with Pasta and Frisée, 87
- Rigatoni with Pork Ragù and Fresh Ricotta, 88
- Orecchiette with Brussels Sprouts and Bacon, 88
- Pasta with Sausage, Basil and Mustard, 89

POULTRY
- Thai Chicken with Mushrooms, Green Beans and Basil, 94
- Vietnamese Lemongrass Chicken with Caramel Sauce, 94
- Roast Chicken with Shallots and Dried Cranberries, 105
- Lemon-Herb Chicken with Roasted Vegetables and Walnuts, 106
- Roast Chicken with Olives and Yogurt, 107
- Roasted Capon Stuffed with Veal and Smoked Ham, 113
- Glazed Cornish Hens with Garlicky Radicchio, 113
- Teriyaki-Glazed Turkey with Shallot Gravy, 117

kitchen notes

favorite recipes _____

favorite menus

index

a

black beans *See also* Beans
Black-Bean Soup Augier, 68, **69**
Mexican Black Bean Soup
with Sausage, 68
Southwestern Bean Gratin, 229
black beans, Chinese fermented
Shrimp in Black Bean Sauce, 188
blackberries *See also* Berries
Blackberry–Cream Cheese Tortilla
Blintzes, 271
Blenders, 64, 71
blueberries *See also* Berries
Old-Fashioned Blueberry
Pie, 274, **274**
Warm Nectarine and Blueberry
Shortcakes, **280**, 281
blue cheese *See also specific kinds*
Fig and Blue Cheese Tarts, 265
Summer Greens and Herbs
with Roasted Beets and
Hazelnuts, **40**, 41
Boar, Wild, Ragù, Fettuccine
with, 145
bocconcini
Grilled Antipasto with Garlicky
Bean Dip, **24**, 32
bok choy
Golden Asian Fish Cakes with
Spicy Slaw, 183
bonito flakes
Dashi, 176
bourbon
Bourbon Pumpkin Pie with Pecan
Streusel, 276
Glazed Beef with Bourbon-
Roquefort Sauce, 126
brandy *See also* Armagnac
Tabla's Tart and Fruity Sangria,
330, 333
bread, recipes using
Baked Apple Tartines with Walnuts
and Armagnac, 270
Banana Brioche Bread
Pudding, 283
Cheese-Fried Piquillo Toasts, 13
Chicken Liver Crostini with
Beet Salsa, 13
Creamy Garlic Soup, 62
Farmer's Salad with Bacon and
Walnuts, 37

Foie Gras French Toast, 256, **257**
Fontina-Gorgonzola
Fonduta, 34, **35**
Fresh Shell Bean Soup with
Pistou, 58
Garden Vegetable Panzanella, 48
Grilled Chorizos with Salsa, 20
Ham and Sausage Strata, 261
Heirloom Tomato Salad with
Parmesan Anchovy Toasts, 48
Lebanese Chicken Salad, 52
Parmesan Garlic Bread, 252
"Red Hot" Beet Salad with Goat
Cheese Toasts, **44**, 45
Roasted Cauliflower and Broccoli
with Curried Croutons, 204
Roasted Pearl Onion Crostini, 13
Sicilian Stuffed Swordfish with
Cherry Tomato Sauce, 173
Spinach-Shiitake Bread
Puddings, 256
Tuscan Fish Stew, 180
Warm White Bean and Calamari
Salad with Garlic Bruschetta,
30, 31
Wild Mushroom Toasts with Ham
and Fried Eggs, **260**, 261
Zucchini Soup with Basil, 64
breads *See also* Biscuits; Bruschetta,
crostini & toasts; Muffins;
Sandwiches; Scones
Bay Leaf–Scented Spoon Rolls,
254, 255
Flat Bread with Feta, Parsley and
Sesame Seeds, 246
Flat Bread with Mixed Greens,
Winter Squash and Cheese, 246
Irish Soda Bread, 268, **269**
Jim Lahey's Pane Casareccio, 253
Multigrain Molasses Bread, 252
Onion-Buttermilk Pinwheels, 253
Pumpkin Seed Bread, 253
Red Pepper Corn Bread,
254, **254**
Soft Pretzels, 256, **256**
Turkish Flat Bread Stuffed with
Cheese, 246, **247**
breakfast & brunch, 258–71
Brie, Prosciutto, and Apple Panini with
Scallion Butter, 248, **248**

broccoli
Broccoli-Leek Soup with Lemon-
Chive Cream, 60
Chicken-Vegetable Shortcakes, 265
Hot and Sour Vegetables, 213
Roasted Broccoli with Ancho
Butter, 204, **204**
Roasted Cauliflower and Broccoli
with Curried Croutons, 204
Tangy Broccoli Salad with
Buttermilk Dressing, 45
Wagon Wheels with Broccoli and
Parmesan Cheese, 77
broccolini
Vegetable Risotto Dressing, 236
broccoli rabe
Bagna Cauda with Crudités, 17
Winter Vegetable Salad with
Bagna Cauda Dressing, 42
bruschetta, crostini & toasts
about, 14
Cheese-Fried Piquillo Toasts, 13
Chicken Liver Crostini with
Beet Salsa, 13
Heirloom Tomato Salad with
Parmesan Anchovy Toasts, 48
Pierogi Crostini with Two
Toppings, 14
"Red Hot" Beet Salad with Goat
Cheese Toasts, **44**, 45
Roasted Pearl Onion Crostini, 13
Warm White Bean and
Calamari Salad with Garlic
Bruschetta, **30**, 31
brussels sprouts
Hot and Sour Vegetables, 213
Lemon-Herb Chicken with
Roasted Vegetables and
Walnuts, 106, **106**
Orecchiette with Brussels Sprouts
and Bacon, 88
bulgur
Bulgur and Fava Bean Soup, 64, **65**
Chicken and Bulgur Salad with
Avocado, **234**, 235
Red Lentil Köfte with Tomato-
Cucumber Salad, 238, **239**
Tabbouleh with Marinated
Artichokes and Baby
Spinach, 233

m

O

oat(s)

r

radicchio
Arugula, Fennel and Dried
Plum Salad, 41
Glazed Cornish Hens with Garlicky
Radicchio, 113
Grilled Pizzas Stuffed with Cheese
and Radicchio Salad, 243
Salade Guarnaschelli with Oregano
Vinaigrette, 40

radishes
Peruvian Bean Cakes with
Cucumber-Radish Salad, 32
Potato Salad with Honey-
Buttermilk Dressing, 227, **227**
Sautéed Skate with Brown
Butter, 176, **177**
Seared Tuna with Radish Salad
and Wasabi Dressing, 169
Ten-Minute Smoked Salmon with
Avocado-Radish Salad, 28
Tomatillo-Quinoa Salad, **222**, 233
Tuna Carpaccio with Citrus-Ginger
Dressing, 28, **29**
Winter Vegetable Salad with Bagna
Cauda Dressing, 42

raisins
Oatmeal with Pineapple and
Golden Raisins, 269, **269**
Seared Duck Breasts with Honey-
Raisin Compote, 121

raspberries *See also* Berries
Linzer Cookies, **302**, 303

raspberry jam
Hazelnut and Raspberry Jam
Linzer Tart, **280**, 281

red snapper
Grilled Red Snapper with Sweet
Garlic Barbecue Sauce, 178
Red Snapper with Sweet-and-Sour
Eggplant, 177

rhubarb
Sautéed Salmon with Rhubarb
Marmalade, 167
Tapioca and Rhubarb Parfait, 286

rice *See also* Risotto
Almost Dirty Pork Rice, 157
Basil Chicken Curry with Coconut
Rice, 100

Crabby Carolina Rice, 200
Dirty Turkey-Rice Purloo, 237
Grilled Seafood Paella, **184**, 193
Hot and Sour Shrimp Soup with
Jasmine Rice, **72**, 73
Italian Baked Stuffed
Tomatoes, 133
Low-Country Shrimp and Rice, 191
Parmesan-Rice Crisps, 10, **10**
Rice-and-Cremini-Stuffed
Cabbage Rolls, 213
Rice and Lentil Stew with Olive
Gremolata, 232
Spicy Chicken and Rice, 110
uses for, 236
Vegetable Pilaf with Pancetta, 236
Winter Vegetable–Chicken
Paella, 237

ricotta cheese
Creamy Ricotta Tart with Pine
Nuts, 279
Flat Bread with Mixed Greens,
Winter Squash and Cheese, 246
Grilled Pizzas Stuffed with Cheese
and Radicchio Salad, 243
Herbed Ricotta with Roasted
Peppers, 37
Lemon-Ricotta Pancakes Drizzled
with Honey, **266**, 267
Rigatoni with Pork Ragù and
Fresh Ricotta, 88
Three-Cheese Baked Pasta, **90**, 91

riesling
Pan-Seared Pork Medallions with
Riesling and Apples, 156
Riesling-Poached Salmon, 168
Ripert, Eric, interview with, 197

risotto
Lemon Sole with Tomato-Olive
Risotto, 178
Meyer Lemon Risotto with
Basil, **234**, 235
Porcini Mushroom Risotto, 236
Shrimp and Goat Cheese
Risotto, 235
Vegetable Risotto Dressing, 236
Rooster Gumbo with Tomatoes
and Okra, 112

roquefort cheese *See also*
Blue cheese

Glazed Beef with Bourbon-
Roquefort Sauce, 126
Tangy Broccoli Salad with
Buttermilk Dressing, 45

rosemary *See also* Herbs
Citrus Salsa with Rosemary,
326, **327**
Garlic, Rosemary and Black Pepper
Marinade, 327
Grilled Sea Bass with
Rosemary, 174
Pan-Fried Veal Chops with Lemon
and Rosemary, 162
Pork Tenderloin with Rosemary
and Applesauce, 150
Rosemary Gin Fizz, 333
Rosemary and Sea Salt Pizza, 244
Rosemary Syrup, 333
Sicilian Lemon Marinade, 328

rum
December Stormy, 333
Hazelnut-Rum Cake, 300
Sereno Cocktails, 334
Tabla's Tart and Fruity Sangria,
330, 333
Watermelon Mojito, 334

s

saffron
Pasta with Mussels, 82
Saffron Shrimp and Stuffed Cherry
Peppers, 29

sage *See also* Herbs
Butternut Squash Soup with
Popcorn and Sage, 60, **61**
Lemon-Herb Chicken with
Roasted Vegetables and
Walnuts, 106, **106**
Pork with Sage and Madeira, 156

salad dressings *See also*
Vinaigrettes
Carrot-Miso Dressing, 326, **327**
Creamy French Dressing, 326
Tangy Ranch Dressing, 326

salads, 38–53
Asian Shrimp Salad with
Snow Peas, Jicama and Bell
Peppers, **192**, 193

Suzanne Goin

contributors

grant achatz was named one of FOOD & WINE's Best New Chefs in 2002. He is the chef at Trio in Evanston, Illinois.

hugh acheson was named one of FOOD & WINE's Best New Chefs in 2002. He is the chef at Five & Ten in Athens, Georgia.

ann chantal altman is the corporate executive chef for Vivendi Universal in New York City.

michael anthony was named one of FOOD & WINE's Best New Chefs in 2002. He is co-chef at Blue Hill in New York City.

alison attenborough is a food stylist in New York City.

dan barber was named one of FOOD & WINE's Best New Chefs in 2002. He is co-chef at Blue Hill in New York City.

serena bass is a caterer, event planner and co-owner of Serena Bar & Lounge in New York City's Chelsea Hotel.

maggie beer is a farmer, cook, writer, businesswoman and vigneron in Australia's Barossa Valley. She has written five cookbooks, including *Maggie's Table, Maggie's Farm* and *Cooking with Verjuice.*

scott bieber is the chef at Taste restaurant in New York City.

jan birnbaum is the chef and owner of Catahoula Restaurant and Saloon in Calistoga, California, and Sazerac in Seattle.

anacleto and tina bleve are the owners of Bottega del Vina in Rome's Jewish Quarter.

jim botsacos is the chef at Molyvos in New York City.

daniel boulud was named one of FOOD & WINE's Best New Chefs in 1988. He is the chef and owner of New York City's Daniel, Café Boulud and db. He has written three cookbooks: *Chef Daniel Boulud: Cooking in New York City, Cooking with Daniel Boulud* and *The Café Boulud Cookbook.*

bob bowe is a researcher at FOOD & WINE Magazine.

olga bravo is co-owner of Olga's Cup and Saucer in Providence, Rhode Island.

terrance brennan was named one of FOOD & WINE's Best New Chefs in 1995. He is the chef and owner of Terrance Brennan's Seafood and Chop House, Picholine and Artisanal in New York City.

frank brigtsen was named one of FOOD & WINE's Best New Chefs in 1988. He is the chef and owner of Brigtsen's in New Orleans.

bill buford is *The New Yorker*'s European correspondent. He is working on a book about being a cook at Babbo in New York City.

andrea buscema is the chef at Uno e Bino, a wine bar in Rome.

anna teresa callen is a food writer and cookbook author and the director of the Anna Teresa Callen Italian Cooking School in New York City. Her books include *Italian Classics in One Pot* and *Food and Memories of Abruzzo.*

floyd cardoz is the chef at Tabla Restaurant and Bread Bar in New York City.

cesare casella is the chef and owner of Beppe in New York City.

joanne chang is the chef and owner of Flour Bakery & Café in Boston.

lauren chattman is a cookbook author. Her titles include *Instant Gratification* and *Icebox Pies.*

pascal chaupitre is the chef and owner of La Maison de Célestin in Vierzon, France.

susan choung is an assistant editor at FOOD & WINE Magazine.

melissa clark is a freelance food writer who regularly contributes to the *New York Times.* She has authored 13 cookbooks.

david colman writes about art, design and fashion for the *New York Times* and is a passionate amateur chef.

patrick coston is the pastry chef at Ilo Restaurant in New York City.

dana cowin is the editor in chief of FOOD & WINE Magazine.

peggy cullen is a baker, candy maker and the author of *Got Milk? The Cookie Book.* She is currently working on *Caramel,* which is due out in summer 2003.

gary danko was named one of FOOD & WINE's Best New Chefs in 1989. He is the chef and owner of Gary Danko restaurant in San Francisco.

giada de laurentiis is a private chef and caterer in Los Angeles and the owner of GDL Foods.

bernardita del campo correa is the wife of Chilean winemaker Aurelio Montes. The Montes family lives in Santiago and owns vineyards in Curicó and Colchagua, Chile.

traci des jardins was named one of FOOD & WINE's Best New Chefs in 1995. She is the chef at Jardinière and Acme Chophouse in San Francisco.

andrew dicataldo is the chef at Patria in New York City.

graziella dionisi is the cook at Podere Zingoni, a rental villa in Sarteano, Tuscany.

paula disbrowe is the chef at Hart & Hind Fitness Ranch in Rio Frio, Texas. Her food and travel articles have appeared in the *New York Times* and FOOD & WINE Magazine.

scott ehrlich is the chef and co-owner of aKa Cafe and Alias in New York City.

paolo fanciulli is a fisherman and environmentalist who leads boat tours along the Tuscan coast.

taylor fladgate, founded in 1692, is in its fourth century as a family-owned and-managed company. Located in Portugal, it is highly regarded for its port.

claudia fleming, formerly the pastry chef at Gramercy Tavern in Manhattan, is the author of the award-winning cookbook *The Last Course* and the director of food development at Pret à Manger in New York City.

ben ford is the chef and owner of Chadwick in Beverly Hills, California.

damon lee fowler is a food journalist and the author of four cookbooks, including *Beans, Greens, and Sweet Georgia Peaches* and *Damon Lee Fowler's New Southern Kitchen.*

gale gand was named one of FOOD & WINE's Best New Chefs in 1994. She is the pastry chef and co-owner of Chicago's Tru restaurant, host of the Food Network's *Sweet Dreams* and the author of three cookbooks, most recently *Gale Gand's Just a Bite: 125 Luscious, Little Desserts.*

suzanne goin was named one of FOOD & WINE's Best New Chefs in 1999. She is the chef and co-owner of Lucques and AOC in Los Angeles.

tim goodell was named one of FOOD & WINE's Best New Chefs in 2000. He is the chef and co-owner of Aubergine in Newport Beach, California. He and his wife also own four other California restaurants: Troquet and The Lodge in Costa Mesa, Red Pearl Kitchen in Huntington Beach and Whist in Santa Monica.

peter gordon is a New Zealander turned Londoner who rose to fame as chef at the Sugar Club. His new restaurant is The Providores.

laurent gras was named one of FOOD & WINE's Best New Chefs in 2002. He is the chef at Fifth Floor in San Francisco.

lauren groveman is a cookbook author and TV and radio personality who has been teaching cooking and baking skills for over a decade.

alexandra guarnaschelli is the chef at Nick & Stef's Steakhouse in New York City and a teacher at the Institute of Culinary Education in New York City.

maria guarnaschelli has edited many of our most influential cookbooks, including *The Modern Art of Chinese Cooking, Authentic Mexican: Regional Cooking from the Heart of Mexico* and the revised *Joy of Cooking.*

david guas is the pastry chef at DC Coast and TenPenh restaurants in Washington, D.C.

kathy gunst is the author of seven cookbooks, most recently *Relax, Company's Coming: 150 Recipes for Stress-Free Entertaining.*

kurt gutenbrunner is the chef at New York City's Wallsé restaurant and Café Sabarsky.

john harris was named one of FOOD & WINE's Best New Chefs in 2002. He is the chef at Lilette in New Orleans.

sam hayward is the chef and co-owner of Fore Street Grill in Portland, Maine.

maida heatter is the author of ten dessert books, including *Maida Heatter's Book of Great Desserts.*

kate heddings is the editor of FOOD & WINE Books and a senior food editor at FOOD & WINE Magazine.

beth hensperger is the author of *The Bread Bible* and *The Ultimate Rice Cooker Cookbook.*

pierre hermé is a fourth-generation pastry chef who worked at Fauchon and Ladurée before opening his boutique, Pierre Hermé, in Paris.

suki hertz, a contributing editor at FOOD & WINE, is a recipe developer, food stylist and nutritionist.

amanda hesser is a reporter for the *New York Times,* a columnist for the *New York Times Magazine* and the author of *The Cook and the Gardener.* Her upcoming book, *Cooking for Mr. Latte,* is due out in spring 2003.

kate hill teaches the cooking of Southwest France at her restored farmhouse in Gascony when she is not traveling across Europe.

tony hill is the founder of World Spice Merchants in Seattle. His first book on exotic spices, herbs and teas is due out in fall 2003.

madhur jaffrey is a cookbook author and actress. Her cookbooks include *Madhur Jaffrey's World Vegetarian* and, most recently, *Madhur Jaffrey's Step-by-Step Cooking.*

nancy harmon jenkins is the author of three Mediterranean cookbooks, including *Flavors of Tuscany.* Her most recent book, *The Essential Mediterranean,* is due to be published in spring 2003.

joseph jiménez de jiménez is the Basque-born chef and co-owner of The Harvest Vine in Seattle.

thomas john was named one of FOOD & WINE's Best New Chefs in 2002. He is the chef at Mantra in Boston.

daniel johnnes is the wine director at Montrachet in New York City, a partner in Myriad Restaurant Group and the founder of the wine importing company Jeroboam Wines.

joyce jue is a cooking teacher and cookbook author. Her latest book is *Savoring Southeast Asia.*

paul kahan was named one of FOOD & WINE's Best New Chefs in 1999. He is the chef and co-owner of Blackbird in Chicago.

wendy kalen is a recipe developer and writer in New York City.

nicole kaplan is the pastry chef at Eleven Madison Park in New York City.

hubert keller was named one of FOOD & WINE's Best New Chefs in 1988. He is the chef and owner of Fleur de Lys in San Francisco.

marcia kiesel is the test kitchen supervisor at FOOD & WINE Magazine and a co-author of *The Simple Art of Vietnamese Cooking.*

eben klemm is a molecular biologist turned bartender who pours his creative cocktails at the New York City restaurant Pico.

peggy knickerbocker is a freelance writer and longtime resident of San Francisco. She is the author of *Olive Oil from Tree to Table* and *The Rose Pistola Cookbook.*

deborah knight was named one of FOOD & WINE's Best New Chefs in 2002. She is the chef and owner of Mosaic in Scottsdale, Arizona.

jim lahey is the founder and head baker of Sullivan Street Bakery in New York City.

annabel langbein is a cookbook author in Auckland, New Zealand. Her most recent book is *Savor Italy: A Discovery of Taste.*

chantal leroux is Butterfield & Robinson's expert historian guide in Burgundy. She lives and cooks in Beaune for her family and friends.

michael leviton was named one of FOOD & WINE's Best New Chefs in 2000. He is the chef and co-owner of Lumière in West Newton, Massachusetts.

ronni lundy is the author of the Southern cookbooks *Shuck Beans, Stack Cakes and Honest Fried Chicken, Butter Beans to Blackberries: Recipes from the Southern Garden* and *The Festive Table.*

pino luongo is a chef and restaurateur in New York City with his own line of packaged foods based on flavors from his Coco Pazzo restaurants. His fourth cookbook, *La Mia Cucina Toscana,* is due out in fall 2003.

natasha macaller is the pastry chef at Union Restaurant in Santa Monica, California.

roberto marchetti is the owner of Al Bric and Al Ciabot wine bars in Rome.

claudia marulanda is a former art designer at FOOD & WINE Magazine.

nobu matsuhisa was named one of FOOD & WINE's Best New Chefs in 1989. He is the owner of 13 restaurants around the world.

nick mautone is a managing partner of New York City's Gramercy Tavern.

robert mcgrath was named one of FOOD & WINE's Best New Chefs in 1988. He is the chef and owner of Roaring Fork in Scottsdale, Arizona.

alice medrich is known for her chocolate expertise. Her latest book is *Bittersweet.*

eric moshier was named one of FOOD & WINE's Best New Chefs in 2000. He is the former pastry chef at Empire Restaurant in Providence, R.I.

elizabeth and sompon nabnian run the Chiang Mai Thai Cookery School in Chiang Mai, Thailand.

carrie nahabedian is the chef and co-owner of Naha in Chicago.

michel nischan is the chef at Heartbeat restaurant in the W New York Hotel.

david norman, former head baker for Bouley Bakery and Danube in New York City, is currently the baker and ranch manager at Hart & Hind Fitness Ranch in Rio Frio, Texas.

richard o'connell is the executive sous chef at Indigo Restaurant in London's One Aldwych Hotel.

gene opton, a cook and gardener in Berkeley, California, is the author of *Honey: A Connoisseur's Guide with Recipes.*

david page is the chef and co-owner of Home restaurant in New York City and co-owner of Shinn Vineyards in Mattituck, Long Island.

charlie palmer is the owner of Aureole in New York City, Dry Creek Kitchen in Healdsburg, California, and the recently opened Kitchen 22 in New York City. He is also the author of *Charlie Palmer's Casual Cooking* and *Great American Food.*

maria paolillo is the chef and co-owner of Enoteca Ferrara in Rome.

grace parisi is the senior test kitchen associate in the FOOD & WINE test kitchen and the author of *The Sauce Bible,* due out in 2004.

claudine peltot has a vast collection of linens and a passion for cooking. She lives in France, where she travels to flea markets and fairs to sell her linens.

jacques pépin, FOOD & WINE contributing editor, master chef, TV personality, food columnist and cooking teacher, is the author of 21 cookbooks, including *Jacques Pépin's Kitchen: Encore with Claudine and Julia* and *Jacques Cooking at Home.* He is also co-host, with his daughter, Claudine, of the PBS television series *Jacques Pépin Celebrates.*

kathy petronella is the chef and owner of Paulie's in Houston, Texas.

jim peyton is a cooking expert, restaurant consultant and cookbook author. His latest title is *Jim Peyton's New Cooking from Old Mexico.*

tasha prysi, formerly a cook at Chez Panisse in Berkeley, California, teaches and writes about cooking. She has contributed to the *Chez Panisse Café Cookbook, Chez Panisse Fruit* and Corby Kummer's *The Pleasures of Slow Food.*

steven raichlen is the award-winning author of *The Barbecue! Bible, How to Grill* and the new *Barbecue USA.* His TV show, *Barbecue University,* based on his popular school at the Greenbrier resort in Virginia, launches in summer 2003 on PBS.

ramey's diner is located in Whitesburg, Kentucky.

sonali rao is the style editor at FOOD & WINE Magazine.

michael recchiuti and his wife, Jacky, own Recchiuti Confections in San Francisco.

pascal rigo is the owner of several bakeries and cafés in San Francisco, including Chez Nous, Galette, Le Petit Robert and Le Table.

eric ripert is the chef and co-owner of New York City's Le Bernardin.

giorgio rivetti is the head winemaker at La Spinetta, one of the most acclaimed wineries in Piedmont, Italy.

michael romano was named one of FOOD & WINE's Best New Chefs in 1991. He is the chef and co-owner of New York City's Union Square Cafe.

anne rosenzweig is co-owner of Inside restaurant in New York City.

photo credits

william abranowicz 357 (bottom right)

antonis achilleos 61, 247 (bottom)

sang an 132 (right), 152

stefan anderson 62 (right), 166 (left), 226 (bottom), 227 (right)

quentin bacon 56 (left), 92, 111, 114, 116, 127, 163, 227 (left), 296 (bottom), 323, 400

james baigrie 10 (right), 18 (left), 79 (top), 99 (both photos), 106 (right), 146, 198 (right), 216, 222, 247 (top), 257 (bottom), 311 (top), 355 (both bottom photos), 357 (top left), 358 (bottom left), 359 (both right photos), 400

mirjam bleeker/taverne agency 76 (right), 172 (left)

jean marie del moral 266 (top)

brian doben 83, 338

jim franco 127 (top)

andrew french 33

dana gallagher 302 (both photos)

gentl and hyers 366

frances janisch 29 (top), 40 (right), 51, 56 (right), 69 (left), 79 (bottom), 122, 142 (bottom), 148 (left), 177 (bottom), 181, 204 (right), 207, 224 (left), 257 (top), 269 (right), 285, 311 (bottom), 358 (bottom right)

richard jung 80, 171 (top), 293

john kernick 29 (bottom), 30 (left), 35 (top), 90 (right), 141, 160 (bottom), 186 (left), 230, 234 (right), 356 (bottom right)

matt and ted lee 274 (right)

lisa linder 124 (left), 272, 354

maura mcevoy 15, 18 (top), 35 (bottom), 47, 65, 160 (top), 208, 211, 239, 332 (right), 336, 347

william meppem 1, 10 (left), 23, 24, 26 (left), 30 (right), 40 (left), 44 (top), 49 (top), 54, 62 (left), 72 (both photos), 74, 94 (both photos), 102, 119, 132 (left), 142 (top), 184, 189, 190, 192 (top), 195, 201, 202, 204 (left), 215, 221, 248 (left), 254 (both photos), 258, 260 (right), 264, 274 (left), 280 (left), 290 (right), 299, 318, 327 (right), 330, 332 (left), 335, 359 (top left)

james merrell cover, 8, 175, 240, 224 (right)

amy neunsinger 38, 164, 280 (right), 407

victoria pearson 90 (left), 260 (left), 269 (left), 290 (left)

eric piasecki 355 (upper left), 357 (bottom left)

david prince 242 (left)

kieran scott 26 (right), 166 (right)

mark seelen 76 (left)

tara sgroi 43, 136, 356 (left), 359 (top left)

petrina tinslay 343

luca trovato 251

mikkel vang 44 (bottom), 124 (right), 177 (top), 186 (right), 365

jonelle weaver 101

wendell t. webber 69 (right), 86, 106 (left), 135, 171 (bottom), 192 (bottom), 198 (left), 296 (top), 314, 320 (both photos), 327 (left)

michael weschler 248 (right), 356 (top right)

anna williams 49 (bottom), 148 (right), 234 (left), 242 (right), 277, 288, 308

roy zipstein 155

jennifer rubell is the co-owner of Rubell Hotels, a Miami-based, family-owned collection that includes the Beach House Bal Harbour in Surfside, Florida, and the Greenview and Albion in South Beach, Florida.

johannes sanzin is the chef and co-owner of Bistro St. Mark's in Brooklyn.

michael schlow was named one of FOOD & WINE's Best New Chefs in 1996. He is the chef and co-owner of Radius and Via Matta in Boston.

mindy segal is the pastry chef and partner at mk restaurant and mk north in Chicago.

dan segall is an aspiring chef living in Singapore and a brilliant sandwich maker.

michelle shih is a senior editor at FOOD & WINE Magazine.

barbara shinn is co-owner of Home restaurant in New York City and Shinn Vineyards in Mattituck, Long Island.

jane sigal is a senior food editor at FOOD & WINE Magazine.

nigel slater is a columnist in London for *The Observer,* a British television host and the author of eight cook-books, including *Nigel Slater's Real Food* and *Appetite.*

john snell is the former owner of the San Francisco restaurant Meeting House.

andré soltner, formerly the executive chef at Lutèce, is a senior lecturer and the master chef at the French Culinary Institute in New York City. He is also the author of *The*

Lutèce Cookbook and co-author of the *French Culinary Institute's Salute to Healthy Cooking.*

ana sortun is the chef and owner of Oleana restaurant in Cambridge, Massachusetts.

robert stehling is the chef and owner of Hominy Grill in Charleston, South Carolina.

fredrika stjärne is the photo editor at FOOD & WINE Magazine.

mark sullivan was named one of FOOD & WINE's Best New Chefs in 2002. He is the chef and co-owner of the Village Pub in Woodside, California.

david tanis, the former head chef at Chez Panisse in Berkeley, California, is currently cooking and writing in Paris.

mory thomas is a recipe developer in the test kitchen at the Food Network.

fabio trabocchi was named one of FOOD & WINE's Best New Chefs in 2002. He is the chef at Maestro in McLean, Virginia.

suzanne tracht was named one of FOOD & WINE's Best New Chefs in 2002. She is the chef at Jar in Los Angeles.

rori trovato is a recipe developer and food stylist.

tina ujlaki is the executive food editor at FOOD & WINE Magazine.

tom valenti was named one of FOOD & WINE's Best New Chefs in 1990. He is the chef and co-owner of Ouest in New York City. He is also the author of *Welcome to My Kitchen.*

ruth van waerebeek is the chef at Chile's biggest winery, Concha y Toro. She is the author of *Everybody Eats Well in Belgium* and *The Chilean Kitchen.*

benedetta vitali is the owner of Zibibbo restaurant outside Florence and the author of *Soffritto: Tradition & Innovation in Tuscan Cooking.*

jean-georges vongerichten, a contributing editor at FOOD & WINE, is the chef and owner of numerous restaurants: Jean Georges, Vong, Mercer Kitchen and JoJo in New York; Market in Paris; Dune in the Bahamas; Prime Steakhouse at the Bellagio in Las Vegas and Vong in Hong Kong, London and Chicago. He has authored or co-authored *Simple Cuisine, Cooking at Home with a Four-Star Chef* and *Simple to Spectacular.*

joanne weir has written 14 cookbooks and hosted her own television show on PBS called *Weir Cooking in Wine Country.* She travels and teaches cooking all around the world.

paula wolfert, a contributing editor at FOOD & WINE, is the author of six cookbooks, including *Mediterranean Cooking* and *Mediterranean Grains and Greens.* Her most recent book is *Mediterranean Slow and Easy.*

diane rossen worthington has written more than 14 cookbooks, including *The Taste of Summer* and, most recently, *Seriously Simple: Easy Recipes for Creative Cooks.*

kazuo yoshida is the chef at Jewel Bako in New York City.

bill yosses is the pastry chef at Citarella in New York City and co-author of *Desserts for Dummies.*